Hope you enjoy this Dad,
from Hamish and Vida
Xmas 1990

D1330999

THE HISTORY OF AYR

The device on the title page is the Coat of Arms of the Royal Burgh of Ayr, from the Lyon Register, 5 September 1673: Gules, a castle triple–towered Argent betwixt a Holy Lamb, cross staff and banner of Saint Andrew, on the dexter, and on the sinister the head of John the Baptist in a charger Proper, in the base the sea Azure.

THE HISTORY OF AYR

Royal Burgh and County Town

JOHN STRAWHORN

JOHN DONALD PUBLISHERS LTD
EDINBURGH

ISBN 0 85976 281 5

Phototypesetting by Quorn Selective Repro, Loughborough.
Printed in Great Britain by The Eagle Press Plc, Glasgow

Preface

'The Clerk laid before the Magistrates and Council a letter from Mr Ebenezer Thomson, Latin Teacher, craving liberty to read and take extracts from some of the old Records of this Burgh to elucidate the laws, manners, customs, liberties and religion of the earlier times. The Magistrates and Council authorise the Clerk to give him from time to time the use of said records, he always returning one volume before getting another, & the Clerk taking care that no injury is done to these old records while he has them.' *Ayr Town Council Minutes, 13 March 1833.*

The writing of Ayr's local history began two hundred years ago. Francis Grose, who inspired Robert Burns to write 'Tam O' Shanter' to accompany a view of Alloway Kirk, himself prepared a description of the Tower of St John's Kirk, adding a relevant charter of 1378 from the burgh archives, these being included among seventeen Ayrshire items in the second volume of his *Antiquities of Scotland*. Shortly after Grose's visit to the west of Scotland in 1789, Rev Drs Dalrymple and McGill when describing Ayr for the *Statistical Account* referred to 'some old papers' and McGill in supplementary particulars included note of the 'Erection Charter of the burgh of Ayr'.

More systematic study of local history had to await George Chalmers who after seventeen years of erudite toil completed in 1824 his four volume *Caledonia*. In this, a mass of historical and antiquarian material was presented in county and parish sections, so providing appropriate bases for later writers. Items from Chalmers were copied, as by the anonymous author of a *Short Account of the Town of Ayr*, published in Edinburgh in 1828. Some additional material was added to Chalmers in Ayr's first real work on local history. In 1830 William McCarter issued from his printing shop the town's first directory, prefaced by *Brief Historical Reminiscences* attributed to 'a Burgess (Guild Brother)', appearing under McCarter's own name in a revised edition of 1832. McCarter included a translation of the foundation charter of the burgh. In 1833 research on the burgh records was undertaken by Ebenezer Thomson — as the quotation heading this preface illustrates — but no publication followed, regrettably, for he had already showed editorial skill in those books he did publish on literature and language. For the *New Statistical Account*, ministers were specifically requested to provide historical information, and writing in 1837 Rev. Alexander Cuthill devoted a large part of his 85 pages to that aspect of Ayr. James

Paterson, in the first volume of his Ayrshire history published in 1847, supplied 130 informative pages on the history of Ayr, another 25 pages on its landed families, and a further 22 pages devoted specifically to Newton-upon-Ayr. Some extracts from Ayr's 16th century burgh records were printed by John Smith in 1835; in 1848 Paterson edited the Obit Book of St John's Church; but not till much later were other records published.

The Ayrshire and Wigtonshire Archaeological Association produced the Charters of the Friars Preachers of Ayr in 1881, Ayr Burgh Charters in 1883, and other local items in its subsequent volumes. D. Murray Lyon in the 1870s and Rev. John H. Pagan in the 1890s also explored burgh and church records of the 17th century in particular. Reminiscences of Howie (1861), Henry Gray (1872), Hugh Allan (1889), J. M. Ferguson (1884, 1907), Miss E. E. Anderson (1919), and Wallace Allan (1929) show an interest in more recent history. Other late 19th century books dealt with special topics ranging from Jane Campbell's *Air Academy and Burgh Schule* to the Marquess of Bute's *The Burning of the Barns of Ayr*.

In the present century, work on the records has been continued, especially George S. Pryde's volume of *Ayr Burgh Accounts* published by the Scottish History Society. Burgh records were transferred to Edinburgh to be catalogued, conserved, and cared for in the Scottish Record Office, but have since been returned to the Carnegie Library in Ayr. Studies have been made of particular periods and special topics, by various authors for different purposes — as may be noted from the Bibliography at the end of this present book. One major work, *The Royal Burgh of Ayr*, was edited by Dr Annie Dunlop for the Ayrshire Archaeological and Natural History Society and sponsored by Ayr Town Council to commemorate the 750th anniversary of the burgh. This took the form of a series of essays on various aspects of Ayr's history by a team of twenty contributors.

Several comments seem necessary on all that has been written on the history of Ayr. First, it is remarkable how high a standard has been maintained by so many writers both in their diligent use of available sources and skilful presentation of fact. Second, less satisfactory, is the neglect of those parts of the extended burgh which lie outwith the confines of the original royal burgh. And third, though so much has been written, it seems curious that no one has ever attempted a History in the form of a sustained chronological account of the development of the town. The author of this present book aspires to continue the tradition in the first respect, to remedy the deficiency secondly noted, and to attempt the third in this History of Ayr, Royal Burgh and County Town.

The writer of local history has numerous considerations to bear in mind, if he is offering more than an anecdotal account of outstanding events which happened to occur in his parish, with eulogies of prominent persons who chanced to have some local association. If instead he is attempting to compose the story of a community's changing life through the centuries, the local historian has particular problems in preparation and presentation. As far as sources are concerned, available evidence includes manuscript and printed records, not all easily available, sometimes difficult to read or too technical to understand; plus reminiscences, memories, and oral traditions which are especially awkward to evaluate. As well as collecting details of the community being studied, the local historian must show awareness of what was happening elsewhere, and attempt to keep abreast of current research in Scottish history and other specialist fields. In the process of assembling material, the local historian shares the common problem that in the long periods up till the 18th century conjecture on the basis of limited evidence is required; after the 18th century the mass of evidence becomes so vast that conclusions must be based on selection from the data available. In presenting a local history, the author is catering for various readers — local people who expect a readable account of how their community has evolved, some who will merely use it to find out what is said about a particular topic, and (hopefully) academic historians for whom local detail may alter preconceived notions and modify accepted opinion.

This History was sponsored by Kyle and Carrick District Council. It was begun during the term of Provost Gibson Macdonald and completed under Provost Dan MacNeill. The Councillors of Kyle and Carrick, as custodians of the Common Good of the former Royal Burgh, most generously financed three years of research as well as arranging for publication. Ayr Carnegie Library, now headquarters of the District Libraries, has admirable resources, and staff to whom the present author has been deeply indebted for a period of more than forty years. Special tribute must be made to those in the Reference Department, particularly Mrs Sheena Andrew and Miss Sheila West who are so cheerfully competent and consistently helpful.

Those who have assisted in various ways include Sheena Andrew, G. W. S. Barrow, Bob Blain, Nancy Brown, T. R. Bruen, Norman Cunningham, John A. Hay, Peter Hemphill, T. A. Hendry, Jean and Robert Kennedy, Ian Levitt, Alistair Lindsay, Donald MacLean, John Pollock, Margaret Sanderson, Ian R. Smillie, C. A. Whatley, and Jack Wild — their particular contributions indicated in the Notes at the end of this book. There also are listed the Sources of Information. These 'Sources' and 'Notes' will, it is hoped, assist local readers to extend their background of knowledge; provide an adequate alternative to footnotes for other historians, and draw attention to particular local works of interest.

The evidence presented in this *History of Ayr, Royal Burgh and County Town* and my previous *History of Irvine, Royal Burgh and New Town* forms a contribution to Scottish urban history. In particular they may suggest a reassessment of the much-maligned burghs before their reform in 1833 and a fuller appreciation of their role until they were, sadly, abolished in 1975. This book does not pretend to exhaust the local records; there is scope for more specialised analyses of particular aspects of burgh administration; various social changes over the last two centuries require elucidation; and my account of 20th century developments will inevitably be superseded. Perhaps this book may stimulate others to study this and similar communities in sufficient detail to produce a completer understanding of our changing ways of life.

JOHN STRAWHORN

Contents

Part One
Early Times

ONE

Origins

Ayr's written history begins in the year 1197, when a royal castle was built by order of William the Lion, King of Scots.

The precise wording of the chronicle – *factum est novum oppidum inter Don et Ar* – indicates that this new castle was erected between the Rivers Doon and Ayr. The place became known as Newcastle-upon-Ayr, and here just eight years later in 1205 a burgh was created, taking its name also from the river beside which it was situated.

The meaning of the name is the first of a series of prehistoric puzzles. It has been interpreted variously as 'rapid river'; 'violent river'; 'shallow river'; or 'clear river' in contrast to the presumed 'dark river' of the Doon. It is a common enough name for a river, for it appears in England as the Aire of Yorkshire; in France, with an Aire in Gascony and another in Artois; in Switzerland as the Aare; in Germany which has an Ahr and an Ahre; in Belgium, where there is the Aar; and in Spain also the Ara. Many river names are very old, in the forgotten language of the first settlers in an area, and the River Ayr must have been so called by pre-Celtic people who lived here long before the name was first recorded in the 12th century.

This is the second puzzle, for there is no clear evidence of who first settled here or when. Elsewhere on the coast, to the south by Ballantrae and Girvan, and to the north at Shewalton and Ardeer, definite traces have been found of mesolithic fishermen who some six thousand years ago wandered along the shoreline in search of a bare subsistence. Flints found at Doonfoot, and others between Heathfield and Monkton, suggest some passing visits. A solitary polished stone axe found in Alloway Street, and another at Doonfoot, provide evidence of a neolithic or later presence. A standing stone south of the Doon may have been set up by some prehistoric people, but no one can tell when or why. To the Bronze Age and possibly between 1500 and 1000 BC have been ascribed several local archaeological finds: burials with food vessels north of the River Ayr at Content; south near the Doon at the cairn which Tam O'Shanter passed; and another cemetery at Doonfoot.

The third puzzle is to assess the significance of these remains. Other Bronze Age finds further up the River Ayr and throughout what is now Ayrshire indicate that the area was extensively settled by people who were cultivating suitable patches of land, could store food in earthenware pots of their own manufacture, and possessed metal implements for peaceful and military purposes. It is known that these pre-Celtic people were joined later by Celts, who were the Welsh-speaking Britons of the Iron Age. Hill forts of that era have been interpreted as part of a process of military conquest. The effect on the local population can only be guessed by noticing that older pre-Celtic place names are joined, or sometimes perhaps superseded, by a range of Cymric names.

The fourth puzzle is a special one. When the Romans penetrated this part of Britain which was peopled by a tribe they called the Damnonii, did they occupy Ayr? We can no longer accept claims made by earlier local historians that there were Roman baths and villas in this area. Though excavation of several native sites has produced a range of Roman items, these were not necessarily acquired locally from Romans. It is known that they had a fort inland near Loudoun Hill, and temporary marching-camps have been found on the coast near Girvan and Largs. It has been guessed that from Loudounhill a military road may have extended towards Irvine or Ayr. There may also have been roads coming from the south, one via Nithsdale, another via the Doon Valley. An old roadway reaching Ayr by this last route was described as a Roman Road on the first edition of the Ordnance Survey Map. Coming up past Dalmellington, it runs east of the Doon to approach Ayr via Cockhill, and seemed to continue past Castlehill (where a modern street has been given the name of Roman Road) and by Forehill into the heart of Ayr. Those traces of roadway which survive

Six thousand years ago this coast was known to Mesolithic fishermen, but not till much later was settled cultivation introduced by Neolithic or Bronze Age people. The site overlooking the sea was occupied by an Iron Age fort long before Greenan Castle was built in the 15th or 16th century.

possess certain Roman characteristics, but recent expert opinion is reluctant to accept it as genuine without any evidence of a Roman fort to which it might be leading. Here, however, is a thoroughfare of some antiquity, and it is difficult to suggest who else, other than the Roman army, might have built such a length of road.

If the Romans did in fact make their military way towards Ayr, part of the puzzle is to identify where a coastal port and harbour might have been located. This requires some assessment of where the coastline would have been in Roman times, rather less than two thousand years ago. It has been estimated that maximum sea level was reached six thousand years ago, when a 40 feet raised beach was formed. Assuming a steady recession of the sea since then, the shore line two thousand years ago would have been approximately sixteen feet above the present level. Some account must also be taken of the windswept sand deposits of later centuries. The mouth of the River Ayr in

Roman times may in fact have been very near where the New Bridge is now situated. If that were so, then any Roman station would have been located in the High Street area, long buried under later buildings. The approach to it may have been by way of Kyle Street rather than Mill Street as has been suggested. But it must be emphasised that without definite finds all this must remain conjecture.

It might be presumed that the beginning of written records would provide us with greater certainty for the period after the Romans. But such annals as survive were composed far away from here, are difficult to interpret, and of doubtful accuracy. Thus the period before the 12th century is appropriately known as the Dark Ages, and filled with more puzzles. It is accepted that the Welsh-speaking (Cymric) Britons of the Damnonii tribe were incorporated in the kingdom of Alcluyd or Strathclyde. It is known that they were in contact during the Dark Ages with Picts to the north; with Gaelic-speaking Scots from Ireland and Argyll;

At the site where Ayr would grow up, four ford crossings have been identified, which continued in use even after the first bridge was built about the year 1236.

with Angles from the Kingdom of Northumbria, which included the Lothians; and with Galloway, home of the Novantae tribe, which extended northwards as far as the River Doon. There survive some reports of conflict. It is possible to accept that in 750 Edbert of Northumbria invaded and occupied Kyle – the first mention of that name. It is reasonable to presume that the first Viking landings on the shores of the Firth of Clyde happened around the year 870. But the rest are garbled accounts of incidents of which not even the dates can be trusted. Thus we have a story, hardly credible, of a battle in the year 360 on the coast between Ayr and Doon, when Picts in alliance with Romans defeated Scots. In the sixth century the legendary Arthur is reputed to have been operating in this area, a cavalry chief leading Britons against invaders, and it has been suggested that he had one of his principal forts where Greenan Castle was later built. In the year 681 the Britons of Strathclyde are said to have repelled Scots from Ireland after a victorious battle at Mauchline – or at a place with a somewhat similar name in Ireland. In 839 an unidentifiable king called Alpin from Argyll landed with an army of Scots near Ayr, laid waste the country around, advanced up the Doon valley, to be defeated and killed near Dalmellington at that place called Laicht Alpin. In ninth century France there was a philosopher called Johannes Scotus Erigena, supposedly a Scot, but to interpret Erigena as 'from Ayr' is far-fetched. In the realm of local legend, the most mysterious local figure is King Coilus, supposed ruler of a sub-kingdom within Strathclyde, from whom may be derived the name of Kyle – and even, some would say, the title of 'Old King Cole, that merry old soul'. Coilus was involved, according to one story, in a battle near Dalrymple with another king called Fergus (after whom Loch Fergus may be named) and both kings were killed. Another version has it that Coilus survived to cross the Water of Coyle, pass Coylton, and reach Coilsholm near Tarbolton. That spot is the site of another supposed battle and the reputed burial place of Coilus. He is presumed to have been a leader of Britons who defeated invaders variously described as Picts, Scots, or Angles. These events have been attributed to the year 702 in one version, to the third century in another, and about 330 BC in a third, so great is the uncertainty.

From the various chronicles we can at least deduce that there were various war-like incursions into this area during the Dark Ages. We may further presume (what is never recorded) a process of considerable immigration and settlement during the first thousand years of the Christian era. From the west came Gaelic speakers from Ireland and Argyll, who have left their mark here in various place names. Other places have names which indicate that from over the sea there later came not only Viking raiders but Norwegian settlers. From the east, Anglian farmers arrived with improved farming techniques; they began clearing the lowland forests, and their language would become the dominant speech, later called Lowland Scots. Again, what is not chronicled, the new religion of Christianity was introduced. It seems to have reached Galloway even before Ninian was preaching at Whithorn in the fourth or fifth century. At what period the faith came to Ayr may be deduced from a sandstone slab with an inscribed cross, found at Cambusdoon not far from Alloway kirk, and displayed within Loudoun Hall. This cross has been attributed by one expert to the period from the fourth to the sixth century – before Columba reached Iona in 563 – which seems reasonable enough, though another authority thinks the Alloway cross belongs to the eighth century or later. Other Celtic crosses have been found in Carrick, and place names prefixed by *kirk-* and *kil-* suggest, in some instances, the possible sites of early Christian churches of chapels.

The peaceful passage of everyday life has never in any age been deemed newsworthy. Yet the area later known as Ayrshire, occupied by only a few thousand people in the first century BC, may have supported a population of 20,000 by 500 AD, and approached a possible 40,000 by 1000 AD.

By that last date, political history has become clearer. In the ninth century Scots and Picts were united under one king. In the 10th century Strathclyde then Lothian were incorporated into that kingdom of Scotland. In the 11th century there was continued instability, as when Duncan was deposed, then his successor Macbeth – though not quite as recounted by Shakespeare. At the beginning of the 12th century this area was settled enough for certain territories to be recorded as church lands belonging to the bishopric of Glasgow. A document of 1114 or thereby lists three such places in Kyle – Sanchar (St Quivox), Camcachecheyn (Camciscan in Craigie parish), and Carcleuien (Carcluie adjoining Alloway). Throughout the 12th century royal power was systematically consolidated by David I (1124–53), Malcolm IV (1153–65), and William the Lion (1165–1214). The south west of Scotland was brought under effective government.

The winning of the west was commenced by David I. He and his successors recruited from Norman England and France warrior barons who helped bring outlying areas under control, were rewarded with generous grants of land, and acted as agents of the crown in the feudal administration which was subsequently created. Strathclyde though part of the Kingdom of Scotland since 1034 remained insecure, and Galloway was still a semi-independent lordship which had to be encompassed. Thus Robert de Brus, a Norman, was awarded Annandale. Hugh de Morville and Richard his son, also Norman, were granted lands in Tweeddale, to which was added the lordship of Cunninghame. Walter Fitzalan, of Breton parentage, received extensive territories including Renfrew and the northern part of the district of Kyle.

We can visualise the frontier being steadily pushed forward. First there was Cunninghame under the de Morvilles, with a castle built at Irvine and vassal knights garrisoning the area north of the River Irvine, their castles being wooden structures erected on artificial or natural mounds. Then came, south of the River Irvine, that part of Kyle which was awarded to Fitzalan, who held high office as Steward of the king, and so his family became known as the Stewarts. From their castle at Dundonald was controlled Stewart Kyle whose southern limit was marked by the course of the Glenmuir

and Lugar Waters and the River Ayr into which they flow. Here were installed military retainers of the Steward, and the names of some of them happen to have survived in various charters – at St Quivox (Hugh Janitoris), Tarbolton (Adam, son of Gilbert), Craigie (Walter Hose), Symington (Simon Loccart), Prestwick (Arnald), Dundonald (Donald, son of Ywen), Crosbie (Henry Croc), Riccarton (Richard Waleys). Some may have been local lords who were allowed to share in the new administration; others were obviously incomers; inevitably there has been argument about the racial origin of the ancestors of William Wallace. South of Stewart Kyle and extending to the River Doon was King's Kyle, so called because that portion of Kyle was purposely retained under direct royal control. For beyond the Doon was Carrick which was part of the hostile lordship of Galloway. Strong points were necessary to guard the river frontier. Mottes – those great artificial mounds upon which wooden castles with encircling stockades were erected – survive at Alloway and upriver at Dalmellington. Other castles were held at intermediate sites like Barbieston, Skeldon, and Kerse. On Loch Doon an early example of a stone-built castle was erected in the 13th or early 14th century. The fortresses of King's Kyle were held by men who owed direct allegiance to the king. Few of their names have survived, save for Dalmellington (Thomas Colville le Scot) and Ochiltree (Philip de Colville). They belonged to a select military force guarding the south western frontier of the kingdom.

Carrick, like all upland areas of Galloway, was difficult of access. That corner of Scotland had an immigrant population with prominent Irish and Scandinavian elements. Gaelic would survive there longer, and the speech which superseded it was later to be described as South Mid Scots as distinct from the West Mid Scots of the rest of Strathclyde. In the year 1160 Malcolm IV launched a military campaign against this dissident lordship, with forces presumably advancing from King's Kyle across the Doon and into Carrick. Fergus, lord of Galloway, was deposed and the conquered lands divided between Fergus's two sons. William the Lion inherited control over Galloway, but when he was taken prisoner by the English in 1174 Galloway burst into revolt. William was able to reassert authority in 1177. But within a few years a grandson of Fergus called Roland emerged as a new and dangerous lord of Galloway. Roland by marrying Elena de Morville was able to inherit in 1196 the extensive possessions of that family. William required to counterbalance Roland's power. So, just the next year, in 1197 he built his

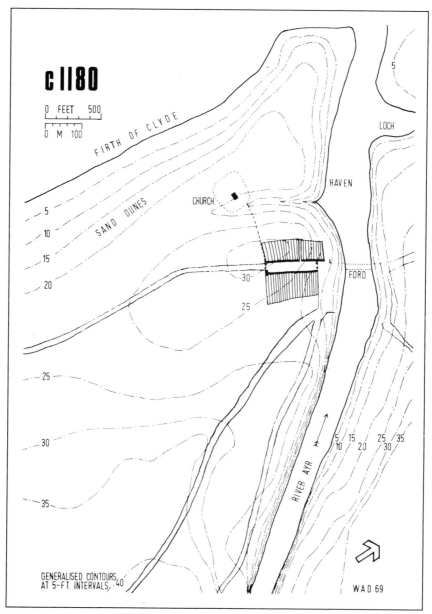

This is first in a series of conjectured plans which William A. Dodd prepared as part of his 'Study of Urban Growth'. It supposes that before the burgh was established in 1205, a settlement existed in what is now the Sandgate. Recently the site of an early chapel has been located upriver; the Church of St John probably followed the building of a Castle in 1197.

new royal castle at Ayr. Carrick was detached from Galloway. Donald, who was Roland's cousin and rival, was obviously won over by the king and created Earl of Carrick. Then in 1207 Carrick was incorporated with Kyle and Cunninghame to form the new sheriffdom of Ayr. Significantly the first recorded sheriff was Reginald de Craufurd from Loudoun, a vassal of the over-mighty lord of Cunninghame and Galloway, but promoted by William the Lion to be a royal official, the

king's representative in Ayrshire, and governor of the royal castle of Ayr.

The Castle of Ayr was located near the mouth of the river, within the area later occupied by Cromwell's fort – whose construction in the 17th century effectively destroyed any surviving remains of the earlier structure. Theories that it was elsewhere may be discounted. Castlehill, despite its name, shows no trace of early fortification; and, like the motte of

Alloway, was too far away from the burgh which would be erected 'at my new castle upon Ayr'. The castle built in 1197 was of wooden construction, replaced by stone just over a century later in 1307. It has been suggested that the burgh coat of arms portrays an exact representation of the later Castle of Ayr. This shows a hexagonal tower, fronted by a curtain wall with two smaller towers, guarding the gateway, and situated beside the sea. Since Roman times the sea level had noticeably dropped, until eight hundred years ago it was a mere six feet higher than at the present day. North of the River Ayr some flat coastal areas in what is now Newton Green were still under water. To the south by the castle, as beyond, the shore line was hardly more than a few yards inland from what it is now. Once (it has been argued) the River Doon found its way across the exposed sands to reach the sea somewhere in the neighbourhood of Blackburn. Topographical evidence has long suggested this as a possibility, and several writers have even traced a presumed route still further, across the Low Green and into the River Ayr. In 1791 Rev Dr McGill was convinced that 'The river Doon, near its mouth, has, at some former period since the division of the county into parishes, altered its channel'. As proof he instanced that Cuningpark was included with lands south of the Doon in the parish of Maybole. Though that was merely circumstantial evidence, later writers have found a further clue in an otherwise-puzzling phrase in the burgh charter. With the burgh bounds defined as following a line 'from Inverdun (the mouth of the Doon) up to Inverpolcurtecan (the mouth of the Curtecan burn)' and thence upstream towards Corton, that stream (later the Slaphouse Burn or the Belleisle Burn) must then have been a tributary of the Doon. Which implies that the meandering River Doon must have formed its modern estuary sometimes after the 13th century. An alternative explanation is that in the 13th century (as much later when Roy's Map was drawn) the area of sands exposed at low tide was much wider than since, and the burn then joined the river on their way across the beach.

The creation of the sheriffdom a decade after the building of the Castle of Ayr signified the consolidation of royal authority. Military occupation was complemented by feudal administration. Warrior barons from their castles exercised justice in the lands which had been allocated to them. Their mottes or mote-hills were sometimes later known as court-hills or law-hills. The baronies which were their responsibility were also the source whence they derived a livelihood and the possibility of increased wealth and welfare. For

their material advancement burghs were sometimes established, as will later appear. For their spiritual welfare they were inspired to generous support of the Church.

The 12th century saw the emergence of a system of parish churches. There already existed many chapels, some of quite ancient origin, and many of them would continue in existence. But it was usual within each barony for one place of worship to become established as a parish church. Barons might endow such a church with a glebe to maintain a parish priest. David I in organising the parish system required that teinds (one tenth of all produce) should be devoted to maintenance of the Church. Part was for parochial provision; the remainder could be appropriated for the support of agencies of the Church elsewhere. The parishes of the sheriffdom of Ayr were administratively grouped into the deaneries of Cunninghame, Kyle, and Carrick, and included within the jurisdiction of the bishop of Glasgow.

In the 12th century the impact of the Church was emphasised by the introduction of regular clergy of the monastic orders who complemented the efforts of the secular clergy of the parish churches. The greater barons, newly installed in Ayrshire, were generous in their awards. In Cunninghame, Kilwinning Abbey was established by Richard de Morville between 1184 and 1189, and its Tyronensian monks of the Benedictine order were supported by the revenues of fourteen parish churches in Cunninghame and six outwith the county. In Stewart Kyle, Walter Fitzalan – who had already founded the great Cluniac house of Paisley Abbey – granted before 1165 to the monks of Melrose that extensive tract of Barmuir and Kylesmuir which stretched from Tarbolton through Mauchline as far as the eastern boundary of Ayrshire. To this was added, between 1165 and 1174, a fishery at the mouth of the River Ayr. Later between 1219 and 1230 a second Walter Fitzalan invited the Gilbertine order of nuns and canons to set themelves up at Dalmilling. When that scheme fell through the lands of Dalmilling in Sanchar or St Quivox parish were awarded to Paisley Abbey, which also acquired the churches of St Quivox, Prestwick, Monkton, Craigie, Auchinleck, Dundonald and its subordinate chapels of Crosbie and Riccarton. Later still in the 13th or 14th century the Order of Holy Trinity for the Redemption of Captives established in Stewart Kyle a house at Fail. These Trinitarians were granted possession of the churches of Symington, Barnweil, Galston, and (for a time) Tarbolton, together with three others outwith Ayrshire. In contrast to this bountiful generosity within Stewart Kyle, there were no similar grants to the monastic orders within the landward area of King's Kyle. To Carrick, however, monks of the Cluniac order were invited by Earl Duncan, and Crossraguel Abbey erected about 1242, with considerable lands and five of the Carrick parish churches. These regular orders which became established within Ayrshire were obviously a civilising influence and, in some instances it would appear, enterprising landowners.

What efforts were made by feudal landowners to develop their estates cannot readily be assessed from charters, which are virtually the only surviving items of evidence. The produce of their lands went mainly to feed them, their families, and retainers; but a surplus was desirable to exchange for what could not be produced by their own dependents. Hence burghs were, by royal authority, instituted as market places where rural produce could be exchanged for items manufactured within the burgh or where possible imported. So Walter Fitzalan established at Prestwick what was Ayrshire's first burgh. He referred to 'my burgh' in a charter dated sometime between 1165 and 1173, which is the earliest definite evidence, even though a later charter imagined an impossibly early date 'beyond the memory of man'. But the baronial burgh of Prestwick failed to develop as an important trading centre. That role was reserved for Ayr, created as a king's burgh in 1205. Ayr was followed by Irvine, founded by the lord of Cunninghame between 1230 and 1249, and later elevated to become a royal burgh and a rival to Ayr. Sometime later, possibly between 1314 and 1371, a fourth coastal burgh was erected at Newton-upon-Ayr, which like Prestwick was another Stewart burgh, and which also failed to develop as a commercial centre. Not till 1491 was Ayrshire's next burgh formed, at Newmilns, first of an extended range of places for trade. But Ayr retained its local pre-eminence, as a royal burgh and the county town.

TWO

Foundation of the Burgh

Is it possible to visualise the local scene at the beginning of the 13th century? The burgh of Ayr was founded in the year 1205 beside the royal castle which had been set up just eight years before. But what lay all around?

We know most, oddly enough, about the area north of the River Ayr, which was part of the territories of the bishop of Glasgow at the beginning of the 12th century and later passed to the Fitzalans. Just a few years after the foundation of the burgh of Ayr, Walter Fitzalan, in his unsuccessful negotiations to establish a Gilbertine monastic house at Dalmilling, described in some detail the attractions of that area. The parish of Sanchar, later St Quivox, within which Dalmilling was situated, extended from the lower reaches of the River Ayr inland as far as Auchincruive and northwards towards Ladykirk. It comprised arable land extending to five ploughgates, about 650 modern acres; pasture land stocked with 300 cows and 2,000 sheep; plus a forested area called then the Wood of Senekacher. Walter could also offer corn mills at Dalmilling and Prestwick, and a share in four fisheries along the coast between Ayr and Irvine. Obviously this was a rich and prosperous area; and that south of the river would presumably be no less so.

Alloway must have been a popular place, even then. It was occupied in the Bronze Age if not before. Even the upland area was quite early inhabited, for there are signs of a crannog lake dwelling on Carcluie loch, and the bishop of Glasgow's possession of Carcluie about 1116 is in fact the earlier documentary reference to any place in the district. The Christian presence at Alloway in the Dark Ages has been noted. To the 12th century may be attributed the Alloway motte. The baron who held it by royal grant required maintenance for his household, and this must have been levied from people who were tilling the land and raising stock on the lands of Alloway, and of Corton and Carcuie which were attached to the barony.

Of the intervening territory between the River Ayr and the Curtecan Burn which became the burgh of Ayr, we have least evidence. The charter clearly defined its boundaries. It extended to the mouth of the Curtecan Burn from the mouth of the Doon (which would thus seem to have been further north than it is now). It continued up the burn which was later known as the Slaphouse or Belleisle Burn, past Corton to Loch Fergus, then found its way northwards towards the River Ayr. Though certain of the place names mentioned in the charter have long since vanished and cannot be precisely located, the boundary clearly followed exactly the line of what was for long afterwards that of the historic parish of Ayr. That area, extending to five pennylands, about 2,300 modern acres, was awarded to the new burgh of Ayr to become its Burrowfield. The charter makes no mention of existing occupants, but it could not have been an uninhabited area awaiting colonisation. Here the land is as fertile as in St Quivox to the north or Alloway to the south, and the sea offered rich fishings. The boundary names suggest human settlement, and reference to ditches implies farm divisions. As with St Quivox and Alloway, some parts were still forested, for there the burgesses might take possession of 'land which they have cleared of wood'. The entire area, according to the charter, 'belonged to the town of Ayr' (*que pertinent ad villam de Are*) and this has suggested that a community of some sort already existed before the foundation of the burgh, perhaps even before the building of the castle, and possibly located in the Sandgate area. Excavation of one area between High Street and the river has quite recently unearthed what may be remains of an early church or chapel ante-dating the foundation of the burgh; and west of Loudoun Hall 'produced evidence of occupation on this site dating back to the 12th century'.

The charter creating the burgh of Ayr was sealed by William the Lion at Lanark in the presence of ten witnesses, most of them royal officials but including three men who had presumably a special interest in this award. Richard de Craufurd had perhaps

CHARTER OF FOUNDATION OF THE BURGH OF AYR, 1205

William, by the grace of God king of Scots, to the bishops, abbots, earls, barons, justiciars, sheriffs, bailies, officials, and all honest men of his whole land, clerical and lay, greeting!

Let those present and to come know that I have made a burgh at my new castle upon Ayr and have granted to the same burgh and to my burgesses dwelling in it all the liberties and all the free customs which my other burghs and my burgesses dwelling in them have throughout my kingdom.

I have also allotted in it a market every Saturday. I have also allotted to the burgesses who shall come thither to inhabit my burgh and settle and dwell there that they be free from toll and from all other custom for their proper goods throughout my whole land. I therefore strictly forbid anyone in my kingdom, on pain of my full forfeiture, to exact from any of them toll or any other custom for their proper goods.

Further, I have granted to the same burgh of mine and to my burgesses who shall settle and dwell in that burgh the five pennylands which belong to the town of Ayr, by the bounds afterwritten, namely from Inverdun up to Inverpolcurtecan, and from Inverpolcurtecan up to Corton, and so by the Curtecan to the head of the Curtecan, and so going up from the head of the Curtecan by Boghesken to Monedamdereg, and so from Monedamdereg by the ditch into Monemethonac, and from Monemethonac by the ditch into Polcleuan, and so by Polcleuan into Loch Fergus, and going down from Loch Fergus into Dufhat, and going down from Dufhat by the ditch to the stream on the east side of Drumnesauel, and going down from Drumnesauel stream into the ditch on the west side of that stream, and so by that ditch into Polclonecrangali into Dufloch, and thence into Polmulin, and so going down by Polmulin into the Ayr, and so going down by the Ayr into the sea.

I have also allowed to my burgesses dwelling there that with each full toft of theirs they may have six acres of land which they have cleared from wood within the foresaid five pennylands, making their own profit therefrom and paying me twelvepence annually for each toft and six acres adjoining it.

I therefore command and strictly order that all men who come to that foresaid burgh of mine with their merchandise to sell and buy have my firm peace and use the market and return well and in peace. I also order strictly that toll and other customs which are owed to the burgh be given and received at Mach, Karnebuth, Loudoun, Crosencon, and Lachtalpin. I also strictly forbid anyone, on pain of my full forfeiture, to presume to carry off beyond the foresaid bounds toll or any other custom which he ought by reason to give to my foresaid burgh. If, however, anyone should presume to carry off beyond the foresaid bounds toll or other custom of my foresaid burgh I strictly order that all men dwelling within the foresaid bounds help my servants to recover my right and to take and arrest the man who has carried off or attempted to carry off beyond the foresaid bounds tolls or any other custom belonging to my foresaid burgh.

Before these witnesses: Florence, bishop elect of Glasgow, my chancellor; Walter and William, my chaplains; Philip de Valence, my chamberlain; Robert of London, my son; William de Bois and Hugh, my clerks; William de Valence; Thomas de Colville; Richard de Craufurd. At Lanark, the twenty first of May.

---

already married the heiress of Loudoun and gained a foothold in Ayrshire, of which county he was soon afterwards appointed sheriff by King William. Thomas de Colville, like another of that family, had been granted lands in King's Kyle. William de Valence was possibly the person elsewhere noted as governor of the Castle of Ayr (*Willelmo vicecomite de novo castello super Ar*). The burgh charter is dated 21 May, but the year is not stated. Early in the 19th century George Chalmers noticed that one of the witnesses, Florence, was bishop elect of Glasgow between 1202 and 1207, which provided an approximation; more recently George Pryde identified the months in which Florence was appointed and resigned, thus narrowing the charter date to between 1203 and 1206; still more recently Geoffrey Barrow's researches into the reign of William have confirmed that the year of Ayr's charter must have been 1205.

While it is possible that there was a town of Ayr before 1205, and possibly even an older castle before the 'new castle' of 1197, it is impossible to accept the theory of a community of freemen which spontaneously evolved into a burgh and was given formal recognition by royal charter. Burghs were in fact the New Towns of the Middle Ages, and a burgh charter was really (in modern parlance) a New Town Designation Order. George Pryde, an authority on burgh history and particularly knowledgeable about Ayr, could state: 'The central fact about the charter is that it is the written record of an act of creation. Something new

At the beginning of the 13th century one river crossing was where the New Bridge would eventually be built, and the coastal route from Doonfoot reached it by way of the wide Sandgate. This photograph was taken about 1860.

had been, was being, and would be brought into being. Men had to be enticed to undertake the adventure of a new life in the new town. If only they would come in and settle as resident burgesses, all sorts of privileges, amenities, and immunities would be theirs – a weekly market, freedom from toll, a 'croft' along with their 'toft', wide common lands for their peat, wood, stone, and heather, and the king's peace to protect their trade'. Nearly thirty king's burghs had already been established by William and his predecessors, almost all located in the east of the kingdom. The extension of royal power into the south west was followed by the creation of king's burghs at Rutherglen, Lanark,

Dumfries, then at Ayr. 'Read in conjunction with other evidence of the period, the charter gives us our clearest picture of the way in which the monarchy imposed its will and its ideas on outlying districts.' So Pryde continued. 'In many ways the charter of erection of the burgh of Ayr is a memorable document, full of interest for the national as well as the local historian. It is the earliest surviving (and may actually have been the first) charter of foundation of what was then called in Scotland a king's burgh (*burgus domini regis*) and, from the fifteenth century, came to be known as a royal burgh (*burgus regalis*).'

How effectively royal policy was coordinated is

The first part of the burgh to be laid out was probably that part of High Street between Sandgate and the Bridge. Properties adjoining the river possessed their own private wharves, as depicted in this 17th century print.

clearly obvious from the establishment of Ayr as a burgh closely associated with a castle; to be followed soon afterwards by the creation of a sheriffdom, also based on Ayr. One can observe the embryo of the shire in that section of the charter which indicates the burgh's trade precinct, with its five toll checkpoints. Mach was by the Maich burn beyond Kilbirnie on the road to Paisley; Karnebuth beyond Stewarton on the way to Glasgow; Loudoun in the upper Irvine Valley on the way towards Lanark and Edinburgh; Crosencon past Cumnock on the Dumfries road; Lachtalpin near Dalmellington on the Doon Valley road. All the main routes through Cunninghame and Kyle were covered save that by Muirkirk, which may have been little used because of a possibly awkward passage across Kylesmuir. No mention was made of traffic southwards through Carrick, which was presumably not yet fully incorporated though soon to become an integral part of the county of Ayr.

The creation of a new town requires – at any period of history – a certain amount of planning. The nature of the proposed layout will be affected by topography, the natural features of the site; and by man-made elements such as existing settlement, land divisions, and thoroughfares. This particular site occupied a peninsula formed by the River Ayr on its way into the sea. Behind the beach a belt of sand dunes provided a suitable open location for the Castle and the Church of St John. Further inland there was flatter and more fertile terrain fronting the river. That river had slowly but perceptibly been changing its character: not only did the continuing recession of the sea push the estuary further out, but the river cut a deeper bed between steeper banks, though two sills of hard dolerite rock would always impede that

process. Eight hundred years ago the river would be much easier to cross. Four ford crossings have been identified: near the Ratton Quay; where the New Bridge would be erected; just upstream from the Auld Brig; and near the site of Turner's Bridge. As the character of the river altered, so too at different times would one or other of these locations be easiest for crossing. From the River Doon, itself fordable near Doonfoot at an early date, the coastal route leading towards the River Ayr diverged as required, and tracks headed towards each of these four crossings: first by way of what is now Fort Street; a second by the Sandgate; a third which crossed towards the line of the later Newmarket Street; the fourth coming by Barns House and through Carrick Street. There were other ancient routes: that coming up the Doon Valley entering by what is now Kyle Street; another from the Cumnock area following the line of Mill Street. There must have been shorter trails – from the Castle by Academy Lane and crossing the Sandgate; and from the Haven by Boat Vennel and the lower stretch of High Street. All suggesting that the principal river crossing at the beginning of the 13th century was that just upstream from the site of the Auld Brig.

It has been suggested that there was a pre-burghal settlement along the line of the Sandgate, perhaps dating back to a time when the ford by the New Bridge was more popular. It has been further argued that the Sandgate site was unsuitable for further development, and the new planned layout of the year 1205 was located in what became the lower end of High Street. These were the conclusions of William Dodd who, skilled in the techniques of urban geography and modern town planning, described the process as follows: 'As Letchworth, Stevenage or Cum-

The first bridge, dating from the 13th century, was replaced by a stone-built one in 1491. As reconstructed in 1588 it survives as the Auld Brig.

bernauld unmistakably show the planning philosophy and technique of their time, Ayr shows the aims and methods of comprehensive planning of its day. From the predicted demand and using a standard width of plot the length of the required main street was determined. Faced with the existing web of routes along the river bank the designer chose a line for the main street sufficiently far from the river to allow space for the plots, and then laid out the boundaries of this civic space-cum-main street so that the space widened or narrowed to suit the proposed function. The whole space was given a subtle double curve along its length, so that when the frontages were built up the overlapping curved facades virtually closed the space. The plot frontages were measured off along the building line and the plot divisions set off parallel with each other and roughly at right angles to the main street frontage. The tails of the plots were lined up and enclosed to prevent illegal entry to the burgh. Where an existing route met this barrier it was diverted as a back road along the outside and given access only by turning at

right angles and running as a narrow vennel parallel with the burgage plots on either side. Care was taken to ensure that no vennel emerged on the high street opposite another vennel. These staggered openings were a further way of maintaining the enclosure of the space as well as aiding traffic and avoiding confusion of direction. Each entry was controlled by a port or gate enclosure, which also stopped the view out'.

Thus, it has been suggested, there was laid out the High Street, extending as far as the port or gateway just beyond the later Wallace Tower; and the earlier settlement in the Sandgate was appropriately incorporated into the new burgh. This would seem an over-ambitious first development. More likely, the initial phase would be that short stretch from the Sandgate towards the principal ford crossing. The first markets would be held within that street area between where the Malt Cross and the Fish Cross were later to be sited. Quite soon, around 1236, a first bridge was erected. Thereafter buildings plots could be laid out further up High Street, on a new axis, allowing a wider street area for the weekly markets, for the annual midsummer fair that was instituted in 1261, and for the construction of a tolbooth at some unrecorded date.

All this is deduced from examination of relatively recent maps and plans which portray long-established thoroughfares and property divisions and suggest others which have been superseded. For more definite evidence we have only incidental references in documents relating to the 14th and later centuries. There are mentions of tenements in streets whose names are unfamiliar or which appear in the quaint latinised versions of medieval scribes. What we know as the Sandgate is first referred to as the Doongate (*vico de done*, 1348; *in lie donis gait*, 1449) leading to the River Doon or – by another interpretation – to the sand dunes. It also appears more exactly as Sandgate (*vicum arena*, 1428) and once as South Street (*vici australis vocati vici arena*, 1427) before its first mention in the vernacular (*sandegat*, 1518). High Street is even later before appearing under that name. In the 14th century there was a Cammergate (*vico de Canniber*, a.1340; *Camyrgate*, c.1340; *le Camyrgat*, c.1348) which may describe the cambers or bends of Ayr High Street. In the next centuries it seems to have become the Marketgate (*vico communi*, 1415; *vico fori*, 1415) then Main Street (*vico principalis*, 1557), King's Street (*vicus regius*, 1548), which name survived (*the Kingis streit*, 1614) after the first appearance of the modern name (*Hie Street*, 1588). Some of the other early street names are less easy to identify. Woodgate is referred to on numerous occasions from the 14th century (*vico nemoris*, a.1340) till the 17th (*abone the auld Tour in the gait callit the Wodgait*, 1614) and may have been Mill Street, for it is more exactly located (*upoun the eist syd of the Kingis streit*, 1614) though there is some doubt (*the Woodgate, on the west side of the king's street*, 1548, 1585). By 1656 it was being described as *the milgait*. There are isolated references to the Seagate (*vico maris*, 1348), which became the Sea Vennel (*the venall passand to the say*, 1533) and then the Boat Vennel; to what became Carrick Street (*Carric Gate*, 1428); to what may have been called Stonygate or Quarrygate (*vico lapidarii*, 1348); to a Fordgate (*in ly vordgait* 1507) which obviously led to the river; and what became Alloway Street is noted by its older name (*le cowgait*, 1499). In the 15th century vennels are named for the first time: the earliest (*una venella*, 1423) unidentified; Mill Vennel is clearly defined (*the commone Vennell descendand to the Freir Furde*, 1491); the Brig Vennel (*commune venallam pontis*, 1492); Giles Vennel (*lie gilis venell tenden ad ecclesiam sci Johanis a fine pretorii*, 1493), with an alternative name (*the Trinity Vennel, which leads to the parish church*, 1580), following the line of the later Newmarket Street from the tolbooth towards the church. There has been much argument about the Foul Vennel. That name was used sometimes in 18th century council minutes to describe Carrick Street. Yet at an earlier date Carrick Street was specifically designated (*Carric Gate*, 1428). At least once (27.8.1794) the name of Foul Vennel was applied to the Cow Vennel. The three earliest references to the Foul Vennel (*le foull venell*, 1496) describe it as running from north to south, two of them indicate it was crossed by another vennel leading to the parish church, and so possibly an earlier name for Fort Street. The name of Foul Vennel thus seems to have been applied to various thoroughfares on the edge of the town and leading to the faulds. The 16th century saw a proliferation of other named vennels, and the first mention of the ports or gateways which guarded the entrances to the burgh.

Though for the earliest years of the burgh street names (and other details) go unrecorded, we can assume for the years after 1205 an influx of incomers. A careful reading of the charter may suggest that it was the written confirmation by the king of a burgh whose creation he had earlier authorised verbally: 'I have made a burgh at my new castle upon Ayr'; there may be a distinction implied between 'my burgessess dwelling in it' and 'the burgesses who shall come thither to inhabit my burgh'. But 1205 was the date when the burgh was formally established. From other parts of Scotland and further afield men with skills were attracted by the facilities which such a new burgh offered for the practice of trade and manufactures. Such immigrants were allocated tofts within the burgh. On each of these allotments of land would be erected a wooden house fronting the street, and behind it a workshop, yard, and usually an arable patch extending in a long tail rig towards the back dyke. A typical toft, for which an annual money rent of five pence was elsewhere paid, has been assessed as an area of one rood (one sixth of an acre) which would imply for a twenty-foot frontage a tailrig of some 700 feet. But there were variations. In Ayr at the lowest end of High Street the tofts backing on to the river were small (approximately 25 × 135 feet) but presumably convenient enough for merchants who could construct their own private wharves for the loading and unloading of their shallow-draught boats. Even further up High Street and away from the river, only a few of the largest tofts (approximately 25 × 500 feet) approached a rood in area. It was usual for burgesses who had been allocated tofts to be allowed

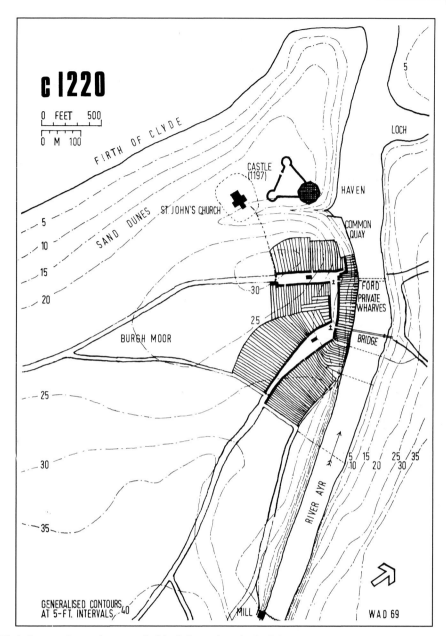

Extension of the High Street shown here probably followed arrival of the Blackfriars in 1230.

a rent-free period for the construction of a dwelling and enclosing dykes – employing others without skills or capital, who could not aspire to become burgesses but who were classed merely as indwellers.

A burgess for the support of his family and dependents would usually require an additional area of farm land to supply immediate needs. So the Ayr charter of 1205 specified that, for an annual rent higher than some other burghs, in addition to the standard toft each burgess might acquire 'six acres of land which they have cleared from wood within the foresaid five pennylands, making their own profit therefrom and paying me twelvepence annually for each toft and six acres adjoining it'. As the five pennylands contained about 2,300 acres, there was ample available. A distant croft, however, was inconvenient for regular cultivation, so places adjacent to the town would be preferred, including land possibly already cleared by existing occupants, who might require to be displaced – though there is no evidence on this point. At any rate, areas round the town suitable for cultivation were acquired, designated as faulds, and in due course enclosed by dykes or ditches. Hence the name of Fauldbacks for that area now occupied by Burns Statue Square. Nearby there were, according to 16th and 17th century records, Snaips Fauld 'in the gait passand to the miln'; Hamfies Fauld 'in the Wodgate'; also the Noltfauld, Freris Fauld, Clerkisfauld. The Foul Calsay, perhaps signifying a road through the faulds, diverged from the Holmston road to take its way past Masonhill towards Loch Fergus. In addition to these arable lands south of the burgh there was the Foul Muir to the west beyond the end of Carrick Street; and, as indicated, the Foul Vennel was probably a road providing access to the faulds.

The burgesses also required pasture for their cattle, and that the town herds led out cattle for grazing by way of what is now Alloway Street is confirmed by its older name of 'the vennel called the Cowgait'. The Burrowfield offered not only ample pasture, but was the source of a wide range of necessary materials. Wood (and later stone) was needed for house-building, turves and heather for roofing, peat for fuel, rushes for floor covering. Demands for timber were insatiable in the medieval economy, since it was an essential element in almost every branch of manufacture. Part of the Burrowfield was wooded (as the charter indicates) and there are references also to the woods of Alloway, Dalrymple, Leglen, and Sanchar over the river – all of which were in course of time cleared away and local supplies of timber exhausted.

Indeed the grant by Alexander II in 1236 of the barony of Alloway may have been specifically designed to provide for the burgh's supply of timber. The burgesses might take 'what is necessary for their own buildings of Ayr, and for making their own boats'. Conservationists would approve the requirement that 'they shall neither burn, nor give away, sell, nor in any wise destroy green wood on the said lands'. This generous award to the new burgh was possibly occasioned by a fortuitous circumstance. We do not know who previously held the barony as vassal of the king and occupied the motte of Alloway, but if he died without issue or tenure otherwise became vacant, some such situation would necessarily precede this new grant. The charter of 1236 gave possession to 'our burgesses of Ayr' in one of the earliest recorded *ad feodofirmam* transactions, conveying the feu of 'five pennyworths of land in Kyle, namely Auilwey, Crottun, and Gortcloy'. These lands of Alloway, Corton, and Carcluie, between the Curtecan Burn and the River Doon, added 2,300 acres to the similar area of the Burrowfield to make Ayr a territorially wealthy burgh.

Notice, however, that while 'our burgesses of Ayr' might take wood from the lands of Alloway, there was no provision for the allocation of arable land or any other rights of use. A later charter of 1324, by which Robert I confirmed that of Alexander II and defined Alloway as a barony, required a three days' supply of fuel and litter for the king's hall, chamber, and kitchen on the occasion of royal visits, these presumably to be obtained from Alloway. But the lands of the barony remained in the possession of residents whose rents from 1236 onwards went to 'our burgesses of Ayr' who were themselves required to pay the crown ten pounds annually on behalf of Alloway. Similarly the crown was entitled to payment from the burgh of the burgesses' annual rents.

When we speak of 'the burgh of Ayr' we tend to think of a kind of self-governing community such as later developed. The designation of 'royal burgh' is proudly accepted as a token of honour and distinction. Yet the term 'royal burgh' and the previous title of 'King's burgh' were precisely used to designate ownership. In the charters of William and later kings reference is always made to 'my burgh' and 'our burgesses' – for the burghs were created by and belonged to the crown, and the burgesses were tenants on crown land. Within the royal administration the sheriff was the king's local representative, acting as military governor, officer of justice, factor of the royal estates, collector of rents and taxes. It was under the close supervision of the Sheriff of Ayr that the new burgh was managed. For purposes of administration, as in any other barony, the superior appointed agents known as bailies, otherwise *ballivi* or *prepositi*. Certain burgesses were chosen by the Sheriff, and – no doubt reluctantly – were made responsible for the thankless tasks of collecting the royal rents and stents; collecting also the petty customs derived from the markets; presiding at the burgh courts as bailies did for so long afterwards; and dealing with an increasing volume of municipal business as the burgh developed.

How burgh affairs were administered can be deduced from passing references. There is a first mention of prepositi in a mandate of Alexander II in 1242 (*prepositi suis de Are*). The first whose names are recorded were Simon Colinson and Adam Petit in 1327. Shortly before 1340 Adam Moor, Sheriff of Ayr, is described as the alderman, with two burgesses acting as bailies. A significant new development ensued. In 1359 though Duncan Wallace was Sheriff, the burgh had its own alderman in Robert Small, a burgess supported by two others as bailies. A further step towards self-government was made by Robert III's charter of

THE FISH CROSS · AYR · 1814 ·

PROVOST DUNLOP,   Mᴿ HUNTER, FANNY COOK,   JENNY BRUCE, NANNIE ROBERTSON, MISS SHAW, Mᴿ PHILIP WHITESIDE (chemist), BROTHERS MORRISON,
                      MARY MORRISON,   DADDY AULD,   LURGAN JOHNNIE (a noted character),

This may have been the original market place, restricted to sale of fish from 1547. The Fish Cross retains its name despite prohibition in 1853 of street sales of fish here.

1400, which introduced a fixed annual payment to the crown known as the *burgh ferme*. Such charters had been granted to various royal burghs since 1319, making them self-governing fiscal units. In the case of Ayr, the 1400 charter confirmed the burgh's rights to its lands, harbour, fishings, mills, petty customs and tolls collected at markets and fair, its burgh court, and converted the rents payable by burgesses into a fixed annual payment of ten pounds. This burgh ferme was supplemented by another ten pounds already payable on behalf of Alloway, and additional stents or levies might of course be required to meet the king's exceptional needs as in time of war. The burgh of Ayr had now an alderman (as the provost was originally entitled) and two bailies, who would soon be assisted by a council, first mentioned in a letter of 1471 from James III to 'the alderman, bailyeis, counsale, and communite of our said burcht of Air'. All burgesses were, like the tenants of any barony,

required to assemble thrice yearly for the head courts of Yule, Whit, and Michaelmas. It became customary for the magistrates and councillors to be nominated at the last of these public assemblies. Though an Act of 1469 attempted to prohibit popular participation, the general body of burgesses in Ayr was – until the 16th century – involved in the election of councillors.

The discovery of fragmentary burgh accounts for the year 1428–29 offers interesting detail of what was going on in Ayr at that time, when the burgh was managed by an alderman and two bailies, with as yet no sign of a council as such. The two bailies, John de Bathgate and Thomas de Carrick, who were responsible for the burgh finances, had to submit to the king's chamberlain a statement of accounts for their year in office. Receipts, though not specified, would include rents from the burgh (*the burgh mails*) and those from Alloway; charges at markets and fairs (*the petty customs*); fines imposed at the burgh and Alloway courts (*unlaws*); minor fees (including *burgess entries*); and what was raised in that year by two special levies (*stents*). Income amounted to £29.0.11d (£29.05). Sums 'awand' were arrears of £1.2.4d (£1.12). This balanced an expenditure of £30.3.3d (£30.17) on items which had to be detailed and provide a most informative list.

Various persons had to be reimbursed for expenses incurred in burgh business. The alderman (who is not named) had to make several journeys, twice making visits to the king. He required 6 merks (£4) 'to passe to the parliament' – and this is the earliest record of Ayr burgh being represented in parliament (as continued till 1707). There are two mysterious payments to 'the aldermannis wyff'. The bailies also had travelling expenses to be paid, one after he 'com ham off cowale', and 15/4 (72½p) when both went to Edinburgh 'qwen thai war sommonit'. There was a town clerk who was paid a fee of 13/4, and if he was 'John Gray, clerk' who was later paid a similar sum, that would give an annual salary of £1.33 in two instalments, plus payments for paper, parchment, and sealing wax. There were also a town's officer (*the serjand*) and another for Alloway, each of whom received 3/4 (17p). In addition there is note of John Lister, an official (*the custumar*) who collected imposts on exports (*the great customs*), an agent of the royal exchequer but paid expenses by the burgh to go 'to the cheker'. There were numerous others obtaining travelling expenses like 'a man til ber a letter till schir jhon kennydy'.

Those were disturbed times requiring payments for guard duty (*the wache*) and for horse patrols (*hors wache that rade*); also purchase of weapons (*14d for twa bows off elm; for half a chaff off arrows 2s and 6d for hedis*); and aid to a French sloop (*wittalyng off a franchs balynger*). Routine expenditure included legal fees (*til a notar for an instrument*), repairing the burgh's money chest (*the byndyn off the common cofer*), checking weights and measures (*selying of the vesel*); also attending to the tolbooth steeple (*burdis to the stepill*), its bell (*byndyn off the commoun bell*) and clock (*a cord to the knoke*). There were contributions to the church, in payments to a chaplain (*to schir davie 13/4, to schir davy 7s*), providing rushes for floor covering (*bent to the kyrk*), and puzzling items (*dychying off the wys of the kyrk*).

There is special human interest in the evidence of sociability associated with business transactions. When the two bailies took over from their predecessors, 6d (2½p) was spent on ale. Entertaining a group of visitors to the town required one shilling's worth of wine. Another six pence was spent sharing a gallon of wine with two bailies from Linlithgow. When a royal official, the Keeper of the Privy Seal, visited Ayr there was a bill of two shillings for wine and fourteen pence for two gallons of ale, amounting in all to 3/4 (17p). The total drinks bill for the year was 15/2, just over 75p and a small sum in modern currency but forming a sizeable 2½% of the burgh budget.

While these burgh accounts reveal some details of municipal administration, another fragmentary contemporary source offers a glimpse of commercial activities. There survives a record of proceedings of the guild court of Ayr for various dates between 1428 and 1432. That guild court was already a century old, for in Robert I's charter of 1325 defining Alloway as a barony there was included an additional award: the master burgesses of Ayr (*dominicis burgensibus nostris*) might have a merchant guild (*gildam suam mercatorium*) with the recognised privileges of foreign trade. That merchants from Ayr were venturing abroad quite soon after the foundation of the burgh is clear. They were involved in the Irish trade by 1237, for in that year Henry II of England instructed the mayor of Drogheda to release the ship and goods of the burgesses of Ayr which had been arrested on suspicion following a robbery at sea. The Exchequer Rolls for 1265 indicate that Ayr was then importing red and white wines from France. Foreign trade was monopolised by those 'master burgesses' who, by paying a quite substantial entry fee, became enrolled in the merchant guild and thus distanced themselves from those other burgesses who were only craftsmen. Many trading enterprises required a pooling of merchants' resources. Thus in 1428 the guild chose five of their number to buy all sea-borne merchandise for equal shares among the guild brethren, and prescribed penalties for individual members who might seek personal profit at the expense of their brethren. Of the five men on the guild committee, four can be identified as having served also as bailies of the burgh. For long afterwards entry to the council was restricted to those burgesses who were members of the merchant guild. Meetings of the guild court were held in the church or the tolbooth, always in the presence of the alderman, with the dean of guild presiding. The dean of guild, elected leader of the merchants, was not yet a member of the burgh council. At the end of the brief surviving record is a list of forty nine guild members, followed by another nineteen who resided outwith the burgh but were recognised as brethren (*confratres gilde extra menentes*).

After its first two centuries of existence, the burgh of Ayr was obviously a thriving community.

THREE

Medieval Church

The parish church of Ayr dedicated to St John the Baptist was an essential adjunct to the burgh founded in the early 13th century. It was situated outwith the burgh precincts – a common enough arrangement – and the substantial structure, as enlarged to provide an appropriate place of worship for three hundred and fifty years, survived to appear on Slezer's view of Ayr in 1693. There it is shown just two hundred yards south west of a mound which marked the site of the long-vanished medieval castle. That castle must have ante-dated the church, which was set up beside the castle, but more than an effective bowshot distant. The church was certainly in existence just a few years after the castle was built in 1197. Within a decade there is mention of Alan the archdeacon in a document dated between 1202 and 1207. In 1225 there was a chapter meeting held in Ayr, which implies the existence of a church. In 1233 there was another meeting, explicitly described as held within the church of Ayr, and involving Alan as *magister scholarum de Are*. The Church of St John may have replaced an earlier chapel which was located further up-river. The first actual mention of its dedication to St John occurs in 1261 when the burgh was granted the privilege of holding an annual fair, appropriately on the feast day of St John the Baptist, 24 June, and for fifteen days following. Veneration of St John was particularly marked in the early 13th century, following the donation of his reputed head on a golden salver to Amiens Cathedral in 1207. So the burgh, sometimes known as Newcastle-upon-Ayr, was otherwise described as St John's Town of Ayr.

The medieval parish church was cruciform in layout and of considerable size and magnificence. Its high altar was near the west end of Citadel Place. At the other end of the nave, above the west door, a circular Gothic window caught the rays of the setting sun – till, perhaps in the 15th century, there was erected a tower which is all that survives of the ancient church. Within the church there were principal altars to the Blessed Virgin, the Holy Rood, the Holy Blood, and the Holy Trinity; with others in the aisles to Saint Michael, Saint Peter, Saint Nicholas, and Saint Ninian. These altars were donated by generous benefactors. Only one is recorded, that of the Holy Trinity founded in 1322 by Simon Loccart of Lee and endowed with ten marks per annum. Later the eight altars were supplemented by another founded, sometime before 1532, by the craftsmen of the burgh to the patron saints of their respective trades. Also, from 1306 till the surprisingly late date of 1599, smaller sums for anniversary masses were provided by devout parishioners. Sixty four such persons recorded in the *Obit Book of St John's* were of middling rank, mostly burgesses (but only two of them wealthier merchants of the guild) plus ten who were apparently not burgesses and another seven who were churchmen. What the medieval Church of St John was like has been described by a local historian in sympathy with the old faith: 'The interior can only be guessed at, but surely it was splendidly in keeping with the importance of this royally-visited kirk with its many altars, its two great bells, its monk-built organ and its band of choristers and clerics chanting the requiem Masses which were so much in demand by the ordinary citizens at the time of the Obit Book. In those far-off days of pageantry and symbolic spectacle, the burgess of Ayr who had donated the small annual rent for an obit Mass thereby assured himself a memorable funeral, with kirk bells tolling, choir singing his 'dirige', and bellmen perambulating to the outmost bounds of the burgh to remind the burgesses to pray for the soul of the departed, and also to call the poor and the leprous to attend Mass and receive the funeral alms'.

The patron of St John's Church was the king, and the teinds from the wealthy parish of Ayr were devoted largely to the support of the Church elsewhere – Glasgow Cathedral from 1327, Melrose Abbey for a time in the 14th century, then from 1502 the Chapel Royal at Stirling. The crown also held the patronage of the much smaller parish church of

The Church of St John the Baptist, first mentioned in 1233, was extended to become an impressive place of worship, as shown in this 17th century print.

Alloway, of which little is known save that it may have been dedicated to St Mungo. Revenues from Alloway were also in the 16th century appropriated to the Chapel Royal, as with other churches in King's Kyle – Dalrymple, Dalmellington, and Coylton. This system of appropriation meant that the person nominated by the crown and appointed by the bishop of Glasgow as Rector of St John's of Ayr would be engaged in duties elsewhere and would seldom if ever minister in Ayr parish. Though a vicar was appointed to deputise, that charge became a sinecure as well. Parochial duties were performed by a curate, maintained by a smaller stipend taken from the residue of the teinds.

The Church of St John as the kirk of the royal burgh of Ayr was served by the curate who was its parish priest, assisted by a parish clerk (first noted in 1449), also eight chaplains and a band of choristers. The chaplains were appointed by and paid by the burgh, which controlled the altar endowments. The chaplains' stipends were derived from the rents of those small properties which had been bequeathed to endow obit masses; augmented by fees for services as notaries, clerks, and teachers. The choir also was supported by many of the donations listed in the *Obit Book*. The choristers were local boys who were provided with appropriate training within the church. As early as 1233 there was mention of Alan as 'master of the schools of Ayr'. These schools were classes in the church where the boys were taught singing; also Latin as used in the Mass, necessary for choristers and any potential priests among them. That the 'schools of Ayr' continued to operate throughout the medieval period is evident. In 1535 the burgh council appointed Robert Paterson 'to play on the organis, sing in quier, and to teiche ane sang scule'. For the teaching of Latin they appointed Andrew McCormyll in 1502 as 'instructor for the time being of grammatical studies in the burgh of Ayr'. One obit of 1524 included gifts to 'poor scholars' as well as to 'the old poor and leprous'. Alms took the form of money, of this order were set up by the king, and of these Ayr seems to have been the first, instituted in 1230.

The Dominican friary of Ayr was provided with a site beside the river, at a time when the burgh was just fifteen years old and in the first phase of development. The original part of High Street extended from the Sandgate parallel to the river. Continued building along that line would have been eventually blocked by the new friary and its grounds, which could explain the sharp turn in the High Street above the Fish Cross, and possibly explains the mysterious name of Cambergate. The site of the friary is commemorated by the name Blackfriars Walk. Of the buildings of the friary there is no trace, though it is known they contained a church dedicated to Saint Katherine, with altars to the Trinity and to Saint Duthac, and within the cloisters was a chapel to Saint Mary. The friary's front entrance was in High Street, just north of where the Wallace Tower would be much later erected. In the grounds of the friary were gardens and an orchard; a cemetery; Saint Katherine's Well, long famed for the remedial properties of its water; and a dovecot which gave its name to the nearby Doocot ford, as the Friars ford was also known.

This Dominican house was served by a prior and other friars, a charter of 1557 naming nine in all at that time. Other documents indicate that some friars were from local families, no doubt trained here, for each Dominican house was required to have its own school. In 1509 one such friar 'renounced all his father's lands, as being dead to the world' – in such terms expressing the loss of secular status by one who had taken the vows of the order. The principal function of the Black friars was preaching and spreading the faith. Thus in 1261 a Dominican from Ayr collected a papal tax to help finance a crusade. They also said prayers and sang Masses for many who chose to be buried in the cemetery of the Blackfriars. One such wealthy burgess in 1348, in return for 'light to be burned on the high altar', bequeathed all his estate to the friars. This comprised six houses and ten plots of land within the burgh, sixty four acres of the Burrowfield, and fishing rights on the River Doon.

The Dominican house in Ayr was initially endowed by Alexander II in 1242 with annual payments of twenty pounds, specifically set aside from the royal revenue as a first charge on the rents the crown derived from the burgh of Ayr – 'out of the readiest fermes of our mills and our burgh of Ayr'. That substantial income was augmented by those donors who rewarded the friary for performing requiem Masses. While obits

The Tower of St John, all that survives of the medieval church, was possibly built in the 15th century with stones from the nearby Castle of Ayr, which had by then been abandoned.

sometimes cake, bread, cheese, fresh fish, or venison. Some obits also included payments to the sacristan, to the ringer of 'the great bells of the church', and to the bellman 'who shall go through the streets with a loud voice' – all this indicating the range of personnel and practice in the medieval parish church of Ayr.

While the secular clergy operated the system of parish churches, their work was complemented by the regular clergy of the various monastic and preaching orders. In the year 1230 Alexander II welcomed into Scotland a body of Friars Preachers who were also known (being followers of Dominic) as Dominicans or (from their robes) as Black Friars. Eight houses

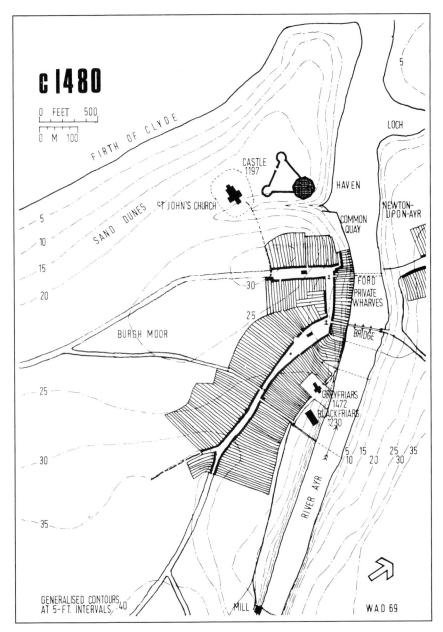

The Blackfriars after several centuries in Ayr acquired extensive properties in the neighbourhood, unlike the later Greyfriars.

in the parish church were financed by annual rents from various properties within the town, those at St Katherine's in the friary attracted also gifts of land. Though the Dominicans were originally a mendicant order, they obtained papal permission to hold temporal property, and the Friars Preachers of Ayr became considerable landowners. Charters record various properties acquired between 1336 and 1541. Neighbouring lairds as well as local burgesses made generous awards. Lands outwith the burgh were obtained, most notably Dankeith in Symington parish from 1411. Eventually there passed into the hands of the Blackfriars a great tract of land extending from the friary upriver and across the Burrowfield beyond Castlehill towards the upland bounds of Ayr parish. The Church of St John, by comparison, possessed only the upland farm of Rudeland and the two small patches of Chapelfauld and Clerksfauld.

The Friars Preachers' original royal endowment in 1242 of an annual £20 was derived partly from the revenue of the burgh mills. In 1328 Robert I further provided the friars with freedom from multures – allowing them to have meal ground without payment; and to have priority over others at the mills. The burgh council argued that this superseded the award of 1242 and allowed the annual payments of £20 to fall into arrears, till in 1389 the rights of the friars were fully upheld. When in 1400 Robert II introduced a burgh ferme, replacing the various rents with a fixed annual payment of £10 to the crown from the burgh, there were arguments as to how the friars' total of £20 should be made up. In 1406 it was finally decided that the Blackfriars should thereafter receive only £10 annually in cash, but would be compensated with ownership of the mills. These were 'the mill of Ayr, of Merlyngburn, and of Lochmylburn, with two cruives in the mill dam of Ayr'. The burgesses and others would pay the friars as multures 'threepence for each boll of corn ground', and the salmon trapped in the cruives would further augment the quite considerable wealth of the Ayr house of Blackfriars.

Another order of friars became established in Ayr in the 15th century. There had arrived in Scotland in 1231, just a year after the Dominicans, those Friars Minor who were known also as Grey Friars or Franciscans. But more than two centuries would pass before their work of evangelism brought them to settle in Ayr. According to a chronicle of the order, 'When the fragrant report which spread abroad concerning the friars who had come to Glasgow, reached the ears of the inhabitants of Ayr, they did not rest until in the year 1474 they possessed a complete monastery for the friars'. That this occurred after the burgh's dispute with the Black Friars had been settled, at the burgh's expense, and perhaps with some continued resentment, is perhaps an explanation of the belated invitation to this other order of friars. As compared with the Dominican Black Friars, who acquired considerable property and wealth, the Franciscan Grey Friars remained faithful to the vows of poverty that their founder Saint Francis of Assisi had preached, especially the Observatine Franciscans who came to Ayr and insisted upon the 'poor and scanty use' of earthly goods. All they required was a restricted site just upriver from the Auld Brig where the pope in 1481 agreed to their building a habitation with church, altars, a little belfry, dormitory, refectory, cemetery, and gardens. 'Thither (according to the chronicle) resorted a great throng of merchants confessing to the fathers, of whom twenty spent their daily life there. In the church of the friars the blessed Virgin May, the mother of God, was worshipped with the

The seal of Robert of Linlithgow, prior of the Blackfriars, from a charter of 1406.

highest veneration by the throng of Christians, and through her prayers and merits many miracles were wrought there'.

The Franciscans settled on a spot where a chapel may have been located before the formation of the burgh, an area under cultivation from the 13th till the 15th century, when it was inundated with wind-blown sand. When an exploratory excavation was undertaken in 1982 (as the Butter Market Close was being cleared for British Home Stores) other finds provided some evidence that despite the waste site the 'Franciscan friary was more resplendent than has hitherto been supposed', with finely-traced glazed windows. For the friars James IV provided a chasuble of rich red cloth with a golden cross, other imported cloth to make an alb, and sufficient silver to make a chalice. There were other gifts of cash and kind from the king – including two bolls of barley yearly. Similar donations came from local landowners, such as a bequest in 1530 of £40 plus two pairs of blankets, three bed rugs, and a needlework bed cover. The burgh council made regular contributions of wine and salt, and was particularly generous in 1537 with three hogsheads of wine costing £12.14/- (£12.70) plus 10/- (50p) in cash. With such gifts, and from begging, the Franciscans lived in austere poverty and gave help to the poor and leprous. They held no property save an acre or so at the friary and (perhaps) as much again at their barns beside the harbour. No documents relating to them have been preserved. The names of only a few of the friars get passing mention in other records. The extent of their local influence can only be guessed.

Another medieval religious establishment was situated outwith the town in the Burrowfield, a hospice or spittal dedicated at St Leonard, at Doonlee on the northern side of the Curtecan burn. Such houses catered for a variety of purposes, and St Leonard's seems to have been a general purpose institution providing for the poor, the sick, the aged and infirm, and for travellers. Who founded it and when is unknown, and how it was staffed is equally uncertain. It must have been in existence long before 1425 when it was 'at present ruinous and endowed with rents so poor that the poor cannot be received and maintained there as was customary'. In that year it was repaired and endowed by John Gray, possibly a native of Ayr, who was a graduate in arts and medicine and holder of various important royal appointments. Among these was archdeacon of Whithorn, and for pilgrims travelling thither St Leonard's could be a convenient place to lodge. From 1425 till 1549 there is record of chaplains or preceptors appointed by the crown to serve here, and in 1546 there is note of adjacent lands which had been donated to St Leonard's. There were forty acres between St Leonard's and 'the Carrouchanburn at its new bridge'; Lampotfauld, three acres in extent, 'between the Sclaitbog, the Spittalbog, the lands of Garrot-roding, and the Twa Stane Croce'; and sixteen acres of Whitestanes.

Lands were possessed also by other agencies of the Church. The Trinitarians of Fail (belonging to the Order of Holy Trinity for the Redemption of Captives) held a piece beside St Leonard's later known as Harperland or Slaphouse; also a tenement in the town in Trinity Vennel, no doubt named after them. In the upland reaches of the parish, Abbothill was held by Crossraguel Abbey, and Melrose Abbey had perhaps a neighbouring patch. In the same area was Nunsland, held for a time by the Nuns of North Berwick who had more extensive properties in Maybole parish, as well as a property within Ayr burgh not far from the Dominican friary. The burgh also contained several Templar tenements. The 12th century crusading Poor Knights of Christ and the Temple of Solomon were awarded properties in all the royal burghs of Scotland and, when that order was suppressed in the 14th century, these and their other possessions were taken over by the Knights of the Hospital of St John of Jerusalem. Though now administered by the Hospitallers, the properties continued to be known as Temple lands, and a list of these made in 1540 included nearly a hundred within Ayrshire. There were a dozen within the royal burgh of Irvine, but only five can be attributed to Ayr, though there was another in Newton and at least two in Prestwick. The

one Templar property which can be precisely located is first noted in 1470 as situated on the east side of the vennel from the market cross to the water, and next to the newly-built house of John Blair of Adamton. In 1521 it was recognised as a place of sanctuary – 'is and has been an asylum girth and refuge to the said man for twenty four hours because it is a Templar Tenement of St John'. There is note of a Templar court held there in 1532, presided over by David Campbell who as templar-bailie was responsible for collecting the rents and administering all the templar properties within the sheriffdom of Ayr.

Throughout Kyle there is further evidence of how highly-organised was the medieval Church. In King's Kyle there were seven parishes – Ayr, Alloway, Dalrymple, Dalmellington, Coylton, Ochiltree, and Cumnock. Each parish church was served by a vicar or curate of the regular clergy, and in each case the teinds were appropriated to finance the Chapel Royal in Stirling (the first five), Melrose Abbey (Ochiltree), or Glasgow Cathedral (Cumnock). But outwith the burgh of Ayr there was no significant presence of the regular orders of monks and friars. It was a rather different situation across the water in Stewart Kyle. In the eastern uplands, Melrose Abbey possessed the wide lands of Barmuir and Kylesmuir and held the parish church of Mauchline. Closer at hand the Trinitarians had their principal Scottish house at Fail near Tarbolton, and these so-called Red Friars held other properties throughout Stewart Kyle, as well as appropriating the churches of Galston, Symington, the now-vanished parish of Barnweil, plus two outwith the county. Tarbolton church itself was held by Fail, then Melrose, and latterly Glasgow Cathedral. All other parishes in Stewart Kyle belonged to Paisley Abbey – Auchinleck, Craigie, Riccarton, Dundonald, Crosbie, Monkton, Prestwick, and St Quivox. Just over the river from the burgh of Ayr, Newton had a chapel, erected at some unknown date, dedicated to the Virgin Mary. Also within the parish of Prestwick was the spittal of Kincase, dedicated to St Ninian, famed as a leper house, and probably established before Robert Bruce reputedly patronised it. In Monkton parish was a celebrated chapel, Our Lady Kirk of Kyle, described as 'a kind of medieval Carfin' to which resorted pilgrims from all parts of Scotland.

One local historian already quoted has looked back to 'the actuality of the past when Ayrshire was part of the universal, everlasting Church and the catholic religion was not something new or foreign, but the original faith and the formative influence of the shire and the nation'. An earlier commentator, though his presbyterian background made him less sympathetic to the old faith, was no less convinced of the important role in society occupied by the medieval Church. In his contribution to the New Statistical Account he wrote: 'From these notices of the religious establishment of Ayr, it would appear that the town had borne its full share in supporting the superstition of the times, and that the people had been by no means lukewarm in the cause of religion, according to the light which they then enjoyed'.

FOUR

Local and National

During the first centuries of the burgh's existence while its institutions were evolving, external events made their impact upon the local scene.

In the early part of the 13th century Ayrshire enjoyed a period of relative peace which allowed the burgh to become securely established, and benefit from the generous royal grants made by Alexander II (1214–49) and Alexander III (1249–86). Between 1205 and 1261 Ayr acquired extensive lands; a weekly market and an annual fair; a harbour with fishing, shipbuilding, and foreign trade; and the town was equipped with parish church, friary, bridge, and corn mills. Details of these follow, in summary form if elsewhere noted. The lands comprised the entire parish of Ayr (as awarded in 1205) to which Alloway was added (in 1236). The weekly market on Saturday (as from 1205) was joined (after 1261) by an annual midsummer fair on 24 June and for fifteen days following. These would be held in the vicinity of the market cross (though such a cross gets no mention before 1460). There is one 13th century hint of a tolbooth and jail in the High Street (though again no definite record before 1427). The burgh acquired the royal fishing rights of Ayr and Doon (1236) to help improve the harbour, while the grant of Alloway in the same year included the provision of wood for shipbuilding. Ships from Ayr are noted as trading with Ireland (1237) and France (1265). The parish church was probably in being before 1205 and the Black Friars arrived in 1230. The bridge is first mentioned in 1236, possibly already built, for the royal fishing rights were to contribute towards its maintenance (*ad sustentationem pontis*). This would be a wooden structure typical of the period. It is difficult to accept a 19th century tradition that ascribes its erection to the munificence of 'two maiden ladies of the name of Lowe, who, commiserating the loss of life occasioned through persons attempting to enter the Town by one or other of the fords then in use, spent their fortune upon the undertaking'. This

story is embroidered in one version which has a knight drowned while crossing to meet his mistress Isobel Lowe; in another version both sisters are in love with two monks who are drowned while crossing over to Newton Castle – whether attempting to escape their clutches or visited by divine retribution is not clear! In 1242 the Black Friars were endowed with some revenue from the royal mills. Of these, that which became known as the Nether Mill was presumably the earliest. Appropriately, on the road leading to that mill there would be erected those Barns where grain could be stored. This catalogue indicates how the burgh had developed before it was affected by its first real crisis.

This did not come, as might have been expected, from trouble in Galloway. When Alan, lord of Galloway, died in 1234 there was certainly dissension and a revolt that had to be quelled. But Ayr seems not to have been directly involved, unless Alexander II's two munificent grants of 1236 were rewards for services rendered by the burgh to the king in his work of pacification. Galloway was again settled. The lordship was awarded to Alan's daughter Dervorguila and her husband John Balliol, parents of the future King John. In Carrick Earl Neil, who died in 1256, was also succeeded by a daughter, Marjorie. For her second husband she would in 1272 choose Robert Bruce, son of the lord of Annandale – literally, according to a legend which says she had him kidnapped. Their son, born at Turnberry in 1274, would eventually win the crown as Robert I.

Alexander II turned from Galloway to the Western Isles which were in Norwegian hands, and advances made in that area brought retaliation in the reign of his son Alexander III. In 1263 King Haakon of Norway brought his fleet into the Firth of Clyde. One account, manifestly exaggerated, has the Norwegians besieging Ayr, storming its castle, and despoiling Carrick and Kyle. The Exchequer Rolls provide more definite evidence. They record Alexander III

A statue to William Wallace near the site of the Old Tolbooth commemorates his reputed imprisonment there and his associations with Ayr during the Wars of Independence.

at Ayr making preparations for defence. Ships were built for the king. How many were provided – at a cost of £60.15.8d (£60.78) – is not detailed, but 200 oars were supplied. The castle was put into a state of readiness. It was defended with the aid of great catapults called ballista. For defenders with crossbows, 1,170 querrellis or bolts were required. That fact suggests there was some fighting, and an account for the repair of buildings within the castle indicates some damage before the attackers were repulsed. The quantity of foodstuffs requisitioned is evidence of a large garrison. One hundred and twenty men had to be supplied for three weeks, in place of the burgesses of Ayr who apparently failed to do guard duty at the castle as the sheriff required. The person appointed to take charge of the castle at this critical time was Walter, Earl of Menteith, to whom the lordship of Arran had been awarded by the king. His expenses included payments to spies who kept watch on the Norwegian fleet anchored in Lamlash bay. Alexander III played

a waiting game, prolonging negotiations till, late in the autumn of 1263, the invasion threat was removed by the battle of Largs.

Before the century was out, Ayr was even more closely involved in a greater national crisis, with the Wars of Scottish Independence. Following upon the death of Alexander III and an uncertain succession, the two most obvious claimants were old Robert Bruce (grandfather of the future king) and John Balliol, both descended from the younger brother of William the Lion. Edward I of England, whose aid was sought as arbiter, in 1291 required fealty to be sworn at various places including what was still called 'the new castle on Ayr'. Here oaths of allegiance to Edward as overlord were administered by Robert Stewart, bishop of Glasgow; James the Stewart, who had recently succeeded Andrew Murray as sheriff of Ayr; and Sir Nicholas Seagrave, the newly-appointed English keeper of the castles of Ayr and Dumbarton. At Berwick, Balliol was chosen and ascended the throne as King John (1292–96). In 1296 Edward I invaded Scotland, forced John's abdication, and imposed English rule through control of the royal castles and sheriffdoms. Ayr merchants, for example, were required to send their wool to the English headquarters at Berwick. The sheriff of Ayr, who was now Sir Reginald Craufurd of Loudoun, had to submit. Discontent was expressed in the rising of 1297.

The resistance movement found its first leader in William Wallace. His father was a vassal of James the Stewart, overlord of Stewart Kyle; his mother was a sister of Sir Reginald Craufurd, the sheriff. He was born at Elderslie in Renfrewshire, or (as local patriots would have it) at Ellerslie in the Kyle parish of Riccarton, which belonged to the Wallace family. Certainly he was closely associated with Kyle. According to one of the numerous legendary tales, his first clash with the English was at Riccarton in a fight with five soldiers while fishing in the River Irvine beside 'the bickering bush'. Further down-river, at some time or another, he is reputed to have fought a pitched battle at Irvine's Puddleford. He took refuge on the banks of the River Ayr (where there are several 'Wallace's Caves') and Leglen on the estate of the the Wallaces of Auchincruive has long been noted. The young Robert Burns 'walked half a dozen miles to pay my respects to the Leglen wood, with as much devout enthusiasm as ever Pilgrim did to Loretto; and ... I explored every den and dell where I could suppose my heroic Countryman to have sheltered'. Appropriately there is a Leglen cairn, erected in 1929 as memorial to both Wallace and Burns.

From Leglen, Wallace made several reputed excursions into the burgh of Ayr, and encounters with soldiers of the English garrison. One braggard he killed with his staff and slew another four companions; on another occasion he knived a greedy and aggressive steward. When he was making an escape upriver, one athletic leap left imprinted in the rock 'Wallace's Heel', still visible beside the River Ayr Walk by Holmston Road. No more credible, one story has him captured and confined within the Castle or (by another version) the tolbooth in High Street. He pined away in captivity on a diet of herrings and water, till he was thought dead and his body thrown over the wall; but rescued and revived by his old nurse. This is commemorated by a statue erected in 1810 by Henry Cowan on the wall of his house in Newmarket Street, near the site of the old Tolbooth. A second statue can be seen further up High Street, installed in 1834 when there was rebuilt the Wallace Tower, which has in fact no known connection with the patriot hero. The most celebrated of Wallace's local exploits is the Burning of the Barns of Ayr. Several of the local gentry were (at some time or another) summoned to a conference in the Castle of Ayr, where (it is said) they were treacherously seized and hanged. In retaliation Wallace and his adherents surrounded the barns where English soldiers were billetted and set them on fire, burning the occupants to death. Other soldiers who were lodged nearby in the house of the Blackfriars were massacred by the holy men in what became known as 'the Friars' Blessing'. The Barns must have been those near the Blackfriars on the road to the mill, that is in Mill Street rather than at Barns Park elsewhere in the town. After the incident Wallace retired to that upland spot where he could observe that 'The Barns of Ayr burn weel!' But the parish of Barnweil almost certainly had that designation before Wallace supposedly gave it a name. The whole story, like many others such as the vision revealed to him in Monkton kirk, contains much that is apocryphal. Certainly William Wallace performed various feats of daring which laid the foundations of his immense and long-lasting popular reputation. In 1297 he slew the English sheriff of Lanark; about the same time he mustered a fighting force at Mauchline; ambushed near Loudoun Hill a convoy of stores on their way to Ayr; and as leader of a company of irregular troops set off to operate elsewhere in Scotland.

Meanwhile young Robert Bruce took action. His aged grandfather had died two years before, and while his father was lord of Annandale the future king was now Earl of Carrick. Twenty-two years old (possibly

The common seal of the burgh, dated before 1340, shows the Castle as a stone-built structure. The previous castle burned down in 1298 by Bruce's orders may have been the original wooden structure. The new stone castle was built and held by the English from 1301 till 1312, when it was taken by Bruce who as King Robert I held parliaments in Ayr in 1312 and in 1315.

four years younger than Wallace) Robert Bruce early in 1297 hurried from Annandale towards Ayrshire: 'I must join my own people and the nation in which I was born'. Wallace's rising was obviously only part of an organised and coordinated scheme. To deal with this an English force under Henry Percy and Robert Clifford was rushed via Annandale and Nithsdale to reach Ayr by the end of June. They found Bruce and his men from Carrick with other magnates near Irvine, and after negotiations arranged for a submission on 9 July. Nevertheless Wallace's victory at Stirling Bridge on 11 September revived hopes. Though Edward I himself came north in 1298 and won a victory at Falkirk, when he reached Ayr at the end of August he found the town evacuated and the Castle burned down by Bruce's orders so that they would be of no use to the English. It has been judged that for the next five years Scotland was effectively freed from English interference. Only in 1303 after two campaigns by Edward I was his control re-established. In 1301 Ayr and Turnberry were taken. English nominees were appointed as sheriff of Ayr (Sir Montesin de Noielan) and governor of Ayr Castle (Sir Edmund de Mauley) and with the aid of Patrick, earl of March, effectively quelled the opposition. In 1302 Bruce again submitted. In 1305 Wallace was captured and executed. For

Bruce is said to have founded the burgh of Newton. It was actually established by a member of the Stewart family between 1314 and 1371. The market cross once stood in the middle of Main Street.

– Dalmilling just outside Ayr. Reinforcements of six men-at-arms and 300 archers were brought in to hold Ayr Castle under James de Dalilegh while another 300 infantry were despatched to hunt for Bruce in Carrick. These were ambushed at Glentrool by Bruce, who broke out and defeated Valence at Loudounhill about 10 May. On 7 July Edward I died on his way north, his army was halted at Cumnock on 25 August, and Edward II retired to England. Bruce undertook the slow process of asserting control over his kingdom. How difficult is evident, for Loch Doon Castle remained in English hands till 1311, and the Castle of Ayr probably till just before a meeting of the Scots parliament at Ayr in 1312. The victory at Bannockburn in 1314 was far from decisive, and the war dragged on till 1328.

In 1315, however, Robert I was securely enough established when he returned to Ayr to hold that parliament in the Church of St John which would settle the succession. If the king died without male heirs, he would be followed by his brother Edward and his heirs; failing whom his daughter Marjorie and her heirs. Edward Bruce in 1316 left Ayr for an expedition to Ireland, where he was killed. When Robert I died at Cardross in 1329, his five-year-old son would succeed as David II (1329–71). Thereafter the crown passed to the first of the Stewart kings, Robert II (1371–90), son of Marjorie Bruce and Walter the Stewart whom she married in 1315, with her father's consent, just after the parliament of Ayr.

From 1312 the burgh of Ayr was released from the pressure of an army of occupation, the repeated disturbances of local military action, and the interruptions to regular commerce. So long as the war continued there was the necessity of military service, which involved not only the feudal landowners who served as cavalry, but the landless men who served as infantry. All able-bodied men were liable, as in 1303 when Bruce as sheriff of Ayr and Lanark was required by Edward I to call up one thousand picked footmen from Kyle, Cunninghame, and Cumnock; plus another thousand as required from Carrick and Galloway. Such a drain of long wars on the economy can be imagined, at a time when the total Ayrshire population was not much more than 40,000. Apart from this, near-normal conditions were restored locally. In 1313 the privileges of royal burghs were confirmed, including exemption of burgesses from military service. Here as elsewhere lands of opponents were confiscated and supporters were rewarded, though only one example is found, in 1317, of a burgess of Ayr being dispossessed. In 1325 Robert I confirmed the burgh's tenure of the barony

eleven years from 1301 till 1312 the castle and burgh of Ayr were in English hands. English records reveal the castle repaired, reinforced, and garrisoned – that masons as well as carpenters were employed in 1307 indicates that the castle was now reconstructed in stone. Arrangements were made for the regular collection of the burgh ferme and the dues from royal lands within King's Kyle. The garrison was supplied with victuals from Ireland.

In 1305 Robert Bruce made his bid for the throne. With benefit of historical hindsight we can present the ensuing events as logical steps towards an inevitable victory. In fact it was a slow and uncertain progression. From Dumfries, where he slew John Comyn, he went to Scone to be enthroned, but before the end of the year he had fled into exile. The castles of Ayr and Turnberry remained in English hands, and Henry Percy made Crossraguel Abbey his headquarters. 1307 saw Bruce's return via Arran to Carrick, whose hill country provided a perilous base. Aymer de Valence, Earl of Pembroke, appointed by Edward I as his governor in Scotland, directed operations from Dalmolin

The mills of Ayr were bestowed by the crown to the Blackfriars, then passed into the hands of the burgh. The original mill of Ayr became known as the Nether Mill after it was joined by others upriver.

of Alloway and extended Ayr's privileges. In 1328 he similarly augmented those of the Friars Preachers.

It appears very likely that at this time there was a new development on the other side of the River Ayr. There seems to have been a community of some sort in the 13th century called the Newton (*novam villam*, 1219 × 1230; *Neuton juxta Are*, c.1280). Tradition has it that this was constituted a burgh by Robert I and its freedom granted to forty eight individuals who had distinguished themselves at Bannockburn. But Newton-upon-Ayr, like Prestwick, was and remained a burgh of barony under the lords of Stewart Kyle. Most likely it was founded sometime between 1314 and 1371 by Walter the Stewart or his son before he ascended the throne as Robert II. The name of Robert I is also closely associated with the spittal of St Ninian at Kincase, which he is supposed to have founded and where there is a Bruce's Well still. The spittal of Kincase was probably already in existence, and it seems that he awarded to it the land of Robertloan, now known as the Loans, in Dundonald parish near Troon. Kincase was a leper house, and Bruce was latterly afflicted with a skin complaint of some sort. One tradition is that he contracted leprosy here while

on a visit; another that he received treatment, which justified his donation.

Before the end of Robert I's reign the local area was thus apparently returning to normality, and though it would be misleading to present a picture of steady progress in the 14th and 15th centuries, there were certainly some notable advances within the burgh.

The institution of a merchant guild by Robert I's charter grant of 1325 allowed the master burgesses who became guild brothers to extend their cooperative ventures in foreign trade. There were (as noted in chapter 2) developments in how the burgh was administered. In 1327 appear Ayr's first named *prepositi*. These bailies were still agents of the sheriff. Sir Adam Moor, referred to as sheriff of Ayr in 1329, was responsible for administration of the extensive royal lands which now included not only King's Kyle, but Bruce's earldom of Carrick, and the bailiary of Cunninghame which had been forfeited to the crown as part of the Balliol estates; he was also (before 1340) officiating as alderman of Ayr burgh, supported by two burgesses who were designated bailies and operated as his agents. A new development towards burghal self-government appeared by 1359

The Overmill may have been built in the 15th century though 1594 is first mention of that name in the burgh records. Demolition in 1963 made way for the Overmills Bridge on the by-pass.

when Duncan Wallace was sheriff, and the alderman (Robert Small) and the two bailies were all burgesses. Fiscal responsibility followed Robert III's charter of 1400 instituting a fixed annual burgh ferme payable to the crown. As alderman Reginald de Fynvyk (1401, 1406) was followed by another of that family, after whom Fenwickland must have been named. Nicholas de Fynvyk in 1415 and 1416 went to the expense of obtaining copies of four old charters, obviously to ascertain the extent of the burgh's privileges. In 1418 a complaint was made 'on behalf of the burgesses and community' that the sheriff of Ayr, Hugh Campbell of Loudoun, had seized goods of burgesses because they had refused to do military service on his instructions, when – it was argued – 'all the burgesses of the king were exempt from the compulsion of the sheriffs'. In 1427 there is note of the alderman and bailies sitting in open court (*in plana curia*) with fifteen of the best men of the town, for the specific purpose of dealing with damage done to the Sandgate by blowing sand. A regular burgh council, elected by the burgesses at the Michaelmas headcourt, replaced government by nominated officials sometime before 1471 (when a council is first noted). There was proof of continued

commercial expansion. James II's charter of 1458 confirmed all previous grants and supplemented the Midsummer Fair (on the Feast Day of St John the Baptist, 24 June, and for fifteen days following) with a Michaelmas Fair (on the Feast Day of St Michael and four days following). Next year the sheriff, Sir George Campbell, attempted to interfere in the running of this new fair and compel attendance at the sheriff court. This resulted in formal recognition of the independence of the burgh court, as the only court to which might be summoned burgesses and indwellers within Ayr and tenants and other inhabitants of the barony of Alloway. So before the end of the 15th century the burgh had won administrative, judicial, fiscal, and commercial independence, and in 1429 – if not before – representation in parliament as one of the royal burghs.

Meanwhile the town was obviously being improved. That the original wooden dwellings were being replaced by more substantial structures is evident from mention of stone houses in documents of 1340 and 1348. Beside the market cross in High Street a Tolbooth was erected. If, as has been guessed, a gaol was here at the time of Wallace, an improved

A notorious occasion in the Ayrshire feuds involved the assassination in 1602 of Sir Thomas Kennedy of Culzean. Coming from Greenan by Doonfoot, he was ambushed among the sand hills near St Leonard's Chapel.

building would be required later. The Tolbooth, first mentioned in 1427, provided a meeting place for the council after it was constituted. A stone-built Auld Brig also dates from the 15th century, for in 1491 masons were at work on it. That they were then engaged in construction rather than repair seems clear, because James IV on pilgrimage to Whithorn that year had to be ferried across the river, and returning on 15 November gave ten shillings 'to the massonis of the bryg off Air'. In the same year is a first mention of 'the quarell of Air', and in 1529 five quarrymasters were working stone beyond the Townhead. Up-river, from 1406 there were three mills to supply the growing town. The Mill of Ayr, as it was then called, became known later (1594) as the Nether Mill. Another nearby, perhaps the waukmill for fulling cloth noted in 1488, was situated beside the Lochmylburn or Lichtmylburn. The Over Mill, so called from 1594, and described as of the Merlyngburn, supplemented the Nether Mill for grinding corn.

That grain production in the area was considerable is evident from the existence of other corn mills in the vicinity – north of the River Ayr at Newton, Dalmilling, and Auchincruive; and Alloway Mill on the River Doon. The rivers which provided water power also produced salmon. To catch them were two cruives by the dam of the Nether Mill. Sea fish were landed at the haven, and there were fishing stations all along the coast. There were five along the Newton shore in the 16th century. The fishing rights on the Ayr shore belonged to the burgh, and those operating 'cobillis upoun the wattir

of Air and Dune' made payments which (since 1236) went towards the upkeep of harbour and bridge. The hinterland of the burgh supplied other products. Thus in 14th century payments from Ayrshire to the royal household, cash was supplemented by kind – herrings, haddocks, salmon, pork, and bacon. 15th century exports from Ayr included some raw wool, loads of untreated sheepskins of various types (in 1497, 1,430 woolfells, 1,520 schorlings, 77 futfalis, 290 lentrinwair); but the most valuable items were treated hides, woollen cloth in increasing quantities, and barrels of salted cod and herring. Ayr was trading with France, the Netherlands, and Scandinavia, and there are passing mentions in the records of ships from Gascony, Sluys, and Denmark, anchored in the haven of Ayr and bringing to the fairs salt, wines, and other items for sale. Though evidence for this period is scanty, Ayr had its crafts, with workers in textiles, leather, wood, and metals – the weavers, dyers, tailors, fleshers, skinners, shoemakers, coopers, squaremen, and hammermen who would form Ayr's nine incorporated trades. That some of the burgesses were acquiring wealth is obvious from their gifts to the Church of St John, to the Black Friars, and their invitation to the Grey Friars to come to Ayr in 1474.

Throughout the Middle Ages, Ayr was the principal seaport of the west of Scotland. This often-quoted fact is undoubtedly correct; but it requires some qualification. Ayr's customs returns for 1327 of just over £3 formed a mere 0.16% of the Scottish total of £1,851, and the eight east coast seaports which outranked Ayr were all far busier. The returns from Berwick

Town House
of the Neills
of Swindridgemuir

in Terry's Close
High Street

Bryden 1887.

Many of the Ayrshire landed families had town houses in the county town.

(£673) and Edinburgh (£439) indicate the relative insignificance of Ayr's share of Scotland's foreign trade. Over the next two centuries, though trade expanded, Ayr's share of the total remained small, and in the 16th century the western ports from Dumfries to Dumbarton produced less than 5% of the national customs revenue. It must be remembered however that foreign trade as recorded in customs returns formed only a fraction of Ayr's maritime commerce. Coastal trade, catering for the whole of the west coast, must have been of far greater volume than in most east coast ports.

Such advances as Ayr made were accomplished in face of difficulties both local and national. Within Ayrshire there was a challenge from the emerging burgh of Irvine. Created as a burgh of barony by the de Morville overlords of Cunninghame some thirty years after William the Lion established Ayr as a king's burgh, in 1323 Robert I awarded Irvine trading rights throughout Cunninghame, thus reducing Ayr's precinct which had until then extended over the entire sheriffdom. In 1372 Robert II elevated Irvine to the status of king's burgh, with all the privileges of foreign trade that Ayr possessed. Irvine's progress was modest, so that Ayr was never seriously threatened. Its trade, as

indicated by customs returns, was consistently smaller, though competing in the same markets. By the 16th century Ayr ranked tenth among the Scottish royal burghs, and Irvine sixteenth, as measured by surviving stent rolls.

One serious local problem emerged towards the end of the 14th century – the blowing of sand, occasioned by heavy western gales. This was sufficiently serious to threaten destruction of the Church of St John in particular and affect the burgh in general. Robert II in a charter of 1380 noted this crisis (*Dum burgus noster de Air, per motionem et agitationem arenae sit quasi totaliter annihilatus et destructus*). An offer of land to those who could reclaim it seems to have had little effect, for in 1425 royal officials inspecting the Sandgate noted a daily inflow of sand which was steadily engulfing it, and ordered the street to be narrowed and straightened. A recent excavation beside the High Street has confirmed that an area beside the river, cultivated from the 13th century, was in the 15th century inundated by sand to a depth of almost one metre; similar evidence appeared also in Garden Street on the opposite bank of the river. The effect of erosion near the shore was to expose the dead in the cemetery beside St John's Church. The Castle of Ayr

This house, built for James Tait in the early 16th century, became known as Loudoun Hall after the hereditary sheriffs of Ayr who owned it until about 1634.

(1329–71) succeeded at the age of five and died aged 46 – his reign included seven years of exile in France and eleven years of captivity in England; the disastrous battles of Dupplin (1332), Halidon Hill (1333) and Neville's Cross (1346); and the Black Death of 1349–60 and 1361–62. During the early part of David's reign, Ayrshire was ravaged by his rival Edward Balliol, and Loch Doon Castle was besieged: in the Battle of Neville's Cross there died several Ayrshire lords, and presumably some lesser men who followed them. The cost of the wars and a king's ransom resulted in heavy taxation and increased customs levied. Such difficulties persisted in the reigns of the Stewart kings who followed David II.

The reign of the first Stewart king Robert II (1371–90) was punctuated by border warfare, with the brief success of Otterburn (1388) followed in his son's reign by defeat at Homildon Hill (1402). Unruly nobles disputed the Stewart succession and in particular the legitimacy of Robert II's heirs through his first marriage. This was to Elizabeth Mure of Rowallan, and the wedding at Lady Kirk in Kyle was not recognised by the Church till many years later. Robert II was 54 when he was enthroned; at the age of 64 he was forced into virtual abdication; and he lived in retirement and died at Dundonald Castle. His son Robert III (1390–1406) succeeded to disorder, which was not quelled when he died at the age of 69. There is a ghastly similarity in the reigns of the next four Stewart kings – James I (1406–37), James II (1437–60), James III (1460–89), James IV (1489–1513). Each succeeded as a minor; each died a violent death; to be succeeded by another minor. At the beginning of seven reigns, including James V (1513–42), Mary (1542–67), and James VI (1567–1625), leading Ayrshire families were involved in the inevitable struggles of Scottish magnates for control of a young monarch. Two Ayrshiremen played major roles during the minority of James III – James Kennedy, bishop of St Andrews, who came from Carrick; then Thomas, Lord Boyd of Kilmarnock. And whenever royal power was weak, the landed families of Ayrshire had scope to advance their own local interests.

The whole of Ayrshire was now part of the royal domain. This included King's Kyle (since the 12th century); the earldom of Carrick (once Bruce ascended the throne); Cunninghame (after he took over the Balliol lands); and Stewart Kyle (when Robert the Steward succeeded as king). Some local families won enhanced status, with lordships from James II and earldoms from James IV. In Cunninghame, the Montgomeries of Eglinton acquired a lordship (1445)

nearby was definitely affected, for in later records there is no further mention of this as one of the royal castles. It certainly ceased to be the headquarters of the sheriff of Ayr. In 1521 there is note of the sheriff court as meeting in the burgh Tolbooth. In 1539 Sir Hugh Campbell was occupying 'the schirefis tenement' which he had purchased from James Tait, and which as Loudoun Hall survives as Ayr's oldest house. If the Castle was dismantled because of the sandstorms, perhaps its stones were used to construct the Tower of St John's about this time, near the end of the 14th or beginning of the 15th century. The fact that Robert II in 1380 was offering land to those willing to reclaim it indicates that the area round the Castle was outwith burghal control, which would prove awkward for the burgh in the 17th century and later.

In Ayr as elsewhere, difficulties were caused by continued wars with England and internal dissensions within Scotland. Robert I's successors were none of them able to cope effectively. His son David II and an earldom (1506); the Cunninghames gained the lordship of Kilmaurs (1454) and the earldom of Glencairn (1488, annulled, restored 1536); the Boyds of Kilmarnock held a lordship (1459–69, restored 1536). In Carrick the Kennedys obtained their lordship (1458) and the earldom of Cassillis (1509). In Kyle, where much land was in the hands of the church, there were no families influential enough to win any such honours. Sir Alan Cathcart of Sundrum, Dalmellington, and Auchincruive gained a lordship (1452); and Andrew Stewart was made Lord Ochiltree (1543): but their main interests were outwith Ayrshire. The Wallaces of Craigie could command no higher status than the provostship of Ayr on occasion. The family of Loudoun, with extensive possessions both in Cunninghame and Kyle, did not achieve their lordship and earldom till the 17th century. But they nevertheless wielded considerable local influence. Craufurds of Loudoun had in the 13th century been the first sheriffs of Ayr. In 1305 their estates passed through a daughter to a branch of the Campbell family. Sometime after 1386 (when William Cunningham held the office) the Campbells of Loudoun became hereditary sheriffs of Ayr. By contrast to their effective influence, when in 1469 it was decreed that the title of earl of Carrick be held thereafter by the eldest son of the monarch – as it still is – that was a symbolic gesture which had no local significance.

The foregoing paragraphs, with their references to people and places outwith the royal burgh, are not really a digression, but provide a necessary background to an important development within Ayr itself. The burgh had since its inception been the headquarters of the sheriff and continued to be so, a centre of royal administration and justice. Now with the emergence of the Ayrshire baronage as just described, Ayr became a county town. The landed families who had their new tower houses in the country also had, many of them, town houses in Ayr. Bargany, Cassillis, and other seven members of the Kennedy clan had their tenements; as had their Carrick neighbours the Mures of Auchendrane and the Blairs of Middle Auchendrane. Kyle lairds with town houses included Wallaces of Craigie, Barnweil, and Carnel, Blair of Adamton, Chalmers of Gadgirth, Cathcart of Carbieston, Dalrymple of Stair, Cunningham of Caprington, Lockhart of Bar, Nisbet of Greenholm, and three Campbell lairds as well as the sheriff Campbell of Loudoun, which was in Cunninghame. The only other laird from north of the River Irvine known to have a town house in

Ayr was Mure of Caldwell. The leading families of Cunninghame had their town houses in Irvine (where Barnweil, Adamton, and Gadgirth also had residences). For the gentry of Kyle and Carrick, Ayr provided a place where they sometimes stayed and met. This was a place for friendships – and enmities. For here could be hatched those plots and intrigues that involved the leading families in the Ayrshire Feuds of the 16th century.

The streets of Ayr witnessed occasional outbursts of violence in which members of landed families were involved. In 1537 Craufurds and Lockharts and a 'Convocation of the lieges in great numbers, within the Burgh of Air' attacked Alexander Kennedy of Bargany, at his house in the Sandgate 'with invasive weapons, and throwing stones at his windows and doors, and breaking and destroying the same'. In 1564 there was another riot when the Fergussons of Kilkerran with a party of over a hundred kinsmen and Kennedys 'arrayed in fashion of war' attacked Craufurds and Campbells in the Tolbooth of Ayr when the sheriff court was in session. In 1567 there was another clash between Kennedys and Craufurds, this time at the horse races on Ayr sands. In 1578 there was a fight 'with pistoletis and land guns' within Ayr churchyard between William Hamilton of Sanchar and John Wallace of Craigie. In 1583 the son of Kennedy of Greenan was released from the Tolbooth by a party of sixty adherents who terrorised the town. But altogether Ayr experienced far less violence than Irvine suffered during the long feud between the Cunninghams of Kilmaurs and the Montgomeries of Eglinton from 1488 till 1528 and again from 1586 till 1606.

That other great feud, with the Craufurds, Campbells, and their allies in Kyle ranged against the Kennedys of Carrick, was fought mainly outwith Ayr, in the east of Kyle and along the banks of the River Doon. In 1511 David Craufurd of Kerse and others seized the royal castle on Loch Doon, whose keeper was Sir David Kennedy. In 1530 John Craufurd of Drongan crossed the river and brought back 125 oxen and cows stolen from James Kennedy of Blairquhan; who quickly retaliated with a raid which took 120 oxen and cows, 200 sheep, and six horses and mares. Here too was located that legendary incident when the Kennedys tethered a sow on the land of Kerse and after a fierce battle the Craufurds made sure that 'the sow was flitted'. The most celebrated incident of the feud occurred in 1527 when Gilbert, earl of Cassillis, was ambushed in the sandhills near Prestwick and killed by a party of

Craufurds and Campbells acting under the instructions of Hugh Campbell of Loudoun, sheriff of Ayr. This however was not especially occasioned by local rivalries, for Loudoun and his followers, numbered at 1,400 armed men, were participating in one of the nationwide conspiracies in the last year of James V's minority.

The third great Ayrshire feud was centred within Carrick, that internecine struggle of the Kennedys between adherents of the earl of Cassilis and the rival Bargany faction. It commenced in 1570 with the roasting of the commendator of Crossraguel at Dunure Castle by the 4th earl of Cassillis. It ended in 1611 with the execution in Edinburgh of John Mure of Auchendrane, prominent supporter of Bargany. That unscrupulous character had in 1597 made a pretended truce with Sir Thomas Kennedy of Culzean, tutor of the young 5th earl. In 1602 Sir Thomas planned a trip to Edinburgh and sent a message proposing to meet Mure on his way past Ayr. On 12 May Sir Thomas, coming from Culzean via Greenan, was met instead by accomplices of Mure, who killed him. Later, to eliminate some evidence, the lad who brought the message to Mure was also murdered, on Girvan beach. The spot where Sir Thomas Kennedy died was 'amang the Sandy-hillis, besyd Sanct Lennardis Cheapell' which was 'near the part where he had trysted to meet ... at the Duppill'.

16th century records of the various affrays may suggest an era of especial violence, but in fact indicate a period of fuller records and increasing efficiency of the justice-ayre courts which met periodically in Ayr. Royal justiciars could deal with serious cases more effectively than the sheriff court, the bailiary courts, the baron courts, or the burgh courts. Trials could be transferred to the High Court of Justiciary in Edinburgh, as in 1539 when the sheriff of Ayr was believed biassed, or as in 1611 with Mure of Auchendrane. Central government under the Stewart kings was exercising increased power. Again, national necessities over-rode local rivalries. Ayrshiremen of different factions and different ranks served and died in the disastrous battles of Flodden (1513), Solway Moss (1542) and Pinkie (1547). The Obit Book of St John's Church records John Dixon, burgess of Ayr, who died 'in the dreadful battle at Flowdon'. At Pinkie, Ayrshire losses included two burgesses from Ayr, Robert Andrew and William Nesbitt. More than forty five Ayrshire 'men of property' fell there, seventeen from Cunninghame, seven from Kyle, and twenty one from Carrick. The total included Montgomeries and Cunninghams,

Campbells, Craufurds, Kennedys, and Mures, who were obviously able on occasion to subordinate local rivalries to common interest. Involvement in national politics brought new alignments, as occurred at the time of the Reformation, and earlier in 1543 when Cassillis and Campbell of Loudoun were both allies of Glencairn and in receipt of English bribes.

The landed families of Ayrshire had other common interests, which illustrate that the feuds were in fact incidental episodes, however horrifying these may at times have been. It is clear that by the 16th century they were making efforts to improve their estates. There is evidence of agricultural improvements in Cunninghame especially and it is likely similar advances were being made in Kyle and parts of Carrick. The heavy demands for wood through successive generations had cleared most of the lowland forests, and Carrick was probably already supplying the rest of Ayrshire from its more considerable surviving resources. To establish crafts and develop local markets there were established new burghs of barony. Landowners in all parts of Ayrshire obtained royal charters. A lead was taken by Campbell of Loudoun at Newmilns (1491) and others in Cunninghame followed at Kilmaurs (1527), Saltcoats (1529), Kilmarnock (1592) and Largs (1595). These were accompanied by similar creations in Kyle – Thomas Boswell at Auchinleck (1507), James Dunbar at Cumnock (1509), the abbot of Melrose at Mauchline (1510); also in Carrick – the 2nd earl of Cassillis at Maybole (1516), Thomas Kennedy of Bargany at Ballantrae (1541). It should be remembered too that the tower houses, most of which were built in the 15th and 16th centuries, were designed not only for defence but for increased domestic comfort. And while some members of the landed landed class are remembered for military exploits, others are renowned for cultural pursuits.

In the Scottish Renaissance, Carrick was neither isolated nor backward. One noted early Scots poet was Walter Kennedy, born at Cassillis about 1460, son of the first Lord Kennedy and nephew of Bishop Kennedy. From Straiton came another makar, Quintin Schaw (1450–1505). Later from Carrick came the celebrated Mark Alexander Boyd of Penkill (1563–1601) and his cousins from Trochrague, Robert Boyd (1578–1627) and Zachary Boyd (1585–1653), poets and Principals of Glasgow University. Quintin Kennedy, last abbot of Crossraguel, was a noted theologican who had studied in Paris, following in the footsteps of George Lockhart (c.1485–1547) that native of Ayr who had an international reputation as a philosopher in the era of Luther and Erasmus. Such take their place beside literary figures from Cunninghame – the 14th century Sir Hew of Eglinton; in the 16th century the 5th earl of Glencairn, Alexander Montgomery, Hew Barclay; in the 17th century Sir William Mure of Rowallan and William Hamilton. Oddly, Kyle produced no poets till the 18th century.

For the landed families of 16th century Ayrshire, life on their estates was enriched by excursions into Ayr. Legal business could be transacted by notaries in the Church of St John or in one of the two friary churches. They could send their sons to the burgh school and, after it moved into new premises in 1602, their daughters also. There were opportunities for sport and recreation and spectacle. Those with town houses could enjoy the sociability of urban life. Some became burgesses, participating in trading ventures and sharing in managing burghal affairs. The landed families who came as visitors or occasional residents augmented the town population and made the royal burgh of Ayr in the 16th century a county town. Bishop Leslie in 1578 could appropriately describe 'the toune of Air, quhilke is called St Johnes toune, illustir and fair anuich baith in riches and biging, and a pleasand situatione, with a prettie seyporte quhair strange natiouns oft arryves and thair lands, the porte is sa commodious'.

FIVE

16th Century Royal Burgh

Ayr in the 16th century was one of about fifty royal burghs. Each of these had originated as a king's burgh (*burgus domini regis*) but from the 15th century came to be known as a royal burgh (*burgus regalis*). The Royal Burgh of Ayr had become a wealthy community. Though its foreign trade was much less than east coast ports, yet when the burghs were assessed for taxation Ayr stood tenth in rank in 1515, ninth in 1557, fifth in 1575, sixth in 1578, and eighth for a long time thereafter. Comparison with other burghs of similar standing suggests that 16th century Ayr must have contained from three to four hundred houses and a population between 1,500 and 2,000.

Such a population would comprise a small number of merchants belonging to the guild and involved in foreign trade (perhaps 50 in number); larger groups of burgess craftsmen in the several trades (perhaps 150); many more employed by them, and other unfree indwellers (around 500); gentry who were not necessarily involved in trading but enrolled as burgesses or guild brethren (say 30); together with wives and children (up to 1,000 or half the total). A century earlier in 1432 there were listed 49 guild brethren plus 19 non-resident members; one might guess no significant increase for a time thereafter; but the burgh accounts which survive from 1534 show a trend of increasing numbers of burgess and guild entries; which would reflect a growth in local trade and population, and so justify an estimated 1,500 at the beginning of the 16th century and 2,000 by 1600.

The extent of the 16th century town can be measured from the location of the ports which were its gateways. Barriers at the main entrances to the burgh, supplemented by the back dykes at the rear of the burgage tofts, were required to prevent unauthorised access; though always necessary, it is only from the early 16th century that they find mention. Four were obviously long-established. At that point where a narrowing of the Sandgate is still obvious, stood the Sandgait Port, thus described in 1605, though

earlier in 1545 called the Carrick Port, for this was a principal route southwards towards the crossing of the River Doon. At the other end of the Sandgate, the way from the harbour was protected by the Sea Port (1545), otherwise the port in the Boat Vennel (1602) or of the Sea Vennel (1610). Up High Street the crossing of the bridge was protected by the Brig Port, as noted in 1547 when a night watch was stationed at the north end of the bridge. Further up High Street, just beyond the present Wallace Tower was the Kyle Port (1513), known also as the South Port (1513) or the Port at the Auld Tour (1543). Beyond that, as building extended into the Townhead there were required an Overport (1546) in what is now Kyle Street; and a Cow Port (1603) in what was the Cowgait (1499), otherwise the Cow Vennel (1656), later Alloway Street. In addition there was a subsidiary port in the Kirk Vennel (1592) as St John Street was then called; and similar yetts would be required in Carrick Vennel and other minor side entrances.

While the burgh in the 16th century had extended into the Townhead, its older precincts were experiencing increased congestion. Buildings fronting the street were joined by back tenements to which access was obtained through narrow and sometimes covered closes. One notable example was the 'new tenement of John Blair of Adamton' built shortly before 1470 in the 'vennel leading from the Market Cross to the Water of Ayr', a building which survived to become Ayr's oldest house until it was demolished in 1972 to make way for Marks and Spencer. There was also building outwards into the streets, to accommodate those booths which replaced earlier temporary stalls where goods were displayed for sale. The widest part of High Street was particularly affected. Beside the Tolbooth, with its own four booths available for let, there grew up a cluster of other houses, forming an isle in what had previously been an open area. This encroachment on the market space left on one side only a narrow passage, now designated Hope Street but still known as

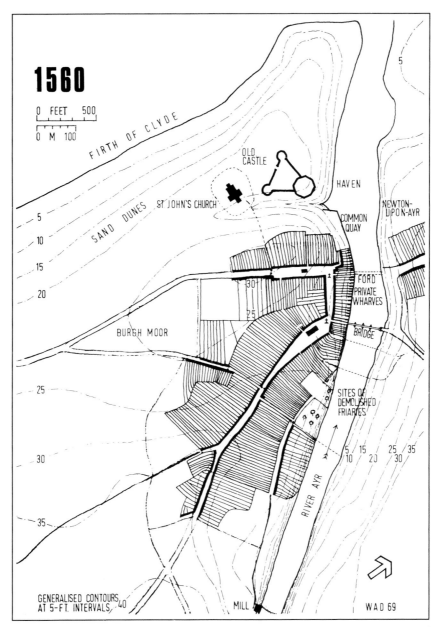

1560

0 FEET 500

0 M 100

FIRTH OF CLYDE

OLD CASTLE

HAVEN

ST JOHN'S CHURCH

SAND DUNES

NEWTON-UPON-AYR

COMMON QUAY

5

10

15

20

FORD
PRIVATE
WHARVES

BURGH MOOR

BRIDGE

25

SITES OF
DEMOLISHED
FRIARIES

25 35

5 15

10 20

30

30

RIVER AYR

25

30

35

GENERALISED CONTOURS
AT 5-FT. INTERVALS
40

MILL

W A D 69

The burgh extended far beyond its original bounds, with a population growing in the 16th century from 1,500 to 2,000.

the Back of the Isle. With the market area restricted, it was decreed in 1547 that 'na kynd of stuff be sauld in tyme comyn at the fyshe cross but fysh'. The malt cross at the Sandgate corner was possibly then established as an alternative site for the sale of certain dry goods. The tron, where produce could be weighed, remained beside the Fish Cross. South of the Tolbooth a meal market was mentioned in 1559 and extended in 1586. Further up High Street there was a sheep market (noted in 1592) and a market for wool (mentioned in

1656). Beyond Townhead, cattle and horses were sold at the Fauldbacks. Ayr High Street must have been a busy place during the Saturday markets and especially at the Midsummer and Michaelmas fairs.

Congestion in High Street no doubt influenced the council decision to have their new tolbooth erected in 1575 on a new site, in the Sandgate. This was a quieter and more open situation, and the inconvenience of blowing sand was one that was being overcome. For at least fifty years work had been proceeding on the reclamation of Sandy lands along the road to the Doon, although in 1575 the council still had to pay 'for taking away the sand from the sand-gait'. Here, however, the council sited their new High Tolbooth in the middle of the street, leaving their former one which was thereafter referred to as the Laigh House. The new High (or Over) Tolbooth was an impressive structure. Constructed of stone from the burgh quarry, it was slated and had three iron-framed windows, glazed, with the burgh coat-of-arms painted on one. The new tolbooth was entered by a flight of stairs, and the Court Hall was furnished with table, benches, a coal fire, and a barrel adapted as 'ane dry privie'. Beneath was the Thieves' Hole. A debtors' prison was attached to the south gable. Outside were stocks and jougs where other miscreants could be tethered. Later in 1615 a bell tower was added, surmounted by a cock weathervane. A bell was then obtained from a foundry in Irvine, and a new town clock constructed locally by John Smyth, who installed below it a device for indicating the phases of the moon. This replaced the old town 'knock' on the Laigh Tolbooth, which previously in 1558 had to be sent to Edinburgh for repair.

The burgh was wealthy enough to provide not only such a fine new tolbooth, but to undertake expensive outlay on other works. Each year necessary repairs and improvements were made at the Church of St John: in 1537 for example the bells required new ropes, the organ was renovated, candles had to be supplied 'to the organis in wynter at the evinsangis', five hundred slates were purchased for roof work, glass and other materials for the windows, and a new altar cloth was provided. This was in addition to the fees paid (from endowments) to the eight chaplains and two sangsters; and annual payments to the Greyfriars and the Blackfriars. There was also regular expenditure on maintaining the haven and repairing its quays, particularly after 1547 when part of the stone work 'past away with the storme'. In 1588 the council obtained crown permission to levy a brig impost, and thereafter dues had to be paid for animals and packs crossing the bridge, and vessels entering the harbour. The proceeds over the next four years went towards an extensive reconstruction of the century-old bridge – requiring turf from Newton Green to build a dam, and use of a pump to keep the foundations drained while work was in progress. The Auld Brig as we know it probably dates from this work in and around 1590. Money was also spent on the haven. A gabbart or lighter was acquired to transport stone downriver from the quarry. In 1599

a further investment was made 'off the stent collectit be the burch of Air amongst thaimselffis' whose main purpose was 'the bigging of the key'. That individual burgesses were also able to afford substantial building on their own behalf is indicated by the construction in High Street beside the Blackfriars of what was even in 1544 known as the Auld Tour, and later in that century as Cathcartis Tour.

As early as the 15th century some burghs found it necessary to borrow to meet their commitments, but Ayr remained virtually debt-free throughout the 16th century. Any loans were small and paid off soon after they were incurred. Burgh revenues between 1534 and 1562 were fairly steady, between £200 and £300 per year. By the last quarter of the century the average had risen to £600, and in some years was twice that, so that (allowing for a 30% devaluation of the currency) the burgh of Ayr's real annual income more than doubled in the 16th century. This was sufficient for councils to cope with extraordinary demands as well as routine expenditure, and allowed them on occasion to be generous and even lavish.

The allocation of burghal revenue varied widely from year to year with changing circumstances, but for the first sixty years of the 16th century the average pattern is clear. Around 40% was devoted to the Church, most of it for what we now call 'statutory' responsibilities, but with a special emphasis on schooling. In 1502 Andrew McCormyll is noted as 'instructor for the time being of grammatical studies in the burgh of Ayr': the 'schools of Ayr' teaching Latin and Music at the Church of St John had presumably been in continuous operation since the one previous mention in 1233. The burgh council which had the responsibility of appointing chaplains to the Church of St John clearly selected (from 1519 if not earlier) persons fitted for teaching. In 1519 for the Latin classes in what would become the grammar school Gavin Ros, a notary, was appointed for one year and later continued for life. For a different clientele, in 1539 Robert Paterson was appointed 'to play on the organis, sing in quier, and to teich ane sang schule'. The master of the sang school was expected to provide elementary schooling in reading and writing. Mr Patrick Anderson (1540) was paid £10 per annum, and supplied with paper and ink 'for to mak sang bukis'. In 1550 the council closed two private schools to encourage attendance at the Church school. To cater for the more secular education required for most sons of burgh merchants and country lairds, the town council in 1556 decreed that the scholars 'be lairned baythe Inglis and Latyne at the optioun and pleasure of the parents'. Already

John Blair's tenement built in the later 15th century survived at 70 High Street till its eventual demolition in 1972.

the calsay on Corpus Christys eyn for honour of the sacrament'. When the street were thus cleared of *red*, and the *middingis* removed, the *puldir* was taken away by Alloway horses to be spread over the sand hills. In 1590, 2/– (10p) was spent on shovelling snow from the streets. In the same year a 'bowat for mirk nychtis' indicates an effort to provide street lighting.

Administration cost around 20% of total expenditure. This included salaries, fees, and wages for those engaged in council business. There were law suits, sometimes costly: legal action had to be taken against those who infringed the rights of the royal burgh, including the sheriff; and against local lairds who were in arrears with dues payable to the burgh. Since Ayr was one of the top ten towns of 16th century Scotland there was the cost of sending magistrates as commissioners to parliament, to the Convention of Royal Burghs, and on other business trips. In 1600, for example, the dean of guild after a ten-day visit to Perth recovered £20 at the basic daily rate of £2 for himself, his man, and his horse. The effective discharge of burgh business required also correspondence, and horse messengers and runners were employed. In one year, 1553, over £32 was spent 'for riding to Edinburgh ... Taking the town's books to Edinburgh ... 13 messengers going or running to Edinburgh ... 5 messengers going or running to Glasgow ... other messengers and boys ... for the hire of horses'. There were also charges, ranging from food for prisoners in the Thieves' Hole to purchasing coals, tar, and timber for the burning of witches in 1587, 1595, 1600, and 1618.

A measure of affluence is shown by the amount spent on hospitality and festivities – averaging 5% in the first half of the 16th century, 9% near the end, and sometimes much more. State occasions were celebrated by bonfires and banquets. Local lairds were often entertained, annually there was a bailies' supper after the Michaelmas elections, and workmen were regularly supplied with ale and bread and drinksilver. Distinguished visitors were lavishly provided with hospitality and gifts. When the Convention of Royal Burghs met in Ayr in 1583, the bill from one tavern keeper amounted to £120. There were royal visits by James V (1527, 1530) and Mary Queen of Scots (1552, 1563). On 2 and 3 August 1563 she had 'soupper et coucher at St Jehan d'Era', at unknown cost, for the burgh accounts of that period are missing. Local festivities included annual Robin Hood plays (till 1560); visits by gipsies as in 1541 when two quarts of wine were given 'to the Egiptianis quhen thai dansit to the baillies'; the wappinschaws when the

before the Protestant Reformation the church school had become a burgh school for which the town council undertook entire responsibility. There were of course occasional difficulties, as in 1542 when the treasurer was required 'not to gif ony money of the commoun purss to ony chaplain' for priority had to be given to 'commoun warkis on hand mair necessair to be done'. Yet George Pryde whose researches into Ayr's history included a detailed analysis of the burgh accounts was impressed by 'a community with many other commitments yet finding the will, the time and the money to maintain its own schools and provide a decent competence for the teachers whom it employed'.

Around 30% of burgh expenditure was devoted to the 'common works', principally maintenance of the bridge and harbour, but where necessary dealing with exceptional crises such as the plague (as described later in this chapter). Routine work included spasmodic efforts at scavenging, as in 1537 'the reddene of burgesses paraded with their weapons, shot at the wooden papingo in contests of archery, or practised gunmanship with their hagbuts. That area from 'the kirkyard dyke to the Blackburne' which includes the modern Low Green was reserved for 'the pastyme of the honest men in gayming according to use and wont'. Here golf could be played – in 1587 the magistrates had to deal with theft of 'ane gad of irn' (iron club) and 'goff ballis'. There was also football, for we learn of a miscreant at Alloway in 1514 who 'plait at the fut ball'. That there was tennis is evident, for in 1519 one of the chaplains had a legal dispute with a laymen whose eye was injured by a ball during a tennis match. There were horse races, as in 1576 when the feuding Kennedys and Craufurds became involved in a clash.

Some 5% remained to be spent on miscellaneous purposes. Though poor relief was principally a concern of the Church, the burgh was ready to supplement this by casual payments. In 1537 they authorised licensed begging by providing lead tokens, paying 2/– (10p) 'to the tynklar for making of v score of lyddin takyngis to the pure folk'. Relief was on occasion provided for former employees, like Stephen Prestoun (1560), sometime town clerk and formerly well-to-do; also 'in support of the drummer being seik' (1559); and the town piper (1555) who was given monetary assistance, then a winding sheet for his burial. Generosity extended to strangers from other parts of Scotland, some Irish and English, French including shipwrecked Bretons, a Norwegian and a Dutchman, while in 1588 shipwrecked sailors of the Spanish Armada were provided with meat, drink, lodgings, and 'four pair of schoone gevin to the saidis four Spainyardis'.

Military obligations involved some expense. Though there had been from 1263 local objections to the sheriff ordering the burgesses to perform military service, it was accepted that the king could in times of war call upon each royal burgh for a quota of armed men. The burghs when possible offered financial aid instead, as in 1578 when Ayr requested 'gif the toun culd be discharget thairof, or uthirwyiss quhidder gif men or money wald serve'. In any circumstances, the burgesses were required to perform military training at the periodic wappinschaws, and the town's military equipment in the 16th century included spears, pikes, those primitive muskets called hagbuts, six pieces of artillery costing £133 which were stored in the Church of St John; plus accoutrements such as trumpets, drum, banners, and a tent. The burgh also had an obligation to contribute to national taxation. Stents included the *cess* as prescribed by parliament; burghal

levies on behalf of the Convention of Royal Burghs; in addition to stents for local purposes. The bailies, with the assistance of burgesses enrolled at stenters, assessed and collected such taxes – which were quite distinct from the burgh revenue. Sometimes there was a surplus which went to augment the Common Good of the burgh; sometimes arrears or deficiencies in national taxes were included as an additional item in regular burgh expenditure.

That a small town like Ayr could afford such extensive and often expensive outlays is an indication of the wealth it derived from its commercial activities. Though its foreign trade with France, the Netherlands, and Scandinavia was only a fraction of that of many Scottish east coast ports, yet it seems to have been regular and profitable. Combines of guild merchants contributed to make up cargoes of wool, hides, cloth, and salted fish, which after payment of export duty – *the great custom* which was collected by the *custumar* on behalf of the crown – were sold in the market of a foreign port. The little sailing ships would return with cargoes of wine, spices, flour, iron, or salt – more suitable for preserving fish than that from the local salt pans. The goods imported would be shared among the partners of the combine for sale at the markets and fairs in Ayr. It was typical when in 1528 Alexander Lockhart travelled to Britanny to purchase a vessel and brought it back with a cargo to be shared with his three partners. That foreign merchants also involved themselves in Ayr's trade is seen, for example, in 1597 when two Flemish merchants brought in a load of salt which three local merchants purchased, with the condition that they could export, freight-free, 'sex ton wecht of retour in the said schip bak frae the port of Air to the portis of France'. During this century there was a new line in exports, with ships from Ayr taking coals to Ireland. The first local mention of coal concerns its use at the saltpans of Prestwick in 1480. Soon afterwards John Wallace of Craigie acquired the rights to 'the coilys contenit in certane bondis of that commun'. In 1509 another member of the Wallace family was working coal at Bruntwood near Galston. In 1528 John's brother, Adam Wallace of Newton, obtained a licence 'to wyn coil and coal hewis quhar ever thai may be apprehendit wythin the barony of Alloway'. Significantly Adam Wallace had been Ayr's provost and would be again, while his partner Stephen Prestoun was a future town clerk. Their Alloway venture seems to have been successful in that an initial seven year lease was renewed before its term was run. Though there is no record of continued working here or in the Burrowfield, the 'wyning of the coil' was

High Street was narrowed when buildings were erected around the tolbooth, forming an Island with on one side only a narrow passage – still known as the Back of the Isle.

certainly continued, for example at Leglane in 1548. The burgh accounts record purchases of coal (both for heating the tolbooth and burning of witches) and by the end of the century it must have superseded peat as a domestic fuel within the town, for in 1593 there was 'a maist exhorbitant derth and skantness of fewall' and a temporary ban was imposed on export 'not onlie be strangeris but alswa be the burgessis, merchands, and traffiqueris'. Beside the foreign trade and coal trade, there was the fishing fleet seeking herring and other fish in the Firth of Clyde and the sea lochs beyond. Ayr, compared to east coast ports, had a relatively large coastal trade serving the whole west of Scotland from the Solway to the Western Isles – not included in the customs returns, so that Ayr harbour was really much busier than these suggest.

A recent study of Ayr's export trade indicates 2,038 tons of coal handled between 1581 and 1598, with a maximum of 343 tons in 1591; approximately 80,000 yards of cloth despatched in the same period, with 7,500 yards in 1583; and sample figures for other principal exports were 4,500 barrels of herrings (1591), 2,300 hides (1582), and 5,600 sheepskins (1598). Ayr also re-exported salt and Spanish and French wines, plus a miscellany of other goods including dyes, brass, iron, bells, olive oil, soap, paper, prunes, whisky (15 gallons of Arran whisky sent to Ireland in 1590), and barrels of 'drywair' containing items like hats, clothes, needles, and playing cards.

Ayr was also important as a naval base from which expeditions were sent to Ireland. In 1513 James IV's *Great Michael* with its complement of 32 guns and one thousand men arrived at Ayr. Ayr was a convenient port of call when passage across the North Sea was awkward, as in 1515 when the Regent Albany arrived in Ayr from France 'with aucht schippis weille furnesit with men, and all kinds of apperell for his honorabill convey'. Robert Jamieson, sometime magistrate of Ayr, was owner of the ship *James Royal* which was hired in 1590 to bring James VI and his queen to Scotland from Norway, and again in 1598 to take the king to Kintyre, 'provydit and furnist with a sufficient nowmer and equippage of the best and maist able marineris within the toun of Air'. Keeping the sea routes free from pirates was at times necessary. In 1590 the burgh provided 'gunpowder and wine to the young men (who) ... gang with boittes sufficientlie furnesit to serche, seik, tak and apprehend the said rubberis ... quha lyis about Ailsay in the middle of the firthe, quha takis, rubbis, and spulzies pure merchand men usand thair lesum tred'. The danger of piracy was a principal reason for the formation in 1580 of the Mariners Society of Ayr for the benefit of seamen and their dependents who might suffer 'sum be pilasing and reiping of thair guidis by pirattes, sum be greit hurt in thair bodies sustenit in defence of thair guidis'. It was financed by levies at the end of 'French weyages, Inglis and Irland weyages'.

The guild merchants plying their 'lesum tred' had foreign wares to sell at the weekly markets and especially the two annual fairs. Here too the craftsmen of the burgh sold their products. Under an Act of 1555 the various trades were formed into associations, each with its deacon, each concerned not only with practice of the craft but with a fund for the support of 'falziet brethren' – on the evidence of the wrights and squaremen, whose minute books from 1556 have survived. Weavers or websters; waulkers of cloth; tailors; skinners; cordiners or shoemakers; squaremen who were stone masons; hammermen who worked in metal – these formed Ayr's seven incorporated trades of the 16th century. Later that number grew to nine with the addition of coopers and fleshers and the replacement of waulkers by dyers. There was some competition from the rival royal burgh of Irvine, where only five of the original seven crafts were able to maintain a continued identity. There was also a threat from lesser burghs and other places where

markets were set up and a limited number of crafts practised. Irvine was concerned about the situation in Cunninghame. Ayr's trading precinct of Kyle and Carrick contained the old burghs of Prestwick and Newton and the new baronial burghs of Auchinleck (1507), Cumnock (1509), Mauchline (1510), Maybole (1516), and Ballantrae (1541). These were slow to develop, and indeed in some cases never became properly established. In 1538 the burgh of Ayr made complaint to the king 'anent chepmen at landwert kirkis'. Later there were more specific charges. In 1583 developments at Mauchline were seen as 'to the dirogatioun of the liberties of this burch'. In 1598 the quiet little burgh of Newton was stirring itself and the merchants of Ayr insisted that when ships came in 'that na guidis be lossit nore discharget on the Newtoun syde'. In 1599 Maybole was infringing Ayr's monopoly by selling foreign goods, which required a costly law suit to win a Court of Session prohibition. Such disputes, however, were incidental signs of an expanding economy, which remained centred in the markets and fairs of the county town.

For management of the markets, fairs, and other aspects of the burgh, municipal organisation had evolved from the 13th century beginning with selected burgesses nominated by the sheriff. By the 15th century an alderman and two bailies were operating as representatives of the burgesses, supported by a council (as first mentioned in 1471). Burgesses had always been expected to attend the head courts at Yule, Easter, and Michaelmas, and it was at the last of these that appointments were customarily made. An Act of 1469 attempted to prohibit choice of councillors by popular election at such assemblies. But the royal burghs were slow in adopting the new regulations. In Ayr it was not till well into the 16th century that there was a belated acceptance of the 1469 Act which excluded the general mass of burgesses from participation, and introduced a system whereby the council in effect renewed itself by cooption. The burgh records which survive from 1580 indicate that by that date the new system was operating. Each Michaelmas, the council convened in the tolbooth and chose five merchants and two craftsmen to be new councillors; at a second meeting, the old and new councillors drew up leets for the appointment of magistrates and other 'officemen'; at a third meeting, the selection was made by the old and new councillors together with seven deacons of crafts. The five new magistrates, the five old ones, and the seven new councillors formed the council of seventeen for the ensuing year. This 16th century *sett* or burghal constitution would operate with only minor modifications till 1833, an elitist system in which the councillors were selected members of the merchant guild plus two hand-picked deacons of crafts, all 'maist meit and convenient'.

The chief magistrate was the provost, as the alderman came to be known in Ayr during the 16th century. That the council was not yet entirely independent and self-reliant is suggested by neighbouring lairds quite often occupying the provost's chair. The imposition of non-resident provosts resulted in popular tumults on at least six occasions in the later part of the century; and in 1587 the council was able successfully to resist a royal nominee. That a provost sometimes served for several years suggests that the prestige, power, and privileges of the office outweighed the burdens which produced among the other magistrates a more rapid change in personnel. One burden which which was often shed by the provost of Ayr in the difficult political circumstances of the later 16th century was representing the burgh in parliament; other magistrates were chosen to serve as parliamentary commissioner.

The two bailies retained certain fiscal responsibilities for collecting the burgh fermes or rents and supervising the collection of royal stents. But a bailie's principal duty was already that of judge in the burgh court. All magistrates were allowed a fee for their services, but the bailies had an additional perquisite in being allowed to pocket such fines as they might impose. Such *unlaws* were however limited to certain offences: like selling goods at prices higher than prescribed by the council each Martinmas, and some breaches of the peace. Offences were more commonly punished by public exposure at the jougs or in the stocks, scourging, branding, temporary imprisonment in the Thieves' Hole followed by banishment or execution. In 1551 two adulterers were sentenced 'to be scurgeit throu the toun'. In 1598 a thief was sentenced 'to be hangit to the deyth'. The gibbet was at one time situated beside the Nether Mill, later at the Knowe in the Burrowfield.

Sometime between 1429 and 1547 a fourth magistrate was appointed, to whom as thesaurer or treasurer was delegated most of the fiscal responsibilities previously exercised by the two bailies. He paid all fees, expenses, and bills, and supervised some of the common works. In this function he had in the 16th century the assistance of a Master of Works who was not a magistrate but shared responsibility for maintenance of the harbour, bridge, tolbooth, and other works. At a date between 1553 and 1580 the dean of guild became recognised as a fifth magistrate.

The merchant guild had existed since 1325; its dean as chosen by the guild brethren became a member ex officio of the town council; latterly the council chose one of its own members to act as dean of guild. He collected the guild entries, took charge of the rents endowed to the Church, and the maintenance of the Church of St John was his principal concern.

The common clerk is first mentioned in 1428, though some such office must have existed from the inception of the burgh. In the 16th century one town clerk was Stephen Prestoun who, when he became a bailie, handed over to his son Henry Prestoun. Later there was Michael Wallace, who was also provost for time. Later still John Masoun, who was related to another bailie, served for thirty nine years from 1586 till 1625. The clerk was paid a fee for his services (as were the magistrates) but was not subject to annual re-election. The clerk kept the burgh accounts (sometimes not very accurately!) and acted also as procurator fiscal, assisted on occasion by other local lawyers and Edinburgh writers. Lesser officials were the four serjeants who were 'ordanit to gang at the Baillies bakis with ane halbert or ax' and who had various duties and perquisities; the burgh 'lockman' who served as hangman when required; the clocksmith 'for keping of the knok'; the drummer and piper who perambulated the town daily at 4 a.m. and 6 p.m., and were fed by the burgesses in rotation; the town herd who looked after the cattle, and the 'poinder' who kept them off the sand hills. Chaplains including the schoolmasters were also salaried employees of the burgh.

Special appointments required to be made on those terrifying occasions when 'the pest' affected the burgh. The Black Death had ravaged Scotland in 1350–51 and 1361–62; there were later epidemics in 1380, 1401, 1430, 1439, 1456; in 1499 and 1500 it is known that Prestwick and Irvine were threatened. Experience no doubt suggested the drastic measures recorded in the burgh records when the pest came to Ayr with dreadful impact in 1545–56; threatened again in 1585, 1587, 1597, and 1601; re-appearing to wreak further havoc in 1606–07 and in 1647. How devastating was the epidemic of 1545–46 can only be guessed. Impressive precautions were taken as soon as the scourge was rumoured. In 1544 the ports were strengthened and manned by watchmen, two vennels were closed up, and thorns and stakes protected 'the oppin partis of the toun'. Despite efforts to exclude infected persons, from September 1545 till the following March 'the pest wis wonder greit' in Ayr as in 'all the burrowis townis of this realm'. The normal burgh

The Auld Brig O' Doon, possibly built in the 15th century, provided the principal link with Carrick and beyond.

organisation broke down. Provost Richard Bannatyne very likely fell victim, as Master of Works Alexander Farquhar certainly did, and possibly other members of the council. In this emergency William Neisbit was appointed 'kepar of the toun' and as 'vice-provost' or 'president' isolated 'the seik folkis upoun the mure' and exercised special disciplinary powers against 'thame that brak rewll in the tyme of the pest'. How ruthlessly the crisis was handled is revealed by an edict of 1585 (probably based on the measures of 1545) that persons entering the town otherwise than by the ports should be scourged and branded; any person communicating with unauthorised visitors would be banished; all infected persons were to be hospitalised in wooden 'ludges' erected on the Foul Mure beyond Carrick Street; if any such re-entered to the town they would be summarily hanged. 'Clengers' were hired to disinfect clothing by boiling in kettles, and to fumigate houses with fire and water. The cost to the town was horrific. Loss of life must have been considerable, including William Neisbit himself. At least £470 was spent over the next few years in connection with the pest, including compensation to persons whose houses were burned down and to the schoolmaster for fees lost 'quhen the schule held not'. It says much for the resilience of the local economy that the burgh finances were soon restored to normalcy.

Collection of the revenues, though the responsibility of the treasurer, was customarily for convenience farmed out. The petty customs charged on stall holders at markets and fairs; the tron custom charged for use of weights and measures; the customs charged on sale of nolt (cattle), sheep, wool, and cloth – instead of the burgh employing men to collect these, there were auctions where the customs were rouped; and individual burgesses, sometimes councillors, bid a sum payable to the treasurer, and were entitled to whatever they might collect. This system of roup and tack was obviously open to abuse, but it provided the burgh with a guaranteed income without the expense of collection, and the system was extended. In 1589 when the bridge impost was introduced, it was let to a tacksman; and in 1609 the successful bidder for the new anchorage dues was designated as water bailie – a confusing title since he was not a magistrate and not necessarily a councillor. Similarly the burgh fishing rights on the Rivers Ayr and Doon were rouped to the highest bidders, as were the quarries and mills.

Taking the period 1539–40 as typical, the treasurer's total income was just over £200. £82 came from the roup of the petty customs (£32), fishings (£8) and the Alloway mills (£42). Another £19 was derived from properties in the town. Two new burgesses, each paying their burgess fine or entry fee of 2 merks contributed less than £2. £108 came from the extensive burgh lands, forming more than half of the treasurer's returns. By the last quarter of the century annual revenues were averaging about £600, never less than £240, once reaching £1,429, and in real terms (allowing for 30% depreciation of the currency) the burgh's income was double what it had been early in the century. Part of this was the result of growing trade; but there were increased returns from the burgh lands which continued as the main source of revenue.

Within the Burrowfield the earliest burgesses had each been allowed by the royal charter of 1205 to acquire 'six acres of land which they have cleared from wood within the foresaid five pennylands, making their own profit therefrom and paying me twelvepence annually for each toft and six acres adjoining it'. Thus burgesses with their tofts within the town acquired 'faulds' in the adjacent area of the Burrowfield, and as the burgh expanded additional small arable plots were acquired. An area of such croft lands to the south east of the town and comprising perhaps 300 acres is suggested by 16th century references to numerous small holdings which were located in that area. All were held by individual tenants and there is no evidence of runrig or cooperative cultivation with rotation of holdings as has been found in Irvine for example. On the outermost extremity of Ayr's arable area was Fynnickland which, though not recorded till 1593, was probably under cultivation in the early 14th century at the time of the two aldermen called Fynvyk. Significantly Fynnickland was 6 acres in extent, the area as stipulated in the 1205 charter. Lands which were of poorer quality, as their names suggest, may have been reclaimed at a later date, but even so probably long before they find first mention in the records: Little Moss (1534); Gawblare (1430) with its 'pete landis' (1560); Sklaitbog (1537); Spittalbog (1540); with 'ane pece new land' (1561).

Other areas closer to the town remained uncultivated – the grazing land reached by the Cow Vennel, the Foul Mure beyond the Carrick Vennel; and south of the Sandgate were 'waste lands leading to the Water of Done' (1599).

The remotest parts of the Burrowfield were the lands on the lower reaches of the Curtecan burn; and that great upland area (forming half of the Burrowfield's 2,300 acres) rising from 100 feet above sea level to near 400 feet in the vicinity of Loch Fergus. Within these two areas were established by the 16th century over thirty separate properties, some of which have survived to become modern farms. In the 16th

century they were contributing nothing towards the burgh revenues, and if it were not for the definition of the Burrowfield boundaries in the 1205 charter and specific later references to individual properties as being within the Burrowfield, we could only guess (as with Irvine) that the the burgh lands originally comprised the entire parish of Ayr. Some were church lands, which we may presume to have been generously donated by the burgh. But in 1336 the Friars Preachers acquired through private gift around 220 acres which had previously belonged to someone called John of Kylmernock. How did so much burgh land pass into private possession between the 13th and 16th centuries? The reason was given in 1581: 'In tymes bigane the provost and baillies of the burt being for the tyme hes wtout consent or knowlege of the counsale throf disponit the townis lands, or at leist consentit to dispositioun of the samen be the tennents and occupiaris'. This was, as the council then agreed, 'to the greit hurt and prejudice of the said burt'.

Earlier in that century the council made a minor though notable acquisition. The lands of 'Cunyne Park lying between the Water of Doon and the burn of Corrochan' had belonged to the laird of Greenan since the 12th century, though sometimes leased, as in 1532 to William Nichol, Ayr merchant and master of works. Soon after that date the portion of Cunning Park known as the Common Isle passed into the possession of the burgh, and so afforded easier access to sea wrack for the tenants of the barony of Alloway. Obviously the 16th century councils were exercising a more effective policy of estate management than some of their predecessors.

Alloway had always been more efficiently controlled. Perhaps it was because this area of 2,000 acres between the Curtecan burn and the River Doon, rising gently towards 300 feet, was considered more valuable than the upper reaches of the Burrowfield. The fact that Alloway was defined as a barony in 1324 imposed special responsibilities upon the burgh authorities. Each year at Yule, Easter, and Michaelmas, a barony court met, originally at the motte of Alloway, latterly within the town of Ayr. The magistrates of Ayr in their capacity as barons-superior of Alloway at these courts renewed leases, adjudicated land disputes, exercised powers of justice. How detailed was their involvement is exemplified by a case in 1516 when one man sued a neighbour for a white hat which he had borrowed but lost at Flodden; and a ruling in 1529 that any tenant guilty of adultery could be deprived of his holding. It is not surprising that under such close management Alloway made regular and considerable contributions to the burgh revenues. In 1539–40, rents from Alloway produced £53 as compared with £50 from the Burrowfield. With these £53 in rents, £40 from Alloway mill, £2 from Alloway waulk mill, and £3 from Doon fishing, the barony in that that year provided just under half the burgh's total income.

There is clear evidence that the Ayr councils of the 16th century were making determined efforts to augment income from its lands and properties. The original burgh mails which the burgh collected on behalf of the crown, commuted into a fixed annual payment of £10 from the bailies to the exchequer, had become so insignificant and awkward to collect that they were ignored, thus burgesses holding older properties became in reality owner-occupiers. All that the council had from properties in the town were those annual rents which certain householders had allocated as endowments on behalf of the church. Similarly many of the faulds and crofts and much of the upland part of the Burrowfield had slipped into private possession. But part of the extensive muir and sandy wasteland was deemed capable of improvement. In 1535 (and possibly before) there was expenditure on spreading wrack and sowing corn 'quhar the sand blew'. In 1552 lands 'of the Sands' extending to 144 acres were leased out in plots on a nineteen-year tack. In 1557 these leases were converted into feus with an expected increased return, never realised, of over £300 per annum. Similarly the burgh accounts show that while some of the smaller properties in the Burrowfield continued to pay the traditional mails (amounting to £12 in 1539–40), others were now being feued at higher annual payments (totalling £18) with additional income from a grassum charged to each new occupant (providing £25 from two that year). A similar transformation in tenure followed at Alloway, there commencing in 1595 when one mailing fell vacant; the new occupant on entry paid a grassum or 'rentall silvir' of nearly £17; and an annual feu duty which was not a fixed money payment but a 'victual ferme' based on the price of barley and so proof against inflation. As other mailings became vacant, similar feus were granted. There were over thirty new entries in 1607–08, probably following deaths from the plague of the previous year. By 1623 Alloway had 56 merklands which had been feued and only 14 still 'unfermit'. With grain prices high, the former produced £504, the latter £16, giving a total ten times what it had been thirty years before. There was one further augmentation of income when after 1560 local church lands passed into the hands of the burgh. Such lands had not, of course, been worked by the churchmen themselves, but leased to laymen whose rents were received by the Church. The nature of such tenures was various and sometimes uncertain. Thus though the list of churchlands transferred to the burgh in 1567 is a lengthy one, no dramatic increase in rental is reflected in the burgh accounts till the first receipts from the mills are included (1577) and some of the larger church properties become vacant and available for feuing on new terms. In 1586 Friars Dankeith in Symington parish was feued by the council in return for annual meal payments. Surprisingly local church lands went for a fixed monetary feu duty, like Friarland in 1585 to David Craufurd of Kerse, Castlehill in 1592 to David Bannatyne, and Roodland in 1607 to John Cunningham.

The surviving records of the 16th century are sufficient to allow us to visualise the appearance of the local landscape. In particular we can refer to the Map of Kyle which appeared in Blaeu's Amsterdam Atlas of 1654, based as it was on surveys made by Timothy Pont a half-century before that great publication appeared. There were still areas of forest, particularly where the Wood of Dalrymple extended into the barony of Alloway beyond Carcluie, and on lower ground beside the River Ayr where Lochyrmoss adjoined Laiglan. Some of the lower ground was badly drained and unfit for cultivation, as again at Lochyrmoss where Pont noted two areas of water, since drained and vanished. The burgh muir provided rough pasture. Near the sea were the sandy lands where efforts at reclamation begun in 1552 had been a limited success because, by 1604, of the 144 acre plots, 58 had been abandoned and their occupants 'nocht weill knawit'. In the upland parts of the Burrowfield there could have been only small areas of arable land separated by wide areas of rough grazing. None of the land holdings was big enough to boast anything as impressive as a tower house. Those whom a later generation would describe as bonnet lairds might afford a decent stone-built home. But the typical rural dwelling was a miserable thatched cottage with low walls of stone or turf, and unglazed windows. Flitting meant removal of the *cuppill* or main roof beam to be used in the construction of a similar shack elsewhere, as is suggested in the Alloway records.

The area was however maintaining a sizeable and probably growing rural population. Traffic was sufficient to justify the bridges as recorded by Pont. Beside the Brig over the River Ayr (as reconstructed in 1588) there was also now the Auld Brig of Doon. This may have been built in the 15th century, traditionally attributed to a bequest from Bishop Kennedy. It gets

Newton Castle was built in the 15th century and its owners thereafter dominated the adjacent Newton burgh.

first mention in the burgh accounts for 1604, and in 1614 masons were employed in its repair. Pont also noted no fewer than five lesser bridges crossing the Curtecan burn boundary between the Burrowfield and Alloway. These indicate the routes taken by local traffic and by travellers passing through. From Coylton, Cumnock, and Nithsdale beyond came the road past Belston, Lochyrmoss, Gaitsyd, the Overmill, and Holmston to cross the Lichtmylburn where in 1582 there was 'an ancient bridge'. From that bridge (near the present Cemetery gate) the road entered the town via Millbrae, the Nether Mill, and what is now Mill Street. This main route was joined near Holmston by that lesser road known as the Foul Calsay, coming down from Loch Fergus, Treis, Rudeland (Wee Macnairston), Macnairston, Blackstob, Crofthead (or Dupholburnhead), and Burnton, by what was later called the Shavin Brae. The long-established road from Dalmellington crossed the Alloway lands of Mosshill and Cockhill, and entering the Burrowfield passed Abbothill, Whythill, Braston, and Bank. A bridge took it over the Glengall burn before it skirted Castlehill, Duppol (later Sandyford), and Little Moss to pass the quarry holes before entering the town by what is now Kyle Street. This road was joined at Little Moss by that other great road from the Brig of Doon. Passing between Alloway Kirk Crofts and the Upper Crofts it crossed the Curtecan burn by the Slaphouse bridge. Beyond was that land once belonging to the Friars of Fail which was renamed Harperland, Slop, or Slaphouse. The road after Slaphouse passed Chapelfauld and Corsmore to reach the Dalmellington road by what is now Inverkar Road.

The last of the important main routes into Ayr was that which ran from the ford at Doonfoot to enter the town by the Sandgate. This shore road crossed the Curtecan burn by a 'new bridge' noted in 1546, its stone work repaired by masons in 1577, 1582, and 1590; further north the Black burn was easily crossed by ford. In addition to these four major routes into the town there were lesser ones serving local needs. There was a track from Doonfoot to Alloway kirk (as joined by Tam O'Shanter at Mungo's Well); this continued past the motte of Alloway where it diverged with branches to Corton and Carcluie. What was known as the Wrack Road came down from Corton past Laigh Glengall, Fynnickland, and Chapelpark to the sea at Blackburn. Another came down from Carcluie past Alloway motte, over the lands later called Rozelle, and across the Slaphouse bridge on the way to Blackburn. Up each of these roads was transported seaweed wrack to manure the inland fields; down came peat (and sometimes coal), and people from Dalrymple on market days. Wrack for the eastern part of the Burrowfield required (in modern parlance) an inner by-pass from Brighouse on the Curtecan; past Cunning Park, St Leonards, Chapelpark; by Spittlebog to Twa Stane Cross and Duppol and past Castlehill – this was the route Sir Thomas Kennedy of Culzean was following in 1602 when he rode into ambush and assassination.

During the 16th century, on the opposite side of the River Ayr, the little burgh of Newton-upon-Ayr had become firmly established. That community had been in existence since the 13th century, when it found brief mention; was created a burgh of barony, probably between 1314 and 1371; and the records of that burgh when they begin in 1595 reveal a small but thriving population of perhaps two hundred persons, making a living principally by farming, supplemented by fishing and a few crafts. The records begin with 'The burrow court of the burgh of Newtoun sett and hailden within Adam Hunter's house', meeting at Whitsun, Beltane, and Michaelmas, or more frequently as required. Business concerned management of the 200 acres of arable and 150 acres of pasture that comprised the burgh, settling disputes over boundaries, imposing fines for unauthorised removal of turf or wrack, or allowing animals to stray, and legislating 'no person to brew ale dearer than 16d a pint'. There was then (or soon afterwards) a market cross and a Wednesday market in the King's Street. Here between two rows of cottages flowed the stream which came from Newton loch and served Newton mill before emptying itself into the River Ayr. The little burgh had an Upgate on the road to Prestwick; on the short track to the Bridge of Ayr was the Doungate (*doun* here meaning down), with a smithy and the Chapel of St Mary on the Chapelland. There were also the West-side port leading to the shore and the East-side port on the road past Newton Castle leading to St Quivox. As compared with the royal burgh of Ayr this was a primitive community. Yet it had a council with as many members of Ayr. A provost, two bailies, and councillors were chosen each Michaelmas, and appointments made of a procurator fiscal, treasurer, officer, four 'liners' who perambulated 'thair haill common lands' each Whitsun; and William Rankin, notary in Ayr, was in 1596 made a burgess and appointed clerk for life.

That Newton was able to operate effectively as a burgh is surprising. Growth was inhibited by the adjacent royal burgh always jealous of its own privileges. Its existence was insecure because of uncertainty over its precise boundaries, and new charters of 1595 and 1600 failed to settle the vexed issue of superiority over this burgh of barony asserted by the owners of the neighbouring lands of St Quivox.

Most of St Quivox parish had in the 13th century been awarded by the Stewart overlords of Kyle to Paisley Abbey following the failure of the Gilbertines to establish themselves at Dalmilling. At that time the eastern corner of the parish was held by Richard Wallace, whose family continued at Auchincruive till 1384 when it was inherited, along with Sundrum and Dalmellington, by Alan de Cathcart. A tower house was noted in 1532 at Auchincruive, which continued in the hands of the Cathcarts till the 18th century. In the 13th century another part of the parish was held

by William 'of Sanchar', forming later the barony of Sanchar-Lindsay which in the 14th century passed with other lands into the hands of the Wallaces of Riccarton who from 1381 made their home at the castle in the parish of Craigie. A branch of that family seems to have installed itself on the western edge of St Quivox parish, for an Adam Wallace of Newton is recorded in 1468. He or one of his immediate predecessors built Newton Castle where the lands of the burgh marched with St Quivox parish, so that there was long uncertainty whether the Castle was sited in that parish or within the parish of Monkton and Prestwick in which Newton burgh then was.

During the 16th century St Quivox experienced dramatic changes in land ownership, involving some remarkable characters. We find Matthew Wallace of Craigie and Adam Wallace of Newton becoming provosts of Ayr. Later came two other men with even wider interests and quite spectacular careers – William Hamilton, followed by James Stewart, Earl of Arran.

William Hamilton, eldest son of John Hamilton of Macnairston in the Burrowfield of Ayr, became a servitor in the household of James V. Early in Mary's reign he was knighted and served abroad as ambassador and at home at governor of Edinburgh Castle. Sometime about 1530 he acquired lands in Symington and Barnweil and took over also the lands of Sanchar-Lindsay. This, renamed Sanchar-Hamilton, included in St Quivox and adjacent parishes the lands of Sanchar (Eister and Wester Sanchar, Foulshaw, Gibbsyard), land on the south side of Sanchar Bog (Knockhill, Knock, Langholm, and part of Mainholm), Sandyford (Stockhill, Sandefurde, Craigisward, Schelbog, and the meadow of Sancharbog), Sancharmuir (with Clune and Prestwickschaws), the bailiary of Kincase and Robertlone, and the sea fishings of Wolquhare, Outcraog, and Welschot on this side of the Pow burn. There was added in 1540 the Castle of Newton with more adjacent lands (Newdykes, Cynungharis, Toscheochill, Cutrudes, Stanehousegreen) and fishings at Ruiff and Sandilshot on the adjacent shore. In 1547 from the abbot of Paisley he feued most of the remainder of St Quivox – Chapelland between Ayr Bridge and Halkhill; the adjoining Blackhouse, Bracanlie, and Barnbog lands; Dalmilling, Dalmilling mill, and Mainholm; Kirkhill and Kirklandholm near St Quivox church. Other lands were acquired in Barmure and Kylesmure in the eastern part of Kyle. He became William Hamilton of Sorn by inheritance from his father, thus also obtaining properties within Ayr Burrowfield, including Abbothill, Jakisfauld, Rough Acres, Twa Stane Cross. He became a a burgess and provost of Ayr, then of Edinburgh. Within thirty years this great estate, with lands elsewhere in Scotland, had passed into other hands, as Hamilton ascendancy over the crown waned. In 1578 there was a dispute between William Hamilton of Sanchar and John Wallace of Craigie and a fight within the church yard of St John's of Ayr. In 1579 the Hamilton lands of St Quivox and neighbourhood passed, temporarily, into the hands of William Cunningham of Caprington. By 1585 they were acquired by another Ayrshireman who like William Hamilton held for a time high office of state – Captain James Stewart, sometime Earl of Arran.

James Stewart, second son of Lord Ochiltree (and brother-in-law to John Knox) served as a soldier of fortune in Holland, France, and Sweden before returning to Scotland in 1579. Favoured by the young James VI he was made earl of Arran, and virtual ruler of the kingdom as Lord High Chancellor from 1583 till 1585 when he was overthrown. During his ascendancy he acquired among other possessions the barony of Sanchar-Hamilton and the Castle of Newton. In 1584 he secured the appointment of his brother Sir William Stewart of Monkton as provost of Ayr. After his deposition Arran retired to Newton (and with his brother was entertained by Ayr town council). He left Ayr by ship for exile in 1586, returned in 1587, whereupon his properties were escheated, and on a subsequent return in 1592 he was assassinated. In 1587 his wife Lady Elizabeth and their infant son (adulterously conceived while his mother was not yet divorced from her previous husband) were put out of Newton Castle, which a year later passed into the hands of John Wallace of Craigie.

Newton Castle became the headquarters of the Wallaces of Craigie from 1588 till 1701. John Wallace's acquisition was not made without some difficulty. There were conflicting claims for various properties, difficult to settle because as yet there was no statutory registration of sasines. Wallace ownership of most of St Quivox parish was confirmed – including the coal noted in East Sanchar. But certain properties remained outwith his control. Auchincruive of course continued with the Cathcarts. Mainholm with Woodhead and Dalmilling from 1579 belonged to George Jamieson who would become provost of Ayr. Boghall belonged successively to John Lockhart who died in 1593, his son Alexander, John who was Alexander's son, then John Lockhart of Bar who

succeeded in 1630 as grandson of Alexander – all four being sometime provosts of Ayr. Their lands included Boghall, part of Dalmilling with its mill, and Chapelland with Dykes and Smiddyhill 'befoir the yett of Newtoun'. The neighbouring lands of Blackhouse with Bracanlie and Barnbog belonged for a time to an Adam Wallace and would pass in 1648, along with Boghall, to a notary from Paisley called Robert Alexander.

There were conflicting claims for control of the burgh of Newton, and because of this the burgesses sought and obtained in 1595 a royal charter as a 'new foundation of the said burgh'. This cost them 800 merks (over £500 Scots) which substantial sum they were able to raise by stenting themselves. The charter, acquired for 'defence against Alexander Lockhart of Boghall' recognised the right of the burgesses to elect their bailies, and in 1596 they chose John Wallace of Craigie as their provost. The charter of 1595 failed to indicate who was the superior of the burgh, and Wallace seized the advantage. In 1600 both Newton and Prestwick had new charters. That of Newton included a warning against any infringement of the privileges of the royal burgh of Ayr. Each burgh was defined as subject to the king's son as Steward of Scotland. This, however, was vague enough to suggest that Wallace had a hand in securing these two charters of 1600, for he obtained for himself in 1599 and 1603 two other charters granting him personal possession of both Newton and Prestwick. The burgesses of Newton in 1602 in desperation turned to Alexander Lockhart of Boghall and his son John, admitted them as burgesses, and chose John Lockhart as their provost 'in respect of the greitt trubile and unkindness done and usit againes thaim by John Wallace of Cragie'. But Wallace was elected provost of Newton in 1603 and of Prestwick in 1605. The hereditary control which ensued has been appropriately described by George Pryde: 'The oppression of the tiny burghs by the Wallaces of Craigie makes a sordid and shameful tale'.

At the beginning of this chapter it was estimated that the 16th century royal burgh of Ayr contained from three to four hundred houses and a population between 1,500 and 2,000. The adult working population comprised approximately 500 unfree indwellers; 150 craftsmen who though burgesses were limited in wealth and influence; 50 merchants involved in foreign trade who were burgesses and guild brethren; 30 neighbouring lairds who were guild brethren, some of whom were actively involved in trade. The leading burgesses who formed the council came from those last select 80 households. It is possible to assemble biographical details of some from council books (surviving from 1547), the accounts (from 1538) and certain national records. It should be particularly interesting to assess the background of those who became the chief magistrates of the burgh, known as aldermen and then (from 1548) as provosts.

Those preceding paragraphs which looked north of the river indicated that a number of aldermen and provosts held lands there. In St Quivox there was Sir William Hamilton of Sanchar, the Lockharts of Bar, George Jamieson of Mainholm, the Wallaces of Newton and Craigie. From an adjacent parish came Stewart of Monkton and Blair of Adamton. But no one landed family was able to dominate Ayr in the way the Montgomeries of Eglinton did for Irvine. Royal influence was equally limited. In the 15th century John Multrar, alderman for a long period, was perhaps a royal nominee holding as he did the crown appointment as Custumar for Ayr, deriving profit from the customs during the period from 1440–80. But a century later there were protests in 1569, 1573, 1578, and 1584, directed against non-resident provosts, and in 1585 a royal nominee was successfully rejected.

Attempts have been made by some historians to distinguish between merchant burgesses (whose main interest lay in making money) and burgess lairds (socially-superior landlords who happened to find it advantageous to become involved in municipal affairs). Ayr had burgesss lairds, but none of them became prominent in running the burgh apart from the Wallaces of Craigie. The Lockharts certainly came from landed stock – the Lockharts of Bar in the parish of Galston – following the not-uncommon pattern of a younger son of the laird taking up a commercial career, whose profits were in due course invested in land. Thus John Lockhart purchased Boghall and bequeathed it to his son and grandson, along with a range of properties in Ayr and its Burrowfield – a tenement near the bridge, another by the Fish Cross, a third near the sheep market, two crofts at the Townhead, three others called Pennybus, Rudeland, and Maryland (in what is now Forehill), four more

to the south including Sklaitbog, Chapelfauld, and Branzanefauld, plus three separate acres of the adjacent Sandy lands. William Hamilton of Sanchar was the son of a burgess, who made his fortune from a career in the royal household. The more usual background for a provost was a successful commercial career. Such was James Tait, a prominent merchant who built then sold what became known as Loudoun Hall, and had other properties including Glengall (Over Clongall). Another was Richard Bannatyne, a recent incomer from Bute, whose son David in 1592 acquired the lands of Castlehill and Crawisland and whose family would in the 18th century produce in John Ballantine one of Ayr's greatest provosts. Another dynasty was that of Archibald Fergushill and his son David, both provosts. The father had shipping interests, the son had other skills for he was involved in building the new tolbooth and the hospital. They were obviously moneyed men, who made substantial loans to the burgh and to private individuals. They had a tenement with two shops, which they let, situated at the meal market in High Street 'at the end of the Tolbooth thereof, between the said Tolbooth on the north, and the well called the new well, and the common street of the burgh, on the south'. They had a barn 'between the common barns of the said burgh, in the vennel which leads to the quarry', a small holding of land beside the Foul Calsay, others at Spittalbog, Corrochan, and the Sandy lands, some other properties held temporarily in wadset as security for loans awaiting redemption, and they may thus have acquired Sauchrie in Maybole parish. There were other well-represented families. Early in the 16th century John Brown and Thomas Brown, both aldermen, may have been related. John Jamieson was followed as provost by George Jamieson, perhaps a son or brother. Another member of the family, Robert Jamieson, son of John Jamieson, was councillor for three spells between 1581 and 1603 and though never a provost was bailie, dean of guild, and served as parliamentary commissioner twice. His ships, which carried James VI on two occasions, were manned by 'the best and maist able marineris within the toun of Air'.

Part Two
Transition

SIX

The Church Reformed

During the 16th century there was for Western Europe an expansion of commerce and in some countries including Scotland more effective central government, bringing social changes which affected Ayr, as suggested in the previous chapter. One particular change now to be specially examined was that which involved the Reformation of the medieval Church and the establishment in various northern countries of new Protestant churches. The first challenge to the Church came in Germany in 1517; the Scottish Reformation followed belatedly in 1560; and more than a hundred years would pass in painful struggle, occupying most of the 17th century, before a religious settlement was achieved. From before 1560 till after 1689 the problems of the Church dominated Ayr's history.

In the 16th century, and indeed earlier, there were widespread criticisms of the church. Both theology and practice were questioned in 1494 by thirty lesser lairds from central and northern Ayrshire led by Adam Reid of Barskimming. These Lollards of Kyle were tried at Glasgow, charged with heresy, and admonished. Local interest in doctrine continued, as instanced by another Ayrshire Lollard who about 1520 prepared a manuscript translation into Scots of a Wyclif New Testament. He was Murdoch Nisbet of Hardhill in the parish of Loudoun, parish clerk and notary, who did business sometimes in Ayr, as in 1536 when the burgh treasurer paid 14s to 'Murdoch Neisbyt, for services to the town'. But another generation would pass before local criticism developed into open protest.

Many who had no time for the new doctrines were nevertheless concerned about the condition of the church, especially disturbed by the way its spiritual effectiveness was limited by secular considerations. The Church by donations and bequests had become a wealthy landed corporation, and some churchmen were inevitably affected. The local jingle (of unknown provenance) may have had some substance:

The Friars of Fail they made guid kale
On Fridays when they fasted,
And they never wanted gear enough
As long as their neighbours' lasted.

The Black Friars of Ayr, as Chapter 3 explained, were a well-off house with their lands and mills. It may have been local hostility to this situation which persuaded the burgesses in 1474 to invite to Ayr the Grey Friars of the Observatine order who were noted for their strict vow of poverty.

Certainly there were many good men in the Church. No better example could be cited than George Lockhart who was born in Ayr about 1485, son of James Lockhart and his wife Mariote Multray. When his mother died in 1500 George and his brother John must still have been at school in Ayr (and thus the first identifiable pupils of that noted establishment). In 1504 they went to continue their studies in Paris. George Lockhart there became a lecturer, and in 1519 Prior of the College of Sorbonne. He was a convinced defender of the traditional doctrines against the new Lutheran ideas. Between 1514 and 1528 he published ten books which won him an international reputation as a philosopher. George Lockhart returned to Scotland between 1522 and 1525 to be Rector of St Andrews University – where he may have tutored young John Knox. He came back again from Paris in 1533 to serve for the last fourteen years of his life as Dean of Glasgow. After his death in 1547 there were regularly celebrated in the Church of St John, as he had arranged, obit masses for his parents, his brother, and himself.

Another Ayrshireman who studied in Paris was Quintin Kennedy, who in 1547 became abbot of Crossraguel, an appointment certainly deserved by merit, but obviously obtained through family influence, as son of the 2nd Earl of Cassillis. This was perhaps the most serious defect in the administration of the church, that many appointments were subject

George Lockhart, a native of Ayr, became Prior of the Sorbonne in Paris and a philosopher whose books defended traditional doctrines against new 16th century Lutheran ideas.

to lay influence and consequently the resources of the church often became diverted to secular ends. The crown in particular took advantage, for the royal exchequer was short of funds in this age of inflation, and the Church was far wealthier that the State. By a papal indult of 1487 the Scottish crown was allowed, when bishoprics and abbacies fell vacant, to leave such offices unfilled for eight months during which appointments acceptable to the king might be made, including commendatory abbots who were sometimes laymen and who like bishops and other ecclesiastics might raise money by feuing church properties. Much of the landed wealth of the church had already been dispersed by feuing, before the Reformation.

Staunch defenders of the old faith like Quintin Kennedy were conscious of an urgent need to reform (from within) the organisation of the church, but though provincial assemblies of the church were convened to consider reforms, secular vested interests remained intact. Quintin Kennedy sadly noted that

'gyf ane benefice vaick (becomes vacant), the gret men of the realme wyll have it for temporale rewarde ... the convent and place quhare God suld be daylie honourit and servit gais clene to rewyne ... Geve (if) the Kirk had the auld ancient libertie ... than sulde all hereseis be flemit (cast out). ... In the mene tyme ... the Kirk is sclanderit, God is dishonorit, all hereseyis, wickitnes, and vise regnis'.

One particular complaint was the neglect of parish churches when available resources were diverted into secular pockets. Teinds were collected from landholders in each parish, but only a portion provided for maintenance of a parish priest. Long before the 16th century the 43 parishes of Ayrshire had all been appropriated to monastic orders or other religious establishments, which were awarded the parish teinds as a means of subsidising their good works. The collection of teinds however was often leased out to local laymen, who out of their takings paid the vicars whom the patrons had appointed as parish priests. Vicars themselves sometimes acquired several parishes and their responsibilities were delegated to curates who were considered poorly-paid and poorly-qualified. From Dundonald parish in the 16th century for example, Paisley Abbey derived £160 plus 2½ chalders of barley; from this £60 went to a non-resident vicar, plus some £13 each to two curates responsible for parochial duties. An example of pluralism in the same period was the man who was simultaneously vicar of Kilmaurs, Dalry, and Monkton. Such typical abuses were to be found in Ayr.

The Church of St John had been appropriated to support Glasgow Cathedral since the 14th century until 1501 when the proceeds of Ayr, Alloway, Coylton, Dalmellington, and Dalrymple were for the most part diverted to help maintain the new Chapel Royal in Stirling. Ostensibly responsible for Ayr parish was a rector, who was seldom if ever resident. This rectorship was held briefly by Henry Stewart (along with other posts from 1528 till he became bishop of Aberdeen); Andrew Lockhart (in 1531); then for fourteen years from 1532 by Gilbert Binning (who was a notary doing business in Glasgow with a chaplaincy in the Cathedral there); followed by David Gibson who held half-a-dozen posts in different parts of Scotland which left him little if any time to devote to Ayr, whose rectorship he held for twenty years after 1546. As deputy for the rector there was a vicar, but once again the vicarage fees for Ayr seem to have been collected by non-resident priests like Michael Cunningham (from 1521), John Campbell (from 1540), Robert Montgomery (from 1546). From

1548 the vicar was Robert Leggat who was also curate at Prestwick and clerk of the burgh court there. The actual care of souls within the parish of Ayr was left in the hand of curates. Henry Hunter was promoted from chaplain to be curate from 1506 till 1535; followed by George Lockhart (1542); then Richard Miller, chaplain at St Peter's altar, became curate in 1551. He was probably Ayr's last parish priest before the Reformation, his duties taken over in 1558 by the vicar Robert Leggat who was sympathetic to Reformed ideas.

Fortunately, burgh churches like Ayr could rely on the services of chaplains who were attached to the various altars. These chaplainries had been endowed by local benefactors, and the burgh council managed the funds and appointed and paid the chaplains. There were by the 16th century eight chaplains attached to the Church of St John. Many seem to have been local men – this provided a good living for the sons of some important burgesses. Their duties were carefully spelled out in the Obit Book. But even here there was slacknesss. Some chaplains acquired vicarages in neighbouring (and even distant) parishes; many acted as notaries. Andrew MacCormyll, son of a burgess family and himself a local property owner, appointed in 1502 as chaplain and 'instructor for the time of the grammar school of Ayr', was from 1488 till his death in 1507 also vicar of Straiton, and active during that period as a notary. Gavin Ros, son of the laird of Hayning in Riccarton parish, graduated at Glasgow University in 1512 and set up as a notary, a business which he continued, operating through Ayrshire and beyond, even after his appointment in 1519 as schoolmaster and chaplain of the Holy Trinity. On several occasions Ayr burgh council had to complain of chaplains breaking their contract of residence. More seriously, there is one instance, in 1475, of the chaplain John McNedar being found guilty as 'a common nycht walker and ane oppressour of the kyngis lieges by common tulze, and a deforsar and defouler of women'.

Efforts made from within the church to deal with acknowledged abuses proved unsuccessful. The new movement, which added objection to church doctrine to these other criticisms, gathered strength.

The first overt action in Ayr occurred in 1533 when Walter Stewart, brother of Andrew Lord Ochiltree, was accused of decapitating an image of the Virgin in the Greyfriars church, signifying opposition to what the reformers regarded as idolatry. Stewart was persuaded to recant, but divine displeasure at this (it was later alleged) was shown when he was drowned

John Welch, son-in-law of John Knox, exercised an enormous influence in Ayr during his brief ministry 1600–1606. His garden behind High Street survived till 1968.

crossing a river on the way home from Glasgow. The year 1544 saw the beginning of an organised movement, with George Wishart's visit to Ayrshire on a preaching tour. Backed by the 3rd Earl of Cassillis and the 4th Earl of Glencairn he proclaimed the new reformed doctrines in sermons at Galston, Mauchline, and Ayr. Two years later Wishart was taken and executed at St Andrews, and the subsequent seizure of St Andrews castle by protestants proved an abortive coup. The movement however continued, supported in particular by the lesser lairds. The household chaplain of George Campbell of Cessnock read the scriptures in English as part of family worship, a practice probably followed in other lairds' houses. Between 1545 and 1548 John Lockhart of Bar and Charles Campbell of Bargower organised a campaign in Ayrshire and adjacent counties, in course of which they violated churches and chapels, despoiling altars, stalls, and glazed windows, seizing eucharistic chalices and other ornaments of the mass. For this they were fined in absentia, but not till 1550. The regents who governed on behalf of the child Queen Mary pursued a vacillating policy, and support for the reformed faith was growing.

A crisis was developing. In 1556 John Knox after his return to Scotland visited Ayrshire to preach at Bar (Galston), Kingencleugh (Mauchline),

Carnell, Ochiltree, Gadgirth, and Ayr. Adherents of the new doctrines were obviously forming themselves into protestant congregations meeting for worship. By 1559 there was complaint that in Ayr John Willock was 'usurping the authority of the church, and for taking upon himself the service thereof, and also for convocation and gathering of the lieges ... haranguing and preaching to the said lieges and persuading and seducing them to his erroneous and seditious doctrines and heresies'. In 1559, on John Knox's second return to Scotland, the rising tide could no longer be stemmed. Ayrshire protestant lords assembled at Craigie – the 5th Earl of Glencairn, Campbell of Loudoun, Boyd of Kilmarnock, Stewart of Ochiltree, Chalmers of Gadgirth. With twelve hundred horse and as many foot they joined the Lords of the Congregation in that brief struggle which, with timely aid from England, won victory for protestantism. In 1560 the Scots parliament rejected the authority of the Pope, celebration of the Mass was forbidden, and a Reformed Confession of Faith was enacted.

The Reformation was accomplished by men whose motives were mixed. Some were obviously actuated by sincere religious beliefs, but the lords whose political actions enabled protestantism to become established were at the same time subject to other inducements. Many had already enriched themselves at the expense of the church and some were no doubt anxious to enrich themselves further. Many were becoming disillusioned with the traditional Auld Alliance with France which involved repeated wars with England and disasters like Solway Moss (1542), the 'Rough Wooing' (1544, 1545) and Pinkie (1547) where Ayrshire losses were so heavy. Ayrshire notables like Cassillis, Glencairn, and Campbell of Loudoun were ready to accept bribes to build up a pro-English party in Scotland – though as ready to turn again to France when political circumstances demanded. England accepted Scottish protestant preachers like John Knox and John Willock till Mary Tudor re-established Catholicism in that country; thereafter they sought refuge in Geneva, home of John Calvin. After the child Mary Queen of Scots succeeded in 1542, the regents who ruled on her behalf adopted towards the protestants changing policies of toleration and repression depending upon the current political situation. What brought matters to a head was the marriage in 1558 of Mary Queen of Scots to the heir to the French throne and an immediate prospect of Scotland becoming a French province; her mother Mary of Guise as regent in Scotland from 1554 now

showing increased hostility towards protestants; and the accession in England, also in 1558, of Elizabeth, whose aid was available to prevent French control over Scotland. What happened in Scotland thereafter has been described as 'a revolt against France as well as Rome'. The Lords of the Congregation took control; foreign troops were withdrawn; protestantism was formally recognised by parliament in 1560. But the Lords of the Congregation had neither the authority, the will, nor the expertise to create a new established church. Its organisation depended upon local initiative and enthusiasm.

That the burgesses of Ayr, or many of them, were anxious for a reformation is apparent. So much so that protestant worship was being conducted, with the cooperation of the burgh council, possibly in 1557, certainly by 1559, and before the parliament of 1560 provided a legal sanction.

The growth of protestantism within Ayr can be traced. Perhaps the first instance was in 1521 when the curate Henry Hunter excommunicated certain burgesses. In 1533 there was that incident when Andrew Stewart from Ochiltree cast down images in the Greyfriars. In 1537 the authorities summoned certain unnamed persons from Ayr while 'serching of the hereticks of the west land' In 1539 a local friar, John Willock, adopted the new faith. It is not clear whether he was Dominican or Franciscan, but he renounced his vows and departed to join other protestants in exile in England. In 1542 the curate of St John's was one George Lockhart, and it is tempting to wonder if this in fact was the philosopher dean of Glasgow returned to spend his last years in his native town attempting to strengthen the old faith. In 1543 when parliament declared it permissible to read the scriptures in English, there was a tumult in Ayr with a Grey friar, John Routh, the central figure in a riot. That he opposed the innovation is the accepted story (though there is some doubt).At any rate the council provided him with expenses to leave the town, and accepted 'the charge to read the scripture in Inglis'. In the following year, 1544, the visit of the protestant preacher George Wishart produced another incident. This required the presence of the bishop of Glasgow to deny him entry into the Church of St John, so that Wishart preached his sermon in the open at the market cross. There was a similar visit by John Knox in 1556. The burgh accounts show the council continuing its routine contributions towards the Church of St John. The treasurer's accounts for 1557–58 however include a novel item, allowing £4 'for the minister's chalmer male' indicating that the council (or a majority of its

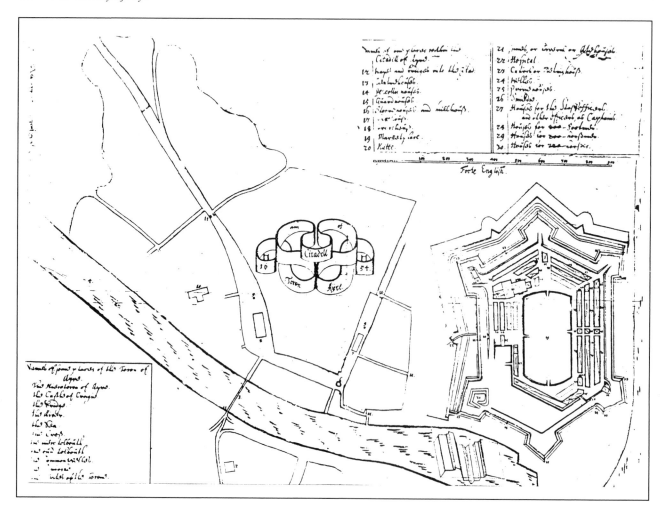

Cromwell's army of occupation 1651–1660 required the construction of a Citadel. Tessin's Plan shows also an outline of the streets at the time, and the site where the parish church was relocated.

members) had agreed to provide accommodation for a protestant preacher. This may have been that native of Ayr, Richard Bannatyne, who became a secretary to John Knox, returned with him in 1556, and perhaps remained in Ayr thereafter, for we find him here in 1559–60. The accounts for 1557–58 indicate a legal dispute with the Black friars, and trouble was brewing at the Church of St John. Early in 1558 Richard Miller gave up his curacy, presumably under pressure from the magistrates, who were cooperating with the vicar Robert Leggat, who had a tenement on the east side of the High Street, and was sympathetic to the reform movement. Leggat is thereafter described as the vicar-curate of Ayr, and was conducting burials here in 1558 though continuing at Prestwick as curate.

In the spring of 1559 events came to a local climax. The ex-friar John Willock returned to Ayr, to preach in the Church of St John. Quintin Kennedy, abbot of Crossraguel, who was 'constrainzit on my conscience to oppone myself to this wickit lymmaris heresie and doctrine' arranged a debate with Willock in the town house of the laird of Carnel, but this was prevented by Willock's supporters, four or five hundred in number. The council entertained the preacher with 'wyne to Johnne Willock' despite instructions brought 'fra the Quene Regent to forbyde the prechouris'. Sometime after Michaelmas 1558, and probably in the summer of 1559, James and George Bannatyne rode to Edinburgh and brought back 'ane preachour', Christopher Goodman, the first protestant incumbent at the Church of St John. Joiner work on the pulpit, as authorised by the burgh treasurer, suggests that the church was being adapted for protestant worship. A further development is indicated by the accounts for

1558–59 showing the usual annual payment to the Greyfriars had ceased, a hint that they had decided to abandon Ayr, for thereafter they find no local mention. The Blackfriars however remained.

In May 1559 the council dismissed the chaplains from the Church of St John and prohibited any further celebration of the mass. In the same month, at Whitsun, as part of a concerted national campaign against friaries, the house of the Blackfriars at Ayr was attacked. According to a poem published in 1595 this was acccomplished without undue rancour. The task was entrusted to Robert Campbell of Kingencleugh and Hew Wallace of Carnel, who gave the friars advance warning and

> Either withe good will or with ill
> The keyes they gave thir twa untill,
> After their gudes they had out tane:
> So greater harm the Friers had nane.

Two of the friars indeed continued in Ayr, and each was allowed by the council £16 a year for his life-time, John Rollie till 1582, David Allasoun till 1618. This might seem surprising, but in 1562 an act concerning the Fruits of Benefices recognised all holders of office within the old church as still legally entitled to two thirds of their dues, providing they did not breach the law of 1560 forbidding the celebration of mass. At the Church of St John some chaplains could be summarily dismissed by the council, though two of them were able to claim the life-rent of their posts. The council took pity on another, Alexander Kerr who had kept the books and vestments for a long period and was offered £10 if he was prepared to serve as bell-ringer and cleaner and 'renunce the Devill, the Paip, and all thair warkis'. Titular office-holders continued to collect their revenues: David Gibson and his successors as rectors of Ayr, and Robert Leggat as vicar. At Alloway the absentee vicar Henry Arnot continued to benefit from 1546 till 1571. Teinds which had been leased to laymen continued to be collected by them. Thus in 1570 Thomas Kennedy of Bargany was tacksman for the parsonage of Ayr and Adam and Cuthbert Wallace for Alloway. John Knox and the protestant churchmen had vainly recommended that all the properties of the old church should be transferred for the use of the new. The unsatisfactory compromise of 1562 provided only for a third of benefices to be taken for the needs of the crown and the maintenance of the ministers of the reformed church. Later as offices fell vacant more of the teinds became available. In the initial stages, responsibility for the maintenance of the new church was willingly undertaken in Ayr by the council.

In 1559 Ayr's protestant congregation had invited Christopher Goodman to be their pastor. He was an Englishman of outstanding ability who had collaborated with John Knox at Geneva in compiling a protestant Book of Common Order. The burgh accounts for 1559–60 indicate the council paying for a new pulpit in St John's Kirk suitable for protestant worship, providing bread and wine for the communion; there was also 'silver gevin to the minister ... ane gowning ... curtenis to the ministeris chalmer'. When Goodman went off with Richard Bannatyne on political business, his travelling expenses were covered, and John Orr, the newly-appointed schoolmaster, required to deputise in the reading of prayers and administering the sacrament. The vicar-curate Robert Leggat was meantime officiating at Prestwick (where he would be appointed protestant 'reader' in 1563) but his continued involvement at Ayr affords (in the words of Dr Sanderson) 'a unique glimpse of the co-existence of the two ecclesistical systems'.

In August 1560, at the Parliament which enacted a Reformed Confession of Faith and prohibited celebration of the Mass, the burgh of Ayr was represented by bailie John Kirkpatrick. At the end of that year Christopher Goodman after his brief ministry in Ayr moved to St Andrews. He was succeeded by Robert Acheson, who was provided by the council with rent, coal, candles and 'all uther necessaris and ane pair of schone to himself and ane uther to his boy'. In the year 1560–61 he was furnished with black clothes adorned with silk buttons, a canvas gown, and shirts; the next year with 'a coat of French black' and £10. In 1562 when 'the disputatioun wes betwein the Abbot and John Knox' there was expenditure on hospitality for the reformer on this his second visit to the town. A three-day debate between him and Abbot Quintin Kennedy took place in Maybole, not, as had been proposed, in Ayr where a bond for the maintenance of the reformed church was subscribed by 'Michael Wallace, provost of Ayr, with fortie more of the honestest burgesses of that town'. Also in Acheson's ministry, in 1567 the burgh was endowed with what became known locally as Queen Mary's Mortification. As part of an unavailing attempt to rally support for the Queen, the extensive lands of the Blackfriars, the few acres of the Greyfriars, and those of St Leonard's Chapel were transferred from the crown to the burgh for the maintenance of the reformed church and provision for poor relief and education. The next minister James Dalrymple entered his charge in 1568 with improved prospects. Mary Queen of Scots had been deposed (for reasons which were only marginally concerned with religion). The advisers of young James VI

The Church where worship was held from 1656 is a fine example of 17th century ecclesiastical architecture.

arranged the first formal recognition of the reformed church and decreed that it might take over benefices as they fell vacant. Thus James Dalrymple was able to acquire the revenues of the vicarage of Ayr (1571), and of Alloway (1573) which he gave up on obtaining the rectory of Ayr (1579); and the burgh made up his stipend. In 1573 he claimed he was entitled to more. But the burgh pointed out that the profits of the friars' lands were still being taken up by tacksmen, and the proceeds of the obits and chaplainries were more than absorbed in upkeep of the kirk, in payments to a reader (or assistant minister), to the clerk of the kirk session who was a 'sangster that takis up the psalmes befoir and eftir the precheing', costs of cleaning and repair, plus £56 towards the poor. Nevertheless before his death in 1580 Dalrymple's stipend for the combined parishes of Ayr and Alloway had risen from £100 to a substantial £150 a year. He had also two assistants in Thomas Greig for Ayr and James Ramsay at Alloway. They were 'readers' qualified to conduct services but not authorised to preach doctrine. Greig who was doctor or second master in the burgh school had a combined basic salary of £20; Ramsay had £17 plus the glebe of Alloway.

James Dalrymple seems to have been a chorister in the Church of St John before the Reformation. Other clergymen from Ayr accepted conversion to the new faith and served within the reformed church. Two chaplains who were schoolmasters found posts outwith Ayrshire – Patrick Anderson and John Buchan. Another, George Cochran, went to St Quivox as reader. Thomas Andrew, another Ayr chaplain, became vicar then reader at Irvine. William Kirkpatrick, brother of bailie John Kirkpatrick of Ayr, was a monk at Kilwinning Abbey who became minister of that parish. David Allasoun, the friar who received a pension from Ayr burgh, may be the person of that name who served as reader at Barnweil then St Quivox. Robert Leggat, the vicar of Ayr who was also curate at Prestwick continued there as reader. If we include the names of Richard Bannatyne and John Willock who were earlier converts, then there is substance in John Knox's description of Kyle as 'a receptacle of God's servants of old'.

Yet only a small number of clergymen conformed. Most preferred to retire, sustained by the life-rents they continued to enjoy, equivalent to two-thirds of their former livings. There was an acute shortage of ministers in the reformed church. In 1574 Ayrshire's 43 parishes were provided with only sixteen fully-qualified ministers, supported by 41 readers. Despite initial difficulties in finding ministers and paying for them, the protestant church established itself, with no evidence of local opposition. Only in Carrick was there any serious attempt to maintain the old faith. In 1563 a convocation of two hundred armed men assembled for mass at Maybole and Kirkoswald. But after Quintin Kennedy's death in 1564, all that survived were those monks continuing at Crossraguel till the last one died in 1607.

The coronation oath of the infant James VI (1567–1625) committed him and his successors to support the reformed church. But how that Church should be organised and what were to be its relations with the State remained unresolved. For more than a century argument raged, and the country would be involved in bitter and sometimes bloody conflict.

The early protestant kirk of Ayr was typically organised on a congregational basis, with ministers chosen by the membership, and having a kirk session of annually-elected elders. Some remote supervision was exercised through meetings of the General Assembly and a Synod of Glasgow, who appointed certain ministers to be superintendents or commissioners – like John Willock who was for a time Superintendent for the West. There were also (elsewhere in Scotland) holders of bishoprics who had conformed and retained their status and titles within the reformed church; the appointment of other bishops would follow – in 1571 John Porterfield, later to be minister of Ayr, was nominated as first protestant bishop of Glasgow. But the choice of bishops by the crown rather than by the General Assembly, and royal involvement in the affairs of the church, were resented by some. Andrew Melville who returned from Geneva in 1574 asserted that church and state were 'Two Kingdoms' and the independence of the kirk required a scheme of presbyterian government. In 1581 the General Assembly ordered the formation of presbyteries composed of ministers and elders, initially in thirteen districts, with the Presbytery of Ayr covering the 24 parishes of Kyle and Carrick, whilst that of Irvine took in those in Cunninghame. In 1584 (when James Stewart, Earl of Arran was in power) the so-called Black Acts re-asserted the authority of the crown over the entire church. In 1592 (when political circumstances allowed) presbyterianism was recognised by the Golden Acts – there should be independent General Assemblies; presbyteries were made effective church courts; and the duties were specified of kirk sessions, whose elders were now to

be appointed for life. But from 1597 James VI was able to re-assert control over the General Assembly and re-introduce episcopacy with the appointment of bishops. After he departed for England to succeed Elizabeth in 1603 as James VI and I he continued to inflame presbyterian resistance by his erastian policies, culminating in the imposition of a new liturgy in 1618. Within Ayr this sequence of national events had their immediate impact.

When Ayr's second protestant minister James Dalrymple died in 1580 the burgh council, despite its earlier dispute with him over the stipend, was generous enough to provide support for 'his widow and fadderless barnes for the ardent luf shown by the said James to the said burgh'. As his successor a call went to John Porterfield, previously minister of Ardrossan. Not only did the council pay for the flitting, sending a man 'to gang about the Ministeris geir', but it spent £20 on a bribe 'to the scribe to the privie counsale to obtain the parsonage and vicarage of Alloway for the minister'. During Porterfield's twenty years as minister of Ayr his stipend rose to £200 from the revenues of Ayr and Alloway parishes and contributions from the council. The ministry was becoming an attractive career, for Porterfield's successors in the 17th century would outdistance inflation to get more than £500 a year. Of John Porterfield's character the evidence suggests he was no zealot. He was friend of 'diverse great men', on Sundays after church service used to shoot at the bow-butts, and though he participated in setting up the presbytery in 1581 he seemingly offered no resistance to the legislation of 1584 which threatened the independence of the church. Nor indeed did Ayr council, for the king's minister who introduced these 'Black Acts' – James Stewart, Earl of Arran – secured the appointment of his brother William Stewart of Monkton as provost of Ayr. Nevertheless, when the archbishop of Glasgow visited Ayr in 1588 he was mobbed in the streets; and in 1593, after presbyterianism had been recognised by the king, Provost George Jamieson and the council guaranteed that it would be 'defendit by thame after thair poweris to the uttermest'.

In 1600 John Welch was unanimously elected Porterfield's assistant and successor. Born at Dunscore about 1570, after a wild boyhood he trained for the ministry in the new university at Edinburgh, was ordained to Selkirk then translated to Kirkcudbright. There he married the youngest daughter of John Knox. In 1596 in a sermon he threatened rebellion against the king and was suspended for six months. This vigorous proponent of the new aggressive pres-

THE AULD KIRK PULPIT, AYR.
erected in 1658 at a cost of £600 Scots,
taken down in 1877.

A central feature of protestant worship was the sermon, emphasised by pulpit and sounding board from the 17th century church.

byterianism was a popular choice for the congregation of Ayr. His preaching and practice confirmed him as 'thair weill-belovit pastor'. The impact of John Welch and the kirk session on the social life of Ayr (as is described in the next chapter) was tremendous. Behind his house in High Street was a garden where he regularly prayed: this John Welch's Garden was preserved as 'one of the most sacred and historic places in Ayr' until built over in 1968.

In 1603 when James VI succeeded as James I of England, the Union of the Crowns was celebrated in Ayr on 25 July, 'to be keipit as an solemn day, be the haill inhabitants of this Burch, Baronie of Alloway, and Burrowfield'. But though there were 'fyres of rejoising' the 'prayers and thanksgiving' were premature. For the king continued his efforts to limit the powers of the Church in Scotland.

Welch succeeded Porterfield when the latter died in 1604. But quite soon, after only five years in Ayr, Welch was removed, never to return. When James VI

attempted to curb the independence of the General Assembly, a number of ministers met in defiance of royal authority. Six including Welch were imprisoned in Blackness castle and banished from the kingdom in 1606. Ayr council was prepared to contribute £10 'To pay the expenses of the minister's wife in going to her husband at Blackness'; and indeed for several years sent his full stipend to Welch in France. There he mastered the language and ministered to continental congregations till he was allowed to come to London, where he died in 1622. His wife Elizabeth Knox died in Ayr in 1625.

After Welch's removal in 1605, the charge remained vacant till George Dunbar was translated from Cumnock in 1608. Though willing to be inducted by episcopal forms he too gave offence and in 1612 was removed and imprisoned in Dumbarton. He was allowed to return in 1613 to occupy the second charge as colleague to the moderate William Birnie who held the first charge from 1612 till his death in 1619. In 1617 Dunbar protested against the proposed innovations in worship, and in 1622 (now promoted to the first charge) he was again deprived and confined in Dumfries. He illegally returned to preach in his own parish, was outlawed, and in 1625 left Ayr for Ireland. Though described then as 'ane aged, decreaped, and puire man, and charged with a great familie', he ministered for twelve years in Larne, then was able to return to Mid Calder.

The archbishop of Glasgow had difficulty in nominating a successor to Dunbar who was acceptable to the local congregation, but in 1624 William Annand from Falkirk was received 'at the speciall requeist of the towne'. His preaching and personality won him initial acceptance. But Charles I who succeeded in 1625 was determined to extend his father's erastian policies and impose changes in the forms of worship. The new ritual Annand was willing enough to introduce. Sir William Brereton who visited Ayr in 1636 was told by his hostess about the minister: 'She complained much against him, because he doth so violently press the ceremonies, especially she instanced in kneeling at the Communion; whereupon Easter day last, so soon as he went to the Communion table, the people all left the Church, and departed, and not one of them stayed, only the pastor alone'. This preceded the introduction in 1637 of a new Prayer Book, which produced widespread outrage. Concurrently with his liturgical innovations, Charles I was attempting to solve the long-standing problem of teinds and church finance, and so threatening the vested interests of those who had acquired church lands. So the National Covenant of 28 February 1638 won broadly-based support, and nobles, lairds, and burgesses combined with presbyterian radicals in signing it. This was a preliminary to open revolt against the king.

When in 1637 William Annand defended the new Prayer Book at the Synod of Glasgow, he was ill received and afterwards the women of that city gave him a rough handling. On his return to Ayr his parishioners resolved 'never more to receive him within their pulpit'. Services in St John's were conducted by the ministers of Kirkoswald and Maybole in the spring of 1638, and on Sunday 8 April the Ayr congregation subscribed to the National Covenant 'men, wemen, and all bothe young and old'. Annand left Ayr, and though he retracted and signed the Covenant, he was deposed by the General Assembly which met in Glasgow to remove all traces of episcopacy from the Church. This was the first General Assembly to meet for twenty years, and it was composed, as for long afterwards, of ministers and elders representing the presbyteries plus commissioners from the royal burghs and universities.

In Ayr as elsewhere those ministers who had favoured episcopacy and been deposed had to be replaced by others who were committed presbyterians. Annand was briefly succeeded by Robert Blair. Though he declared that 'I had rather lay downe my life nor be separat from my flock at Air', he was by order of the General Assembly in 1639 transferred to St Andrews 'for the good of their Universitie'. Opportunity was taken to provide Ayr with two ministers, as apparently authorised in 1567 but previously possible only from 1613–19. To the first charge (with a stipend of £600 plus glebe) there was called from Ochiltree John Fergushill, a native of Ayr and son of a former provost, who had earlier suffered imprisonment for opposing the introduction of bishops. To the second charge (whose stipend of £500 depended on a burgh subsidy and voluntary contributions) was inducted William Adair, whose career would be long and eventful.

William Adair, son of a Portpatrick laird, had been a soldier before entering the ministry. In 1639, the year of his arrival in Ayr, Scotland became involved in a long and complex series of political and military struggles. Charles I refused to ratify the acts of the Glasgow Assembly; a Covenanting army occupied the north of England in the Bishops' Wars of 1640–41. Charles I, by this time also seriously in dispute with his English parliament, attempted to compromise with the Scottish Covenanters. He nominated as Chancellor the Earl of Loudoun, a signatory to

the National Covenant – the sheriff of Ayr whose father Hugh Campbell had been granted a lordship in 1601 and was himself ennobled in 1633. When civil war broke out in England in 1642 the parliamentary party appealed to the Scots for help and a Solemn League and Covenant sealed their alliance in 1643. During this period the Ayr kirk session minutes record special services with fasts and blessings in support of the Covenanting cause, and thanksgiving when in 1644 the king was defeated at Marston Moor, with the earls of Eglinton, Loudoun, and Cassillis among the victors. War came closer to home in 1645 when a royalist force of highlanders under the Marquis of Montrose won temporary control of the lowlands, and in Ayr there was 'no session keipit because of the present trouble' and 'absence of the minister and session who went out to the expedition'. Adair had in 1644 been sent by the General Assembly to administer the Solemn League and Covenant to the Scots army in Ireland; he was recognised as a zealot, and after his return became Moderator of Ayr presbytery in 1646. Two years before, the minister of the first charge had died, and Adair was promoted. Several moderates nominated for the second charge were reluctant to become colleague to the notoriously fanatical Adair, so until 1656 when William Eccles from Kildonan was inducted, he served alone.

In 1646 Charles I surrendered and was handed over to the English parliament, which now refused to introduce presbyterianism into England as promised by the Solemn League and Covenant. Scottish royalists and moderate presbyterians entered into a secret Engagement with the captive king and planned an invasion of England on his behalf. William Adair, of course, was opposed to these 'malignant, ungodly designs', though there were moderates in his kirk session who disagreed with him. In June 1648 Adair and six other Ayrshire ministers assembled at Mauchline with 1,200 horsemen and 800 others who were committed Anti-Engagers. They were dispersed at the Battle of Mauchline Muir. Prisoners were brought to Ayr, and the Tolbooth was so filled that the council had to meet in the provost's house. Adair was charged with treason, but the west of Scotland was 'very ready for new commotions'. When the Scottish army organised by the malignant Engagers was defeated by Cromwell at Preston, opportunity was taken by Loudoun, Eglinton, and Cassillis to march on Edinburgh in the 'Whiggamore Raid'; with their success Adair was exonerated. The Engagers however recovered power, and after the execution of Charles I in London in 1649 that faction reached agreement with his son who was proclaimed Charles II. But the dissidents of Ayrshire and adjoining counties formed a Western Association, originally constituted at Ayr at the end of 1648 and revived in 1650 under James Fullarton of Crosbie, with a military force controlling the south west of Scotland. William Adair was closely involved, 'appointed to go out to the Associat Army and to attend the same'. Now aged 35 he married a daughter of Boyd of Trochrague in 1651, and a second time in 1653 when he wed another laird's daughter, the widow of a brother minister.

With the Scots divided, Cromwell swept into Scotland in 1651 and established military control. At Ayr and four other strategic centres citadels were erected and military rule enforced. A force of 500 men was stationed here from 1651 till 1661, garrisoned in the Citadel which was constructed between 1652 and 1654, reputedly using stones transported from Ardrossan Castle. The army of occupation could at times become disorderly – in 1656 there was a riot between garrison soldiers and a regiment embarking for Jamaica – and the session records indicate they were not always puritanical in their behaviour. Fraternisation is indicated by a surviving marriage contract of 1657 recording the union of Abe Shockley, one of Cromwell's soldiers, with Margaret Campbell of Ayr. And some demobilised soldiers chose to settle in Ayr.

As far as the Church was concerned, during the Cromwellian occupation of Scotland the General Assembly, Synods, and presbyteries were prohibited from meeting, though kirk sessions could continue. When the Ayr session met, two army officers attended as observers 'whereupon the minister protested', but to no avail. Nor could Adair approve the toleration allowed to all protestant sectaries, committed as he was to presbyterianism as the only true form of church government. But when construction of the Cromwellian Citadel required the annexation of St John's kirk, opportunity could be seized for a desirable replacement. In 1612 that 13th century place of worship had been deemed 'presently ruynous' and there was complaint in 1649 of the 'want of ane orderlie building'. The congregation which was displaced in 1652 from St John's met in the adjacent grammar school till a new church was erected, with a subsidy from the army of a third of the cost. In this church, built on the riverside site where the Greyfriars had once lodged, William Adair on 22 September 1656 celebrated communion, with the newly-appointed minister of the second charge William Eccles.

Restoration of Charles II in 1660 brought no relief, but rather an aggravation of the religious disputes.

William Adair who was minister in Ayr between 1639 and 1682 played a prominent part in the bitter religious disputes of his time.

Royal authority over the church was re-imposed and episcopacy re-introduced. Ministers who had taken up a charge since 1649 required to have their appointment confirmed, and thirty ministers within the presbyteries of Ayr and Irvine who refused to submit to the Archbishop of Glasgow were deprived of their charges, including William Eccles. William Adair whose appointment dated from 1639 escaped this requirement, and though he was forbidden to preach outwith his own parish, and suspended in 1668, he was re-instated because of his 'peaceable deportment' and 'aversion to all illegal disordoures and clandestine meetings'. It would seem, in the words of a contemporary, that he had declined 'from his former zeal and forwardness'. He accepted as colleagues those episcopal curates who were appointed to replace the deposed Eccles – George Whyte from 1664 and William Waltersone from 1682. Indeed in 1670 he found Whyte 'ane godlie, pious, and discreet man' and refused to 'baptise any children upon the north syd of the toun, quhilk he called Mr George Whyte's syd'. Only in his last years did Adair's rebellious spirit re-assert itself. He was temporarlily suspended in 1681, then deposed in 1682 'becaus he would not conform which is now the fourtie-third year current of his ministrie in Air'. He was replaced in the first charge by Alexander Gregory from St Quivox, and died in 1684 aged 69.

The scene in Ayrshire from 1660 till 1689 is often portrayed as a continuous and bitter struggle between a populace totally committed to the Covenanted cause and a crown relentlessly determined to enforce episcopacy. In fact, government policies vacillated clumsily between repression and compromise. Growing numbers of local people were prepared to conform. Ministers like Adair accepted government indulgences. Most councillors in Ayr, as the burgh records show, followed opportunist policies and so seem often quite inconsistent in their attitudes. It was a minority who remained resolutely committed to the belief that the only scripturally acceptable form of church was presbyterian.

The Restoration of Charles II in 1660 was not unanimously welcomed by the garrison in Ayr Citadel, many of whom were religious sectaries. Some elected to be discharged in Ayr and these 'severall English fanaticks who had served during the rebellione under the usurper in that place' contributed to unrest which brought the Privy Council to Ayr in 1662. The Privy Councillors and their retinue were remembered, because their 'daily and nightly drunkenness resembling a heathen bacchanal brought shame unspeakable upon the Christian religion' and it was also reported that in a midnight spree at the market cross the devil's health was drunk. Possibly as a result, the trades demonstrated 'in ane mutinous and seditious way'. In 1664 when councillors were required to abjure the Covenants, Provost William Cunningham and nine others submitted, but the other eight refused and had to be replaced. When the council as patron appointed George Whyte as a 'king's curate', attendance at church services dropped, and private worship in conventicles became common, though declared illegal. In 1666 rebellion broke out in Dumfriessshire, spread to Ayrshire, and Colonel James Wallace of Auchans led 2,000 armed Covenanters from Ayr towards Edinburgh and defeat at Rullion Green in this so-called Pentlands Rising. Among prisoners taken some were hanged in Edinburgh, including one Ayr merchant. After trials in Ayr twelve were sentenced, eight of them to be hanged here. Neither the hangman from Ayr (who fled) nor the one from Irvine (who refused, even under duress) would perform these executions; which were done by the one local man among the prisoners (who was promised reprieve and filled with brandy). To settle the local population 450 troopers were quartered in the town, with Newton Castle as their headquarters. For a period thereafter there was leniency – 'the Blink' – when a blind eye was turned on conventicles. But repression returned. In 1675, 1677, and 1680 three local schoolmasters were dismissed for reasons of their religion. In 1678 the 'Highland Host' and other troops were quartered in Alloway and the Burrowfield as a punitive measure. But conventicles continued and in 1678 the magistrates even allowed Mr John Brown, one of the Covenanting 'vagrant preachers', to conduct services within the parish church for several Sundays, which attracted 'a large multitude'. In 1679 a second rising commenced with a skirmish at Drumclog; some of the victorious Covenanters visited Ayr to be welcomed by the town council; prisoners were released from the tolbooth; the heads of those who had been executed were removed from above the town ports and given decent burial. But soon the Covenanters were defeated at Bothwell Bridge: several Ayr burgesses (including a schoolmaster) were apprehended; two were among those sentenced to transportation. Ayr town council had ignominiously to make John Graham of Claverhouse and his associates honorary burgesses and guild brethren. But there was amnesty for those who pledged themselves not to rise in arms again, and an indulgence to all ministers who guaranteed their 'peaceable behaviour'. This was sufficient to satisfy a majority of presbyterians. Only a minority continued resistance, those extremists known variously as Cameronians, Cargillites, Societymen, or Hillmen, some of whom were taken in a clash at Airdsmoss in 1680.

The Test Act of 1680 produced unnecessary complications. That oath to be taken by all holders of public office was so badly worded as to offend not only presbyterians but even episcopalians and Catholics. Initial refusal was often followed by a reluctant acceptance to allow business to be conducted. Rev. William Adair, who refused to take the test, was suspended, restored, then finally deposed in 1682. Two schoolmasters had to demit office. The merchants at their guild court and the trades meeting to elect their deacons were required to take the test. Those freemen of Newton who refused the test could be deprived of the land and liberties which constituted their livelihood. In practice it proved impossible to enforce religious conformity. Over the next few years the Privy Council nominated a succession of new magistrates for Ayr. This has been interpreted as a ruthless royal authority spitefully depriving the burgh of its self government, deposing from the council those honest men of principle who refused to take the test. In fact the Privy Council intervened only when the councillors refused to take the test in 1681 and all abdicated. But after this initial stand, nearly all the local politicians took the test when it seemed advantageous to further the interests of their own faction. The complex and sordid story of the faction fight for control of the council remains to be told in the next chapter. Here it can be noted that each faction sought to advance its cause by complaining to the Privy Council about the others. The leaders of three factions, Robert Hunter, William Brisbane, and William Cunningham junior accused one another of bribery, corrupt practices, threats, and violence; also of giving aid to dissidents by such methods as supporting rebels, allowing unlicensed preachers to operate in Ayr, failing to enforce the taking of the test, and (in the case of Brisbane) bringing into the council in 1683 'several English fanaticks'. All this is useful evidence, for if one ignores the abuse one can detect a burgh where the population remained sympathetic to presbyterian forms of worship, where Covenanting preachers could move around freely, even allowed access to prisoners in the tolbooth, preaching to field conventicles at Alloway (Gearholm), Prestwick, and within Ayr itself – in private houses, at the Citadel, and several times 'in the toun kirk to a large multitude'.

The moderate majority was irritated by the return of Graham of Claverhouse in 1682 with instructions to check on possible suspects such as those who had withdrawn from attendance at church. In 1684 Ayrshire landowners (except some who had sought refuge in exile) were confined in Ayr's old church and in the tolbooth till they attested and were freed from suspicion of harbouring rebels. By such means the populace was cowed into submission. Only the Hillmen remained obdurate. All who disagreed with them they regarded as 'enemies of God' and when James VII and II succeeded to the throne in 1685, 'a professed papist and excommunicate person', they as 'the contending and suffering remnant of the true presbyterians' renounced allegiance to the civil authority. Those taken by Claverhouse and his dragoons refused to take the test; when they further refused to abjure the Apologetical Declaration they were liable to summary execution. There followed the Killing Year of 1685. Of 54 Ayrshire names on the county's numerous memorials to Covenanting martyrs, 25 died in that year.

In 1687 William Wallace of Craigie, a Roman Catholic, was appointed provost of Ayr. In that year presbyterians (except the Hillmen) took advantage of the king's new policy of religious toleration. Designed to accommodate his co-religionists, it allowed others 'to meet and serve God in their own way'. So Ex-provost John Mure and his friends were able to purchase the old St John's Kirk, re-open it as a place of worship, and brought back William Eccles (who had been deposed in 1662) to serve as their minister. A separate kirk session also was instituted, and this presbyterian congregation outnumbered those attending the episcopal services in the parish church. Even the beggars seeking relief resorted to the door of the presbyterian St John's Kirk.

Late in 1688 events in the south resulted in the expulsion of James VI and II by the Glorious Revolution which brought William and Mary to the throne. Ayr, it is said, was the first town in Scotland to proclaim its adherence to the new dynasty, with John Mure as the new provost. Before the Scots parliament could attempt a religious settlement, the episcopalian ministers Alexander Gregory and William Walterstone were expelled from Ayr. After 10 January 1689 there was no episcopal service in Ayr 'because both ministers were discharged upon their perill to preach, either by themselves or others, by ane armed partie of rebellious hilmen'. This 'rabbling of the curates' was followed by the installation of William Eccles in the parish church. In 1690 an act of the Scots parliament established presbyterian government within the Church of Scotland. The era of violence was mercifully at an end.

SEVEN

17th Century Social Aspects

The story of the religious conflicts of the 17th century has often overshadowed other aspects of the period, in particular social and economic developments. It seems to have been a time of mixed fortunes. The community, though faced with a number of problems, was making continued progress in various respects.

The problems which beset 17th century Ayr included natural disasters, economic difficulties, social and political upsets. These may appear to us more serious than previous generations had encountered, though very likely just because we have more evidence of the 17th than earlier centuries. The plagues of 1606–07 and 1647 were familiar repetitions of those of earlier times. The famine which brought the century to a close with the 'Seven Ill Years' was not a novel experience, though worse than the dearth of 1602 at the opening of the century. Trading ventures continued to be threatened by shipwreck and piracy. From various contemporary comments about trade in general and the harbour in particular, it has sometimes been suggested that for Ayr this was a period of decline, particularly after 1660. But some of the complaints seem to have been exaggerated. Ayr's 17th century merchants have been described as 'lively, adventurous, and bold in the face of adversity', by an author (T.C.Smout) who argues that they were doing reasonably well in foreign business till the French connection was broken by the wars after 1689.

That a general air of settled prosperity persisted from the 16th into the 17th century is suggested by visitors' comments. Bishop Leslie in 1578 described 'the toune of Air, quhilke is called S. Johnes toune, illustir and fair anuich baith in riches and biging, and a pleasand situatione, with a prettie sey porte quhair strange natiouns oft arryveues and thair landes, the porte is sa commodious'. Sir William Brereton in 1636 found Ayr 'a dainty, pleasant-seated town; much plain rich corn land about it; and better haven, there being a river, whereon it is placed, which flows much higher than the bridge, which is a great and fair neat bridge.'

Though it was 'but a bare naked haven, no pier, nor defence against the storms and weather' nevertheless it had a 'better store of shipping' than Irvine. 'Most inhabiting in the town are merchants trading unto and bred in France'. Brereton found good lodgings with 'a cleanly neat hostess, victuals handsomely cooked'. Ayr council in an address to the king in 1610 proudly boasted that 'the towne, which is so ancient, and for civilitie, bewtye, buildingis, and good governement may be reckyned amangis the best and worthiest of this kingdom ... for nomber of goode schippes and skilfull and able marinaris it is the best in this your maiesties kingdome, Leyth and Dundee onlie except'. At that time work was in progress in 'reparation of the herbery'. This was financed by crown grant in 1588 of an impost for nineteen years on ships entering the harbour; and stents on the inhabitants in 1599 and 1604 for 'bigging of the key'. Foreign traders were 'arryvand within this harbery and seyport with wyne, salt, victuall, oranges, tymber, coles, hydes and other gudes'. Already in the first half of the 17th century, at least two Ayr merchants – William Kelso and Robert Rolland – had commenced a transatlantic tobacco trade.

After mid-century various difficulties were reported. In 1656 Thomas Tucker described Ayr as 'groweing every day worse and worse, by reason of theyr harbours being clogged and filled up with sand'. But this was written during a depression which proved temporary. Despite obvious problems arising from the Cromwellian occupation, the opening of English and colonial markets stimulated local trade, and indeed there was formed in 1655 a Merchant Company, followed by Merchant Adventurers and Sailors Company and a Concord Company. Some of these proved as short-lived as the free trade of the Cromwellian union. But the local economy was healthy enough for 28 'Inglis traderers and breweres', as listed in a stent roll of 1657, to have remained as permanent residents, as well as some soldiers, like

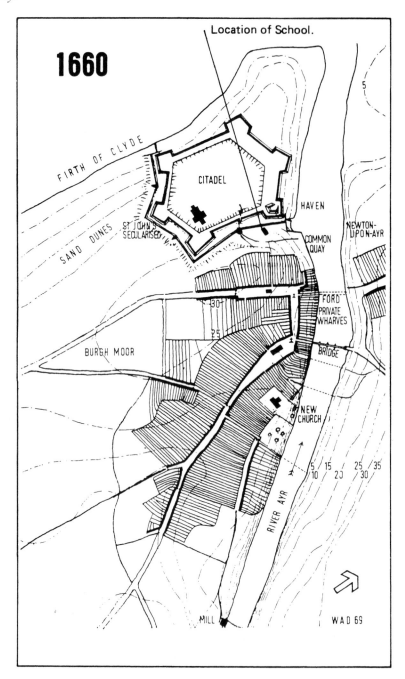

Location of School.

1660

FIRTH OF CLYDE

CITADEL

HAVEN

ST JOHN'S
SECULARISED

NEWTON-
UPON-AYR

SAND DUNES

COMMON
QUAY

30

FORD
PRIVATE
WHARVES

25

BRIDGE

BURGH MOOR

NEW
CHURCH

5 / 15 / 25 / 35
10 / 20 / 30

RIVER AYR

MILL

WAD 69

Despite various difficulties, Ayr's population grew to near 3,000 by 1700.

Vaxley Robieson, later provost. That Ayr could in the later 17th century provide business for the silversmith Matthew Colquhoun suggests a certain affluence. The Restoration of 1660 meant the end of free trade with England and its colonies; but when ten years later the council complained that trade had collapsed, that was to justify their paying nothing to assist Dundee. So it would be unwise to accept literally the colourful description of 1670: 'Our harbour is totally ruined and decayed quhilk we are not abill in the least to maintain. Our bridge daylie failing by great spaits, and yce coming down in the winter tyme on it.' In fact, increase in trade is suggested by the division, sometime between 1673 and 1677, of the county into two precincts for customs purposes, with separate offices in Ayr and Irvine. The harbour was well enough maintained: to supplement the anchorage dues and a share of the 'Brig penny' the council arranged in 1668 for a stent of 1,000 merks for harbour repairs; in 1677 over £1,000 was spent on the north and south dykes of the river; and in 1678 a further £400. Urgent repairs were promptly executed. In 1681 for example the north and south dykes were renewed following damage just months earlier by *The James of Ayr*. When *The Margaret of Queensferry* was wrecked in October 1683 and blocked the harbour, the council – despite its current religious problems – hired in June 1684 a Glasgow engineer called Peter Bruce to clear the harbour, which was done by the end of August.

During the depression of 1692 a questionnaire from the Convention of Royal Burghs produced a return from Ayr council lamenting (as so many other councils did) 'the decay of trade and poverty of the inhabitants'. Here was a harbour which was 'almost altogether ruinous', and a town containing 'about ane hundreth and fourty waste houses besides sewerall ruinous houses and particularly tuo great tenements on each syde of the marcat cross both ruinous'. The details of trade as supplied by the council are so dubious as to produce (from T.C.Smout) comments like 'demonstrably false' and 'deliberately falsified'. More reliable was the account of Thomas Morer made in 1689 which described Ayr as 'pretty enough' with 'a good bridge upheld by four arches'. It had 'formerly a very great trade'. Recent losses Morer attributed to 'the success of Glasgow' and because they 'chuse rather to freight other men's ships, than be at the hazard to build any of their own'. Ayr had twenty ships in 1638; six by 1645; three in 1656 (as compared to five from Glasgow, the only others on the Firth of Clyde over 30 tons). A List of Seamen supplied to the privy council by the burgh provides details of the situation in 1665. There were three ships: *Unicorn*, 60 tons, with nine of a crew, sailing to the West Indies; *Lyon* and *Marie*, each of 20 tons with five of a crew, on voyages to Spain and Bristol. There were also four barques of 6 or 7 tons which plied to Belfast or Loch Fyne. There were attached to the port 3 skippers, 26 seamen, and 16 boatmen. But, as Morer implied, the number of ships registered at Ayr does not represent the volume of trade. For (T.C.Smout argues) 'the customs books and the commercial letters of the period do not support this picture of a senile and collapsing burgh'. The customs records for Ayr show, during a period 1681–85, ships arriving from and departing

A splendid Malt Cross was set up in 1697, at the junction of Sandgate and High Street.

to Ireland (17, 42), England (2, 2), France (32, 39), Holland (8, 14), Norway (7, 0), America (2, 4). In an average year eight ships continued the traditional trade between Ayr and the French ports of St Nazaire, Nantes, La Rochelle, and Bordeaux, exporting herrings, coal, wool, some manufactured textiles like woollen plaidings and coarse linen; importing salt for fish curing and tanning of leather, wine, prunes, chestnuts, and manufactured goods. There was the occasional ship bringing timber from Scandinavia. There were few cargoes for the Netherlands, but there was an important new trade involving Ayr (and Kilmarnock) merchants sending loads overland by packhorse for export through Bo'ness to Rotterdam. Cloth and hides could thus be carried abroad, also Ayrshire and Irish butter; dried fruits, seeds, dyes, and ironmongery were imported. These facts are revealed in the correspondence of Andrew Russell, principal Scottish factor in Rotterdam. He was in 1680 doing business with sixteen merchants from Ayr, more than from any other place except Edinburgh and Glasgow. Ayr's trade with America was bringing in sugar and dyes from the West Indies, tobacco from Virginia; though small in scale, it was regular, and involved not only larger ships from 40 to 140 tons, but even *The Swan* of 14 tons, which was lost en route to the West Indies. Ayr merchants and skippers were indeed adventurous, and cosmopolitan in their outlook. In addition there was a limited trade with Ireland in ships averaging 15 tons, less with England, but a steady coastal trade catering for most of the west of Scotland, and fishing on the Clyde.

Ayr in the 17th century was still ahead of the other royal burgh of Irvine. The traditional rivalry between them was superseded as both now faced an apparent threat to their commercial privileges from the other burghs of the county. Prestwick and Newton-upon-Ayr were too insignificant to worry about. But the more recently-chartered burghs of barony – Newmilns (1491), Auchinleck (1507), Cumnock (1509), Mauchline (1510), Maybole (1516), Kilmaurs (1527), Saltcoats (1529), Ballantrae (1541), Kilmarnock (1592), Largs (1595), Fairlie (1601) – had in many cases become busy market centres where various crafts were being energetically developed. Now they were being joined by others – Dalmellington (1607), Dundonald (1638), Riccarton (1638), Kilbirnie (1642), Montgomeriestoun (1663), Girvan (1668), Tarbolton (1671), Fullarton (1707). In some cases though charters were granted no organised burgh was ever constituted. This was the case with the charter for Montgomeriestoun which Hugh, 7th earl of Eglinton, was impudent enough to obtain and the representatives of the crown stupid enough to grant. For Montgomeriestoun was the area of Cromwell's Ayr Citadel which the earl was granted as compensation for losses. He did initiate some manufacturing which caused Ayr town council some concern, but the threat of a rival burgh with rival markets and fairs on Ayr's doorstep fortunately came to nothing. More serious was competition from burghs of barony like Mauchline and Maybole, and from landward markets which were being held in almost every parish. The most serious challenge of all was to the monopoly of foreign trade which the royal burghs held. Within the county Kilmarnock, established as a burgh as recently as 1592, had a meteoric growth in its first century. Taking advantage of acts of 1672 and 1693, enterprising Kilmarnock merchants by 1700 had developed

trading links with France, Holland, Norway, Virginia, England, and Ireland – 'above half of the trade of both of the Burghs of Ayr and Irvine', as these two royal burghs complained. Similarly Glasgow, taking 10th place in 1564 to Ayr's 9th in the burgh stent roll, had within a century far outranked Ayr. By 1670, Glasgow was 2nd in Scotland and Ayr now only 12th. The relative commercial importance of the various places may be indicated by noting the investments each made in 1696 in the Company of Scotland's Darien colonial scheme. Ayr contributed £2,800; Irvine £1,200; Kilmarnock £1,800. Glasgow merchants alone contributed over £26,000 to the grand total of £400,000.

It can be concluded that while 17th century Ayr continued to make progress, it was far more modest than was being achieved elsewhere, How Ayr was losing some ground is emphasised by its declining status among all the royal burghs as measured by their contributions in tax, recorded in the stent rolls. In the 16th century Ayr stood as 9th (1564) and 8th (1597); in the 17th century Ayr's position dropped to 13th (1649), 12th (1670), and 10th (1683); by the 18th there would be a more decided change to 14th (1705), 15th (1718), 17th (1730).

The other problem which affected Ayr, those disputes which racked the church for most of the 17th century, did not seriously interrupt the continuity of congregational worship. Nor did the various amendments to the presbyterian system affect the operation of the kirk session. This, the church court with the longest continuous history, exercised its discipline throughout the entire period, whether subject to supervision by presbytery, bishop, or the Cromwellian army.

The authority of the kirk session seems tacitly to have been accepted even by those who had to endure its penalties. Little more than a generation after the pre-reformation church had been overthrown, the divine right its priests had claimed was now vested in the persons of the minister and elders who formed the kirk session. At any rate, this was the case in Ayr, where John Welch's brief ministry from 1600 till 1605 was dramatically effective. As a preacher, he was so popular that the need for a bigger church was felt. As a pastor, he armed himself with helmet and intervened to break up fights between contending groups in the streets of Ayr. As a man of God, he was held in awe not only for his devoutness, but for the second sight he was reputed to possess. When the plague was threatened in 1600, Welch advised that certain pedlars should not be admitted to the

The Auld Tour in High Street was purchased by the burgh in 1673, and was mysteriously renamed Wallace Tower in 1774.

town; they went instead to Cumnock, which became infected. So long as the plague threatened, crowds attended church. In 1602 the tolbooth was adapted 'to be ane place of the common prayers ilk morning and evening'. In 1603 the Sunday services were so crowded that the building of a new church was suggested. In 1604 when the plague was affecting Glasgow and Edinburgh, Welch preached, 'Repent, repent, or else it shall be so with you as it was with them'. In 1606, after Welch had departed, the plague reached Ayr. The council took measures similar to those in the great epidemic of 1545–46, 'seeing it hes plesit the almytie god to veseit this sinfull toun with the seiknes of the pest justlie deservit for the sinnes therof and contempt of his word'. The plague returned to Ayr in 1647 when once again the council took the usual measures of appointing quartermasters, cleaners, and erecting isolation quarters on the Burrowfield. Once again there was a call to repentance. This time the call was made by the zealous William Adair, and to great effect. He convened separate meetings of the

kirk session, the council, each of the trades, then the merchants and the sailors; he addressed them in turn; each re-assembled to draw up its confessions of corporate failings; after a week of soul-searchings, the following Sunday the confessions were read out in full from the pulpit by Adair, and engrossed in the Session books 'for the use of posteritie'.

While it is easy enough to explain away religious enthusiasm in time of crisis as mass hysteria, it is less easy for 20th century minds to appreciate the fervour with which quite soon after the Reformation there were accepted the new Calvinist theology preached in sermons, the new liturgy associated with presbyterianism, and the discipline imposed by the kirk session. The earliest reference to Ayr kirk session is in the Register of the Privy Council where under the year 1568 Bailie George Lockhart was accused of 'irreverent and contemptuous disobeying of the commandment of the minister, elders, and deacons of the Kirk of Ayr'. In 1582 an offender who was 'convict before the kirk' was dealt with by the magistrates, which became a common procedure. The earliest extant records of Ayr kirk session cover that brief period from 1604–05 when John Welch was sole minister, and there were twenty elders and nine deacons. The minutes commence with a list of 'Penalties for Violation of the Sabbath' and indeed this seems to have been the principal offence, apart from a few cases of squabbling, slander, and one of pre-marital fornication, that sin so diligently pursued by later sessions. Punishment might be by 'publik confession', standing at the kirk door, or 'in the pillar', which was the place of repentance within the kirk. Sometimes a fine had to be paid, this contributing to poor relief. The care of 'the pure folk' was in 1604 as always a concern of the kirk session. In this they collaborated with the council, as they did with recalcitrant offenders, who were 'deliverit to the magistrates for their disobedience'. Such collaboration was normally effective, since many of the elders were also councillors. John Welch's session of 1603 contained, for example, Ex-provost Alexander Lockhart of Boghall and John Mason, town clerk. William Adair's first session in 1639 contained 30 elders and deacons, including at least thirteen identifiable as current or former councillors, among them the aged Lockhart and Mason. Virtually the only occasions when council and session clashed was over the appointment (by the session) of session clerk, reader, and precentor, which posts were filled by teachers in the burgh school (who were appointed by the council).

Unanimity, however, was the norm in one field

in which church and state collaborated zealously. The Scots parliament in 1563 declared witchcraft a capital offence, thus participating in a campaign of extirpation which involved the execution of thousands throughout Europe and America in the course of the 17th century. What modern minds would describe as superstition involved kirk session and presbytery examining suspects; burgh magistrates confirming findings; then crown approval for a trial; followed, if found guilty, by public execution by burning. The first recorded in Ayr was in 1586 when the burgh treasurer paid out 'in expenssis sustenit in the burning of the witche of Barnweill, in candillis, hir meit and drink, pyk barrellis, colis, rosat, heddir, treis and utheris necessaris, £7. 3s. 8d'. Other victims followed: Marion Grieff, 1595; Janet Young, 1599; Bessie Bell and others, 1613; Maly Wilson, 1618; Janet McAllister, 1618; Margaret Wallace, 1629. Others were cited in 1643 and 1650, and in 1658 a Cromwellian colonel wrote (with some disgust) of Janet Saers who was strangled at the stake then burned to ashes. The total number in Ayr who suffered as condemned witches cannot be ascertained, but almost certainly as many as in Irvine where more than twenty were executed. There is no record of Maggie Osborne, Ayr's best-known but unidentifiable witch. Her reputed exploits included dealing with persons who had offended her by burying them under snow or by raising a storm to wreck a ship in Ayr bay. One story has it that she was the daughter of a warlock laird of Fail who married and kept a tavern in Ayr. An alternative version is that she was a member of the well-known merchant family, the Osbornes who lived in 76–78 High Street opposite the Fish Cross; suffering from brain fever she was found guilty of possession by the devil and executed as a witch. Not all accused of witchcraft were found guilty; some escaped with lesser punishments as spaewives or fortune tellers. The most determined efforts were made to ensure witches did not evade discovery. In 1650 for example, round-the-clock interrogation was practised in Ayr when 'elders and deacons shall for the space twentie four hours per vices both in the day and in the night, shall oversie the said prisoners to exhort them to confessione'. One who suffered particularly was Janet Smyllie. In 1613 for making filthy slanderous speeches she was gagged with the branks at the Fish Cross. In 1621 she had to do penance in church. In 1628 she was confined to the women's cell under the tolbooth stairs. In 1629 she was tried on suspicion of witchcraft, and banished. In 1649 she was back in Ayr, once again confined to the tolbooth, where she died. Whereupon the council

'with advyse of Mr William Adair, minister', ordained that the corpse of Janet Smyllie 'salbe drawin upoun a slaid to the gallowis foot and brunt in asches'. That would take place at the common place of execution beyond Mill Street.

The parish minister and session were of course concerned with the more routine business of preaching the Word. During John Welch's ministry the Sunday services were supplemented with 'common prayers ilk morning and evening'; in 1621 these were restricted to 'begin at sevin hoors in the morning daylie, and the preaching at a quarter afoir aucht; and the haill action of preaching to be endit afor nyne hoors'; about 1650 daily services were replaced by preachings on Tuesdays and Thursday; these were discontinued in 1662 but recommenced in 1690. Sunday worship was heralded by the tolbooth bell ringing at 6 a.m., after which family worship was to be held as preparation for the public worship to follow. Church service commenced at 8 a.m. after the first morning bell as rung both at tolbooth and church. For the first hour it was the duty of the reader or precentor 'to conceive prayers, read the scripture, and raise the psalmes'. After the second morning bell at 9 o'clock the school children were catechised. The eleven o'clock or third morning bell was the summons to divine service led by the minister. This service was centred on the sermon wherein doctrine was expounded at length. While that at the weekday service was restricted to one sand-glass measuring a half-hour, the Sunday sermon required at least an hour, so that after prayer and benediction the service would end about 12.30 p.m., when another bell marked the end of the forenoon and the commencement of the afternoon services. The second afternoon bell at quarter past one summoned the scholars again, and the third afternoon bell at quarter to two preceded the afternoon worship. During the long services most had to stand, or squat on portable stools. The Church of St John had no fixed seats save those for the scholars till lofts were erected to accommodate the magistrates (1594), the trades (1603), and the sailors (1623). When the congregation moved into the new parish church in 1656 there were also pews for those who had contributed £12 towards the building (as considered later in this chapter). Many still had to stand, and naturally there was sometimes inattention, misbehaviour, and even disorder. Holy Communion was celebrated thrice yearly at Martinmas, Candlemas, and Beltane at the beginning of the century, though apparently not at all between 1642–47 and 1649–56. Each sacrament was preceded by a week of fast days, with preparatory services, catechising, and issue of tokens to those deemed fit to come to the tables. On communion Sunday there might be (as in 1619) nine tables (or communion services) with over 100 persons at each, continuing from 9 a.m. till 4 p.m.

The changing political circumstances of the 17th century involved Ayr's council in various difficulties and at times interfered with its operations. Nevertheless, the burgh continued in good financial heart throughout. Despite inflation, heavier taxation, and extraordinary military and other burdens the council could afford to undertake new commitments and maintain them successfully.

At the Reformation, the protestant church inherited and willingly assumed responsibility for the provision of poor relief and schooling; and the council's involvement in each was extended.

The council continued to cope with the deserving poor by licensing beggars – the treasurer paying for a supply of lead tokens in 1537 and again in 1602. The distribution of alms to those who were aged or infirm and without family to assist was the responsibility of the church. The church collections, fines imposed by the session, legacies, and the alms-boxes carried on all local ships – these provided a fund for payment of pensions to the regular poor and donations to the casual poor. Ayr session also showed compassion by gifts to strangers in distress, though like other sessions it required the expulsion of 'strange beggers'. The burgh complemented the work of the session by providing from its own poors box for some exceptional cases, such as shipwrecked sailors, vagrants deserving of pity, and even a few local persons awarded special treatment. Burgh and kirk collaborated in making new provision for the poor by the construction in 1604 of a 'hospital'. The Queen Mary Mortification of 1567 allowed for 'the support of an hospital for the poor, mutilated, and distressed persons, orphans, and infants forsaken by their parents'. It took some time before there was any return from the properties which the Mortification awarded to the burgh, but by 1604 construction was in hand and Provost Fergushill supervised the expenditure of about £350 on a building which was possibly ready in time for the plague of 1606. The hospital was built of stone brought from Alloway, and was slated. It was presumably in Mill Street on the site of the later 18th century poors house. Though financed by the burgh, the hospital was managed by the session. In January 1655 in an unexpected cold spell the session 'Lent to the toune to buy coales for the hospital, 40s'. The session arranged for admissions. Some entered voluntarily, as 'Bessie Hunter, a pure bedrell was upone

her humble sute admitted'; others were reluctant, but 'pensioners salbe dischairgit of thair pensioune, quha will not enter as they salbe commandit'. The session arranged for Sunday services and required (in 1653) that all patients should know 'at least the Lord's Prayer, the beliefe, and Ten Commandments, togidder with some knowledge of the Catechisme'.

There was similar collaboration between council and session in educational provision. At the Church of St John there had been a school since 1233 and the burgh appointed in 1519 (and possibly on earlier occasions) a chaplain to take charge of 'grammatical studies' and teach Latin; and another to 'teach a sang schule', with reading and writing as important as music. Already before the Reformation the school at St John's was in process of being converted into a burgh school, catering for the sons of burgh merchants and sons of lairds from the landward area. In 1559 the town council, complaining of 'the great hurt and misgovernance of the infants and bairns of this burgh this long time' appointed John Orr to give instruction to 'bairns of the town and to others repairing thereto'. His duties were 'to teach them in manners and the art and science of the Latin tongue and grammar'. As a protestant he could supply the appropriate religious instruction to provide them with 'manners' while the teaching of reading and writing was a necessary preliminary to study of the classics. John Orr was first of a new type of schoolmaster, no longer clergymen for whom this was a subsidiary duty but laymen for whom teaching was a career. The council was not merely maintaining the old church school under its own auspices. It was making a deliberate attempt to extend its facilities. In 1582 there was a proposal to appoint 'ane skillit doctour' as assistant teacher. The master of the grammar school could concentrate on the teaching of classics to lads o' pairts aiming at the ministry; while reading and writing were left to the doctor. There was also the sang schule, known also as the Scots or English school, a kind of elementary department whose master had 'to learne the bairns that sings to read and write Inglis'.

In 1600 there was a new departure, with schooling offered to girls. The council decreed that 'the lasses that learnis to reid and write to be put to the maister of the Sang Schule to that effect, becaus it is not seemlie that sic lasses suld be in the Grammar Schule amang the lads'. Segregation of the sexes was confirmed in 1604 when 'all maill children are to be taichit only in the Grammar Schule, except sic as plesis to learn musik at the music-scule'. Girls were restricted to the sang schule 'or any other school' – for private schools

John Slezer in 1694 provided two views of Ayr. This one shows the skyline dominated by the new High Tolbooth, erected in 1575 in the centre of the Sandgate, and surmounted in 1615 by a bell tower. The old tolbooth in High Street may be the square building shown.

for girls were permitted by the council. Private schools for boys were rigorously prohibited by the council for two hundred years from 1550 when the burgh school monopoly was first recorded.

For the enlarged school improved accommodation was required. Throughout the 16th century the school continued at the Kirk of St John, but that part of it which formed the 'scule hous' had by 1599 been allowed to 'decay untheikit'. So the Ayr burgh school moved into rented premises. In 1602 the town council 'Aggreis with Johne Osburne for his hous in the Sandgait to be ane schulehous for ane year'. Payment to Osburne continued only till 1607. After that the school moved to premises at the other end of the School Vennel, a two-roomed cottage where the academy was later to be built.

The school had to undergo a series of difficulties in the course of the 17th century. There were staffing difficulties to begin with. Not till 1603 was a doctor regularly employed, and from 1606 till 1613 the sang schule seems to have been without a master. In 1606 and 1647 schooling was disrupted by the plague. In 1654 when Cromwell's army took over the Church of St John to include within the new Citadel, church services were held in the cramped conditions of the grammar school till the new church was ready in 1656. After 1660 the work of the school suffered more serious interruptions as a result of the religious conflict. When Mr William Wallace retired in 1675 because of 'old age and infirmity' there were difficulties because his successor Mr David Skeoch was unwilling to undertake in an episcopalian church the master of the grammar school's usual duties. The following year James Anderson, master of the sang scule, was suspended because as precentor he refused to sing the Doxology in church. Later in 1682 the two masters, Mr William Rankin and George Adamson, were suspended till they took the test. Rankin before

This second 'Prospect' shows the Church of St John, where there had been a school as far back as 1233. The 17th century burgh school occupied that isolated cottage at the end of the School Vennel, overlooking the harbour. The harbour was sometimes busier – as in the picture opposite – with ships trading to America and the West Indies as well as Europe from Baltic to Mediterranean.

he came to Ayr is reputed to have taken part in the 1679 rising, and an unidentified master of Ayr was involved in the rising of 1666.

In normal circumstances, the three teachers worked a ten-hour day seven-day week, for on Sundays they had to supervise their pupils in church, where they had additional duties with the master of the grammar school serving usually as clerk to the kirk session, he or the doctor as reader, and the master of the sang schule as precentor. At the beginning of the century the grammar school master was paid £40 with an additional £10 as reader; the doctor received £20; the sang schule master received £40 inclusive. Of course they were entitled to school fees paid by parents. In the grammar school the master received £1 and the doctor 8s from burgh pupils; double that if from the landward area. Fees in the sang schule were paid quarterly, for a time 5s for English, 6/8 for singing, 13/4 for lessons on the spinet. To attract well-qualified staff the council

paid 'chamber mail' for house rent, occasionally paid for clothing, sometimes removal expenses, with free meals from parents in times of difficulty. By the 1620s basic salaries had been increased to £80 and £30 in the grammar school, while the master of music had a generous £100 plus 50 merks from the session. Though the Queen Mary Mortification had not specified education as one of its purposes, it became used for that purpose. By 1692, out of its income of £1,285, nearly all was spent on salaries: 'to the second minister, £666.13.4; for his house rent, £60; to the master of the grammar school, £200; to the doctor of the said school, £100; to the Scots schoolmaster, £52; to him as precenter in the church, £66.13.4'.

The council was involved in the provision of a new church built to replace the old Church of St John which was requisitioned by Cromwell's army to become part of the Citadel. The construction of that vast fortress covering seventeen acres required the transportation of stone by sea from Ardrossan Castle. It was a military undertaking, and compensation was paid for the loss of the parish kirk. The subsidy of

one thousand merks sterling covered just about one third of the total cost of £20,827 Scots whose sterling equivalent was £1,733. The considerable remaining sum was to come from council funds, supplemented 'be voluntar contribution or be stent as shall be thought most expedient'. The contracts were signed by the minister William Adair acting 'with the express advice and consent of the Town Council, kirk session, commonality, haill parochiners and inhabitants of the burgh and paroch'. There were purchased in 1653 four parcels of ground comprising the Friars Yeardis beside 'the kirk of auld callit St Kathareing the Virgin' and 'the common wai that tends to the water of Air by the well'. The body of the kirk was to be 'four score and ten foot in length, without the walls; in breadth thirty foot within the walls; and to fix and build thereto an isle of the length of three score six foot from the pulpit to the gavell thereof'. The building work was undertaken, at a price of ten thousand pounds, by Theophilus Rankin, smith, with John Mason, mason, and John Smith, mason from Kilmaurs. There was additional expenditure on levelling the churchyard, building a dyke, and (sparing no expense) erecting in 1656 the 'porche' or archway at one of the three entrances to the churchyard. The interior of the church was generously furnished with a pavement floor, and with woodwork much of which remains intact, a tribute to the workmanship of John Hunter, carpenter. The original pulpit survives, with a sounding board and screen removed in 1882 but restored in 1952. There was a reader's desk or 'laitron', now gone, like the seat of repentance. Also remaining are the Sailors Loft to the right of the pulpit, the Trades Loft to the left, and facing the pulpit is the Merchants Loft, where the session held their meetings, and occupied latterly also by the council. The original Magistrates Loft was adjacent, a semi-circular projection, with the scholars' seat behind, and entered by an outside stair. Contributions for these lofts from the merchants, the trades, and the sailors society were augmented by contributions from parishioners who might rent one of the sixty pews which were erected, or one of the fifty-four placings where seating had to be privately provided. The seats were allocated in March 1656, suggesting that congregational worship began soon afterwards, some months before the celebration of communion in the new church on 21 September 1656.

The provision of this splendid new church confirms that 17th century Ayr was a wealthy community. Despite the various troubles, the council could increase its commitments with expenditure on hospital, school, and church. Because of the plague, the council in 1607 engaged its first town surgeon, James Harper, and continued him on a yearly fee of 50 merks. There were other signs of affluence. The tolbooth in the Sandgate, erected in 1575, was improved in 1615 by the construction of a wooden spire and bell tower, surmounted by a cock weather vane. In 1616 a new bell was obtained from a foundry in Irvine, and a new clock made locally by John Smyth, snapmaker. Later in the century, in 1662 the meal market in High Street was reconstructed. Then in 1663 the council appointed John Harper and Arthur Scott 'to be foot poasts betwixt Edinburgh and Air' leaving on Mondays and returning on Saturdays. The postmaster at Edinburgh was for a number of years commissioned to send 'to the magistrats the weiklie gazet and news lettres'. About the same time, at the junction of Sandgate with High Street, the Malt Cross was enhanced by the construction of a replica of Edinburgh's mercat cross. This has been attributed to the reign of Charles II; but the likely date would seem to be 1697 after John Anderson, mason, was admitted burgess and gild brother, 'and has gottin Libertie to oppin the quarrie of this Burgh upon the termes following ... that he is to cast the Kings armes in stoune and put the same upon the Croce of this burgh wher they ar now set upe in timber as also that he shall mend the tackleing about the said Croce ...' In 1673 the Auld Tour in High Street, formerly the property of Robert Cathcart of Carbieston and now belonging to Ex-provost Adam Ritchie was purchased by the council to be converted into 'ane correctione house'. The burgh accounts show money being spent lavishly. Anyone of importance who happened to visit Ayr was made a burgess and guild brother 'for good deids done and to be done' and bills for hospitality could amount to 10% of council expenditure. One obviously riotous occasion in 1687 is indicated by a bill of '£38. 11s for wyne drunkin by the Magistrats and Counsell upon the threttieth day of May instant and' – the damning evidence – 'for brokin glasses'. Local festivities were supported. Though some like the Robin Hood plays had gone out with the Reformation, new ones were introduced. Regularly from 1609 grants were made 'for the bend of the papingo' – a band or sash which was the prize in annual archery contests for young men. The council patronised the races, as in 1593, 1609 ('the Golden Bell horse race' on 10 May) and 1610 (the 'gold raiss'); and in 1698 presented a silver cup 'to the valew of betwixt seven and eight pounds sterling ... as ane pryse to be run for upon the nynth of August nixt to cum, att a horse race in the Sands of Ayre'.

To pay for all this, burgh revenues had to be augmented. Income had increased in the 16th century from an average £250 in the period before the Reformation to £600 afterwards; in the early decades of the 17th century it was always more than £1,000, occasionally exceeded £2,000, and averaged £1,600. Allowing for inflation, revenue had increased six and a half times in a century. In the course of the 17th century annual income approximately doubled, reaching £3,000 by 1692. Of this, £1,285 was the money of the Queen Mary Mortification as derived from the corn mills. The remaining £1,770 was not much more than before. Petty customs produced £860; rents from Alloway nearly £600; feu duties from the Burrowfield among the remaining minor items. Whenever income was insufficient to cover expenditure, stents could be levied for local purposes in addition to those imposed by the crown as the burgh's taxes. But in the 17th century there was an increased reliance on loans. At the beginning of the 17th century Ayr was virtually debt-free; by the 1620s there was a debt of £2,000; in 1692 the debt had increased to £7,750 with another £2,000 in dispute. In that year the council had to pay, at 6%, interest amounting to £465, which was 15% of burgh expenditure. This situation was not peculiar to Ayr. 'During the seventeeenth century most of the royal burghs became deeply involved in debt ... many towns had got their finances into a sorry muddle'. This disapproving comment (by G.S.Pryde) on 'the ways of the improvident' needs reassessment if only because attitudes to public (and private) finance have changed drastically since it was made fifty years ago. It no longer seems immoral for Ayr's 17th century council to have taken out a mortgage on the security of the burgh's resources. Those who lent the money obviously felt that it was (especially in the absence of banks) a good and safe investment. The fact that there was money available for lending and borrowing is one final piece of evidence that this was a wealthy community.

It is possible to get some impression of the distribution of wealth in 17th century Ayr from several mid-century stent rolls which happen to have survived, recording the amount of tax 'payabill be the whole inhabitantis'. One of November 1656 records £1,742. 15. 4d as due for the second half of that year. This figure included £96 payable by the burgh for Alloway; £112 which was the responsibility of a dozen owners of land in the Burrowfield; £1,535 was accountable to 421 persons within the town itself. The stent roll was drawn up by a committee of burgesses nominated by the burgh council. These stenters were also responsible for the collection, which was probably still made, as during the previous century, in the 'pailyeoun' or tent which the burgh owned. The burgh was divided into four quarters: apparently the seaward side of Sandgate plus the river side of High Street as far as the bridge; that same side of High Street from the bridge to the Wallace Tower; the Townhead; High Street from the Carrick Vennel down that side to the Sandgate and continuing along the landward side of Sandgate. How the stenters in 1656 calculated the amounts to be levied is not clear. They had abandoned the system of a generation earlier whereby each craft made a contribution. The stent in 1656 was levied on houses, lands, trade, and brewing, or combinations thereof, so that the number of persons stented may be taken as approximately equivalent to the number of households. This figure of 421 households suggests a population of around 2,500.

The most substantial people of the town were obviously included among 80 persons paying £5 or more in the stent. Some of these are designated in the roll as merchants, some as magistrates like Bailie James Cochrane who paid £40. But only a few names on the stent rolls have occupations shown, which makes it difficult to be precise. Also there are other merchants and magistrates who paid less than £5, which is a reminder that amounts paid in tax may then (as now) only hint at individuals' total wealth. Yet the stent rolls do indicate a pyramid of wealth. The 80 persons paying £5 or more, the top 20% of tax-payers, provided 50% of the total tax amount. 38 of them who formed the top 9% were responsible for 30% of the total.

The list includes 213 persons whose assessments specifically mention payment 'for traid'. Allowing for others who happen to be designated as craftsmen, we can make comparison with our previous estimate for the 16th century to suggest an increase since then from 50 to 70 guild merchants and an increase from 150 to 200 burgess craftsmen.

There must have been wide variations in wealth. That is suggested by the stents charged to merchants ranging from £40 to £1.10s. Similarly with those who can be allocated to one of the seven incorporated crafts. Only one hammerman was listed, a smith, at £8. Weavers ranged from £5 to £1.4s; tailors from £3.10s to 12s. Squaremen included masons at £8 – £1.4s, wrights at £2 to £1.4s, one slater at £3. Shoemakers or cordiners ranged from £5.16s to £2; Skinners from £4.10s to £1; Waulkers from £4 to £1.16. This last was in process of being superseded as an organised craft by Dyers, though none was listed as such in this stent roll. Two other new crafts were becoming organised – Coopers (incorporated as an eighth craft before 1647), ranging from £2.2s–£1.4s; and Fleshers, from £5–12s. These figures of taxes paid may suggest relative prosperity of members of the various crafts, and of others belonging to non-incorporated trades. Sailors ranged from £10 to £1.4; Bakers or baxters from £6.16 to 18s. John Mason, notary, paid £5.7s; John Reid, surgeon, paid £4.10s; ministers and teachers occupied rented accommodation and paid no stent so cannot be compared. Other occupations included glover £4.14s, miller £4.11s, maltman £4, candlemaker £3, pipemaker £2, fuller £1.10, messengers £1.4s, tinkler 18s, and coblers at 18s to 16s.

The burgh population in mid-century included guild merchants (perhaps 70), burgess craftsmen (perhaps 200), those employed by them (at a guess, 600, not included on the stent roll) and other 'unfree' and unprivileged indwellers (say 130 including nearly all the 49 who paid less than £1 and most of the 118 paying less than £2 in stent). To this total of 1,000 add at least as many for dependent wives and children, to give 2,500. In 1600 there had been possibly 2,000. Natural increase was perhaps inhibited by dearth (in 1583 and 1602) and plague (in 1606 and 1647) though it would be dangerous to attempt a calculation when local losses from plague on those occasions were said to be 2,000 and 34 respectively. The population was augmented by immigration, including English who settled permanently during the Cromwellian occupation, and French protestants escaping from Louis XIV's persecution after 1685. In this period country lairds seem to have found town houses in Ayr less attractive. The Blairs of Adamton had sold their house to David Wallace, a burgess, before 1585. Another belonging to Thomas Cunningham in 1656 had been 'bought fra mylnquarter'. Also in 1656 Thomas Blair owned 'the houses somtyme the Laird of gaitgirthes'; and Theophilus Rankin was occupying Ardmillan's house in the Kirk Vennel. The first Earl of Loudoun, after he ceased to be sheriff, by selling the hereditary sheriffdom to the crown in 1634, disposed of Loudoun Hall. In 1656 there is note of 'My Lord Lowdoune for his tenement in the Sea Vennell' which was then 'possest be Margaret Bannatyne'. It was acquired by James Chalmer of Gadgirth; who in 1666 sold it to James Mure of Park, merchant, councillor, and later provost. Only four lairds' town houses are found in the 1656 'Roll of Ground Annuals': Kennedy of Bargany's in the Sandgate; Gilbert Richart of Barskimming

in 'the quyht hous in the fleshemercatt'; William Hunter of Drumdow's 'Land in the Wollmercat'; Lady Shewalton's house, formerly belonging to the laird of Craigie, was probably in the Sandgate. Late in the century the decline of the French trade must have limited Ayr's growth. The severe famine which ravaged Scotland in the last years of the 17th century caused loss of life which was remembered in the county a century later, though the royal burghs of Ayr and Irvine were in an advantageous position for importing grain from Ireland. Thus it is possible that by 1700 the burgh population was approaching 3,000.

For the 17th century it becomes possible to get a glimpse of what Ayr looked like. In 1654 Cromwell's engineer Hans Ewald Tessin drew a plan of the Citadel, which included an outline of the adjacent town. There are marked (in the Sandgate) 'the town hall'; and (in High Street) 'the old town hall' and 'the new town church' The old ports which were gateways to the burgh are shown, though un-named. Building has extended beyond the Sandgate port; and in High Street beyond the port at the Auld Tour and even beyond the later Overport, so that the Townhead stretched into what would become Kyle and Alloway Streets. From the main streets building obviously extended along those vennels shown, which would be later known as Mill Street, Carrick Street, Kirk Port, Old and New Bridge Streets, Boat Vennel, Academy Lane, St John's Lane. This compact and somewhat cramped town is even more clearly revealed to our vision in the two drawings by the Dutchman John Slezer, published in 1694 and presenting views from the opposite side of the river. 'The Town of Aire from the House of Newtowne' shows the recently-built Church; adjacent properties with tree-lined gardens backing on to the river; some indication of the Doocot ford upriver and that other on this side of the Auld Brig; beyond which are the masts of a fleet of substantial ships occupying the harbour. The other 'Prospect of the Town of Air from the East' illustrates the harbour at a quieter spell with some smaller vessels at anchor and a couple of fishing cobles at work. There is a clear view of the walls of the dismantled Citadel; the buildings where after 1660 the Earl of Eglinton had set up a brewery and woollen manufactory, purchased in 1687 by John Mure along with the Church of St John; that church with its outbuildings and prominent tower still intact though disused and isolated from the town. On the edge of the town proper is a detached building which has been identified as the burgh school; the spire of the Sandgate tolbooth crowns the skyline; and from the ford at the Ratton Quay up towards the Auld Brig the river is lined with private wharves, each attached to warehouses which fill up the spaces behind the dwellings and booths of that part of High Street.

There are no comparable means of visualising the Burrowfield and Alloway, apart from the map published by Blaeu in 1654 but based on information supplied by Timothy Pont a half-century earlier. We can guess at improved cultivation in the barony of Alloway, sufficient to provide the increased revenues which the burgh collected in the 17th century. The stent of £96 which the burgh paid for Alloway in 1656 was less than £112 to be collected from the Burrowfield. Which indicates that the Burrowfield was by no means waste land as might be imagined from its paltry contributions to the burgh revenues. The stent roll of 1656 lists a dozen payments for lands in the Burrowfield, ranging from £22.16s to 18s. Alexander Campbell paid that maximum sum for Macnairston and adjacent lands of Belsbank, Bankheid, Duphoilburn, and Byrestoun. Lochrymos, belonging to William Caldwell in 1600, paid £19.10s. Holmstoun belonged to the Wallaces, a branch of the Craigie family, and was charged £12.13s. Lochfergus, which the Earl of Loudoun had sold to William Cunningham of Enterkin, paid £13.13s. Clongall, which went through various changes of ownership, paid £10.2s.6d. Gawblair (£6.12s) and Duphoil (£4.1s) were two smaller named properties. The sizeable Castlehill estate, which in 1656 was held by Agnes Lockhart, relict of William Kelso, was acquired in 1676 by John Fergusson, writer. Castlehill is not listed; nor any of the numerous smaller properties in the Burrowfield, such as Barns. Barns House, still occupied, includes a part which obviously dates back to the 17th century. The apparent incompleteness of the roll suggests that burgesses who paid for houses, trade, brewing, and land had included in the last item not only burgage plots but their holdings in the Burrowfield – which would therefore be much more valuable than the £112 noted. A list in the council minutes for 1684 indicates 25 holdings within the Burrowfield and 19 in the barony of Alloway.

As in the 16th century, trade and land each contributed to the wealth of those merchants who played such a prominent role in the municipal life of Ayr burgh. In this century, Ayr was served by thirty provosts; for more than half the time by sixteen men who belonged to one of six leading families. Most of these municipal dynasties derived from landed families. But they were principally merchants, often only distantly related to their country cousins, and the land they possessed was usually recently acquired as an investment. Thus Lockharts came from Barr in Galston parish to be merchants in Ayr and acquired Boghall in St Quivox parish, contributing three provosts, two near the beginning of the 17th century. Of the remaining five families, those provosts who were Kennedys had ancestors who came from Bargany, Cunninghams from Kilmaurs, Mures from Rowallan, and Hunters from Hunterston.

One whose antecedents are obscure was John Osborne. His forbears were well-established locally, Alexander Osborne in 1501 occupying the family tenement in the vennel leading from the Fish Cross to the river. John Osborne was a merchant and shipowner trading in timber and wine; he married Elizabeth Fergushill, two of whose family had been provosts; he became provost for the first time in 1611 by royal recommendation; he (and his wife) died in February 1633. His son John, trained to be skipper of one of his father's ships, was wealthy enough in 1620 to lend the burgh £2,000 and astute enough to charge 10%. He was a councillor for most of the next twenty years, and provost six times during a period of national crisis. The son of one provost, he married Janet Ritchie, daughter of another. Late in the century a namesake twice became provost. A quite similar pattern was followed by three provosts of the Kennedy family, who were also shipowners. Hew Kennedy, who married Susanna Bannatyne, was provost five times, and died in 1623 while still a councillor. Hew Kennedy, his elder son, was provost seven times. In his capacity as Ayr's commissioner to parliament he was one of those sent to England to negotiate with Charles I. He no doubt profitted in 1643 and 1644 from supplying the Scots army in Ireland with meal and with 'tua thousand paire of good and sufficient double soled shoes of elleven twelffe or threeene inches'. He benefitted from his marriage in 1649 to Jean Bryson by obtaining as a dowry Clongall and other lands. His younger brother John also joined the council about 1630, married Margaret Bannatyne, became provost for one term, and died in 1648, possibly a result of the plague. Of the four members of the Cunningham clan who served as provosts in the 17th century, William Cunningham (1628–29) and John Cunningham (1675–76) were much less prominent than the others. William Cunningham of Brounhill became provost in 1665 for the first of ten terms, and in the awkward years when Charles II was re-introducing episcopacy Cunningham was reliable enough to be continued in office by royal authority from 1660 till 1667 and again from 1669 till 1671. In

1662 he acquired Mylnequarter in St Quivox and in 1667 the lands of Brownhill in Tarbolton parish. He died in 1686, after continuing to serve on the council during the first of his son's provostships, 1678–81.

John Mure, the founder of a longer dynasty, was provost briefly from 1673–75 when indulgence was temporarily granted to committed presbyterians. In 1664 Mure had been suspended from the council for refusing to abjure the covenants, and was suspended again in 1675 because he would not sign the 'band against conventicles'. In 1677 he was alleged to have withdrawn from the parish church to participate in field and house conventicles, one at Prestwick, one within the Citadel, four within his own house where he sheltered vagrant preachers who were rebels. In 1689 following the Glorious Revolution when James VII and II was replaced by William and Mary, nominated councils were replaced by new ones specially elected 'by poll of the burgesses'. John Mure was elected, serving as provost for five terms between 1689 and 1707 and as councillor till his death in 1709 or 1710. He was married to Janet Doock and two of their sons became provosts – Robert, various years between 1695 and 1719, Samuel between 1710 and 1714. John Mure inherited Park in Tarbolton parish, purchased Loudoun Hall, then the Citadel (so that services could be held in the Church of St John, as permitted in 1687). His son Provost Robert Mure would acquire the estate of Blairston.

Robert Hunter was provost briefly from 1684 till 1686. Though his grandson would in the 18th century also be provost for a little longer, this would seem scant excuse for special and detailed mention were it not for the involvement of so many Hunters in late 17th century Ayr, with a web of family connections which would extend still further in later generations. The progenitor of the Ayr Hunters seems to have been James Hunter, a younger son from Hunterston in West Kilbride, who acquired Abbothill around 1569. By the end of that century members of the family were tenanting Corton, Broomberry, and Holmston, some were in Newton-upon-Ayr, others were set up in the royal burgh as webster, glover, cooper, smith, and quarrier, providing the council with one magistrate (1574–75) and another (1611–12, 1623–24). Robert Hunter who would become provost served on the council from 1663; he was sometimes described as Robert Hunter of Dogland, suggesting that he was country laird, but this was a mere three acre holding near St Leonard's which the Ayr merchant possessed. On the council with him for a long spell was his elder brother Adam Hunter, also a merchant, who succeeded to Abbothill when their eldest brother John Hunter died after 1685. From 1678 till 1686 Robert Hunter's career is worth following in some detail as a case study in 17th century local politics.

Robert Hunter is noted in the minutes of 1678 as the leader of a faction opposed to Robert Doock and William Cunningham junior. What had precipitated the breach between the Hunters and the Cunninghams is not known. It was certainly not religious principles: both were alleged to have sympathies with the Covenanters; both followed an opportunist policy of compromise with the government as convenient to their interests. The basic dispute may have been a family one, for William Cunningham's mother was a Barbara Hunter. On 17 September 1678 Hunter protested in council that 'no man sould have voyce in the Electione bot onlie wha wald or have givin obedience to the Law'; but he was overruled by the provost, excluded from the council in 1679, then re-admitted in 1680 and elected bailie. The imposition of the Test in 1681 resulted in the eight persons (from both factions) at the election meeting on 3 October 'upone severall reasones and consideratiapplapples refuissed the samen' and 'in respect that they were not ane competent number' adjourned. They then 'did most presumptuously in face of the people, at the foot of the tolbooth stair, call for the toune officers and dismiss them, telling them there was to be no more government in that place'. Ayr was thus left without a council till 2 January 1682, when it was reconstituted with members nominated by the Privy Council. The new provost was Vaxley Robson, a former Cromwellian officer settled in Ayr; and among the other nominees were Robert and Adam Hunter – who now took the test. Those coopted to make up the council's number were another brother, Mr James Hunter; and a cousin William Hunter, tailor and late deacon convener.

In September 1682 troops were sent into Ayr by the Privy Council, which rightly feared 'differences and tumult likely to fall out at the election'. At the Michaelmas meetings the faction led by Provost Robson and Bailie William Brisbane physically ejected the seven members of the Hunter faction who were deemed to have behaved 'in ane tumultous and seditious manner'; and successfully prevented the entry of that other faction led by an unruly William Cunningham. There was difficulty in making up the council's numbers, especially selecting the two craft councillors. For William Hunter persuaded the trades to boycott the meeting to choose their conveners. In doing this in the spring of 1683 William Hunter 'did give in ane seditious and mutinous paiper' for which he was imprisoned, had his burgess ticket 'lacerat and riven at the mercat croce', was fined 500 merks, and threatened with banishment. He acknowledged fault as 'ane poor illiterat tredsman'.

In August 1683 the Hunter faction successfully re-established itself. Robert Hunter was able to persuade the Privy Council that he and his friends had been put off the council 'in ane illegall and tumultuous way'; and the Privy Council authorised the restoration of six Ayr councillors including three Hunters, though not William. At the 1683 Michaelmas elections Adam Hunter was the only one re-elected and William Brisbane as provost succeeded Robson who had died in office. Robert Hunter however continued through 1684 his tactics of appeal to the Privy Council. His case against Brisbane was found not proven; William Cunningham was adjudged unfit for public office; and Robert Hunter was nominated as provost from November 1684. His council included six of the clan: brothers Adam and Mr James, his eldest son James, his son-in-law Robert Fullarton, and his cousin William (to whom all privileges were restored). In 1685 this council was continued unchanged. At the Michaelmas meetings William Cunningham had been 'useing fraudulent and sinistrous designes to get himself elected Proveist for the ensueing yeir and had endangered the peace and quiet of the Burgh and raised a tumult at the electing'. But Cunninghame was able to turn the tables. He proved to the Privy Council that Robert Hunter had won by guile – claiming that as provost he had two votes – and by coercion – one witness declaring that 'he saw Robert Huntar, provest, get up on the table with his feet and say ... "Get you gone villianes" and caused turne them out by force'. In March 1686 the Privy Council nominated a new council with William Cunningham as provost, though Adam and Robert Hunter were retained as councillors. Ex-provost Robert Hunter died in 1692. How many Hunters were involved in the complex story may be indicated from several other items from 1686. James Hunter, miller, was made a guild brother (27 April); as was his son John Hunter, town officer (14 December) along with William Hunter, merchant, son of the late John Hunter, tailor. Then (on 28 December) John Hunter, officer, was cashiered and dismissed for 'abuseing the Inhabitants'.

On the opposite side of the river the Wallaces of Craigie were the dominant family. In St Quivox parish the Cathcarts continued in ownership of Auchincruive; Robert Alexander in 1648 formed his Blackhouse estate including Boghall, Chapelland, Dyke, Smiddyhill, Dalmilling mill, to which in 1668 was added Woodquarter or Thornyflat; Robert Shaw was owner of Mainholm at the beginning of the 17th century. Most of the rest of St Quivox belonged to John Wallace of Craigie who resided in Newton Castle and acquired effective possession of the whole of Newton-upon-Ayr when he was recognised as hereditary provost of that burgh in 1603. He was succeeded (before 1614) by his son Hew Wallace, a royalist who was knighted by Charles II, fought in Montrose's army, and forced to accept a humiliating pardon. His grand nephew succeeded to the estate in 1663, was awarded a baronetcy by Charles II in 1670, and as Sir Thomas Wallace of Craigie became Lord Justice Clerk in 1675. When his son Sir William Wallace succeeded in 1680, because he was a Roman Catholic there was an attempt to deprive him of the provostship of Newton. Ayr's ex-provost John Osborne who (like several other Ayr burgesses) was a freeman of Newton was elected its provost but deposed within months; and ironically six years later Sir William Wallace of Craigie, hereditary provost of Newton, was by royal command of the Roman Catholic James VII and II made also provost of the royal burgh of Ayr.

As in Ayr, the council of Newton was appointed annually at Michaelmas. In Newton the procedure was superficially more democratic, in that all 48 freemen participated in the election 'inquest', though (as the events of 1680 showed) Wallace of Craigie as superior had to approve. Two bailies were annually appointed, supported by a treasurer, procurator fiscal, and councillors varying in number from four to fourteeen. A notary from Ayr acted as clerk, and selected freemen had to act as officers, eveners (who apportioned lands), lyners (who checked boundaries), poinders (who impounded stray animals), tasters of ale and beer, visitors of the seaside, and collectors to assist the bailies with stents and feu duties payable to Wallace. The council met as required throughout the year, with head courts at Beltane and Michaelmas. Much of the business concerned management of the land. The Sea Daills, the Lang Daills, and the West Daills which formed the three main arable areas were divided for allocation to the freemen each eleven years from 1604. Disputes over land had to be settled, including use of the common land for pasture. There was a toun herd, and fines for those who allowed their beasts to stray. The gathering of seaweed 'wrack' from the shore required the super-vision of the 'visitors of the seaside'. Punishments for breach of the 'old acts' were normally fines, as in 1660 when someone was 'unlawed 10 groats for casting and taking away diffots to big an unfreeeman's house'.

Criminal offences were dealt with severely. In 1681 a woman guilty of 'scandalous carriage and calumnating' was 'To be put in juggs Saturday next at ten o'clock to remain an hour, a paper of capital letters on her face. Meantime imprisoned, thereafter banished the toun, never to re-enter, and to have the spurr in her mouth, when she is in the juggs. Also fined £10.' The usual punishment for theft was banishment, and for assault a period in the stocks at the cross.

Though the freemen depended on the land, few of them restricted themselves to farming. In 1671 Newton council indicated that 'the employment, substance, and livelihood of the most part of the inhabitants consists in salmon fishing in the mouth of the water of Ayr' insisting on their monopoly of fishing 'between the mouth of the barr of Ayr and the Pow Burn'. Indeed each August when the main summer catch of salmon had been salted or smoked there would follow the Kipper Fair, which became Newton's principal festival. There was a modest range of crafts – websters (weavers), litsters (dyers), tailors, wrights, cordiners (shoemakers), carpenters, masons, brewers, and coal hewers. These last are noted in 1656, no doubt involved in the coastal salt pans. Later in 1672 Sir Thomas Wallace began searching for coal inland on the east side of Newton loch.

This small community's problems were sometimes the same as in Ayr. The plague in 1605 and 1646 required 'uncouth persons' to be kept out, and quarter masters to isolate infected persons and goods 'at the loch head beside the burn foot' during this sign of 'goddis anger'. In 1650 one Bessie McCallan was imprisoned as a suspected witch, and may have been executed. In 1665 when seamen were being conscripted for the Dutch War a number of Newton fishermen fled to escape. After 1681 there were difficulties with freemen refusing to take the Test and having their privileges nullified; and it was ordained that anyone protesting should be scourged, jouged, then banished. One special problem for Newton was the distance from the parish church in Prestwick, which persuaded some to worship in Ayr, though they and others from St Quivox were in 1639 required to return to 'thair awin paroche kirks'. Proximity to Ayr had also the odd consequence of Newton council occasionally meeting in Ayr tolbooth.

Like Ayr, Newton in the 17th century seems to have experienced some improvements. It still remained small, with a few hundred inhabitants in the double row of houses which formed the King's Street. Some at least of these were two-storyed, and new houses were being constructed. The houses were set widely apart on both sides of the lade which ran down from the loch into the River Ayr at Newton Mill. The inhabitants were prohibited from washing their clothes or other items in the lade, and obliged (1680) to 'keep all their middens and dunghills in the backside of their houses that the high street of the toun be not any more damnified by them'. In 1667 Sir Thomas Craigie began enclosing the land around Newton Castle and obtained Privy Council permission to divert the public highway from Kilmarnock and Irvine which ran through his grounds towards the Auld Brig. To provide an alternative route through Newton, he persuaded the 'haill freemen and inhabitants' to repair the road on the south side of the mill lade 'fit for passing of horses and carts', promising to remit his feu duties, whereupon 'all in one voice agreed'. The following year he attempted to close up the former 'common way' to the Auld Brig past Newton Castle. But the road through Newton was still 'so narrow, and a mill-laid running through it, rendered it impossible that cairtes or slaides could pass that way' and 'the tide in winter came so close up to Craigie yard dyke' as to make it impassable then. So a new track running east of Newton Castle had to be formed (later Wallace Street). In 1672 the inhabitants of Newton were required to lay a causey as a private road from the bridgend to the entry of the Castle (Garden Street). In 1686 advantage was taken by Sir William Wallace of a new parliamentary act to require of each inhabitant six days statute labour on the repair of highways.

One notable improvement in Newton was provision of a tolbooth. From 1596 the first recorded meeting of the council took place 'within Adam Hunter's house'. Later they met in the homes of other freeman, and once in 1605 'on Newtoun Green'. There was certainly a place called a tolbooth but really only a prison until a new building was erected for the first meeting of the 'Court in Newtoun Tolbooth' in October 1647. This was located in the main street opposite the mercat cross where the weekly markets were held. We can guess that nearby was the school mentioned in 1643 and 1664, one further sign of social advance in the 17th century.

EIGHT

The 18th Century Burgh Council

The sett of the burgh, as attested in 1713, defines how the council was then constituted:

SETT OF THE BURGH OF AIR.

Air, ninth July jm vijc and thirteen years.

The constitution and sett of the magistrats of the burgh of Air and the manner of their election is as follows, viz.:

There is the provost, tuo baillies, dean of gild, treasurer, ten merchant and tuo trades councilers, in all seventeen, which are elected at the times and in manner aftermentioned, to witt

upon Wednesday before Michalmass the saids provost, baillies, dean of gild, treasurer, ten merchant and tuo trades councilers meet within the tolbuith and elect four other merchant and tuo trades, all of different deaconries and crafts, who are to be members of the council for the subsequent year, and

upon Friday immediately before Michalmass day the old and new council, consisting of tuenty three in number, chose and elect the persons who are to be on the leits for provost, baillies, dean of gild, and treasurer, three persons of the said tuenty three being on the leits for provost, six for baillies, three for dean of gild, and three for treasurer.

Upon Munday immediately after Michalmass day the said old and new council meet with the remaining three deacons of the other crafts, consisting in all of tuenty six in number, within the said tolbuith, about ten of the clock before noon, and betuixt and tuelve of the clock at noon. elect out of the said leits the provost, baillies, dean of gild, treasurer, with the tuelve councilers, four of the merchants and tuo of the trades of the old council necessary falling off.

This attested by, *sic subscribitur*, Jo. Hunter, Clerk depute

This 18th century constitution was one which operated, with few changes, for more than two hundred and fifty years from the 16th century (sometime before 1580) till the 19th (with the Burgh Reform Acts of 1833). Indeed until 1949 when council elections were transferred to May from November, the municipal calendar continued the long tradition of the burgh year commencing after Michaelmas.

With Michaelmas on 29 September the three 'election meetings' took place at the end of that month, sometimes extending into October. At the first (Wednesday) meeting, the old council of five magistrates and twelve councillors convened in the tolbooth, as they had done in the late 16th century 'according to the ordour obseruit thairanent' and 'eftir sage and lang aduisment' nominated new councillors, seven in the 16th and 17th centuries, six after 1689. All but two of these had to be members of the merchant guild. The other two had to be deacons of crafts. There were seven crafts (tailors, waulkers, cordiners, skinners, websters, hammermen, and masons or squaremen) and the old council, which contained two deacons of crafts, made choice from the other five craft deacons. Though fleshers and coopers became incorporated crafts in the 17th century, their deacons were never recognised for representation on the council. At the second (Friday) meeting the old council and the nominated new councillors – 23 in all – drew up leets or short lists of three candidates for appointment as the new magistrates – provost, two bailies, dean of guild, and treasurer. At the third (Monday) meeting the old council, the new councillors, plus the remaining three deacons of crafts ('the extraordinary deacons') made up an assembly of twenty six who selected by vote the five new magistrates. The council for the ensuing year comprised (a) the five new magistrates; (b) the five old magistrates; (c) the seven new councillors; and quite often (d) if any old magistrate or new councillor were chosen as a new magistrate, sufficient old councillors were retained to make up the total of seventeen. In the course of the 18th century it became customary to have one 'old councillor' selected by his colleagues as being preferred for this purpose.

This replaced the system of the early 16th century when councillors, varying in number from fourteen to twenty one, were apparently elected by popular acclaim, together with four magistrates; the dean of guild was not then a magistrate, but chosen by the members as dean of the court of the merchant guild. The abandonment of election by 'ane multitude' was ordered by the crown in an Act of 1469, but the introduction of the system of self-elective councils was not implemented in Ayr till a century later. Thereafter the rule of a merchant oligarchy was secure. Continuity was ensured by the retention of old magistrates for the ensuing year, and by the choice of some of the old councillors as new ones. Yet there was, as Pryde has shown for the late 16th century, a real change in personnel with an average of six new recruits each year. This included the trades councillors who were annually changed, presumably to prevent any mere craftsman becoming too influential. There was a somewhat similar limitation of magistrates' terms of office, though here the ostensible reason was to prevent overwork. In 1602 annual changes of magistrates were ordered since 'euerie honest man of the toun aucht of dewitie to beir his equall burdene yeirlie about'. By the 18th century this restriction had been abandoned, though provosts could now serve only for two consecutive years, with the possibility of re-appointment after an interval. The normal routine was upset in the awkward political circumstances of the late 17th century, when (as the last chapter showed) the system broke down in 1681, and the Privy Council nominated magistrates and councillors for several years. After the deposition of James VII and II in 1688, there was a similar deposition on 1 January 1689 of Provost William Wallace of Craigie 'in regard he is ane papist', and on 16 May there was 'ane new electione of Magistrats and Counsell', as the Convention of Royal Burghs had recommended 'by the Pole of the burgesss', deciding 'by the pluralitie of their number'. In this isolated opportunity for popular participation, only the dean of guild and one councillor were acceptable enough to be continued in office. At Michaelmas 1689 there was a reversion to the traditional system of renewing the council by cooption. The practice thereafter was to choose six rather than seven new councillors each year, and the council continued to have a membership of seventeen.

The council required a number of 'officemen' to carry out various duties. In the 1580s appointments seem to have been made by the old and new councillors at the Friday meeting before Michaelmas, and included a master of works, a water bailie, procurator fiscal, and quartermasters – all of whom may have been councillors; also officers and other paid employees. The office of town clerk was in practice an appointment for life. In the 17th and 18th centuries it was left to the new council to choose annually one of its members as procurator fiscal; appoint whenever required a master of works and a water bailie; and

continue from year to year employees such as the herd, the keeper of the knock, and the four town officers. The locksman or hangman was appointed 'dureing the Magistrats and Counsells pleasure' as in 1688 when William Meldrum was equipped with a long coat, breeches, hose, and shoes, and promised 12s for putting miscreants in the juggs, 30s for a whipping, and £3 for an execution. Each new council was required to enrol some burgesses to undertake various duties. Stentmasters and collectors were required for valuation and collection of taxes. The markets and fairs required constables (usually 2 for each quarter of the town); clothmetsters otherwise cloth measurers, also saltmetsters in the 17th century; and visitors to inspect the meal and flesh markets.

Quite soon after its appointment each new council summoned the burgesses to Michaelmas Head Court, held early in October. All burgesses were supposed to attend; but when fifty or more were present (as sometimes happened) the tolbooth must have been overcrowded; and it is difficult to imagine 221 'within the tolbooth' on one occasion in 1688. Other head courts were originally held at Yule and Easter, but that at Michaelmas alone remained as a fixed occasion, when the new council assembled in presence of the burgesses, and the annual statutes were enacted or renewed – no doubt after opportunity for expression of opinion. From the 16th century (if not before) till the 19th, prices were fixed for ale, bread, corn, hay, and candles. For example, in 1678 ale and beer were priced at 20 pence per pint; white bread at 12 pence per 14 ounce; grey bread at 12 pence for 24 ounces; oat bread at eighteen pence per oatcake; candles at four shillings per pound; corn for horses at four shillings a peck; three shillings for a 24-hour supply of hay or straw for a horse. A century later in 1782 a pint of ale was to be charged at 24 pence, and beer at forty eight pence, still reckoned in Scots measure; a table was now required because of the several varieties of wheaten and household bread on sale. Oatcakes, at one half-penny sterling per pound troy, were oddly enough one of the few items accepting the English measures statutorily introduced in 1707 by the Act of Union, articles 16 and 17. Candles at 7s 4d per stone had dropped in price, but hay and straw for horses followed the more usual pattern of inflation to seven and three shillings respectively. Corn for horses was sold at 12 shillings per half bushel when the price was twelve shillings the boll – confusing enough to be superseded by the English Winchester bushel.

Also at Michaelmas, the 'town acts' were made. In the 16th century these regulated the marketing

The Tolbooth in the Sandgate, reconstructed in 1754, provided a court hall for meetings, with prison accommodation for debtors and criminals.

of flesh, fish, wool, butter, and cheese; prohibited re-grating, which was purchasing in bulk for resale at a profit; forbade the keeping of swine; and ordered 'myddingis' to be removed from the streets weekly. Each year the old acts were ratified and by the 18th century a busier town is suggested by the long list of additional measures, no doubt the result of popular complaints made at the Michaelmas head courts. 'The middings be removed off the streets on Saturday' was accompanied by penalties against dropping dung within ten yards of a public well. Horses had not to be left unattended in the street, nor driven furiously. There was to be no overnight parking of carts, and dead horses were not to be left unburied. Bonfires in the streets were prohibited, and chimneys had to be swept regularly, Swine had to be kept in styes; neither swine nor sheep might be pastured on the common; cattle and horses only under care of the town herd. Dogs were not allowed to stray at night and were to be destroyed if they attacked anyone. No whin burning without permisssion, nor keeping whins stacked near houses. Victuals could be sold only at the markets, and coals only at the harbour by the Shore Barrel of 6 Winchester bushels.

The risk of fire, which these Town Acts recognised, persuaded the council to make special provision. Something had obviously been attempted before 1796 when it was noted that 'the fire engines' were insufficient, and it was decided to purchase a new one from London, similar to that which the army had in the new barracks, and which had efficiently extinguished a recent conflagation in the town.

The council was busy with meetings throughout the year. Regular weekly meetings were enacted, on Wednesdays from 1583, Tuesdays from 1602. By the 18th century Wednesday was again the preferred day, though they did not meet every week, and chose other days when business was pressing. Hurriedly-convened brief meetings seem to have given way to longer and more formal meetings – 76 meetings were required in 1582/3, 51 in 1682/3, only 22 in 1782/3.

Throughout the year the minutes record the admission of new burgesses. While originally burgesses were required to take up residence and occupy a burgage plot, with the passage of time all that was required was payment of an entry fee called the burgess fine. This varied according to the applicant, and at the end of the 16th century there were six different rates for burgess entries and three for guild entries. A hundred years later there were simplified scales, which were continued into the 18th century with some modifications. There was a nominal payment of three pounds to become a burgess or (with a supplementary guild entry of £4.50) become a guild brother – if you were the son of one, or even a son-in-law through the daughter 'in hir poor virginitie'. Any other indweller or an incomer who wished to become a burgess and practise a craft had to pay over ten times as much as his burgess fine – 50 merks (approximately £33.30). Such a person aspiring to become a guild brother in order to trade locally as a merchant was charged 100 merks (about £66.65); and even a craftsman burgess was required to pay that amount to be admitted into the select circle of the merchant guild. Distinguished visitors to the town were made burgesses and guild brethren without fee 'for good deids done and to be done to the burgh' and their servants were sometimes also made honorary burgesses. To avoid offending any stranger who might turn out to have influence, practically everyone of any standing who visited the town was so honoured, and often entertained lavishly. In the last forty years of the unreformed burgh (1793–1833) there were admitted 375 burgesses, 322 guild brethren, and 96 honorary burgesses. By that period it was proving difficult to prevent unfree traders – in the later 18th century lists had to be drawn up periodically of 'persons carrying

The Sandgate tolbooth was exposed to wider view after 1788 when the New Bridge was opened and the Malt Cross demolished.

on trade, traffick, or business without being freemen', and in 1763 for example, 43 such 'were warned'. In the previous century unfree persons daring to import salt, or even ale from the Citadel brewery, had been more ruthlessly dealt with by fine, imprisonment, and banishment.

The second head court of the burgh year was by the 17th and 18th centuries held at the end of April or the beginning of May. This was for 'the Rouping of the Customs', when burgesses bid in an auction for the right to collect tolls for the ensuing year from first June. The most profitable always fetched the highest bids. These were the Meal Market (£185 in 1678; £276 in 1783), the Tron for weighing other items from wool to iron (£205, £213), the Bridge (£118, £206). Tolls levied on 'nolt' (cattle), 'scheip' (sheep), and 'Fish, flesh, and Loads' became more profitable (altogether £112 in 1678, £747 in 1783), but less so with the fairs (£50, £61). On the same occasion there were let by auction the three vaults under the tolbooth and the right to pasture on 'the grass of the hills'. Altogether these petty customs and other items rouped produced a total of £32 in 1539, £635 in 1678, £1,747 in 1783, all in Scots, rising to £562 sterling in the early 19th century.

There was often held soon afterwards a third court, usually the best attended, for this was when – following the provost's return from the Convention of Royal Burghs – the council proposed and the community had to accept the necessity of a stent or levy to meet the burgh's share of national taxation or finance some local project. Stentmasters were appointed from among the burgesses to assess payments from individual householders, and collectors responsible for each of the town's four quarters. The quarters of the town (as defined in 1776) were (1) the seaward side of Sandgate and the river side of High Street as far as the bridge; (2) the river side of High Street from the bridge to the Wallace Tower; (3) the Townhead; (4) High Street from the Carrick Vennel down to the Sandgate plus the landward side of Sandgate. Separate arrangements were made for collecting the stent levied on the rentallers of Alloway. In August came the court where there was rouped 'the merk to be exactit aff everie boll malt to be grund at the mylnes of Air and Alloway'. This was the burgh's most valuable item of revenue, producing in the later 17th century over £2,000 each year.

Throughout the year there was routine business to be dealt with. The ceremony of taking sasine had to be performed whenever land in the Burrowfield was transferred by purchase or inheritance to a new

In 1767 work began on a street which in the 19th century would be named Newmarket Street. After a period of decline, the royal burgh doubled its population in fifty years to reach 4,000 before the end of the 18th century.

occupant. In the barony of Alloway new rentallers had to be approved of, and regulations made at the Alloway head courts. The magistrates as patrons of the church had responsibility (1712–1874) for choice of the minister of the second charge, while the crown held patronage of the first charge. The council was also responsible for maintaining the church and churchyard, allocating seats within the church, and making arrangements for communion services in February and August. Royal burghs were entitled to representation in the General Assembly of the Church, and Ayr council in this period normally nominated someone with a local connection resident in Edinburgh, a writer to the signet, the burgh's town agent, for several years after 1776 Professor Dugald Stewart, then from 1784 till 1822 George Fergusson from Kilkerran who became Lord Hermand. Similarly the school and schoolmasters were managed by the council, which (as will appear) continued from the 17th into the 18th century its concern for educational advance.

The burgh's 'public works' included maintenance of the highways. In 1763 the Sandgate and Townhead

Ports were demolished, because these 'Two Porches' were deemed 'useless and Cramp the passage of the Street at these places and Limite the Views'; similarly in 1788 the Malt Cross was removed to provide improved access across the New Bridge. In 1767 work was commenced on 'the New Street' from Sandgate to the Meal market, which would become Cross Street and later Newmarket Street. The cleansing of the streets was provided for by the annual 'rouping of the toun's redd'. As the century advanced the six street lamps provided in 1747 were supplemented by others, as were the two public wells in High Street and Townhead. The tolbooth, harbour, bridge, and the three mills had to be maintained (as well as church and school). The tolbooth indeed required considerable work to complete the steeple; this was accomplished after 1727 with a gift to the council of one quarter of the stones of the derelict St John's Church; the tolbooth however required virtual reconstruction in 1754. The council had also acquired (in 1673) the Auld Tour in High Street and, with help of public subscription, added in 1731 two upper storeys to provide a belfry with clock for the benefit of residents at the Townhead. In 1749 it was in use as a prison (perhaps until the tolbooth was reconstructed) and in 1774 it is noted in the council minutes by the new and puzzling title of Wallace Tower. The council added to its list of public properties with the building of a slaughterhouse beside the river, 1747; a Fleshmarket beside it, 1764; a poorshouse adjoining, 1755; a powder house at the Citadel, 1766; a washing house on the green, 1767; a new schoolhouse behind Wallace Tower, 1773; the new Bridge, 1788, of which more later; then purchased in 1786 the hospital of Kincase at Prestwick, with the right to nominate a number of poor persons to be accommodated there as inmates. At the corner of Sandgate and High Street the council acquired (before 1773) premises known as the Assembly Room which 'though not large, is very neat and convenient for an ordinary company', and was let to James Gregg, land surveyor and dancing master, for classes in country dancing. The court hall at the tolbooth was adjudged 'tolerably large and commodious'. Here was held the sheriff court, which gained increased status after the abolition of heritable jurisdictions in 1747. The court hall was also a meeting place for the Ayrshire Freeholders' annual Michaelmas head court, and when they assembled on occasion to choose the county member of parliament; and for meetings of those other county authorities, the Commissioners of Supply and the Turnpike Trustees. Here too met the Circuit Court of Justiciary where in 1785, for example, Lord Braxfield sentenced three persons 'to be hanged, and hung in Chains, in the common muir of the Burrow'. The council had to erect the gibbet and provide the hangman; the magistrates were required to attend the execution, accompanied on that occasion by 120 citizens forming a guard. This was a remnant of the council's former judicial responsibilities; after 1747 the bailies in the burgh court dealt only with minor charges. At a session of the Circuit Court in Ayr on 12 April 1787 there was an innovation when Thomas Winstanly, late soldier in the 12th Regiment of Foot, being found guilty of theft was sentenced 'to be transported beyond Seas' for a period of fourteen years. He may have been among the 736 convicts who left Portsmouth on 13 May on the First Fleet which arrived in Australia on 26 January 1788.

The council was involved in what is now called planning consent. Thus in 1775 there was in High Street an old building 'of a timber Construction, and was now become old and ruinous'; the owner proposed to 'rebuild it in a modern and uniform manner' and assured the council that it would 'Ornament and beautify that part of the street'. In the same year Charles Dalrymple of Orangefield sought permission to build houses on both sides of the new straight road leading out of Sandgate. He hoped to purchase land additional to the three acres he already feued between the end of Sandgate and the lands of Patrick McNeight of Barns, lying between the new road in a straight line from the Sandgate and the 'old road or loaning, which formerly was used as a road to the lower part of the barony of Alloway by the Bridgehouse, but which was now in disuse'. Other examples of plans authorised by the council were a customs house (1775), a course for horse racing on the Town's Common (1770), a Viewhouse at that racecourse (1787); and a Lodge for the Ayr Squaremen Freemasons (1769). Work on one new thoroughfare – 1767, Newmarket Street – was followed in 1781 by that other, now called Fort Street. In those new streets ground was feued for house-building; other plots were made available 'near the Shore', including one (in 1799) between the Citadel and the sea on ground 'of no earthly use to the community'; and in 1799 a plan was made for feuing the area of the Green.

As well as domestic business, the council was necessarily involved in affairs of the outside world. Each year a representative was sent, usually the provost, to the Convention of Royal Burghs. Ayr like all other royal burghs was represented in the Scots Parliament, also usually by the provost. The last so to do was Provost John Mure, who participated in the final sessions when that parliament approved of the Treaty of Union in 1707. An address to parliament from Ayr council dated 30 November 1706 was anxious for 'rectification of the articles of Union' and another of 3 December 1706 'on behalf of the merchants, deacons and other inhabitants of the burgh' also expressed opposition to 'an Union with England in the terms of the articles'. Yet in the critical parliamentary votes quite soon afterwards Provost Mure was among the majority of burgh commissioners who decided 33–29 in favour of the Act of Union. In the United Kingdom parliament, Edinburgh was the only Scots burgh important enough to be allowed separate representation. All the others were combined into fourteen groups. Ayr was thus associated with Irvine, Rothesay, Campbeltown, and Inveraray, and, whenever elections were called, commissioners nominated by the councils of these royal burghs met, and the five of them chose the MP for Ayr Burghs. There was also an MP for Ayrshire, one of Scotland's thirty county members, chosen at a meeting in the county town by the freeholders of Ayrshire – 97 of them in 1759 rising to a maximum of 235 in 1781. With such

Ayr, 30 January 1793.

The General annual Meeting of the Ayr Library Society, convened in Mrs White's the following Members, viz.

Mr William Bowie

Mr John Murdoch

Mr John Ballantine

Capt Robt Gardner

Mr Alexr Forsyth

Mr David Limond

Mr John Hunter

Dr Paterson

Mr William Tennant

Mr James Dowie

Mr David Tennant

Mr Charles Shaw

The Revd Mr William Peebles

Mr Patrick McKnight

Mr Robert Aiken

Mr David McWhinnie

The Revd Mr James Taylor

Mr George Dunlop

Mr David Ewen

Mr Robert Miller

Mr James Pearson

Mr Gilbert McClure

and

Mr John Hunter.

The Meeting unanimously elected Capt Robert Gardner their Præses, and continued Mr Eb. Shaw Librarian, and Mr David Tennant Treasurer.

The Treasurer's Accounts examined and balance was found in his hand and one pen

Eodem Die.

Mr Charles Shaw having moved, That as the writings of Thomas Paine have been found by the Judicial Power of this Country to contain treasonable and seditious Doctrines, the Committee at their first Meeting shall destroy such of the said writings as are in the Library. which motion was without a Vote agreed to by the Meeting.

Mr Quintin

as Members being paid £1..11 each and six shillings

Ayr 6 February 1793.

This day Paine's Books, agreeably to the order of last General Meeting, were burned in the presence of the Committee.

admitted by transfer from Mr Ferguson, and Mr McKenzie writing Master by transfer from Mr

To prevent circulation of dangerous democratic ideas the government declared Thomas Paine's writings to be seditious, so the Ayr Library Society was required to destroy its copies of his books.

a restricted franchise, the earls of Cassillis, Eglinton, Loudoun, and Glencairn were able to exercise their 'interest' and play an influential part in selection of the county member. As far as the MP for Ayr Burghs was concerned, Inveraray and Campbeltown were controlled by the Duke of Argyll, Rothesay by the Earl of Bute, Irvine by the Earl of Eglinton. The role of Ayr's commissioner alongside the other four was often crucial. The three members for Ayr Burghs between 1722 and 1741 were proteges of Argyll; two from 1749 till 1761 were nominees of Bute. In 1761 there was a pact that the Bute – Eglinton candidate for the county seat, Archibald Montgomerie, should not be opposed by the Argyll – Loudoun faction, whose nominee, Lord Frederick Campbell, should be returned unopposed in Ayr Burghs. The Earl of Loudoun had already used his influence and at the Michaelmas elections in 1760 'turned out of the Ayr Council' some possible opponents, and 'endeavoured to get a magistrasy that should be united among themselves'. But the council, instead of humbly accepting the nominee of their betters, proposed a candidate of their own in Sir Adam Fergusson of Kilkerran. Loudoun advised Bute that the councillors of Ayr were 'a better sort of Men than those in the small burrows usually are and they are proud of their town, never having been venal so that the Highest Bribe to them is being taken notice of'. They were 'in a very bad temper from the threats made against them'. But if bribery could not in this instance influence Ayr councillors, threats were more effective. At a midnight meeting in an Ayr tavern the Earl of Eglinton browbeat them into nominating a commissioner who would vote for Lord Frederick Campbell. The episode has been described (by W.L.Burn) as 'this comedy'. A recent commentator (Bruce Lenman) has aptly summarised the occasion: 'Ayr town council became heartily sick of the antics of the rival noble lords and made them squirm at the end by being thoroughly obstructive towards the delicate process of setting up a satisfactory compromise'. But, significantly, the council's attempt to pursue an independent policy in parliamentary politics proved a failure. From 1707 till 1832 the choice of MP for Ayr Burghs was not really made by the five commissioners of the group of burghs, nor by the councils which nominated these commissioners, but depended upon the current relationship between Argyll, Bute, and their noble friends. This was tacitly accepted, for in 1785 Ayr council unanimously agreed that reform would have 'many hurtfull and mischievous consequences'.

Loyalty to the constitution was unquestioned. The accession of George I in 1714 was greeted in Ayr by ringing of bells, bonfires, and 'train bands discharging volleys at the cross'. These train bands were the armed men of the burgh between the ages of sixteen and sixty, formed when invasion was threatened in 1696, reconstituted in 1704, and in readiness for the first serious Jacobite rising in 1715. On that occasion two companies each of sixty eight officers and men were specially recruited for active service against the rebels. In the later rebellion of 1745 there was alarm at Prince Charles's initial success in taking Edinburgh. A missive from Holyrood dated 27 September demanded financial aid 'for his Highness's use'. Ayr council took the unprecedented step of augmenting its numbers by coopting a number of former councillors and other burgesses. On 15 October a message was received that 'part of the Highland army were last night in the town of Douglas, and their route uncertain'. James Hunter and Elias Cathcart were despatched to Holyrood to arrange for immediate payment of £172.3.3 as demanded, to avoid threat of military occupation. But the Jacobite army was heading south. When they retreated from Derby in December in apparent disarray, the council called out the able-bodied men from sixteen to sixty. These assembled on the school green on 16 December – there were 346 men from the burgh, 26 from the Burrowfield, and 41 from the barony of Alloway, armed with 133 fire-locks, many 'not in order', so fortunately not required. A company of infantry was recruited and properly equipped for service in the campaign which ended with the defeat of the Jacobites at Culloden. As in 1715, volunteers were paid by the council and were to be made burgesses on their return. There was no sympathy for the Jacobite cause in Ayrshire. The only local man having a known association with the exiled Stuarts was Andrew Ramsay. Born in 1686, the son of a baker who lived near the Fish Cross, he was educated in Ayr burgh school then at Edinburgh University. He travelled abroad as tutor, soldier, and scholar, and the publication in 1723 of *The Life of Fenelon* by the Chevalier Ramsay (as he was now entitled) was followed by two years in Rome as tutor to Prince Charles Edward. Thereafter he returned to England, to be honoured by the Royal Society and by Oxford University. Ramsay wrote various works on philosophy, education, and literature, but even his most popular book on *The Travels of Cyrus* is seldom read now. He spent his last years in France, died in 1743, and was buried in Saint-Germain-en-Laye – with which French town Ayr is now appropriately twinned.

A further threat of invasion by French forces

Thomas Garvine, who became provost of Ayr after a career as surgeon in Russia and China.

appeared in 1760. In May arms were despatched from London to threatened coastal burghs, those for Ayr being sent via Leith. They comprised 8 chests containing 200 short muskets with bayonets and cartridge boxes; 9 boxes each containing a hundredweight of musket shot; a bag with 800 flints; and 3½ barrels of gunpowder. In June arrangements were made for all fencible men to be trained by a sergeant (who was recompensed with drink money). After the end of this war in 1763 the gunpowder in the tolbooth was sold off. In 1776 the town suffered from a fire followed by an explosion in which two men were killed. This incident persuaded the council to establish a Powder House in the Citadel which was ready the following year for the use of quarriers, coalmasters, and for storing military equipment in any emergency. In 1766 local merchants trading with the colonies in America expressed apprehension over

disturbances there following the Stamp Act; nine years later when rebellion broke out there the council sent a loyal address regretting the 'alarming situation' caused by 'these unhappy and deluded People'. Bounties were offered by the council and also by the trades to men enlisting in the army or navy against 'the unnatural Rebellion in America'. In 1777 panic seized the town at word of 'American Privateers being upon the coast'. All fit to bear arms were to be trained 'by the Dragoons now lying in Ayr'; the council furnished 'the Towns Militia with bonnets and feathers'; and a night guard was mounted in fear of 'a descent upon this Coast, from the American or other Enemies ships' – for the privateer John Paul Jones was then threatening shipping.

Next in the series of 18th century wars against France began in 1792, complicated by the French Revolution of 1789. That aroused initial sympathy and continued interest. The Ayr Library Society, for example, acquired between 1790 and 1792 Thomas Paine's *Rights of Man*, Burke's *Reflections on the Present Revolution*, Priestley's *Letters in Answer to Burke and Paine*, McIntosh's *Vindiciae Gallicae*, Christie's *Answer to Burke*, Rabaut's *History of the French Revolution*. But with the outbreak of war and the government's repressive measures, the Library Society on 30 January 1793 ordered the destruction of Paine's seditious works, which were in fact 'burned in the presence of the committee' on 6 February. Ayr Town Council, alarmed at 'illegal associations against the present happy constitution', called a public meeting in December 1792 to approve a loyal address. The council two months later mourned 'the attrocious murder of the late Lewis the Sixteenth, King of France'. Threatened invasion was met by the formation in 1793 of the West Lowland Fencibles (under Colonel Hugh Montgomerie of Coilsfield, afterwards 12th Earl of Eglinton), disbanded in 1797 for riotous behaviour; the Ayrshire Fencible Cavalry (under Captain Andrew Dunlop) superseded in 1798 by the Ayrshire Yeomanry (under Archibald, Lord Kennedy, later Earl of Carrick); and an Ayrshire Militia in 1797. Proposals for the formation of a militia in Scotland had been made to the government in 1772 with the support of Ayr burgh council, but then turned down for fears of Jacobitism. Now in 1797 the formation of militia units in Scotland was met with some resistance because of compulsory registration. But the militia units in 1797 did become permanently established. In 1798 Ayr Town Council contributed £200 for defence against 'their present inveterate and implacable enemy'. As well as infantry units there was a corps

John Ballantine, the celebrated provost of Ayr who planned the building of the New Brig and the opening of the Academy.

of Artillery. The Major Commandant of the Artillery unit was John Loudon McAdam of Sauchrie, who was enrolled as a burgess of Ayr in 1789, and served as a councillor in 1793–94.

Throughout the long war, the town council offered bounties to encourage local men to enlist in the army and navy. In 1796 the burgh had to provide a quota of five men or £25 sterling as an equivalent. There was the additional burden of quartering troops who were stationed in this coastal county town. In 1791 it was noted that according to 'ancient practice' soldiers were billetted upon innkeepers, butchers, brewers, bakers, and others in a descending order of priority. Some relief from this imposition came in 1794 when the government feued from the council an area of ground at the shore, and the empty Sugar House was converted into Barracks – to serve as such until 1873. As a garrison town, Ayr experienced recurring difficulties, like the 'riotous and mutinous conduct of a great number of Irish recruits' in 1794 and the local gaol filled with 'deserters from the Glasgow Regiment' in 1795.

As each municipal year drew towards its close, in September the Treasurer presented his annual accounts. By 1753 the total income was £6,000 Scots. which was almost completely taken up in payment of salaries, expenses, bills for necessary works, and interest on the town's debt of £8,200. The tolbooth was in urgent need of rebuilding; the bridge was damaged by ice and in a dangerous condition; and with trade recovering improvements at the harbour were necessary. To afford such public works, a new source of income had to be tapped. Thus in 1752 a special committee recommended the feuing of the lands of Alloway when the tacks to the rentallers expired in 1754. The barony, of 2,335 imperial acres, was then divided into twenty eight lots, which were auctioned on 5 June 1754. These were acquired by ten local purchasers, realizing £7,190 sterling initially and annual return in feuduty of £116.12.9. The 'grassum' or initial payment to allow entry was equivalent to £86,280 Scots, and the annual income from feu duty also twelve times its sterling value when converted into Scots. So the rouping of the lands of Alloway provided the burgh of Ayr with sufficient capital to pay off its debt and undertake a series of expensive projects. Not till 1792 did the council require to borrow, but thereafter municipal debt steadily increased till it was almost £20,000 sterling in 1837. The writer of the New Statistical Account then lamented the sale of the lands of Alloway for 'a fair price at the time, but what we would reckon trifling compared with the present value of landed property. Had they been retained, they might have now yielded to the town a rental of betwixt £8,000 and £10,000 a year'. This regret has been repeated more recently by a historian (Pryde) who condemned the council of 1754 for its 'irresponsible government' which allowed the 'wanton alienation of burgh lands' in an unsuccessful attempt to solve the problem of 'chronic financial insolvency', one which was indeed common to all the royal burghs of 18th century Scotland.

From 1689 till 1722 Ayr town council was in the hands of the Mure family. John Mure who had served as provost from 1673 to 1675 was the local hero of the Glorious Revolution and was chosen as provost for eight terms between then and 1707 when he represented Ayr in the last Scots parliament. In the intervening periods and thereafter the provost's chair was often occupied by John Mure's sons Robert or Samuel, so that there was a Provost Mure for twenty five out of thirty three years. Then the Mures were ousted for alleged maladministration. For the next generation James Montgomerie was provost for nine terms, and Thomas Garvine won the appointment on no fewer than fourteen occasions between 1724 and 1755. This followed a remarkable earlier career. Garvine was a native of Kilmarnock who trained as a surgeon; went to Russia to serve Peter the Great at the St Petersburg Hospital; from 1715 till 1718 was in China, travelling by way of Siberia to Pekin by invitation of the Manchu emperor K'ang Hsi; then returned from St Petersburg to practise as a surgeon in Ayr. He purchased Camsiscan in Craigie parish c.1727, and married a daughter of Hugh Montgomerie of Coilsfield, who long survived him as a childless widow. For the rest of the century there was a much greater number sharing the provostship, with Fergussons and Ballantines the only ones achieving more than the customary two years. David Fergusson of Castlehill was first appointed in 1766 and in 1785 after ten years as provost he was presented with a silver cup. His wife's brother John Ballantine would follow him both at Castlehill and in the provost's chair. As will appear in later chapters, he was remembered as one of the burgh's most outstanding civic heads. His father William Ballantine and his uncle Patrick Ballantine were partners in a firm importing wood and tobacco. Son John became a banker, eventually a partner in Hunter's Bank. He entered the council in 1780, a year later he became dean of guild, a position he held till his selection as provost in 1787. He served three two-year terms as provost over the next ten years, during which time Ayr acquired a New Bridge and an Academy. 'The former was erected during his Administration; and of the latter, he may be said to have been The Founder.' Thus he was praised after his death in 1812, described also as 'a Gentleman who was not more endeared to his private friends by his Unassuming Manners, and Amiable Dispositions, than to the Community of which he was long the Head, by his Exertions for the Improvement of his Native Place'.

The council records of the 18th century witness a gradual introduction of the new spelling of Ayr, which first appears in that form in the minutes for 1713. For long after, however, the old usage continued. In 1791 the Statistical Account, after remarking that 'The ancient name of this parish, as appears from some old papers, was Are' noted that 'the modern name is Air or Ayr'. In 1803 the town's first newspaper took the title of Air Advertiser and only in 1839 did it belatedly follow fashion. The New Statistical Account in 1837 indicated that 'since the end of the last century, Ayr has very generally been adopted, and is likely now to be permanent'.

NINE

18th Century Commerce

Ayr's 18th century record is one of decline followed by recovery. In 1723 a passing traveller, Captain J. Mackie, remarked: 'From Kilmarnock in eight miles I crossed the river of Air over a fair stone bridge, to the town of Air which looks like a fine beauty in decay. Here are the ruins of an ancient trading town; the market-place and two streets show what it hath been, but everything is now out of order'. This impression was confirmed when a year later the Convention of Royal Burghs sent commissioners to assess if Ayr (like Dundee) required assistance. They found Ayr harbour 'very much out of order, and in an insufficient condition, occasioned mostly by the decay of the north and south dykes of their river'. Trade was 'very low and much decayed, and ... only two barques, one of about thretty tons, and the other of about twenty, belonging thereto'. Many houses in the town were 'ruinous and waste'; the walls of the tolbooth seemed 'likely to fall'; fortunately the bridge seemed in good repair though requiring 'to be calseyed of new'. The burgh's annual revenue amounted to some £2,500 Scots but routine expenditure (including interest on £5,780 debt) left a balance of just under £500. Since this was quite insufficient for necessary repairs, the burgh was awarded £40 Sterling, the equivalent to £480 Scots, towards renovation of the harbour. Thus the Convention of Royal Burghs assisted in 'supporting the honour and dignity of the burgh'. In the same year (1725–26), it is perhaps worth noting, the council paid out nearly £300 Scots on one wine bill.

The comments on Ayr's difficulties in the 1720s were made by persons who had no reason to exaggerate. The principal cause of decline was obviously the sudden collapse of Ayr's trade with France at the turn of the century. That French trade was the most important foreign business conducted by Ayr merchants. Indeed Ayr was third in rank of Scottish ports trading with France, taking 10% of all vessels arriving and departing. No Scottish burgh would lose more than Ayr out of interruption of trade with France. The first setback to Scottish merchants was the introduction by the French government in the late 17th century of mercantilist restrictions on imports of foreign goods. Trading with France was also made more difficult by the series of French wars which began in 1689–96 and would continue throughout the 18th century, 1703–14, 1740–48, 1756–63, 1778–83, 1792–1815. Permanent damage was done by the English Methuen Act of 1703 whose terms were extended to Scotland after 1707, by which Portuguese and Spanish wines were given preferential treatment as imports. There was an inevitable slump in the importation of French wines, in particular the favoured Scots drink of claret from Bordeaux. How great the local wine trade had been is suggested by the amount for which Ayr traders paid import duty, the average for the years 1685–88 being 50 tuns, that is to say 200 hogsheads or 45,000 litres per year, selling at perhaps £17,000 Scots. In the 18th century the importation of French wines continued, by merchants who contrived to evade the prohibitive import dues by pretending the wines came from Spain or Portugal; or by smugglers operating in war as in peace, but obviously landing their wines and brandies elsewhere on the Ayrshire coast than the port of Ayr. The slump in legitimate trade was perhaps signified by a proposal in 1714 to dismantle 'the three old ships in the harbour, called the *Unicorn*, the *Hopewell*, and the *Success*'.

The collapse of Ayr's French trade was accompanied by an apparent decline in the burgh population. Later in the 18th century it could be written (in the *Statistical Account*) that 'when wine was imported at Ayr from France, the population was much greater than at present'. Numbers in 1700 were (according to the estimate in Chapter 7) approaching 3,000. In 1755 (according to Webster's enumeration of the Scottish population) Ayr parish contained fewer than that, and the burgh itself probably not many more than 2,000. One may guess what this decline meant, in terms of bankrupt businesses, upset families, widespread poverty, and increased human misery. Ayr indeed was 'a fair beauty in decay' (1723); 'many of the houses on the fore street of the said burgh are ruinous and waste' (1724); and there were fears (1725) that the Customs might make Ayr a subordinate port under Irvine. For by contrast, the royal burgh of Irvine was continuing to grow, with a population of some 1,500 in 1700 doubling in fifty years to surpass Ayr with near 3,000 by 1755. Irvine was less dependent on French trade; its coal exports to Ireland were increasing and would continue to do so. Though its transatlantic trade like that of Ayr was limited before 1707, thereafter for a brief period some Glasgow merchants found it convenient to land American imports at Irvine and transport them overland to the city.

Ayr however recovered its lead. In the second half of the 18th century the burgh population was rising again, and markedly enough to double the number of inhabitants within the royal burgh, which were 3,871 in a survey of 1791. This reflects renewed commercial expansion in and around the county town.

What has always kept the harbour of Ayr open were the fisheries. In the difficult times at the beginning of the 18th century the herring remained plentiful, and indeed the first harbour light was in 1712 put 'on the south stob, for directing the fishers in outgoing and returning'. A series of law suits from 1711 till 1719 confirmed the privileges of the burgh of Ayr by prohibiting landings on the Newton side of the river. Herring were still being caught in mid-century, with record catches from 1747 till 1750, selling from 3d to 6d per hundred. Fish offal also provided oil for tanners. In 1713, to avoid fires, the council prohibited 'boiling herring gutts, to make oil, within any dwelling or under any roof'. After 1763, 'since the herrings left', haddock and cod were caught. By 1791 this white fishing was 'mostly carried on by a society of people from Aberdeen' who supplied Irvine, Kilmarnock, Paisley, and Glasgow from Ayr, and the price increased from 1d to 1½d per English pound. There were seven fishing boats plus nine belonging to Newton, each with a crew of four. There was also salmon fishing, with three cobles on the Ayr and four on the Doon river, at four men in each boat. The fishing at at the mouth of the Doon, and a cruive six miles upriver, belonged to the Earl of Cassillis. The fishing on the River Ayr and the Newton shore had originally belonged to the burgh of Newton, but Sir Thomas Wallace of Craigie purchased the fishing or (as the *Statistical Account* drily put it) 'otherwise got possession'; by whom it was sold to the Society of Writers in Ayr. The price of salmon was sometimes as high as 6d per pound.

The harbour continued its coastal and foreign trade. Ayr's wine trade enjoyed a curious recovery after 1765. In that year the crown took control over the Isle of Man from which base many of the smugglers had previously operated. A number of such merchants now found it convenient to transfer from Douglas to Ayr, where they combined legitimate trade with continued smuggling. The business commenced by Alexander Oliphant and Company in 1766 still operates, but under more respectable auspices than originally, for recent research has concluded that 'the Oliphant partnership seems to have been a front for organising the growing smuggling trade on the Ayrshire coast'. In its early years, as the firm's letter book shows, the company had agents in Madeira, Cadiz, Lisbon, Oporto, Barcelona, Bordeaux, and Guernsey; cellars in Ayr, Kilmarnock, Glasgow, Moffat, and Stranraer; and customers from the north of England to the West Indies. Expensive vintage clarets were handled (up to 46s or £2.30 per dozen bottles) but efforts had obviously been made to extend the Spanish and Portuguese trade; and indeed Ayrshire established close links with Madeira. Smuggling ventures are obviously less well recorded, but in the next chapter are noted some of the 'honest men' who were involved.

During the 18th century Ayr's transatlantic trade continued. The importation of tobacco is recorded in the 17th century. In 1679 for example, Robert Fullarton, second son of the minister of Coylton, was licensed to sell tobacco in Ayr. In 1733 the town was excited by reports that Ayr was to be excluded from the list of nominated ports for importation of tobacco and wines; but this was successfully altered. In 1739 a brick warehouse was built within the Citadel near the harbour by Hunter, Ballantine, and Company, who traded with America. The partners were John Hunter, the brothers Patrick and William Ballantine, William Cunningham, and William Campbell. In 1749 they built an extension 'fronting the big key'. In 1750 storehouses were built for another firm in the tobacco trade, that of David Galloway and Samuel Cuthbert. After mid-century the following Ayr merchants appear in the customs records as importers of tobacco: William Alexander, William and Patrick Ballantine, John Borland, William Campbell, Elias Cathcart, William Cunningham, James Ferguson, John Glasgow, James and John Hunter, George Hutchison, Gilbert McAdam, David McClure, Alexander Morris, William Stewart. The trade of importing tobacco and re-exporting it to Europe ended with American Independence. But in 1785 there were still six Ayr merchants dealing in tobacco and concerned at new laws concerning its importation. These were John Ballantine, Thomas Clark, David Ewen, David McClure, John McClure, William Reid. Ballantine and some others however became more interested in timber from Canada, for use especially in shipbuilding, along with fir from Danzig and English oak. One shipbuilder, John Fraser, built in 1767 a fifty ton sloop for Alexander Oliphant and Company's fleet. On the Newton shore shipbuilding on a large scale was commenced in the 18th century, employing fifty hands in 1791, with another ten in an adjacent ropework, using hemp from Russia.

The exportation of coal would also become important enough to involve both sides of the river. Even after 1771 when a quay on the north bank was provided, the Auld Brig and High Street remained busy with loads of coal from St Quivox, Coylton, Cumnock, and local pits which had their coal rees on the south side of the river. The first of these coal yards 'at that pairt of the citadel next to the water' had been provided in 1710, 'which will be encouraging to the trade of the place, now so much decayed'. While the Irish market was supplied chiefly from Saltcoats and Irvine, Ayr's contribution became increasingly important. In mid-century only 6% of Ayrshire coal exports left Ayr harbour, about 600 tons annually. By the 1790s that proportion had risen to 25% with over 9,000 tons being shipped from Ayr.

Ayr town council had concerned itself with the working of coal since the 16th century. In 1528 it granted a lease 'to wyn coil' within the barony of Alloway. In 1611 the council invited investments for the sinking of a coal pit 'at the waterside'. Municipal enterprise continued. In 1700 the council resolved 'to sett down and shank a coall heugh on the toun lands', but though coal was discovered at the head of the Mill Vennel, working proved difficult and uneconomic. Private enterprise followed in 1728 when a company of 'Undertakers of Coal at Alloway' was formed by 23 merchants and another 17 local men, with Provost James Montgomerie as president. After eighteen months activity, with shanking at Broomberry and Clongall, their project was abandoned. There was however an outcrop at Broomberry, and a coal heugh was worked (before 1754) by the rentallers of Corton who, for its use, had to supply annually the magistrates of Ayr with eighty carts of coal — a perquisite, for which loss the magistrates had to be compensated after the sale of the barony lands in 1754. Coal continued to be worked there, fuelling the Broomberry lime kiln a century later. Other small scale attempts to work coal within Ayr were made. In

1775 Dr John Campbell of Wellwood was taking coal from his garden adjoining the churchyard. From this era may be dated several pits near the South Quay – their remains were later discovered at the Slip Dock, at the gas works in Cromwell Road, and a third near the Fort wall. These provided fuel for 'the old salt pans' which were abandoned by 1772 (when they were so described); and later supplied a lime kiln which was set up at the South Quay in 1787. Another lime kiln (whose remains are still visible on River Ayr Walk) was fuelled by coal from Holmston (on the site of Kyle Academy). Here coal was being worked from 1759 when the kirk session complained that 'Holmston's Colliers are exceedingly disorderly in their behaviour, especially on the Lord's Day'. But elsewhere in Ayr parish, hopes of large-scale local developments came to nothing, despite a renewed exploration in 1796.

There were, however, better prospects over the river. In 1764 Newton-upon-Ayr council appointed John Scott of Gadgirth to search for coal, and invited subscriptions. Ayr town council in 1765 subscribed £50 'to assist the town of Newton in boring for coals, as it would be a conveniency to the burgh, and perhaps lead to exportation of coals'. Another £50 was contributed to try to deal with flooding which was troubling the two pits sunk in Newton Green. Then in 1767 Ayr council gave a loan of £150 towards a very expensive steam pump to drain the workings – a 'Fire Engine' which cost at least £880. David Dick from Gorbals who had a 19-year lease from the council sublet his tack in 1769 to James Montgomerie and Company. The chief partners in this company were Dr James Campbell and William Fullarton of Rosemount, and they invested heavily in the project, Campbell borrowing £11,500 from the Ayr Bank. Though some of the coal was for use in the saltpans on the Newton shore, or for sale locally as domestic fuel, the bulk was destined for export to Ireland. With the approval of Ayr town council, a wharf was in 1771 erected on the north bank of the river and an 800 yard waggonway brought the coals down to this North Quay. In 1777 Campbell, now sole partner, became involved in a dispute with his colliers which culminated in the closure of the pits in 1780. They were re-opened in 1786 by a 'company of Edinburgh gentlemen' led by John Taylor, Writer to the Signet, who took up residence at Newark. Between 1786 and 1790 coal production in Newton was around 1,200 tons per annum, and Newton council benefitted by £300 each year.

More substantial exploitation was being undertaken in the adjoining inland parish of St Quivox. In 1729 collieries were noted at Milnquarter and Milrig near

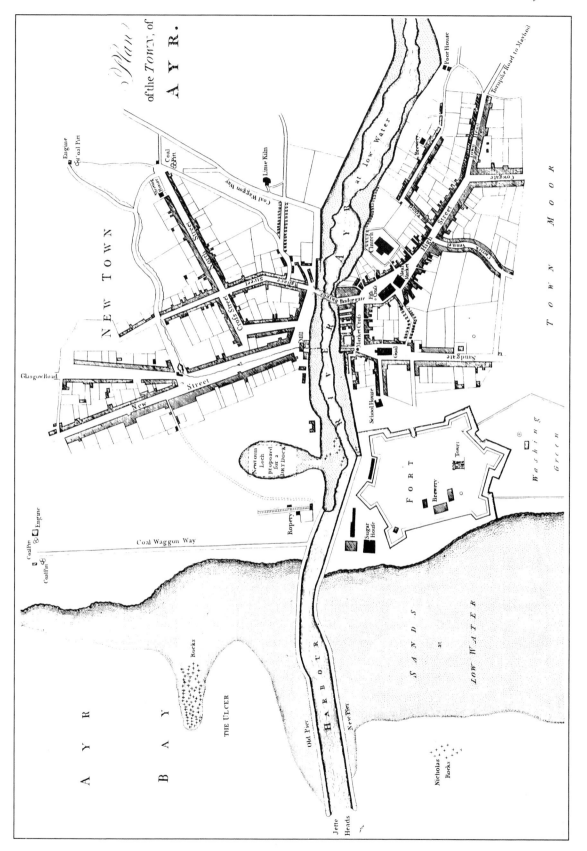

A reduced version of one of six sheets on Ayrshire by A.& M. Armstrong, 1775. This exhibits commercial developments in Newton and the new community of Wallacetown.

Ayr. In 1765 Ayr town council contributed £50 from its Common Good towards the repair of the 'roads from the several Coal Pits in the parish of St Quivox'. Robert Paterson Wallace of Holmston was working coal across the river at Mainholm, and in 1775 it was being worked also downriver near the end of the Auld Brig. A major development followed the acquisition in 1764 of Auchincruive estate and adjoining lands of Mainholm and Braehead by Richard Oswald, a wealthy merchant with American connections. The long tenure of that estate by the Wallaces (till 1374) and the Cathcarts (till 1758) was followed, after the brief ownership of James Murray of Broughton, by the Oswalds from 1764 till 1925. Following Richard Oswald's purchase of this extensive estate occupying two thirds of St Quivox parish, a new mansion house was completed by the Adam brothers in 1767. Also in 1766 Auchincruive Coal Works were being managed by Robert Doak. In 1781 after the death of Robert Paterson Wallace the lands of Holmston were added to the Auchincruive estate. This facilitated the construction, probably before Richard Oswald's death in 1784, of an 'iron railway' from the Auchincruive pits over a bridge to Holmston and down the river side 'to near the town of Ayr; but could not obtain liberty to carry it through the Burgh-acres to the harbour'.

Apart from Auchincruive, which was inherited by Richard Oswald's nephew George Oswald, the rest of St Quivox parish was divided among two substantial and five minor heritors. The Craigie estate continued for most of the 18th century in Wallace hands. Sir Thomas Wallace (successor to that Sir William who was sometime provost of Ayr) was an advocate, as was his namesake son who succeeded him as fifth baronet about 1730. Their legal careers kept them much in Edinburgh, so they were not noticeably inconvenienced when Newton Castle had to be demolished in 1701 after being 'blown down on Friday (3 October) by the violence of the storm'. The fifth baronet built (in 1730, it is guessed) the mansion house of Craigie, upriver and away from the new community of Wallacetown which he laid out about 1760. This Sir Thomas was abandoned by his wife, leaving him with a son who died in 1758 aged twenty seven, and a daughter born in 1730. This Frances Ann Wallace eloped at the age of sixteen with John Dunlop of Dunlop, was widowed in 1785, and found consolation in the poetry of Robert Burns with whom she became a principal correspondent. Her eldest son on inheriting Craigie from his grandfather in 1771 took the title and name of Sir Thomas Dunlop-Wallace. But he ran into debt

and had to sell Craigie in 1783. The new owner William Campbell had made his fortune in India, and followed the purchase of Craigie with Dalmilling in 1790. But Craigie's coal resources remained unexploited till the 1850s.

On the estate of Blackhouse there were major developments. This estate was inherited in 1769 by Robert Alexander, an Edinburgh merchant. He engaged as manager of the Boghall Coal Works an experienced mining engineer John Beaumont who brought in colliers from his native Newcastle. By 1771 Alexander had 'a pretty extensive Coalwork' when he obtained from Ayr council permission to erect a shed at the South Quay. A small steam engine for pumping was installed in 1770 followed by a larger one in 1775. A waggonway was constructed to convey the coals from Boghall down to the river whence they were (inconveniently) taken over the Auld Brig and down High Street for export via the South Quay. Alexander and Beaumont were both in debt to the Ayr Bank, which collapsed in 1772; it took years for the creditors to deal with the bank's affairs, but when settlements were made Beaumont went bankrupt in 1781 and Alexander in 1784. They were both running the coal works when James Hutton the geologist inspected them during his visit to Ayrshire in 1786; and Beaumont was still employed at Newton in 1790. But the Blackhouse estate was sold in 1787 to the Ayr Coal Company and its principal partner was John Taylor who already had acquired the Newton pits. The Blackhouse estate comprised Boghall and Dalmelling, including lands known as Jasper Humstead, Smiddycroft part of Chapel Lands, Mailings, Greystack, part of Woodquarter called Thornyflat, Dykes and Smiddyhill, and fishings.

Blackhouse, which was producing 15,000 tons annually, provided most of the coal for the export trade. Other contributions came from Newton, Auchincruive, Holmston, Drongan, and from the Sanquhar pits worked in 1788 by William Forbes of Callendar. The *Statistical Account* remarked in 1791 that 'The demand of late for exportation is so great, that oft times scarce any are left for home use'. The fifth Earl of Dumfries tried to augment the supply with coals from his Cumnock estate, but transport proved difficult. More successful was Mungo Smith of Drongan. In 1784 he had a coal ree at the South Quay and in that year he was elected one of the eight Harbour Trustees. Again the *Statistical Account*, reporting the price of coal as from 2s 3d to 2s 6d per cart, pointed out 'That at Drungan, in the parish of Stair, though a little dearer, is undoubtedly the best'. In 1796 Ayr

RIVER WALK, AYR.   30

On the River Ayr Walk is one surviving trace of 18th century coal mining – a limekiln, which was fuelled by Holmston pits.

town council noted that Newton or Blackhouse coal was available at 1/6d per ton.

Rev Dr McGill could also write in the *Statistical Account* that 'The exportation of coal to Ireland is the principal branch of trade carried on at this port', with 12,627 tons for 1790, carried mainly in Irish vessels which brought limestone in return. Rev William Peebles of Newton supplemented this by noting that more than 300 vessels were employed, trading with Dublin, Belfast, Larne, and other places in Ireland. It was a seasonal trade, for as a local coalmaster complained in 1770, 'In every Winter there are weeks together when none can be shipped: and indeed the Bulk of it must, and will of Necessity be shipped in Summer'. In December 1789 when attempting to enter the harbour a dozen ships were stranded on the beach, one was totally wrecked, and a number of lives lost, prompting the coalmasters to erect lights at their own expense.

Despite its financial problems at the beginning of the 18th century, the council never ceased in its efforts to maintain the harbour. Parts of 'the big key' were rebuilt in 1713 and 1715. In 1724 and 1728 masons were employed to improve the 'north dyke' on the other side of the river. In 1730 a sandbank at the harbour mouth was removed after the council ordered it dredged by 'a drag like that used in Dublin, for keeping the harbour free of banks; which, with the assistance of three or four men, and

a boat or gabbart, in proper seasons, will effectually clean the same'. Little more than routine work was attempted in subsequent years. Nothing was done about the difficult access. In 1712 a light had been provided for the herring fishing, but this seems to have been a temporary arrangement. Navigators had to rely on features which happened to be visible. In 1769 the council contributed £10 to a fund raised by William Fullarton of Rosemount, to repair the Tower of St John's as a monument and as a landmark for shipping. The revival of trade persuaded the council in 1772 to secure an act of parliament for improving the harbour. This legislation, renewed and extended in 1794 and 1817, empowered the council to borrow sums up to £15,000, and required the appointment of eight harbour trustees to manage the undertaking. Stone piers were constructed along both sides, with breakwaters extending beyond the river mouth. But even so the harbour entry remained unmarked till the installation by the coalmasters in 1790 of two reflecting lights on the Newton side, following the shipwrecks of 1789.

By 1790 the harbour was busy with 33 vessels belonging to the port. 18 of these, each averaging 105 tons and manned by a crew of seven, were engaged in foreign trade, with 8 in the coastal trade (average 41 tons, crew of 4) and 7 at the fisheries (average 38 tons, crew of 4). Two packet boats plied to Greenock, one to

Liverpool, and another occasionally to Campbeltown. But there was limited scope for further development, for the harbour entrance could not hope to admit ships of more than 250 tons.

As Ayr was able in the 18th century to recover from the loss of its French trade, so it was not seriously incommoded by two financial crises. The first occurred at the very end of the 17th century. In 1696 there was projected in Edinburgh a Company of Scotland trading with Africa and the Indies, with a capital of £400,000. Sixty seven subscribers from Ayrshire contributed just over £13,000. That included £1,200 from the council and eleven persons of Irvine; £2,400 from the council and twenty two persons of Ayr; and £1,700 from 13 persons in Kilmarnock. Various ventures of the Company, including its Darien colonial scheme, proved unsuccessful. The existence of the Company of Scotland was a continuing threat to the English East India Company and a nuisance to the London government. Hence the Act of Union provided for the dissolution of the Company of Scotland; and provided shareholders with welcome recompense. This must have predisposed towards a grateful acceptance of the Union the twenty two subscribers from Ayr. These were John Ballantine, Mungo Campbell, Elias Cathcart, William Chalmer, Hew Crawfurd, Patrick Coltrane, David Fergusson, Hugh Hay, Robert Hunter, James Hutchison, Charles Logan, Thomas McJarrow, John Millikine, John Moore, Robert Moore, Samuel Moore, William Robine, John Vans, James Wallace, all merchants; John Fergusson, skipper; James Stevenson, surgeon apothecary; and Rev Patrick Liston. All of whom recovered their investment of £100 – thanks to one of their number John Moore (or Mure) who as provost and parliamentary commissioner in 1706–7 voted in favour of the Act of Union.

The collapse of the Ayr Bank in 1772 had more than local impact. The firm of Douglas, Heron, and Company was formed in 1769. It took over John Macadam and Co., which had done banking business in Ayr since 1763, and became known as the Ayr Bank, though it had offices also in Dumfries and Edinburgh, and agencies elsewhere in Scotland. Douglas, Heron, and Company was founded chiefly by landed interests and had a capital of £150,000. Its shareholders (including two dukes, a duchess, and two earls) numbered 260. 20% came from Ayrshire, 20% from Dumfries and Galloway, 20% from Edinburgh and the Borders, 15% from Glasgow and neighbouring counties, 5% from other parts of Scotland; the remaining 20% included eleven from furth of Scotland and 38 unidentified. Of those 57 from Ayrshire, nearly all were landowners, some of them having business connections with Ayr, and associated with them were a dozen residents of Ayr itself. These were merchants like John Christian, David Ferguson, George Macree, David McClure, Robert Whiteside; lawyers like John Boswell, John Murdoch, Robert Ferguson of Castlehill; Patrick Douglas, surgeon; George Dunlop of McNairston, bank teller; Claud Thomson, Collector of Excise; and Rev. William McGill. The Ayr Bank's policy was to lend money generously, which resulted in extensive estate improvements and the expansion of various merchant companies. When a banking house in London failed, Douglas Heron and Company followed on 'Black Monday' 12 June 1772, and closed its doors on 12 August 1773. That was before the era of limited liability companies, so that the Ayr Bank's debts of nearly £700,000 became the responsibility of its shareholders. The slow process of winding up the affairs of Douglas, Heron, and Company was not completed till 1804. It was in the 1780s that effects of the bank collapse became obvious through the sale of numerous Ayrshire estates, the transfer of various companies to new owners, the impoverishment of all shareholders to some extent – but with few apparent cases of outright ruin. The bank of James Hunter and Co. was set up in 1773 by the provost's son who had been cashier in John McAdam's bank and continued under Douglas, Heron and Co. Hunter's Bank had a capital of £10,000 and business was conducted on more prudent lines. It was able successfully to compete against the Bank of Scotland which set up a branch in Ayr in 1775. These banks provided the finance necessary for further improvements in commerce, agriculture, and manufacturing.

Towards the end of the century Rev. Dr McGill indicated that 'Manufactures are not carried on to any great extent in this parish'. Of the burgh's nine Incorporated Trades, some had declined. The Skinners and Dyers together employed only sixteen persons by 1791; the Coopers only 22; the Tailors had 57. In each of these four trades masters outnumbered those enrolled as journeymen and apprentices – an ominous situation. A healthier pattern was showed by the Hammermen (with 24 masters, 16 journeymen, 24 apprentices), the Squaremen (34, 68, 33), the Fleshers (14, 16, 4); and by the two principal manufacturing trades of Weavers (61, 89, 36) and Shoemakers (25, 27, 10). Shoemaking expanded in the second half of the 18th century. The erection of a slaughterhouse in Mill Street in 1747 (after thirteen years of argument) was followed by a tanyard behind the Wallace Tower in

1761, and a tannery in Mill Street which would operate for the next two centuries. By the 1790s an average of 3,000 hides were tanned annually and twice as many calf skins, providing materials for the shoemakers and saddlers of the town whose products were in demand for export. The weaving trade also enjoyed development. In 1749 William Duff set up a building in Mill Street as a linen manufactory, but this early attempt at mass production by handlooms did not succeed. The linen industry was freed from craft restriction by a parliamentary act of 1751, which allowed manufacture outwith burghs, and this may have contributed to Duff's failure. Unauthorised weaving of woollens in the town and across the river was complained of by Ayr's incorporated Weavers in 1767, but it was difficult to limit a quickly expanding trade. In 1776 the number of handlooms 'in Ayr and district' was about 200 for woollen cloth and linens, about 60 for silk, and 15 stocking frames. Those within the burgh were chiefly employed in weaving plaidings and other traditional coarse woollens. There were experiments with cotton. In 1765 a Glasgow ship coming from Virginia landed at Ayr 140 pounds of cotton 'wooll'. In 1780, £4 was spent installing in the Poorshouse a spinning jenny described as 'a machine for the throwing of thirty threads of cotton or woollen yarn at one time and by the hand of one spinner, either a boy or a girl'. Cotton was eagerly taken up in Newton and Wallacetown. Within the royal burgh there must have been some resistance, and difficulty in setting up new businesses. Yet by 1791 Dr McGill could state that Ayr had 'weavers of all kinds' and many must have turned to cotton for they had 'most of them employment from Glasgow and Paisley'. And recently, he continued enthusiastically, there were 'many female children happily engaged in the tambouring business', doing intricate embroidery work on cotton muslins. There were thus many more employed in the textile industry than the 186 who belonged to the incorporation of Weavers. It remained a domestic industry. In 1790 when William Neil abandoned the Wallace Tower schoolhouse in favour of a more convenient location, the council leased it to John Sword, a Glasgow muslin manufacturer. He planned to employ there from fifty to a hundred girls between the ages of eleven and sixteen on tambouring. Also in 1790 there was an abortive scheme, as noted in the next paragraph, for a large cotton factory near the harbour. Then in 1794 'ground was feued for a cotton manufactory, adjoining the citadel, and between it and the washing house'. This small spinning mill was actually built, on the west side of Fort Street. It proved unsuccessful; but

The cellars, still in use, of a wine importing firm which was founded in 1766 and engaged in the profitable smuggling trade.

early in the 19th century it would be converted into a woollen mill; then acquired by James Templeton.

Few new manufactures were commenced within the burgh in the 18th century. There was a brewery in Mill Street in 1775 and another later nearby in Mill Vennel. There were two soap manufactories. One was in High Street beside the river. The other was in old buildings taken over about 1770 by James Gibb from Mauchline who had a grocer's business at the Fish Cross. Gibb's soap factory can be precisely located for its owner later built Dalblair House alongside; indeed in 1785 he agreed with the town council to share with Patrick McNeight of Barns the repair of what is now Dalblair Road 'from the end of Carrick Vennel past James Gibb's soap works and the lime kiln into the great road from Townhead of Ayr to the Old Bridge of Doon'. An ambitious plan introduced a new industry when the seven-storey Sugar House was built in 1772 between the harbour storehouses and the old salt pans. But sugar refining proved unrewarding, and after a few years the building was derelict, useful only as a guide for navigators. In 1790 there was a scheme to convert the Sugar House into a cotton factory with 60 jeanies spinning yarn and 170 persons employed, but this came to nothing. In 1794 the building was acquired for use as military barracks.

Various attempts had been made to establish manufacturing businesses within the Citadel, ever since 1663 when that area was designated as outwith the authority of Ayr burgh, a situation which was confirmed by the Court of Session in 1787. Hugh, 7th Earl of Eglinton, who obtained a royal charter in

1663, failed to develop his burgh of Montgomerieston here, but he did set up a cloth manufactory by 1662 – in which year Irvine burgh council paid to send there 'twa poor boys' as apprentices. In 1681 the earl was empowered to arrest and employ vagrants from Ayrshire, Renfrewshire, and Galloway. Malting was also being carried out at the Citadel, to the annoyance of Ayr town council, which objected repeatedly, as in 1681, to the 'bringing in of wirt aill and beir out of the citedaill'. In 1687 the citadel area was purchased by John Mure to obtain use of the Church of St John for worship. In 1727 ownership passed to Susannah, Countess of Eglinton. This celebrated beauty, to whom Allan Ramsay had dedicated his *Gentle Shepherd* just a year before, erected in 1734 a building for the distillation of whisky and various infusions; but by 1754 these premises were leased as a brewery. In 1755 Countess Susannah (who was by birth a Kennedy) disposed of the Citadel and its brewery to her relative Sir Thomas Kennedy who would soon become 9th Earl of Cassillis, by which family the Citadel was retained till 1854. In 1768 the citadel was rented by an Ayr Wine Company which gave up brewing but continued malting; then soap-boiling was undertaken for some time, probably in adjacent premises; from 1781 cattle were slaughtered in the Citadel and the beef cured for exportation; in 1787 brewing was recommenced, and Ayr town council was unsuccessful in its case against the Earl of Cassillis.

Conservatism and vested interest are sometimes blamed for the failure of royal burghs to develop industrially, but this was not the only factor. The Citadel area was outwith the burgh of Ayr, and most conveniently located beside the harbour; but failed to acquire more than a brewery. Most large-scale manufacturing enterprises required water power. This was available on the River Ayr at the Overmill, where corn milling was supplemented in 1761 with a waulk mill for processing cloth; and the Nethermill where new installations handled barley from 1794 and snuff a year later. But the provision of water power within the burgh proper (or within the Citadel) would have been difficult. On the River Doon there had been a corn mill and waulk mill in the 16th century. By 1754 grain was processed at Alloway Mill. Upriver was the Dutch Mill. This is supposed to be so-called from its construction by a company from Holland who wrought a lead mine at Brown Carrick Hill. All that is definitely known is that it belonged to Lord Stair before becoming part of Doonside estate in 1754: in 1775 Ayr town council noted the transfer of the 'Waulk miln of Alloway now called Waulk miln of Doon' from John Dalrymple of

Stair to John Crawford of Doonside. Later and shortly before 1790 a paper mill was established by David, 10th Earl of Cassillis at Doonfoot, on the south bank near the river mouth.

The major area for economic growth in the later 18th century seemed to be north of the River Ayr, within the parishes of Newton-upon-Ayr and St Quivox. That is suggested by population trends. Between 1755 and 1791 numbers in the parish of Ayr increased by 57%; Newton and St Quivox each by 290%. At the earlier date Ayr burgh contained about 2,000 inhabitants with about a thousand more in the landward parts of the parish; Newton and St Quivox together held another thousand, mostly involved in farming. By the later date there were three sizeable urban communities: Ayr burgh (3,871), Newton (1,689) and Wallacetown (960). An analysis of the Newton population showed how the some traditional trades had grown. As well as 60 fishermen (many of whom were also farmers) there were 14 shipmasters and 51 sailors. The most popular trade was weaving, with 40 masters, 40 journeymen, and 21 apprentices. The other crafts of wrights, carpenters, shoemakers, smiths, stocking weavers, coopers, and bakers had among them 32 masters, 31 journeymen, and 17 apprentices. Together these accounted for 80 persons, fewer than the 101 involved in handloom weaving of cotton as well as the customary work. Another 81 persons were in the coal business, 24 colliers (who were skilled men) and 57 labourers at the collieries, these employed in the Newton and Blackhouse pits, with some at the long-established saltpans. The ropework employed 10 men. There were listed another 89 men engaged mainly in service occupations, who lived in Newton but some of whom may have worked within Ayr, as did some of the 59 'female servants, many of whom reside with their parents'. There are no equivalent statistics for St Quivox parish, but Rev. William McQuhae attributed the growth of Wallacetown to four groups of immigrants. There were those who came to work in the Blackhouse and Newton pits. A number of well-to-do farmers displaced from their farms set up businesses here as dealers in farm produce. A third important group settled in Wallacetown – 'Mechanics of all sorts flocked into it, and feued houses, or rented those that were built by others, with a view to profit. They are here exempt from the laws or regulations of the incorporated trades in the adjoining royal burgh of Ayr'. A last group came from Ireland and the West Highlands, some being disorderly vagrants, others however settling as weavers or labourers.

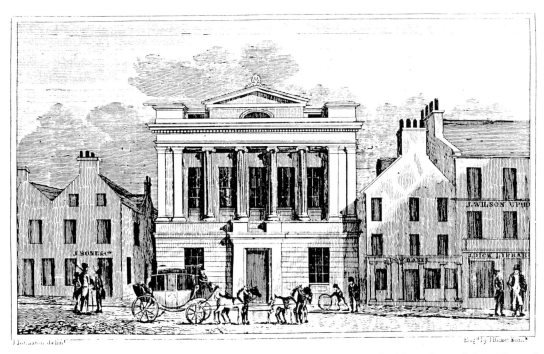

The Ayrshire Banking Company set up in 1830 on a site in the Sandgate where had been located the offices of the ill-fated Ayr Bank which collapsed in 1772.

In both St Quivox and Newton the only large scale businesses were the coal pits. The coalmasters brought in workers, and had the technical expertise to introduce steam pumps for drainage and iron railways for transport. By contrast, growth in the manufacturing trades like weaving was simply by increased numbers arriving on their own initiative to set up in business and undertake traditional processes in domestic conditions. So far from water power being more fully exploited, the Dalmilling waulk mill was closed before 1761, and Newton Mill was abandoned some years after the opening in 1788 of the New Bridge across the River Ayr. The more rapid population growth on the north side of the river should not therefore be attributed to a greater spirit of enterprise than within the royal burgh. There was the geological accident that coal was available for exploitation and export. There was in Newton less restriction and in Wallacetown positive encouragement for incomers to settle freely. But many of the new residents north of the river obviously worked within the royal burgh, so that it was – in modern parlance – a new dormitory suburb for the royal burgh. Rev. William Peebles had this in mind in 1791 when he wrote: 'The inhabitants of the town of Ayr, amounting to 3,871 souls, and that of Newton, which may be called its Southwark, to 1,689,

the capital of Ayrshire may be said to contain, in all, 5,470 souls'.

Ayr remained 'the capital of Ayrshire'. As a manufacturing centre it had been overtaken by Kilmarnock (which had 5,670 inhabitants in 1791). Ayr, however, was also the county town. As such it was a seat of justice – with burgh court, sheriff court, and High Court on circuit – and meeting place for such administrative assemblies as there were in the 18th century – Freeholders of the shire, Justices of the Peace meeting in quarter sessions, Commissioners of Supply, Turnpike Trustees. It also remained an important market town whose business developed considerably in the course of the 18th century.

Between 1755 and 1791 the population of Ayrshire increased from 59,000 to 75,000 which meant many more mouths to feed. And a predominantly rural population in this period gave way to one where towns and villages accommodated more than half of the inhabitants. There was thus an enormously increased market demand for farm-produced foodstuffs. Also, merchants were exporting more textiles and leather goods, keeping busy the weavers and shoemakers, and the farmers who produced the wool, flax, and leather which were their raw materials. The 18th century agricultural revolution converted a traditional and basically-subsistence system into the modern commercial farming. Thus for St Quivox at the end of the century, 'The whole parish has been inclosed with hedge and ditch within the last 30 or 40 years'. There were thirty families who lived by farming, leasing the improved farms on 19 year tacks, and paying rents ranging from 12s to £3 an acre, averaging about £1. Oats, bear (barley), and potatoes were the principal crops, grown in a specified rotation, with the land ploughed, limed and dunged as required, cropped then left in pasture for a period of years. Specialisation in dairy farming had been established locally. There were 350 milch cows (valued at £2,000); each produced, beside her calf, from £3 to £4 per year from sales of butter at 9d, and cheese at 2½d to 6d per pound (of 24 ounces). There were 200 calves worth £2 each, 200 cattle being fattened worth £5 each, and occasionally a few sheep. The farms were equipped with 132 horses worth £11 each, men servants paid £6 to £8 per year, women servants from £3 to £4, and labourers at a shilling a day. Such features of improved farming in St Quivox were typical of the Ayrshire lowlands – with the exception of Newton, where 'the whole parish is open and unsheltered ... not a tree to be found, and no thorn hedge of any growth'. This was blamed on the severe westerly winds which blew the sandy soils; but the lack of improvement was attributed (by Sir John Sinclair) to the constitution of the burgh which though 'founded on the generous principles of equality and independence' and (as noted earlier) allowed industrial development, nevertheless and paradoxically remained backward agriculturally. The arable land was divided among the 48 freeman into 4 acre lots where some oats, bear, and potatoes could be grown, and there was pasture on the 150 acre common; but though allocation of the 'daills' or lots was in 1771 extended from seven to fifty seven years, few improvements could be implemented.

By contrast, across the river in the Burrowfield of Ayr and barony of Alloway, agriculture 'has made great progress here ... within the last thirty or forty years'. The most awkward area was that part of the Burrowfield adjacent to the sea. In 1687 Ayr council had leased the hills and links 'almost lost by the constant blowing of sand' to Ralph Holland, paying him 100 merks for nine years to make improvements, and for 21 years thereafter he would be charged an annual rent of £40. By 1725 the council was again concerned about the 'excessive blowing of the sand, as it hath done of late years' so that there were 'severall acres of the laigh and mid-sands much damnified'. The laigh sands comprised the area on the seaward side of the

Cottages in the appropriately-named Weaver Street are relics of the 18th and early 19th century when domestic handloom weaving of cotton was a principal local manufacture.

road from Sandgate towards Blackburn, Bridgehouse, and the Carrick shore, that is the present Racecourse Road. The mid sands extended from that road inland towards the road from Cow Vennel towards Alloway, that is the present Carrick Road. The laigh sands were in 1725 leased again to tacksmen. These were Colonel Charles Cathcart, later 8th Lord Cathcart, and Captain Lawrence Nugent, Customs Officer and owner of the estate of Galrigs or Newfield in the parish of Dundonald. Between 1725 and 1735 they levelled the sand dunes, ploughed certain areas, consolidated ground with 'the wreck and rubbish of the town', and sowed clover and grass seeds. The area thus reclaimed extended from the 'west part of the suburbs without the Sandgate Port, and from thence by the north west of the laigh sands towards the Blackburn'. These lands were further levelled by the council in 1747; but they remained part of the 'pasturage of the hills' and unsuitable for regular cropping. As far as Alloway was concerned, when the barony was feued in 1754, the new owners not only 'adorned with plantations' their country seats, but within thirty years 'the lands have been brought into good cultivation, and are now finely inclosed'. The council was content thereafter to collect its feu duties annually. In the inland and cultivable part of the Burrowfield, 'alienated from the town at some far distant period ... though they pay a feu-duty it is a mere trifle', Ayr council in 1766 noted that William Donald junior wished to enclose his lands near Light Mile burn; and this was approved because others had already done so without seeking permission. The council really concerned itself only with the common land nearer the sea. In 1770 the council was approached by a committee of gentlemen seeking permission to form a race course on the common, to supersede the horse racing on the sands. This was approved. In 1787 they were allowed to erect a stand or viewhouse on the west side of the road from Ayr to the New Bridge of Doon. In 1788 the council enclosed the race course by a circular stone dyke, rooted out the whins, to provide pasture for 'the town's milk-kye'. These sixty three imperial acres were leased in 1791 but retained in municipal ownership. An adjoining thirty three imperial acres of the mid sands, in two lots, were in 1788 disposed of 'between the Common and John Campbell's house for pasture and ... between Campbell's house and Barns for cultivation'. When in the same year the Common Isle and four other small patches around the Race course were disposed of, all that was left of the town common was the area which became known as the Low Green.

Dr McGill in 1791 could boast that 'There is scarce any part of the parish which is not arable, and most of it actually bears crops, chiefly of oats'. Yet the population of town and parish was now too great to be self-sufficient. 'Large supplies, both of vegetable and animal food, are brought in from all the neighbouring country, from Galloway, and often from Ireland'. In 1774 the town council noted 'severe distress for want of oatmeal' and arranged for cargoes of 120 tons and 46 tons to be imported. Such recurring dearths and fears of famine would soon be a thing of the past. When the potato became part of the staple diet in Ayrshire, the disastrously bad harvest of 1782 required no exceptional measures. For as Colonel William Fullarton observed in 1793, 'of all the benefits the lower classes have acquired within the present century in this county, the general cultivation of potatoes is probably the most important'. Yet a century after the famines at the end of the 17th century, history repeated itself with bad harvests in 1799 and 1800, shortage of meal in the market, high prices, a 'distressed situation' for 'the labouring part of the community', and a council proposal in 1801 that distillation of grain should be (temporarily) prohibited throughout Scotland.

The traditional fairs and markets of Ayr continued to operate, busier than ever. At the beginning of the 18th century Ayr had two annual fairs. There was the Midsummer Fair, deriving from the royal charter of 1271 granting Ayr a fair on the feast day of St John's nativity and for fifteen following days; from 1690 it was held on the last Tuesday of June and for the rest of the week. There was the Michaelmas Fair, from the 1458 royal charter providing a second fair on St Michael's day and four days afterwards; from 1690 held on the last Tuesday of October and for the rest of that week. In 1701 by Act of Parliament a third fair was added on the first Tuesday of January. Later in the century the Palm Fair was added on the first Tuesday of April. So by 1791, wrote Dr McGill, 'we have four fairs in the year, one every quarter. At the beginning of each fair, coarse raw woollen cloths, manufactured in this, and the neighbouring parishes, are sold to merchants from Glasgow, Paisley, etc., to the amount of £4,000 or upwards yearly, at the four fairs.' These Web Fairs were held on Tuesdays, for the Glasgow customers found Mondays inconvenient. At three of the fairs, 'when the cloth market is over, is a large horse market, chiefly of Irish horses.' The January Fair became known specially as the Horse Fair, and early in the 19th century there were added a Cattle Fair on the last Friday of April and a Wool Fair on the third Tuesday of July. Fairs continued to provide opportunity for periodic and specialised commercial transactions; and were, as always, occasions for jollification and spending on the little luxuries that travelling vendors had on offer.

More important for regular consumer purchases were the weekly markets. These were originally held on Saturday; moved to Friday in 1690; and by 1791 'There are two market days in the town every week, Tuesday and Friday'. In the High Street south of the old tolbooth was the Meal Market, where oats, barley, pease, meal, and malt were bought and sold. The Meal Market, mentioned in 1559, was extended in 1586, and was replaced by a covered building which lasted from 1662 till 1843. Adjacent were the Wool market, and the Web market for homespun plaiding. In 1785 the council planned a market 'for poultry, butter, cheese, and other vivers' in the new Cross Street between High Street and Sandgate; but not till 1814 did this Buttermarket open in what was thereafter known as Newmarket Street. Earlier in 1747 a slaughterhouse had been built in Mill Street by the riverside, and in 1764 a Fleshmarket was provided beside it. That replaced the previous fleshmarket beside the meal market, where beasts had once been slaughtered in the street. In the early part of the 18th century this was only about fifty in any one year, so little was the consumption of butcher meat then. By the end of the century several thousand cattle and great numbers of sheep were slaughtered and sold in Ayr Fleshmarket. The Cattle Market, for sale of live beasts,

After opening of the New Bridge in 1788, a daily mail coach service between Glasgow and Ayr was inaugurated.

was traditionally beyond Townhead at the Fauldbacks, of necessity a wide area including what is now Burns Statue Square and adjoining properties. In 1690 there was an attempt to remove the 'noutt mercat from the Townheid to Ralph Holland's fauld in the Sandgate' but by 1694 it had returned to the Fauldbacks. In 1700 the annual sales of cattle were moved from the first Tuesday of November to the second Tuesday of October. The horse fair, instituted in 1700, was also held in the area which has continued as the location of Ayr's market for livestock. Notice how in course of the 18th century marketing migrated south along High Street. The Malt Cross could be removed from the Sandgate – High Street corner in 1788 because by then it seemed no more than a barrier to traffic over the New Bridge. In the same year it was noted that business at the Fish Cross was suffering from 'Sellers of Fish at Second hand from hawking'; ten years later there was no recovery of business at the Fish Cross; in 1801 the council accepted the inevitable and built a Fish Market at the harbour 'at the head of the Little Quay'.

However busy the markets were in the 18th century, they were already superseded for the sale of certain goods. Booths temporarily erected outside merchants' and craftsmen's houses were being replaced by shops. The earliest noted local example is of a newly-built fore shop ('new biget foir chop') as listed in the Roll of Ground Annuals for 1656. In 1688 John Campbell, merchant, obtained the council's leave to 'build two little houses or Schops within his own property under the forestare upon the Backsyd of the Isle'. By 1791, according to Dr McGill, 'Of retail shops in the town of Ayr, besides a few of inconsiderable note, there may at present be reckoned thirty-six. Twenty-one of which are furnished with articles of grocery, four with hardware, two with saddlery, and nine with broad cloth and haberdashery.' So originated Ayr's new role as a shopping centre.

From the same source we are informed that 'The price of provisions is more than doubled within these last 50 years. Beef and mutton is now from 4d to 5d per lib. Lamb is from 1s 3d to 2s 6d per quarter; pork 6d per lib.; veal from 4d to 6d; pigs from 2s

6d to 3s; geese 2s; ducks from 9d to 1s; chickens 4d and sometimes less; rabbits 9d; butter from 6d to 8d per lib.; cheese from 4d to 6d; wheat from 21s to 25s per boll; barley from 18s to 20s; oats from 16s to 18s.' Any arithmetically-minded housewife who cares may translate these into modern currency at 240d or 20s per £. Wages, of course, were correspondingly low, as Dr McGill illustrated. 'A labourer, with a wife and 5 children, is able to earn 7s per week, and sometimes a little more. At an average, he purchases 3 pecks of meal, and a greater quantity of potatoes, half a cart of coals, and soap to the value of 2d per week; 3 stone of wool, at 7s 6d the stone, for clothing, and 10 lib. of lint, at 10d per lib. per annum. His wife's attendance on the children prevents her from earning much. This may serve as a general specimen of the wages and expenses of a labourer's family. A shoemaker, if industrious, gets from 1s 2d to 1s 8d a day; a mason from 1s 3d to 1s 8d; a wright from 1s 3d to 1s 9d; a taylor 1s 2d'.

TEN

Auld Ayr and its Honest Men

Robert Burns spent the first eighteen years of his life resident within the parish of Ayr, from 1759 till 1766 in the cottage at Alloway, then on Mount Oliphant farm till 1777. While dwelling thereafter in the nearby parishes of Tarbolton and Mauchline, he must regularly have revisited the town. A visit on 26 March 1788 was the last recorded occasion. It is unlikely that he attended as planned the Ayr horse fair on New Years Day 1789. That he sometime paid a visit to his place of birth was later asserted by Miller Goudie who occupied the Cottage at Alloway. During the latter years of his short life Ayr was less accessible. But for twenty eight years he was intimately acquainted with Ayr, at that critical time in the later 18th century when the royal burgh was shedding some of its medieval characteristics and entering its modern era.

> Auld Ayr, wham ne'er a town surpasses,
> For honest men and bonny lasses.

The Auld Ayr that Tam O' Shanter knew, and his dramatic homeward ride past Alloway's auld haunted kirk, were set by Robert Burns in a vanished past. There still continued to be honest men and bonnie lasses. The latter get scant attention from the historian, for those women who happen to find mention in surviving records tend to be witches or wealthy widows, with little reported of their wisdom, wit, or winsomeness. Taking Burns himself as evidence, he found his first 'bonny lass' in Nell Kilpatrick, at Mount Oliphant during the harvest 'in my fifteenth autumn'. For her he composed a song, 'O once I loved a bonnie lass', a significant event in his career, for 'Thus with me began Love and Poesy'. It is easier perhaps to identify the honest men. Among these Robert Burns counted 'Dalrymple mild', who had baptised him; 'glib-tongu'd Aiken', the lawyer who befriended him; and his other patron John Ballantine who as 'Provost John' promoted the New Bridge and the Academy and did so much to advance Ayr's progress.

'Tam O' Shanter' was a tribute to the Auld Ayr

that was disappearing. By contrast, 'The Brigs of Ayr' which Burns appropriately dedicated to Ballantine presents a dialogue between the Auld and the New bridges, tradition versus progress, with the 'auld warld squad' on the council who 'in all the pomp of ignorant conceit' accuse the new men of spending 'weel-hained gear on damn'd new Brigs and Harbours'.

In 'The Brigs of Ayr' the poet lightly sketched in the background of the town he knew so well:

> The drowsy Dungeon-clock had number'd two,
> And Wallace Tow'r had sworn the fact was true.

The Dungeon-clock was set above the Tolbooth in the Sandgate; the Wallace Tower had, for the benefit of residents in that part of High Street and Townhead, been supplied in 1731 with a belfry and clock, and for their greater convenience the clock was fitted with minute hands in 1779. The royal burgh, with its twin main streets, had now in each a set of clock and bells, and this duality was emphasised with the recent growth of a fashionable west end and an industrial east end.

In the Sandgate most of the county gentry had their town houses – until the 17th century when Edinburgh became the place for them to spend the winter season, and the 18th century when London displaced Edinburgh for the most select. However, lairds with regular business in Ayr retained residences. Some widowed gentlewomen preferred Ayr, and at times in the 18th century Sandgate had among its residents Lady Dunduff, Lady Orangefield, and Lady Cathcart. In 1756 John Loudon McAdam was born here, his parents renting Lord Cathcart's house, moving in 1760 to another off St John Street; in 1770 he was sent to an uncle's in New York; returning in 1783 to purchase Sauchrie. In 1763 the Sandgate Port was removed, principally because it did 'Cramp the passage of the Street' but also for a novel reason that it did 'Limite the Views'. In 1765 Provost William Fergusson built a new house for himself on the west side of the street

MURDOCH'S HOUSE
Sandgate.
where Burns had lessons in French.

In the Sandgate lived John Murdoch who tutored Robert Burns. This was the fashionable part of Ayr in the 18th century.

outwith that Sandgate port, by the vennel 'leading from the said porch towards the Citydale', later the Collector's Vennel, now St John Street. About that time the School Vennel (now Academy Lane) was favoured for fashionable new residences by Hamilton of Bargany and Lady Dumfries. Only towards the end of the 18th century would Cathcart Street be opened up, taking its name probably from the adjacent house of Lady Cathcart. The Boat Vennel with its huddle of old houses and harbour traffic had declined in prestige; Loudoun Hall was let after the death of John Mure of Blairston in 1744, sold by his son Dr Robert Mure in 1770, and thereafter converted into a tenement of rented dwellings. The laying out after 1767 of what became Newmarket Street provided attractive sites for new building. It meant however the removal in 1777 of the houses of Lady Dunduff, Lady Orangefield, and the latter's relative Rev. William Dalrymple. His was an old house 'built with mudd, and not with lime' which had previously belonged to Sir David Cunningham of Milncraig. Dr Dalrymple (as he would become in 1779) took a feu on the north-east part of the new street. His colleague in the second charge Rev William McGill acquired a building plot also in 1777 but on the 'south east corner of the Citadel, north east of the Washing Green'. This

was the real west end, where in 1781 the town council laid out 'a regular street' – soon to be called Academy Street and now Fort Street. Fashionable dwellings were erected there and 'at the Shore'; in 1799 the town council made a plan for feuing the Green, and in 1800 the Earl of Cassillis considered the possibilities of building within his Citadel grounds. Earlier in 1775 Charles Dalrymple of Orangefield had feued 3½ acres of the laigh sands betwixt the end of Sandgate and the lands of Patrick McNeight of Barns and the following year sought to acquire more to build houses. Already at Sandgatehead where the street narrows still, outwith the old port, on the eastern inland side stood Sandgate House, recently erected by the lawyer John Boswell whose little estate would become known as Boswell Park. On the opposite side of Sandgatehead was the more modest dwelling where for three weeks in 1773 Robert Burns lodged with his teacher John Murdoch. One week before harvest was spent at the burgh school 'to revise his English grammar'; for two weeks after the harvest he 'was engaged in learning French', and this (as brother Gilbert also recalled) 'procured him the acquaintance of several lads in Ayr ... and the notice of some families'.

The Sandgate was proving to be not only an attractive residential area, but an appropriate place of

High Street remained the centre of commercial life, as in this imaginative view of the Fish Cross.

business for many of the burgh's sixteen solicitors and five physicians and surgeons (in 1791), for the ill-fated Ayr Bank from 1770 and the Bank of Scotland from 1775. Another convenient facility was the Assembly Room which James Gregg was able to rent in 1773 and later years for his popular classes in country dancing. Near the Malt Cross Alexander Forsyth had his book shop, as noted in 1780. At the far end of the School Vennel was the burgh school which was converted in 1796 into Ayr Academy. The Sandgate was indeed a most convenient part of Ayr, especially after the opening of the New Bridge in 1788, as later described. The only drawback was the tolbooth in the middle of the street. When the celebrated architect Robert Adam visited Ayr in 1785 he proposed redesigning it in classical style; but the council which had virtually rebuilt it as recently as 1754 took no action.

By contrast the High Street was a busier, noisier, smellier place. Before 1788 all traffic for the harbour crossed the Auld Brig and turned down High Street; through traffic continued to traverse High Street and Townhead if heading into Carrick and beyond to Portpatrick for Ireland. Opposite the Fish Cross, McAdam's bank was sited 1763–1771 and Hunter's Bank after 1774. Nearby in Gadgirth Vennel were the old houses of Osborne and Blair, the latter for

a time occupied by John Mair of the burgh school. During the three or four annual fairs the whole of High Street was thronged, though on the weekly Tuesday and Friday markets most business became concentrated beyond the old tolbooth. Congestion continued despite efforts at dispersion. In 1747 slaughtering of cattle in the street was prohibited after the construction of a slaughterhouse beside the river, and in 1764 the flesh market was moved to an adjacent site. In 1785 a New Market was planned for the sale of poultry, butter, cheese, and other foodstuffs. The sale of cattle, horse, and sheep was effectively restricted to the distant Fauldbacks beyond Townhead.

In High Street, many of the long 13th century burgage plots were filled with back tenements reached through pends. By the 16th century the town had extended beyond the Kyle Port to form Townhead, leading to the Overport (in what is Kyle Street), with a branch to the Cow Port in the Cow Vennel (later Alloway Street). By the middle of the 18th century these streets were almost entirely built up along their length – as indicated on Roy's map. So was Carrick Vennel, sometimes known in this period as the Foul Vennel. The Mill Vennel and Mill Street were to be filled up within the next twenty years – as shown by the Armstrong map of 1775. Here were located

The Kings Arms was conveniently situated as a coaching inn for traffic crossing the New Bridge and heading up High Street towards the Brig O' Doon.

the slaughterhouse (1747), the Fleshmarket (1764), a tannery (1761), a brewery (before 1775), Campbell's coal pit (1775) beside the churchyard, with coal also brought down from Holmston and (after 1775) from Auchincruive. There was also traffic to and from the Nethermill and Overmill and from the freestone quarry. At this end of the town were accommodated many of the increasingly numerous weavers and shoemakers, while west of the Cow Vennel were Gibb's soap works and a lime kiln. The Townhead area thus formed the main industrial zone of the burgh – and here the Poorshouse was opened in 1756 at the end of Mill Street. Elsewhere in the town the harbour held warehouses and coal rees; and near the end of the century depots for the Muirkirk Iron company and McAdam's tar works; the Citadel had little more then a brewery; the textile manufactory in Fort Street was an isolated novelty.

Across the river were Newton-upon-Ayr and Wallacetown. These Burns failed to mention by name in 'The Brigs of Ayr' though the 'simple Bard' of the poem went 'down by Simpson's'. This was a tavern just opposite the Auld Brig, conveniently situated as a posting house for the coaches which were operating on the new turnpike roads, improved in Newton and St Quivox parishes after the 1767 Act. At Simpson's Inn in September 1782, William Burnes the poet's father and David McClure of Shawwood had failed to settle their dispute over the Lochlea rent. Four years later in September 1786 Robert Burns sent from here a note to John Ballantine. He would have come down from Mauchline past Auchincruive, by Mainholm, skirting the Blackhouse pits before entering the busy new community of Wallacetown. Laid out quite recently, about 1760, it would soon have a thousand of a population. These included weavers, miners, respectable retired farmers, and less reputable ne'er do weels who found Wallacetown a convenient howff, unpoliced and outwith authority of the Ayr magistrates. Here presumably was one of 'only two houses of ill-fame on both sides of the river' whose existence was noted by J.M.Ferguson a century later. Wallace Street was the principal thoroughfare, named after Sir Thomas Wallace of Craigie who had founded the town. There was a transverse street – North Street till the cross roads, then Cross Street which turned down to the river as Garden Street. From Simpson's Inn the coaches would travel by Wallace Street and North Street towards Mauchline for Muirkirk and Lanark, others by Galston ¯for Strathaven. Those for Glasgow by Irvine or Kilmarnock after leaving Simpson's passed the end of Garden Street to make their way through Newton.

Newton was growing rapidly, from some 500 to 1,700 in the second half of the 18th century, with fishermen, colliers, weavers, and other tradesmen becoming tenants of the forty eight freemen of the burgh. Almost all were accommodated on the one large main street, about 680 yards in length, 80 feet in breadth, through which ran the stream from Newton loch to power Newton mill before the water fell into the River Ayr. About thirty new houses were built in the 1780s, mostly at the north end beyond the Damside, forming a New Street and an appropriately-named Weaver Street. There was no direct link with Garden Street or Cross Street in Wallacetown – which lands were presumed to be part of the parish of Monkton and Prestwick, to which Newton-upon-Ayr was attached until 1779.

The council of the burgh of Newton made some valiant attempts to adjust to new circumstances. From 1666 till 1771 the lands were re-divided among the forty eight freemen every seven years, which made agricultural improvements virtually impossible; in 1771 the 'daills' were allocated for a period of fifty seven years, which was a step in the right direction. In 1764 Newton council initiated a plan to exploit its coal resources, and the prospect of revenue from royalties encouraged them to further ventures. In 1777 a church was built; in 1778 Rev. William Peebles was called to this chapel of ease; in 1779 Newton-upon-Ayr was disjoined from the parish of Monkton and Prestwick; and the patronage of the church was purchased for the burgh and its inhabitants. In 1780 they provided a glebe of 6½ acres and in 1787 a manse for their minister, whom Burns commemorated as 'Poet Willie' and 'Peebles, frae the water-fit'. The provision of a church within Newton was a facility appreciated by the people who had previously to go as far as their parish church at Prestwick, or cross the Auld Brig to worship in Ayr. It proved convenient also for the people of

Wallacetown whose parish church was three miles away at St Quivox; though from 1770 there was at the end of North Street (later King Street) a meeting place for Anti-burghers belonging to the General Associate Synod. Towards the end of the century Newton council, after some years when expensive outlays seemed to threaten bankruptcy, were rewarded with coal royalties which enabled them to support schooling and in 1795 built the impressive Newton Steeple to provide improved chambers for the council and a dignified frontage for the church.

Newton looked across the river to the Ratton-key, the little landing place just down from Ayr burgh school; Wallacetown was opposite the ford by the Ducat-stream, which Burns also mentioned. Between was the Auld Brig, a 'ruin'd, formless bulk o' stane and lime', quite unsuitable for modern traffic, 'Where twa wheel-barrows tremble when they meet'. John Ballantine became a councillor in 1780, was dean of guild from 1782 till 1787, when he became provost. In 1782 he commissioned a report which found that the bridge was in 'a very precarious position'; minor repairs were carried out; efforts to involve the county Commissioners of Supply proved unsuccessful; a private act of parliament would be required to authorise the rebuilding of the bridge. In 1785 Provost William Campbell and Dean of Guild John Ballantine were despatched to London, and Ballantine stayed there throughout May and June to help the passage of the bill; in July the council, as authorised by the new Act, replaced the traditional bridge custom by a new toll to be collected on the Newton side of the bridge; and the Bridge committee considered various proposed designs for a new bridge. Ballantine, while in London, had commissioned Robert Adam, the fashionable architect, to prepare plans:

> New Brig was buskit in a braw, new coat,
> That he, at Lon'on, frae ane Adams got.

The original idea had been to demolish the Auld Brig and replace it with a new structure on the same site. But Ballantine had another idea, possibly coming from Adam himself who had been in Ayr that year, having just completed the building of Dalquharran and now planning his new major commission at Culzean. In August Ballantine persuaded the council that 'the best place for building the bridge is from the Water Vennel to the street of the Old Newton'; the Auld Brig could conveniently continue in use during its construction and thereafter be retained for foot passengers only. There is some mystery about what happened next. The council decided to make use of

Though Newton was growing, its nucleus remained the two rows of cottages between which an open stream supplied water power for Newton Mill. The Freemen of Newton provided their own church in 1779, fronted in 1795 by a townhouse with steeple.

freestone from their own quarry instead of granite or limestone from a distance; Adam apparently modified his plans; these were implemented by another architect Alexander Stevens, who in April 1786 made a contract to complete it for £4,000. Construction proceeded slowly. Work commenced in May 1786; but not till August 1787 was the keystone of the middle arch secured; and it was November 1788 before the bridge was open for traffic, appropriately during John Ballantine's provostship. Also in 1788 the Malt Cross was removed to allow free access through New Bridge Street which superseded the Water Vennel. The new bridge of five arches afforded a more direct entry from the north, and more convenient access to the harbour was provided after purchase and demolition of some riverside houses in 1789. However, when Burns wrote 'The Brigs of Ayr' in September 1788, work had scarcely begun, and as James A. Morris pointed out, 'very little even of the "rising piers" could have been visible and the "Braw new coat" then existed only on the contract drawings or in the poet's imagination'. One line in the poem has often been quoted, when the auld brig advises the new

that 'I'll be a Brig when you're a shapeless cairn!' for in 1877 the new bridge was damaged by flood and had to be rebuilt. In this prophecy Burns may have been echoing Ballantine's possible misgivings when the council abandoned Adam's original plans and produced a cheaper version, which as so often turns out was a false economy.

If in 'The Brigs of Ayr' Burns was looking into the future, in 'Tam O' Shanter' he was recreating the past. Not the distant past, for Alloway Kirk ceased to be a place of worship only in 1690, but sometime before 1754 when the roup of the lands of Alloway began the transformation of that area. In 1771 the modern direct route to Alloway was opened up leading from the Cow Vennel (Alloway Street) towards Slaphouse (by Carrick Road). Previously there was one way via Townhead (Kyle Street) and the road to Dalmellington (Castlehill Road) branching off (at Inverkar Road) towards the Slaphouse road (Carrick Road) east of the Town Common. Another old route left by the Carrick Vennel (Carrick Street) which continued past Barns and the Mid Sands (by Racecourse Road) towards the Town Common (the Old Racecourse). Tam did not leave the town by this way. The Carrick Vennel was (in 1753 at least) called the Foul Vennel, and troubled with flooding, hence the name of Stank Acre for a nearby part of Barns estate. That estate was in process of improvement by its owner Patrick McNeight. The flooding here was the result of water from his Culross Moss (formerly Spittalbog) being diverted past Killoch instead of into the Black Burn as formerly. Similar improvements in the Mid Sands between Barns and the Town Common, and earlier levelling of the Laigh Sands (by Cathcart and Nugent) had also interfered with drainage there and created the short-lived Katy Lake. A.L. Taylor has pointed out that it would be too difficult to imagine what this area had been like before the improvements. It would be easier to envisage Tam leaving by the Cow Vennel and making his way across the Town Muir before the new Carrick road was made. Tam was 'Weel mounted on his gray mare, Meg' and crossing the town's pastures he 'skelpit on through dub and mire'. En route he would pass the Knowe (located in Midton Road) where the town gibbet was located, and the ruins of St Leonard's Chapel (beyond Chapelpark Road) but these go unmentioned for (as A.L. Taylor reminded us in his survey of Tam's route) 'murderer's bans in gibbet-airns' were saved up for the climax and there was no room in the poem for more than one ruined church. Tam continued across the Town Common (used as a racecourse since 1770 but not enclosed by a dyke till 1788); then went over the

The New Bridge was based on a design by Robert Adam which was modified for reasons of economy. Burns's prophecy of its future collapse probably echoed Provost Ballantine's fears.

Slaphouse burn (not by either of the two bridges but on an older route) by 'the ford, Whare, in the snaw, the chapman smoor'd'. Tam passed the 'meikle stane, Whare drunken Charlie brak's neck-bane': that must have disappeared when the policies of Belleisle were planted (after 1754); conversely there is no mention of crossing a road (namely Greenfield Avenue, laid out by William Burnes in 1756). The 'cairn, Whare hunters fand the murder'd bairn' can still be located (in Cairn Crescent); then in a direct line 'Before him Doon pours all his floods'. Thereafter Tam continued on the old track upriver to the still-surviving St Mungo's well 'Whare Mungo's mither hang'd hersel'. Thus he reached to Kirk Alloway and there facing him was auld Nick in 'a winnock bunker in the east'. Whence he was pursued by the witches to 'win the key-stane of the brig', and escape over the River Doon into Carrick, leaving Alloway behind.

The 'mosses, waters, slaps, and styles' that lay between the town of Ayr and the River Doon were in the later 18th century being transformed from a barren landscape into one enhanced by woodlands and improved fields. The roup in 1754 of the barony of Alloway divided it among purchasers, several of whom wished to set themselves up as landed gentlemen. But only those with considerable resources were successful in laying out the new estates and building stylish mansion houses.

Doonholm, which would become the largest with around one thousand acres, began very modestly. In 1754 two farms called Berriesden and Warlockholm, amounting to 40 acres, were purchased by James Neill, who sold them to another merchant David Mitchell, from whom they were acquired in 1756 by someone with more capital. A relative of the Fergussons of Castlehill called Dr William Fergusson had been a physician in London and now retired to become a landowner, and in due course provost of Ayr. He named the small estate Doonholm, which he enlarged and improved. In 1756 he purchased (from John

Crawford of Doonside) those 222 adjacent acres in Alloway called Upper Crofts, Loaning or Clochranhill including the clachan of Alloway, Dumfries Park, Fieldheads and Whinknow. In 1758 he purchased (from James McDermeit Fergushill, writer) another 363 acres of farmland with South High Corton (renamed Mount Oliphant), High Broomberry Yards (Pleasantfield), and High Carcluie. In 1766 he completed his purchases with 337 acres (from William Donald, merchant) comprising High Muir of Corton (Cockhill and Mount Fergusson) and Riddick's Moss (Mosshill). On Provost Fergusson's death in 1776 Doonholm estate was inherited by a daughter, whence it was purchased in 1783 by her cousin John Fergusson who returned from India with a fortune, much of which was bequeathed to found Ayr Academy and support local charities. The estate was purchased in 1796 by John Hunter, WS, who had married the second daughter of Dr Fergusson. Like his father he had been Ayr's town agent in Edinburgh; like his cousin James Hunter Blair, Lord Provost of Edinburgh, he was a grandson of James Hunter of Abbothill, writer in Ayr; and distantly related to the two Hunters who had been provosts of Ayr.

Rozelle was formed from the largest initial purchase of 676 imperial acres by Robert Hamilton of Bourtreehill. He had been born in Ayr in 1698, eldest son of Hugh Hamilton of Clongall, merchant, and Jean Fergusson of Castlehill; he had made a fortune in Jamaica, where the estate of Pemberton Valley was owned by Robert and a younger brother John (who died by drowning and for whose infant son Sundrum was acquired). In 1748 Robert Hamilton acquired Bourtreehill in Irvine parish and he now added this larger estate of Rozelle, originally Rochelle, named after a property in Jamaica. The mansion house was built in 1770. The estate contained the farms of Broomberry, South Laigh Corton, North Laigh Corton, North High Corton; to which in 1789 were added Over Glengall, and parts of Crawisland and Slaphouse. Robert Hamilton's eldest daughter Jean married George, 3rd Viscount Garnock, later Earl of Crawford; she succeeded to her father's estates after his death in 1773; widowed in 1781, the Countess of Crawford resided at Rozelle till her death in 1809.

That part of the Netherton of Alloway bounded on the north by the Slaphouse Burn and on the south by the Sergeant's Burn amounting to 194 acres became the estate of Belleisle. These lands were acquired in 1754 by Dr Alexander Campbell and William Donald, merchant; the former's share passed in 1765 to his brother Archibald Campbell of Grimmet, writer in

Edinburgh; then in 1775 to a nephew Dr John Campbell. Dr Campbell was a physician in Ayr; owner of Wellwood estate in Muirkirk parish, commended as a noted improver; also a coalmaster, being a principal partner in the Newton pits; a partner in Alexander Oliphant's wine importing business; and deeply involved as shareholder, director, and debtor of the Ayr Bank; he was gaoled for debt in 1780. In 1787 his and Donald's holdings (described as Belisle and Summerfield) were purchased by Hugh Hamilton of Pinmore. Son of a Girvan minister, he had done well in Jamaica with his uncle Robert, late of Rozelle. He purchased Pinmore in Colmonell parish in 1781, and now in 1787 added not only Belleisle but also some adjacent lands of the Burrowfield including Bridgehouse. Hugh Hamilton of Pinmore built the mansion house of Belleisle and laid out the policies. Though married he died without issue, and his estates went to Colonel Alexander Hamilton, second son of his cousin John Hamilton of Sundrum.

There were several smaller estates formed within the barony of Alloway. Cambusdoon originated when the Nethercrofts and Kirk Crofts, together amounting to 79 acres, were acquired by Elias Cathcart to form an estate he called Greenfield. Elias Cathcart was a merchant involved in the wine and tobacco trades, and as provost of Ayr promoted the building of the Poorshouse. His son David Cathcart (1763–1829), who trained as an advocate and became Lord Alloway in 1813, inherited the estate in 1776, and by his marriage to Margaret Mure acquired also Blairston in 1801. The neighbouring part of the Netherton of Alloway called Dykehead Moss and Park, with the mill of Alloway, formed an estate of 30 acres acquired by Charles Dalrymple of Orangefield, who immodestly designated it Mount Charles. After his death in 1781 the little mansion house was occupied for a time by his brother Rev. William Dalrymple. Mount Charles in 1787 was sold to Captain Robert Gairdner, but with Alloway Mill going to David, 10th Earl of Cassillis. Adjacent was the last of Alloway's little estates, the 20 acres of Gearholm purchased in 1754 by Hugh Whitefoord Dalrymple to add to Cunningpark and Windyhall already owned; sold in 1772 to John Christian; after whose bankruptcy in 1785 they were mostly acquired by David, 10th Earl of Cassillis.

Within the Burrowfield there were several sizeable established estates. In the immediate vicinity of the town was the property known as Barns and Jamieson's Acres. This was acquired in 1727 by Patrick McNeight, described as a land labourer. His son and namesake succeeded in 1775, and built an 18th century house as

Alloway ceased to be a separate parish in 1690. The ruined kirk was featured in Francis Grose's *Antiquities of Scotland* and Burns wrote 'Tam O' Shanter' to accompany this illustration in the book.

an extension to the original 17th century one. He also made a considerable series of land purchases. His son Lieutenant Colonel Patrick McNeight in the service of the East India Company inherited in 1800 an estate on which would be built Fullarton Street, Barns Street, Alloway Place, Miller Road, Killoch Place, and had detached portions extending as far south as Windyhall beside the racecourse, which lands were also available for 19th century feuing. Holmston, on the river side, was occupied by Wallaces from at least the beginning of the 17th century. Robert Wallace in 1719 added the adjacent lands of Gawblair to Holmston and Maryland he already possessed. Robert Paterson Wallace, WS, succeeded his uncle in 1754; his son, an Edinburgh banker, in 1781 disposed of Holmston estate to Richard Oswald of Auchincruive. Castlehill with Crawisland or Whinmuir had existed as a distinct property since the end of the 16th century, when it

was tenanted by David Bannatyne from Bute. During the 17th and most of the 18th century it was in the possession of the Fergussons who provided Ayr with several provosts and numerous lawyers. From 1766 till 1779 the owner was Robert Fergusson of Castlehill, but he had to dispose of his estate because of liabilities following the collapse of the Ayr Bank. The house may have been tenanted thereafter, perhaps by Provost David Fergusson till 1791. Before the end of the century it was acquired by Patrick Ballantine, who built the new mansion house in 1804. It was inherited in 1810 by his brother Ex-provost John Ballantine, the banker, who lived in Townhead and had purchased Sandyford and adjacent lands in the Burrowfield. He died unmarried in 1812.

Some other such little estates were in process of creation in the 18th century. Adjacent to Castlehill was Bank, to which James Fergusson, lawyer and town clerk, added parts of Whitestones and Braston in 1768. In 1771 he became provost, after relinquishing the office of town clerk to his son and namesake. That James Fergusson continued as town clerk till he was succeeded (by David Limond) in 1787; in which year he succeeded his father in the estate, to be followed in turn by his son James in 1792. The upland property of Macnairston passed into the hands of the Dunlop family and was inherited in 1764 by George Dunlop, Controller of Customs, banker, provost, bibliophile, and antiquarian. In 1775 the lawyer Robert Aiken acquired Hole of Macnairston or Thornhill; and in 1778 on the opposite side of the Dalmellington road set himself up in Whitehill, later Glenpark. Other parcels of land in the Burrowfield were possessed by local merchants. Some parts were acquired by county landowners. David, 10th Earl of Cassillis, who lived in his favoured residence of Newark just across the Doon, in 1787 obtained Loch Fergus, Knocksoul, and Rudeland or Wee Macnairston in the Burrowfield, as well as Cunning Park, plus Gairholm and Alloway Mill in the barony of Alloway. Richard Oswald of Auchincruive who owned two third of St Quivox parish extended south of the river to acquire Laigland, with Lochyrmoss, Gateside, Bellston, and Holmshill, from William Cunningham of Enterkin, 1764; and Holmston, with Maryland, Gawblair, and Duphold from Robert Paterson Wallace, 1781. The small property of Bridgehouse was sold in 1763 by Andrew Cochrane (1692–1777), an Ayr merchant who became provost of Glasgow; in 1785 it was added to Belleisle. In 1789 the Common Isle was sold by the town to David Cathcart of Greenfield.

There were numerous examples of moneyed men from Ayr investing in small parcels of land elsewhere in the county. Thus James Neill, writer, (properties in Prestwick, 1782 and 1783); John Hutchison, merchant, (Mauchline, 1783); James Bone, surgeon, (Mauchline, 1785); Alexander Forsyth, bookseller, (Fenwick, 1785); George Charles, surgeon, (Stair, 1786). A few were wealthy enough to purchase estates in adjacent parishes. Two were notable examples of local men who made fortunes in India. James Macrae spent part of his childhood in Ayr where his widowed mother Bell Gairdner earned a bare living as a washerwoman; on his return to this country in 1731 he set himself up in the estate of Blackheath in Kent. Visiting Ayr in 1733 'James Macrae, late Governor of Madras' was admitted as honorary burgess. He found all his relatives dead except a cousin married to Hugh McGuire, a carpenter in Newton who had some local repute for playing the fiddle. In 1734 Macrae

presented a statue of William of Orange to Glasgow; and between 1736 and 1739 he purchased a number of estates for McGuire and his children. Drumdow in Stair was presented to Hugh McGuire; Ochiltree to the daughter Elizabeth McGuire who in 1744 married the Earl of Glencairn; Houston in Renfrewshire to James McGuire who took the name James Macrae and turned out to be rather a nasty character; Alva near Stirling to Margaret McGuire who married James Erskine, later Lord Barjarg and Lord Alva; to a third daughter would be given the Monkton estate which he had renamed Orangefield, and this Macrae McGuire married Charles Dalrymple, who was Sheriff Clerk of Ayrshire, as was their son James who followed him in 1785. James Macrae himself lived at Orangefield, in 1745 lending Glasgow £1.500 for the levy made on that city by Prince Charles Edward, and it was at Orangefield that he died just a year later. Another local 'nabob' was Claud Alexander, younger brother of Robert Alexander of Blackhouse, who returned after a career with the East India Company. In 1786 he acquired the estate of Ballochmyle near Mauchline, and married in 1788. In association with David Dale he set up on the banks of the River Ayr the cotton spinning factory and new town of Catrine. Another who made a fortune abroad was John Loudon McAdam, born in Ayr Sandgate in 1756; in New York from 1770 till 1783 built up a successful business and made a fortunate marriage; he returned to become laird of Sauchrie in Maybole parish, partner of the 9th earl of Dundonald in the British Coal Tar Company, member of the Ayrshire Turnpike Trustees, a Deputy Lieutenant, briefly councillor in Ayr burgh; before going south in 1798 to win fame as a roadmaker before his death in 1836.

Two rare and differing examples of other local men wealthy enough to set up as landowners in neighbouring parishes may be cited. Provost Robert Mure, who became a rich man trading in wine and tobacco, in 1698 acquired Blairston, formerly Middle Auchendrane, across the Doon in Maybole parish. It remained in the family: by direct inheritance in 1734 to John Mure; in 1744 to Dr Robert Mure; and in 1801 to Mary Mure who in 1793 had married David Cathcart of Greenfield, later Lord Alloway. A less permanent acquisition was that of Shawwood in Tarbolton parish by David McClure. He came from Dailly and as a self-made man of business became a burgess and guild brother of Ayr in 1759 at the age of twenty six. He was involved in several shipping firms, but as well as legitimate business he seems to have become heavily involved in the profitable smuggling

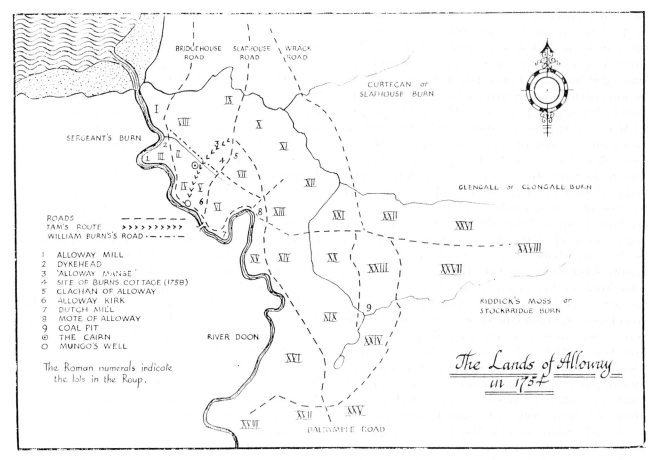

The Barony of Alloway was transformed after 1754 when Ayr town council rouped its 2,335 acres, realizing £7,190 and annual feu duties of £116.12.9d. The lots were numbered as shown, sometimes named, and modern names are added (in brackets):

I. Gearholm
II. Dykehead Moss and Park (Mount Charles)
III. Alloway Miln
IV. Alloway Nether Crofts (Cambusdoon West)
V. Alloway Kirk Crofts (Cambusdoon East)
VI. Alloway Upper Crofts (Alloway Cottage field)
VII. Alloway Lonings and Glebe (Clochranhill)
VIII. Part of Netherton of Alloway (Belleisle West)
IX. (Belleisle East)
X, XI. (Rozelle)
XII. (Rozelle and Doonholm)
XIII. (Dumfries Park)
XIV. Fieldheads and Whinknow (Doonholm)
XV. Berriesdam and Warlockholm (Doonholm)

XVI. Barrhill
XVII. Nether Carclowie (Carcluie)
XVIII. Skellydub (Blackhill)
XIX. Laigh Broomberry Yards (Broomberry)
XX. South Laigh Corton (South Corton)
XXI. North Laigh Corton (North Corton)
XXII. North High Corton (High Corton)
XXIII. South High Corton (Mount Oliphant)
XXIV. High Broomberry Yards (Pleasantfield)
XXV. High Carclowie (Pleasantfield and Carcluie)
XXVI. North High Muir of Corton (Cockhill)
XXVII. South High Muir of Corton (Mount Fergusson)
XXVIII. Riddick's Moss Muir (Mosshill)

trade, among his associates being Robert Whiteside and John Christian from the Isle of Man, Andrew McCulloch in Ayr, Douglas Graham from Shanter in Kirkoswald, and Matthew Hay in Dundonald. He did well enough to build a house for himself near the school in 1767. In 1769 he became a shareholder in the ill-fated Ayr Bank, in 1770 in association with George McCree of Pitcon and Dr John Campbell of Wellwood he began purchasing lands in Tarbolton parish and set himself up in Shawwood. He served on Ayr town council for ten years between 1761 and 1783. But Bailie McClure's estate was in that year sequestered and his debts assessed at £45,000 because of his liabilities to the Ayr Bank. He left Ayr in 1787 to set up in business anew in Liverpool; and died in Toxteth in 1799 'much and justly regretted by a numerous acquaintance'.

McClure on several occasions had been nominated but never achieved the provostship. One suspects that nouveaux riches with shady business connections were not altogether acceptable to the established families who composed the local establishment. The Fergussons and the Ballantines were the most substantial families in the second half of the 18th century, providing provosts for thirty one of those fifty years. The Dalrymples were less in evidence in municipal affairs, but Rev. William Dalrymple was well-connected. His only brother was Charles Dalrymple, who succeeded his father as sheriff clerk of Ayr, and whose marriage to the wealthy Macrae McGuire brought him Orangefield and made him brother-in-law to the earl of Glencairn. Of their six Dalrymple sisters, four married. Sarah married John Aiken, shipmaster and father of the influential lawyer Robert Aiken; Margaret married John Smith, shipmaster and benefactor; Marion married Rev. David Shaw of Coylton, whose lawyer son would become Provost Charles Shaw; Catherine married the master of the grammar school David Tennant, whose family was doing well. John Tennant, an elder brother and childhood friend of Elizabeth McGuire, was, after she became Countess of Glencairn, appointed factor of her Ochiltree estate, as later noted. Burns knew him as 'Guid Auld Glen' and his large family included Charles Tennant who would found St Rollox Chemical Works. The Hunter family continued to be prominent in Ayr. James Hunter, a grandson of the 17th century provost Robert Hunter, was himself provost for four years between 1736 and 1742. His eldest son James Hunter set up his successful banking company in Ayr in 1774; a younger son John Hunter founded Ayr Hill in Virginia. The Hunters extended their influence to Edinburgh. James Hunter, WS, who died in 1739 had succeeded to the little family estate of Abbothill and added to it other properties, including Park in Tarbolton parish acquired from the Mures. His brother John Hunter was a prominent merchant in Ayr, whose son Robert Hunter became Professor of Greek in Edinburgh University. James Hunter's own eldest son Andrew Hunter, also a Writer to the Signet in Edinburgh, was Ayr's town agent till his death in 1770; he had ten of a family. The eldest son Rev. Dr Andrew Hunter sold off Abbothill in 1772, before he became Professor of

Divinity at Edinburgh University; the younger son John Hunter was a lawyer in Edinburgh, succeeding his father as town agent, and returned to Ayr as owner of Doonholm in 1796; his sister Janet married Robert Aiken who had trained with her father in Edinburgh. James Hunter, WS, had another son, John Hunter of Mainholm and Milnquarter, whose youngest son was especially successful: this James Hunter, born in Ayr in 1741, became an Edinburgh banker, married an heiress in 1777, adopted her name, as James Hunter Blair became MP for Edinburgh 1781–84, the city's Lord Provost 1784–85, and was created baronet shortly before his death in 1787. His aunt Janet, daughter of James Hunter, WS, married her half-cousin Provost James Hunter of Ayr. If the reader has been able to penetrate this genealogical jungle thus far, at least one thing will be clear – the far-reaching connections of this important Ayr family. How important were family relationships can sometimes be guessed. For example, when the kind but not very popular Calvinistic Rev. Andrew Hunter was appointed professor in 1779 by Edinburgh town council, the influence of his cousin James Hunter Blair was detected. How closely related were certain members of Ayr's various principal families may already have been noticed. Two final examples: in 1750 James Hunter, banker, married Sarah Ballantine, daughter of Patrick Ballantine and cousin of John Ballantine, banker; in 1773 John Hunter, WS, married Jane Fergusson, younger daughter of Provost William Fergusson, a previous owner of Doonholm.

It is usually less easy to trace the career of lesser folk, but the celebrity of Robert Burns and the diligence of many of his admirers enables the historian to examine the circumstances of his upbringing within the parish of Ayr. William Burnes from Kincardineshire arrived in Ayr in or about 1752. He was an experienced estate worker, who had worked at the Meadows in Edinburgh before coming west in 1750 into the employment of Alexander Fairlie of Fairlie, one of Ayrshire's leading agricultural improvers. He then moved to Doonside, working for John Craufurd and lodging at the Dutch Mill. In 1754 when the lands of Alloway were rouped, Ayr town council required a new road to be made and William Burnes was well enough thought of by Ayr town council to be awarded the contract for laying out what became Greenfield Avenue. For this work he received from the council a final payment on 7 June 1756; and a fortnight later he purchased from Dr Alexander Campbell, owner of the new estate of Belleisle, a feu of seven acres to form his own small holding. He probably intended to

Doonholm became the largest of the new estates created after the roup of the lands of Alloway. The Poet's father William Burnes was employed as gardener and overseer of the estate.

employ himself full-time at these 'New Gardens' and leave Doonside where Craufurd was selling off some of his lands. But, on evidence supplied by Gilbert Burns, 'Before William Burnes had made much progress in preparing his nursery, he was withdrawn from that undertaking by Mr Fergusson, who purchased the estate of Doonholm, in the immediate neighbourhood, and engaged him as his gardener and overseer'. In 1756 William Burnes met Agnes Broun at Maybole fair, set about building a cottage on his Alloway holding, and married her on 15 December 1757. He was aged 38, she was 27. Robert was born on 25 January 1759, followed by Gilbert in 1760, Agnes in 1762, and Annabella in 1764. Mrs Burns kept a dairy while raising the family; William Burnes was fully employed at Doonholm in his capacity as overseer. It is clear he was not, as sometimes supposed, a menial labourer, but a skilled worker of the type much in demand for laying out of parks and gardens, planting of avenues of trees, construction of roads, replanning of farms. In 1765, on behalf of a group of parents, he selected John Murdoch as a teacher for their children, for there had been no school at Alloway since William Campbell gave up teaching at Alloway Mill to become superintendent of Ayr Poors House. In February 1767, because cattle were straying from Elias Cathcart's fields into the unenclosed churchyard of Alloway, William Burnes in association with William Reid in Doonside mill and John Tennant, blacksmith, obtained from Ayr town council permission to build a stone dyke at their own expense. He had moved to Mount Oliphant farm in 1766 as tenant of Dr Fergusson, a 'generous master' who lent £100 to stock the farm. In May 1768 when the council proposed a census of residents, those from the barony of Alloway nominated to collect the information were William Reid in Doonside mill and 'William Burns in High Corton' – as the farm was then called. At Mount Oliphant there were additions to the family with William in 1767, John in 1769, and Isabella in 1771.

Rozelle House, built in 1770, was after two centuries in Hamilton hands gifted to the burgh of Ayr in 1966.

Robert and Gilbert continued to attend Murdoch's school at Alloway till 1768 when their teacher went off to Dumfries; thereafter it was possible for them to take some lessons at Dalrymple in the summer of 1772; and Robert would attend Ayr burgh school for three weeks in 1772 under Murdoch who had returned there as English master; followed in the summer of 1775 by a surveying course at Kirkoswald. But after Provost Fergusson's death in 1775, as Robert recalled, 'we fell into the hands of a factor ... and, to weather these two years, we retrenched our expenses'. In 1777 the Burnes family moved from Ayr parish to Tarbolton. There William Burnes leased the farm of Lochlea from David McClure of Shawwood who was enthusiastically making improvements, and because of the expenses of renovation, the terms of let were necessarily vague. McClure and Burnes were initially on very friendly terms, and Robert remembered that

'For four years we lived comfortably here'. But when McClure found himself in financial difficulties, in 1781 he began to press William Burnes, who from 1782 was in failing health. McClure's claims were not sustained by litigation, but all the resources of the Burns family were swallowed up by the time of William Burnes's death in February 1784. This account of William Burnes's career disproves the occasional unwarranted assumptions that he was merely a common labourer lacking ability to make a success as a farmer. William Burnes was a skilled, competent, and respected man who was perhaps over-ambitious, but whose ultimate failure was because those upon whom he was dependent found themselves in financial difficulties.

There are misconceptions about his social as well as his economic circumstances. He is commonly but

Burns Cottage was erected in 1756 by William Burnes who feued the ground from Dr Alexander Campbell of Belleisle.

mistakenly viewed as a solitary incomer from the east of Scotland, marrying a lass from Carrick, and setting up home at Alloway among strangers, a lonely life which became lonelier still when they moved to Mount Oliphant. But though William Burnes left behind relations in Stonehaven and Montrose, linked only by letters, brother Robert and his family in Stewarton were near enough to exchange visits. There was much coming and going with the Brouns from Kirkoswald. The relations of Mrs Burnes included Andrew McCulloch, who kept a tea shop in Ayr and whom Gilbert later admitted 'made a little money in the contraband trade'. One of McCulloch's smuggling associates was a James Young, quite possibly the person of that name who was a witness at the baptism of Robert Burns on 26 January 1759. The other signatory was John Tennant, either the blacksmith at Alloway or his nephew. The latter, John Tennant (1725–1810) who would become factor to the Ochiltree estate as already noted, was born at Bridgend Mains on Doonside estate, set up farming on his own behalf at Laigh Corton, where he took in his widowed mother, brothers and sisters, and had as neighbours from 1766 the Burnes family in Mount Oliphant. The young brother David Tennant (1734–1823) in 1755

became English teacher in Ayr burgh school: it was he who in 1765 advised William Burnes to appoint John Murdoch as teacher in Alloway. William Burnes was also on close terms with Alexander Paterson, rector of Ayr burgh school, possibly because they both came from the north east. Even after Paterson's death in 1768, Mr and Mrs Burnes were welcomed by the widow into her home after Sunday church service, and continued to borrow books from her husband's library. In 1772 when David Tennant succeeded to the mastership of the burgh school, John Murdoch returned from Dumfries to become English teacher. John Tennant in 1769 left Laigh Corton to become factor of the Countess of Glencairn's Ochiltree estate and moved to Glenconner, but friendship was maintained with 'Guid Auld Glen'. He had sixteen of a family from two of his three marriages, and the fourth son John remembered Robert Burns attending Ayr burgh school with him in 1773. Among acquaintances young Robert Burns then made were George Charles, later surgeon and provost. Others would emigrate, like some of his McCulloch cousins, and William McClure, son of the laird of Shawwood who was also attending the burgh school at this time. Gilbert Burns recalled that his brother was already 'considered as a sort of prodigy' at the burgh school.

Ayr Poorshouse was located in Mill Street from 1756 till 1860.

The master, David Tennant, had married Catherine Dalrymple in 1762. This made him a brother-in-law of Rev. William Dalrymple, an uncle of Robert Aiken, and also uncle of James Dalrymple who would soon succeed to Orangefield. Robert Aiken would be legal adviser both to William Burnes at Lochlea and Robert Burns at Mossgiel, and the 'first poetic patron' of the Kilmarnock edition. Dalrymple and his brother-in-law the Earl of Glencairn would make possible the success of the subsequent Edinburgh Edition. Robert Burns later recalled how in Ayr he 'formed several connections' and emphasised that 'My vicinity to Ayr was of some advantage to me'.

While it has been possible thus to examine one family from Alloway with a rural background, for the majority of 'honest men' who lived in the town and were neither merchants nor professional people there is no comparable evidence of their circumstances. One small group can however be dealt with, the very poorest who were confined to the poorshouse.

Ayr Poorshouse was managed by a Board of thirty three Directors with members from the town council and kirk session, and smaller numbers representing the Merchants, the Trades, the Sailors, and the lawyers of the Writers Society. A committee of five met weekly to superintend the Master William Campbell who was responsible for discipline, worship, and schooling and a woman employed (designated as the Mistress) who did the cleaning and cooking. The Poorshouse, in Mill Street, was opened in November 1756 and admitted 24 paupers. There were 7 men and 2 boys sharing five beds, and 13 women and 2 girls in another eight beds. Accommodation was increased to sixty, and indeed by 1781 there were 65 inmates. The number of old folk had not noticeably increased, but many more children were being catered for. To begin with they were apprenticed to local traders, but in 1786 there was a new departure when ten children were indentured for four years at the Rothesay Cotton Works. These included orphans already in the poorshouse: John Wood; John Galloway, a sailor's son; Gavin and Robert Strawthorns, 'sons of the deceased John Strawthorns, late in Dutchmiln'; another three orphans including one from Maybole; also the son of an impoverished barber and the son and daughter of the farmer in Sessionfield. The older women in the Poorshouse were employed in spinning, sewing, and assisting the Mistress in cleaning and cooking; the men picked oakum and may have done some shoemaking. It cost just under one shilling (5p) per day to feed each inmate. The menu was specified in 1756. For breakfast daily and for supper each evening except Sunday there was porridge with ale or milk. For the midday dinner meal there was on Monday and Thursday herring and potatoes or salmon and bread; on Tuesday and Saturday there was broth with bread and cheese or butter; on Wednesday there was broth, bread, and meat – the same as for Sunday supper; on Sunday between the church services the dinner was bread with ale or milk. Purchases were made in bulk. Thus (on occasions during 1757 and 1758) were bought 2 carcasses of beef (at 2/6 per stone), 10 sheep (at 2/4 each carcass), 30 pecks of meal (at 11/– per peck), 25 stones of cheese (at 3/– per stone), and 1,800 herrings (at 18d per hundred). Salmon was purchased so long as it remained cheaper than ¾d per pound. Expenditure proved greater than contributions from the bodies represented on the Board, and levy of a poors rate was notoriously difficult to collect, so that economies had to be made. Thus in 1784 the menu was modified, with meat only once a week, herring the only fish, and helpings of some items reduced.

Porridge was restricted to a mutchkin with 1 gill of ale or milk; bread was reduced from 4 ounces to 3; cheese from 4 ounces to 2; butter from 2 ounces to 1; meat from 3 ounces to 2. The boys and girls got full helpings for breakfast and supper, but only half at dinner-time. Monotony for the old folk was lessened by supplies of tobacco and snuff. Rev Dr McGill reported (in 1791) that 'many of the poor chuse rather to receive a small weekly allotment'. There is a list (for 1777) of forty three such out-pensioners, most allowed around one shilling per week either in cash or partly in oatmeal. Dr McGill concluded that 'Our poor are, upon the whole, well provided for'. In St Quivox the poors allowance was only 2/– per month. As a result, he continued, 'the poor of neighbouring parishes ... flock in upon us from every side, but do not complain of want, till they have made there a three year residence in the place, after which they are reckoned its own proper poor'. He also noted that Ayr gaol had during 1790 to cope with 40 vagrants in addition to 70 debtors and 73 criminals. He indicated a further problem. 'We are likewise oppressed with unfortunate women, who bring forth numbers of illegitimate children, whom they cannot find fathers to own, (these being generally sailors or soldiers, previously gone away to distant places,) and who must therefore be either maintained by the public, or suffered to starve'.

The Church found it impossible to exercise effective discipline over a parish which by 1791 contained 4,647 inhabitants, fewer than half of whom were natives. Some indeed were 'strangers and not of this communion'. In 1743 an episcopalian congregation was formed; their first resident clergyman left to support the Jacobite rebellion in 1745; thereafter episcopalian clergy were under suspicion, but a small congregation met in various buildings, served by an intermittent ministry. In 1765 a Moravian missionary arrived in Ayr from Ireland, sympathisers formed a Moravian Society, a meeting house was built in Mill Street in 1780, and this became a firmly-established congregation whose preachers enjoyed cordial relations with other churches. In 1785 Methodism was introduced by an English soldier who was a lay preacher, and the following year a meeting place in Carrick Vennel was acquired and a minister appointed. These new congregations were associated with incomers. Elsewhere in Scotland seceders were leaving the established church to set up separate congregation. There was a small group of such seceders in Ayr in 1755 but no church was formed for 'it was difficult for them to obtain a piece of ground'. After 1770 such of them as were Anti-burgher seceders could worship in

In the 18th century new congregations were formed outwith the Established Church. The Moravian Union had a place of worship in Mill Street from 1768 till 1916.

St Quivox in a church with their own minister, attached to the General Associate Synod. That first church was built at the top of King Street beside their Wallacetown cemetery which was long afterwards known as the Seceders' Graveyard. In 1779 they moved to a new church in George Street. Nearby in 1799 the rival Burgher seceders of the Associate Synod built a church in Wallace Street. But none of the new congregations north or south of the river was large. There were few dissenters in 18th century Ayr. However, the church historian Wodrow noted with disapproval that in 1729 there was in Ayr a group of seven or eight men 'who deserve little better name than that of atheists', one of them being James Dalrymple, clerk, described as 'a drunken, loose man'.

The secessions in the 18th century Church of Scotland were occasioned by objections to the Patronage Act of 1712 by which congregations lost their powers in choosing a minister, and by objections to new Moderate views which some ministers in their sermons preferred to the traditional Calvinist theology. In Ayr several circumstances contributed to the weakness of dissent. First, because of the longevity of certain ministers, the only presentations of new ministers were five between 1746 and 1761 and none after that when disturbances took place in other parishes. Also, the parishioners and kirk session of Ayr claimed some continuing share in the choice of minister, for the town council was the patron selecting the minister of the second charge; and when there was a vacancy in the first charge the crown simply promoted the minister of the second charge. The first minister of

the new parish of Newton-upon-Ayr was appointed in 1778 by delegates representating the congregation and the community. In St Quivox, where the laird of Auchincruive presented the minister, William McQuhae was ordained in 1764 and served till 1823. There were thus few occasions for objection to unpopular presentations; and few locally seemed to be critical of the ministers thus appointed, for Ayr was fortunate in the calibre of its clergy.

Rev John Hunter who was born in Liberton and studied in Edinburgh had apparently no connection with the Hunters of Ayr. He was ordained to the second charge in 1696, translated to the first charge in 1701, and died as Father of the Church in 1756 after his 60 years of ministry in Ayr. He wrote *A New Method of Teaching the Latin Tongue*, published in 1711, with rules in rhyme; and he was also acquainted with French and Italian. According to his grandson George Dunlop he was 'most earnest' in pastoral duties, while his sermons were 'eloquent' and delivered 'with much animation'. He was amazingly far ahead of his times in one respect. He was 'enthusiastically fond of Music. The Organ was his favourite instrument, one of which, of considerable power, he kept for practice in his own house, by himself or some of his family. He incurred the displeasure of some of his more austere brethren by a wish he expressed of having this instrument introduced into the church service'.

Rev. William Dalrymple, who served in Ayr for 68 years, was a son of John Dalrymple, Sheriff Clerk of Ayr, and married his cousin Susannah Hunter. A graduate of Glasgow, he was ordained to Ayr second charge in 1746 and succeeded his uncle and father-in-law as minister of the first charge in 1756. He wrote several minor publications, was awarded a doctorate by St Andrews in 1779, served as Moderator of the General Assembly in 1781, and died in 1814 at the age of 91. C.D.Gairdner, a grand-nephew, remembered that 'his sermons and services gave great satisfaction to his people' and 'he had the mildness and simplicity of a child', thus confirming Burns' description of 'Dalrymple mild'. Gairdner told an appropriate anecdote of Dalrymple returning home from afternoon service one Sunday and when he took off his gown he was seen to be without a shirt. Mrs Dalrymple was puzzled. 'Dear me, you surely had a sark on in the morning. What in the world is become of it?' The minister explained that in the mid-day interval between services he had visited the home of a dying parishioner. 'Weel, the truth is that I found the poor man was gone and his family in such grief and poverty I gave them my shirt to dress the corpse'.

Rev William McGill, son of a Wigtonshire farmer, graduated at Glasgow and was assistant in Kilwinning before coming to Ayr. After Dalrymple had been translated from the second charge, there had been two unusually brief ministries, to be followed by the long occupancy by McGill of 47 years from 1760 till he died in 1807 aged 84. Gairdner thought McGill was abler than Dalrymple, and indeed various publications won him a doctorate from Glasgow in 1785. A year later his *Practical Essay on the Death of Jesus Christ* was followed by a charge of heresy. That book and a reply in 1788 to Rev William Pebbles of Newton-upon-Ayr were said to 'contain doctrines contrary to the word of God, the Confession of Faith, and his ordination vows'. The issue was debated by Presbytery, Synod, and General Assembly over three years. The case for the defence of McGill was made in the General Assembly of 1791 by a young lawyer, Thomas Muir of Huntershill, who would soon himself be sentenced to transportation for advanced views on political reform. McGill was exonerated in 1791, having been supported throughout by his colleague Dr Dalrymple, the entire kirk session, and by the town council. McGill was 'universally beloved by his people on account of his piety and dutiful attention to the parish'. Gairdner recalled 'his affectionate interest in the young people connected with his church' and his monthly Wednesday meetings where he 'led us, in spite of ourselves, to listen to his addresses'. His racy conversation and witty repartee made him 'attractive to every grade of society', whether visiting Lady Crawford at Rozelle

or playing his daily round of golf in all weathers (excepting only those weekdays when there were services in connection with the Sacrament).

The ministers of Ayr were quite wealthy men. Rev. Patrick Liston had subscribed to the Darien company and Rev. William McGill would be a shareholder in the Ayr Bank. Dr Dalrymple as minister of the first charge had a stipend from the teinds, based on grain prices, valued at £130 in 1790; plus Alloway glebe; and twelve guineas in lieu of a manse. Dr McGill in the second charge had a stipend derived from mill rents, with a supplement from the council, amounting in all to £112, with twelve guineas extra too. The stipend of Rev. William McQuhae in St Quivox was raised in 1787 to £120; that of Rev William Peebles in Newton-upon-Ayr was only £75, raised to £75, supplemented by a glebe valued at five guineas, and a manse. In 'The Kirk's Alarm' Robert Burns gently chided 'Poet Willie' of Newton for his verses critical of McGill, whom Burns applauded (along with Dalrymple, John Ballantine, and Robert Aiken). In 'The Twa Herds' we find McGill and Dalrymple castigated along with the minister of St Quivox – 'that curst rascal ca'd Mcquhey'. But it has to be remembered that the poet is here affecting that Auld Licht Calvinistic view from Kilmarnock which in 'The Ordination' could refer to the county town as 'the wicked town of Ayr'.

The kirk session could certainly no longer exercise effective discipline over the enlarged population of the parish of Ayr. Before the Sacraments in February or March and August the elders perambulated the quarters into which the town was divided and distributed communion tokens to those free from censure, but there were many 'strangers'. There were services on Friday and Saturday before, and on Monday after, as well as the sacramental Sunday, and twelve elders officiated. They had in their number magistrates and burgesses, and a list of new elders proposed in 1781 included a merchant, baker, tailor, weaver, miller, and farmer – which may be typical. At meetings of the kirk session (held in the merchants' loft within the kirk) routine business included matters of discipline. The most commonly-reported offence was that of ante-nuptial fornication, as proven by 'a child in uncleanness'. It was sometimes still feasible to require three appearances in church for public rebuke. But often the session was content to accept a guinea for the poor and administer a private sessional rebuke. The reduced power of the session can be gauged by their failure to deal with sabbath breaking. In 1753 there was a complaint that persons from Townhead were among those 'guilty of most profane abuse of the Lord's Day by going to the

Troon ... for carrying away of run spirits'. Note that the offence is not smuggling, but practising it upon Sunday. In 1759 the colliers at Holmston were accused of being 'exceedingly disorderly in their behaviour, especially on the Lord's Day'. In 1781 there was more widespread misbehaviour with 'children on Sabbath diverting themselves upon the Quay, the Bridge, and the Banks of the Miln Dam with not a few of the old people giving the countenance of their example and some of the young swimming in the sea and elsewhere both in time of divine service and afterwards'. Clearly the theocratic society of the 17th century had been superseded by one of increased secularism.

Ayr burgh school had been under the secular control of the town council since the 16th century. The kirk session expected to be consulted in the appointment of those masters who would serve also as session clerk and precentor in the church; the presbytery of Ayr exercised inspection of schools. But the limited influence of the church can be illustrated. Rev John Hunter was unsuccessful in having his *New Method of Teaching the Latin Tongue* introduced into the burgh school; despite persistent efforts from 1714 till 1732, when in obvious exasperation it was described as 'greatly defective and in many things erroneous' by Mr James Fergusson, the aged master, and young John Mair, his assistant, also decided 'it will never answer the designed end'.

Through the 18th century successive councils continued a policy of extending educational provision. The two-roomed school on the green beside the citadel was extended in 1721 and 1747, augmented in 1773 by a schoolhouse in the High Street, and replaced by a new academy building in 1800. At the beginning of the 18th century the master of the grammar school and the doctor who was his assistant shared two rooms with the master of the sang school. In 1721 an additional room was added to be the Mathematical School where the doctor could specialise for 'the mathematical part of learning is a principal part of a gentleman's education'. Already one master of the sang school who was responsible for reading and writing had added arithmetic in 1673 and a successor introduced book-keeping in 1716. In the grammar school Latin was the principal subject, and there is mention of Greek in 1727. When John Fergusson retired in 1746 after fifty years as doctor, then master in the grammar school, the council took this opportunity to make some major alterations. John Mair, a graduate of St Andrews, had been doctor since 1727 and added geography and navigation to the mathematical curriculum. The council now accepted

Of those who left Ayr, William Maclure was one who won fortune and fame overseas.

his proposals to convert the burgh school into what he called 'a sort of academy'. He himself, with the new title of rector, taught arithmetic, book-keeping, geography, navigation, surveying, geometry, algebra, some natural philosophy, as well as the top class in Latin. A second master (the old title of doctor was dropped) would be responsible for five junior classes in Latin and for Greek. The English master (as the master of the sang school would now be known) taught reading, using 'the new method'. The Writing Master (a new post) would provide elementary instruction in reading, writing, vulgar arithmetic, and music. The two-roomed grammar school and the mathematical school were joined by a newly-built English school to provide four classrooms. It required careful time-tabling to fit in the various subjects, in a school day from 7 a.m. to 5 p.m., with pupils attending for their own subjects only, with French and astronomy available in the evenings after 1761. John Mair was obviously a most competent and enthusiastic innovator, able to offer as wide a range of subjects as was available anywhere in Scotland. His *Introduction to Latin Syntax* went through many editions; at Ayr he pioneered the teaching of science; and modern accountancy owes much to a textbook on book-keeping by Mair. He left in 1761 to take charge of the new Perth Academy, the first Scottish school to be so designated, introducing the educational ideas he had already tested in his 'sort of academy' at Ayr.

Mair's departure was followed by a generation

of setbacks. Alexander Paterson retained the title of rector with the power of 'Inspection of the School' but after his death in 1768 his successor was appointed only as master of the grammar school with no authority over the other departments. Thus David Tennant, virtually self-taught, and English master since 1755, though promoted in 1772 to become master of the grammar school, was simply the teacher in charge of classics. The other masters, competing against one another to secure pupils, tended to neglect their specialist subjects, and the advanced mathematical and scientific studies initiated by Mair languished. In 1773, to extend facilities, a second English master was appointed to take charge of a new school erected behind the Wallace Tower; but the master in 1775 found this inconvenient and took his pupils down High Street to be taught in his own house at the Fish Cross. John Murdoch, the other English master, was perhaps annoyed at the competition, and when 'overtaken in liquor' he called Rev William Dalrymple 'a Lyar or a damned lyar', which earned his dismissal in 1776. George Douglas who had studied at Edinburgh University and was the author of a book on *The Elements of Euclid* was appointed Mathematics master in 1768, but he was found wanting as a teacher; he was spending too much time in private tutoring, suspended in 1784 for 'want of authority', and dismissed in 1791. A Writing master had to be asked to retire in 1790, and in 1792 the Mathematics master and the two English masters were told to desist from teaching writing, which elementary work they were obviously undertaking to augment their fees. One of the masters in 1787 pointed out that 'the value of every Article of life had of late very much increased' so that what fifty years before had been a 'decent and comfortable appointment' was now quite inadequately recompensed; and the town council agreed to an increase in 'school wages' as the fees paid by parents were called. In 1790 the Classics master with a salary of £20 and 40 pupils at 5/– per quarter had an annual income of £60; the Mathematics master had a similar salary, though possibly less from fees. The two English masters had each £15 plus about 40 pupils at 3/– per quarter, bringing them a total approaching £40 each. The two Writing masters earned still less, one having £10 salary, the other depending entirely on fees. Ministers were clearly much better off than teachers; yet those in Ayr were better paid than many schoolmasters in country parishes. The highest recorded elsewhere in Ayrshire was £50 a year; the national average was £13.

The burgh school was overcrowded; two of its masters were operating in the High Street school rooms at the Wallace Tower and the Fish Cross; the Mathematics master was (in 1787) occupying the room below the Assembly Hall. There were in 1790 three other private 'English schools' where reading and writing were taught, plus the free school for paupers in the Poorshouse. There were special schools for girls: in 1764 the council granted Christian Laidler £3 a year to 'provide herself with a sufficient room' for teaching sewing and embroidery; between 1782 and 1789 the Misses Smith maintained a boarding school for girls which was 'a convenience to the neighbourhood' and received £15 a year from the council as an 'encouragement'. Several persons gave private lessons in French. In Newton-upon-Ayr there was a parish school with up to 50 scholars learning reading, writing, and arithmetic; and also private schools. In St Quivox these subjects were taught by a 'well qualified' parish schoolmaster whose whole income was about £24 plus a house and garden.

Before the end of the century a new beginning was made in Ayr. That became possible after 1791 with an educational bequest of £1,000 from John Fergusson of Doonholm, former Calcutta merchant and grandson of the former master of the grammar school. In 1794 Provost John Ballantine issued Proposals for establishing an academy. This would be 'furnished with teachers of approved ability' and provide 'the most necessary and useful parts of learning' as would be suitable for 'the great bulk of the people in a commercial country'. The pupils would remain 'under the observation of their parents and friends' as compared with those at university who undertake 'tedious and expensive' studies and learn 'speculative and indolent habits'. This echoes John Mair's prophetic vision in 1746 of 'a sort of academy where almost every sort of the more useful kinds of Literature will be taught and the want of College education will in great measure be supplied'. The town council, persuaded by Ballantine, promised £100 a year to supplement the Fergusson bequest, and public subscriptions were invited. Over two hundred persons contributed a total of £7,000: a third of the subscribers came from Ayr itself; another third were county gentry; the others were old boys living elsewhere, many of them in India and Jamaica. Ballantine and other fifty five gentlemen (tempted by the promise of hereditary directorships) donated £50 each. In 1798 a royal charter for the establishment of 'the Academy of Air' was granted on behalf of King George III to John Ballantine, who was elected first chairman of the Board of Directors. It was his drive and enthusiasm which brought to reality the academy as first conceived by John Mair. Already on 1 August 1796 the first session of Ayr Academy had begun in the old burgh school, while new premises were building behind. William Meikleham from Kilmarnock was appointed rector at an attractive £80 per year plus £20 for taking in boarders, plus his share of fees; succeeded in 1799 by Thomas Jackson, another highly-qualified scientist who after nine years would also depart to become a university professor. Some continuity was provided by David Tennant who was kept on as Classical master till he retired in 1811. New men were appointed as masters of Writing, Mathematics, English and French. The two former English masters were not accepted as members of the academy staff, but continued in the High Street premises, now elementary schools under the patronage of the town council, while the fine new Ayr Academy was managed by its Board of Directors.

By the end of the 18th century the community was enjoying a range of other new facilities. The race course was laid out in 1770 and the earliest recorded race on it was on 10 October 1775 for a purse of £50. In 1787 a wooden grandstand or viewhouse was erected on the western side, the weighing room and judges box was on the east, while to the south space was reserved for carriages and tents. In 1791 an Airshire Hunt was formed. There was as yet no organised form of golf, which was played on the laigh sands, as were archery, bowls, and quoits (until the last was prohibited in 1800 as damaging the pastures). Sea bathing was now fashionable, and recommended for its therapeutic effects. Children played handball, whereby (in 1775) 'the slates and windows of the schools are not only damaged, but the children frequently get themselves hurt'. A novel form of entertainment for Ayr was promised when in 1789 George Stephens Sutherland, manager of 'a Company of Comedians' sought ground for a Playhouse, but in fact he set up his theatre in Dumfries. In 1796 a 'Party of Players' performed in the Wallace Tower schoolhouse.

New organisations were being formed to join the long-established ones of the merchants and trades. The Merchant Guild, formed in 1325, since 1655 operated a Merchants' Company which maintained their gallery in the church and provided occasional gratuities to members in distress. The nine Incorporated Trades were now principally benevolent societies as the Sailors' Society had always necessarily been since its inception in 1581. In 1710 the local lawyers were formed into a Writers' Society with the initial title of the Fraternity of Procurators in Ayr. In 1773 its

fifteen members initiated a scheme of annuities for their widows and children, their funds from 1784 till 1806 invested in salmon fishing rights on the River Ayr. Several lodges of freemasons were now formed. The Mother Lodge Kilwinning chartered in 1765 Squaremen's Ayr Kilwinning, and in 1771 St James Kilwinning in Newton-upon-Ayr; the Grand Lodge of Scotland chartered in 1776 Ayr Operative, in 1786 Ayr Royal Arch, and in 1799 Ayr St Paul.

In 1762 there was established an 'Air Library Society' for the benefit of those 'anxious to obtain access to books, the source of all knowledge and true pleasure'. Its founding members included three ministers – Dalrymple, McGill, and Shaw of Coylton; John Murdoch and Robert Millar, writers; James Hunter, banker; Patrick Douglas, surgeon; David McClure, merchant; James Gregg, land surveyor and dancing master; David Tennant, schoolmaster, who would be librarian till 1786; and possibly some others such as Dr John Campbell. The Society numbered 47 in 1777 (when records begin) and thirty years later reached a peak membership of just over a hundred. As well as merchants and professional people of the town, some neighbouring lairds joined (like John Loudon McAdam of Sauchrie) and at one point five ladies. A high entry fee kept the society select, enabled two dozen books to be purchased some years, and the library had 700 titles by 1804. These included the *Encyclopedia Britannica*, the *Scots Magazine*, Sinclair's *Statistical Account*, and a range of books including travel, history, some literature, selected items of theology, a good deal of philosophy, and miscellaneous works on subjects ranging from natural history to sea bathing. The Ayr Library was supplied for a time by William Creech, the Edinburgh bookseller, and the members who attended the twice-yearly meetings in Mrs Limond's tavern were obviously well-informed. In 1776 were published three books which have become famous – Lord Kames, *The Gentleman Farmer*; Adam Smith's *The Wealth of Nations*; and the first volume of Gibbon's *Decline and Fall of the Roman Empire*: all three were purchased by the Ayr Library Society in the year of publication. New ideas were reaching Ayr, and that they were diffused beyond the narrow membership of the Library Society is suggested by two examples. David Tennant the librarian was a close friend of the Burnes family and it seems likely that through him Robert Burns had access to some of the many books he knew. He was sufficiently impressed with the value of libraries as himself to organise one later at Mauchline and another at Dunscore in Dumfriesshire. The Ayr Library had eventually an even wider influence. David

McClure, one of the founder members, had a son William who must have had access to the library books at home and possibly in the burgh school where they were stored. William Maclure was a pupil in the classes of George Douglas when Burns more briefly attended as a pupil of John Murdoch. Leaving Ayr for the United States, Maclure made a fortune before he was forty years of age and devoted the rest of his life to scientific and educational pursuits. Surveys he made in America and Europe earned him the title of 'father of American geology'. He played a prominent part in establishing the American Philosophical Society, the Philadelphia Academy of Natural Sciences, and organising with Robert Owen the utopian socialist community of New Harmony. When he died in Mexico in 1840, aged 76 and a bachelor, he left most of his fortune for the foundation of libraries in Indiana and Illinois. Many like him had had to leave Ayr in their youth. In 1774 the council noted 'a Spirit of Emigration ... had Seized the People'. Robert Burns recalled, 'Parting with these young friends and benefactors, as they occasionally went off for the East or West Indies, was often to me a sore affliction'.

Part Three
The Nineteenth Century

ELEVEN

Old into New

The *Air Advertiser*, which commenced publication in 1803, had much to report in its first decades. The naval victory of Trafalgar (1805), then the final defeat of Napoleon at Waterloo (1815), followed by post-war problems and demands for political reform. George III (1760–1820) was after 1810 known to be unfit to rule; the son who acted as Prince Regent and succeeded as George IV was noted as an extravagant rake; the accession in 1830 of his brother as William IV was widely welcomed. During these eventful decades of war and peace at the beginning of the 19th century the character of auld Ayr was quite changed.

It was remarked (in the *Advertiser*, 3.4.1828, 11.11.1828) that Ayr 'has been asleep' and any advances had been trivial till twenty or thirty years previously; since when 'the town has extended itself greatly'. Rev. Alexander Cuthill in 1837 made the same point in the *New Statistical Account*: 'Few places have undergone a greater change for the better than this town has done, within the last twenty years. During that time, it has made greater advances in architectural and other improvements, than it had done perhaps during a century before'.

At the first official Census in 1801 the population of the parish of Ayr was 5,492, Newton was 1,724, St Quivox was 2,070. The combined population of 9,286 increased at succeeding decennial censuses to 12,805, 16,874, and 16,915 in 1831. Even so, these figures failed to match the continued growth of Kilmarnock, though Ayr's old rival royal burgh of Irvine was being left far behind. We can guess that the population of the built-up area north and south of the river increased from 8,000 inhabitants (in 1801) to nearly 15,000 (in 1831). Newton's parish population more than doubled, reaching 4,020 (133%); as did St Quivox, rising to 5,289 (155%). Ayr parish showed a more modest increase to 7,606 (38%), with numbers within the royal burgh rising from from about 5,000 to 6,500.

It was already an accepted fact that Ayr comprised more than the royal burgh. The Armstrong Map of 1775 included the 'New Town' north of the river in its 'Plan of Ayr.' In 1791 Rev William Peebles referred to 'the capital of Ayrshire' as containing his own parish of Newton. Though John Wood in his map of 1818 chose as a title, 'Plan of the Towns and part of the Parishes ...' the three constituent units were regarded as parts of one greater community. William McCarter's first local directory in 1830 covered 'Ayr, Newton, and Wallacetown', as did several voluntary organisations set up in the first decades of the 19th century.

It was north of the river that there was most building of new houses. This was especially true of Newton. Wood's Plan showed new building west of Main Street, on the Back Riggs and beside the Green. In 1828 the lands were after 57 years reallocated to the forty eight freemen, and the new arrangement to apply (with dubious legality) for 999 years facilitated further building. The minister of Newton, Rev. James Stevenson, had to admit in 1837 that 'few of the houses in it can be said to be elegant'. Most were erected to house the growing numbers of industrial workers. Further out along the Prestwick road by 1837 (it was left to the Ayr ministers to report) 'the eye is gratified with small well-cultivated inclosures, neat cotages and gardens, and handsome villas with ornamental avenues and shrubberies'. East of Newton in St Quivox parish, Wallacetown was extending, with a network of new streets beyond George Street. Wood's Plan of 1818 showed alongside these a proposed street obviously designed for superior building, extending upriver from the Auld Brig as far as the Physic Well; and beyond that Content House was already built. But in fact by 1837 housing of low quality became uniform, for 'The inhabitants of Wallacetown and Content belong chiefly to the poor class of Irish settlers'.

South of the river, Wood's Plan outlined developments of a different character.

Ayr town council had in the 18th century begun

Air Advertiser, or, West Country Journal.

THURSDAY, NOVEMBER 14, 1805.

LONDON.

WEDNESDAY, Nov. 6.

TOTAL DEFEAT

OF THE

COMBINED FLEET.

Death of Lord Nelson!!

LONDON GAZETTE EXTRAORDINARY

The *Ayr Advertiser* founded in 1803 departed from custom by printing on its front page news of the Battle of Trafalgar (21 October) just received (14 November).

feuing building plots to form what was called Academy Street (from 1800) until (by 1830) it became Fort Street. Land on the southern edge of the town was in private hands. Dalblair House, erected by James Gibb, grocer and soap manufacturer, and acquired by Provost David Limond, was bounded by the more extensive Barns estate. Lieutenant Colonel Patrick McNeight of the East India Company, who inherited Barns from his father in 1800, began to dispose of land for house building. The northern edge of his property formed the south side of a new street (to be named after Provost William Fullarton). From the Carrick Vennel to 'the high Road leading from the sand gate of Ayr to the new Bridge of Doon' there was laid out what became Barns Street. In 1806 Ex-provost Shaw obtained from the town council a lease of part of the Green, built a residence on what was originally a westward extension of Barns Street, and the town council in 1807 offered feus for 'Houses on the same side as Mr Shaw's house'. In 1808 when a nearby site for proposed County Buildings was granted to the Commissioners of Supply by Ayr town council, plans were made to convert the area facing it into a square. On what would become the eastern side of that square, Hon. Roger Rollo took a feu from Patrick McNeight in 1808, and would be joined there soon by John Ballantine of Castlehill (who died in 1812) and before 1814 by Dr George Charles. The first of the three ex-provosts to reside in this new and fashionable square, Charles Shaw, named his residence Wellington House, presumably following the Peninsular War hero Arthur Wellesley's creation as Duke of Wellington in 1809. Wellington Square took that name after his victory at Waterloo in 1815, was so designated in Wood's map of 1818, and was described in Pigot's Directory of 1820 as having 'very handsome houses ... now nearly finished'. In Barns Street, the lawyer Quintin Johnstone had a house on the south corner before 1808, but there would be no further building on that side till after 1830 – which would then involve the closure of the old road from Carrick Vennel past Barns House. On the north side of Barns Street, a feu was taken in 1814 by Miss Jean Younger, and No.2 Barns Street became part of what has been described as Ayr's first terrace. So many of its houses were occupied by genteel ladies that this became known as Maidens' Row. In 1813, after feuing a plot for a Methodist Chapel, the council helped to lay out what was (before 1815) named Charlotte Street, presumably after Queen Charlotte Sophia (1744–1818) or her grand-daughter Princes Charlotte Augusta (1796–1817). To the south of Wellington Square another square had been planned by Lord Alloway in 1799; and though portrayed in Wood's plan of 1818 and Milliken's copy of 1832, only Alloway Place was actually built.

Meanwhile most of Sandgate and the lower parts of High Street were in process of being rebuilt. In 1822 Peter McTaggart and Son, merchants, obtained council permission to erect columns at the sides of doors and windows of premises at the Fish Cross which was 'a great improvement to that part of the Street, and an Ornament to the House'. Some shops (in 1825) were allowed 'projecting screens' to protect goods from the sun. Cross Street – renamed Newmarket Street when the Buttermarket was eventually established there in 1814 – was lined with new shops and dwellings. Where Newmarket Street reached High Street, premises on the site of the old tolbooth were rebuilt in 1810 by Henry Cowan. It is uncertain whether this was the grocer and spirits dealer known as 'Whisky Henry' or his banker son. In any case he replaced an old effigy of William Wallace with another which was in 1820 disparagingly described as of 'a Pigmy Giant'. In this period, the main thoroughfares were cobbled and provided with open sewers to carry off rainwater. Efforts were made by the town council and the Road Trustees to improve access to the town, in particular by widening Townhead, Alloway Street, and Kyle Street. In 1824 the British Gas Company had from the council a feu of land beyond the Citadel to erect plant and gasometer, so that after 1826 the main streets, some shops, and modern homes had improved illumination. Less successful was Bailie Andrew Williamson, wine merchant, in having implemented his proposals of 1829 for an improved water supply. In 1828 a less expensive improvement was the naming of all streets. One, it would seem, was then named after Provost William Fullarton, the first local dignitary to be so honoured. Houses were also numbered, and appropriate signs painted.

Great pride was taken in the new public buildings. Ayr Academy, opened in 1796 within the old burgh school, moved on the last day of 1799 into the new building erected beside it designed by John Robertson of Glasgow. Further along that street Ayr Library Society in 1804 built a modest house for its librarian and the stock of 700 titles; Ayr New Church was designed by David Hamilton and opened in 1810 with two thousand seats to supplement as many in the Auld Kirk; the Relief Church opposite was built in 1816; a Methodist Church at the head of Charlotte Street in 1813; and the Theatre Royal in 1815. In the vicinity, prominently situated at the end of Wellington Square, there was erected between 1812 and 1822 the County Buildings, comprising Court House, County Hall, with offices, and a gaol added to the rear. The architect was Robert Wallace and the project was a joint undertaking of Ayr town council and the Commissioners of Supply for the county. This was hardly complete when the council planned its own new Town Buildings. The tolbooth in the middle of the Sandgate had been judged unsafe in 1803 but plans to replace it were deferred till 1823 when there were warnings of 'daily danger' from the Steeple's 'insecure and dangerous state'; in 1824 demolition could no longer be safely delayed; in 1826 the materials from the steeple, tolbooth, courthouse, cellar, and two houses attached were sold to John Robb of Blackburn for £100, whose property was thus enclosed with stones some of which had belonged successively to Ardrossan Castle, Ayr Citadel, and the Sandgate Steeple. Demolition of the tolbooth not only removed 'obstructions in the passage to the Bridge' but as the town council also realised 'the Sandgate Street would be materially improved and beautified'. After much argument, the site of the old assembly rooms and adjoining properties at the corner of High Street was selected as the best available, and plans prepared by Thomas Hamilton, the eminent

Edinburgh architect. The foundations were laid in 1828 and the buildings opened in 1830, complete with shops, coffee room, card room, supper room, assembly room, and surmounted by a splendid 225 foot spire. While work was in progress on the Town Buildings, concern was felt at the burgh's other property in High Street. In 1808 the Wallace Tower had been reconstructed, but on old inadequate foundations, so that Thomas Hamilton who was called in advised that 'the old Wallace Tower was in various places fast giving way to the weight of the new'. So he was commissioned to design a replacement, which handsome edifice with 115 foot Gothic tower was completed in 1831; but (as the Commissioners on Municipal Corporations reported) 'either from a deficiency in the specifications at first given, or from faulty work, the building first erected gave way, and it had to be entirely rebuilt.' This expensive reconstruction was completed in 1834. In the new Wallace Tower a niche was left for a statue of William Wallace by James Thom, sponsored by David Auld and provided by public subscription. The charge on the council funds of so much building was substantial, contributing to a debt of over £20,000 incurred between 1792 and 1835. The burgh had to pay £10,000 for the Town Buildings, £6,000 for the New Church, and £2,200 for the Wallace Tower – £1,500 more than had been estimated; plus a share in the £30,000 County Buildings, and contributions towards the £3,000 Academy. In 1814 it was agreed to subscribe, more modestly, ten guineas (£10.50) towards the erection of a Burns Monument – provided it was erected at Alloway. Of the buildings listed in this paragraph, all survive intact save the Academy, rebuilt in 1880; and the gaol replaced by an extension to the County Buildings in 1931. The three churches have been converted to secular purposes; conversely the Theatre Royal after a period as the Queen's Rooms has become the Baptist Church.

The Burns Monument erected on the banks of the Doon was provided by public subscription raised by a committee chaired by Sir Alexander Boswell of Auchinleck, who inspired and directed the project. Succeeding his famous father in 1795 at the age of twenty, he was not only an admirer of Burns but a poet himself, an antiquarian, and printed some rare works on his private press at Auchinleck; also a member of parliament for Plympton Earle, colonel commanding the Ayrshire Yeomanry Cavalry, helping crush the Radical Rising of 1820, rewarded the next year by a baronetcy, and died in 1821, shot in a duel with a political opponent. He thus did not survive for the opening of the Monument on 4 July 1823.

But he organised the first meeting in 1814 and presided at the ceremonial laying of the foundation stone on 25 January 1820. The subscribers ranged from the Prince Regent to the architect Thomas Hamilton of Edinburgh who returned his fee of £20 as a contribution to the fund. The elegant classical monument was set in pleasant grounds, in one corner of which were displayed figures of Tam O' Shanter and Souter Johnny designed by James Thom, the self-taught sculptor. The Auld Brig O' Doon, replaced by a new bridge in 1816, was saved from demolition by Rev Hamilton Paul, editor of the *Advertiser*.

Pigot's Commercial Directory of 1820 and the first local directories published in 1830 and 1832 by William McCarter record a full range of local facilities. Hunter's Bank was situated in High Street, where Ayr's first bank had been located, opposite the Fish Cross. It was managed by William Cowan who in 1816 organised a savings bank, which by 1830 attracted nearly 500 depositors. In 1830 Quintin Kennedy left to found the Ayrshire Banking Company, which built fine new premises in the Sandgate; these were beside Academy Lane where the town clerk's office had been and before that the head office of the ill-fated Douglas and Heron bank. Further along the Sandgate was a branch of the Bank of Scotland. In Newmarket Street a private bank was conducted by Henry Cowan and, on his retiral in 1830, taken over by the Union Bank. How shopping facilities had been extended may be computed from examining the 1820 Directory which lists, for example, 59 grocers in Ayr, Newton, and Wallacetown. In addition to 46 of those who were also spirit dealers, there were three vintners, including Anthony Whiteside who had succeeded to Oliphant's wine cellars in Academy Street. There were 40 taverns, six of them in Newton, and several inns as well. The best-appointed were the King's Arms at the foot of High Street, an old building which William Noble renewed after fire in 1833; over the river James Watling ran the Black Bull in the premises Burns had known as Simpson's Inn; George Dunn's Crown Inn, 129 High Street, was a new establishment – it had a ballroom, unlike the rebuilt King's Arms. There was a coffee room in Harbour Street, which moved into the Town Buildings in 1830, and another (also providing newspapers) off the yard fronting the King's Arms.

There were obviously ample facilities for the various clubs and societies which now flourished in Ayr. There were in 1830 six lodges of freemasons – Ayr Kilwinning 123 (Provost Fullarton, Grand Master). Royal Arch 163, and Ayr and Renfrew

Wood's Plan of 1818 . . .

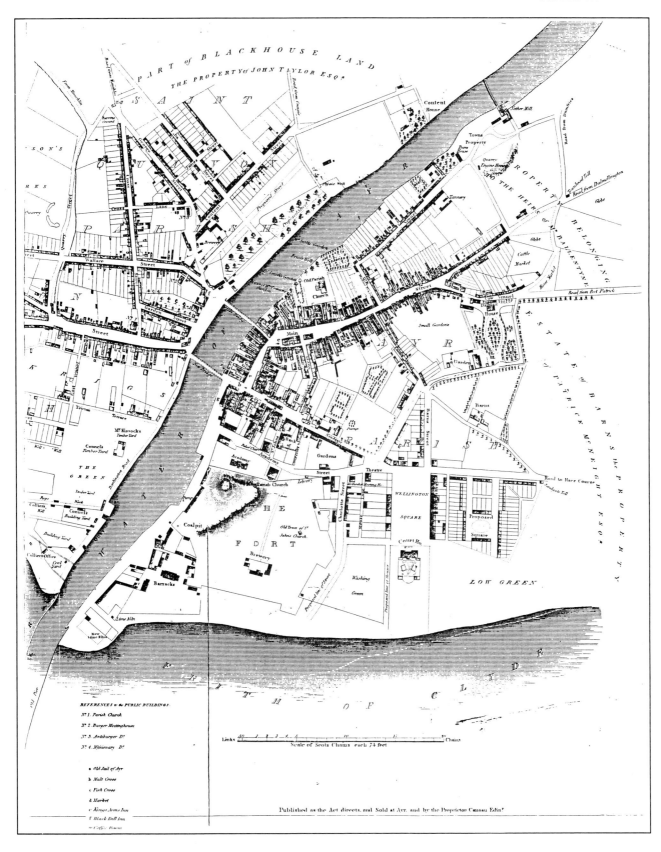

Wellington Square was named after Arthur Wellesley who was created Duke of Wellington in 1809 and won Waterloo in 1815. Construction of the County Buildings was completed in 1822.

St Paul's 203, meeting within the royal burgh; as well as Newton St James's 124, Newton St Andrew 299, and Ayr Operatives 126. There were numerous informal gentlemen's drinking clubs (like those in Edinburgh), and – a novelty – Burns clubs. The first recorded Burns Supper was held in the Cottage at Alloway in the summer of 1801, attended by John Ballantine, Robert Aiken, Patrick Douglas, and others personally acquainted with the Poet. The cottage had been purchased from William Burnes in 1781 by the Incorporation of Shoemakers, who retained it for exactly one hundred years. It was rented as a tavern (the Burns Head Inn) and occupied by James ('Miller') Goudie when that first supper was followed (from 29 January 1802) by annual celebrations of the poet's birthday. As well as this Burns Club, styled 'the original' in the 1830 Directory, other groups organised celebrations in various inns, like the Air Burns Club formed in 1819. Other new organisations were the Ayrshire Horticultural Society formed in 1815 with annual competitions; a Society for the Competition of Flowers, Fruits, and Vegetables, instituted in the 1820s and meeting six times a year in the King's Arms;

and to cater for this widening interest in gardening, a Horticultural library from 1827 in McCarter's shop in New Bridge Street, and Thomas Imrie who from 1820 sold seeds in his High Street shop, and with an extensive nursery at Little Moss between the Cumnock and Dalmellington roads. A different interest was provided by an Ayr Medico Chirurgical Association formed in 1830 and containing most of the town's thirteen medical practitioners. There were the old-established Sailors' Society (1581) and the Merchants' Company (1655), this latter by 1830 'open to all men of business'. These were principally benefit societies as were also the the Incorporated Trades, and the Whipmen's Society formed in 1765 and chartered by the council in 1808, which last paraded on Friday each Midsummer Fair. In 1835 the Commissioner on Municipal Corporations described such organisations as 'decayed and useless'. The Squaremen (51 members), Hammerman (24), Tailors (21), Skinners (3), Coopers (6), Weavers (42), Shoemakers (27), Dyers (4), Fleshers (15) possessed funds ranging from £50 to £1,500. The three skinners had by 'a manifest and ill-disguised manoeuvre' helped themselves to the funds, taking £130 each; copied by the coopers, who had only £40 to share.

Among Ayr's newer facilities was the theatre. In 1802 Mr Beaumont, manager of an itinerant company of players, leased the Wallace Tower schoolroom for a year; by 1809 he had moved into Gibb's old soapworks by Dalblair House. Later companies established themselves in Content Street in Wallacetown, and continued under Henry Erskine Johnston till 1815. In that year Roger Rollo, Collector of Customs, obtained from the council (7 June) on behalf of a committee of gentlemen a feu on which to build a theatre as 'an Ornament to the Town'. This 'small, but handsome' Theatre Royal at Sandgatehead would present celebrities like Mrs Siddons, Edmund Kean, and Paganini, as well as 'Signior Blitz, the prince of conjurers' and other now-forgotten entertainers. But in 1830 there was 'comparatively little encouragement in Ayr even for the first rate stars', and the theatre was used for 'worship, dances, etc.' which were presumably less affected by the 'intolerable' smell of gas. In 1816 a different sort of entertainment was provided by a two-day visit from Polito's menagerie from Exeter, exhibiting a range of animals including elephant, zebra, lion and lioness, hyena, and polar bear. For those seeking literary culture, the Library Society provided its members (a maximum of 105 in 1808) for an entry fee of five guineas (£5.25) and annual subscription of ten shillings (50p) access to 700 titles in more than three thousand volumes, stored in their new premises in Fort Street. The Air, Newton, and Wallacetown Library formed in 1806 was select (with 35 members) but cheap (about 30p annually). The Mechanics Institution founded in 1825 had around 150 members (paying £1.20 per annum) attending its lectures and able to borrow from its library of 2,500 books. There were also specialist libraries catering for members of the horticultural and medical societies, and one connected with Newton parish church. For lighter reading there were circulating libraries belonging to the three local booksellers.

An anonymous *Short Account of the Town of Ayr* published in Edinburgh in 1828 described the town as 'a gay and fashionable place. Its annual Horse Races, patronised by the Nobility and Gentry of Ayrshire, and the neighbouring Counties, under the lately adopted name of the Western Meeting, are accompanied by the usual amusements, and are numerously attended. It is also, at times, one of the places appointed for the meeting of the Caledonian Hunt'. The Western Meeting had actually been instituted in September 1824, with an annual donation of £25 from the town

NEW STEEPLE OF AYR.

Ayr Town Buildings with its splendid spire was completed in 1830, following demolition of the ruinous Sandgate tolbooth.

council. Ayr Gold Cup, the premier award, was provided by subscriptions – as solicited by advertisement on 24 November 1803, in the earliest surviving issue (no.17) of the *Air Advertiser* – and first competed for in 1808. An enlarged Viewhouse grandstand was installed in 1817. For the *New Statistical Account*, Rev. Alexander Cuthill added in 1837 that 'the Caledonian Hunt assembles here every five years. There are two packs of fox hounds and one of harriers kept in the neighbourhood, for the amusement of those who are fond of such sport; and angling and shooting may be easily practised by such as feel inclined.' Though he was obviously not himself a sportsman, he approved of such pastimes as 'enable the inhabitants to pass their hours of relaxation very agreeably, and help to maintain a steady cheerfulness of temperament, a dignified sociability of character, and a pleasant and frank demeanour towards one another'. He might have added an archery club (noted 1823); a quoiting club (formed 1829); a curling club with a membership restricted to fifty, having a pond at the race course in 1831, then one adjoining the Townhead Washing House in 1832. The writer of 1828 noted the Green 'affording to the Inhabitants the most commodious walks and rides, and extensive links or downs for the exercise of the favourite Scotch Game of Golf'. One indoor sport had fluctuating popularity: two billiard rooms 'discontinued, from want of encouragement' in 1830, were reopened by 1832. In 1825 'several Gentlemen' obtained permission to erect a 'Set of Baths', but this was apparently not implemented till 1839 when a feu was obtained in what would be named Bath Place. In 1831 there were bathing machines on the beach.

One of the most significant events of the period was the commencement of the weekly *Air Advertiser* in 1803. In 1790 John Wilson, after seven years in Kilmarnock printing a score of publications of varying merit, decided for reasons unknown to transfer his press to Ayr. He remained in charge of his bookshop in Kilmarnock, while his brother Peter ran the printing shop at 23 High Street, Ayr. The Wilson brothers published around seventy works between 1790 and 1810 – principally religious, literary, and educational books. On Thursday 5 August 1803 appeared the first issue of their *Air Advertiser or West Country Journal*. After a difficult first year, it hoped for 'a growing circulation through every town in the County'. But sales were limited by the expensive sixpence per copy (2½p); there was 'no immmediate prospect of profit', as newspaper tax increased from 1½d to 2½d per copy in 1804 and 4d in 1815. Rev. Hamilton Paul who succeeded Peter Wilson as partner and editor in 1810 continued the initial policy (during the 1812 election) 'that friendly intercourse will never be interrupted by political rivalship'. Only after John Wilson's death in 1821 and complete control passed (following a law suit) into the hands of McCormick and Carnie, Adam Carnie as editor from 1816 till 1833 advocated the popular policies of liberal reform. The *Advertiser* devoted most of its four folio pages to national and international news. There were full accounts of the campaigns against Napoleon until 1815, and parliamentary debates were fully reported, especially those leading up to the Reform Act of 1832. Advertisements appeared on the front page; some letters to the editor were included inside; on part of the back page were news items, usually brief, relating to town and county.

The Wallace Tower was completed in 1834.

A Tory competitor appeared in the *Ayr and Wigtownshire Courier* established in 1818 by Maxwell Dick and Rev. Alexander Cuthill. This failed in 1825, though the *Ayr Observer* which followed in 1832 was more successful. There was a number of short-lived periodicals, commencing with two issues of a *Juvenile and Literary Miscellany* published in 1822 by D.McCarter. Between 1824 and 1828 various publishers followed one another in attempting magazines, usually fortnightly, containing tales (some about Ayrshire), verses, reviews, anecdotes, and brief local notes. These were *Ayr Correspondent*, eleven issues; *Ayrshire Independent and Literary Gleaner*, four issues; *The Ayrshire Magnet*, twenty monthly issues; *The Gaberlunzie*, fourteen issues. The *Advertiser* press

The Burns Monument at Alloway was opened in 1823.

now produced fewer books, but had some notable publications, such as an edition of Burns' *Poems and Songs* with a biography by Hamilton Paul, 1819; and a scholarly edition of James I's *The Kings Quair* with notes by Ebenezer Thomson of the Academy, 1813 and 1815. An innovative publication came from William McCarter in 1830 – *Brief Historical Reminiscences of the County and Town of Ayr ... to which is added ... a Post Office Directory ... by a Burgess*. This was intended especially for 'Travellers and Tourists who, during all seasons of the year have of late visited the Land of Burns'. A revised edition with additional illustrations appeared in 1832.

Among the facilities Ayr had to offer was the Academy in its new building from 1800. 'Its success has surpassed expectation' was the opinion of 1820. The roll grew from 374 scholars in the first session to a maximum of 594 in 1829. A description in 1828 of 'this valuable institution' advertised that 'Here are taught the English, Latin, Greek, Anglo-Saxon, French, Italian, German, and Oriental languages, – writing, arithmetic, drawing, mathematics, navigation, geography, logic, rhetoric, botany, chemistry, and natural philosophy. This Academy has acquired a high degree of celebrity from the abilities of its teachers'.

The first rectors of the academy served briefly before promotion to university professorships; the third had a longer term, but terminated by fraud and bankruptcy. There followed (1826–44) the remarkable Dr John Memes, a 'gentleman of varied and elegant accomplishments' who took over just after his thirty-first birthday and after eighteen years and several disappointments departed to become a parish minister in Hamilton. He was competent in all the subjects just listed (save perhaps one) and was also able to instruct the 'lowest in the first formation of their letters'. His enormous energies were recalled by pupils. 'We have seen him meet his classes at extra hours, so early as six a.m., teach for twelve hours with trifling intervals – sketch large maps for his Geographical classes till eight at night – meet the Library society at that hour – superintend all their arrangements – direct their views – solve their difficulties, and sum up their debate to the admiration of all, and dismiss them between ten and eleven at night. Next morning, at four or five o'clock, he was to be found actively engaged with his Mathematics class, making plans of the Town harbour'. He also conducted evening classes in astronomy, provided gratuitous instruction to the Mechanics Institution, and delivered Sunday evening lectures on Christianity to packed congregations in Wallacetown Chapel. He assisted the Ayr Medico-Chirurgical Association with his knowledge of anatomy; he aided the Sheriff of Ayr by calculating the trajectory of a bullet; he provided surveys for the proposed Glasgow – Ayr railway and for a projected water supply from Brown Carrick Hill. In January 1836 he proposed the Immortal Memory at the Burns Club supper in Alloway; a few days later, after a severe storm when the Town Buildings were struck by lightning, Dr Memes 'quieted public alarm' by climbing the steeple and assessing that the structure was safe. In his spare time he had published books on sculpture, architecture, poetry, biography, and his translation in 1839 of Daguerre's book popularised photography in this country. As rector he had only 'general supervision' and 'little connection with the masters' who were in virtually independent control of their own classes. Several outstanding members con-

The theatre opened in 1815 was acquired by the Baptist Church in 1887.

tributed to the academy's reputation. Classics master (1811–38) was the erudite Ebenezer Thomson, author of an Anglo-Saxon grammar and editor of *The Kings Quhair*. James Ridley (1819–34) was a distinguished teacher of English and elocution. Mathematics was taught by James Gray (1809–46). For an even longer period (1794–1855) Robert Taylor taught writing and drawing, remembered especially by C.D.Gairdner for the fifty lashes from his 'formidable whip' after truanting at the Ayr Races of 1807. From 1797 till 1854 there was a policy of employing foreigners to teach modern languages, notably a refugee French priest, Abbé Francois Nicolas (1802–10), followed by Solomon Gross (1811–38).

Some scholars of this era – local boys and incomers – had distingushed careers. Following in the footsteps of David Cathcart (1763–1829) who became Lord Alloway, two others became judges, – John Cowan (1798–1878) as Lord Cowan, James Crawford (1805–76) as Lord Ardmillan. There were two minor authors – Hew Ainslie (1792–1878) and Andrew Kennedy Hutchison Boyd (1825–99) who wrote as 'AKHB'. There were two men of action – Admiral Sir John Ross (1777–1856), the Arctic explorer; and General James George Smith Neill (1810–57), a hero of the Indian Mutiny, whose statue stands in Wellington Square near his birthplace. One

scientist of minor importance was Dr Thomas Clark (1801–67), whose mother is credited with having invented Ayrshire Needlework, and who himself made some original contributions to medicine and chemistry.

In Ayr Academy there were some separate classes for girls in English, Writing, Arithmetic, and French. More however attended private schools, which ranged in character from several for young ladies to sewing lessons for girls from poorer families. Parents who could not afford the high fees for Academy classes might choose one of the cheaper private schools or Ayr's other parochial school. This branch of the burgh school in a schoolhouse behind Wallace Tower was continued after the Academy was established, moving soon afterwards to the Fish Cross. Additional provision followed Captain John Smith's bequest of £2,000 to found a school for children whose parents could not afford school fees. Smith's Institution opened within the Poorshouse in 1825. Pupils were to be taught only 'to read English, Writing, and what is called the Five common Rules of Arithmetic ... fitted for the common occupations of life'; but assistance should be provided for any with 'uncommon ability and strong inclination for Learning'. Altogether by 1837 there were over a dozen schools within Ayr, plus two in the country parts of the parish, and with over 1,100 scholars, 'there are few other parishes now in Scotland that can boast of a greater proportion'. In Newton, there were in 1837 five schools. Two of these were 'of a very imperfect description; being taught by elderly women in the humbler walks of life'. One of the other private schools was 'for the education of young ladies – and in it English, writing, music, drawing, and fancy-work are taught in moderate terms.' In Newton Parish School John Gemmell, appointed after public examination in 1802, expressed in 56 lines of verse appreciation at a rent allowance of eight guineas to augment his income from scholars' fees; but it needed a lawsuit from 1814 till 1818 and a Court of Session judgment to award him the statutory minimum of a parish schoolmaster. In return for this £16.13.4 per annum plus fees (from 91 scholars in 1837) he taught Latin, French, and mathematics in addition to the basic subjects. There were few children in Newton who could not read or write. Though only 250 children were then enrolled in the five local schools, many more were sent to schools in Ayr or in Wallacetown, both places offering better facilities. In St Quivox, apart from 'some of the Irish settlers, and a few of the younger members of their families', it was claimed that 'the whole of the native population can read'. One can believe that 'In general,

Ayr Academy, opened in 1796, moved into this new building in 1800 – here drawn by Robert Taylor, writing master for sixty one years.

education is sought after' – for in addition to the St Quivox parish school (where the salary was £30 per annum) there were eight unendowed schools. Classes in Latin, mathematics, book-keeping, and geography were available after William Watson established his private Wallacetown Academy in John Street in 1833 or 1834.

In the early decades of the 19th century the established Church continued to lose its ascendancy. The Church of Ayr, dating back to 1654, was too small to cope with the town's increased population. Pews which became available were expensive to purchase, and many preferred in any case to cross the river to worship under the evangelical Rev William Peebles in Newton Parish Church. With the opening in 1810 of Ayr New Church, adequate accommodation became available, with over 2,000 sittings in each. There on alternate Sundays preached Rev Robert Auld (1814–53), successor to the aged Dr Dalrymple in the first charge; and the minister of the second charge, Alexander Cuthill (1814–52). Dr Auld, son of a Mauchline farmer, received a doctorate from St Andrews in 1815; but he is chiefly distinguished by his campaign of litigation from 1814 till 1825 when the House of Lords required the town council to provide him with a manse. Mr Cuthill was author of several books of discourses plus the detailed description of Ayr in the *New Statistical Account*. Neither seems to

have had much impact upon the community. Auld was remembered as 'a meek, gentle person' and his colleague as 'of a bashful, retiring disposition'. That local worthy Rab Hamilton cheekily told Auld that he dreamed of being welcomed into Heaven by St Peter thus: 'Glad to see you, Robin, for there hasna been a soul come here frae the auld town o' Ayr this forty years'. Newton Parish Church, enlarged to accommodate a congregation of just over a thousand, continued to attract communicants from across the river – in 1836 there were 1,794 in Ayr's two parish churches; 251 from Ayr joined 500 others in Newton Parish Church. Those who lived in Wallacetown had for long enough to choose Newton, for St Quivox Parish Church was three miles away and even after renovation in 1820 still held only 500. Not till 1835 was a Wallacetown Chapel provided by public subscription for adherents of the established Church, and this attracted others (obviously dissatisfied with Auld and Cuthill) 'who sought spiritual ministrations in Wallacetown rather than in the two parochial churches of the town of Ayr'.

How far the Established Church had lost its hold is revealed in the *New Statistical Account*. By 1836, within Ayr parish 5,000 persons belonged to the Established Church and 2,400 to other denominations. Relative figures for Newton were 3,000 and 1,000 persons; for St Quivox, 724 families and 422 families. The

Dr John Memes, the remarkable rector of Ayr Academy 1826–1844.

other denominations now claimed in these parishes 32.4%, 25%, and 36.8% of support.

A third of the population were now attached to other denominations. Within the royal burgh the Moravian Church in Mill Street since 1778 was well enough established to open a school in 1816, though its congregation was small, fewer than 200 in 1836. The town council in 1813 agreed to feu a plot in the Green (where Charlotte Street would meet Fort Street) for a Methodist Church, which attracted over 300 adherents by 1836. The council also feued a plot for the erection in 1816 of a Relief Church. This denomination – formed in 1752 'for the relief of Christians ... and their natural right to choose a pastor' – found local adherents after the death in 1814 of Rev Dr Dalrymple. It soon became the largest congregation, having a thousand local members and

as many coming to worship from adjacent parishes. With its Sunday School, library, and Penny Society for sick members, it appealed to many, some of them quite well-off, who were not prepared to join one of the more extreme sects across the river. There in George Street the Antiburghers of the General Associate Synod maintained their separateness, after 1827 within the Original Secession Church. The rival Burghers had since 1799 a church in Wallace Street, attached to the Associate Synod, after 1820 known as the United Secession Church – in 1836 having around 800 adherents as compared with 600 of the rival sect. Also in Wallacetown, these Seceders were joined by a varied range of other religious bodies. In 1805 in River Street a Tabernacle was set up by independent Congregationalists, fewer than a hundred in 1836. A group of Macmillanites, deriving from the Cameronian Covenanters who had never accepted the church settlement of 1689, formed a congregation in an old brewery in Content Street from 1828 and built their Reformed Presbyterian Church in 1832 at the corner of John Street and George Street, attracting over 100 adherents by 1836. There were other two groups, whose origins were regarded as alien. What was described in the 1832 directory as the 'English Chapel' was set up that year in Content Street 'with an English clergyman from Whitsun next'. Adherents of the Scottish Episcopal communion had been meeting irregularly since 1826 in the Barracks hospital, and after seven years in their own little chapel, the congregation now numbering more than 300 (and including some of the county gentry) found in 1838 a more fashionable place of worship, within the royal burgh in Fullarton Street. In 1827 in Wallacetown there was set up in John Street by the Roman Catholic Church what was accepted as 'the handsomest church in Ayr'. From the commencement of the 19th century there had been a massive influx of Irish immigrants. Pastoral work among them was undertaken by Abbé Francis Nicolas, the refugee French priest who taught in Ayr Academy from 1802 till 1812. There was an established mission from 1822, with its priest William Thomson regularly celebrating mass in the Hammermen's hall at Boar's Head Close. By his exertions St Margaret's Church was built and had by 1836 a congregation of a thousand, including 200 from over the river. Mr Thomson (as he was always designated) had to provide for all of the faith within the whole of Ayrshire till 1845, and died in 1859 'worn out with long years of labour'.

Roman Catholic emancipation was authorised by parliament in 1829, and accepted without any local rancour. In 1824 a proposal to build the chapel on the Green had been turned down by Ayr town council on the lame excuse that there was 'no ground eligible for feuing to the extent Mr Thomson specifies'. Nevertheless, the foundation stone of St Margaret's was laid in the presence of the provost, magistrates, and gentlemen of Ayr, including office-bearers of the lodges of freemasons! Sectarian ill-feeling was more obvious between certain of the protestant churches, though there was some cooperation in such organisations as the Ayr Sabbath School Union Society formed in 1821 and the Ayrshire Bible Society reconstituted in 1828. The Established Church still had precedence within the burgh. The magistrates were responsible for maintenance of the parish church (and building a second one), contributing towards the stipends of both ministers, after 1825 providing (grudgingly) a manse for the minister of the first charge, retaining responsibility for appointments to the second charge, and continuing as a royal burgh to be represented at the General Assembly of the Church. But not all councillors were members of that Church, and in 1819 the council agreed to a petition from the seceders that the burgess oath should be abolished. No longer were those enrolling as burgesses required to 'profess and allow within my heart the true Religion which at this present is publickly preached within this Kingdom and authorized by the Laws thereof'.

Despite so many innovations in the century's first decades, there was little industrial development, whose limited extent is revealed in Wood's town plan of 1818. Beyond Townhead there was a tannery in Mill Street; a quarry with engine house between the Poorshouse and the Nether Mill; beyond the Cow Vennel were horse and sheep markets. In the Fort, as well as the long-established brewery there was a coal pit. By the harbour were two lime kilns; and from 1818 till 1832 coal was worked outside the fort wall by the Newton colliery company. The barracks, put up for sale by the crown after the war ended in 1815, failed to attract business interests. Ayr's most important manufacturing premises, at the top of Charlotte Street, is marked on Wood's plan though not named. That cotton mill of 1794 was converted to woollens. It was owned by James Dick and Company in 1804, then by Alexander Gibson and Company who operated also at Doonside and Kilmarnock until the company failed in 1815. Provost Dr Charles then took over this spinning mill, employing orphan children. In 1827 it was acquired by his manager James Templeton, who with his son manufactured blankets, then carpets from 1832. The works were extended and over a hundred hands

JAMIE HENDRY
of the Newton Whipmen.

The Whipmen's Society of Newton organised annual Cadgers Races which ensured the survival for a time of the Kipper Fair.

employed in Fort Street and in a new bleachwork and dye-house built beside the river in Mill Street. A brother, Alexander Templeton, took over the Dutch Mill on the Doon, employing 30 in blanket making.

The Newton side of the harbour showed on Wood's plan two timber yards, Connel's shipbuilding yard, Ayr Rope Work, a lime kiln and saltfield, and the Colliery Office and coal yard at the end of the rail road from the Salt works and Newton colliery beyond. By the time of the *New Statistical Account*, the shipyard was owned by Cowan and Sloan, who had installed a patent slip in 1831. Though never as busy as wartime, when two hundred men were employed, there were

50 men shipbuilding and another 10 ropemaking, and the firm was enjoying a growing reputation for its wooden sailing vessels, building fast clippers for the East India trade – though significantly for Greenock rather than local merchants. Associated trades were developing in Newton Green, including four small foundries working iron and brass. Wallacetown in 1818 had a brewery; a coal pit on Allison's Park with others (not shown) on 'Blackhouse land, the property of John Taylor'. In 1837 there were 'three coal pits constantly worked' and the 'thriving village of Whitelets' is noted.

John Taylor worked the Newton and Blackhouse collieries till his death. Two brothers seem to have shared the inheritance with his eldest son, to whom was bequeathed the Blackhouse estate. William Taylor extended the mining interests in the Irvine area. George Taylor took over the Newton pits: the one on Newton Green as shown on Wood's plan, plus the Annpit at Heathfield, both linked to the harbour by the waggonway constructed in 1807. These pits were worked out in 1832, but there continued the associated salt works where were also manufactured magnesia, epsom and glauber salts, vitriol and marine acid. John Taylor who inherited the Blackhouse estate disposed of it in 1826 on coming of age, his considerable fortune being spent thereafter on radical politics. John Taylor Gordon, who came from Aberdeenshire, a trained advocate and possibly a distant relative, arrived in 1832 and acquired the Newton saltworks and Blackhouse mineral rights. The pits in Newton itself were worked out – the Green Pit by Newton Lodge and the Ann Pit by Heathfield before 1832, and others of uncertain date being the Allison Pit near Russell Street, Newtonhead Pit, Saltfield Pit ('by Hunter's Folly'), Williamfield Pit between Newton Lodge and Bellrock, Prestwick Pit at New Prestwick, Hawkhill Pit. Coal was also worked early in the century on the farms of Sanquhar and Noltmire. John Taylor Gordon constructed what was in 1836 described as a 'railroad from Whitelets to the harbour of Ayr'. It served initially two pits on Sanquhar estate – Crooks Moss by Noltmire, and March Pit behind Braehead farm – and ran westwards via Hawkhill towards what is still called Waggon Road to link up with the earlier Newton waggonway which, with the salt works, had been acquired by Gordon, who lived there at Newton Lodge. In 1836 it was reported that 'One hundred waggon-loads are daily conveyed to the port along a railway, from the coal-mines in the parish of St Quivox'. Hugh Allan later recalled that 'They were drawn by horses, a train consisting of four two or

three ton waggons'. The yearly exportation from Ayr harbour increased from 40,000 tons (1836) to 50,000 tons (1837, 1838) and 70,000 tons (1839) – this not counting what was consumed locally. In addition to Gordon's two pits, St Quivox had in 1836 one other 'constantly worked'. It was possibly that pit (Allison Street) mapped in 1818 and again in 1830. Richard Alexander Oswald, owner of Auchincruive between 1819 and 1842, worked coal intermittently during the 1830s, near the mansion house, on Mainholm farm, and at Holmston.

Domestic manufactures (which obviously could not be indicated on Wood's plan) were of considerable importance, and noted in the *New Statistical Account*. In 1837 Newton had about 400 handloom weavers and perhaps 700 women hand-sewing Ayrshire embroidery. Within the royal burgh there were 250 and 300 in these groups, plus 200 shoemakers. The manufacture of shoes had employed far more during the war; by this date only one firm had a large export business. Members of the Incorporated Trades were almost entirely engaged in supplying the local market.

The council was involved with trade as far as the markets, fairs, and harbour were concerned. In 1827 a committee collected evidence of fairs throughout the south west of Scotland which might clash with those of Ayr, and the council made appropriate alterations to the local dates. These re-allocated the New Years Day Fair (Thursday and Friday before the second Wednesday of January, which was a Glasgow fair); Palm Fair (first Tuesday in April); Midsummer Fair (Thursday and Friday before the second Monday in July which was the Glasgow Fair), and the Michaelmas Fair (second Thursday and Friday in October). At the three principal fairs, Thursday was for woollen goods and Friday for horses. There was also as before a cattle sale on the last Friday in April. Tuesday was the weekly market day. Though the meal market was discontinued, from 1819 sales were conducted by Adam Hutcheson. The cattle market was at the Fauldbacks. The butter and cheese market was held at the foot of High Street near the King's Arms till 1814 when the long-planned move was made to what now became Newmarket Street, with sales there on Tuesdays and Fridays.

Because of the popularity of the fairs and markets in the royal burgh, those of Newton became 'merely nominal'. Wallace Allan remembered a 'Knout Fair' for sale of cattle in River Street. The 'Kipper Fair', on the first Friday after 12 August, survived under new auspices. There were fewer fishermen, and kippered mackerel substituted for kippered salmon. The Fair was perpetuated by the Whipmen's Society of Newton and St Quivox, formed in 1838, which organised annual Cadgers Races on fair day. Hugh Allan quoted from the reminiscences of an older resident: 'From early morn the various stables were busy scenes. The horses were groomed as they never were groomed before, and their forelocks, manes, and tails were decorated with a profusion of flowers and ribbons in every colour. The carters themselves, dressed in holiday attire, with huge light blue Kilmarnock bonnets with huge scarlet 'toories' and long fliers of light blue ribbon, when mounted on their chargers were "prood, prood men that day". The muster generally took place in front of the house of the president of the Carters' Society for the year. Here was unfurled the flag of the Corporation, and borne aloft on poles the saddle, bridle, and spurs, the prizes of the race. To the music of Fifer Jamie and a rattle drum, the cavalcade marched through the streets to the Newton shore, where the race took place when the tide was out. On the return march the procession halted and formed up in front of the houses of the winners of the prizes, and whangs of cheese and bread and whisky were handed round, so that by the close of the day many of the men were exceedingly hilarious'. David Caldwell recalled that the carters crossed the river to visit all the public houses of Ayr; and the day was enlivened by scurrilous bills produced by 'Treacle Doup' Connel the printer.

The Act of 1772 for improving the harbour was renewed in 1794, 1817, and 1835. The harbour trustees – representing the councils of Ayr and Newton plus shipowners and merchants – commissioned surveys by Watt (1771), Smeaton (1772), Rennie (1805), Stevenson (1830), and Gibb (1836). The north pier was extended in 1800 and again in 1830, as was the south pier in 1825, while a breakwater would be added after 1836. Nevertheless, access remained awkward because of the harbour bar, so that it was impossible for ships over 220 tons. In 1803 a life boat station was established, and a ten-oared boat acquired following a grant of £50 from Lloyd's Society. In 1791 Ayr had 18 ships employed in foreign trade, 8 in coastal trade, and 16 fishing vessels. By 1837 the total number of vessels belonging to the port was reduced to 11 in coastal and Irish trade, with seven for fishing. Local merchants, perhaps disconcerted by wartime maritime difficulties, were forsaking overseas trading ventures and were content to serve the local market as shopkeepers. In 1827 Ayr town council was alarmed by a decision to move the Customs House from Ayr to Irvine. After intensive lobbying this was rescinded in 1829 – even

though in a recent year the port's foreign trade had been only nine incoming and six outgoing cargoes. By 1837, the *New Statistical Account* reported that 'About sixteen vessels arrive annually' with imports of timber, hemp, tar, and iron from the Baltic, and 'from twelve to seventeen sail to foreign countries with cargoes of coals, cordage, leather, cotton and woollen goods, &c'. There were about 300 coastal arrivals with general traffic, and about 1,100 departures including what was now Ayr's principal export of from fifty to sixty thousand tons of coal annually, mostly to Ireland. Ayr, was 'long the principal fishing station on the west coast' but with improved facilities elsewhere on the Firth 'many fishers have removed thither from this place', and the Ayr fishing fleet was reduced to seven Newton boats with four men in each, supplying the local market with white fish. Salmon from the Doon and Ayr rivers and the coast as far as the Pow Burn were netted by men employed by the tacksman, who supplied Glasgow, Edinburgh, and even London.

Ayr was benefitting from improved road communications. Over thirty carriers were by 1820 transporting goods to and from Ayr by horse and cart. Such carters were serving Ayrshire – to Kilmarnock (3), Irvine (2), and Saltcoats in Cuninghame; to Troon, Tarbolton, Mauchline, Catrine, Ochiltree, Cumnock (2), and Dalmellington in Kyle; Maybole (2), Straiton, Dailly, and Girvan in Carrick. Others plied further afield to Glasgow (3) and Edinburgh, and into Galloway for Dumfries, Castle Douglas and Kirkcudbright (3), Newton Stewart (2) and Stranraer. Four-horse passenger coaches for Kilmarnock and Glasgow left twice daily from the King's Arms or the Black Bull on alternate months, with the *Telegraph* coach carrying the mail. There were also twice weekly services to Greenock via Irvine, to Portpatrick (for Ireland), and in summer to Newton Stewart. In 1831 the *Marquis of Hastings* coach from the Crown Inn began a direct daily service via Strathaven to Edinburgh. Ayr thus obtained a twice-daily mail delivery from Edinburgh and Glasgow, and for an extra half-penny letters were delivered through Ayr and Newton from the post office, which moved from Newmarket Street (1820) to 7 High Street (1830). By 1836 it was possible 'to go from this to Edinburgh by coach, at five different times each lawful day'. By then too there were regular packet boats from the harbour to Glasgow, Liverpool, and Dublin. Steam packet boats left Ayr daily for Glasgow, touching at intervening harbours, and there was a weekly service to Stranraer for Ireland. The story of these improved coastal communications began in 1822 when the old slow packet boats were superseded by a clipper-built yacht purchased by a consortium of local merchants for a weekly service to Glasgow. This vessel known as *The Ayr of Ayr* was replaced by a steam vessel of the same name, built in 1825 to travel twice weekly to Glasgow. It proved a success – surviving an accidental collision with *The Comet II*, sixty of whose passengers were lost. In 1826, its first year in service, it provided also summer pleasure cruises to Arran, Ailsa Craig, and the Kyles of Bute, with some excursions to Campbeltown, Stranraer, and Belfast. From 1831 there was competition from the *Countess of Glasgow* which offered a twice-weekly service to Glasgow on alternate days, with 'superior speed, comfort and accommodation' and 'an excellent Table with Wines and Liquors of the best description'. By 1834 the *Ben Ledi* advertised day trips down the Clyde to the Western Meeting and the 'Land of Burns'. The *Ayr Advertiser* noticed that by choice of boats 'men of business, too, have it in their power to visit their friends in Greenock and to return home the same evening'.

The various social advances described in this chapter are easily enough recognised in retrospect. Contemporaries, however, can never enjoy the benefit of historical perspective. To those living in the first decades of the 19th century other events to be noted in the following chapter may have assumed greater significance; and for some the Reform Act of 1832 seemed the culmination of a generation of struggle.

TWELVE

The Coming of Reform

Early 19th century Ayr was a deeply divided community. The royal burgh had always had its social divisions, but merchant guild brethren, craft burgesses, and indwellers had formerly all lived together in High Street and Sandgate. Now members of different classes were becoming segregated, and the difference between rich and poor was almost certainly widening. Those improved facilities described in the previous chapter were in many cases enjoyed only by a minority of Ayr's inhabitants. There remained to be solved certain social problems which vexed various sections of the population, and political differences which culminated in parliamentary and municipal reform.

The fashionable part of the royal burgh included the lower part of High Street, Sandgate, and the new residential areas to west and south. Rev. Alexander Cuthill observed in the *New Statistical Account* that 'The society in Ayr, taking it all in all, is as agreeable and well-regulated and as fashionable as can be met with, in any other county town.' He noted that 'among the higher and middle ranks in particular, social intercourse is conducted with urbanity and easy politeness'. The county gentry who frequented the town and patronised the balls, particularly during the Western Meeting, no doubt inspired what Cuthill called 'a natural propensity to press upwards' among the middle class residents. Well-to-do people began to settle in Ayr's new residential district 'to enjoy the agreeable society of the place' and the local climate which 'although variable and moist, is comparatively genial and salubrious'. Some came 'for the sake of education for their children at the Academy'. There were 'gentlemen of independent fortune' and retired army officers in Wellington Square especially; Barns Street was known as Maidens' Row because so many of means lived in this pleasant area. The 1820 Directory listed also 33 lawyers (still called writers), the principal group among the professional people. There were only 16 persons described specifically as 'Merchants and Ship Owners', and these bore little

resemblance to the venturers who once engaged in foreign trade. Most members of Ayr's merchant guild were now shopkeepers, profitably catering for their affluent local customers. Significantly, no one engaged in commerce occupied the provost's chair. John Ballantine was followed by other bankers like George Dunlop (later Collector of Customs), William Cowan, Hugh Cowan, and Quintin Kennedy; Charles Shaw and David Limond were lawyers; David Charles was a physician; William Fullarton of Skeldon was a landowner. Buying and selling had become a less-highly regarded occupation. The local aristocracy were those families who had made their money in trade and set themselves up as landed gentry in the estates fringing Ayr. Such were the Hamiltons of Belleisle and of Rozelle, Cathcarts of Greenfield, Ballantines of Castlehill, Hunters of Doonholm, Robb of Blackburn, Oswald of Auchincruive, Campbell of Craigie, Taylor of Blackhouse. Despite subtle social distinctions, all those noted were, in Cuthill's opinion, 'much given to hospitality and kindly fellowship with one another'. They formed a small well-knit group. Henry Gray recalled that 'Powdered hair, knee breeches, and even the pig-tail hanging from the head, gave a rather picturesque appearance to those moving amongst the most respectable class of society'. Gray noted the popularity of gentlemen's drinking clubs and other places of meeting. He told of old Dr Philip Whiteside who lived at the centre of things, looking up High Street from his house in New Bridge Street. Dr Whiteside frequented the nearby reading room beside the King's Arms Hotel, and after the mail coach came in with the London papers he would emerge to read the latest news to the assembled crowd.

Henry Gray recorded that 'One part of the town long existed as a separate community, and that is what is called the Townhead.' Those of native stock were old-fashioned enough still to celebrate New Year according to the old style calendar (which had been superseded in 1752), and some had been

Alloway Place exemplified the impressive facade of Georgian architecture which catered for a comfortable middle class . . .

'noted smugglers'. They all lived 'in a very plain and frugal manner'. Cuthill as a contemporary observer remarked on 'the sturdy feelings of independence, for which Scotchmen, until of late, had been so much distinguished'. But there were 'some families of Irish labourers of the poorer classs, who have been induced to become resident here ... from no strong temptation as to remunerative employment, but because any change whatever from their miserable condition in their own country was likely to be a change for the better'. The town council in 1804 and again in 1822 were worried by the influx of such immigrants, who might become a charge on the poors fund. Some needy persons had in fact contrived to settle within Ayr because of its more generous provision of poor relief than in neighbouring parishes. This, it was alleged, persuaded local persons to claim from charities 'in which they think they have a better right to participate than strangers'. It was calculated in 1837 that one in twenty-three of Ayr's population was a pauper, compared with Glasgow's one in forty.

In Newton by contrast, the freemen were 'highly respectable', mostly 'in comfortable circumstances', and 'much above mediocrity in wealth, education, and intelligence'. Others of humbler station were also described by Rev. James Stevenson in 1836 as 'comfortable' and living in their own houses. The number of persons in extreme poverty was relatively small. The fishermen still wore traditional costume though some were 'not so attentive as could be wished to cleanliness in their habits'. Rev. Stair

McQuhae of St Quivox described the population of Wallacetown as containing some artisans and shopkeepers, but composed chiefly of 'the poorer class of Irish settlers' employed as colliers, labourers, and weavers, plus other 'strangers from Ireland', who lived cheaply here and went begging in Ayr.

The *Advertiser* noted (3.4.1828) that 'the town has extended itself greatly', yet in the older part of Ayr there remained 'antique and shapeless houses'. The Fish Cross in particular (11.11.1828) was 'a dirty, awkward and confined corner' and vegetables and fruit were sold nearby 'over two common sewers or principal gutters'. Butchers had abandoned the fleshmarket and hung carcases outside their shops 'to the disgust of those having an appetite as well as those who have none' – which would be a long-continued practice. Of the burgh's twenty five wells, the water was deemed unsuitable for drinking, culinary purposes, or washing, not even 'proper or safe for a horse' (20.11.28) – though by repute that from the well on the washing green was best for infusing tea. While the houses in some areas were 'well-aired' yet (7.3.1833) 'in the Townhead of Ayr, and the greater part of Newton and St Quivox, the streets and particularly the lanes, are in a very filthy state ... each family having a separate, and in general, openly exposed dungstead'. A visitor (10.10.1831) remarked that 'though much seems to have been done to improve and ornament the other parts of the town' he was particularly revolted by 'the unmentionable pollutions that disgrace the south bank of the river'; he compared Ayr to a peacock which 'presents his unadorned rear to the spectator'!

What occasioned unusual concern about sanitary conditions was the cholera epidemic of 1832. The *Advertiser* noted it in the north of England (10.11.1831) and reported in its next issue a meeting on 14 November of invited inhabitants of Ayr, Newton, and Wallacetown called by Provost Fullarton, and the formation, following Privy Council advice, of a local Board of Health. This was composed of magistrates, medical practitioners, ministers ('of all denominations'), and representatives of various bodies; it would take responsibility for the three parishes; with committees to raise subscriptions and report on developments at weekly meetings. In April 1832 it was reconstituted after a more representative meeting of householders. Meantime in January 1832 a soup kitchen was established by 'several Gentlemen' and operated by a committee which also supplied clothing to the needy, while the Board of Health recommended to the town council immediate action against insanitary 'filth and stagnant water' in the Carrick Vennel. Cholera was reported at Doura near Irvine (1.3.32), reached Kilmarnock (12.7.32), and was brought to Ayr on 19 July by a woman who came from Glasgow and died within twenty four hours. This was initially diagnosed as typhus, locally prevalent the previous winter and spring. But this first case (in Isle Lane) was followed by others which spread 'alarm' and 'terror' through the town. In its first month there were 82 cases, involving 31 deaths. During the next week from 15 till 21 August new cases totalled 229 (43 of them on 20 August) and there were 79 deaths (a maximum 14 on 18 August). New cases continued to be reported till 11 October. The Board of Health had provided a hospital at the Secession Church in Wallacetown but no more than thirty were admitted, for 'the prejudices of the people rendered the hospital provided of no avail'. A House of Seclusion was provided on the South Quay (for relatives of those infected) and of 214 admitted only seven took cholera. Of fourteen medical attendants, not one was affected, though a medical student serving in the Dispensary died. Copying 17th century precautions against the plague, the Board of Health instituted a watch to prevent entry of vagrants and other suspects. So long as the pestilence raged, tar barrels and torches were kept burning by day and night, and those who could escaped to the country. Even Whitletts was relatively safe. Throughout the months of crisis, the streets were strangely quiet, with the 'dead cart' taking corpses to the 'dead house' by night, and by day the sparsely-attended funeral processions to the extended graveyard east of the Auld Kirk. Initially guards were placed to prevent anyone leaving or entering infected houses, but of necessity this had to be superseded by 'SICK' marked on the door, replaced after a death by 'CAUTION' and treatment by chloride of lime. There was a final count of 205 deaths from over 400 cases. This was almost as bad as Kilmarnock's 250 deaths, and much worse than Irvine's 21. Ayr's Board of Health was finally disbanded in February 1834 after disposing of equipment by public roup, and gift of four surplus coffins to the Poorshouse.

There was another but less general panic around this time, occasioned by fears of the resurrectionists. The trial in 1813 of the Glasgow body-snatcher Granville Sharp Pattison was the prelude to later alarms. The *Advertiser* (6.11.1828) noted the arrest in Edinburgh of a man 'called Burke or Burt' on suspicion of selling corpses to a lecturer in anatomy, and in following issues reported on his trial for 'the West Port Murders'. William Burke was hanged on 28

. . . But well-off families and their domestic staff had to make do with limited facilities, like the dry closets and ashpits to the rear of the premises.

January 1829 and his accomplice William Hare who turned king's evidence was released. The *Advertiser* (11.11.1828) contained reports of churchyards being violated in Paisley and Dublin. So in Ayr as elsewhere a night watch was organised, with relatives taking turns to guard graves where corpses had been recently interred. Some graves were protected by mortsafes, examples of which have been preserved within the archway at the entrance to the Auld Kirk yard. In December 1829 there was a macabre incident in Newton. Boxes landed from a Stranraer boat for transportation to Glasgow were discovered by the carrier to contain three bodies. These, as the *Advertiser* reported (17.12.1829) had been purchased in Ireland for dissection at Glasgow University. But James Howie, writing 'from personal recollection' in a chapter of his *Historical Account*, tell that the party from Glasgow to collect the corpses were presumed to be body snatchers. Some locals seized the bodies and interred them on Newton shore, then for their greater safety exhumed them for burial at sea. Much later the *Advertiser* reported (9.6.1831) on 'Resurrectionists at Newton' when graves were disturbed and coffins found to be empty.

Newton Main Street and most other places north of the river suffered particularly from the deprivation that stimulated radical demands for reform.

Throughout the early part of the 19th century – as before and after – there were the continuing problems of poverty. Bad harvests in 1799 and 1800 were followed by inflated grain prices in the first year of the new century, requiring a council committee to collect contributions for the poor, and even a petition to parliament proposing the prohibition – for a limited period – of distillation of grain into spirits. In 1812 there was a riot because of the shortage of meal, and another one in June 1816. On the latter occasion a crowd of colliers and others from Newton and Wallacetown crossed the new weir and attacked the Nether Mill. The store of meal and flour was divided among the women, and everything else damaged or broken. Several shops were also gutted. There was further distress among unemployed weavers in 1819 and again in 1832; and in 1822 among colliers of Newton, who went on strike and were imprisoned for illegal combination.

In general, as Rev. Alexander Cuthill reported in 1837, the people were 'happy, orderly, and respectable', and he included 'the lower orders of

society'. Since 1796 fifteen friendly societies had been formed in the three parishes, as well as several female societies, and a local health service was provided by the Ayr, Newton, and Wallacetown Dispensary formed in 1817. Over 500 families paying five shillings per year could obtain treatment from five of the local doctors. For poor relief, an improved system of management was instituted in 1817. Before then the kirk session made provision from the regular church collections, the rent of the farm of Sessionfield, and various mortifications; the town council had a separate fund and managed numerous charitable bequests (listed in the *New Statistical Account*) including since 1786 an endowment from the now-defunct Kingcase hospice. The Poors House had a Board of Directors composed of representatives of the council and several local bodies, and was financed by their contributions plus a levy on the inhabitants. This Board was enlarged in 1817 to include also the session and the twelve major landed proprietors, and make more comprehensive provision. The Board of about sixty directors and a smaller standing committee thereafter with the aid of a Superintendent of Poor admitted from 20 to 25 inmates to the Poors House and allowed from 6d to 3s weekly to 300 out-pensioners. Comparable figures for the same year (1836) were 47 in Newton and about 80 in St Quivox.

According to Rev Mr Cuthill there were 'few instances of open crime among even the lowest of the population' and he boasted that 'The streets, and lanes, and suburbs, may be traversed at all hours of the night in perfect safety'. There were occasional pitched battles between the boys of Ayr and Newton, some drunken scenes in Wallacetown, and when boats from Arran arrived at the Midsummer Fair with illicit whisky. More serious cases were dealt with by the Sheriff Court, and those sentenced were lodged within the County Gaol after 1822. Thus when James Auld, the burgh hangman died in 1824, no successor was required. In the burgh court, the magistrates had only about a dozen cases each year. There was no regular police system, apart from those burgesses annually appointed as constables, and these, the council admitted in 1831, were 'not well organised'. Earlier in the century a group of young men set themselves up as what would later and elsewhere be called vigilantes, but this Black Gang become something of nuisance before its members settled down to respectability. In 1837 Cuthill admitted that there had been 'fermentation and excitement, occasioned by the agitation of questions of reform in Church and State; but' – and here he was not quite accurate – 'these have never been carried the length of making them forget the ordinary proprieties of life'.

During the recent war, units had been raised for home defence against threatened invasion. The only action in which they participated was the suppression of local radicals and reformers. In 1794 the West Lowland Fencibles were raised and commanded by Colonel Hugh Montgomerie of Coilsfield, who in 1796 became 12th Earl of Eglinton. These patriotic volunteers were supplemented in 1797 by an Ayrshire Militia composed of 436 men conscripted by local ballots. There had been a militia in England since 1757 but continued anti-jacobite fears postponed for forty years a Scots Militia Act. There was some resistance to serving in the militia, and the Fencibles were despatched from Ayr to Ochiltree where two days were spent in quelling anti-militia riots. The Fencible infantry were soon afterwards disbanded, allegedly for riotous behaviour. In 1803 an Armed Association was formed, equipped with one thousand pikes to deter possible invaders. There was also (1795–1800) a

regiment of Fencible Cavalry under Colonel Andrew Dunlop, superseded by a more permanent force. The Carrick troop of Yeomanry Horse was raised in 1798 by Archibald, 12th Earl of Cassillis. In 1801 command passed to Richard Alexander Oswald of Auchincruive, and became the Ayrshire Yeomanry Cavalry when the Carrick troop was augmented (1803) by an Ayr troop and a Cumnock troop, with annual parades on Ayr Green. From 1794 when the government established its Barracks, regular troops had been stationed at Ayr, but after the end of the war in 1815, the barracks were closed and offered for sale. In 1816 because of post-war disturbances the Ayrshire Yeomanry was increased to two corps of four troops each, and Alexander Boswell of Auchinleck succeeded as commanding colonel. In June 1816, after the Ayr meal riot, a detachment under Captain Alexander Gairdner was placed on duty for eight days to prevent further disorders.

There was increased political activity, with revived demands for parliamentary and burgh reform. In November 1817 the Guild Brethren and Trades presented a resolution to Ayr town council, suggesting wider participation in the choice of councillors. The council, while not unsympathetic, expressed the view that 'mature deliberation' was required and no local urgency, though elsewhere there might be 'mismanagement and neglect'. In 1818 a Radical Association was formed, composed mainly of weavers and shoemakers. James Howie has recorded details of government plots to provoke the radicals into law-breaking, naming one James Logan as an agent who actually became secretary of the local association. In November 1819 a county demonstration was organised in Wallacetown. Hustings were erected on the Back Riggs between Wallace Street and Limond's Wynd. Bands of radicals arrived, to the music of fifes and drums, carrying banners with revolutionary slogans, the cap of liberty borne on a pole by 'a masculine, good-looking amazon' from Kilmarnock. Two troops of the Yeomanry under Colonel Boswell were on duty; but the meeting was peaceful and the crowds dispersed quietly.

Early in 1820 rumours were circulating of an imminent and widespread radical uprising. The Yeomanry were called out for five days at the beginning of March. Weeks later there appeared mysterious placards calling from Glasgow for a kind of general strike after Saturday 1st April 'By Order of the Committee of organization for forming a Provisional Government'. The *Advertiser* found these 'inflammatory and treasonable beyond any thing perhaps ever circulated in this quarter'. The same issue revealed that 'a person who took an active part in the Radical Meeting at Wallacetown' hoped to recruit a leader for a local uprising and 'waited upon a gentleman of great consequence in the county'. But that noted reformer – elsewhere identified as Richard Alexander Oswald of Auchincruive – reported this to the Sheriff, shrewdly suspecting a plot to implicate him. Precautions against the anticipated revolution in the west of Scotland involved the re-opening of Ayr Barracks, where were stationed the 10th Hussars and the 4th Royal Veteran Battalion. The disciplinary floggings several of these regulars had to endure scandalised some local people. Middle class young lawyers and shopkeepers joined the Armed Association which was revived in 1819, known officially as the Loyal Air Volunteers and popularly as the 'Dandies'. As their commander Lieutenant Colonel Alexander West Hamilton of Rozelle was succeeded by Major Dugald Campbell of Thornyflat, a veteran who had served in the Peninsular and Waterloo campaigns. Ayr town council deplored 'the late alarming and treasonable conduct of a number of deluded persons in this quarter of the country'. They agreed to compensate those enrolled in the 'corps of citizens' who had lost work, including 'several Mechanics'. The constables of the Town Guard patrolled the streets at night as a precaution against a threatened attack on the banks. On Sunday 2 April, alarm bells were rung and the churches emptied at news of a reported rising in Lanarkshire. That afternoon the Royal Veterans marched out of the Barracks, following the Hussars which had mustered outside the King's Arms. The Dandies were assembled in the Academy playground to assume, along with Militia staff, responsibility for the safety of the town. On Monday 3rd, 'a great part of the inhabitants of Air, and the other towns and villages in the county, did little else but stand in the streets and converse on the subject of the the alarms'. But the *Advertiser* was 'persuaded, however, that this general stoppage of work proceeded more from the irresistiblle curiosity of knowing what was going on, than from any inclination to obey the injunction of the placard, or any fear of the consequence of disobedience'. On Monday at noon the entire two corps of the Ayrshire Yeomanry – each of four troops of fifty horse – assembled at mustering points throughout the county 'in marching order, with necessaries'. Three troops were despatched to Glasgow, two to Paisley. The remaining three, for service within the county, paraded in Ayr Sandgate to be issued with ammunition. On Monday afternoon

Dr John Taylor, Chartist leader.

one troop led by Lieutenant A.C.Gairdner departed for Stewarton to disperse Radicals assembled there. As these troopers rode through Wallacetown, stones, bottles, and mud were thrown by a mob, chiefly of women and boys. Within a week disturbances in Glasgow and Paisley had been subdued and most of the Ayrshire Yeomanry stood down by 8 August. The Edinburgh Yeomanry, however, came to patrol Kilmarnock in their 'Western Campaign'. Detachments of Ayrshire Yeomanry were still required at Ayr, Mauchline, and Galston, and on 22 April Mauchline was surrounded by the Yeomanry's 2nd troop and a detachment of the Royal Veterans. Thirty Radicals were arrested and arms seized. The Radical Rising was followed by treason trials conducted by Special Commissioners. That in Ayr was held within the New Church and seventeen were indicted, nearly all weavers, from Stewarton (7), Galston (7), and Mauchline (2). All but four absconded, and the trial continued throughout July and August. Thomas McKay of Stewarton was sentenced to death, but this was remitted and all four were released. Nationally, of twenty four sentenced to death, three were hanged, at Glasgow (James Wilson) and Stirling (Andrew Hardie and John Baird).

Ayr was also agitated in 1820 by a political controversy of a different calibre. The marriage of the Prince Regent to Princess Caroline of Brunswick in 1795 had been followed by separation a year later. After his accession as George IV in January 1820, he began divorce proceedings in June. The estranged wife returned from abroad and won much popular support. In London, 'If anyone was so contumacious as not to take off his hat and huzza for the Queen ... he was liberally bespattered with mud'. This was quoted in the *Advertiser* whose columns that autumn were almost entirely given over to verbatim reports of parliamentary debates on the divorce. When the government felt it politic to drop the divorce bill in November 1820 there was widespread rejoicing. In Ayr the *Advertiser* reported excitement 'after the arrival of this gratifying intelligence'. The town council – most of whom were 'King's Men' – prohibited public celebration. But the magistrates were unable to prevent Captain Reid from illuminating his vessel *Active* anchored in Ayr harbour. There were numerous bonfires lit by 'Queen's Men' in Newton and Wallacetown. At Cowan and Sloan's quay in Newton the *Commerce* had just arrived from Archangel. A mob of boys purloined from it tar barrels and other combustible materials, dragged them in a fishing boat across the New Bridge, and defied the council with a great bonfire on the site of the Malt Cross. Three lads were charged in the burgh court; Bailie Donaldson (who was sympathetic) fined them each ten shillings, to be paid when they were able (which they never were). In July 1821 for the coronation of George IV (from which Queen Caroline was forcibly excluded) Ayr town council ordered 'ringing of Bells and a bonfire at the Mercat Cross'. The inhabitants were restricted to displaying flowers in their windows, as on royal birthdays. A year later in July 1822 during George IV's famous Royal Visit to Edinburgh, at a levee in Holyrood Provost David Limond presented a loyal address and kissed the royal hand. The council subscribed ten guineas towards a commemorative equestrian statue.

A movement for parliamentary and burgh reform was sponsored within Ayr by the burgesses and guildry through annual meetings from 1817 till 1824, followed by a lapse till renewed interest was shown in and after 1830. In that year the accession of William IV (in July) was followed by a general election, and by November the tory Duke of Wellington was replaced as prime minister by the whig Earl Grey. The Ayrshire Yeomanry whose cadre was increased from 400 to 640 were called out to reform demonstrations at Girvan in September and at Ayr in December. A reform bill introduced into the Commons (March 1831) was thrown out, and the king dissolved parliament for another general election, amid popular excitement. On the day before that election, two troops of dragoons arrived to occupy Ayr's deserted barracks, in anticipation of trouble. The choice of a county member of parliament was in the hands of 135 freeholders, and made by an open vote at a meeting in the County Buildings on 18 May. The Sheriff called for the election of a chairman of the proceedings. A show of hands for this, rather than a protracted roll call vote for the candidates, showed that the tory Colonel William Blair of Blair had defeated the whig Richard Alexander Oswald of Auchincruive by 73 to 36 votes. The crowds in the gallery and outside expressed their disapproval by throwing missiles. The popular loser was cheered as he left by coach. All others had to await the arrival from the barracks of the dragoons, who conveyed the new MP to the harbour, whence, cut and bruised, he escaped by steamboat to Ardrossan. The crowd smashed windows of Tory supporters in and around Wellington Square. Election of the burgh member caused less furore. Commissioners from the five burghs met later that month in Ayr to re-elect Thomas F. Kennedy of Dunure. Born at Greenan in 1788, he was admitted to the bar in 1811, and in 1818 (on the recommendation of the Duke of Argyll) was elected MP for Ayr Burghs, with the support of Ayr town council. He would continue as member till he retired in 1834, became a privy councillor in 1837, and survived till 1879. Kennedy was committed to parliamentary reform and – as important – so was Ayr burgh council, which in November 1830 unanimously accepted the principle of municipal reform and in March 1831 sent an address to the king advocating parliamentary reform. A second Reform Bill introduced to the Commons in June 1831 was thrown out by the Lords in October. Ayr town council followed up a petition to the king and the Lords in August by another to the king in October regarding this 'alarming crisis', which was not resolved till the following summer. Another reform bill passed by the Commons in May 1832 was halted by a hostile amendment in the Lords, this followed by the resignation of Earl Grey as prime minister; he was reinstated eight days later on 15 May and the Lords coerced into accepting a third bill, which would provide for a redistribution of seats in the Commons and an extension of the franchise. When news reached Ayr of Earl Grey's reinstatement, guns were fired,

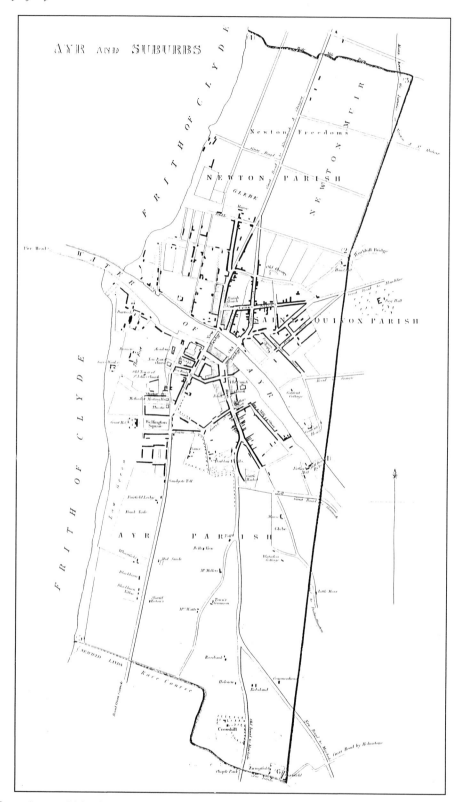

By the 1832 Reform Act wealthier householders in Ayr and Newton were granted the right to vote; but there were only 291 such local electors, who joined with others in Irvine, Campbeltown, Inveraray, and Oban in the choice of MP for Ayr Burghs.

squibs exploded, and a bonfire lit at the Cross – with the town council's approval. After the English bill passed on 7 June, a crowd paraded round the homes of leading local Tories, but doing little damage – three panes of glass were broken. After the passage of the Scottish bill on 17 July, in Ayr 'The people gave vent to their joy and their satisfaction in a manner they never did before, and which has never occurred since' – as James Howie later noted. A grand celebration was planned for Friday 10 August, too late to be postponed despite news that Kilmarnock was in the grip of cholera and five local cases had been reported.

The entire town was decorated with flowers and foliage and the streets crossed by triumphal arches. The Grand Procession was headed by the Reform Committee led by Provost William Fullarton and his nephew Dr John Taylor. There followed the Whipmen, Town Councillors, Hammermen, Weavers and Spinners, Engineers and Colliers, Gardeners, Painters, Shoemakers, Tailors, Squaremen, Bakers, Newton Weavers, Fleshers of Ayr and Newton, neighbouring Tenantry – many with flags and banners. The route was from County Buildings past Wellington Square, Barns Street, Dalblair Road, Alloway Street, High Street, New Bridge into Newton, then back by Sandgate to Wellington Square. There was a Boat Race on the river; a Public Dinner in the Assembly Rooms (4 p.m., tickets 9/–) and others in almost very inn; bonfires; fireworks outside the County Buildings; and a Grand Illuminated Arch of Gas Lamps at Deacon Convener McIlwraith's house at 32 High Street. One observer, who was then more concerned with the threat of cholera, later referred (*Advertiser* 7.3.1833) to the 'rejoicings, which in this part of the world means hard drinking'.

The first parliamentary election under the new franchise, in December 1832, naturally evinced great public interest, though that franchise had not been extended as widely as many had hoped. In the counties it went to proprietors of land valued at £10 per annum and well-off tenants paying £50 rent; in the burghs to householders whose property was valued at the considerable £10 per annum. In the county election, Oswald now obtained an overwhelming 2,152 votes against Blair's 324. The burgh seat was retained by the whig T.F.Kennedy with 375 votes; the radical Dr John Taylor had 163, and the tory James Cruikshanks a mere 33. This Western Burghs constituency still comprised five burghs – Ayr, Irvine, Campbeltown, Inveraray, with Oban replacing Rothesay. The member was no longer selected by a clique of five burgh commissioners but by the electors of designated areas. The parliamentary burgh of Ayr contained the royal burgh south to Seafield, east to the Overmill; plus Newton, Wallacetown, and Content as far as the Half-mile Burn and Hawkhill. Of an estimated population of 14,817 the number of electors enrolled in 1832 was 291. Of these, 154 voted for Kennedy, 41 for Taylor, 22 for Cruikshanks. After the result was announced, stones were thrown at the houses of presumed radicals who had voted for Kennedy. But the *Advertiser* was pleased to note how little disorder there had been.

At the beginning of 1834 Kennedy announced his withdrawal because of ill health. In the subsequent by-election of March 1834, there was elected Lord James Stuart, the Marquess of Bute's brother who would represent the whig liberal interest as burgh MP till 1852. On this occasion there was a straight fight and Stuart obtained 305 votes as against 213 for Taylor, including 111 against 76 among Ayr voters. This time feelings ran high. A Yeomanry troop coming from Monkton on the day of the election had forcibly to clear a way through Newton. When it became obvious that Taylor could not win, the radicals were disappointed, and a pitched battle developed in River Street. The Yeomanry, supported by special constables posted on the bridges, prevented a crossing of the river. But the Yeomanry failed to disperse the radicals who formed themselves into three parties, those in Main Street sheltering behind the old Newton Mill (which was still standing), the others at the foot of Wallace Street and Garden Street 'following a well-known continental fashion' setting up barricades and defending themselves with stones till it was safe to withdraw at midnight.

Dr John Taylor, that popular local hero, was born at Newark on 16 September 1805. He became a naval surgeon, and associated with republicans and democrats in France and Greece. He is said to have spent his twenty-first birthday in a French gaol. Certainly that year, soon after he came of age, he disposed of Blackhouse estate, which he had inherited from his father. Most of the £30,000 realised is said to have been spent fitting out a ship to assist the Greeks in their war of liberation. Dr Taylor practised as a surgeon in Cathcart Street. After his unsuccessful candidature in the 1832 election he founded and edited the short-lived *Ayrshire Reformer and Kilmarnock Gazette*, which foundered after a libel suit by T.F.Kennedy, who was challenged to a duel. For this 'Breach of the Peace by sending a challenge to fight a Duel' there was incarcerated in Ayr prison 'John Taylor of the Ayr Chemical Works and residing in Newton upon Ayr' from 12 till 25 September 1833, when he was released on pledging his good behaviour. Despite his second electoral failure in the 1834 by-election, Taylor continued a political career. This affected Ayr only marginally (as noticed in Chapter 13), but won him a wide reputation before his death in Larne on 4 December 1842. In an obituary notice, the *Advertiser* described him as he had been 'on the platform, his full black eye kindled with his subject and his long dark hair in graceful curls on his shoulders'.

He was generously praised for 'talents of a very high order, to which study and travel had imparted great polish and versatility, and with an eloquence which made him the idol of the people and the admiration of many an audience'. By public subscription there was erected in 1850 in Wallacetown cemetery a statue of 'John Taylor, Esq., of Blackhouse, M.D., ... Professionally, he was alike the poor man's generous friend and physician; Politically, he was the eloquent and unflinching advocate of the People's Cause ...'

THIRTEEN

The 19th Century Burgh Council

In the course of the 19th century Ayr widened its boundaries. In 1832 the parliamentary burgh was formed as a constituency comprising the royal burgh and the built-up areas north of the river. Ayr and Newton however retained their own town councils. Then from 1873, for municipal as well as parliamentary purposes, the Burgh of Ayr encompassed much of Ayr parish and most of the parishes of Newton and St Quivox, with the subsequent demise of Newton burgh council. In 1885 the municipal burgh boundaries were further extended to include more of Ayr and St Quivox parishes and all of Newton. In 1895 these latter two parishes were incorporated within an extended Ayr parish, though Whitletts and Alloway remained outwith Ayr's municipal jurisdiction till 1935.

During the 19th century there was increased popular participation in burgh affairs, as the franchise was extended for municipal as for parliamentary purposes. Ayr's first burgh election was in 1833, when 280 owners and tenants of property rented at more than £10 became entitled to vote. In 1868 the electorate was significantly augmented when suffrage was granted to nearly all ratepaying householders plus some lodgers, so that when the municipal burgh was extended in 1873 nearly 2,500 were eligible to elect its councillors, and did so by secret ballot, which was introduced in 1872. In 1884 the franchise was further widened to include most householders and some others, so that most adult males were now eligible.

For one third of the century the burgh remained unreformed. During more than 250 years, the council had annually renewed itself by a process of cooption. Sometime in the 16th century before 1580 the Act of 1479 had been belatedly adopted, abandoning the previous system of selecting councillors by popular choice at the Michaelmas assembly of all burgesses. The municipal oligarchy was composed of fifteen councillors selected from the brethren of the merchant guild, the other two being deacons of crafts. Only once, in the exceptional political circumstances of 1689, did the general mass of burgesses participate in choosing the burgh council. A century after that, radical opinion was beginning to advocate reform of both parliamentary and municipal representation, to be eventually and respectively accomplished by the Reform Act (Scotland) of 1832 and the three Burgh Reform Acts of 1833.

Criticisms of the unreformed burghs made early in the 19th century by the advocates of change have been uncritically accepted by most historians ever since. Yet an examination of Ayr's record shows the council of this royal burgh not lacking in enterprise. In the latter years of the 18th century Ayr council took the initiative in providing the New Bridge, improving the Harbour, establishing an Academy, followed in the early decades of the 19th century by the construction of a New Church, the County Buildings, and its own Town Buildings. The council in 1825 arranged for the streets to be lit by gas, which a private company supplied. In 1829 a public water supply was planned, though its provision was slow in coming. In other ways – as detailed in the preceding chapters – successive councils were improving the town. Sometimes intricate (and expensive) dealings, not only locally but in London, were necessary preliminaries, as when parliamentary approval was required. The council was aware that its powers were limited, as in 1826 when the private gas company tried to sell its two-year-old works to the town, an offer turned down for it was 'entirely out of their line to interfere in any such commercial speculation'. The council in Ayr – as in the neighbouring royal burgh of Irvine – valiantly attempted to cope with various serious problems. Where it lacked powers to operate on its own authority, an effective technique frequently exercised was to cooperate with local voluntary agencies. Thus it shared in the administration of the Poorshouse and the Academy. So it cooperated in forming committees to raise subscriptions for the poor in 1801 when grain prices were abnormally

Ayr Town Council, an elected body after 1833, was responsible only for the royal burgh south of the river until 1873. Newton retained its own town council. The Ordnance Survey shows the situation in 1855.

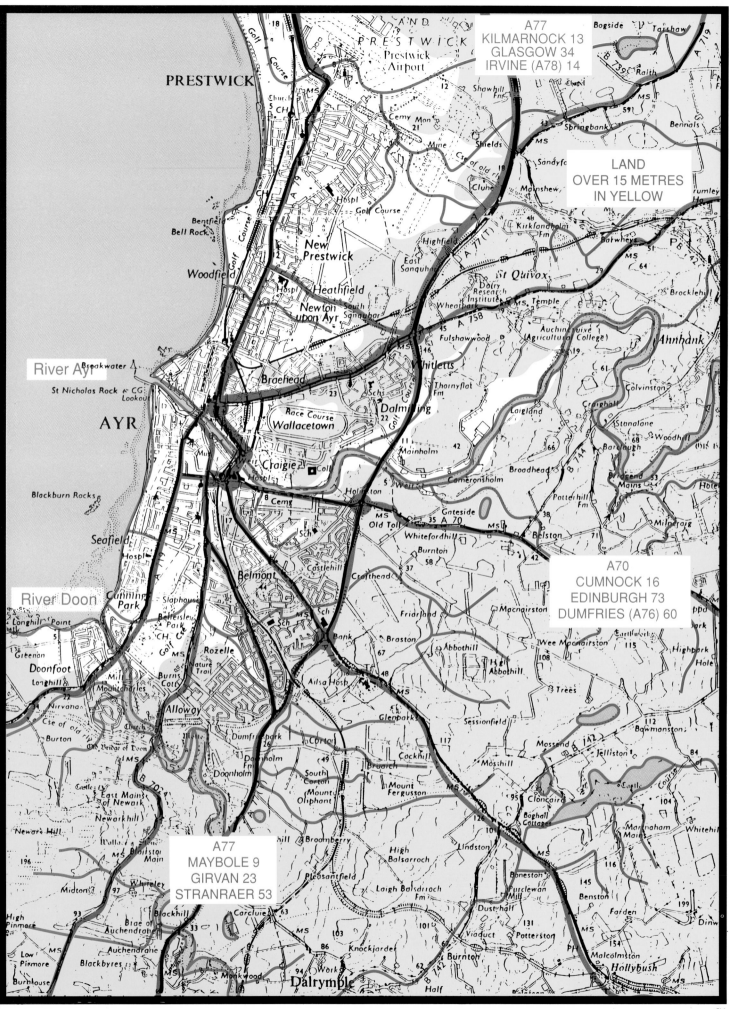

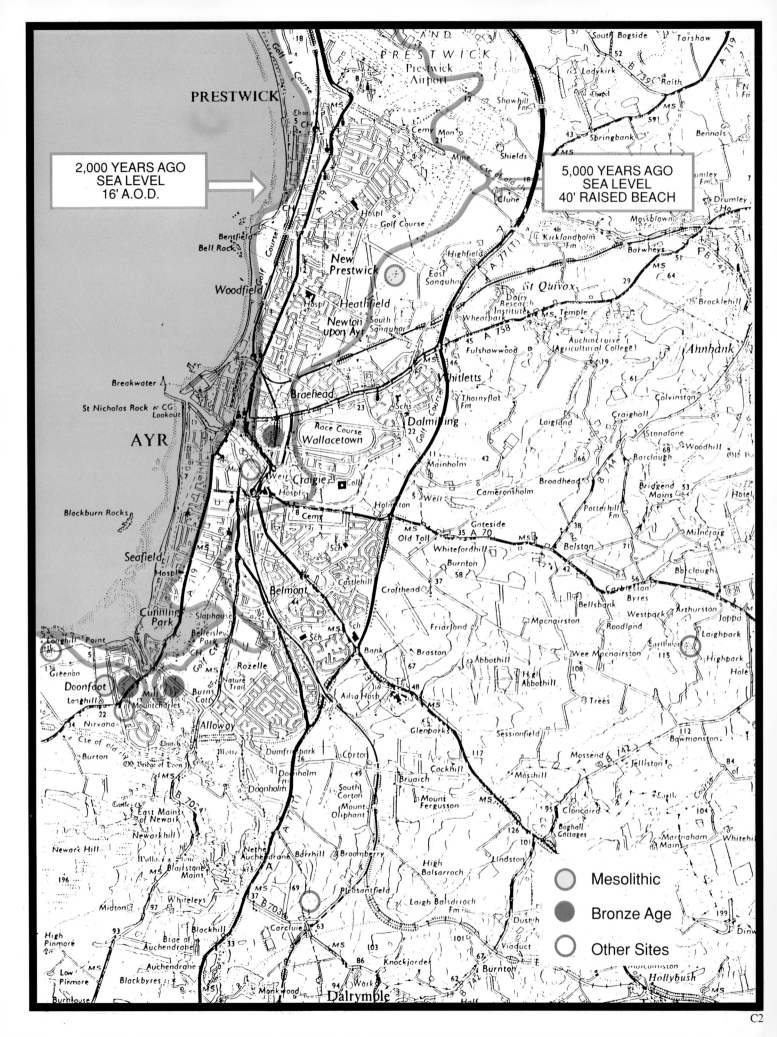

PRESTWICK

2,000 YEARS AGO
SEA LEVEL
16' A.O.D.

5,000 YEARS AGO
SEA LEVEL
40' RAISED BEACH

AYR

Mesolithic

Bronze Age

Other Sites

C2

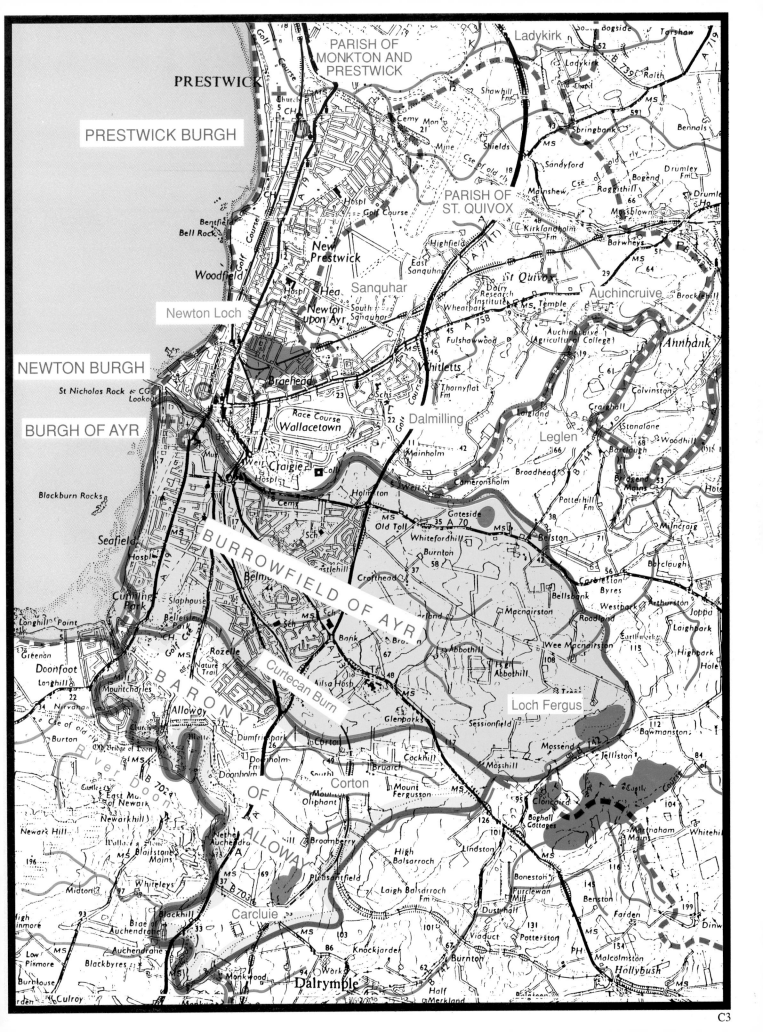

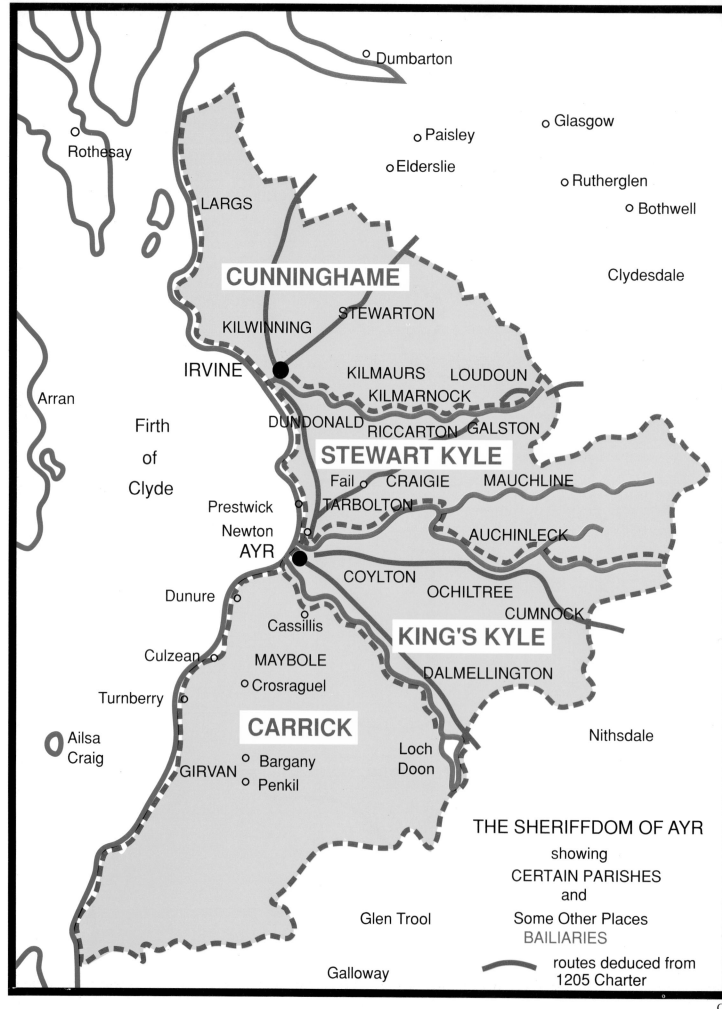

Dumbarton

Rothesay

Glasgow

Paisley

Elderslie

Rutherglen

Bothwell

LARGS

Clydesdale

CUNNINGHAME

STEWARTON

KILWINNING

IRVINE

KILMAURS   LOUDOUN

KILMARNOCK

Arran

Firth

of

Clyde

DUNDONALD

RICCARTON   GALSTON

STEWART KYLE

Fail   CRAIGIE   MAUCHLINE

Prestwick

TARBOLTON

Newton

AUCHINLECK

AYR

COYLTON

Dunure

OCHILTREE

Cassillis

CUMNOCK

KING'S KYLE

Culzean

MAYBOLE

Crosraguel

DALMELLINGTON

Turnberry

Ailsa

Craig

CARRICK

Nithsdale

Loch

Doon

GIRVAN   Bargany

Penkil

THE SHERIFFDOM OF AYR

showing

CERTAIN PARISHES

and

Some Other Places

BAILIARIES

routes deduced from

Glen Trool

1205 Charter

Galloway

C4

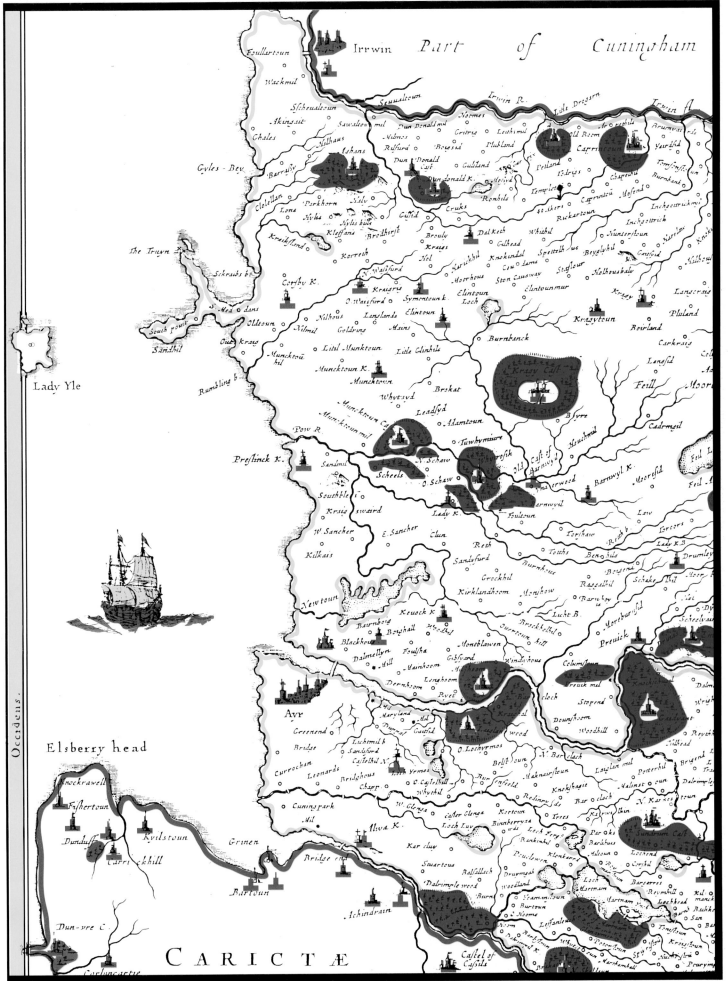

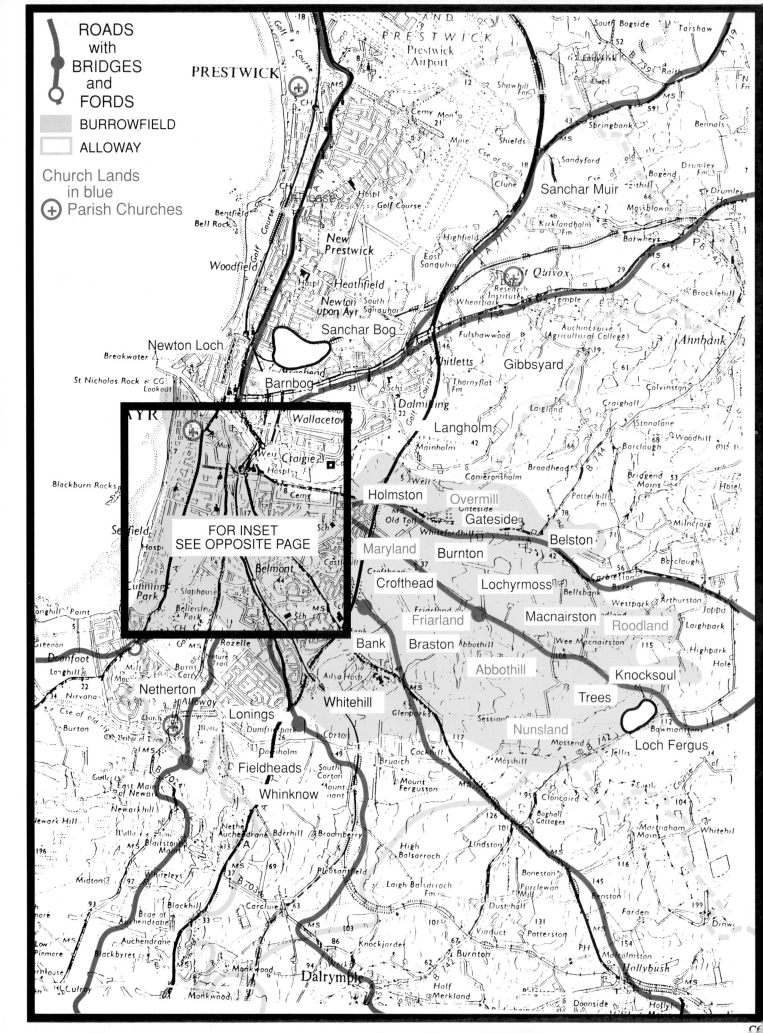

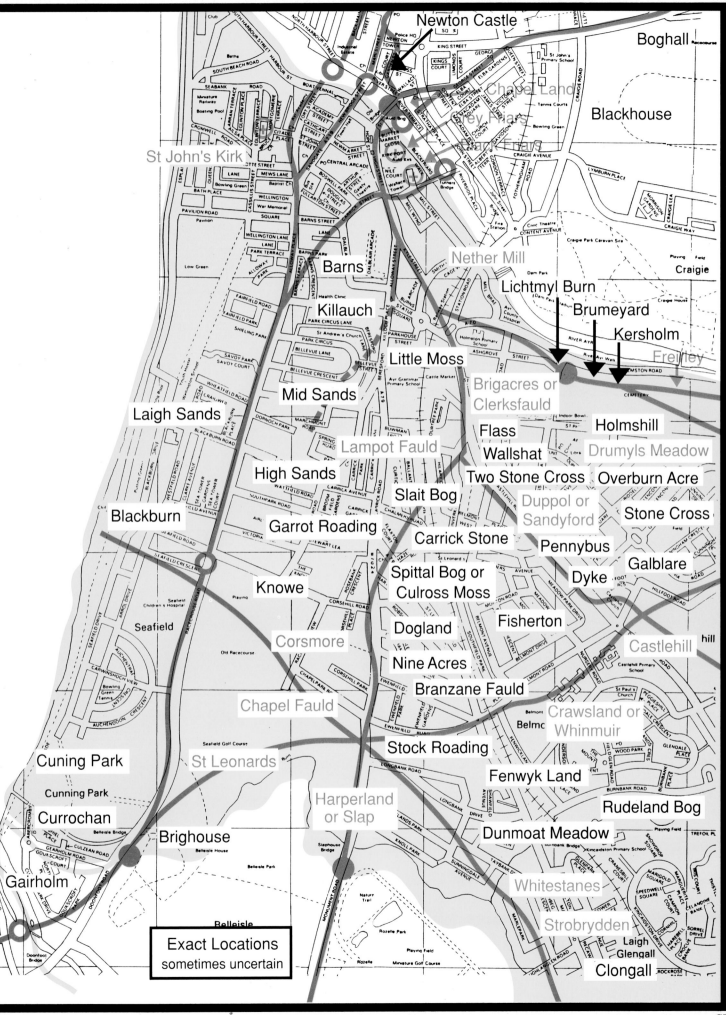

Newton Castle

Boghall

Blackhouse

St John's Kirk

Nether Mill

Craigie

Barns

Lichtmyl Burn

Brumeyard

Kersholm

Killauch

Little Moss

Frenney

Mid Sands

Brigacres or Clerksfauld

Holmshill

Laigh Sands

Flass

Drumyls Meadow

Lampot Fauld

Wallshat

High Sands

Two Stone Cross

Overburn Acre

Slait Bog

Duppol or Sandyford

Stone Cross

Blackburn

Garrot Roading

Carrick Stone

Pennybus

Galblare

Dyke

Knowe

Spittal Bog or Culross Moss

Fisherton

Corsmore

Dogland

Castlehill

Seafield

Nine Acres

Branzane Fauld

Crawsland or Whinmuir

Chapel Fauld

Belmc

Stock Roading

St Leonards

Fenwyk Land

Cuning Park

Harperland or Slap

Rudeland Bog

Currochan

Dunmoat Meadow

Brighouse

Whitestanes

Gairholm

Strobrydden

Laigh Glengall

Exact Locations
sometimes uncertain

Clongall

C7

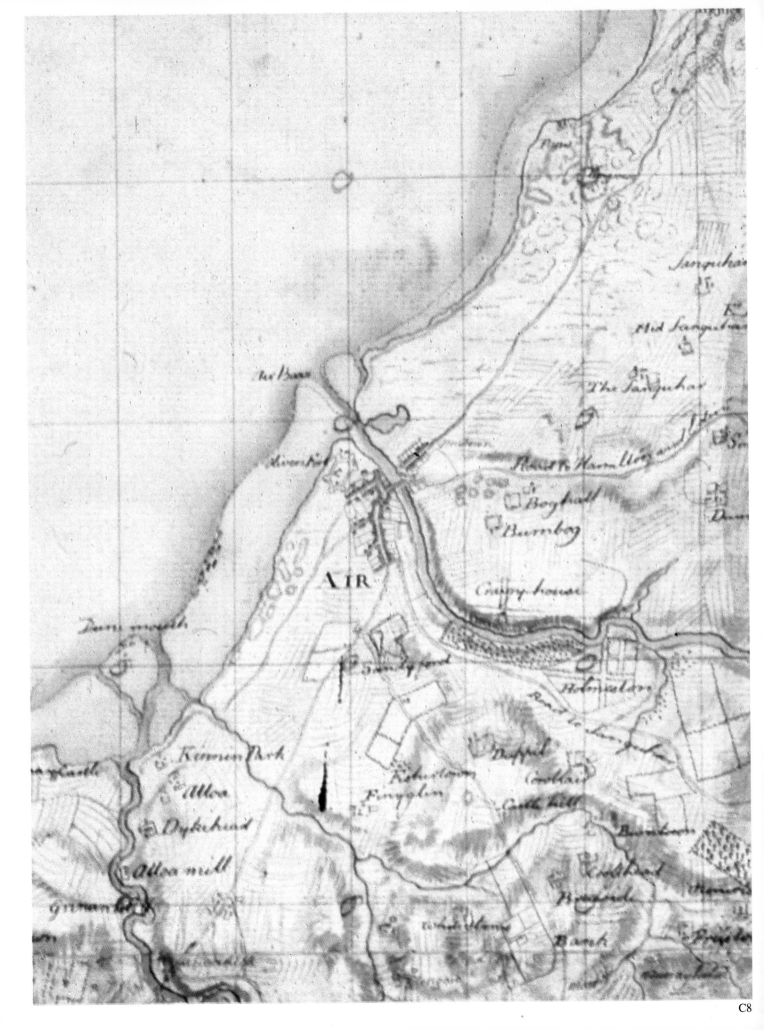

AIR

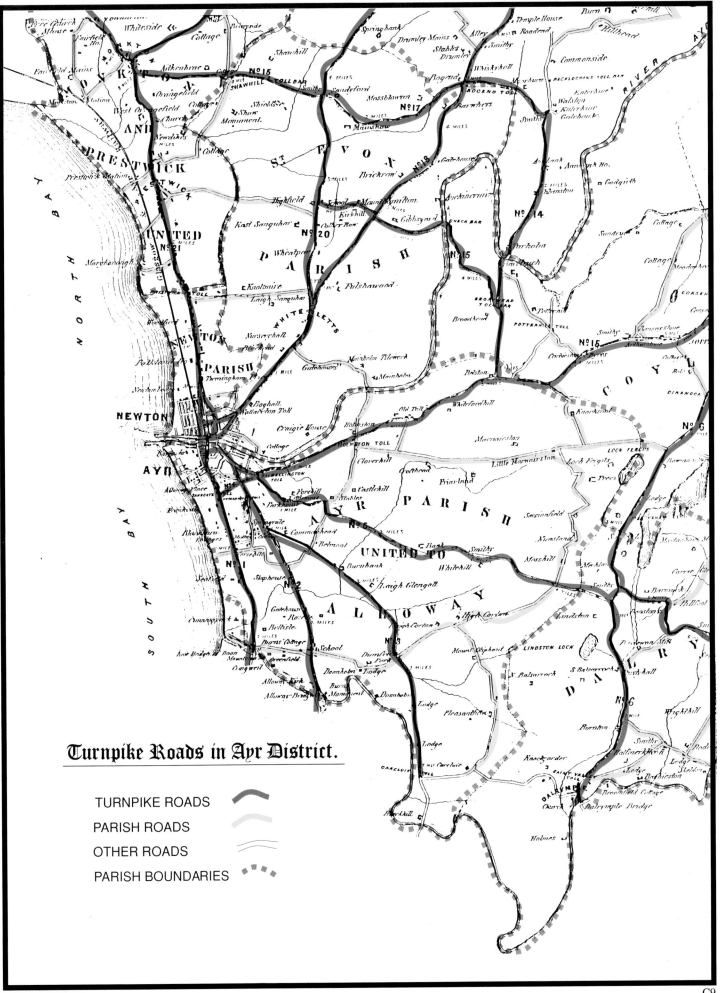

Turnpike Roads in Ayr District.

TURNPIKE ROADS

PARISH ROADS

OTHER ROADS

PARISH BOUNDARIES

C9

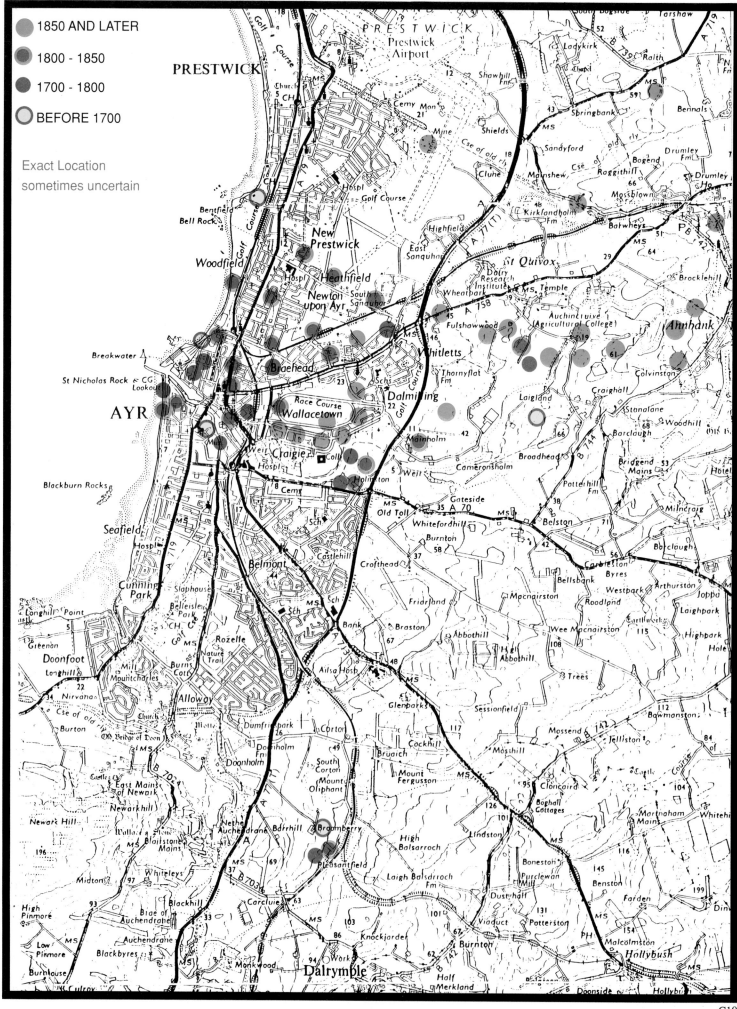

1850 AND LATER

1800 - 1850

1700 - 1800

BEFORE 1700

Exact Location
sometimes uncertain

PRESTWICK

C10

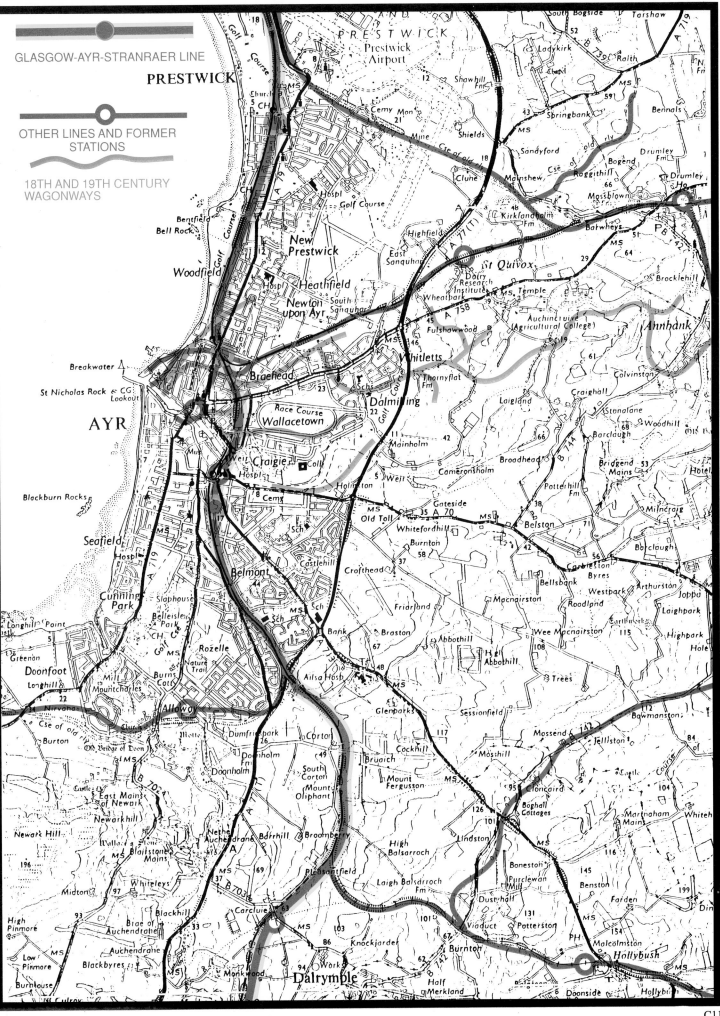

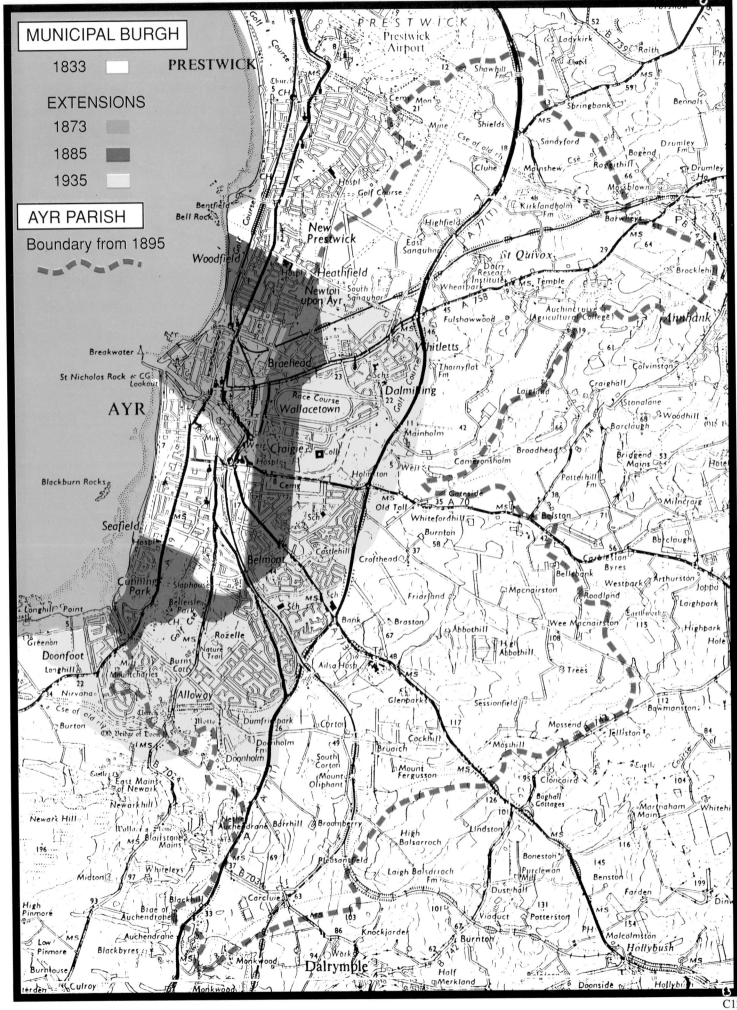

AYR IS
AN HISTORIC
TOWN

WALLACE STATUE

AYR TOWN HALL

MILLER'S FOLLY

AULD BRIG

LOUDOUN HALL

ST. JOHN'S TOWER

FISH CROSS

KIRK PORT

C13

HEART OF THE BURNS COUNTRY

BURNS COTTAGE

THE ANNUAL TAM O'SHANTER RIDE

BANKS AND BRAES OF BONNIE DOON

TO ALLOWAY'S AULD HAUNTED KIRK

BURNS MONUMENT

AND ACROSS THE BRIG O' DOON

HOLIDAY RESORT

AYR BEACH

THE HARBOUR

THE LOW GREEN

AYR RACES

CRUISES ON " THE WAVERLEY"

CRAIGIE CARAVAN PARK

GAIETY THEATRE

A PLACE FOR LIVING

HIGH STREET

SANDGATE

THE RIVER AYR

PARK CIRCUS

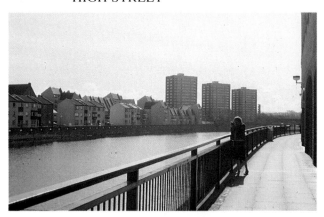

ROZELLE

MACLAURIN ART GALLERY

COUNTY BUILDINGS

MOSSHILL INDUSTRIAL ESTATE

C16

high; in 1819 when so many of the stocking weavers were unemployed; and again in 1832 when weavers and labourers were out of work. So in the cholera epidemic of 1832, the council promoted a Board of Health to handle the crisis. In the management of its own affairs, it had since 1778 annnually appointed a local lawyer to be procurator fiscal, rather than one of the councillors as previously; also in the later years of that century work on the new bridge had suggested a council committee on public works, which became a permanent arrangement, joined early in the 19th century by a committee on law matters and by another on the annual accounts. Criticisms of the unreformed burgh's lack of enterprise would seem to be unwarranted.

Another criticism of the unreformed burghs is of their finances. Close examination of the records would probably reveal corrupt practices – but it seems unfair to single out the burghs for what was then endemic in parliament and most other institutions, and not unknown even in 20th century local government. Nor is it fair to blame the unreformed councils for failing to balance their budgets when the government itself was then steadily increasing that National Debt which remains still with us. The Commissioners on Municipal Corporations reported Ayr's net debt in 1833 as just about £19,000, all contracted since 1792. The only specified imprudent expenditure had been on the Wallace Tower, whose rebuilding cost £2,200, more than twice what had been estimated. The council was also criticised for its management of the Bridge Trust: tolls had long since paid off the cost of building the New Bridge but were still being levied (quite illegally) to help pay for other public works. Expenditure for the year 1832–33 amounted to £3,395, including £512 on salaries, with the bulk devoted to public works – £730 on 'ordinary disbursements' and £1,525 on 'incidental discharge and disbursement, including repairs' – plus £616 for interest on borrowed money. Revenue was never sufficient to cover expenditure: from £740 in 1792 income had risen in forty years to just over £2,000 by 1833, most of this coming from rents (£973), feu duties (£304) and the town customs (£563). The only assessments imposed upon the inhabitants were £109 for Cess annually payable to the government and £608 for Poor's money in 1832. In 1818 Ayr council proposed obtaining a parliamentary Police Act with powers to levy rates for local services. (These 'police' powers we should define rather as 'political' powers or powers to enforce 'policy', for what we now call 'police' was then known as 'watching'.) Such provisions had been acquired in Glasgow (1800), Edinburgh (1805),

Paisley (1806) and Kilmarnock (1810). But in Ayr the proposed bill had to be dropped, in view of a public petition expressing massive public opposition. As will become obvious later, the unreformed burgh council of Ayr was indeed unrepresentative – in that it could be more progressive than those who would form its future electorate.

In 1785 the Ayr council had roundly condemned the 'visionary schemes' of 'certain discontented people in the different Boroughs'. In 1817 the movement for burgh reform was revived; a general meeting of the burgesses petitioned Ayr council. The councillors were now more favourably disposed than their predecessors, though they opined that there was no urgency, since locally neither mismanagement nor neglect could be alleged. In 1818 the council chose a commissioner who helped elect, as Ayr Burghs MP, T.F.Kennedy who was an enthusiast for reform. In 1819 the council replaced the traditional oath for those enrolling as burgesses with a declaration acceptable to seceders of the Anti-burgher persuasion and a growing number of others. There followed a decade in which the council proved less flexible. In 1820 the council held a majority of 'King's men' at the time of the Queen Caroline affair. In 1822 Provost Limond obsequiously kissed the royal hand at Holyrood. In 1824 Provost Cowan's council ungraciously refused to feu ground for a Roman Catholic chapel. Later in the decade there was much argument before it was agreed by ten votes to six to proceed with the Town's Building. By 1830 (when the reform movement revived) Provost Quintin Kennedy declared that disorders of past generations had then justified the 'system of self election', but now the franchise should be extended to all tax payers. A petition to this effect was unanimously approved by the council. In 1831 three separate petitions were addressed to King William in support of the Reform bill, while an historic innovation was made on 24 August that year when 'Reporters for the newspapers' were admitted to council meetings. The passing of the Reform Act was celebrated (despite the cholera epidemic) by a Grand Procession led by Provost Fullarton. In 1833 a petition to the House of Commons from the inhabitants of Ayr regarding municipal reform was endorsed by the council, and in terms of the Burgh Reform Acts the first municipal election was held on 5 November.

Details of this election are hard to come by. The *Advertiser* reported that it took place on 'Tuesday last' between 8 a.m. and 4 p.m. at the Court House in Wellington Square, when 'each Elector handed his list, on which were the names of the seventeen individuals whom he proposed as Councillors, to the Town Clerk or the Provost, who read the list aloud, when the Clerks in attendance marked the names proposed.' But neither of the local newspapers nor the council minutes record how many candidates there were. A main issue seems to have concerned the office of Treasurer and Collector of Taxes, which had some monetary perquisites. It was held by Thomas McClelland, one of two councillors who in 1817 had opposed burgh reform, and in 1825 had (unsuccessfully) opposed the re-election to parliament of Thomas Kennedy. So it was alleged in addresses to electors by Hugh Reid and John McCubbin, two candidates who were 'avowed friends and supporters of reform'. Neither of these two was elected.

In the burgh of Irvine where the unreformed council had been as progressive as that of Ayr, the 1833 election had six members of the old council re-elected plus three who had previously served, to form a majority in the council of seventeen. The pattern was almost exactly similar at Ayr, with five re-elected members, four who had previously served, and again only eight new men. Provost William Fullarton topped the poll with 174 votes, closely followed by Thomas McClelland with 167 votes. Also re-elected were Ex-provost Quintin Kennedy (5th, 127 votes), Bailie Andrew Williamson (7th, 107), Councillor Hugh Miller (12th, 96). The four who returned after an interval were Dr Philip Whiteside (3rd, 147) who had served 1825–28; John McIlwraith (11th, 100) who had been chosen as one of the two trades councillors on alternate years 1824–1830; Adam McHutcheon (13th, 92) who had been on the council for nine years between 1818 and 1829, and four years a bailie; David Limond of Dalblair (14th, 88) who had less support than might have been expected of one who had been councillor 1820–25, provost for three of these and another six to follow. Of the eight members first elected to the council in 1833, none was influential enough ever to attain the provostship.

The *Advertiser* (10.10.1833) on the eve of that election had 'waited with patience till the Reform Bill should cleanse the old system of all its impurities'. But there was no significant change in personnel. And though the *Advertiser* also predicted that 'a new era is about to commence in our Burgh politics', the new council continued to operate just as its predecessors had done. There were no dramatic changes. At the first meeting on 7 November, William Fullarton was continued as provost, and all but one of those chosen as magistrates had served previously in that capacity. Thomas McClelland retained the positions he had held

WILLIAM McGILL
WILLIAM McMURTRIE
JAMES McDERMENT

HUGH REID, TOWN CLERK.
HUGH MILLER, PROVOST.
JOSEPH ERSKINE, TREASURER.

OF AYR.

Ancient municipal traditions survived the reforms of the 19th century, though the regular Sunday parade with halberdiers to the Auld Kirk gave way to an annual Kirking of the Council.

since 1827, continuing to receive £20 as Treasurer, £10 as Collector of the Cess, and £5 as treasurer of the Bridge Trust. As officials, Andrew Murdoch was retained as town clerk, and Hugh Reid, writer, as procurator fiscal, both with nominal salaries, which were supplemented by fees for their various duties. There were still four town's officers and two bell-ringers; there had been no burgh hangman since 1824. The council continued to pay for a water bailie, a keeper of the clocks, precentors, various minor offices, and contribute to ministers' stipends and to the academy. Following established routine, certain inhabitants were nominated as Constables of the Four Divisions (Townhead, 27; Wallace Tower, 18; Fish Cross, 23; New Bridge, 20) and Visitors to the Markets (for Meal, Bear and Barley, Flesh). Councillors were selected as Directors of the Academy and of the Poors House; the Guild Court was constituted of 'Such of the Members of Council as are Guild Brethren', no longer necessarily fifteen as in the former councils; the Committees on Public Works and on Law Matters were continued. The Town Acts were given their annual renewal. Subsequently the council agreed to admit to their meetings 'such of the public as choose to attend', confirming the presence of reporters as allowed since 1831. Council meetings, formerly every third Wednesday, were (1834) to be fortnightly. These were still to be in the Court House (in Wellington

Square) though it was decided (1838) to meet during the winter months in the Town's Assembly Rooms.

The councils were predominantly Liberal – not till 1888 was there a provost who was a Conservative. On Earl Grey's visit to Edinburgh in 1834, an address commending his work for reform was personally presented by Provost Fullarton, and later that year a letter was sent to the king deploring the dismissal of Melbourne's ministry. But the later Conservative Provost J.M.Ferguson noted the 'bye-word that to be a Liberal in politics by no means indicated a liberal person'. The historic legislation of 1832 which is supposed to have ushered in an 'Age of Reform' was followed locally by a period in which municipal enterprise stagnated.

There was one significant difference in the character of the new councils after 1833. Councillors now represented the £10 householders, who were the wealthier burgesses, professional people, and gentlemen of means who had settled in the town. A list of those enrolled as electors in 1835 records a total of 235, located variously in High Street (128); New Bridge Street, Harbour Street and the Quay (22); with few in Mill Street (6); more in the fashionable Sandgate, Academy Street, and Cathcart Street (27), Wellington Square and nearby (36), and Newmarket Street (16). The unreformed councils had previously been unrepresentative; but that meant they could if they wished be independent. Councillors were now conscious of an electorate closely scrutinising their decisions and expenditure, in a community still small enough for frequent personal contacts; and their policies were consequently inhibited.

The council before the end of 1833 appointed a special committee to survey burgh property. In 1834 the annual £25 in support of the Races was (temporarily) discontinued. Provost Fullarton, who died in 1835, was later described (by Hugh L.Allan) as 'a pleasant, gentlemanly man, who left the management of the town's affairs very much in the hands of the Bailies'. David Limond of Dalblair returned to the provost's chair as his successor. In 1836 after the steeple of the Town's Building was damaged by lightning, it was decided to economise and it took a public petition to persuade the council to restore the vane, considered necessary in a coastal town. Plans which had been prepared by the old council (1832, 1833) for a public water supply were dropped. The *Advertiser* agreed (31.10.1833) that it was inappropriate to spend the town's funds on such a project; and it was left to the private enterprise of an Ayr Water Company to apply in 1836 for an Act, which

was obtained in 1840. When a Scottish Municipal Bill suggested union with Newton-upon-Ayr it was decided (1837) that a proposed joint meeting 'would not serve any good'. The Liberal councillors who formed the majority were divided into factions, and when Limond was ousted in 1841 he resigned.

Hugh Miller who followed was another of the old regime – he had entered the council in 1832 – and retained the provostship for a record fourteen years from 1841 till 1855. Miller was, in the opinion of an opponent (J.M.Ferguson), 'a decent High Street merchant. ... He held office for a long time more on account of the way he pulled the municipal strings than from any great merit he had ... but he has had one of the finest roads in Ayr named after him'. A less critical commentator (H.L.Allan) admitted that Miller was a 'smallish-sized and unpretentious looking man' but was however 'the greatest civic ruler in many respects that Ayr ever possessed'. 'His principal aim', according to Allan, 'was to bring the finances of the burgh into a healthy condition'. According to Ferguson, this meant that now 'Ayr did not progress at all', which was less than fair to Miller. For in 1850 his council, immediately after Lock's Police and Improvement Act was passed, applied and obtained from the Sheriff powers to establish a Burgh Constabulary, and the councillors as Police Commissioners acquired other responsibilities. In 1850 Donald McDonald of the County Constabulary was appointed Superintendent in charge of eight constables. In 1851 James Inglis McDerment was appointed Surveyor of Works and Inspector of Nuisances. Licences were now required for lodging houses, pawnbrokers, and hackney carriages. By-laws were drawn up, replacing the old Town Acts. In 1853 the sale of fish at the Fish Cross was prohibited! The councillors in their capacity as Police Commissioners took over responsibility for streets, lighting, and drainage. But they eschewed any special assessment – expenditure was covered by an annual grant from the Common Good fund, which was kept solvent by feuing of plots of burgh land for house-building.

Primrose William Kennedy who followed, 1855–61, was (even Ferguson agreed) 'the beau ideal in many respects of a Provost for the county town. He was the leading Banker in the county, was well known and highly respected, and could take his place in any company; accomplished, a good speaker, and really a most amiable personage'. But during his provostship there still continued 'the rule of quietness' and 'Public improvements did not bulk largely in the public view. One of the most momentous brought forward was the purchase of a water-cart to water the streets.' Kennedy

MATTHEW·BELLAMY·
·THE·AYR·TOWN·DRUMMER·

Death in 1888 of the last town drummer ended another tradition.

(as Allan had to admit) 'lived much in the company of his own thoughts'.

In parliamentary as in municipal elections, this was a period of Liberal ascendancy, Ayr Burghs being represented by Lord James Stuart (1834–52) and E.H.J.Crawford of Auchenames (1852–74). Stuart's only competition in 1834 and 1835 was from Radical candidates, and in 1841 and 1847 he was actually returned unopposed. Though Dr John Taylor did not contest the seat after 1834, he continued politically active, as editor of the Glasgow *Liberator*, chairman of the Scottish Radical Association, and gaining national prominence as a Chartist. At the Chartist Convention of 1839, Taylor represented Newcastle, Renfrewshire, and four other English and Scottish constituencies; Ayrshire's representative was Hugh Craig of Kilmarnock, though the Ayr and Cumnock groups would have preferred Taylor. On 13 December 1838 at a meeting in Wallace Tower hall Taylor founded the first-ever Dhurna Society whose Chartist members pledged themselves to follow an Indian technique of refusing to purchase heavily-taxed items like liquor, tea, and tobacco, so impoverishing the government and enriching themselves. But while accepting such policies of 'moral force' Taylor became associated with those Chartists who were prepared if necessary to adopt 'physical force'. In 1839 he was twice arrested, suspected of sedition; and somehow associated with abortive risings in Yorkshire and Wales in 1840. But by this time his health was fast deteriorating and he died of tuberculosis in his brother-in-law's Larne home on 4 December 1842. The Chartist movement revived in 1848, when there were meetings in Ayr in connection with the national petition for universal suffrage. But the Chartists made little impact upon parliamentary politics. When Lord James Stuart stood down in 1852, E.H.J.Crawford who was nominated to succeed him belonged to the radical wing of the Liberals. He was opposed by a Conservative candidate, Archibald Thomas Boyle, son of the Lord Justice General. Crawford won by only nine votes, and Boyle is reputed to have lost because of Robert Bone, the Newton saddler, poet, and political heckler. When in an election speech Boyle happened to use the phrase 'I draw the line ...' he was interrupted by Bone: 'Is the line the candidate for the Ayr District o' Burghs speaks o' the one his faither hung the Radicals wi'?' The uproar which followed was not untypical of political meetings of that era. The *Mustard Blister*, a four-page monthly commenced in 1850 by Bone and printed by James Connell, contained local political verse satires of a type then popular in Ayr. For example, Henry Gray (noted in the next paragraph) was addressed in 'Pious Henry's Prayer' as Holy Willie had been by Robert Burns, one verse being:

An' tae this end I humbly pray,
That Thou shalt on an early day,
Confoun' and blast the senseless fae
Wha'd ever dare,
Tae keep thy servant Henry Gray,
Frae ruling Ayr.

E.H.J.Crawford continued as member of parliament, returned unopposed in 1857 and 1859, facing rival

Liberals in 1865 and (after the 1867 extension of the franchise) in 1868, until he was defeated in 1874, which ended a Liberal ascendancy in Ayr Burghs of 56 years since 1818. Kilmarnock Burghs, a new constituency created in 1832, continued (except 1837–41) consistently Liberal. The County constituency showed pronounced variation: Liberal only 1832–39, 1857–59; then after the 1867 Reform Act (when as well as an extension of the franchise there was a redistribution of seats) Liberals took the new seats of North and South Ayrshire, but lost them both in 1874.

In municipal affairs impending changes were foreshadowed by increased factionalism in the 1860s. When Provost Andrew Paterson resigned after only three years, the 1864 election was won by William Pollock and his supporters; but opponents were able to have John Macneille elected as provost. After the 1868 election, six councillors of one faction resigned in protest following the appointment as bailie of Archibald Rae, a worthy though colourful character. One of those who then resigned was Henry C. Gray (parodied above) who was fiercely involved in every local controversy, political and ecclesiastical, and who in 1872 produced that useful account of *The Auld Toun O' Ayr and its History since 1800*. He unsuccessfully opposed the undue influence over the council being exercised at that period by the officials. The Burgh Surveyor James McDerment (son of the Poorshouse schoolmaster) was appropriately nicknamed 'The Maister', for he effectively managed committees and even freely participated in council debates and at municipal elections. Less influential in this period were those lawyers who served as town clerks. David Limond had served for 34 years from 1783 till 1817 and died two years later 'at an advanced age'. He was followed by Alexander Murdoch, then Hugh Reid, John Gray, and John Pollock. In 1871 salaries were, for the Town Chamberlain £40, Town Clerk £30; Inspector of Public Works £20; and – a quaint survival – for the Water Bailie five shillings, six and eight twelfth pence.

Council business after 1833 was largely as it had been before, dealing for example with roads ('Macadamizing New Market Street' 1833; street dung let again to the tenants of Whitehill, 1835); harbour (with the 1817 Act replaced by a new Harbour Act of 1835); continuing to enrol burgesses (including Janet Ballantine as a freewoman, 1837) even after 1846 when parliament abolished their exclusive right to trading within royal burghs; until then dealing with unfree traders (as in 1835 'to be wrote to', 'to

be summoned', then 'to prosecute'); equipping the three Town's Officers with blue uniforms as worn by the Glasgow police (1836, though retaining the 'antiquated and conspicuous red colored coat' for Sabbath days and ceremonial occasions); sponsoring public subscriptions (as for unemployed handloom weavers, 1837); introducing an annual Wool Fair in July 1838 (as proposed by the Agricultural Association); continuing to manage the church (for example by appointing a new sexton, 1839). Involvement of the council in the established church was causing increasing difficulties: in 1834 petitioning against Church Patronage; in 1835 forming a committee to lower seat rents; in 1837 deciding by nine votes to three that the burgh commissioner to the General Assembly should support abolition of Church Patronage. Some councillors belonged to other denominations, and P.W.Kennedy before he became provost seldom attended church for 'he had many things to think about, and he preferred to think about them out in the green fields', according to Ferguson. The regular Sunday walk to church of the magistrates, with halberdiers in attendance, was abandoned, and replaced by an annual Kirking of the Council after the November election, apart from special occasions.

One tradition continued was that of dispensing and enjoying the hospitality: the celebration arranged by the provost following each municipal election; entertainment of teachers and clergy after the annual examination of the Academy classes; an annual dinner to celebrate the monarch's birthday (since 1810 replacing publicly drinking a loyal toast at the Cross); every six months the visit of the Circuit Court was accompanied by a levee, procession, and dinner; latterly there would be annual visits to the Barnweil Monument and in 1887 a first trip to inspect the Loch Finlas waterworks. But for conviviality the councillors of Newton were particularly noted.

£10 householders resident within Newton acquired in 1832 the right of voting in parliamentary elections to choose the member for Ayr Burghs – there were 44 such registered as voters in 1835. But the Burgh Reform Acts of 1833, which allowed £10 householders within the royal burgh of Ayr municipal voting rights also, did not extend to minor burghs of barony such as Newton-upon-Ayr. Such burghs had been too insignificant in 1469 to be included in the act prohibiting popular election of councils in royal burghs; so did not require provision for restoration in 1833. Each Michaelmas the forty eight burgesses of Newton, with such of their eldest sons as were entered as young freeman, assembled to elect two bailies, a treasurer, and six councillors. The three magistrates each received £5 yearly; the town clerk got £10, the officer got 5 guineas (£5.25), both plus 2/6 (12½p) on the entry of each freeman. Each May at the Beltane Court the burgh laws were made. The daills or lots of 6–10 acres were re-allocated every seven years before 1771, then extended to forty seven years, till 1829 when it became 999 years. In 1833 the freemen were authorised to convert these shares into feus, giving permanent possession by a process which the Commissioners on Municipal Corporations considered in 1834 to be of dubious legality. Also, many of the freedoms had been sold, at prices rising from £70 to £500 after the working of coal from 1765 and the extended tenures as just noted. Only sons or sons-in-law were supposed to be eligible for admission as new freemen, but in practice the freedoms were at the disposal of the council, on payment of 30/– entry money to the community. The council, willing to accept such new freemen into the community, was from the later 18th century equally prepared to allow unfreemen to trade or manufacture within the burgh, without licence or fee. There were no incorporated trades surviving to enjoy exclusive privileges. The weekly market was no longer held, and the Kipper Fair was of social rather than commercial importance. The burgh finances, though including a debt of £1,300, were (for the year 1831–32) in a healthy condition. Stipends to minister (£160) and schoolmaster (£40), salaries to magistrates and officers (£30), repairs (£65) and interest on debt (£52) contributed to an annual expenditure of £347, comfortably balanced by revenue of £437 from feu duties (£90), rents (£135), and church seat rents (£212). Rent of the common land plus coal royalties could be distributed among the freemen each Michaelmas: thus in 1845 'Freemen attending the Ensuing Election shall each receive 5/– as usual'. The only assessments upon inhabitants were a trifling cess levied by the County Collector and Poor's money from occupiers of houses above £2. From all this it is obvious that business at Newton Council meetings was minimal, except when there were negotiations with coal, gas, shipbuilding, or railway companies. The town clerk is reputed to have prepared the minutes of most meetings while the members were assembling in the Council House, leaving blanks to be filled in when decisions were made 'farther up' in Cuthbert's tavern. J.M.Ferguson (who was a magistrate in both burghs!) had 'no hesitation in saying that ten out of the twelve popular ministers of Newton Parish Church were actually elected in this public-house', and Thomas McCosh, the lawyer who

[36 & 37 VICT.]   *The Ayr Burgh Act, 1873.*   [Ch. cc.]

CHAPTER cc.

An Act for extending the Municipal and Police Boundaries of   A.D. 1873.
    the Burgh of Ayr; for dividing the extended Burgh for   —
    Municipal and Police purposes into Wards; for regulating
    the Number and Election and defining the Powers of the
    Magistrates and Town Councillors of the extended Burgh;
    for regulating the Common Good of the Burgh; for
    abolishing the Petty Customs now levied therein; for
    empowering the Magistrates and Town Council to improve
    certain Streets, to extend the Market Places and Slaughter-
    houses, to purchase the Undertakings of the Companies
    which now supply the Burgh with Gas and Water, and to
    supply Gas and Water to the extended Burgh; and for
    other purposes.   [28th July 1873.]

WHEREAS "The General Police and Improvement (Scotland)   25 & 26 Vict.
    Act, 1862," has been adopted in the burgh of Ayr, and the   c. 101.
provisions of that Act are now in force within the burgh: *(Public.)*
    And whereas it is expedient that the municipal boundaries of the
burgh should be enlarged and made co-extensive with the parliamentary boundaries thereof, and that the extended burgh should
for municipal and police purposes be divided into wards:
    And whereas it is expedient that the number of the magistrates
and town councillors of the extended burgh, herein-after called
"the Corporation," should be fixed and their powers defined, and
that provision should be made for their qualification and election,
and for the qualification of electors for municipal purposes within
the extended burgh:
    And whereas it is expedient that provision should be made for
regulating the common good of the burgh and the purposes to
which the same shall be applied, and that the petty customs
hitherto levied in the burgh should be abolished:
    And whereas it is expedient that the Corporation should be
empowered to improve certain streets, and to regulate and extend

[*Local.–200.*]   A   1

Ayr Burgh Act of 1873 widened the burgh boundaries to include an area north of the river, and extended the powers of the reorganised town council.

was town clerk of Newton from 1845 till 1864, had an obvious influence in the management of its affairs.

The extension of the franchise in 1867 marked the beginning of a new era which would within less than a decade transform completely municipal administration locally.

One of the Acts of 1833 allowed royal burghs and burghs of barony to adopt what was known as a 'police system' with powers to levy a rate to provide various local public services. Neither of Ayrshire's two royal burghs was disposed to do so, though Kilmarnock had obtained its own Police Act in 1801. Further acts of 1850 and 1862 extended such permissive powers to 'populous places'. Ayr (as has been noticed) took advantage in 1850, but only three other Ayrshire towns became police burghs before 1870, with police commissioners administering services, though none (except Ayr) was big enough to have its own constabulary. Of those north Ayrshire burghs of barony which continued to function, Newmilns became a police burgh in 1872, Ardrossan (belatedly chartered as a burgh in 1846) became a police burgh in 1877, Kilmaurs never did so; other populous places which became police burghs were Stewarton (1868), Darvel (1873), Largs (1876), Saltcoats (1885), Kilwinning (1889), and Stevenston (1952). In south Ayrshire both surviving burghs of barony became police burghs, Maybole (1857) and Girvan (1889). The pattern in Kyle was quite peculiar: police burghs were established at Galston (1862), Cumnock (1866), and Troon (1896); Prestwick, the county's oldest burgh of barony, became a police burgh eventually in 1903; Tarbolton never assumed additional powers but has contrived uniquely to survive as a burgh of barony; Newton-upon-Ayr's days were numbered in 1873 when the Ayr Burgh Act extended the royal burgh's authority.

Burghs as established by royal charter were created as commercial centres; their councils, responsible primarily for organising markets and fairs, became in course of time incidentally involved in administering various basic local services. But such duties, unmentioned in burgh charters, could not be made mandatory by 19th century parliaments, and (as has just been noticed) permissive legislation was slow to be accepted. Parliament was compelled to use other agencies.

The Commissioners of Supply were those landowners first appointed in the 17th century to make assessments and arrange for the collection of the land tax, which was supplemented by additional taxes such as the window tax (1711–1851). The Commissioners had also responsibility for 'bridge money', though the urgent need for improved communications persuaded Ayrshire landowners to have set up from 1767 Road Trustees to construct and administer separately new turnpike roads. The Commissioners of Supply were also required to collect 'rogue money' for the apprehension of criminals, holding them in prison, and cooperating with the sheriff and justices of the peace. The County Buildings and Gaol, opened in 1822, were financed by the Commissioners of Supply, in association with Ayr burgh council whose tolbooth required urgent replacement. In 1830 the Commissioners appointed three constables, to Girvan, Newmilns, and Beith; in 1839 they organised a County Constabulary with an initial complement of fifteen; by 1858 when the Charlotte Street headquarters was opened, numbers

had increased to 60. An outside body exercising authority within the royal burgh was never welcome, so that in 1850 a separate Ayr Burgh Constabulary was instituted, with Superintendent Donald McDonald of the County Constabulary appointed by the council to take charge, later succeeded by Captain McKay.

Poor relief was a problem which required parliament to establish a new system. Kirk sessions were supposed to have the cooperation of magistrates in the royal burghs and landowners in heritors committees elsewhere. But in 1811 Ayr, Kilmarnock, and Loudoun were the only Ayrshire parishes where a poors rate was regularly levied. With existing agencies unable to cope with an increasingly pressing (and potentially dangerous) problem, the Scottish Poor Law Amendment Act of 1845 established Parochial Boards charged with administration of relief through a mandatory assessment levied on owners of property and their tenants. Ayr Parochial Board comprised the provost, bailies, six kirk elders, all major landowners, and elected representatives of owners of smaller properties. Archibald Hamilton of Rozelle was the first chairman, followed by three provosts and two solicitors. Annual expenditure rose from £1,009 (1846) to a peak £3,861 (1870) with the number of registered poor increasing from 241 to a maximum of 563; but costs and numbers were thereafter drastically reduced to 158 costing £2,577 in 1893. This was the result of a 'poorshouse test' which cut down outdoor relief to casual poor by requiring all applicants to accept indoor relief in the poorshouse if offered. The Poorshouse in Mill Street was in 1860 superseded by the Kyle Combination Poorshouse, built in Holmston Road by Ayr and seven neighbouring parish councils to provide for 150 inmates.

A renewed threat of cholera inspired the Public Health (Scotland) Act of 1867 which empowered town councils and parochial boards to deal with nuisances and take more positive steps to social improvement. As a result of this, the *Ayrshire Express* could proudly announce in 1870 (in *Ayr as a Summer Residence*) the water supply had been extended with new reservoirs; the town was divided into drainage districts and the principal sewers 'entirely renewed', supplementing 'the great natural sewer' which was the River Ayr.

Another act of that year – which extended the franchise, municipal as well as parliamentary – created an electorate amenable to further reforms. To ensure that future electors would all be literate was a principal purpose of the Education (Scotland) Act of 1872 which established elected parish school boards to take over existing schools and build more as required.

George Street, Ayr.

Wallacetown remained the poorest part of the town.

When in 1878 road tolls were abolished, the new County Road Trustees comprised some elected by ratepayers. In 1889 an elected Ayr County Council was established as an authority for the landward area, responsible for roads, public health, and police (though management of this last could not be trusted entirely to elected members, who had to share with the Commissioners of Supply till 1929). In 1874 parliament abolished patronage in the Church, allowing an element of democratic control in the appointment of ministers thereafter. In 1894 parish councils replaced the parochial boards as responsible for poor relief: these were entirely composed of elected members; and in 1895 Ayr Parish Council absorbed those for Newton and St Quivox, which parishes ceased thereafter to exist. Nationally, the franchise, extended in 1867, had been further widened in 1884, while introduction of the secret ballot in 1872 eliminated intimidation. It was within this political environment of widening popular participation that the Ayr Burgh Act of 1873 was brought into operation.

The impetus towards change came not from within the burgh but (as in 1850) from the county authority responsible for police. In December 1871 the anomaly of two separate police forces within the parliamentary burgh of Ayr was pointed out to Ayr town council. Wallacetown had been 'a harbour for dangerous gangs of criminals, and in every respect a nursery for crime' until 1858 when the County Constabulary was

properly constituted, but even since then the situation had been 'never satisfactory'. Some ratepayers in Newton and Wallacetown proposed adopting the 1862 Act to form a new police burgh north of the river. An alternative proposal was considered in Ayr town council to adopt that act by extending the royal burgh's boundaries to include the whole of the parliamentary burgh. 'The whole Inhabitants of the Parliamentary Burgh are so mixed up in their social and business life that to sever them for local government is unworthy an advanced intelligence and enlightened civilization'. This point made in council was supported by ratepayers and electors in public meetings. The only serious issue was insistence that the royal burgh should retain its Common Good. A private bill proved necessary.

The Ayr Burgh Act of 1873 gave parliamentary sanction to widen Ayr's municipal boundaries to those of the parliamentary constituency. The extended burgh was divided into six wards, each represented by three councillors. The town council would thus now be composed of eighteen members, of whom one third would retire annually, and would include a provost, four bailies, and a treasurer. The extended burgh would continue to have the status of a royal burgh, and surviving burgess rights would be preserved. The burgh would retain its property and other funds which comprised the Common Good, but income would be diminished by abolition of the petty customs as

In 1877 a flood destroyed the New Bridge (as Burns had prophesied).

levied at markets and fairs. Borrowing would still be permissible, but householders would be required to pay rates to finance the various local public services. In particular, the council as a Corporation could take over those private companies which provided water and gas, and widen and improve High Street and Kyle Street, with powers of compulsory purchase.

Contrary to common belief, this Act did not specify the abolition of the Burgh of Newton-upon-Ayr. Its area was of course incorporated within the extended burgh as fifth of the six wards. But the burgh of Newton-upon-Ayr is nowhere mentioned in the Act, and indeed continued to exist. As a public body it had lost most of its purpose. In the 19th century its markets were no longer held, and the Kipper Fair was only a social occasion. The last vestiges of authority disappeared when control over schooling was handed to a Newton school board in 1873, and patronage of Newton Church was lost in 1874. The freemen of the burgh had in 1828 become virtual

proprietors of their 'daills' and in 1872 they shared out the sum of £1,200 which comprised the burgh funds. Significantly, of the 39 freemen then listed, only fourteen had an address in Newton. After 1873 magistrates were still elected – J M.Ferguson, bailie and later provost of Ayr, was also treasurer of Newton burgh. Liners, visitors, and poinders of outer town bestial continued to be appointed, and the annual acts were reiterated regarding such things as herding of cattle, collection of sea wrack, expulsion of vagabonds. Newton freemen were still owners of communal land and of the Newton council house. Extant minutes continue until a meeting of the Beltan Court on 26 May 1896. Membership of Newton Town Council was listed in local directories after that, the last being the Directory for 1910–11. The Valuation Rolls continued to list the Burgh of Newton as owner of properties till 30 November 1940 when Ayr Town Council obtained a court ruling to 'have the sole right, title and interest in and to the properties held formerly by the Freemen of the Burgh of Newton-on-Ayr'. This was, remarked the *Ayrshire Post*, the 'End of an Auld Sang'.

Ayr Town Council was constituted in its new form following the municipal election on Tuesday 4 November 1873. There were contests in each of the six wards, with 34 candidates competing for the eighteen seats. Of the seventeen members of the old council, thirteen sought re-election, but only seven were successful. Most members of the reconstituted council were thus newcomers. The majority were Liberals and as expected Robert Goudie was the unopposed choice for provost as successor to John Macneille who retired after nine years' occupancy of the chair, in which he had negotiated the plans for burgh expansion. Two bailies were re-appointed and two new ones created. The treasurer was a new man. The former dean of guild was made master of works for the extended burgh. Altogether the council continued to operate as previously. After the new councillors took the traditional oath of loyalty, those who were not burgesses paid £1 each to be enrolled, continuing a tradition initiated in 1833. The council continued medieval ritual by nominating two Visitors to the Meal Market, re-appointing the harbourmaster as water bailie, and a local watchmaker as Keeper of the Town Clocks. The principal officials were retained, despite an attempt to oust the officious Burgh Surveyor. That so little was changed can be explained by the balance of electoral forces. The old royal burgh was divided into a First Ward (south of the town) with 135 electors; Second (Townhead) with 419; Third (High Street and Sandgate) with 331; Fourth (Fort) with 156. These four wards, with twelve councillors represented a total of 1,051 electors. North of the river there were 1,368 electors, but represented only by six councillors from the fifth (Newton) and 6th (Wallacetown) wards.

The new council did however from the beginning realise the need for certain adjustments. The Law and Finance committees were continued; but the Works Committee was divided into two, the new one taking responsibility for north of the river; and a Water committee was initiated. Provost Robert Goudie laid plans for improvements in water, drainage, and the harbour. Under Provost Thomas Steele the wet dock was completed, work commenced on the slip dock and the esplanade, and the Town Hall opened. In 1877 a flood destroyed the New Bridge, necessitating its replacement by a five-span structure 88 yards long and 50 feet wide, this noticed further in Chapter 15. A private act of parliament was necessary in 1877 to allow the rebuilding of the bridge, and a further Ayr Bridge

Act was required in 1884 during the provostship of William Kilpatrick.

Extension of the franchise in 1884 was followed by another Ayr Burgh Act of 1885 which extended the municipal boundaries and provided additional powers, as utilised in 1887 for the Loch Finlas water scheme. Wallace Allan long afterwards described the 1885 election as marking 'a new era in municipal ventures'. Seeking election himself, he held public meetings, which was an innovation appropriate to the new situation of a mass electorate. As a councillor he found the burgh finances in some disorder because an antiquated accounting system survived. As an example, John Pollock for his traditional duties as town clerk was paid a salary of £318, but was able to charge the council for supplementary tasks, which fees and commissions brought his annual income towards £2,000, or so Wallace Allan alleged.

Liberal ascendancy in the burgh came to an end when James Murray Ferguson became provost in 1888. The son of a tobacconist, he abandoned that trade to become owner of the *Observer*. He was renowned for 'his geniality and his pleasure in the company of his fellows'. He was a Freeman and magistrate of Newton, Session clerk of Newton Parish Church, chairman of Newton Parochial Board for its last twenty years. As provost of Ayr he significantly expanded local services. The *Ayrshire Post* commented that 'in some respects he was too daring a municipalist'. During his provostship (1888–91) an Order was obtained to erect a generating station and provide a supply of electricity; also in 1890 were instituted those proposals which resulted in the opening of the Ayr Carnegie Library in 1893. The Electricity Works in Mill Street became operational in 1896. In that year too, the town surveyor John Eaglesham was authorised to undertake a twelve-year programme which completely reconstructed the town's system of drainage and disposal of sewage, with outfalls at the Euchar and St Nicholas Rocks. In 1898 an additional river crossing was provided by the Victoria Bridge, 70 yards long and 38 feet wide. In 1899 another Ayr Burgh Act was obtained, promising new developments in the following century.

Provost Ferguson was editor of the Conservative *Ayr Observer* at a time of intense political controversy. Locally the Liberals had long been split between Radicals and the Old Whigs. In parliament Gladstone's Irish Home Rule Bill of 1886 resulted in the secession of Liberal Unionists. The Independent Labour Party founded by Keir Hardie in 1893 would begin to deprive the Liberals of working class support. In

The first issue of the *Ayrshire Post* had to be produced by a rival's printing press.

general elections before 1874 the Liberals normally sank their local differences when faced with Conservative opposition. But in 1874 the sitting Liberal member lost Ayr Burghs by seventeen votes to Sir William Montgomerie Cunningham of Corshill, described by the Whig *Advertiser* as 'a Tory of the Tories'. In 1880 however the seat was easily recovered for the Liberals by R.F.F. Campbell of Craigie; retained in 1885 despite most of the newly-enfranchised working class voters apparently voting Conservative; and held by him again as a Liberal Unionist in 1886, till his death caused a by-election in 1888. For a spell thereafter Ayr Burghs became a marginal seat, characterised by what was then called 'wobbling'. It was won by Rev.J.Sinclair, Liberal, 1888; J. Somervell of Sorn, Conservative, 1890; W. Birkmyre, Liberal, 1892, by seven votes; C.L. Orr Ewing, Conservative, 1895 and 1890.

The number of electors in the entire Ayr Burghs parliamentary constituency was increased by extensions of the franchise in 1867 and 1883 and by boundary alteration in 1873, rising from 631 (in 1832) to 1,340 (1865), 2,655 (1868), 4,297 (1880), and 5,449 (1885). By the end of the century the political parties sought to organise the new mass electorate through local associations and the 1900–01 Directory lists also a Junior Conservative Club in Newmarket Street, a Junior Liberal Club in Sandgate, a Newton Liberal Club in Main Street, and a Working Men's Unionist Club opened 1891 in New Road.

Political controversy was the lifeblood of the 19th century local press. The *Air Advertiser*, founded in 1803, began in 1816 advocating Whiggish policies of reform. In 1832 came the first of successive enlargements, and with Thomas McMillan Gemmell as proprietor, and editor from 1833 till 1853, its circulation increased from 600 in 1837 to 2,100 by 1853. Its support for Liberal policies won it readership in other Ayrshire towns. Radical views were expressed by the *Ayrshire Express* which was published from 1857 till 1871. The *Ayr Observer* which began in 1832 appealed to the landed gentry and those of Conservative opinions. It had a rapid succession of editors (including Rev. N.Cuthill and the historian James Paterson) and various owners till it became firmly established, in the ownership of John Dick and later W.M.Dick. Other papers proved short-lived – a Conservative *Ayr and Wigtownshire Courier*, 1818–25; the Free Church *Western Watchman* 1842–46; in the sixties an *Ayrshire Weekly News*, another *Ayrshire Courier*, and the *Western Argus* as a penny Friday edition of the *Observer*. In 1871 there were five local papers: *Ayr Observer*, Tuesday, J.M.Ferguson, 49 Newmarket Street; *Ayrshire Courier*, Tuesday, W.McIlwraith, 53–55 Newmarket Street; *Ayr Advertiser*, Thursday, T.M.Gemmell, 108

High Street; *Western Argus*, Saturday, J.M Ferguson; *Ayrshire Express*, Saturday, W.McIlwraith. In 1871 the *Express* absorbed the *Courier* and in 1872 amalgamated with the *Argus*, then merged with the *Observer*, which became a bi-weekly with Tuesday and Saturday editions competing with Thursday's *Advertiser*.

During the fifties and sixties political life in Ayr was enlivened by keen rivalry between the newspapers. In desperation to publish the most up-to-date news, speeches were sometimes reported before they had been delivered, and on one occasion a curling match was vividly described although it had been cancelled because of a thaw. There were hard-hitting leading articles, and items which were often scurrilous, though sometimes tinged with humour. T.M.Gemmell of the *Advertiser* was first attacked in 1857 by William Buchanan, an ex-minister who edited the *Observer* and who for a time formed an unholy alliance with Robert Howie Smith of the *Express* who had been sacked from the *Advertiser* for his vicious lampoons. This friendship ended when Smith was too drunk to write his leading article and Buchanan obliged, resulting in a Conservative policy being that week advocated in the Radical paper. Journalistic vituperation, like political rowdiness, declined in the last decades of the century. After the abolition of stamp duty on newspapers (1855) and on paper (1861) cheap daily newspapers obtained a national circulation, and the local weeklies devoted more space to local news and local topics. J M.Ferguson included in the *Observer* his 'Reminiscences of Auld Ayr' (later published in book form) and Hugh L. Allan in the *Advertiser* had a series on 'Ayr Half a Century Ago and Since'.

With the *Ayr Advertiser* adopting Liberal Unionist views, a rival Liberal weekly paper, the *Ayrshire Post*, appeared in 1880. Difficulty with its press threatened the initial publication, but there were generous offers from the two established competitors, and the *Post*'s first issue was produced by the *Observer* printing works. The first owners, who included William Robertson, found things difficult till a consortium of local Liberals took over. The *Advertiser* became the leading exponent of the Unionist cause, and in 1909 would absorb the *Observer*.

FOURTEEN

The Railway Age

Ayr entered the Railway Age in 1840 with the Glasgow-Ayr line opened under the auspices of the Glasgow, Paisley, Kilmarnock, and Ayr Railway Company. Local people were of course already familiar with the waggonways for transportation of coal from the pits of Newton and St Quivox to the harbour, and were no doubt aware that such horse-drawn waggons had been used between Kilmarnock and Troon as early as 1814 for the conveyance of passengers, and a steam locomotive tried (though without success) on that line in 1816. In 1824 Ayr town council welcomed a proposal (which was never implemented) for a rail road from Edinburgh to Troon, promising to subscribe if it were extended to Ayr. It was in April 1836 that a prospectus was issued for what became the Glasgow, Paisley, Kilmarnock, and Ayr railway. The promoters, mainly Glasgow businessmen, found no difficulty in raising the necessary capital of 11,000 shares of £50 at an initial 5% deposit. Among the five Directors appointed in July 1836 were two Ayrshiremen, both landowners, Archibald Hamilton of Rozelle and William Campbell of Netherplace. The original plans by Edinburgh civil engineers Grainger and Miller were for the route eventually followed from Glasgow to Paisley (a joint line with the Glasgow-Greenock company), rising gently thereafter towards Kilbirnie and a summit only 95 feet above sea level, then down the Garnock valley and along the coast to Ayr, with a branch from Dalry to Kilmarnock. This route was preferred by George Stephenson who was called in as arbiter after a Kilmarnock group of shareholders commissioned the survey of a more direct (but difficult) route to Ayr via Kilmarnock. Plans of the approved line were in December 1836 inspected by Ayr town council with 'approbation' of this project 'of great public utility'. In January 1837 the council petitioned parliament in support of the requisite private bill, which was enacted in July 1837. Exactly two years later in July 1839 a special train took the railway directors on a trip from the terminus at Ayr North Harbour over the newly-completed line to Irvine. In the interim ambitious plans were being made to extend the railway southwards. Dumfries town council was in September 1837 ready to accept any route whether from Kilmarnock or Ayr. Ayr council in November 1838 was pleased to note that as part of the proposed Dumfries-Glasgow line, a link from Cumnock to Ayr would have fewer engineering difficulties than the alternative between Cumnock to Kilmarnock. Which was undoubtedly the case, but Kilmarnock would win this round of the contest. Meantime constructional work was continuing, allowing the opening of regular services between Ayr and Irvine (August 1839 in time for the Eglinton Tournament); reaching Kilwinning (March 1840) and Beith (July 1840); with the Glasgow-Paisley line (opened July 1840) extending to Howwood, linked up (27 July) and opened throughout 12 August 1840. The waggonway between Kilwinning and Ardrossan was adapted as a branch line (July 1840) and the line from Dalry to Kilmarnock was completed (April 1843). The old Kilmarnock-Troon waggonway was taken over (1847) and converted to provide a more direct link between Ayr and Kilmarnock. The main line south from Kilmarnock to Dumfries, opened in October 1850, allowed travel by rail between Ayr and London. This was previously only possible via Glasgow (since 1848) on the rival Caledonian Railway Company's Beattock line to Carlisle. The Glasgow, Paisley, Kilmarnock and Ayr Railway Company and its associates, operating over 171¾ miles of track, were in 1850 incorporated to form the Glasgow and South Western Railway Company.

The local press greeted with lyrical enthusiasm the official inauguration of the Glasgow-Ayr railway on 11 August 1840. 'It is impossible to foresee the full extent of the revolution which this new facility for transit is destined to produce', commented the *Observer*, which could report only 'Just as we are going to press, we observe that the procession of gaily fitted

The Glasgow–Ayr Railway was inaugurated on 11 August 1840 with the official train arriving at the North Harbour.

carriages has arrived'. The *Observer* on this occasion was upstaged by its rival *Advertiser* whose issue of Thursday 13 August could describe the occasion in flowerly detail. 'Seldom has it been our lot to witness a scene more truly animating. The Union Jack flaunted from the Wallace Tower – the Town's bells were ringing – the Kilwinning band was playing *Ayrshire Lasses* with exquisite taste – banners of every size and hue streamed from at least a dozen heights about the Station – a splendid arch of evergreens, mixed with beautiful plants and flowers, suspending the Railway Arms, and surmounted by a floral crown, was thrown across the approach – the walls on both sides of the line as far as the eye could reach were crowded by spectators – every eminence in the vicinity was clad with men, women, and children'.

At the Glasgow terminus in Bridge Street, though the Station-house was not completed, a temporary wooden building had been erected, and 'the rain, which throughout the morning had at intervals fallen copiously, had completely subsided, and the prospect afforded was accordingly that of an afternoon's almost unalloyed delight'. Over 350 invited guests had assembled, 'a great part of whom were ladies, whose variety and gaiety of dress formed a principal part of the attraction of the scene, and whose movements and graceful vivacity showed how strong was the feeling of pleasure with which they contemplated the occasion of their assembling'. The eleven first-class and ten second-class carriages were decorated with

evergreens and flags, as were the two locomotives heading this long train. The *Cutty Sark* and *Bruce* were their appropriate though incongruously mismatched names. (For the information of railway enthusiasts, the specifications were that the former was a 2–2–0 by E.Bury & Co., with round-top fire-box and bar frames; the latter a 2–2–2 by Kinmond, Hutton, & Steel, to J.Miller's specifications, having a raised fire-box with combined dome and safety-valve on the front ring of the boiler, with a second safety-valve over the fire-box, and double frames and cylinders inside.)

'Precisely at one, the screech of the engines told that all was ready, the gasping monsters felt their freedom, the loudness of their snorting bespoke their power, and instantly the train sped along majestically'. Proceeding at a 'moderately rapid pace', Paisley was reached in exactly twenty minutes, and 'the town appeared to be in a state of general excitement; the streets were lined with people, the road had its eager crowd, and even the roof of the gaol bore its quota'. At Beith the Ayrshire shareholders and their guests awaited, most of them earlier brought up from Ayr by special train. There were nearly a hundred; not all could be taken on board; and a few had to await a later train. A more serious delay occurred after passing Irvine. One of the locomotives lost power. The engineman who had negligently allowed the boiler to run dry was summarily dismissed. The train completed its last seven miles 'at a very slow pace', arriving at quarter to four, after a journey

The original railway station continued in use for goods traffic after the opening of new Townhead stations in 1857 and 1886. A line was driven through the old station building in 1899 to take an extension by bridge to the south harbour.

of 2¾ hours. 'On the arrival of the long train of glittering carriages, with their gaily attired inmates, we have seldom if ever heard such a loud and long continued peal of welcome. ... although the patience of the assembled spectators was slightly tested, ample compensation was made, on its arrival, in the grandeur of the spectacle at the Station'.

Two sheds beside the Station were fitted out as Pavilions, with crimson festooned drapery on a white and crimson ground, and fountains (fitted by Mr McIlwraith, plumber). 450 invited guests partook of a collation of cold viands, followed by fruits and confectionery, with 'the choicest wines in abundance' (all very creditable to Mr Wilson of the Ayr Arms Hotel). A series of appropriate toasts followed in each room (simultaneously with different proposers), with hurried speeches and sudden departure of the guests,

'intimation having been given of the immediate return of the train to Glasgow'.

The railway in its first decade made a speedy and profitable expansion. William Johnstone was its forceful general manager from 1841 till 1875. He and his subordinates, as pioneers in a novel enterprise, regarded themselves as 'men of importance': stationmasters, clerks, porters, engine drivers, ticket collectors, and guards all 'treated the public with some little contempt', and also in J.M.Ferguson's opinion, 'Complaints were treated as pertaining to insolence'. Nevertheless, the utility of the railway is indicated by the 1850 statistics of rolling stock. Four locomotives originally purchased and used in ballasting the line were supplemented by another four for the first regular services. By 1850 the number of locomotives had increased to 73. All of these had been built elsewhere,

The harbour was completely renewed during the 19th century to cope with increased trade. In 1880, 40 sailing vessels and 8 steamers belonged to the port. Overlooking the harbour is Miller's Folly, creation of the owner of Fort Castle.

transported by sea to be unloaded and assembled at Ayr or Glasgow. Not till 1856 did the G. & S.W. R. build its own locomotives (at Kilmarnock). How passenger traffic had grown is evident from 236 coaches in use by 1850. The earliest of these (also imported by sea) were 1st and 2nd class of three compartments, and (on some trains only) 3rd class without roofs or seats. A variety of colours and coats of arms was superseded in 1847 by a more economical and uniform green. This became the traditional G.&S.W. colour, retained on locomotives after 1884 when maroon was adopted for carriages. New customers of different types were attracted by 1st and 2nd class season tickets from 1843, and cheap day tickets from 1845. In 1840 trains left Ayr for Glasgow at 8 and 10 a.m., 4 and 6 p.m.; leaving Glasgow Bridge Street for Ayr at 8 and 10 a.m., 2, 4, and 6 p.m. No smoking was allowed on trains or in stations. The journey of about two hours, so much faster than five to eight hours by steamship or an entire day by stagecoach, was steadily reduced to a record 50 minutes for a non-stop service in the years 1905–10. Goods trains were introduced in 1841, and the range and extent of the traffic may be gauged from the statistics of 1850 when there were nearly 400

goods waggons, about 280 others for horses and cattle, plus 1,800 for the profitable mineral traffic in coal and pig iron.

Ayr's first railway station was actually outwith the royal burgh, within Newton at the North Harbour, where there had stood a three-storey house called Lottery Hall. It was convenient enough for business, professional, and residential groups within Ayr, for the south end of the New Bridge was the hub of the town. It was convenient for coaches which continued to leave the nearby inns for places in south Ayrshire. It was convenient for connections with steamships leaving Ayr harbour for Stranraer, Belfast, and Liverpool – this last being the quickest way from Glasgow to London in that short period from 1840-1848. The situation of the railway station was less convenient (after 1849) for the Dalmellington Iron Company carts conveying lime and iron ore early each morning, returning each evening with loads of pig iron; on each occasion rows of carts were parked in High Street, while the horses were rested and the carters refreshed themselves in convenient taverns. Nor was the railway station particularly convenient for tourists following the advertised trips to the Land of

Burns, though hostelries en route to Alloway no doubt benefitted from the passing trade. In particular, one at 138 High Street acquired by James Kerr in 1837 had the name 'Tam O' Shanter Tavern' first attached to it in the 1841-42 directory which appeared not long after the railway opened.

When the railway station was transferred to Townhead in 1857, according to J.M.Ferguson 'a great part of the inhabitants thought it was a great piece of nonsense'. This however was a consequence of the continued expansion of the G. & S.W. railway network. Coal mining and manufacturing, then centred in north Ayrshire, were served by new branches from Kilmarnock to Irvine (1848) and to Newmilns (1850), and on the Kilmarnock-Dumfries line from Auchinleck (1848) to the ironworks of Lugar and Muirkirk. There followed southern and eastern extensions from Ayr, beginning with lines to Dalmellington (1856), and to Maybole (1856) and Girvan (1860) for steamers to Ireland. Ayr's new Townhead station (entered from Kyle Street) was more suitable for this extended network. The old terminus was retained for goods and mineral traffic, with a line driven through the station building and across a railway bridge to the south quay in 1899. The new main line diverged at Falkland junction and would eventually have a Newton-upon-Ayr station (1886). To carry Prestwick road over the new line, 'Tam's Brig' had to be constructed. Its name has never been satisfactorily explained; it had certainly nothing to do with Tam O'Shanter; it may have been called after the builder or, some say, a signalman; the most reasonable theory credits it to the farmer from nearby Bellesleyhill, Tam McCreath. The line (on which work began in 1853) required a series of other road bridges at Hawkhill and Whitletts road; level crossings at Viewfield and Craigie roads for the existing waggonways; and a bridge over the River Ayr. The line then crossed Mill Street on a bridge between the Poorshouse and Templeton's dye works to reach the Townhead station. Just beyond were two new bridges: one carried the Dalmellington road over to Kyle Street, by the other the Holmston road was continued westwards into Miller Road.

Such alterations, which brought no special local benefits, aroused only grumbles. There were general complaints, which the *Observer* summed up: 'That Company have had Ayrshire at their command for twenty years, and they have made their passenger fares and their goods rates so heavy as to be almost unbearable. ... By their table of rates they virtually offer a premium on goods directed away from Ayr

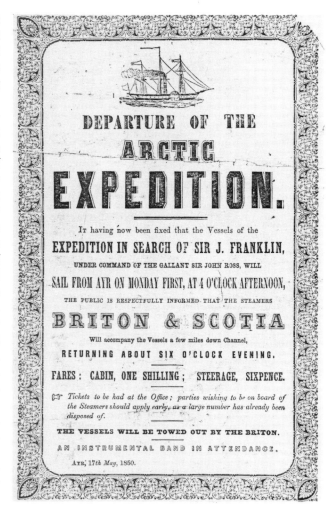

DEPARTURE OF THE ARCTIC EXPEDITION.

It having now been fixed that the Vessels of the

EXPEDITION IN SEARCH OF SIR J. FRANKLIN,

UNDER COMMAND OF THE GALLANT SIR JOHN ROSS, WILL

SAIL FROM AYR ON MONDAY FIRST, AT 4 O'CLOCK AFTERNOON,

THE PUBLIC IS RESPECTFULLY INFORMED THAT THE STEAMERS

BRITON & SCOTIA

Will accompany the Vessels a few miles down Channel,

RETURNING ABOUT SIX O'CLOCK EVENING.

FARES : CABIN, ONE SHILLING ; STEERAGE, SIXPENCE.

☞ *Tickets to be had at the Office ; parties wishing to be on board of the Steamers should apply early, as a large number has already been disposed of.*

THE VESSELS WILL BE TOWED OUT BY THE BRITON.

AN INSTRUMENTAL BAND IN ATTENDANCE.

AYR, *17th May*, 1850.

Admiral Sir John Ross was educated in Ayr, and it was from Ayr he set out in 1850 on his third Arctic expedition.

Harbour to the Harbour of Ardrossan. ... their sole supremacy in the county is a public evil'. Hopes were temporarily entertained of competition from the Caledonian Railway Company. That rival enterprise surveyed a route from Ayr through Mauchline and Muirkirk to Douglas, with the intention of providing thereby a direct link between Ayr and Edinburgh; but that plan was dropped. Later in 1883 the Caledonian company produced an alternative scheme, which was partially realised. Lines from Lugton were constructed to serve Ardrossan (1888), Kilbirnie (1889), and Irvine (1890). But plans to extend that line from Irvine through Troon to a Caledonian Railway station off Ayr High Street never materialised.

The Glasgow and South Western Railway Company continued to expand its services from Ayr. Branch lines from Hawkhill junction were opened

**TO AND FROM GREENOCK AND GLASGOW,
WITH GOODS AND PASSENGERS.**

The Steam-Packet. "AYR," Capt. M'ARTHUR, sails from
Ayr to Glasgow every Monday and Thursday, and returns
every Wednesday and Saturday, during the Summer Months;
and sails from Ayr to Glasgow every Tuesday, and returns on
Fridays, during the Winter season, with Goods and Passengers
calling at Troon, Ardrossan, Largs, Gourock and Greenock
in passing, weather permitting.

Hours of sailing to be seen on the Boards.

Cabin Fares to Glasgow,........Gs.
Steerage   do.   do.   ....4s.

AGENTS.
ANDREW PATERSON, Ayr.
ARCHIBALD BLACK, Greenock.
JAMES & GEORGE BURNS, Glasgow.

☞ *A board is put up at the corner of Mr Ewing's House,
New-bridge street, and at the Coffee-Room.*

WITH GOODS TO AND FROM GLASGOW.
The "SWIFT" Packet, Capt. LOGAN, sails regularly
Summer and Winter, from Ayr to Glasgow with Goods,
calling at Greenock.
Freight Moderate.

AGENTS. Messrs COWAN & SLOAN, Ayr.

Regular steamboat services were introduced in 1825.

to Mauchline (1870), and to Cumnock and Cronberry (1872), allowing through trains from Ayr to Edinburgh (1879–1914 and later). The main line was continued south to Stranraer (1876). Locomotive sheds were erected in 1877 at the Hawkhill junction. In Glasgow a new terminus was provided with St Enoch Station coming into use in 1876, and completed with its hotel in 1879. In Ayr, a more commodious station was then felt necessary. The adjacent site chosen required replacement of the two existing railway bridges with a new one, redirection of road traffic, and Kyle Street ceasing to be a main exit from the town. But 1886 provided Ayr with a more impressive station on this third site, with its Station Hotel opened the same year. The *'Thorough' Guide* of 1890 advertised 'Fares from Glasgow to Troon, Prestwick or Ayr:- 1st Class, 5s., Return, 7s.6d.; 3rd Class, 2s.6d. Return, 3s.9d.' and noted that 'The G. & S. W. Company have recently

built a large hotel at Ayr Station. Coupons for board and lodging and including a first-class railway journey from and to Glasgow are issued as follows: Sat. to Mon. morn., 25s.; Fri. to Mon. morn., 35s.; one week, 70s.' For those wishing to travel elsewhere, the directories at the end of the century still advertised coaches (each Tuesday) to Kirkmichael and Straiton, and to Ochiltree and Cumnock.

'Nothing has contributed more to the changes which have taken place in all departments of life during the last eighty years than railways'. That assessment by J.M.Ferguson in 1907 was undoubtedly correct. Many social and economic features were affected. The impact of improved communications on local industries was however less dramatic than might have been assumed.

The harbour certainly enjoyed an expansion of its trade. In 1835 the number of Harbour Trustees was increased to allow fuller representation of the shipping interests. The 18th century lighthouse was replaced in 1843 by one which has since been retained as a museum piece. Ayr's first lifeboat of 1803, renewed in 1819, was superseded when the Royal National Lifeboat Institution made its first local provision in 1859; in 1867 the *Janet Hoyle* was endowed by Thomas Hardie of London; and replaced by another of the same name in 1910. Before the end of the century, as Hugh Allan recollected, virtually every quay wall was rebuilt by the Harbour Trustees. The north breakwater and south pierhead were reconstructed in 1869; at the north harbour there was installed, with financial backing of James Baird of Cambusdoon, an eight acre wet dock which was opened in 1878; and the south harbour thereafter acquired a slip dock, which involved removal of the old wooden pilot house, the lime kilns, and Paton's saw mill; near the Ratton Quay, a row of dilapidated cottages made way for new large warehouse stores. Reconstruction of the harbour involved the closure in the 1880s of the Newton yard of Sloan and Gemmell where wooden vessels had been built, including the *Felix* launched in 1850 for the Arctic explorer Sir John Ross to go in search of Sir John Franklin. The tradition of shipbuilding, dating back to 1236, was however continued by iron paddle steamers built and repaired by Samuel McKnight & Co. commencing in 1883 and ten years later employing over 600 hands. In fifty years (c.1830–1880) vessels registered as belonging to the port increased from 18 of just over 2,000 tonnage to 40 sailing vessels of 13,200 tons and 8 steamers of 900 tons. That corresponded with a general increase in trade, as indicated by statistics of tonnage of ships clearing the port in the years 1856 and 1880: to other British ports, 101,059 and 220,825; to foreign and colonial ports, 187 and 7,259. The fishing trade revived, employing 270 boats of 800 tons in 1880. In 1878 the Ayr Steam Shipping Company commenced a regular service to Belfast and Larne. There were also regular steamer sailings to Greenock, Glasgow, Campbeltown, Girvan, Stranraer, and Liverpool. Though most passenger traffic had been lost to the railways, save for summer pleasure cruises, there was substantial trade in general cargo. Ayr's chief imports (in 1880) were beef, butter, barley, yarn, linen, limestone, whiting, and porter from Ireland; slates and bark from Wales; whisky from Campbeltown; tar and pitch from Archangel; timber from the Baltic and North America; guano and bones from South America for agricultural fertilisers. The chief exports were coal, pig iron, farm produce, leather, ale, and manufactured goods. Coal was the chief export, 384,846 tons in 1878, mostly to Ireland, with 10,368 tons sold on foreign markets.

The export of coal from Ayr, which in the 1830s was 70,000 tons, by the sixties regularly surpassed 100,000 tons, in the eighties reached 400,000 tons, and in the year 1900 amounted to just over 500,000 tons. This was almost entirely brought to the harbour by rail, carried on the branch lines from Dalmellington and Cumnock which were specifically designed for such mineral traffic. As Ayr harbour trade expanded, there was an increased involvement in its operation by coalmasters (like James Baird and J.T.Gordon) and also by the G. & S. W. Railway Company (which from 1873 was associated with the reconstituted Harbour Trustees). Additional facilities ranged from the bucket-dredger *Kyle* (1885) and the paddle-tug *Ayr* (1897) to a new railway bridge (1899) which served the south harbour.

There were only limited developments possible in coal mining in the immediate vicinity of Ayr. The major local coalmaster was John Taylor Gordon, who operated the Ayr Colliery Company on the estates of Newton, Blackhouse, Sanquhar, and Auchincruive. The pits in Newton itself were worked out before Gordon took over in 1832. He opened up new pits on Sanquhar estate, served by waggonway to the harbour. Around 1840 he purchased the estate of Blackhouse and moved there from his former residence at Newton Lodge. In 1841 he was employing over 700 persons, some resident in Wallacetown and New Prestwick, but mostly in the rapidly-expanding mining community of Whitletts. The wages of his men averaged from 1/6 to 2/– (10p) per day and boys from 6d (2½p) to 1/8. Regulations dated 1837 strictly defined conditions

DANIEL MAIN, FOR 50 YEARS COXSWAIN OF AYR LIFEBOAT.   DIED 1895, AGED 69.

A ten-oared lifeboat of 1803 was replaced by others, like the *Janet Hoyle* from 1867.

of employment and prohibited membership of 'any union or association of working men'. In 1842 compulsory insurance of the Ayr colliers through membership of a friendly society was imposed, and the consequent deductions from wages may have sparked off the bitter strike of that year. James Howie, who was a contemporary, described Gordon as 'of a haughty, tyrannical disposition, often at variance with his workmen. He would not listen to any complaint they had to make, reasonable or unreasonable'. When the dispute arose in 1842, Gordon's employees were immediately 'sent adrift', to be replaced with 'men unaccustomed to the trade' and he 'hired at high rates of wages some experienced workmen to act as guides and instructors to the new hands.' A riot ensued. One of the strike-breakers – known as 'nobs' or 'black-nebs' – was shot dead, the Ayrshire Yeomanry was called out 'in consequence of the riotous conduct of the turn-out colliers', and after thirty three days order was restored in December 1842. Gordon was now developing the resources of his Blackhouse estate.

The Ordnance Survey portrayed the heart of the town in mid-century.

"Tam o' Shanter" Inn, Ayr

The Tam O' Shanter Inn took that name in the 1840s to attract tourists on the way to Alloway passing up High Street after arriving at the harbour railway terminus.

His waggonway to the north harbour was extended across Whitletts road at Nurseryhall, to serve two pits at Dalmilling. By mid-century, as the Ordnance Survey reveals, the waggonway reached new pits being worked at Wheatpark, Fulshawwood, Gibsyard, Laigh Thornyflat, and beside Oswald Bridge. Gordon had overcome earlier resistance from Alexander Oswald and was now exploiting the coal resources of Auchincruive. A separate development began in 1855 when James Campbell of Craigie leased his mineral rights to Robert Brown from New Cumnock, and six pits (on the south of the present racecourse) were worked till 1865, served by a waggonway leading as far as Content Street in Wallacetown. J.T.Gordon extended his empire further. In 1858 he acquired the Enterkine pits; in 1860 the new mining village of Annbank was created comprising 233 houses; his waggonway now stretched 6½ miles from Annbank to the north quay, crossing the River Ayr twice, replacing the level crossing at Whitletts Road by an underpass, and with steam locomotives superseding horse traction, possibly from 1855. The Auchincruive pits became worked out before 1870, but to those at Annbank Gordon had in 1863 added others at Sundrum, and in 1865 at Gadgirth. In 1870 the G. & S. W. Railway line reached Mossblown and from Annbank Station the Cumnock branch from

1872 was available to serve Gordon's pits, rendering the private waggonway redundant. Though coal was no longer worked in the vicinity of Ayr, some of those employed at Annbank colliery lived in Whitletts and in Ayr itself. Under the terms of their employment they were (until 1869) required to purchase provisions in the company store, which meant carrying them four miles home. The labour force at Annbank colliery fluctuated between 200 and 900 men, and fifty were dismissed between 1859 and 1863 simply for 'sloping', i.e. not making purchases in the store.

The parishes of Newton and St Quivox each showed a decline in population in the 1820s and again in the 1860s – perhaps in part due to pit closures, but certainly affected by decay of the cotton trade, which early in the century had employed many in handloom weaving and embroidery work. During the American Civil War (1861–65) the supply of cotton was cut off by the blockade of Confederate ports by Union naval vessels – ironically many of them were former Clyde paddle steamers. The cotton trade in Scotland never recovered, though some local weavers and muslin flowerers were able to survive through the later decades of the century.

There were some compensatory developments in the woollens branch of textile manufacturing. The firm of James Templeton and Son continued to

When Ayr's railway station was moved to the Townhead the upper part of High Street became busier and more popular for shopping.

weave carpets. By 1876 there were employed 170 male weavers and over 200 women and girls preparing the wool, in four tall buildings at the corner of Fort Street and Charlotte Street. On 16 June that year, a fire broke out about eleven in the morning and within two hours the entire complex was gutted. Twenty nine persons died, trapped in the blazing interior – 28 girls aged 13 to 21, and their foreman. A new mill was built in 1878 off Kyle Street, not far from the firm's riverside dye works; abandoning carpet weaving to specialise in the production of woollen yarns. Some smaller woollen factories in Wallacetown made blankets, flannels, plaidings, none employing more than 35 persons till William C. Gray, a cashier in Templeton's, started in 1876 his own carpet-making business. Beginning in Carrick Street with two looms and twelve employees, he moved to a purpose-built building off Prestwick Road. In that Newton Carpet Factory, modern equipment produced a range of quality carpets which reached a wide market.

Other traditional trades contrived to survive. Provosts Paterson and Macneille each managed tanneries in Mill Street, which at the end of the century were still operating, as were two in Newton, though another off High Street had closed. The Newton Shoe Factory opened in 1883 continued that craft on a mechanised basis. Though the brewery at the Fort closed in 1869, others continued at Mill Street, in Cross Street, and the Newton Brewery in Main Street. About 1880 this last was taken over by A.M.Turner and to the brewing of beer he added the manufacture of aerated waters, soon outstripping four firms already established in the 1870s. Before mid-century, work ceased at the three Townhead quarries, though stone was worked till later in the century at Content and Allison Park. Sawmilling was carried on by two firms founded in the 1830s. In Wallacetown, William Alexander from Kilkerran set up his sawmills in 1836. James Paton & Sons, founded in 1837, moved to the north quay in 1881 when their yard on the south side was taken over for the new slip dock.

The early 19th century saw the establishment of

several small foundries. The mid-century Ordnance Survey showed the Ayr Foundry in Green Street, Vulcan Foundry in Newton Green, Wallacetown Foundry in Limond's Wynd; and two others south of the river – the Townhead Engine Works established by J. & A. Taylor in 1848, and the adjoining Kyle Foundry of J. & M. Rodger. Several of these specialised in farm machinery, with J. & T. Young making threshing machines at the Vulcan Foundry. Farming was also catered for by Taylor's Newton saltworks which in 1838 began crushing bones to produce bonemeal fertiliser. In the same area A. Weir and Co took over Miller's Foundry in 1860 and began to manufacture superphosphate, this firm being taken over by Daniel Wyllie & Co. in 1880. The chemical industry included the gas companies of Ayr (1826) and Newton (1845); supplemented by Starch Works beside John Street; and by W. G. Walker & Sons producing asphalt at their Hawkhill Works.

By the end of the century, industry south of the river was concentrated in Townhead, with two tanneries, a woollen factory, two engineering works, the slaughterhouse (in the old Poorshouse), the electricity generating station – all situated near the new railway station. Nearby were the Ayr Mills, as the Nethermill was sometimes now designated; the steam-operated Victoria Mills complex of 1886; and upriver were the Overmills (before the 19th century called only the Overmill). Other industrial establishments were adjacent to the harbour or distributed throughout Newton, with William C. Gray and W. G. Walker & Sons colonising a remoter area which would become a main industrial area of the 20th century.

Though Ayr did not develop into a major industrial centre in the 19th century, it did make substantial advances – for the railway contributed to its growth as a residential and holiday town, and emphasised its continued importance as county town.

For a place whose population in the course of the century had risen from 8,000 to 30,000 there was an appropriate range of trades. From the Directory for 1892–3 some sample details have been assembled. Building and maintenance of property required 5 architects; 12 builders; 4 cement merchants; 23 joiners; 4 plasterers; 12 plumbers; 4 gas fitters; 17 slaters, but now only 2 thatchers; 11 painters and paper hangers; 4 chimney sweeps; 11 house factors; 5 registry offices for servants. 16 washerwomen faced competition from the Hugh Wallace's American Steam Laundry, newly-established in Wallace Street, and followed four years later by the Greenan Laundry at Doonfoot. For alimentary needs there were 16 bakers;

23 fleshers; 5 fishmongers; 15 fruiterers; 64 grocers – 18 of them selling spirits, supplemented by 43 wine and spirit dealers. Shoppers from the town and from central and south Ayrshire were catered for also by 30 drapers; 47 dressmakers; 22 tailors; 6 hatters; 4 outfitters; 3 umbrella makers; 15 wool and hosiery shops; and 23 shoemakers (despite that name, now only selling and repairing). Other wares were provided by 17 booksellers and stationers; 11 tobacconists; 11 chemists and druggists; 7 china dealers; 16 cabinetmakers and upholsterers; 8 ironmongers; 4 toy merchants; 11 watchmakers and jewellers. Specialised services were provided by 4 dentists; 11 physicians and surgeons; 5 photographers; 5 pawnbrokers (2 in Cross Street, 3 in High Street); 9 hairdressers; 10 nurserymen and seedsmen; 4 pianoforte and music sellers; 8 printers; and the ultimate service provided by 4 sculptors who would design tombstones for erection in the New Cemetery which was opened in 1860.

One of the most noticeable changes that Hugh Allan had noticed in his lifetime was the transfer of trading from stalls in the High Street into shops. He recalled the noisy fishwives behind their creels at the Fish Cross, 'all of weather-beaten visage, arrayed in big blue pilot jackets, brown petticoats, and striped woollen aprons, with a *mutch* or handkerchief about their heads'. On the opposite side of the street in a row from the Old Bridgend upwards a row of covered carts dispensed vegetables, supplemented in summer by farmers bringing in cart loads of early potatoes. Street markets in High Street came to an end in mid-century. In 1853 the sale of fish at the Fish Cross was prohibited, and in the same year the old one-storey meal market was demolished to make way for the Winton Buildings. Shops as then existed were low-roofed, dingy and stuffy, with small windows until plate glass windows became more common. When a young man named Brown opened a new grocery shop at the corner of Kirkport, 'his window was a nine days' wonder'. Despite introducing new wares, he did not succeed. Neither did the Ayr Economical Society, a cooperative society formed in Newton which for a time around mid-century operated shops in Main Street, in Wallacetown and High Street. Nevertheless, the older type of shopkeeper was being superseded, for as Hugh Allan wrote towards the end of the century, 'in comparatively few instances are the leading merchants of the present day the lineal descendants, or even family connections.'

Ayr retained its importance as a market town. There were still six fairs: these survived for the sale of cattle and horses and (in April and October) for hiring

Ayr's first departmental store was David Hourston's draper's emporium in Alloway Street opened in 1896.

of farm servants. Regular weekly markets were held on Tuesdays and Fridays. Though the street markets ceased, alternative provision was made, between High Street and the river, by a Corn Exchange, and an adjoining Fish and Vegetable Market. A Buttermarket Hall was also provided there when the old site in Newmarket Street was acquired in 1869 for the Macneille Buildings. Cattle continued to be sold at the Fauldbacks near the head of Alloway Street till construction of the new railway station in 1886, and the subsequent formation of Burns Statue Square. The new Cattle Market was located beyond the railway. James Craig began operating as auctioneer of livestock in the old market in 1889, and after a few months moved to the nearby site where his firm still operates.

Certain trades (as recorded in the 1892–3 Directory) catered particularly for county and farming customers: 7 auctioneers; 10 blacksmiths; 6 cab and carriage proprietors; 5 coach builders; 11 grain merchants; 4 millers; 4 ham curers; 1 gunsmith; 4 saddlers; 10 carters; 12 carriers of goods to outlying parts; 2 veterinary surgeons; and there were 21 cowfeeders who kept a few beasts for milk sold around the town.

In the course of the 19th century, Ayrshire dairy farms expanded their production to supply local demands and, by railway, transport produce to more distant markets. The *New Statistical Account* reported on the agricultural improvements being made in the parish of Ayr – tile-draining, deep ploughing, and use of clay to consolidate the lighter soils; Ayrshire cattle

'brought to great perfection'; Leicester and Cheviot sheep lately introduced on the upland farms. In St Quivox parish in particular, 'Husbandry is in a flourishing state, and the land, in possession of a very intelligent and industrious tenantry, has of late years been much improved'. Some farms marketed butter and cheese in Glasgow and Edinburgh, others fattened beef cattle. Even in the parish of Newton, since the tenures of the freemen had been extended there was 'a complete revolution in the rural economy'. Rent of farm land in the vicinity of Ayr varied from 10/– (50p) to £5 per acre. Farm servants were paid about £12 a year plus bed and board, women half that; labourers' wages ranged from 8/– to 10/– per week, and at harvest time sometimes as high as 2/6 (12½p) per day. The continued advance of farming was encouraged by the Ayrshire Agricultural Association which was formed in 1835. It held shows in various parts of the county until 1852; then annually in Ayr in Beresford Park until 1896, in which year the Association purchased Dam Park as its own showground.

As the county town, Ayr was served (1892–93) by no fewer than 49 solicitors, 4 accountants, agents for 81 insurance companies, and 7 banks. Each of the three local banking companies had been taken over. In 1831 Cowan's bank, then in 1843 Hunter's bank, were absorbed within the Union Bank of Scotland, which thereafter operated in High Street on its south side, then crossing the street to new premises. The Ayrshire Banking Company in 1845 became part of the Western Bank, which failed in 1857, after which the National

Bank in 1859 took over its building in New Bridge Street. The Bank of Scotland continued in Sandgate, opening new premises in 1877. The Clydesdale bank opened a branch in 1843, taking over Cowan's old Glasgow Union office in Newmarket Street before moving into the new Winton Buildings in High Street in 1856. In 1855 the Royal Bank opened a branch at the corner of Newmarket Street and Sandgate, with Primrose Kennedy as its agent; he, other staff in Ayrshire, and most customers, luckily decided to abandon the Western Bank just two years before it collapsed. The Commercial Bank also arrived in Sandgate in 1855. The British Linen Bank from 1874 operated in Newmarket Street till 1902, then moved into a new building in High Street on the site of a former Union Bank. There was also a City of Glasgow Bank, first located in Sandgate, then in Newmarket Street until its disastrous collapse in 1878. The proliferation of banks would continue into the next century with the Mercantile Bank of Scotland opening in Newmarket Street in 1903 and the North of Scotland Bank in New Bridge Street in 1909.

The railways after 1840 had speeded the transport of goods and passengers. Communications were also facilitated by the Penny Post (introduced in 1840) and by the British Electric Telegraph Company which (from 1853) provided immediate contact between the railway station and distant places. In 1872 the post office was transferred, despite protests, from Sandgate to Newmarket Street, but returned in 1893 to the new Post Office building at 45 Sandgate – open 7 a.m. till 9 p.m. daily, 9 till 10 a.m. on Sunday. In 1900 Postmaster Robert Ramsay was responsible also for sub-offices at High Street, Newtonhead, George Street, Ayr Docks, and for 25 pillar and wall letter boxes. In 1872, a new facility was introduced by the National Telephone Company. But commmercial life remained quite leisurely despite this new-fangled invention. In 1892 there were still only 36 subscribers attached to the Ayr Exchange. Some major manufacturers (like Templeton) felt a telephone unnecessary, unlike smaller firms such as T. Hyland & Co., starch and gum manufacturers, River Terrace, Tel. Ayr No.1. It had obvious advantages for agents handling cargoes (there were 9 numbers at North Quay addresses) and other firms like W.G.Walker & Sons, Hawkhill Chemical Works. Several businessmen, like James Craig, cattle dealer, and Walter Mitchell, ham curer, found it advantageous to have both home and office numbers. The only shopkeeepers were two fishmongers, Mrs A. Allan of New Bridge Street, and P.B.Hill, 65 High Street; and two grocers, Logan Bros of Newmarket Street, and Robert Wallace, 5–9 High Street. The County Hospital was connected, but only two of the eleven general practitioners. County and Burgh Police Offices were connected, as was the County Buildings (Tel. No.3) but not the Town Buildings. Only four private householders were subscribers. The *Observer* was the sole newspaper to have a phone installed – providing a call office at its Kyle Street premises, as Logan Bros. did in their Newmarket shop. Neither banks nor hotels as yet found the telephone to be necessary.

FIFTEEN

The Victorian Town

A description of Ayr, appearing in Groome's *Ordnance Gazetteer* of 1885, waxed lyrical about the 'the singularly brilliant and imposing picture' from Brown Carrick Hill of the town, which was 'screened all round by gently-rising heights' and whose 'outskirts and environs, and many of its streets and houses, command a magnificent view over a large expanse of the Firth of Clyde, to Ailsa Craig, (and) the alps of Arran'. The town was characterised by 'Suburban villas and blocks of buildings, all more or less shaded by plantations ... the Gothic mass of Wallace Tower, and the lofty tapering spire of the Town's Buildings ... the chimney tops and gable ends of the old parts of the town'. Indeed, it was concluded, 'the entire place sits so grandly on the front of the great amphitheatre, with the firth sweeping round it in a great crescent blocked on the further side by the peaks of Arran, as to look like the proud metropolis of an extensive and highly attractive region'.

Among the attractions Ayr had to offer to well-off families choosing to settle here were the choice sites available for building. Already before the railway brought Glasgow within convenient daily travelling time, there were attractive new terraces in Fort Street, Charlotte Street, Wellington Square, Fullarton Street, Barns Street, Alloway Place. To the south of Barns House, Dalblair House, and Parkhouse, feus were available in that fashionable area extending towards the racecourse and the grand estates just beyond. Before 1830, villas like Fairfield Lodge, Wheatfield, and Midsands had been built in Racecourse Road; Bellvue was the first in Midton Road; Corsehill and Ewenfield further out on Carrick Road leading to Alloway. A score more followed in the next decade; the Ordnance Survey maps of 1857 and 1897 indicate how steadily this suburban building was progressing. Some features deemed to disfigure the fashionable residential area were removed. Such was the Washing Green on Midton Road; old cottages like Broseyland at Corsehill, Shawfield at Ewenfield, others at Belleisle

– including one at Bridgehouse where lived Robert Burns's sister, the widowed Isabella Burns Begg, from 1843 till her death in 1858, and her two daughters who died in 1883 and 1886.

On the great estates which ringed Ayr the mansion houses were most of them rebuilt or improved to Victorian standards of gracious opulence. Ownership was retained by members of the families of Hamilton (Rozelle), Campbell (Craigie), Oswald (Auchincruive) and Ballantine (proprietors of Castlehill till 1909). Mount Charles which was acquired by Lieutenant General John Hughes in 1827 passed by his nephew to the Hughes Onslow line. Doonholm after the death of Alexander Hunter in 1858 was purchased by Sir Colin Blackburn, and before the end of the century went from that family to James Kennedy. Belleisle similarly passed from Hamilton hands to William Smith Dixon, a Glasgow ironmaster, then in 1886 to George Coats, Paisley thread manufacturer. Barns estate after the death of Patrick McNeight in 1840 was shared among relatives; J.C.Nicolson who married one of the legatees occupied Barns House which became surrounded with 19th century villas and terraces built upon land feued from this once-extensive estate.

The great estates with their impressive mansion houses were joined by several new but more modest little estates. Gearholm and Gowkscroft were purchased from the Marquess of Ailsa by William Stewart, returned from India. His neighbour at Seafield was Captain J.O.McTaggart of the East India Company, followed by Sir William Arrol who in 1888 purchased its 50 acres and built a new house. William Arrol (1839–1913), born at Houston in Renfrewshire, was owner of the Dalmarnock ironworks, knighted in 1890 for his notable work as bridge-builder, and MP for South Ayrshire from 1895 till 1903. At Blackburn John Robb in 1826 enclosed his property with a wall made with stone from the old tolbooth, and according to the *New Statistical Account* 'may be said to have "new made" his

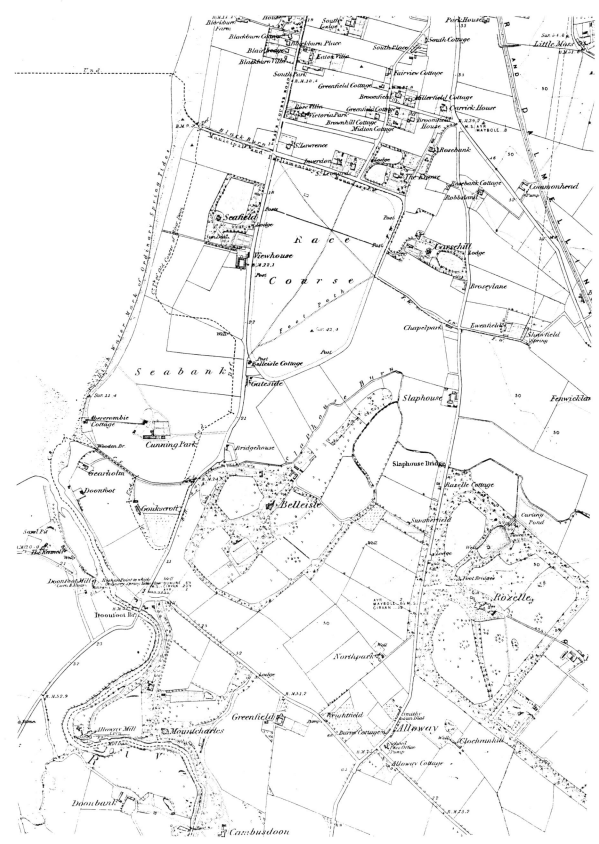

By mid-century villas were being established in the area south of the town. The fashionable Ayr Races were held here from 1787 till 1906.

small estate'. Belmont House was erected in 1843 for James Morton, a lawyer who was eccentric enough to have erected before his death a handsome tombstone in the New Cemetery. In 1853 James Baird acquired Greenfield, alias Craigwell, built a new house, and renamed the estate Cambusdoon. That outstanding industrialist, born in Lanarkshire in 1802, extended his business interests into Ayrshire in 1844 and by 1865 could boast of employing 25,000 persons producing coal and iron, with 14 blast furnaces at Gartsherrie, 4 at Dalry, 8 at Kilwinning, 6 at Hurlford, 4 at Lugar, and 3 at Muirkirk. To his Cambusdoon estate he added those of Auchendrane (1862), Muirkirk (1863), Drumellan (1866), and Wellwood (1873), making him a major landowner with nearly 20,000 acres in Ayrshire alone. But this tough Scots-speaking industrialist was not socially acceptable to certain persons within the royal burgh. According to J.M.Ferguson, when the chairman and engineer of Ayr Water Company sought to acquire Milton Springs to augment their supply, they succeeded only in antagonising Baird by their patronising approach. At a subsequent parliamentary election, Baird was howled down when he spoke in support of the Conservative candidate. Perhaps because of this, Ayr gained nothing from Baird till he guaranteed £165,000 for the construction of a wet dock – opened in 1878, after his death. As a staunch member of the Kirk, Baird financed in 1858 the building of a church at Alloway, which was erected into a separate parish in 1860 after being annexed to Ayr since 1690. This aroused protests, directed against Baird, for the new church was said to spoil the view of the Burns Monument. Later Baird gifted £500,000 to the Church of Scotland. This, donated just two years before his death in 1876, was unkindly described by Baird's critics as the largest fire insurance premium on record.

The built-up area adjacent to the town was quite slowly extended. What became Miller Road was laid out and named (after the provost) only in 1854. The OS map of 1855 shows building beginning there, at Killoch Place, and in Dalblair Road. Other modest developments of terraced and detached houses were commencing in Bath Place and in the Fort area. This last property was purchased in 1853 from the Kennedys by John Miller, an eccentric gunsmith and antiquarian who made a fortune in Calcutta and converted the Tower of St John's into a Gothic-style Fort Castle residence where he lived as 'Baron Miller' till his death in 1910, during his time creating 'Miller's Folly' which still overlooks the South harbour.

Improvements were carried out by the Police Commissioners (as the town council constituted itself after 1850 for such purposes). In 1854 for example, twenty two additional street lamps were erected to illuminate Racecourse Road, Midton Road, Maybole Road, and Dalmellington Road – with two provided outside Provost Miller's residence, Midton Cottage. The Surveyor of Works and Inspector of Nuisances, James McDerment, was responsible also for cleaning up the older parts of the burgh. Streets and pavements were repaired (1851), lodging houses licensed (1851), and Isle Lane renamed Hope Street as part of council policy to 'remove the bad characters who were located in this lane'.

Practically all of High Street, Hugh Allan recalled, was rebuilt in the second half of the 19th century. Beyond the Wallace Tower a medieval townscape had long survived – 'small one-storey thatched houses stood with their gable ends out to the edge of the gutter', and 'closes which had been built at right angles to the line of street'. That part of High Street and Alloway Street were widened, and lined with fashionable shops following the opening of the new railway station in 1886 and the naming of Burns Statue Square in 1897. The lower part of High Street, Newmarket Street, and Sandgate were embellished by new buildings, with the several banking companies vying to emphasise their solid reliability. The house at 78 High Street where the reputed witch Maggie Osborne had lived was replaced in 1881. The Town Buildings were extended in 1880. In Wellington Square statues were erected to Brigadier General George Smith Neill (1810–57) who was born in the Square and died at Lucknow; Archibald William, Earl of Eglinton (1812–61); and Sir James Fergusson of Kilkerran (1832–1907). These supplemented the two older statues to William Wallace in the High Street; that at Townhead to Robert Burns (1891) which complemented the Burns Monument at Alloway (1823); and one to Dr John Taylor, the Ayrshire Chartist, erected (1850) in the remote Wallacetown Cemetery. Provost Primrose Kennedy (1800–63) was commemorated by a fountain at Sandgatehead, and A.M.Turner of Newton Brewery by a steel footbridge which he donated (1900). That new creation of 1788, the New Bridge, was widened and improved in 1840, and tolls abolished in 1850. As prophesied by Burns in 'The Brigs of Ayr', that bridge gave way in severe floods of 1877 (which the Auld Brig withstood). A finer structure costing £15,000 was opened in 1878. Some decorative parts of the first New Bridge were rescued – one of four stone plaques was installed at the corner of Monument and Chapelpark Roads; and when the Pavilion was built on the Low Green the bal-

Ayr attracted wealthy incomers, like the ironmaster James Baird who built Cambusdoon in 1853.

ustrades from the bridge were incorporated. In 1898 an additional road crossing was provided upriver by the Victoria Bridge.

On the other side of the water, the old mill house which impeded access to the bridge was acquired by the Road Trustees in 1834 as a prelude to demolition. The open lade which ran down the middle of Main Street was covered in, and Newton mercat cross had to be removed. This lay in the adjacent kirkyard from about 1860 till about 1905 when it was re-erected near the New Bridge, and moved aside in 1913 to accommodate the branch tramway line to Hawkhill. The OS map of 1855 shows New Road opened to replace Weaver Street as the principal exit to the north, and villas extending along Prestwick Road. There already in 1837, as Rev. Alexander Cuthill noticed, there were 'neat cottages' and 'handsome villas' where previously there had been only 'wreaths of barren sand'. In St Quivox there were the 18th century mansion houses of Craigie and Auchincruive, and the more modest Content House and Blackhouse.

There was (before 1873) no public authority north of the river competent to undertake improvements to the environment. Thereafter the Town Council of the extended burgh meeting as Police Commissioners operated as a Local Authority responsible (under appropriate Acts of Parliament) for various public health functions. Nevertheless the general situation north of the river was deplorable. Dr H.J.Littlejohn, Medical Officer of the government's Board of Supervision, reported in 1878 after a visit of inspection that Wallacetown was 'inhabited by a low class of the population ... the houses were of poor description ... the clauses relating to Common Lodging Houses were not enforced ... this at one time outlying country district still maintains the characteristics of a dirty village. ... The cottages have manure in all directions in their back courts, ill-kept piggeries abound, and privy accommodation is either totally awanting or of the most offensive description. Ayr itself is one of our cleanest Scotch towns and such adjuncts as Wallacetown must be made to conform to the usages'. The Census report of 1891 indicated overcrowding in Ward 6 (Wallacetown) and Ward 5 (Newton) of 1.94 and 1.92 persons per room, as compared with south of the river where wards 1 to 4 had respectively 0.71, 1.1, 1.23, 0.97. Of Ayr's 5,376 families, 22% were living in single-ends and another 35% in two-roomed dwellings – and we can guess that most of these were north of the river.

The Tower of St John was converted by the eccentric John Miller into a residence called Fort Castle.

Dr Littlejohn returned in 1892, following a typhus epidemic the previous year in which there were 29 cases. 'With the exception of this last case (which was that of the respected Medical Officer of Health, Dr Dobbie), all the cases occurred in the poorer districts of the Burgh, viz. in Newton and Wallacetown'. Dr Littlejohn commented that unlike Edinburgh, in Ayr 'all its attractions can be seen and enjoyed without the poverty and wretchedness of many of its poorer inhabitants being obtruded on the visitor'. His report was critical of arrangements to quarantine infected families. 'The Reception House provided by the Local Authority is a mere makeshift, and is of no use for the purpose. I should say that it would be impossible to induce any family, even the poorest, to undertake the perilous journey necessary to reach, at the extremity of the Docks, this haven of refuge which, when arrived at, anyone would, in my opinion, be justified in refusing to enter'. It was recommended that special hospital provision be made.

Various public authorities had combined to provide the Kyle Combination Poors House at Holmston Road in 1860 with accommodation for 168 paupers, and housing 124 in 1891; and a district lunatic asylum at Glengall Asylum in 1866, extended to care for 355 inmates by 1891. It was left to voluntary effort to provide infirmaries. A little fever hospital was opened in 1844 at Townhead, with twenty beds, managed by a committee. It was superseded by the County Hospital in Holmston Road, opened in 1883 for 44 patients in the general hospital and 20 in the separate fever ward. But as the Board of Supervision later advised: 'A favourite residential town like Ayr with a permanent population of about 25,000 and a much greater summer population, cannot safely depend upon a County Hospital; nor should the arrangements be such as may tend to discourage full advantage being taken of the hospital by all classes of the community'. In the repeated outbreaks of smallpox in the last decade of the century, the only

(Ayrshire Post Photo.)
THE PASSING OF BARON MILLER.

The death early on Tuesday morning of Mr John Watson Miller, of the "Fort Castle," Ayr, in his 90th year, removes from the county town of Ayrshire its most picturesque figure. For sometime Mr Miller had been in poor health, and the end was not altogether unexpected. For about sixty years Mr Miller had been a familiar figure in the streets of the burgh, to which he was devotedly attached, and in the progress and prosperity of which he always evinced a keen interest. He was popularly known as "Baron Miller," from the fact that he was proprietor of the lands which were formerly known as the Barony of Montgomerieston. With a twinkle in his eyes, he would occasionally remark that he had as much right to the title of Baron as many of the members of the House of Lords. The Baron was a quaint figure as he strode along the streets of Ayr, generally on his way to or from one of the auction rooms

'Baron' Miller developed the Fort area and constructed 'Miller's Folly' overlooking the harbour.

provision was a two-roomed wooden Reception House in the grounds of the County Hospital, initially without water supply or drainage. Even though it was rebuilt in 1896, this was deemed 'wholly unsuitable', for the Local Authority had 'deliberately neglected the lessons of their own experience and the protestations of the Board'. Eventually in 1903 a little smallpox hospital was built at Crofthead and in 1905 an Infectious Diseases Hospital at Heathfield.

While some Victorians were especially concerned about Cleanliness, it was invariably regarded as subordinate to Godliness. The impressive range of church buildings which still grace the town is witness to Victorian piety. Some emphasised continued doctrinal differences. Others were the product of ecclesiastical controversy about relations between the State and the Established Church – the great Disruption of 1843 when the Free Church was formed.

Within Ayr Parish, neither the Old nor the New Church was much affected by the Disruption; Dr Auld and Mr Cuthill continued in their charges till their deaths in 1853 and 1851 respectively. At Newton Parish Church however, the scholarly and revered Rev James Stevenson with seven of his eight elders and almost the whole of his congregation left in 1843 to form Newton Free Church, building within months their first place of worship beside the parish church, replaced by a new one there in 1863. Similarly in Wallacetown, the newly-ordained Rev William Grant with five of the six elders and most of the congregation left the Church of Scotland to celebrate his first communion in Alexander's woodyard. William Alexander was a typical adherent of the new Free Church, who provided also a wooden place of worship in Alloway Place till Ayr Free Church in the Sandgate was opened in 1845. Those who preferred to continue worshipping in Wallacetown did so in the Wooden Kirk in Limond's Wynd till a Wallacetown Free Church was built in 1860 on the south side of John Street. When in 1876 the majority of the Reformed Presbyterian Church decided to join the Free Church, their local congregation of Cameronians became the Martyrs Free Church, continuing in their place of worship at the corner of George Street and John Street. A fifth local congregation of the Free Church originated in a local dispute within Wallacetown Free in 1889: dissidents formed a separate congregation in the Artillery Hall, Newmarket Street, and in 1893 built St Andrew's Church in Park Circus.

Meantime the seceding sects which had originated in the 18th century were most of them drawing closer together. The local congregation of Anti-burghers, however, obdurately refused to participate in successive arranged unions, but continued worshipping in George Street, attached to the Synod of Original Seceders. By contrast, the Burghers from 1820 belonged to the Wallacetown United Secession

Church; participated in the union of 1847 with the Relief Church to form the United Presbyterian Church; and this Wallacetown U.P.Church in 1860 left Wallace Street to become Darlington Place U.P.Church. In 1865 their premises were acquired by congregationalists of the Evangelical Union, whose Wallace Street E.U.Church chose in 1898 to become the Wallace Street U.P.Church. South of the river, the Relief Church became from 1847 the Cathcart Street U.P.Church. In 1898 Trinity U.P.Church originated with meetings in a hall in Midton Road.

The Established Church recovered from the Disruption. The Parish Churches of Ayr (Old and New), Newton, St Quivox, and Wallacetown Chapel were indeed supplemented by additional places of worship to supply the extending town. A new church was provided at Alloway in 1858, enlarged in 1891. St Leonard's Church was commenced in 1886 beside Carrick Road, its name recalling the medieval foundation of that vicinity. North of the river, Newton Parish Church sponsored in 1885 a separate North Newton congregation which would become St James's Parish Church in 1904. Wallacetown Chapel became a Parish Church disjoined from St Quivox in 1874. At St Quivox there was remarkable continuity in one respect. Rev William McQuhae, minister for the long period from 1764 till 1820 was followed by his youngest son Rev Stair Park McQuhae, who retired in 1859. An even longer family connection was provided by Rev James Wilson (1859–1906), his eldest son Rev James Peter Wilson (1906–41), then the latter's nephew Rev William Lyle Brown Wilson.

All those eighteen congregations so far listed were organised on a presbyterian basis, eight attached to the Established Church, five belonging to the Free Church, four U.P., and one O.S. Other denominations followed their separate traditions. The Moravian Church in Mill Street and the Methodist Church in Charlotte Street each continued with limited support, but the Independent Tabernacle in River Street closed by 1878. Other congregationalists who first met in 1844 formed in 1865 the Wallace Street E.U.Church; though that congregation joined the U.P.Church in 1898, a separate faction attached itself to the Congregational Union. Baptists, after an unsuccessful earlier attempt, became established, in 1884 purchased the Queen's Rooms, and converted that theatre into a place of worship; in 1889 another congregation of Baptists began to meet at Prestwick Road. The Roman Catholic community was served by St Margaret's Church in John Street, their numbers augmented by continued Irish immigration, Rev

The Kyle Combination Poorshouse in 1860 superseded the 18th century Mill Street institution.

William Thomson and his successors able to shepherd local adherents more effectively after 1847 when Ayr ceased to be their only church in Ayrshire. The Scottish Episcopal Church moved into Fullarton Street in 1838, with its minister Rev. W.S.Wilson elevated in 1859 to be Bishop of Glasgow. His vigorous promotion of episcopacy was evident locally when the Trinity Chapel had to be enlarged in 1852. By 1884 when Bishop Wilson retired from the incumbency of Ayr, the congregation had outgrown the existing building. In 1888 the aged bishop dedicated a new chancel which was joined to the existing nave, which was itself extended to form Holy Trinity Church as dedicated in 1908.

An unofficial census of church attendance one Sunday in 1876 revealed some interesting figures for Ayr. 1,857 attended Church of Scotland services: in the Old Church, 478; New Church, 476; Newton, 544; Wallacetown, 359. 2,843 attended so-called Dissenting churches: Ayr Free, 461; Newton Free, 530; Wallacetown Free, 273; Cathcart Street U.P., 423; Darlington Place U.P., 347; Original Seceders, 330; Reformed Presbyterians, 47; Evangelical Union, 140; Methodists, 61; Moravians, 34; Episcopalians, 197. Add to the total of 4,700 persons those belonging to the Roman Catholic Church and members of various small sects, and it is clear that those who were involved formed a minority of the 18,000 population of the parliamentary burgh at that period.

Ayr County Hospital of 1883 replaced a fever hospital at Townhead.

New sects proliferated in the second half of the 19th century. Following the Religious Revival of 1859 the Christian Brethren, who had originated in Plymouth and were nicknamed the Dippers, baptised their first local converts on the Newton shore, and became formally organised by 1864. The Moody-Sankey Revival of 1874 enthused others. After a third Revival in 1878 an Ayrshire Christian Union was formed, and in 1881 services began in the Wooden Kirk. The Salvation Army reached Ayr in 1884. A Hebrew congregation has been noted about 1880.

Though many of the separate sects were the product of dissension, in time initial bitterness tended to diminish. The several presbyterian churches cooperated in evangelical work. The first joint undertaking is said to have been a series of Sabbath evening lectures in 1851 on the subject of Papal Aggression. Anti-Catholic fears were at the time aroused by the influx of Irish immigrants and an obvious increase in strength of that Church, facilitated by the Catholic Emancipation Act of 1829 and culminating in the re-establishment of a Church Hierarchy in 1878. Yet overt anti-Catholic feeling seems to have been restricted to immigrant Ulster Protestants, and five local Orange Lodges which had a brief existence in the 1870s were concerned about Irish politics as much as religion. Cooperation among presbyterian congregations in 1851 involved ministers exchanging pulpits, and during the 1859 Revival ministers took part in united meetings in their several churches. There was also cooperation in such bodies as the Sabbath School Union Society (1821) which by 1841 had 21 affiliated Sunday schools in Ayr, Newton, St Quivox, and Monkton. There was the long-established Ayrshire Bible Society (1828).

A Total Abstinence Society (1838) was forerunner of the wider Temperance movement, in which U.P. ministers took a leading part, with support from the Free Church, though less from the Auld Kirk. The Forbes Mackenzie Act of 1853 defined licensing hours. Thereafter the Temperance movement continued active, represented by the Good Templars, the Rechabites, and the Band of Hope. Church cooperation was obvious in managing the industrial school, whose directors were the ministers of the Established, Free, U.P., R.P., O.S., and Independent churches; and when the first Burgh School Board was elected in 1873 the *Advertiser* was pleased to note the absence of sectarian rancour. With so much emphasis on evangelism, traditional Calvinist theology was less atttended to in many pulpits. In 1865 the Cathcart Street minister warned of 'certain tendencies abroad which are to be watched with great earnestness if not with sharp suspicion, tendencies with regard to the question of the inspiration of scripture, of the nature of the Atonement, of the duration of future punishments, of the observance of the Sabbath'. In 1841 Rev James Morison was expelled from the Kilmarnock United Secession Church for preaching heresy. But before the end of the century Morisonian concepts of Atonement were tacitly superseding the Calvinist doctrine of Election in presbyterian as well as congregational sermons; though a minority insisted on emphasising traditional doctrines and practices.

Another thing that modified former differences was the obvious loosening of ties between the Civil authorities and the Established Church. That Church had once had prime responsibility for poor relief, education, and discipline, its kirk session sharing duties only with the town council of the royal burgh. As people forsook that Church it lost its dominance, and 19th century parliaments were now legislating for an augmented population, arranging for provision which could no longer be effectively made by churches or other private agencies. Complementing the Church's declining role in public affairs was Ayr Town Council's withdrawal from involvement in the Church. The traditional parade of the councillors to the Auld Kirk each Sunday was abandoned during the regime of Provost Kennedy, not from lack of piety, but councillors who belonged to other denominations refused to allow the established church special recognition. The town council was statutorily involved in choice of the minister of the second charge, but from 1850 sought the advice of members of the congregation, and when a minister was required for the first charge conveyed such recommendations to the crown, which held the patronage. But when the town council arranged an ordination dinner for Rev John Sinclair in 1871 there were objections. In 1874 parliament abolished patronage, thus ending resentment that had lasted since 1712. The council continued to retain responsibility for the fabric and grounds of the Old and New Churches, and the continued privilege of appointing an elder to represent the royal burgh annually at the General Assembly of the Church.

In previous centuries, prominent parish ministers had made their impact. In the 19th century ministers of various denominations won widespread respect, in particular Mr Thomson of St Margaret's, Bishop Wilson of Trinity, and Rev John Robertson of the Original Seceders. Rev William Shaw who served the Auld Kirk from 1851 till 1863 was (in Hugh Allan's words) 'a man of scholarly culture, a graceful preacher, and possessed social gifts which increased his hold on the better class of society'; but it was his successor Rev Thomas Dykes who from 1854 till 1909 revived that church and (according to J.M.Ferguson) helped 'tone down sectarian feeling' and won 'the general respect of the whole community'. As compared with Dr Dykes's long tenure, there was in Newton Parish Church a rapid succession of short ministries – most of them able young men chosen by the representatives of the Newton Freemen, at the beginning of distinguished careers. Rev James Stevenson of Newton and Rev William Grant of Wallacetown were powerful enough to lead most of their elders and congregation into the new Free Church. The latter helped form a Young Men's Christian Association which contained members from various denominations. Rev John Graham, though with a mere handful of adherents in the Reformed Presbyterian Church, attracted packed attendances to his monthly Sabbath evening lectures. Especial zeal was exhibited by the Salvation Army and other groups who conducted street services. Even before their time there were 'street preachers who figured in the town ... who took to it on their own account with no coadjutors' and Hugh Allan remembered Colonel M. Shaw, a retired army officer with strong opinions on most subjects who carried around a wooden rostrum to set up at various street corners; Johnnie Borland, an itinerant umbrella mender who on a Sunday evening at the Fish Cross could repeat in his stentorian voice almost word for word the sermon he had heard that morning in the Moravian church; and Willie Justice, a Newton shoemaker who with great fervour warned about the Wrath to Come.

A changed attitude to religion is evidenced by the character of new places of worship erected in the Victorian era. The rectangular boxes of the early part of the 19th century were succeeded by edifices of greater architectural merit, and designs of the Gothic revival were commissioned by all save the most conservative denominations. The older places of worship were renovated. Rev Dr Thomas Dykes recalled that the Old Church after two hundred years was 'very picturesque and interesting' but 'there was no flooring in the area, the pews resting on the earth, with foot boards in front to enable the sitters to keep their feet off the ground'; the galleries were only partially floored, and the wooden ceiling was patched with canvas. Improvements were financed by congregational contributions, as with the installation of gas into the Old Church (1844) and the New (1865). The Old Church acquired stained glass windows in 1878.

The character of the church services was embellished with musical innovations. In 1821 the town council was advised that 'Several young Gentlemen and Ladies propose to form themselves into a Band for improving the Psalmody in the Old Church of Ayr'. In fact it was in the New Church that a choir became established. The Free Churches from their beginning were concerned with improving psalmody, and Ayr Free Church in 1846 hired a teacher of music. The formation of choirs in other congregations was stimulated by two lectures on psalmody delivered in Cathcart Street Church in 1854 by Rev Neil Livingstone of Stair Free Church. In 1868 an innovation was made in the Old and New Churches of reversing the traditional practice of sitting while singing, and standing for prayer. The old regime continued in Newton Parish Church till the end of the century. The introduction of instrumental music into church was pioneered by a harmonium in the New Church in 1871, and a pipe organ in 1874. Installation of a pipe organ in the Old Church in 1882 sadly involved destruction of some of the handsome woodwork: the 17th century pulpit was saved, but it lost its sounding board and screen. Ayr Free Church, much more conservative, did not acquire a harmonium till 1893 nor a pipe organ till 1896. With the introduction of organs, precentors were superseded by organist-choirmasters, the first being J. Butler Cowap in the New Church. Praise was diversified by the introduction of hymns into Ayr Free Church in 1884, a year ahead of the Old and New Churches.

Regular Sunday worship was altered, with shorter services, and the second afternoon service replaced by an evening service in the Old Church in 1886. Until late in the century the half-yearly Sacrament

The Relief Kirk built in 1816 typified the plain stern style of the various seceding congregations.

involved Fast days (which were public holidays) with services of preparation preceding the Sunday Sacrament, followed by a Monday thanksgiving service. One other change within the established churches was the disappearance of the repentance stool and the abandonment by most denominations of public rebuke. It was no longer feasible for a kirk session to exercise such discipline when membership was voluntary. And evangelism was concerned with bringing in rather than driving out. In 1868 a bazaar raised funds for the building of a parish Mission Hall in Carrick Street, and other denominations followed in providing meeting places for Sunday schools and other organisations, with midweek services, lectures, and soirees which outsiders might be persuaded to attend. At the Jubilee service in connection with Cathcart Street U.P.Church in 1865, Rev. W.Morrison noticed that 'Sabbath schools, libraries, missions to the heathen, home missions, temperance societies, church extension, ragged schools, the operations of Biblewomen – all these have either originated or been greatly developed within half a century'. By 1893 there was even an Ayr Guild Swimming Club for young men attached to the Established Church. The Boys Brigade, which was formed by William Smith in Glasgow in 1883, reached Ayr in 1886 when in Cathcart Street Church hall was formed the first of three local companies recruited that year.

The enthusiasm with which new churches were

erected in the Victorian era was paralleled by developments within the sphere of education. Existing facilities were found insufficient (in coping with the increased number of children in the extended town) and inadequate (in catering for the needs of certain groups of children).

The system of parochial schools which had served Scotland well in the 18th century could not effectively be adapted to 19th century urban industrial communities. To meet local needs, Ayr burgh school had been converted into an Academy, which was initially successful. But even before the departure of Dr Memes in 1844 a declining roll was evidence that all was not well. The teaching of science, pioneered here in the 18th century, had almost disappeared by 1834. The teaching of Classics was in 1838 taken over by the rector and ceased to be a separate department. The experiment of foreigners providing instruction in modern languages was abandoned in 1854. During the rectorship of Dr William Hunter (1844–62) the various masters, who operated virtually independent departments, devoted most of their time to elementary classes – or, in the case of the English Master Arthur Lang (1838–88), to profitable dealings in local property. Because of its relatively high fees Ayr Academy could cater for only a small proportion of the younger children of the town. An official report of 1868 described the Academy as containing a 'genuine middle class population', half of them 'children of shopkeepers and clerks'. Those of higher social class included boys sent to Ayr to board with one of the masters. There was only a score of 'children of artisans, labourers, etc.', nearly all those being free scholars benefitting from the endowments by Fergusson of Doonholm (1794) and Hamilton of Pinmore (1829). 120 girls formed a third of the total roll of 362 that session. Ayr Academy was managed by a Board of Directors, on which the town council was represented; but it had obviously ceased in function as in name to be the burgh school.

The Established Church could in parish schools now make provision only for a minority, despite the availability from 1833 of Privy Council funds for building new schools. In St Quivox a parish school catered for the rural population in the east of the parish; augmented by a school attached to Wallacetown chapel which was erected in 1837. In Newton-upon-Ayr the school held in the Council room could take few children, though adjudged by the Court of Session in 1818 to be a parish school. In 1847, however, the Freemen opened a new school in Green Street, which though teaching only elementary

St Andrew's Free Church, built in 1893 in Gothic style, exemplified changing features in worship.

classes, cheekily took the name of Newton Academy; and with low fees and sufficient reputation attracted pupils from as far away as Alloway. Following the establishment of a separate parish of Alloway in 1860, the Church took over (from 1863) the provision of schooling.

That the parish and burgh schools were statutorily associated with the Established Church persuaded various denominations to provide schools in which adherents' children could be nurtured in what was deemed to be the true faith. The Moravians in 1816 opened such a school beside their Mill Street church. The Roman Catholic Church was able, following the Emancipation Act of 1829, to open its own school beside St Margaret's Church. Sometime after 1839 a school was provided by the Episcopal congregation of Trinity Chapel. Following the Disruption of 1843 each of the new Free Church congregations set up schools, staffed by teachers who having left the Established Church had to resign their posts in parish schools. Such schools were formed in Ayr at the former Fish Cross School, in Newton beside the Free Church in Main Street, and in Wallacetown Weaver Street.

Other schools were provided by various agencies. An Ayrshire Educational Society was formed in 1840 for the establishment of schools in destitute localities.

Already since 1825 there was in Ayr Poorshouse a school provided for by Captain John Smith's bequest; there William McDerment single-handed taught 245 pupils (in 1838) until in 1842 Smith's Institution was opened nearby, 'one of the largest and most commodious schoolrooms in the County' measuring 54' × 26' × 17', to which a second storey was added in 1867; by which time 300 scholars paying a penny a week and 70 poor children enrolled free were taught by a staff of three teachers and two pupil teachers. In 1843 another charity school for infants and juveniles was opened in Charlotte Street. It was initiated by a gift from Archibald Hamilton of Rozelle and named after his wife the Lady Jane Hamilton's School. It took 200 to 300 pupils from Ayr, Newton, and Wallactown. In the early 1850s a School of Industry, under patronage of the Earl of Eglinton, was established on the west side of Carrick Street. There was also a Ragged School in Newton.

There were schools which depended entirely upon fees. In Content Street, William Watson taught science, languages, and classics – effectively, as revealed by the careers of some of his former pupils, particularly those sons of Bailie John McIlwraith who prospered in Australia, John McIlwraith (1832–1902) as Mayor of Melbourne and Sir Thomas McIlwraith (1835–1900)

Holmston School was one of many rebuilt by Ayr Burgh School Board. Originally a charity school it retained the name of Smith's Institution till 1930.

as prime minister of Queensland. Watson with one assistant enrolled 300 pupils in 1841, but when Watson retired, this so-called Wallacetown Academy closed, sometime in the 1850s. Also in Wallacetown the cripple poet John Callaghan maintained a small private school before turning to tutoring. On both sides of the river there were other 'adventure schools' most of them providing cheaply instruction in reading and writing, or sewing for girls, At Alloway a school was opened in 1848, supported by the laird of Rozelle. At Whitletts there was by the sixties a school provided by the feuars. There were several exclusive establishments in Ayr, as in Charlotte Street. In 1836 there was a Charlotte Street Academy taught by Mr Potts; Milrig was for a time a boarding school for young ladies managed by the Misses Baird; with Mr Johnstone teaching boys in an adjoining property. In Wellington Square in 1839 a boarding school for young ladies was opened which would prove to be long-lasting. It was set up by the wife of Solomon Gross who had just retired from teaching languages at the Academy from 1811–38. Mrs Gross taught twenty 'young ladies of quality', instructing them in French, history, elocution, pianoforte, and embroidery. There was however a demand in the town for something else. At a public meeting in 1867 arrangements were made for establishing what was called a Middle school, whose fees should be lower than at Ayr Academy though higher than Smith's Institution. A field by the Horsemarket was acquired

and Ayr Grammar School built at a cost of £1,300 raised by sale of £1 shares, and without seeking a government grant which might involve some loss of independence. This school opened in 1868, with a master (£250 per annum) and two assistants (£80 each), and a scale of fees from 3/6 to 10/6 per quarter – less than half what the Academy required.

Ayr Academy benefitted from major reorganisation initiated by Dr James MacDonald (1862–83). A modern-style time table and planned curriculum were introduced. There were five preparatory classes for pupils between the ages of six and ten. In the Higher School pupils continued on a common course for two years then for their final two or three years chose either the Classical or Modern section. No longer was a pupil enrolled only for certain classes, but for a year's course – in preparatory classes from 7/6 to £1.12.6 per quarter, in the Higher school from £2 to £2.15/–. Ayr Academy retained its superior middle-class character, but despite the high fees the roll began to increase and the school's reputation recovered.

The Education (Scotland) Act of 1872 introduced a new era. A nation-wide system of schools was established. From 1873 there was compulsory education for all children between the ages of five and thirteen. The anomaly of parents who could not or would not pay was resolved in 1889 when fees were abolished in elementary schools. In 1908 further advances would be made by raising the school leaving age to fourteen

Ayr Academy was rebuilt in 1880.

and providing free books and jotters. A significant number of young people who had left school for work were catered for by 'night school' classes. Between 1873 and 1919 the schools were managed by elected parish school boards, and financed mainly by a rate levied on owners and occupiers of property. Ayr Burgh School Board constituted in 1873 consisted of nine members, with Rev Dr Dykes as its first chairman. Existing schools which applied were taken over to become public schools. A massive building programme was undertaken to replace old schools and build new ones. Newtonhead (1874) replaced the former Free Church schools in Main Street and Weaver Street. A new Wallacetown School (1875) replaced the old one in Cross Street. Ayr Academy was rebuilt (1880). Smith's Institution moved (1884) into new premises in Holmston Road. A new school was opened at Russell Street (1890). Old small schools in High Street and Carrick Street were closed down after 1873; Lady Jane Hamilton's School was extended. Ayr Landward School Board replaced Alloway School (1896). In that other area outwith Ayr burgh, a third School Board

– for the landward part of St Quivox parish – took over the little St Quivox parish school and also the former subscription school at Whitletts. There were also the Episcopal School in Fullarton Street and the R.C. school in Elba Street with an extension opened in Whitletts Road in 1893 – these by choice remained outwith Board control and had no support from the rates, though they obtained some government aid and so were subject to inspection. For those unfortunate children who were orphaned or otherwise in need of care, the ragged schools were superseded in 1874 by a School of Industry for boys and another for girls. These were built at Commonhead (by St Leonard's) and in 1891 contained 93 and 44 'inmates'. As private schools, the 1900 Directory named Wellington School at 22 Wellington Square and Newnham House School in Fullarton Street.

Ayr Burgh School Board experienced some difficulty because no provision was made in the legislation of 1872 for maintaining or replacing a 'higher class school' like Ayr Academy which provided post-elementary instruction. Yet the Board which

Andrew Carnegie turned down an invitation to lecture in Ayr, but offered instead £10,000 to help build the Carnegie Library which was opened in 1893.

superseded the Directors was enthusiastic enough to spend £9,000 in providing a new building in 1880, and supported improvements initiated by Dr MacDonald and his successor William Maybin (1883–1910). Additional staff were appointed for specific new tasks like a Lady Superintendent (1880) and Infants Mistress (1895); and to develop new subjects like sewing and knitting (1880), shorthand (1891), piano (1895) and singing (1906), gymnastics (1897), woodwork (1907). In 1896 a Science department was formed. A new 'direct method' of teaching Modern Languages was pioneered by Duncan MacKay (1880–1914). Robert Taylor who had been appointed Writing Master in the 18th century was followed by Laurence Anderson (1858–1902), who continued teaching into the 20th century, and more important, he developed a flourishing Art Department. All this required an extension to the academy in 1895, financed by a three-day bazaar, whose proceeds supplemented a government grant which was by then available for 'higher class schools'. From 1886 the Academy was subject to inspection by the Scotch Education Department, and presented candidates for the S.E.D.'s Leaving Certificate examinations which were

instituted in 1888. The Academy at the turn of the century continued to charge high fees (from about £4 per session in the first classes to around £10 in the highest); yet the roll continued to increase. Various bursaries augmented the number of free places, so that this became in essence a county academy specialising in post-elementary studies, as the foundation charter had envisaged. In 1876 there were 253 local pupils and 166 others who either travelled daily by train or lodged in Ayr. Of the 419 pupils on the roll, 316 were over the age of twelve. Of this latter figure there were 63 local and 38 other girls. In addition to all these, there were others who enrolled in the Academy's evening classes, especially in science and art.

That there was opportunity for the poor lad o' pairts is confirmed by the career of George Douglas Brown, who has won a place in Scottish literature as author of *The House with the Green Shutters*. Ayr Academy records for 1884 show enrolment into the Higher Fourth Class of fifteen-year-old 'George Brown', son of 'Miss Sarah Gemmell, Dairy, Kayshill, Stair', with fees generously abated by the masters. A distinguished career was cut short by untimely death in 1902, just a year after the publication of his now-famous novel, which he affec-

The Hungarian patriot Louis Kossuth lectured in Ayr in 1856, and left a message in the visitors book of Burns Cottage – which was a tavern from 1781 till 1881.

tionately dedicated to William Maybin, Rector of Ayr Academy.

As the end of the century approached, Ayr Burgh School Board (now with William Robertson as chairman) was in the fortunate position of having replaced all its school buildings except Lady Jane Hamilton's; and with spaces for 4,222 pupils could accommodate 3,871 enrolled in its elementary schools. In October 1899 the rolls were: Grammar, 406; Newton Academy, 551; Smith's Institution, 363; Newtonhead, 744; Wallacetown, 418; Lady Jane Hamilton's, 256; Russell Street, 1,133. There were 408 pupils in the R.C. schools and 322 in the Episcopal school. Also, under separate Boards, were schools at Alloway (with 117 pupils in 1879); St Quivox and Whitletts (64 and 106 pupils in 1884); these able to accommodate 159, 94, and 180 respectively. Schools apart from Ayr Academy were developing post-elementary studies, obtaining grants for teaching 'specific subjects'. During the 1890s, Ayr Academy had twenty nine successful candidates in the Glasgow University bursary competitions; Ayr Grammar and Ayr Newtonhead had also one each.

Hugh Allan, editor of the *Advertiser*, writing in 1889 of 'Ayr Half a Century Ago and Since' noted with appreciation 'the prodigious change that has taken place in the social and material condition of the people of our towns and villages, and of their moral and intellectual condition as well. I can remember the times when a bad harvest in Scotland simply meant starvation to many families, when wages were low, and food and clothing were dear; when butcher meat was scarcely seen on a working man's table; when loaf bread and butter and tea and sugar were things tasted only on Sunday or on special occasions; when oatmeal and potatoes were the common diet. How much better are we off now. Within the last fifty years wages on an average are double what they were in these old times ... Compared with the old times, we live in a golden age'. While this seems generally true, he had forgotten that in trade depression in the eighties, soup kitchens had to be provided for the needy in Ayr, Newton, and Wallacetown. J.M.Ferguson of the rival *Observer*, dealing with the same era in his *Reminiscences of Auld Ayr*, doubted if 'with an advanced education and refinement we are any better or happier or even more respectable members of society' but he had no doubt of 'what may now be considered quaint and savouring of the primitive and commonplace compared with what we may consider the higher-class civilisation of this more staid day of the present day'. Wallace Allan, recalling his childhood in mid-century, noted Auld Ord's open-air circus annually at the Fauldbacks, a 'geggie' theatre rigged up where Darlington Church would later be built, cock-fighting at Lovers Lane on the site of the later Somerset Park, and Saturday-night 'penny readings' in the Good Templars Hall in the Sandgate. He remembered the queen's birthday being celebrated each year with a bonfire in Bridge Street, and a burning boat dragged through the streets – a custom last noted in 1888.

Miss E.E.Anderson, a pupil of the school in Wellington Square, whose memories went back to 1849, could vividly recall some incidents which made a particular impact: knitting mittens and scarves for the sailors on the *Felix* going off to the Arctic with Sir John Ross in 1850; hearing in Mr Grant's church in December 1856 Louis Kossuth lecturing (in splendid English) on the Hungarian revolution; the capture, 1855, of Sebastopol in the Crimean

To cater for a developing holiday trade, the town council from 1880 began work in providing an esplanade at the beach.

War, celebrated by a bonfire in Wellington Square; the horror aroused in 1857 by news of the massacre at Cawnpore in the Indian Mutiny. She had much to write about schooldays at No.19 Wellington Square, holidays at Mauchline, and changes in fashion. She patronised Robert Maclehose's bookshop in Sandgate with its 'excellent library'. Nearby lived Miss Tennant, dressmaker, Burns's 'cousin Kate', who spoke 'the purest Scotch to be heard in the town of Ayr'. Miss Anderson had music lessons in Academy Street from John Hall who had learned fiddling from Neil Gow. She commented that around 1850 the town was still a small place where the building of a new house or the advent of a stranger was the subject of local gossip, for 'Auld Ayr was very conservative in those days'.

The Ayr which Miss Anderson knew best was the area south of the river. The old royal burgh contained just over 5,000 people in 1851. That close-knit community doubled its numbers in the next fifty years. Its population of 10,237 was however by then incorporated within a conurbation which was anything but compact. The parliamentary burgh, which in 1851 contained 17,624 persons, was then simply an electoral unit. That area was chosen in 1873 to constitute the extended municipal burgh. These municipal boundaries were widened in 1885 to include, by 1901, 28,697 persons within the Burgh of Ayr. It was of that greater Ayr that Dr Littlejohn

remarked in 1892 that 'all its attractions can be seen and enjoyed without the poverty and wretchedness of many of its poorer inhabitants being obtruded on the visitor'. The decennial Census reports provide statistical evidence that despite general improvements, a dichotomy persisted even though the communities of either side of the river had been united under one municipal authority. The working class areas north of the river with their generally-larger families and less healthy domestic and working conditions continued to have more children and fewer old people. As earlier noticed, overcrowding was worse north of the river, which was home for most of the 6,212 persons (4,432 male, 1,780 female) working (1891) in industrial occupations. South of the river lived most of the 1,017 professional people (748, 269); 1,532 engaged in commerce (1,433, 99); and nearly all 1,577 domestic servants (93, 1,484), most of them girls who formed one of the town's largest occupational groups. Those whom the Census report of 1891 classified as 'unoccupied' included most old people over the age of 65, children below the age of 13 when many left school to start work, and 4,580 women between the ages of 15 and 65. Most married women were 'unoccupied' housewives, no matter which area they lived in.

There was one changed feature of local life. The influx of Irish immigrants early in the century had ceased. The 1891 Census report indicates 99% of the population as Scots-born, with only a thousand or so Irish, almost as many English, and a handful of foreigners. Compulsory registration of births, marriages, and deaths as introduced in 1854 produced vital statistics which would indicate as general trends a high birth rate which began to decline in the last decades of the 19th century; more or less continuous decline in the death rate; always a natural increase by excess of births over deaths; comparison with the actual increase indicating net gain or loss through migration. While lack of uniformity in the statistics over the period makes it impossible to supply actual figures, it would appear that Ayr suffered heavy losses through emigration in mid-century when Scotland experienced the collapse of the cotton trade. Though emigration continued, in the last three decades of the century Ayr was again experiencing an inward trend, with incomers from nearby parts. Of those who left Ayr, several won prominence in other parts of Britain and abroad. John Young (1811–78) became a Canadian statesman; William Schaw Lindsay (1816–77), London shipowner and member of parliament; Captain William Greig (1821–92) sailed the Pacific Ocean and developed the guano trade; Sir Thomas McIlwraith (1835–1900) and his brothers played an important role in Australian development; Sir Thomas Oliver (1853–1942) a native of St Quivox became professor of medicine at Newcastle and an authority on public health; there were Scottish law lords like Andrew Jamieson (1845–1911) who became Lord Ardwall, and William Hunter (1865–1957), Lord Hunter; prominent churchmen like Henry Cowan (1844–1932) who was professor of church history at Aberdeen, and John McMurtrie (1831–1912), a leading Edinburgh minister. In addition to those natives of Ayr, others who spent some early years here included John William Mackail from Ascog (1859–1945), professor of poetry at Oxford; David Patrick from Ochiltree (1849–1914), historian and encyclopedist; the novelist George Douglas Brown also from Ochiltree (1869–1902); and making a career overseas, Sir John Woodburn (1834–1902) born in India of a Dalmellington family became Lieutenant Governor of Bengal. Most of those going overseas were lesser folk who settled in Canada, United States, Australia, and New Zealand. The name of Ayr was transplanted: in 18th century Virginia when John Hunter, son of a provost and younger brother of the banker, built a house and village called Ayr Hill in what is now the middle of the town of Vienna; in Canada, Robert Wyllie in 1840 gave Mudge's Mill in Ontario the name of Ayr which that community still retains; in Australia the town of Ayr in Queensland was so designated in 1882 by Sir Thomas McIlwraith.

Miss Anderson thought of Ayr's 19th century development that 'If the mercantile development was awanting there was no lack of intellectual or professional life'. It is true that Ayr acquired additional social facilities during the Victorian era. But progress in this respect was hardly commensurate with the town's growth: they were nearly all located south of the river, patronised mainly or entirely by the middle class, and did not always attract adequate support.

The development of organised sports reveals how fashions sometimes changed. Ayr Bowling Club (1834) was joined much later in the century by others at the Citadel (for a time), at Hawkhill, then at Wattfield (1882), There were four curling clubs in the 1840s, and from time to time skating was also available at Castlehill, Rozelle, and on the river above the dam. In the sixties there were five cricket clubs as well as three junior clubs. Ayr Cricket Club, which was instituted in 1858, played first on the Low Green, from 1883 at the Cattle Market park, from 1888 at Northfield in Newton Park, then (1898–1935) at Dam Park. There was an Ayr Bathing Club. Equally select was croquet in Wel-

lington Square (1870) and after 1890 lawn tennis clubs with courts at Southpark Road and Ballantine Drive. The only golf available was with one of the two clubs at Prestwick. There was a quoiting club in 1870. By that date there was extended leisure time for the majority (of men), after the introduction of Saturday half-day working for most workers and mid-week merchants holidays for some others – as compared with two decades before when Wallace Allan as apprentice to watchmaker Robert Templeton worked twelve hours daily, continuing an extra hour till 9 p.m. on Saturdays. In the last three decades of the century, there developed through the west of Scotland a craze for the new sport known as association football. In 1872 an Ayr Thistle Football Club was playing at Robbsland park, Maybole Road; the following year boys from Ayr Academy played on the Low Green against an Ayr Fort team of soldiers from the Barracks; in 1875 an Ayr Eglinton Club was formed, joined in succeeding years by Ayr Albert, Ayr Victoria, and Ayr Parkhouse. In 1876 Ayr Academy and Ayr Eglinton amalgamated to form Ayr Academicals, which in 1879 joined with the older Ayr Thistle to form Ayr F.C.(at Somerset Park), which would combine with Ayr Parkhouse (Beresford Park) to form Ayr United in 1910. Long before this Ayr Academy had adopted the other code, by 1889 arranging regular fixtures with schools in Beith, Greenock, and Glasgow, and an Ayr Rugby Club was playing at Dam Park in 1900. Organised athletics began with Ayr Academical Athletic Club holding a Sports Day in Springvale Park in 1877, which developed after a few years into separate school sports and open amateur meetings. These for a time involved bicycle races, and current demand required a specialist shop (the West of Scotland Cycle Depot in Carrick Street); there was a Cycle track on vacant ground where Boswell Park would later be formed; and another track at Somerset Park.

Recreational activities of a cultural nature were surprisingly sparse. The story of libraries shows what problems had to be overcome. The Ayr Library Society had its own premises in Fort Street since 1804, but as a select body with just over 100 members failed to compete with the lending libraries of the various booksellers. The Mechanics Institution had a library in High Street (1825–52) then in New Bridge Street, but not more than 150 members. In 1869 a public meeting decided there was insufficient support for a public library funded by the ratepayers. Nevertheless in 1870 a committee rented a room in the new Macneille's Buildings in Newmarket Street and opened an Ayr Public Library. It was given the books and cases of

The Burns Statue erected in 1891 welcomed visitors arriving at the new station which had been opened just five years before.

– in 1873 ranging from operatic singers to American Minstrels and Temperance Handbell Ringers – till it was closed and converted into Ayr Baptist Church in 1887.

Music in Ayr was little appreciated till after 1850. In the fifties concerts were given by the New Church choir, conducted by John Fraser. Various groups were formed for private practice of cantatas and the like – as Robert Andrew's Harmonic Society in Wallace Street U.P.Church, John Brown's Choral Society, and Mrs Peter Cowan's ladies group. An Ayr Musical Association comprising five vocalists and an orchestra of twelve provided two amateur concerts in the Assembly Rooms in the winter of 1855–56. But it was still necessary for music-lovers to travel to concerts in Glasgow and Kilmarnock. In Kilmarnock where a philharmonic society had been formed in 1845, Miss Anderson enjoyed oratorios 'long before they were heard in Ayr'. In 1859 Hugh Allan of the *Advertiser* began teaching the new tonic sol-fa system. In 1862 a Choral Union was formed, but this lapsed after a couple of years. There was no music shop till Paterson, Sons, and Company opened a branch in Ayr in 1867. In 1871 a Glee Club was commenced by J.Butler Cowap, the New Church organist. At last in October 1876 a more successful chapter commenced when the Ayr Choral Union was formed by amalgamation of several surviving though languishing groups – Ayr Musical Association, Harmonic Society, Choral Society, Glee Club. Hugh McNabb was appointed conductor (and continued as such for thirty three years). For the first concert (in February 1878) it proved impossible to obtain the use of the New Church – the only one with an organ – so the alternative had to be a skating hall in Dalblair Road. Thereafter the Queens Rooms were used. In 1881 the new Town Hall, complete with pipe organ, became available; but for only a few years, because the Town Hall was burned down in 1897 and the Ayr Choral Union had to wait six years for it to be rebuilt. During this period there came to an end that long tradition (as noted in 1598) of 'the common minstrels of the toun, pyper and drummer, gang dayly ilk day through the toun'. Hugh Allan recalled hearing 'the strains of Willie Brodie's fife and Johnnie Scoffel's kettle-drum' on their way to the race course. The last town drummer, Matthew Bellamy, who perambulated the town making public announcements, used a hand-bell; he died in 1888 aged 69. Efforts to establish brass bands locally proved unsuccessful. There was a Band in 1838, but its practising was, in the town council minutes, deemed 'a nuisance', and a

the Mechanics Institution, the small library of the Ayr Young Men's Association, in 1876 the stock of the Ayr Library Society, and in 1885 the books of the little Newton parish library were added. By that date the Library had 10,000 books, the subscriptions of the 400 members being supplemented by popular (and profitable) public lectures. When the millionaire-philanthropist Andrew Carnegie was invited to lecture, he offered instead to donate £10,000 towards a building, if the ratepayers agreed to maintain a free library. In 1882 such a proposal to adopt the Public Libraries Act had been turned down after an 'exceedingly stormy' meeting, but that decision was now reversed, a site was chosen on the Newton side of the New Bridge, and on 2 September 1893 Ayr Carnegie Library was opened. Less successful was Ayr's attempt to maintain a theatre. The Queen's Rooms in Fort Street accommodated occasional touring companies band from Kilwinning had to be brought to Ayr for the opening of the railway in 1840. In 1887 a football match was organised to raise money for a bandstand, and a burgh band performed at the Queen's Jubilee that year – as did a choir of 1,500 children attached to the Band of Hope.

19th century Ayr produced no creative artists of consequence. A local essay on 'Some Eminent Men' has concluded that 'The contribution of Ayr men to pictorial art has not been one of great distinction'. In an earlier generation John Caldwell (1738–1829) gained some reputation as a miniaturist, and John Wilson (1774–1855) was a pupil of Alexander Nasmyth and was 'Auld Jock' to more famous Scottish painters. John Stevens (1793–1868), William Crawford (1811–69), James Wright (1876–1947) also made careers outwith Ayr. Two others who were not practitioners became better known. James Fergusson (1808–86) was an Indian planter, interested as an amateur in archaeology and antiquities, who became a recognised authority on architecture. Sir James Lewis Caw (1864–1950) began as an apprentice engineer with J. & A. Taylor, but went on to become author of books on Scottish art, Curator of the Scottish National Portrait Gallery (1895–1907) and the first director of the National Galleries of Scotland (1907–1930). More local impact was made by architects like James A. Morris (1857–1942), a sculptor like James Thom of Tarbolton (1799–1850), and Lawrence Anderson who between 1858 and 1902 developed the Art Department of Ayr Academy. In depiction of local scenes, outstanding work was done by Robert Bryden (1865–1939). Born in Coylton, he began as apprentice architect in Ayr before going to study art in London, where he worked for many years before returning to Ayr. In 1895 there was sufficient local interest for an Ayr Fine Arts Exhibition held in the Public Library. Among nearly 400 exhibits there were only a couple of dozen by local painters (including Bryden) but the show, lasting a month, proved worth repeating in 1898 and subsequent occasions. Sir William Arrol, one of the patrons, could at Seafield enjoy his fine collection of paintings and listen to operatic records on a gramophone, and in these respects was typical of Ayr's better-off inhabitants. The majority of households had to make do with photographs, because they were cheaper.

That novel 19th century invention was publicised by Dr John Memes whose *Daguerre's History and Practice of Photogenic Drawing* (1839) went through several editions, this translation being the first book to make the French inventor's techniques familiar in Britain.

A former pupil of Ayr Academy, Dr John McCosh of Kirkmichael (1805–85) is now recognised as having made a notable contribution to the development of photography as an art form. McCosh (who must have left school before Memes arrived in 1826) trained at Glasgow University (1827–30) and for a time during his final year served in Dr Ronald's Apothecaries' Hall at 60 High Street, Ayr. In 1831 he went to India as an hospital surgeon. Shipwreck on a trip to Tasmania inspired his first travel book in 1836, followed by *The Topography of Assam* in 1837. He returned to complete his medical education in Edinburgh (1840–41) and was awarded an MD degree in 1841. Before returning to India he had published *Medical Advice to the Indian Stranger*, and became acquainted with the caloptype process of photography. As an army surgeon he produced between 1843 and 1856 a series of 'very bright life-like calotypes with a direct and natural style, marking him as a photographer of considerable talent'. In his *Advice to Young Officers in India*, 1856, which contains a reference to photography, he describes himself as member of the Royal College of Surgeons, Edinburgh; member of the Photographic Society, London; and late of the Bengal Medical Staff. In his retiral he made trips through France, Switzerland, and Italy as recounted in a poem of ten cantos called *Nuova Italia*: a first volume of this appeared anonymously in 1872, but he included in his presentation copy a signed photograph of himself; the second volume (1875) he dedicated to Lord Ardmillan and members of the Edinburgh Ayrshire Club of which he had been elected a honorary member, though for health reasons he was residing in the 'sunny south'. The poem was reprinted (1881) as *Grand Tours in Many Lands* by John McCosh, M.D.Edin., H.E.I.C.S., F.R.G.S., which work was described as 'a very tolerable volume of neat and sprightly verse'. None of McCosh's photographs seems to have survived locally. In his will he bequeathed to Ayr Academy the McCosh Bursary fund now incorporated in the Ayrshire Educational Trust. Commercial photography began in Ayr with the appearance in the 1864 Directory of Hugh Murdoch, photographer, Beresford Terrace; within the next thirty years there were five photographers in the town, and notable visiting photographic artists included George Washington Wilson, James Valentine, James Craig Annan, and Francis Frith.

As far as creative writing was concerned, none of the local versifiers deserves special recognition. Ayr has some claim to the novelist George Douglas Brown who was a pupil at Ayr Academy 1884–87, living with his mother in a cottage at Crofthead

Dalblair was first of the many large private houses converted into hotels.

farm, and would be buried in Ayr Cemetery. James Paterson (1805–76) from Kilmarnock was for a time editor of the *Ayrshire Observer* which published in 1846 the first of his two series of collected *Ballads and Songs of Ayrshire*, and an 1895 edition of his *History of the County of Ayr*. Ayrshire's other historian, William Robertson (1848–1924), son of Rev. John Robertson, born in the Original Seceder manse in King Street, was a sailor on windjammers before turning to local journalism, with the *Observer* and *Express* before involvement with the new *Ayrshire Post* of which he was for a time editor and joint proprietor. He was elected to Ayr Parochial Board and Ayr Burgh School Board and as a Liberal parliamentary candidate contested North Ayrshire, 1895; Ayr Burghs, 1910 twice; South Ayrshire, 1918. His *Historical Tales and Legends of Ayrshire*, 1889, was followed by several historical romances and books of local lore; two volumes of *Historic Ayrshire*, 1891, 1894; and his *Ayrshire, Its History and Historic Families*, 2 volumes 1908. Significantly, only two of his smaller works could be printed and published in Ayr.

Those facts already remarked upon, that most social facilities were located south of the river, catering for the middle class, suggest that the royal burgh retained a social identity after the municipal boundaries were extended in 1873. This may be exemplified by examining various other organisations, which also showed uncertain growth. The long-established Sailors' Society (1581) and Merchants' Company (1655) survived

only as benefit clubs among the more numerous friendly societies and insurance companies. Even after the exclusive privileges of the burgesses were abolished, the brethren of the merchant guild continued to meet as the Guildry of Ayr; and others joined the Incorporated Trades, known before the end of the century as the Trades House, with only four surviving sections – hammermen, tailors, shoemakers, and squaremen. These burghal organisations no longer practised their traditional public pageantry. Other forms of ritual were maintained by the lodges of Freemasons, five of which maintained continuous existence till the end of the century. Less exclusive, and appealing to artisans and lower middle class, were new national mass organisations which combined ceremonial and sociability with mutual benefit and dedication to some common purpose, The Oddfellows formed locally in 1841 continued throughout the century, joined by Foresters, Free Gardeners, and Ancient Shepherds. Also operating at the end of the century in Ayr were five lodges of Good Templars and two tents of Rechabites, these specifically devoted to temperance. An Ayr tent of the Independent Order of Rechabites was set up in 1842 but next year like many others collapsed; it was resuscitated in 1881 for another brief spell; and more firmly established in 1891, with a juvenile tent added in 1892, and joined by a Newton tent in 1896.

The Forbes Mackenzie Act of 1853 by introducing licensing hours put an end to the many gentlemen's drinking clubs of the early part of the century, including the earliest local Burns clubs. The recently-opened railway brought an estimated 80,000 persons in 1844 to a Burns Festival at Alloway, where in a tented pavilion the Earl of Eglinton presided over a grand banquet, with the three sons of the Poet as principal guests. Beside Burns Cottage, which was still a public tavern, a hall was erected in 1847, and there was celebrated in 1859 the Centenary of the Poet's birth. In 1881 the Cottage was purchased from the Incorporation of Shoemakers by the Trustees of the Burns Monument, and for visitors an adjoining museum was erected in 1900. In none of these projects did the initiative come from within Ayr. The Burns Federation, formed in Kilmarnock in 1885, appointed Ex-provost Robert Goudie of Ayr as one of its five Vice-Presidents. He was instrumental in convening a Meeting of Gentlemen in the King's Arms, resulting in the establishment of an Ayr Burns Club in 1886. In its first year the Club organised a Burns Choir of 450 voices and an open air concert helped raise money for the Robert Burns statue erected at Townhead in 1891 – belatedly following Edinburgh (1839), Glasgow (1877), Kilmarnock (1879), Dundee (1880), Dumfries (1882), London (1884), New Zealand at Dunedin (1887), Australia at Camperdown (1885) and Ballarat (1887), and the United States at New York (1880) and Albany (1888).

Those organisations which catered for a clientele wider than the town did well. Ayr Races, and the Western Meeting in particular, attracted the horse racing fraternity from all parts of Britain following the completion of the railway network. From all over the county and beyond came farming folk to the cattle shows which the Ayrshire Agricultural Association held annually in Ayr from 1852. Ayr became the headquarters of the Ayrshire Cattle Herd Book Society formed in 1877. The long-established Ayrshire Horticultural and Agricultural Society continued, and there was also an Ornithological Society which had (in 1900) a show of poultry, pigeons, canaries, and parrots. The newspapers printed in Ayr (as noticed in Chapter 13) found readers throughout most of Ayrshire. A meeting in the County Buildings in 1877 inaugurated an Archaeological Association for the counties of Ayr and Wigton, which produced eighteen impressive volumes in the twenty years of the society's life. For the county gentry an Ayr County Club was formed in 1872, with impressive premises at 41 Sandgate; and also a Town and Country Club at 26 Wellington Square.

In 1873 Ayr as a county town augmented its attributes when it was nominated as headquarters of the Royal North British Fusiliers, which had originated in 1678 as the Earl of Mar's Regiment. This involved renovation of the Ayr Barracks, which then comprised a block thrown up in 1858 to supplement the 18th century Sugar House, which latter was gutted by fire in 1873. In 1881 the county regiment (with most recruits now from this area) was renamed the Royal Scots Fusiliers. Militarily, Ayr enjoyed each summer that week when the Ayrshire Yeomanry were quartered for training, and parades were followed by balls and other evening functions. The Yeomanry as a cavalry unit attracted young men who were mainly from the country. In 1859 young townsmen got their opportunity when Volunteers were organised. These were fashionable units too, for Riflemen were required to pay an entry fee of £2.10/–. The Artillery Volunteers, paying only £1, were for better-off 'artisans and mechanics'. Though there was no lack of enthusiasm, the county town was also in this respect slow in taking action, following Kilmarnock and Irvine, so that the Ayr Riflemen were only No.3 Company. The Ayrshire Rifle Volunteers also had annual camps at Ayr from 1873 till 1890 – at the Racecourse, later Greenan, then Castlehill before a move to Troon. At the battalion inspection of 1873 there paraded 14 companies with a complement of 800 men. In 1879 they were reformed into two corps, with headquarters at Ayr and Kilmarnock. Less fashionable was the militia, though composed of volunteers after 1852. The Ayrshire and Wigtownshire Militia in 1881 was attached to the renamed Royal Scots Fusiliers. In 1887 the Rifle Volunteers were formed into two Volunteer battalions of the RSF, after which it became less than fashionable to serve in the ranks. The Ayr Company of the 1st Ayr and Galloway Volunteer Artillery were attached to the Royal Artillery.

Looking back to mid-century, Miss Anderson realised that 'Glasgow had not discovered then what a charm is to be found in the ozone of the Western Sea'. For a time at the end of the 18th century sea-bathing had been a fashionable cure for various ailments. People had been attracted to settle here because of the purity of the air, so that Rev William Peebles could claim in 1791 that 'this part of the country has, with some justice, been called the Montpelier of Scotland'. A generation later Rev Alexander Cuthill could compare Ayr with the Bay of Naples in respect of its scenic attraction. A *Guide to the Glasgow and Ayrshire Railway* published in 1841, the year after its opening, included also a guide 'to Ayr and its environs, and to the Land of Burns'. The opportunity afforded by the railway was not followed by an immediate expansion of the holiday trade. In 1870 the *Ayrshire Express* published a fourpenny brochure reprinting articles on *Ayr as a Summer Residence*. It gave prominence to 'Sanitary Aspects' noting 'no large manufactories or chemical works to poison it with carbonic acid gas, or rob it of its oxygen', also 'new reservoirs' and 'entirely renewed' sewers', and (just in case) 'a well-managed hospital'. Attractions included 'fancy warehouses and extensive drapery establishments', several reading clubs, and in summer 'artistes and troupes of performers'. There were 'varied and harmless sources of amusement', and the sports listed included boating and angling, though the River Ayr was 'fished and poached out' and Loch Doon was recommended. More serious visitors were advised of a range of possible studies from antiquities to zoology. Middle class families could be 'established in delightful summer quarters for a month or so' with gentlemen of the family taking advantage of cheap railway season tickets to 'attend to their business'. For trippers, the *Vale of Clyde* steamer left Glasgow daily at 7 a.m., reached Ayr by 12.30, allowed two hours for a trip to the Banks of Doon, then left Ayr at 2.30 to arrive back in Glasgow at 8 p.m. More popular were the cheap excursions by train each Saturday in July and August. In July 1873 the *Advertiser* could report an 'enormous influx of visitors' by train and steamer at the Glasgow Fair, and the following month give results of the Glasgow – Ayrshire bowling matches which had been instituted each summer.

Ayr Town council in 1880 commenced making the beach more attractive. When the slip dock at the harbour was constructed, a concrete sea wall was built on the shore side. This was in 1881 extended southwards as far as the County Buildings and Gaol; though washed away in 1882 it was restored and further extended in 1893. Already the undulating hillocks of the Low Green had been flattened, for as Hugh Allan recalled, 'somewhere about 25 or 30 years ago, when there was a dulness in the carpet weaving and other trades, a fund was raised and was expended in paying for the labour of large gangs of unemployed who were set to work levelling the green'. Thus improved, there was scope for games of various kinds, until these were banned as interfering with pedestrians enjoying walks on the green. The Low Green was enhanced by a fountain presented in 1892 by Hugh Steven of Skeldon. But in 1893 a letter in the *Advertiser* complained of 'the erection in our Low Green of that wooden hut which is to be dignified with the name of restaurant. It might do very well for such a purpose in the backwoods of America or far out in the Australian bush.' This hut let to Petro Brucciano for the sale of ice cream was, the Court of Session agreed, 'a grievance and an eyesore'. By contrast, on the banks of the Doon there were attractive gardens which had been laid out by David Auld of Doonbrae, first custodian of the Monument and patron of the sculptor James Thom. For Ayr beach, plans were prepared in 1899 for a pier extending into the sea with a bandstand at the end – so that Ayr could equal popular English resorts. Though these and other ambitious projects were never implemented, visitors had a fair range of facilities. The 1892–3 Directory listed 28 hotels and inns, and a dozen of these could be described as high-class establishments. There were three temperance hotels, as well as a Working Man's Public House provided in 1880 by the ironmasters H. & W. Houldsworth. In 1882 Fleury Meng who came from Switzerland via Sunderland opened his restaurant in Newmarket Street and soon, according to J.M.Ferguson, there were 'nearly fifty places now where a comfortable cup of tea may be had, and other refreshments.' Such was the 'Salon' in Old Bridge Street where (by 1892) Joseph Rossi from Glasgow sold 'Italian Ice Cream', and also 'Iced Drinks 1d and 2d, Botanic Beer and Ginger Beer at 1d per Bottle'. For the entertainment of visitors, a regatta was organised in 1886. In 1893 four-in-hand Charabanc rides were offered (weather permitting) to Straiton (4/–), Culzean (5/–), and Ballochmyle (4/–). The Glasgow and South Western Railway Co., empowered in 1891 to operate steamships, introduced the *Juno* which provided Ayr with pleasure cruises from 1898 till 1932. The Ayr Steam Shipping Company operated its regular services to Belfast, Larne, and Campbeltown. Every other year local printers issued revised editions of their penny guides to this popular holiday town.

Part Four
The Twentieth Century

SIXTEEN

A New Age

'The New Century dawned upon us amid open weather', announced the *Advertiser* on 3 January 1901. A large crowd followed tradition and gathered 'at the steeple', where buglers sounded a salute and some ill-mannered persons threw squibs. The same issue reported heavy flooding in the English Midlands, and the failure of sixteen London stock exchange firms. Overseas the Australian Commonwealth was inaugurated; in South Africa, after fifteen months of fighting the Boers, there were continued setbacks. The latest casualty list included a trooper serving with the Ayrshire Yeomanry who had died 'in the service of Queen and Country'. Locally there was an account of a brawl and murder in a Wallace Street household. The New Year's Horse fair would be held on 3 January, and 'Aladdin' was being performed at the theatre in Carrick Street.

Three weeks later the *Advertiser* carried a black border in mourning for the death of Queen Victoria on 22 January – 'the saddest bit of news of its kind that it has ever been our lot to record'. During the short reign of Edward VII, and the years following George V's accession in 1910, it was obvious that many changes were afoot.

The *Ayrshire Post* prophetically announced (30.5.1903) that 'The motor has come to stay – so much is clear as clear can be. Evil-smelling, dust-compelling, unpleasantly palpitating, very frequently recklessly driven, it has nevertheless all the elements of permanency about it'. Only a few years later in August 1910 flying machines were on view at the Lanark Aviation Meeting. World records were made with a speed of 75 miles and an altitude of 6,750 feet. The *Advertiser* found it 'gratifying' that there had been no accidents, and commmented that 'Flights lasting for hours have excited no surprise'. Crowds of trippers were transported to Lanark in special excursion trains. However, the railways seemed likely to remain the popular form of transport: indeed the Glasgow and South Western Railway Company extended its network with the opening in 1906 of a coastal route from Ayr through Alloway and Dunure to serve the railway company's new Turnberry Hotel. Another 20th century novelty was presented in September 1906, when a cinematograph entertainment was offered in the Town Hall. There were performances also in the Wallace Tower Hall in 1908, and regularly from 1909 at the Scottish Electric Picture Palace in the Drill Hall, 2 Burns Statue Square.

In the first decade of the 20th century the population of Ayr municipal burgh rose from 28,700 to 33,000 in 1911. The industrial town of Kilmarnock in the same period made only a slight increase from 34,200 to 34,700, which was an index of contemporary economic difficulties. Though depression of trade affected Ayr too, there was actually some industrial expansion. At Townhead, there were still Templeton's worsted spinning mill and two tanneries in Mill Street; the foundries of J. & A. Taylor and J.M. Rodger were joined in 1904 by John Wallace and Sons' Agricultural Implement Works; by 1914 A.M. Turner's Ayr and Newton Breweries extended over the river from Main Street in Newton into Mill Street and South Harbour Street (with Turner's Bridge an appropriate benefaction). At the harbour, Ailsa Shipbuilding Company in 1902 took over the construction of paddle steamers and coasters. North of the river, saw milling continued, two sail makers survived, several of Newton's small foundries, the starch factory at the river side, and at Falkland junction Wyllie's Chemical Works were firmly established. The area of most significant development was off McCall's Avenue. There beside Gray's Carpet factory were set up Andrew Lees and Sons' St Crispin's Works and another manufactory of boots and shoes. In West Sanquhar Road, near W.G. Walker & Co.'s Hawkhill Chemical Works was established in 1900 the Neptune Works of the new Scottish Stamping Company, and the Victoria Stamping Works of James Dickie & Co. followed in Somerset Road, both specialising in drop forgings.

The railway remained the principal means of transport, and Alloway acquired a station on the new line opened in 1906.

The growth of Ayr's population was due largely to the town's continuing popularity as a holiday and residential town. The Directory of 1913–14 reveals a significant expansion of the local building trade (compared with 1892–93 as noted in Chapter 15) with now 9 architects, 23 builders' firms, 32 joiners, 20 plumbers, and increases in most other trades. The Mercantile Bank of Scotland (1903), the North of Scotland Bank (1909), and a revived Ayr Savings Bank (1909) supplemented those facilities already provided in Ayr by the Bank of Scotland, Royal Bank, Union Bank, National Bank, Commercial Bank, British Linen Bank, and Clydesdale Bank. Between 1901 and 1911 the number of inhabited houses increased from 5,871 to 6,866. There were some fine new villas in the exclusive area south of Miller Road; modest private houses by Dalmellington Road, as on the former Little Moss nursery; and especially east of Prestwick Road in that area taking its name from the recently-created Newton Park. It was becoming less profitable to build houses to rent, though in King Street there was one lofty tenement planned in 1896 and ready to acquire

in 1900 its nickname from the battle at Spion Kop. There was a shortage of decent working class housing. The burgh average of 1.31 persons per room in 1901 disguised severe overcrowding, and showed an actual deterioration over the next decade to 1.32 in 1911. The wards (whose boundaries were redrawn in 1903) contained most of them a variety of housing types, but the First Ward (south of Charlotte Street, Fullarton Street, and Dalblair Road) had an admirable ratio of 0.6; while in the Third Ward of Wallacetown (south of Cross Street and Hawkhill) the figure was 1.76. In the slum areas of Wallacetown, Newton Green, and Townhead were to be found 767 one-roomed dwellings in which 2,277 persons lived – in one instance ten persons occupying such a single-end. 318 men and 23 women found accommodation as inmates of common lodging houses, including the Trades Hotel in York Street. Yet despite continued overcrowding, the general situation in 1911 (as compared with 1891) showed improvement with far fewer in single-ends (7% instead of 22%) and more (37% instead of 35%) in two-apartments.

Ayr town council had to some degree ameliorated conditions by provision of environmental services. John Young, Town Surveyor, described in 1908 *Some of the Municipal Works of Ayr* – one of the Carnegie Library series of public lectures 'illustrated by lime-light views', and informative enough to be printed in the *Ayr Observer* and reprinted as a pamphlet. The waterworks established in 1842 had been municipalised in 1873, the Milton springs on Carrick Hill springs augmented by the Loch Finlas scheme in 1886, and mains from the Knockjarder reservoir supplied Ayr, Alloway, Doonfoot, Whitletts, and New Prestwick. The council minutes of 1908 indicate connections to R.A.Oswald's farms of Pleasantfield, Mount Oliphant, and Mainholm. By 1908 a twelve year scheme to reconstruct the burgh sewers had been completed. For refuse disposal the Annpit quarry was used till it was filled up in 1903, after which a Refuse Destructor was installed in Mill Street, adjoining the Electricity Generating Works which had commenced in 1898 and later extended. The Town Council was also responsible for 39 miles of roads, with six miles of granite or whinstone setts and the rest tarmacadamed. The most recent municipal service was a tramway system, authorised by the Ayr Burgh Act of 1899 and commencing operations in 1901. Young calculated that the burgh had spent £151,200 on water supply, £85,000 on drainage, £14,000 on refuse disposal plant, £103,000 on electricity works, £80,000 to date on tramways, £28,000 on bridges, £19,000 on cattle market and slaughterhouse improvements. In addition there was expenditure on the small Crofthead Smallpox Hospital which was erected in 1903, share in the Heathfield Infectious Diseases Hospital opened in 1905, and in the Glenafton Sanatorium for pulmonary cases opened in 1907. In municipal administration, important roles were occupied by the Town Clerk, A.G.Young, who succeeded John Pollock in 1888 and was himself followed by P.A.Thomson in 1906; by the Town Surveyor, John Eaglesham from 1890 and John Young from 1900; and the Chief Constable, James Lowdon from 1903.

Though this was a period when nationally there was keen rivalry between the two main political parties, there was oddly enough less controversy in municipal affairs. In 1910 there were two General Elections, but at the elections to Ayr Town Council in November, candidates in five wards were returned unopposed and at the only contest, in the Second Ward, there were 'no difference on questions of policy'. John Neil, a tailor who now represented the Sixth Ward, was the first Labour member in Ayr Town Council. He

Summer shows were provided in the Pavilion, which the town council built in 1911 to attract visitors.

remained a councillor from 1910 till 1919, resigned to become a trade union organiser, but returned to the council from 1936 till his death in 1941, aged 72.

When in 1903 there was a proposal to purchase the Fort Castle, one councillor insisted that it was 'no part of our duty to acquire such subjects' and expressed current opinion that 'Our principal duty as a Town Council is to attend to the watching, lighting, and cleansing of the streets, as well as the preservation of the health of the community and the keeping of the roads in good order.' In fact it was only some fifty years since such a 'principal duty' had been assumed. Powers allowed under the Burgh Reform Acts of 1833, Lock's Act of 1850, and Lindsay's Act of 1862 were adopted in Ayr in 1850 and 1873. The Burgh Police (Scotland) Act of 1892 and the Town Councils (Scotland) Act of 1900 consolidated the new system of municipal government which was created in the 19th century. As a consequence, one vestige of the past disappeared. At John Neil's first council meeting in November 1910 he was required to subscribe £1 to the Common Good for admission as a burgess to become recognised as a councillor. Within the following year the town clerk belatedly discovered that councillors no longer need be burgesses – an essential qualification before 1833, and continuing

The town council introduced trams, which operated from 1901 till 1931.

as a quaint survival locally till 1911. How the work of the council had expanded by the 1900s is indicated by its sixteen committees and sub-committees. While the 'principal duty' of the council was the provision of certain mandatory services for the benefit of the ratepayers, a policy was being followed of introducing improvements calculated also to attract visitors to this holiday town. In 1881 a beginning was made with a stretch of esplanade at the beach (as an adjunct to the slip dock being constructed). This was extended and the Low Green improved (hiring unemployed men as a relief measure). Plans were prepared in 1899 for a pier, and in 1904 and 1908 for a swimming pond and baths – but these projects were not carried through. In 1902 the council formed an Attractions Commmittee at a time when it was argued in the *Ayrshire Post* that 'the coast-going public are drifting away from Ayr'. The sea front was improved with shelters, lavatory accommodation, bathing machines, and permission granted for boating, ice cream vendors, and automatic sweetmeat vending machines. In 1907 the recently-formed burgh band was taken under town council control, providing summer concerts at the bandstand on the Low Green and in the Tea Gardens at Alloway. A major new facility was provided with the opening in 1911 of the Pavilion, seating 1,500, from 1913 leased to Ben Popplewell for summer variety shows. A proposal in 1903 to create a Pleasure Ground at Carrick Hill came to nothing. But in 1910 a River Ayr Walk was formed on the south bank between the Cemetery and

the Overmill – despite initial reluctance of R.A.Oswald of Auchincruive and J.A.Campbell of Craigie. Easier to implement was the provision of municipal golf on the old racecourse in 1906. North of the river facilities for other sports were provided, but Newton Park like the Newton shore was patronised mainly by residents of the immediate vicinity. There were signs that Ayr was beginning to attract new types of visitor. In 1903 it was conference centre for the Master Painters of Scotland and also the Scottish Trades Union Congress. The council provided hospitality in 1909 to Canadian curlers and in 1912 to Australian bowlers.

A steady stream continued to visit the Land of Burns, to inspect the various places associated with the Poet. It was thus with universal dismay that in 1905 the Auld Brig had to be closed. Since 1868 the town council had made repeated attempts to reinforce the piers, but these were being dangerously undermined by the increased scour of the river as the harbour was deepened by dredging. The Burgh Surveyor John Eaglesham proposed dismantling the bridge and rebuilding upon new foundations. This solution was also advocated in a report by the architect Hall Blyth and supported by Sir William Arrol of Seafield – acknowledged expert who had built the new Tay Bridge, the Forth Bridge, and London Tower Bridge. But there were complications. Robert Templeton, a watchmaker who died in 1879, had left £10,000 for 'rebuilding the Old Bridge of Ayr when such a thing may be required'; and legal

Summer pleasure cruises were provided by the *Juno* from 1898 till 1931.

judgment was precise in its definition of 'rebuilding'. Local architect James A. Morris argued that it was practicable to retain the existing bridge by supporting the superstructure while the piers were renewed. This alternative won the enthusiastic support of Honorary President of the Burns Federation Lord Rosebery; a local Voluntary Committee led by R.A.Oswald of Auchincruive promised to raise the necessary funds; the town council was persuaded; between 1907 and 1910 restoration was undertaken at a cost of £10,000, paid for by the Voluntary Committee. On 19 July 1910 the Auld Brig was reopened, and Rosebery and Oswald awarded the freedom of the burgh. Following upon this there was a proposal in 1912, never implemented, to restore the Malt Cross. In 1911, following the death of 'Baron' Miller, the council again decided against purchase of the Fort Castle. In 1914 it was acquired by the Marquess of Bute, stripped of its 19th century accretions, and restored as the Tower of St John.

In the council's minutes can be noticed stray references that remind of the range of its operations: purchase of a tar spraying machine, 1912; organising a Titanic Disaster Fund, 1912; permission granted for a Royal Flying Corps machine to land on the

Low Green, 1913; purchase from Glasgow of a second-hand steam pump fire engine, drawn by two horses, 1913; obtaining a motor to draw it, 1914; conducting a public enquiry into the Housing of the Working Classes, 1914. One item of business so far only mentioned merits separate consideration – the Ayr Corporation Tramways.

In 1898 an Ayr and District Tramway Company raised capital but hopes of providing horse-cars were abandoned in 1888. In 1898 after the opening of the burgh electricity works, an English company proposed a tramway system for Ayr. This inspired the hurried inclusion in the Ayr Burgh Act of 1899 of powers for constructing and operating a system under municipal auspices. In 1900 the council formed a Tramways Committee; it took seven and a half months in 1901 to lay four miles of 4 feet 8½ inch gauge track from Prestwick to St Leonard's Church in Ayr; a manager and thirty five employees were hired; the five first open-top double-decker tramcars delivered; and the line officially opened on 26 September 1901. From the first the line proved popular and showed a working profit, which encouraged extensions. The line was continued from St Leonard's Church to the Burns Monument at Alloway, opened on 1 June 1902

Ayr Races in 1906, their last year on the Old Race Course.

in good time for summer holiday-makers and for the Ayr Races in September. A Confirmation Act of 1904 allowed double track to be laid through the town. Another Act of 1908 authorised a branch line from the north end of the New Bridge through Wallacetown to Hawkhill. This went as far as the New Racecourse which was opened in 1907; it served also Somerset Park where from 1910 the 'Honest Men' of Ayr United Football Club would play senior matches; and the line brought a little nearer to Ayr the people of Whitletts.

The New Racecourse in Whitletts Road (where the Blackhouse estate had once been) was financed and managed by the committee of the Western Meeting. As a purpose-built private enclosure it was quite superior to the Old Racecourse, which the council could now devote to golf and other sports, and the fashionable residential area rid of the September Shows which could be relocated on the Low Green or Newton Park. The race meetings brought visitors to the town in May, July, August, and September. Visitors were now coming to Ayr in increased numbers each summer to enjoy those attractions provided variously by Nature, by the Town Council, and by private auspices. Summer pleasure cruises were supplied by the Glasgow and South Western Railway Company's *Juno*, daily; by the Caledonian Railway Company's *Duchess of Montrose* on Tuesday, Wednesday and Thursday; and on the Ayr Steam Shipping Company's regular trips to Belfast, Larne, and Campbeltown. At the

beach entertainment was provided by pierrots, and in the Pavilion from 1911. On one special occasion three special trains brought Buffalo Bill's Wild West Show, with 800 of a cast and 500 horses; there were two performances at Newton Park on 12 September 1904, and the 16,000 seats were filled.

Dramatic entertainment in the town had once been provided in the original Theatre 1815–1887, in the Town Hall from 1881 till it was burned down in 1897; thereafter in the wooden Caledonian Theatre in Carrick Street, which was replaced in 1902 by the Gaiety Theatre. An extensive fire in 1903 required virtual reconstruction but after that the New Gaiety Theatre proved popular and successful, presenting plays, operettas, variety shows, and some cinematograph performances. In the summer of 1913 the Town Hall was also offering a Vaudeville Show featuring J.M. Hamilton, the celebrated 'Scotch Tenor'. Regular cinematograph shows were from 1910 presented in the Ayr Picture Palace in Burns Statue Square; joined by Green's Picturedrome in that building at Boswell Park which had been operating as a roller skating rink; and by Newton Picture Palace in the Unionist Rooms in Main Street.

Catering more specifically for residents was an enhanced range of clubs and societies providing recreational facilities. The 1913–14 Directory listed 4 bowling clubs (Ayr, Craigie, Hawkhill, Wattfield), Ayr Cricket Club (Dam Park), 5 curling clubs (including Rozelle Tarmac), Ayr and Castlehill lawn tennis

The impressive roller skating rink, later converted into a cinema called Green's Picturedrome.

clubs, a quoiting club, Ayr United Football Club, Ayr Rugby Football Club, an angling club, a motor cycle club; elsewhere there was note of a Rifle Association, Model Yacht Club, Swimming Club, Athletic Sports, and roller skating. The Sports Page was now a regular feature in the local newspapers. Ayr United, formed in 1910 by amalgamation of Ayr Parkhouse and Ayr F.C., was after three seasons promoted to the First Division in Scottish senior football. There was also an Ayr and District Junior Football League formed in 1904, which one season had ten local teams. Other interests were catered for by the Ayr Chrysanthemum Society which supplemented the continuing Ayrshire Horticultural and Agricultural Society; Ayr and District Canine Club and a Collie Club. There were now four Burns Clubs; Ayr (1886), Newton-upon-Ayr (1904), Ayr Tam O' Shanter (1906), and Alloway (1908). Public lectures were provided by the Carnegie Library (which was managed by equal numbers of councillors and ratepayers). One week in March 1903 there were Health lectures in the New Gaiety Theatre; a Conversazione and two concerts in the Drill Hall (opened 1902) at Burns Statue Square; an organ recital in the New Church; and a Chamber Concert by Mr Newsome's Amateur Orchestra in the Council Chambers. During a previous week (February 1903) there was a singing competition in the Drill Hall which attracted 1,200 contestants from all over Scotland. The Town Hall was re-opened in 1904 with Ayr Choral Union in 'The

Messiah'. By this period music was also provided by an Ayr Burgh Choir, Ayr Presbytery Choir Union, Ayr Philharmonic Society, Ayr Amateur Opera Company, Ayr Burgh Band, R.S.F. bands, the Industrial School Band, and Ayr Boys Brigade Bugle band. In 1912 the Ayrshire Music Festival was instituted by Frederick Ely. If music was now well catered for, so was drama with visiting companies in the New Gaiety Theatre. Ayr Fine Art Exhibitions of 1895 and 1898 were followed by others in 1905, 1906, 1910, 1914, and for practitioners the Ayr Sketch Club was formed in 1901, and an Ayr Amateur Photographic Society in 1905.

This remarkable growth of social activities made Ayr attractive to middle class incomers who continued to settle here, in pleasant surroundings, with an excellent railway service for daily commuters to Glasgow. Of those 32,986 persons resident in Ayr at the time of the 1911 Census, 16,474 (only 50%) were natives of the town; 5,839 (17%) had been born elsewhere in Ayrshire, females forming two thirds of those because of the influx of girls from the mining areas to enter domestic service; from other parts of Scotland no fewer than 8,065 (24%) had come to live in Ayr, plus 1,334 English, 820 Irish, and 567 from abroad.

How facilities for shopping had been enhanced may be seen by comparison of successive local directories. The Directory for 1913–14 shows certain types of business which had made a disproportionate

The view across the river was of unsightly residential and industrial properties.

expansion since twenty years previously, like furniture dealers, laundries, music teachers, photographers, and opticians; and some which had not then existed – antique dealers, fancy warehouses, picture frame makers, cycle agents, motor works and garages, electrical engineers, typewriting offices. Occupying a less prominent place in the life of the extended community were the agricultural connections. There were however still market days each Tuesday, four annual fairs for sale of horses and cattle (January, April, July, and October), hiring fairs (April, May, October, November), the April Show of the Ayrshire Agricultural Association (which had acquired Dam Park in 1897); and the town provided headquarters not only for the Ayrshire Cattle Herd Book Society but now also for the Ayrshire Dairy Instruction Society, the Scottish Milk Records Committee, and the Ayr Ram Society. Sixteen carriers still operated, to Glasgow (2) daily, and Maybole (2) daily, the rest to country towns, mostly on Tuesdays and Thursdays, five of these leaving from the Sun Inn in High Street. There were also coaches to Annbank, Tarbolton, Coyton, and Straiton on Tuesdays and Saturdays. The Whitletts Coach leaving the Black Bull Hotel each Saturday night hourly from 6 till 10 p.m. catered for the shoppers who now frequented Ayr on Saturday afternoons and evenings. What is described as the Ochiltree 'Bus left the Ayrshire and Galloway Hotel

each Tuesday at 3 p.m. This was probably a horse bus. About the beginning of the century a Daimler waggonette with solid tyres, chain drive, and tiller steering was operating between Prestwick and Burns Monument. In 1912 James Dodd of Troon began a Saturday service between Troon and Ayr with his chain-driven Argyll motor waggonette. In 1908 Ayr's first motor lorry was acquired by G.& J.Girdwood, bakers.

The King's Arms Hotel at 14 High Street and the Black Bull Hotel in River Street survived from the 18th century. The Ayrshire and Galloway Hotel in Beresford Terrace and the Ayr Arms Hotel at 209 High Street were more recent. Newer creations still were the Station Hotel, the Burns Statue Hotel, and the Kyle Hotel nearby. The trend of converting mansion houses and larger villas into hotels commenced with the Hotel Dalblair in Alloway Street and Milrig Hotel in Charlotte Street. Other new features were seven Temperance Hotels (located mostly near the harbour or the railway station) and eight boarding houses (near the beach). There were now seventeen restaurants, and High Street by 1913 contained almost as many tea rooms as public bars.

The new century was preceded by the merger in 1900 of the United Presbyterian and Free Churches. To the new United Free Church were initially attached nine local congregations. Cathcart Street U.P. had

North of the river remained a predominantly working class area. A tenement built in 1900 was known as Spion Kop from a battle in the Boer War.

originated in 1816 as a Relief Church; Darlington U.P. derived from the Burgher Kirk of 1797 in Wallace Street; Trinity U.P., recently formed, would build its church in Midton Road in 1902; Ayr Free, built in the Sandgate in 1845, was renamed Ayr West U.F.; Wallacetown Free became St John's U.F.Church briefly till 1904, resuming the name of Wallacetown U.F. when joined by the congregation of Martyrs Free Church (former Cameronians) and some from the Wallace Street U.F.Church; Newton-on-Ayr Free on becoming a U.F. church was from 1905 till 1907 interdicted from using its own place of worship; St Andrew's Free was that separate congregation which built its church in Park Circus in 1893. The Established Church had eight congregations with Ayr Old and New, St Leonard's, Alloway, Newton-on-Ayr, St James (disjoined from Newton in 1904), St Quivox, and Wallacetown. Its adherents were fewer, often less enthusiastic, and some would in 1908 be embarrassed when Rev William Cairns Duncan of the Auld Kirk was tried before the presbytery. More zeal was exhibited by the smaller denominations. Those members of the

Free Church who were dissatisfied with the Union of 1900 formed in 1905 a separate congregation, meeting in the Wallace Tower, then in Newton U.F.Church (of which they took legal possession, despite riotous opposition in July 1905), then in the former Martyrs church in George Street (which was allocated to them in 1907) as the Martyrs Free Church congregation of the continuing separate Free Church. The Original Seceders moved in 1901 from their 1779 church in George Street to the new Robertson Memorial O.S.Church at Craigie Road. Their old church was taken over by the Morison Congregational Church. The Wallace Street E.U.Church dating from 1844 became a U.P. congregation in 1898, and so entered the U.F.Church in 1900, but seceded in 1904 to join the Congregational Union under its original name. The Baptist Church of Ayr was reconstituted in 1904; the second congregation built its New Prestwick Baptist Church in 1900. Smaller numbers found spiritual solace with the Christian Brethren in their Ebenezer Hall at Tam's Brig, or at the Gospel Hall in James Street, the Bethel Mission of the inter-denominational Ayrshire Christian Union in Green Street, the Wooden Kirk Mission in Limond's Wynd, at the Salvation Army Citadel built 1905 in New Road – all north of the river, or among the Irvingites at the Catholic Apostolic Church in Sandgate (that sect whose ministry in Edinburgh had been joined by Rev John Sinclair after he gave up Ayr Auld Kirk Second Charge in 1885). The Methodist congregation in Charlotte Street ceased to exist in 1909, and the Moravian Church in Mill Street in 1916. The two other larger bodies continued to be well-supported. The Episcopal Church in Scotland's Holy Trinity Church was, after twenty years of rebuilding, consecrated in 1908. Their St John Mission in James Street was extended in 1904; but their church school in Fullarton Street was closed in 1907. St Margaret's Roman Catholic Church in John Street, built in 1826 when its parish priest William Thomson was responsible for all of that faith throughout Ayrshire, was by 1900 joined by a score of other chapels in the county, most recently by Annbank in 1898, so that Canon Daniel Collins (1894–1914) had ultimately a more manageable parish encompassing the town of Ayr and its immediate vicinity.

Despite the number of places of worship, in the *Advertiser* of March 1903 fears were expressed of 'The Decline of the Churches'. Just a year before, though more than seven thousand signatures had been collected in mass petition against Sunday operation of the new trams, a public poll (by secret ballot) had voted 1,252 for and only 433 against. There

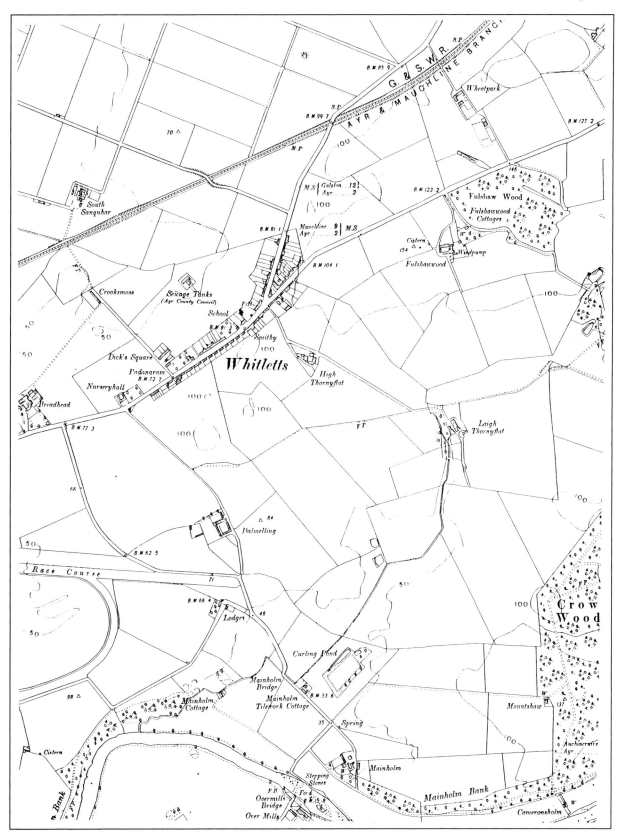

Whitletts in the early 20th century remained a distant and isolated village.

were still religious bodies like the Ayr, Newton, and Wallacetown Tract Society, an Ayr Colportage Society, a branch of the National Bible Society, Ayr and District Sabbath Union, Ayr Boys and Girls Religious Society, Church of Scotland Labour Home, and the Young Men's Christian Association with premises at 138 High Street. But a continuing concern with good works was expressed rather in that growing number of voluntary organisations of diverse purpose and secular character: Ayrshire Mission to the Deaf and Dumb, Mission to the Outdoor Blind, St Andrew's Ambulance Association, National Society for Prevention of Cruelty to Children, Ayrshire branch of the Society for Prevention of Cruelty to Animals, Association to Provide Trained Nurses for the Sick Poor, Ayr Day Nursery 90 Wallace Street, Ayr and District Charity Organisation Society, an Ayr Council for Social Service formed in 1906, a local Old Age Pension Committee (after the introduction of Old Age Pensions in 1909), an Ayr branch of the Royal Lifeboat Institution, Soldiers and Sailors Families Association, a National Service League, Ayr Citizens League, Vigilance Society, Ayr Working Girls Institute and Club in James Street, Scottish Girls Friendly Society, Ayr battalion of the Boys Brigade (with 415 officers and boys in 1903), Boy Scouts (formed in 1907), and British Women's Temperance Society. There continued for self-help 7 masonic lodges; 13 lodges of friendly societies – Good Templars, Foresters, Free Gardeners, Oddfellows, Ancient Shepherds, and Rechabites; Ayr Guildry; and the surviving Trades of Hammermen, Tailors, Shoemakers, and Squaremen.

Part of the zeal once devoted to matters theological and ecclesiastical was now directed into political controversy at a time when parties were keenly divided. In 1895 the Liberals lost Ayr Burghs to C.L. Orr Ewing who in 1900 (during the Boer War when imperial feelings were high) increased his slender majority from 335 to 590. The South Ayrshire constituency was on both occasions held for the Liberal Unionists by Sir William Arrol. When Orr Ewing died in 1904 Ayr Burghs was in the subsequent by-election taken by the Liberal Joseph Dobbie by 44 votes. There was a national swing to the Liberals at the 1906 General Election, with a Liberal gain in South Ayrshire. But in Ayr Burghs the Conservative candidate George Younger was successful at this his second contest. Lloyd George's Budget of 1909 and the ensuing conflict involving the House of Lords brought political excitement to fever pitch in the two general elections of 1910. In January, Younger's previous majority was reduced from 261 to 53, but in December he increased it to 232 in a heavy poll when there voted 90.7% of the electors in that widely-dispersed constituency which included the towns of Ayr, Irvine, Inveraray, Campbeltown, and Oban. Within Ayr, there was an array of political bodies. The Unionists (so-called after the merger in 1912 of the Scottish Conservatives with the more numerous Liberal Unionists) had the support of Ayr Unionist Central Council, Ayr Liberal Unionist Association, South Ayrshire Unionist Association, Women's Unionist Association, the Junior Unionist Club at 20 Cathcart Street, a Working men's Unionist Club in New Road, two Ayr branches of the Unionist Workers League, and the Tariff Reform League. Now less well represented were Ayr Liberal Association, Ayr and South Ayrshire Liberal Club, and the Women's Liberal Association. There was an Ayr branch of the Young Scots Society (who resented Victoria's successor being numbered Edward VII). Another offshoot from the Liberals originated with Keir Hardie's breakaway in 1893 to form the Independent Labour Party; Ayr from 1905 had ILP rooms at 9 New Bridge Street.

Local radical activity had not survived the collapse of the Chartist movement. Three unsuccessful efforts had been made in mid-19th century Ayr to form a Cooperative Society; failure in native initiative was redressed by Kilmarnock Equitable Cooperative Society (established 1860) which opened branch shops in North Harbour Street (1896), Allison Street (1898), Main Street (1899) and began manufacturing bakery products in McCall's Avenue in 1908. More enterprise was exhibited in trade union branches being formed in Ayr by engineers (1852), printing workers (1859), slaters (1866), boilermakers (1883), shipwrights (1885), until the directory of 1913 listed eighteen branches plus an Ayr Workers Representation Committee and an Ayrshire Trades Council. The local Clerical Workers Union obtained a noteworthy member in Mary Macarthur. The daughter of a local draper, she enjoyed an expensive education in Glasgow and Germany before taking a job in her father's shop. She became active in trade union affairs, in 1903 was a delegate to the TUC, then moved south to organise the National Federation of Women Workers and the Women's Trade Union League. As a member of the ILP Mary Macarthur was elected to the Executive of the Labour Party. In 1911 she married W.C. Anderson, a Labour MP, was left a widow in 1919 and herself died in 1921. In the early years of the century Robert Smillie was campaigning as prospective Labour candidate for South Ayrshire, but in fact neither that nor Ayr Burghs seat was as yet contested. More political impact was being made by the suffragettes, whose advocacy of votes for women involved militant strangers burning down the grandstand at Ayr's new racecourse (April 1913) and attempting to set fire to Burns Cottage (July 1914). Less dramatically, Miss Jane Campbell was three times elected to Ayr School Board, topping the poll in 1903, and serving from 1897–1900 and 1903–09.

The first decade of the 20th century saw continued extension of educational provision, with especial developments in post-primary schooling. A change in the government grants system was accompanied by the establishment in 1894 of an Ayrshire Secondary Committee, which among other things introduced into Ayr Academy a number of free places open to competition, and from 1898 by subsidies allowed Academy fees to be drastically reduced. The roll of fewer than 400 in 1900 rose beyond 500 within ten years. Ayr School Board made lavish provision of improved premises: an initial £9,000 on the new building of 1880 was supplemented by further outlays of £3,000 (1895), £8,000 (1907), and £12,000 (1912). The extension of 1895 was partially financed by a bazaar; the School Board provided a new block for the teaching of art and other practical subjects, opened in 1907, this designed also by James A. Morris; who had a third important commission in 1912 when the entire interior was reconstructed with a central hall and 26 classrooms supplemented by facilities for a wider variety of subjects. An equally drastic reorganisation of teaching followed the appointment of Alexander Emslie (1910–1918) as the Academy's first non-teaching rector. Hitherto there survived the obsolete system condemned in 1906 as still 'Really six schools housed in one building' in which 'the control of the Rector is more nominal than real'. Emslie was authorised by the Board to 'exercise a general authority over and be responsible for the conduct, management, and discipline of the whole school'. There were six heads of department (English, Classics, Mathematics, Modern Languages, Science, Art) with fifteen assistants, plus others responsible for special subjects, and four teachers in the separate primary department.

Ayr School Board's principal responsibility of providing free elementary education increased after 1908 when the school leaving age was raised to fourteen. North of the river the opening of Newton Park School (1905) relieved pressure on Newtonhead, Russell Street and Wallacetown schools, and Newton Academy was rebuilt (1911). South of the river Smith's Institution (not renamed Holmston School till 1930) and Lady Jane Hamilton's School (that other former charity school) provided for those unable or unwilling to pay the fees levied in the Academy and also in the Grammar School. This last, though select and long regarded as the town's premier elementary school, occupied premises which in 1898 were described as incomparably the worst in town; not till 1909 was the Grammar School reconstructed and extended. In that same year the Roman Catholic School in Whitletts Road was extended to accommodate all their pupils; the Episcopalian church school closed down in 1907.

As a preliminary to the raising of the school leaving age, elementary schools from 1903 were able to introduce 'supplementary courses for pupils between twelve and fourteen who had finished a primary and do not want a secondary course'; and several would develop into Higher Grade Schools offering three-year post-primary courses. Another new development was the Education (Scotland) Act of 1908 which, as well as raising the school leaving age to fourteen and allowing free provision of books and jotters, extended the powers of the School Boards and required some concern with the social welfare of the pupils. That concepts of education were changing is otherwise indicated by the formation in 1904 by some enthusiastic teachers of an Ayr Schools Football Association. Extra-mural activities were particularly expanded in Ayr Academy. Organised sporting activities were developed after the appointment of gymnastic instructors for boys (1897) and girls (1907). During Emslie's rectorship, rugby, cricket, and hockey were joined by golf, tennis, swimming, and cycling clubs; there were formed a literary and debating society, a field club, a camera club; a magazine commenced annual publication in 1909. In that same year was formed an Ayr Academy Cadet Corps, attached to the Officers Training Corps then instituted as part of the government's military preparations. Seventy boys over the age of thirteen were uniformed, drilled, and in 1912 inspected by the Secretary for War, Lord Haldane.

It was Haldane who, inspired by the experience of the Boer War and the growing threat of a major European conflict, introduced the Territorial and Reserve Forces Act of 1907 which reorganised the British army. The Royal Scots Fusiliers, Ayr county's regiment from 1873, had since served in the Zulu War 1879, the Transvaal campaign 1880, in Burma 1886, and in the Boer War 1899–1902, suffering severe losses at Spion Kop in January 1900, as recorded on the RSF Monument in Burns Statue Square which was unveiled in November 1902. In 1907 to the two regular battalions RSF were attached a 3rd Special Reserve battalion formed from the militia; and 4th and 5th territorial battalions composed of the two former volunteer units, with the 'Ayr Jockies' forming A Company of the 5th RSF. The volunteer gunners became a territorial unit of the Royal Horse Artillery. The Ayrshire Yeomanry Cavalry, some of whom had served in South Africa within the Imperial Yeomanry, also became a constituent part of the new territorial army as the Ayrshire (Earl of Carrick's Own) Yeomanry. Annual camps, with leisurely parades and social functions, were superseded by more rigorous training. In July 1913 14,000 officers and men carried out military manoeuvres in the Dundonald-Craigie area. A year later just after the annual camps, the order came on Tuesday 4 August 1914 for mobilisation.

SEVENTEEN

The First War and After

The *Advertiser* of 30 July 1914 announced entertainments at Ayr Pavilion and the Ayr Picture Palace, Summer Sales at Hourston & Sons (blouses 1/11d each), Open and Closed Cars for hire at the King's Garage in Holmston Road, daily pleasure cruises on the *Juno*, and Holiday Tours organised by James Scott of Newmarket Street to places ranging from the West Highlands to France, Switzerland, and the Rhine. There were reports of the death of Rev Dr Dykes, a motor car accident in Prestwick, an American tourist fined £25 for stealing a brass handle from Burns Cottage, a first exhibition of the recently-formed Ayrshire Sweet Pea Society, and the 5th RSF in summer camp at Doonfoot. There was the usual page of 'Sports and Pastimes' with notices on cricket, junior football, bowling, golf, quoits, shooting, horse racing, athletics, polo, and a column of 'Games, Puzzles, and Frolics'. It was noted that the brilliant weather was still continuing and, in the outside world, the Buckingham Palace Conference on Irish Home Rule was in progress. Leading articles announced that 'A state of war has been proclaimed again in the Near East ... greater seriousness ... the lamentable assassination at Sarajevo ... the menace that is offered to the peace of Europe'.

Before the next issue, war on Germany had been declared on Tuesday 4 August. The previous Saturday the Territorials of the 4th and 5th RSF and the 4th KOSB had finished their summer training at Doonfoot. On Sunday an ILP meeting on the Low Green had called upon 'all sections of the workers to bring pressure to bear on the Government for the preservation of peace'. Then 'Something approaching a state of panic seized the public on Monday and Tuesday' with fears of food shortage, and the price of sugar rose from 2d to 6d a pound. On Wednesday, Royal proclamations were posted at Ayr Town Hall, horses and stables were commandeered, public houses were closed, a number of Germans resident in Ayr left for their own country, and two who had been here for

twenty years belatedly and 'in something of a panic' paid £10 to apply for naturalisation. Also on Wednesday, the 3rd (Special Reserve) territorial battalion RSF, led by pipes and drums, paraded from Ayr Academy (where they were billetted) to the Railway Station, en route to Gosport for attachment to the regulars of the 1st RSF who had just returned from South Africa. RN reservists entrained for Portsmouth. 'Some pathetic scenes were witnessed at the station', reported the *Advertiser*, whose leading articles were on 'Britain at War', 'United We Stand', 'The Citizens's Duty', and 'All for each'.

Within a week the territorials of the 5th RSF had left in three special trains, as had advance parties of the Artillery and the Yeomanry. 'A Call to Arms' was advertised: each recruit aged 19 to 30 was offered '11d per day, after being fully clothed and fed; he will also receive a full kit free'. A married man would supplement his weekly pay (32p) with an allowance for wife (35p) and each child (6p). The food panic had subsided, an Ayrshire Relief Fund for soldiers and sailors was planned at a meeting in the County Buildings, and the *Advertiser* announced a Sixpenny Fund for small subscribers. Ayr Town Council at its monthly meeting continued routine business, but noted six tramway employees away on active service, four horses of the cleansing department commandeered, and agreed to postpone the annual visit of inspection to the Barnweil Monument. At Ayr Picture Palace (admission 4d, 6d, and 9d) a War Gazette was included in the programme; a travelling Vaudeville company in the Town Hall invited patrons to 'Come and Hear Burns's "Soldier's Return" '; the Gaiety Theatre would open its season on 10 August with Dr Walford Bodie the illusionist. One August occasion was upset for, as the *Advertiser* remarked, 'the outbreak of war has had a serious effect on grouse shooting'.

The impact of war made itself felt in the following months. Schools and other organisations held concerts to raise money for war funds, women and

Territorial army units from 1907 underwent rigorous training at their annual camps.

girls knitted garments and provided comforts for the troops, a Belgian Flag Day was first of a series. Local doctors offered to attend without charge the wives and children of servicemen. The Carnegie Library arranged a lecture on 'The Rise of Prussia'. Ploughing matches, Burns Suppers, and other regular functions were abandoned. At the November municipal election there were no contests. Lord Kitchener's Appeal for 100,000 men and local recruiting meetings brought 2,600 volunteers to the RSF depot at Ayr Barracks before the end of August. For soldiers and sailors stationed in Ayr a recreation hall was provided in part of Green's Picturedrome, and a Union Jack Club opened in Dam Park pavilion. In September came the first lists of casualties among the 1st RSF who as part of the British Expeditionary Force were engaged at Mons, on the Marne, and at Ypres. In November there arrived a first batch of wounded men, mostly Belgians, 20 accommodated in the County Hospital and 50 at the Red Cross hospital in Carrick House which was lent by Mrs Thomas Arthur.

By the end of 1914 the anticipated speedy victory was recognised as an illusion and the pages of the local press in the subsequent years of war register increasing gloom and disillusionment, punctuated sometimes by distress, occasionally by hysteria. In 1915 attacks on the Western Front proved unsuccessful, the expedition

to Gallipoli was a disaster, and the sinking of the *Lusitania* signalled a growing threat from German U-boats; in 1916 reverses in Mesopotamia and the indecisive naval Battle of Jutland were followed by the Battle of the Somme and lengthening lists of casualties; 1917 brought the 3rd Battle of Ypres with more dead in the mud of Passchendaele, and though the entry of USA into the war promised eventual victory, the immediate situation was critical after the collapse of Russia in revolution. Throughout the war, the 1st and 2nd battalions of the RSF served on the Western Front, the territorials of the 4th and 5th had their first action at Gallipoli, and the regiment was eventually expanded to include twelve battalions, with the 6th RSF on the Western Front for a time commanded by Winston Churchill. The Ayrshire Yeomanry, converted into an infantry unit, served in Gallipoli, Egypt, Palestine, then on the Western Front.

The Coalition government formed in 1915 introduced military conscription the following year. A local tribunal considered applications for exemption, which was granted for some on business or domestic grounds. Conscientious objectors included pacifists with religious principles and some members of the ILP who were politically opposed to the war: all had to submit to cross-examination, a few claims were allowed, some were allocated to non-combatant

Some members of Ayr Academy Cadet Corps. Most of these boys would be among those 817 from Ayr who lost their lives in the First World War.

duties, some were gaoled. Others also were victims of a surfeit of patriotic zeal – a Glasgow photographer fined for being with a camera near the coast (*Advertiser* 28.1.15); a local pianoforte dealer rumoured to be a German spy (11.2.15); and when lighting restrictions were imposed the first offender was fined £1 at Ayr Sheriff Court (16.3.16) – this was a farmer whose car lights were presumed powerful enough to be observed by hostile aircraft or submarines – while driving in the Main Street of Barrhill! An advertisement before Christmas 1916 advertised 'Santa Claus at Hourston's' with what seems to have been a necessary explanation: 'Where did Santa Claus come from? This is a question which is much exercising the minds of the kiddies ... There seems to be a ridiculous suspicion about, that Santa Claus was "made in Germany" – this is absolute nonsense. ... No, it is really to Russia that we owe the true spirit of Santa Claus ...and is not Russia our ally?' By 1917 a main concern on the home front was the shortage of imported supplies occasioned by the U-boat campaign. There were exhortations to grow more food, and purchasing was restricted. A housewife who bought 65 pounds of sugar (ostensibly to preserve rhubarb from her garden) was fined £2 (11.10.17); readers were urged to 'Avoid the Second Helping', 'Eat Less Bread', and 'Eat like a Patriot' (24.11.17); and further advised that 'Economy in the use of food is a vital necessity' (3.1.18). There were limitations on meals 'served or consumed in any public eating place' (24.1.18). In February 1918 a measure of food rationing was imposed (and continued till 1921).

Lloyd George, who had been Minister of Munitions in Asquith's Coalition government, became prime minister in December 1916. A year later the war seemed no nearer a conclusion, when for a fourth time Christmas treats had to be organised. These were provided for convalescent soldiers in the Carrick House Hospital, and in the Union Jack Club for RSF and Royal Flying Corps personnel plus some discharged servicemen. The Flying Corps (which became the RAF in 1917) had a training unit at Ayr Racecourse; Newton Park was requisitioned from 1915 till 1922 to provide billets for the RSF, the Newfoundland Regiment, and American troops. Sir Edward Morris, prime minister of Newfoundland, on a visit of inspection, was presented with the Freedom of the burgh in September 1916. A similar award went to Ayr's First V.C. This was Lieutenant Robert Shankland who in January 1918 was honoured by Ayr Town Council. The new honorary burgess was a native of Ayr, educated at Smith's Institution and a member of Ayr B.B.; he had emigrated to Canada, volunteered for the Canadian Cameron Highlanders, in 1915 was promoted from the ranks, and won his Victoria Cross 'For Valour' in the battle of Passchendaele.

'Peace at Last' was how the *Advertiser* greeted the armistice of Monday 11 November 1918. Work was abandoned, flags and bunting displayed, bells rang, crowds rejoiced, and the trams were lit up again. On Wednesday, declared a public holiday, a Thanksgiving Service was held in Ayr Auld Kirk. Then, five years after the outbreak of war, 4 August 1919 was designated as Peace Day to celebrate victory. In Ayr there was a parade from the Low Green to the Racecourse (with motor cars to transport disabled ex-servicemen) followed by various functions and distribution of gifts. As visible reminders of the war there were later displayed captured guns and tank. Each 11 November there was two minutes' silence at 11 a.m., and remembrance services, as in Wellington Square at the War Memorial which was unveiled in 1924. The cost of the war in lives was revealed with a total for Ayr of 817. Of these 272 had been with the RSF. Some of those who survived became members of an Ex-Service Men's Club, in Cathcart Street till 1955; or joined the British Legion branch which was formed there in 1928 and acquired its own first premises in Kyle Street.

War had its inevitable effects on local industry. Businesses, many kept busy by wartime demands, suffered in the post-war slump. In the interwar period the Scottish economy in general was especially affected by loss of financial control, foreign competition, and difficulties because of changes in demand. Local trades were affected in various ways. The Ailsa Shipbuilding Company ceased work at Ayr in 1929. The Scottish Stamping and Engineering Company and James Dickie's Victoria Stamping Works, faced with fewer orders from shipyards, successfully found new markets for their forgings, particularly in the motor industry. Most of the smaller engineering firms continued – like J.M.Rodger, John Wallace and Sons, and the Wallacetown Engineering Company in Viewfield Road – but some foundered

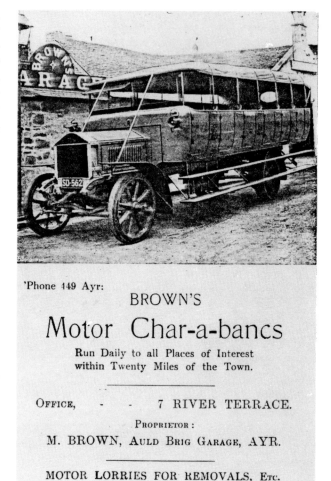

Matthew Brown was a local pioneer of motor bus services, which rapidly developed in the twenties.

– like J. & A. Taylor. Despite difficulties in the textile trade, the two main local firms continued to market their specialised products – Gray's carpets and Templeton's knitting wools. Two other firms – Andrew Lees and Sons, Cuthbert and Son – met the continuing though limited demand for heavy boots, and the firm of Harry Beebee kept open in Mill Street the solitary surviving tannery. Expanded demands for asphalt and tarmacadam ensured work for W.G.Walker's Hawkhill Chemical Works; in 1928 D.Wyllie's firm was merged in Scottish Agricultural Industries Ltd; but Hyland's starch factory closed. Turner's continued to manufacture aerated waters. Several old trades contrived to survive – in 1930 there were still two sailmakers and one cooper. But for cornmilling only the Overmill remained in operation. Overall development of local industry

Holidaymakers were catered for in various ways.

may be gauged by reference to the 1911 and 1931 census reports. Total population of the municipal burgh grew from 32,986 to 36,783; those gainfully employed from about 14,000 to 17,000; numbers employed in manufacturing industries from about 3,100 (2,100 male, 1,000 females) to 3,800 (2,600, 1,200): the proportion of the total population thus engaged in manufacturing actually increased from 9.5% to 10.4% between 1911 and 1931.

Politics was now increasingly concerned with economic problems. By the Representation of the People Act of 1918 the franchise was extended to all men over 21 and – an innovation – women over 30. There was also a redistribution of parliamentary constituencies, which abolished that consortium of widely separated burghs as created in 1707 and modified in 1832. Ayr and Irvine were no longer associated with Campbeltown, Inveraray and Oban; the new constituency of Ayr Burghs comprised the closely-adjoining coastal burghs of Ayr, Prestwick, Troon, Irvine, Saltcoats, Ardrossan. At the general election in December 1918 this seat was retained by Sir George Younger (who had been created a baronet in 1911). It remained in Unionist hands when won by Sir John L. Baird in 1922, 1923, and 1924, and by Colonel Thomas Moore in 1925, 1927, 1929, 1931, 1935, and five later elections until he retired in 1964. In 1918 the opposition (51% of those voting) was evenly split between the Liberals and Labour's first-ever candidate for this seat; from 1923 the Labour Party took second place. In 1924, 1931, and later when it was a straight fight, the Unionist majority over Labour was augmented by many former Liberal supporters, plus a share of the new electors after 1929 when the

franchise was extended to women over the age of 21. In 1935 Colonel Moore had a commanding majority with 25,893 votes against 13,274 for Labour's Arthur Brady. It was different story in the South Ayrshire constituency, which was won in 1918 by Labour at their first attempt and held thereafter with only a brief Unionist interregnum from 1931 to 1935. James Brown, South Ayrshire's MP for over twenty years, was born in Whitletts in 1862, moving shortly afterwards to Annbank which would remain his home till he died in 1939. He began work in the pits at the age of 12, but continued to attend night school. After the sixteen week strike of 1894 he became president of the Ayrshire Miners Union, and from 1904 a full-time miners agent, as well as serving on the Tarbolton school board, parish council, kirk session, and as lay preacher for the Ayrshire Christian Union. As Labour candidate he fought North Ayrshire unsuccessfully in 1906 and 1910; after winning South Ayrshire he was member during the two Labour governments of Ramsay Macdonald, when he most appropriately was appointed Lord High Commissioner to the General Assembly of the Church of Scotland in 1924, 1930, and 1931. From Westminster he returned each weekend to his home at No.56 Annbank, to worship in Annbank Church and still teach in its Sunday school. In 1930 he was made a burgess of Ayr and granted the freedom of the burgh.

In municipal affairs, elections had been suspended for the duration of the war. Provost John Mitchell continued to occupy that office from 1912 till 1918. He had come from Symington as a child when his father set up in Ayr a successful ham-curing business, in which the provost and his brother became partners. Most other 20th century Ayr provosts were incomers to the town. J.M.Mathie Morton who became provost in 1918 was a native of Kilmarnock who in 1867 inherited Belmont from his great-grand-uncle, first entered the council in 1881, then took a medical degree and served as a ships doctor, afterwards in 1891 returning to the council, to become provost at the age of 69. During wartime, casual vacancies on the council were filled by cooption. It was by this method, following recommendation of the 6th Ward Committee, that the council on 28 August 1919 replaced John Neil with another Labour member, Thomas Paterson, engine driver. At the first postwar municipal election soon afterwards in November he won his first election and was joined by William Logan, grocery manager, as a second Labour representative of the 6th ward.

Ayr Town Council was already committed to a programme of building houses for rent. In February 1914

Ayr Gaol did not enhance the sea front – it was removed in 1930.

the Public Health Committee decided to investigate local need, and evidence was heard at a public inquiry. The outbreak of war forced postponement. Inflation persuaded private landlords to increase house rents in 1915; the local Labour party organisation (known as Ayr Labour Council) organised a protest led by Thomas Paterson; and later that year suggested to the town council that plans should be prepared for a scheme of council houses to be built after the war. In 1917 a Royal Commission on the Housing of the Industrial Population of Scotland issued its damning report, and Ayr Town Council in October of that year decided to have plans prepared for a scheme of council houses. In December 1918 immediately after the war ended, a plan (as modified by the Local Government Board) was implemented for building in George's Avenue six blocks of houses designed by J.K.Hunter, to provide accommodation for 24 families. The first of these houses was let in 1921, and plans approved for further building on the grounds of Woodfield House which had been purchased in 1919. Yet despite government subsidies as an encouragement, Ayr in the twenties made little advance in municipal housing. In 1924 it was decided to build at Lochside, but after three years' preparatory work that site was abandoned in favour of Heathfield. This was contrary to the mind of Thomas Paterson, who though appointed Housing Convener by his fellow-councillors could be and often was over-ruled by them. Running sand at Heathfield made it impossible to complete the scheme there, so in 1929 the plans for Lochside were brought out again, but it was 1932 before building could commence there. According to the census reports there was an apparent

deterioration from 1.32 persons per room in 1911 to 1.44 in 1921; however, the figures for that latter year were assessed in June and so distorted by the presence of summer visitors. By 1931 the census reported Ayr burgh as having 8,169 houses for a population of 36,783, with 1.26 persons per room average. That was an improvement, though there was continued variation between the extremes of 1st Ward (0.57 persons per room) and the 3rd Ward (1.7). While the number of one-roomed dwellings had been reduced in twenty years, more people were now crammed into them – 2,589 in 707 as compared with 2,277 in 767; almost half of these single-ends (332) housed four or more persons, in two instances eleven persons. Slums and overcrowding were problems which would be slow to eradicate.

The functions of Ayr town council were changing in other respects. The harbour, a burgh responsibility since the 13th century, and from 1772 managed by a harbour trust, was in 1919 transferred into the sole control of the railway company. Another (but more recent) burgh undertaking was the electricity works which were also disposed of; in this case Ayr and Kilmarnock town councils collaborating with Ayr County Council to set up in 1924 an Ayrshire Electricity Board; the generating station at Ayr was closed and the Kilmarnock station developed as a sole source of supply, after 1932 connected with the Grid of the Central Electricity Board. Another public utility soon to be given up was the tramway system. Its financial returns were causing concern in 1925 when reduction of employees' wages and hours from 48 to 44 per week resulted in a strike. During the General

George's Avenue, Ayr's first council houses.

Strike of 1926 however, the trams kept running, and the *Advertiser* (on 20 May after missing two weeks' publication) reported in the town 'a marked absence of any disorder, and not a single unpleasant incident'. But afterwards a rise in the price of coal meant a rise in cost of electricity and an increase in fares which resulted in annual deficits; there was now more political hostility to 'municipal trading', so that the tramway system was sold in 1932 to the SMT company for replacement with buses. Concern at expenditure which would produce an increase in the rates meant that in 1920 the council gave up a plan to provide a maternity home (after Seafield was acquired for such a purpose by the County Council); in 1922 and again in 1928 the council turned down proposals to provide a swimming pool, and the only significant effort to attract holidaymakers was an extension of the esplanade in 1925. There was some return to ratepayers from leasing part of the seafront to Codona's Shows and even allowing aeroplanes to use the sands for pleasure flights (at £1.15/- per week's rent). One major project (of benefit to residents as much as visitors) was the purchase of Belleisle estate in 1925 to develop as a park, with two golf courses opened in 1927: the purchase price of £25,000 was not a burden on the rates, since it was covered by the Templeton Trust which the council administered as part of the Common Good. The town council of course continued to maintain its traditional services, extending them when essential. Thus the first motor fire engine purchased in 1914 was supplemented by two others, acquired in 1921 and 1927.

There was an obvious division of opinion within the community between those benefitting from the holiday trade and the others for whom visitors could be a nuisance. This was perhaps reflected by the choice of provosts in the twenties and thirties – Donald McDonald, retired from the licensed trade; J.R.Gould, credit draper; John S. Stewart, builder and shopkeeper; Thomas Wilson, Glasgow warehouseman; Thomas Galloway and James Wills, both in the furniture trade.

The other local authority was Ayr Parish Council, responsible for poor relief, which in 1926 after the General Strike earned some unpopularity for refusing relief to dependents of striking miners. Ayr School Board, which in 1873 had taken over from the town council responsibility for schools, was itself abolished in 1918 when an elected Ayrshire Education Authority was formed. This *ad hoc* body administered the county's schools and provided in particular an integrated system of secondary education. A new primary school for Heathfield was opened in 1931. Newton Academy, Newton Park, Russell Street and Grammar Schools developed secondary courses. At Ayr Academy (whose rector Alexander Emslie was dismissed by the School Board in 1918) the Education Authority confirmed the odd arrangement of William Dick and Hugh Jamieson as joint rectors. Fees were entirely abolished for the secondary classes of the Academy in 1927, and its clientele altered. The 900 pupils now came from a more limited area once full secondary courses were offered at Girvan, Maybole, and Cumnock. The Ayrshire Education Authority was also responsible for St Margaret's School which from 1918, like all other R.C. 'transferred schools', came under public control. In the various schools there was organised a system of evening Continuation Classes. Provision was made for a 'Special School for Defective Children' in Green Street Lane, superseded by St Leonard's Special School in premises previously occupied by the now-defunct Boys' Industrial School. Education had become the principal item of public expenditure. Municipal rates, as based on rateable values, in the year 1927–28 were 1/7 per £ for owners and 5/9¾ for occupiers (actually less than for 1921–22); to which each ratepayer had to add 8¾d poors rate and 1/7¾ for education. For those parents who preferred private schools there were Ayr Preparatory School (at Cambusdoon from 1926); Newnham House School (Fullarton Street and Barns Street); and for girls at Wellington School, which moved in 1923 from 22 Wellington Square to Carleton Turrets. Lessons in shorthand and typing were available in Short's and McGeachie's commercial schools.

A noticeable feature of the twenties was the rapid development of motor bus services. One local pioneer was Matthew Brown, coal merchant of 5–7 River Terrace, who set up as a motor hirer in 1913. After the war Brown's motor charabancs (as advertised in 1920) ran 'Daily to all Places of Interest within Twenty Miles of the Town'. Ayr and District Motor Services, Fullarton Street, in 1922 began operating services to Mauchline, New Cumnock, and intermediate places. In 1923 James Dodd recommenced an irregular service between Troon and Ayr 'as traffic required'. In 1924 the Scottish Transport Motor Services set up their headquarters in Kilmarnock and opened a depot in Ayr's Sandgate, with services to Kilmarnock and Dalmellington. Ayr Pullman Motor Services operated to Girvan and Newton Stewart. Shorter routes (some in competition with the trams) were served by Percy Hull (to Annbank), Walter Scott (to Tarbolton), Watson's and Duncan's buses (to Coylton), Rolph's (to Glenburn), Law's (Prestwick to Burns Monument), William Young (Glenburn to Monument and Doonfoot), Frank Kerr (Dundonald – Prestwick – Monument). In 1927 the Midland and Southern bus companies introduced the first direct services between Glasgow and Ayr; then Currie and Thomson between Airdrie and Ayr. For holidaymakers coming to Ayr from inland parts of Ayrshire and beyond, the railway was still the more popular means of travel. In 1923 the Glasgow and South Western Railway Company was merged in the London, Midland, and Scottish Railway Company. To compete with those bus companies which now offered tours to places of interest, the LMSR company introduced day excursions from Ayr to Edinburgh (4/6 return) and via Stranraer to Bangor (9/–). The railway steamer *Juno*, which had returned from wartime duties in 1920, offered cruises each day, now even on Sundays (at 3/6).

For holidaymakers, by 1930 there were 11 restaurants, 15 hotels, 14 boarding houses, and numerous private householders offering lodgings with or without meals. The once-popular inns had become taverns for casual drinking. The long-established King's Arms near the foot of High Street was closed and demolished in 1925; in its place appeared F.W.Woolworth's as first of the major chain stores to be represented in Ayr. Popular entertainment was provided in the Pavilion at the beach and the Gaiety Theatre in Carrick Street. Ben Popplewell (1870–1950), a Yorkshire stockbroker with interest in show business, leased the Pavilion from 1913 till 1918. Ben Popplewell and Sons took it over again in 1922 and continued till 1967; the Gaiety Theatre they acquired in 1925 and operated till 1972; the Palace Cinema in Burns Statue Square they converted into a Palais de Danse to cater for

the inter-war popularity of ballroom dancing; later the Pavilion also provided dancing and in 1929 the 'Latest Craze' of roller skating. At Green's Playhouse in Boswell Park silent films were accompanied by a 'Super Cinema Orchestra' while the Picture House in High Street, opened in 1921, boasted an organ. Both introduced the new 'talkies' in the summer of 1929. In September that year Green's Playhouse was burned down, but the Picture House's monopoly was for a time challenged by thrice-weekly shows in the Town Hall of 'Silent Pictures and a real Orchestra ... No "Amurican" Accents'.

The widening range of facilities included some which were viable because they were patronised by visitors as well as residents; others catered mainly or entirely for the local population. The Ayr Choral Union, Ayr Burgh Choir, Ayr Presbytery Choir Union, Ayr Amateur Orchestral Society, Ayr Amateur Opera Company, Ayr Sketch Club, Ayr Amateur Photographic Society – these were revived after the war and joined by a diversity of new bodies such as the Ayr Readers Union; branches of the League of Nations Union and the British-Israel World Federation; and short-lived dramatic societies like the Ayr Amateur Players (1925) followed by the Ayr Badgers (1926–30). The various sporting organisations were also revived. Ayr United, despite temporary relegation to the Second Division from 1925 to 1928, attracted much support, which however meant less for Ayr Fort and the few other junior football clubs that were re-formed. This was an era when uniformed youth organisations flourished, and as well as one BB battalion there were by 1928 three troops of Boy Scouts, thirteen Girl Guide companies and five packs of Brownies. Many of these youth organisations were attached to the churches, which were recovering from wartime difficulties and trying to cope with postwar disillusionment and secularism. The various charitable organisations and friendly societies continued their good works.

The character of Ayr as a county town was in some respects changing. Ayr was ceasing to be centre for the county gentry. Under pressure of heavy taxation, many country estates were being broken up and the ranks of the landed gentry were depleted. In the immediate vicinity, Seafield became a county council maternity home in 1920; Cambusdoon became a private school in 1926; Belleisle was acquired in 1925 by the town council; and when the extensive Auchincruive estate was broken up in 1925, the House and adjacent lands were purchased by John M.Hannah of Girvan Mains and gifted by him for the use of the West of Scotland Agricultural College and creation also in 1931 of the nearby Hannah Dairy Research Institute. There continued in Ayr the County Club in Sandgate, Town and County Club in Wellington Square, and the Ayr Club in Alloway Street. The county gentry no longer dominated the scene at the Ayr Races. Correspondingly Ayr was changing as a market town. The presence of the farming folk was at any rate no longer so obvious in the town, for horse-drawn carts and waggons were being replaced by motor cars and lorries; the traditional fairs of the burgh survived only as special sales of horse and cattle at the Market; and market day was noticed only because the shops were busier on Tuesdays. Similarly Ayr was changing as a garrison town. After the war the depot of the RSF at Ayr Barracks was less busy, with the regiment reduced to two regular battalions, the territorials forming a 4/5th battalion with headquarters in Wellington Square, the Field Artillery unit in South Harbour Street and the Yeomanry at Citadel Place. Ayr was also changing as

a seaport. Imports of iron ore and limestone declined as heavy industry decayed, but annual exports of coal from just over 500,000 tons in 1900 had doubled by 1920 and reached a peak 1¾ million tons in 1939; the fishing fleet continued to make landings; there were sailings to Belfast three of four times a week by steamers of the Burns and Laird line which was formed in 1922. Ayr continued its role as a judicial and administrative centre, with courts meeting in the County Buildings; but the County Gaol would soon be closed; and the County Council – meeting only three times a year in May, October, and December – would soon assume far greater responsibilities. Last in this assessment of Ayr's changing role as a county town, it had with improved transport facilities become busier than ever with shoppers, day trippers, football fans, race-goers, and summer visitors; and in closer touch with the outside world thanks to increased circulation of national newspapers (including Sunday papers introduced during the war) and 'the wireless' after BBC broadcasts began in 1922.

EIGHTEEN

The Large Burgh and the Second War

By the Local Government (Scotland) Act of 1929, Ayr was designated as a Large Burgh. Those with a population less than 20,000 were reduced in powers and status to 'small burghs', and those fourteen in Ayrshire included the royal burgh of Irvine. Ayr and Kilmarnock as 'large burghs' kept control of water and lighting, streets and highways, fire service, housing, planning, public health; retained a burgh police force separate from the county constabulary; and took over poor relief (renamed public assistance) from parish councils, which were abolished by the same Act.

In 1935 Ayr burgh bounds were extended to take in the two diverse communities of Alloway and Whitletts. These, containing about 1,000 inhabitants each, were in so many ways becoming more closely attached to the large burgh, whose augmented population was thereby increased beyond 39,000. The area of the burgh was more than doubled from 2,000 to 4,600 acres, occupying a third of the parish of Ayr. To the south there were included Rozelle, Belleisle, all the western part of the ancient barony of Alloway, and across the River Doon into Maybole parish towards Greenan Castle to annexe Doonfoot. To south east and east Fenwickland, Kincaidston, Laigh Glengall, Belmont, Castlehill, Holmston, and Overmills – all that part of the old Burrowfield now became part of the burgh itself. To north east, beyond the River Ayr were added Craigie estate, Braehead, Sanquhar, and Whitletts. A projected further northward acquisition was prevented when in 1933 the electors of the small burgh of Prestwick voted against amalgamation with Ayr. Extension of the burgh involved no significant change in its social composition, for the addition of the predominantly working class population of Whitletts was more than equated by the middle class residents of Alloway and of new bungalows built in areas like Seafield and Forehill.

Ayr town council in the thirties thus changed little in character or composition. The Labour Party made little headway and by 1935 had only three members in the council of eighteen; with one further gain thereafter despite rival candidates presented by the ILP which had disaffiliated from the Labour Party. To counter allegedly extravagant Socialist policies, the majority of councillors formed themselves into a Moderate group, dedicated to keeping the rates as low as practicable. The consolidated rates for 1937–38 were for owners 4/1 in the £ and for occupiers 6/– plus a water rate of 1/5, these based upon the burgh's rateable value of just under £400,000.

Though the council sold off its tramway system in 1932, there was nevertheless a resurgence of municipal activity, as exemplified by the opening of a new Fire Station in Sandgate in 1930, inauguration of the Loch Recawr water scheme in 1933, extending the Carnegie Library in 1934, beginning work in 1939 on a maternity home at Thornyflat, also in 1939 purchasing the Craigie estate. To make up for previously inconsiderable efforts, work was commenced in 1932 on the Lochside housing scheme, followed by building at Dalmilling and Mill Street. Demolition orders on more than 500 houses cleared the worst slum properties from Newton Green. In the twenty year period before 1939 Ayr town council completed a total of 2,141 houses, as compared with 1,446 houses privately built. But in December 1938 it was estimated that with 460 houses unfit and another 2,160 overcrowded, 1,310 more council houses were still required.

There was a continuing reluctance to spend money, even to help conserve the burgh's past. Back in 1910 the Auld Brig had been preserved only by voluntary effort and despite a half-hearted council; in 1921 James A. Morris had failed to prevent demolition of the Old Poorshouse building; in 1929 a proposal to remove the Wallace Tower was fortunately thwarted; in 1933 the little John Welch garden behind High Street was restored, thanks to Rev. Archibald MacKenzie; who also in 1937 halted the council's planned demolition of Loudoun Hall, which

Ayr County Council acquired extended powers in 1929, and its new County Buildings were opened in 1935 on the site of the former gaol.

was taken over by the Marquess of Bute, who already had care of the Tower of St John.

The council made some limited efforts to attract holiday visitors. No major capital expenditure was ventured, so that Ayr remained without anything to match the outdoor swimming pools provided by the small burghs of Prestwick (1931), Troon (1931), and Saltcoats (1933), and a belated proposal to copy them was turned down in 1935. In that year an Ayr Attractions Committee sponsored by the Guildry was granted £200 from the Common Good, but only after several close votes. Improvements were made at the Low Green and Belleisle Park. It was considered sufficient to offer (in 1939) 'a long stretch of fine sand at the beach, equipped with bathing bungalows, rowing boats, motor boats, donkeys and ponies for children, and an esplanade almost two miles in length (which) offers a fine walk under most bracing circumstances.' The Low Green was advertised simply as 'a large tract of green grass on the sea front, greatly appreciated and enjoyed', having a bandstand, a shelter, and 'beautiful Rock Gardens'. Nearer the harbour were a putting green, kiddie's playgrounds, boating pond, miniature motor track, and a car park. There were sandbuilding contests in July and August. Special attractions depended on voluntary efforts. It was the Guildry of Ayr which sponsored a ceremony of crowning the Queen of Bonnie Lasses in June 1933

on the Low Green, which was repeated on several occasions. The Guildry also conceived a Pageant of Ayrshire in Dam Park in 1934, whose organisation involved contributions from all parts of the county.

Private enterprise was expected to take the principal part in catering for (and profiting from) the holidaymakers. As with Ayrshire's other coastal resorts, excursions and tours were offered by the bus and railway companies. The *Juno*, which had provided pleasure cruises since 1898, was replaced by the *Duchess of Hamilton* in 1932. The summer variety shows and equally popular ballroom dancing available in Largs, Saltcoats, and Troon were more than equalled by Ayr. Ben Popplewell and Sons provided dancing and other entertainment in the Pavilion; and instituted in the summer of 1931 the annual 'Gaiety Whirl' in which many stage stars made their debut. Their Palais de Danse became Bobby Jones' Ballroom. The cinema was now so popular that the Picture House and Green's Playhouse (reopened in 1931) were joined by the Orient (1932), Regal (1933), Ritz (1936), and Odeon (1938). For those keen to participate in sports, there were bowling greens (with annual open tournaments instituted in 1932), tennis courts, and the two Belleisle golf courses. Those established facilities were now supplemented by Indoor Bowling at Lothian Road and an Ice Rink for skating, curling, and ice hockey opened at Beresford Park in 1939. Spectators could watch Ayr

There was an increasing number of day trippers to Ayr beach in the 1930s.

United playing senior football at Somerset Park – in the First Division 1913–25, 1928–36, 1937–38; Ayr Cricket Club at Cambusdoon from 1935; Ayr Rugby Club at the Old Racecourse; Ayr Races in April, June, July, and September; and a greyhound racing track was opened in 1934.

Mainly patronised by residents were those additional sporting facilities provided by clubs for athletics, boxing, swimming, badminton, ladies hockey, motor racing, and two horse riding schools. The range of other local societies was widened. Ayr Amateur Opera Company, revived in 1927, was joined in 1933 by Ayr Philharmonic Opera Society. Amateur drama was extended by the Ayr Repertory Players formed in 1931. New ventures were Coila's Minstrel Choir, Land of Burns Strathspey and Reel Society, and there was an Ayr Pipe band and an Ayr Military band. Various interests were catered for now by Rotary, the Townswomen's Guild, the Field Club, and a Canine Club. Among long-established organisations, the Guildry continued to operate (as already noted) and three surviving Trades of Tailors, Shoemakers, and Squaremen.

In High Street there was around a score of branches of various chain stores, though still outnumbered by local traders. Of the banks represented in Ayr, some had now more than one branch – Clydesale (3); Bank of Scotland, Royal, Union, British Linen (2 each); there were also branches of the Commercial, National, and North of Scotland banks; the Glasgow Savings Bank in 1932 absorbed the Ayr Trustee Savings Bank. The 1938 Directory listed 37 hotels and boarding houses, more than a dozen of them in or near Racecourse Road, several being imposing 19th century villas which until recently had been private residences. Similarly Belleisle House and Sundrum Castle were converted into hotels. Cambusdoon, Seafield, and Auchincruive had been adapted in the twenties for other purposes. There continued in private occupation Rozelle (Hamilton), Doonholm (Kennedy), Belmont (Morton), Castlehill (Wilson), and Mount Charles (which was rented). At Craigie, James A. Campbell, fifth of that family, died in 1939, when this became the second estate to be purchased by the town council. Sandgate House, built on the edge of the town in the 1780s, home of a branch of the Boswell family, was sold in 1936 to be demolished. To complete this miscellany of contemporary change, 1930 witnessed the last issue of the 98 year old *Ayr Observer*, which had been acquired in 1909 by T.M.Gemmell & Son who continued to publish the *Ayr Advertiser* in competition with the *Ayrshire Post*.

In the thirties the pattern of traffic began to change. This was the last decade in which the railway was of prime importance. The LMSR company brought nearly all of those who chose to spend their summer

Buses brought more shoppers into Ayr.

holiday in Ayr; the mass of trippers from Glasgow and inland Ayrshire, whether by regular passenger service, day excursions, or 'Evening Breathers'; most of the freight for town and harbour; and conveyed a growing number of those whom a later generation would call commuters. Nevertheless, for local travel to work or for pleasure, and for many special excursions, the buses were proving more convenient. After intense competition between operators in the twenties, there was consolidation. In 1932 the Scottish Transport Motor Services merged with several other companies to form the Western Scottish Motor Traction Co. Ltd., with its headquarters in Kilmarnock. This Western SMT in that year introduced in Ayr a bus service as replacement for the tramway system they had bought out; and took over also from the Ayr and District Motor Services. Some of the smaller operators combined in 1926 to form Ayrshire Bus Owners Ltd, whose A 1 buses provided services in north Ayrshire. Another such federation was created in 1930 with A.A. Motor Services Ltd. operating between Ayr and

Ardrossan; this undertaking, with which James Dodd of Troon was associated, acquired in 1931 their depot at Boswell Park, and in 1934 took over Percy Hull's run to Annbank and Tarholm. The roads were becoming much busier. In 1903, the first year of registration, 37 vehicles were registered in the County of Ayr; in 1923 the number was 5,438; by 1938 the figure had risen to 14,518. On the county's busiest road – between Kilmarnock and Ayr – the average number of vehicles passing daily increased from 1,203 in 1925 to 4,467 in 1938. To cope with increased traffic within Ayr, the town council installed vehicle-actuated traffic lights in January 1933 – the first town in Scotland to be so equipped. One set was at the junction of Wellington Square and Barns Street; the second along Alloway Place at the foot of Miller Road. It was somehow appropriate that on the centenary of his death a memorial was unveiled in Wellington Square to John Loudon McAdam, that native of Ayr who became renowned as a roadmaker.

The powers of Ayr County Council were greatly

increased by the Local Government (Scotland) Act of 1929. To provide appropriate administrative headquarters, the County Buildings were considerably extended. The former County Gaol was demolished, a foundation stone laid in 1931 by the Duke of York (later George VI), and by 1935 the completed block in classical style admirably blended with the original County Buildings (where the law courts continued to be held) and afforded a more dignified adjunct to the Low Green. As director of the extended administration, James Edward Shaw of High Greenan (1872–1954) was appointed as County Clerk on a full-time basis. He was solicitor, banker, and estate factor, and had also performed the duties of county clerk on a part-time basis since 1902 when he succeeded his father, Charles G. Shaw. They were descended from Rev. David Shaw who came to Ayrshire in 1749 as minister of Coylton, and intermarriage with prominent local families provided other forbears who held posts in local administration since the 17th century. From 1929 till his retiral in 1939, J.E.Shaw was a dominant figure in the county.

Ayr County Council was responsible for all local services in the landward parts of the county (save for some minor functions delegated to ten district councils). It was responsible for most services in the fourteen small burghs (leaving their town councils to provide housing and some lesser services). It was responsible for education throughout Ayrshire. 41 county councillors were elected every three years by the voters in the landward districts; 26 were nominated by the town councils of the small burghs to share in administering such services as the County Council provided for them; another twelve each by the town councils of Ayr and Kilmarnock, participating only in respect of educational provision.

Ayr County Council Education Committee comprised 32 councillors plus 8 other coopted members, four of them representing the Church of Scotland and two from the Roman Catholic Church in respect of their 'transferred schools'. This superseded the Ayrshire Education Authority which was abolished after a decade's brief existence. In 1932 when the joint rectors of Ayr Academy retired simultaneously, the appointment of a successor was (for the first time ever) outwith local hands. Dr James Ritchie (1932–45) admirably sustained the excellence of the Academy record as a selective senior secondary school; he introduced school uniform, a system of prefects and houses, acquired facilities for sports at the Old Racecourse, and developed extramural activities. Ayr Academy celebrated its 700th anniversary in 1933

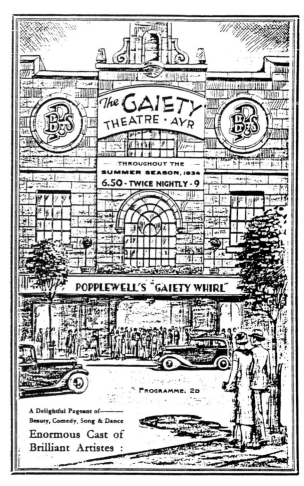

The Gaiety summer shows extended their popularity.

with a pageant on the Low Green and was honoured the following year by a visit from the Prince of Wales (later Edward VIII). The school roll comprised 300 fee-paying primary pupils and 700 secondary pupils. In the secondary department were those promoted from the primary department, some selected from the various local schools, and others from Dalmellington, Prestwick, and (until 1935) from Troon. Increased numbers taking a six year secondary course required the commencement in 1936 of another major extension to supply additional classrooms and laboratories. Apart from an addition to Wallacetown School in 1935, the other local schools could cope adequately with the majority of children who started school at the age of five and left on reaching fourteen. There was an expansion of evening continuation courses and the beginning of adult education classes in current affairs, literature, and the like. There were private schools at Cambusdoon, Monument Road, and at Wellington School for boarding and day girls; and

The popular bus tours as advertised in 1934.

three commercial schools teaching shorthand and typing.

A long-anticipated reunion of churches in 1929 was made possible by decline of theological controversy and erosion of former differences. The established church had been freed from patronage in 1874 and in 1930 a last vestige of secular control was removed when there was abolished the long-established practice of royal burghs (and universities) being represented at the General Assembly of the Church; and there could be little objection to local authorities continuing to maintain the churchyards. The Union brought within the Church of Scotland fifteen local congregations. Those from the established Church were (with names sometimes amended) the Church of St John Old and New, Newton Old, Wallacetown North, Alloway, St James, St Leonard's, and St Quivox; the former U.F. congregations were those of Cathcart Street, Darlington Place, Trinity, Newton New, Sandgate, Wallacetown South, St Andrew's. To provide for the new housing area, a Church extension charge was authorised for Lochside in 1934 in a newly-built hall, and a church dedicated in 1940. Several presbyterian congregations remained separate – the Robertson Memorial Original Seceders Church (of those who did not enter a Union with the Free Church in 1852); Ayr Free Church (formed by those who remained outwith the Union of 1900); joined now by Ayr U.F.Church

(with a church built in 1930 in Kirkholm Avenue by those opposed to the Union of 1929). Beyond the presbyterian fold there remained the congregationalists of the Wallacetown E.U. Church and the Morison Congregational Church in George Street; the Ayr and New Prestwick Baptist Churches; the Christian Brethren in three separate assemblies; the Salvation Army; the missions of the Ayrshire Christian Union and of the Wooden Kirk; a United Evangelist assembly in Mill Street; and a Christian Scientists Society in Citadel Place. The Catholic Apostolic sect ceased meeting and in 1940 its hall was converted by local Jews into a synagogue, which had a brief existence. Apart from such small groups there were of course the more prominent churches of episcopalian form – St Margaret's Roman Catholic Church; and the Scottish Episcopalians worshipping in Holy Trinity Church at Fullarton Street, or in St John's Mission Church built in James Street in 1934.

The outbreak of war on 3 September 1939 bore little resemblance to what had occurred in 1914. The population through newspaper and BBC radio news bulletins could closely follow the series of European crises in the later thirties that proceeded with horrid inevitability towards Chamberlain's reluctant declaration of war on Hitler's Germany. The prospect was accepted with grim determination. Already certain preparations had been made, prompted by experi-

ence of what had happened in the last war, and by
anticipation of what might be different this time.

Ayr remained the headquarters of the Royal Scots
Fusiliers. But links with the regiment were less close.
While Ayr Barracks remained their depot, since 1919
the 1st battalion had been stationed in Ireland,
Glasgow, Portsmouth and Bordon before overseas
service from 1932 in Palestine, Egypt, and India;
the 2nd battalion, after service against Bolshevik
Russia, went to India and Shanghai before returning
in 1932 to Catterick, Aldershot, then Edinburgh. In
the peaceful interwar atmosphere there was limited
enthusiasm for the territorial units. The 4/5 battalion
RSF had headquarters in Wellington Square, the Royal
Artillery unit at South Harbour Street, the Ayrshire
Yeomanry in Citadel Place. Recruitment brought these
up to strength in time for mobilisation. Others preferred to volunteer for the RAF or for a specialist unit,
in advance of call-up. For compulsory military service
was introduced with 'militia-men' in the summer of
1939, and afterwards extended. Successive age groups
from Ayr and around were medically examined in
the Carrick Street halls and thereafter – apart from
those unfit, in a reserved job, or with a recognised
conscientious objection – were allocated to appropriate units. There was a deliberate policy of dispersion
to avoid those sudden heavy losses sustained by some
communities when local regiments were decimated in
first world war battles.

An initial concern in 1939 was the novel one of
threatened air attacks on the population at large.
Thus in 1938 Ayr Town Council was required by the
government to make necessary Air Raid Precautions.
Wardens, special constables, and auxiliary firemen
were enrolled, gas masks issued, an emergency council
committee formed. Air raid sirens were installed and
tested, and when war came a black-out was imposed,
places of entertainment were temporarily closed, and
continuation classes cancelled. The *Advertiser* of 7
September reported the cooption by the council of
certain persons to a committee responsible for food
control; church halls were taken over as ARP posts;
Rev Archibald MacKenzie protested at the proposed
desecration of the John Welch garden by air raid shelters; W.H.Dunlop as a Yeomanry captain resigned his
council seat; building work was halted on the Mill Street
and Dalmilling housing schemes. The principal news
concerned the arrival of school children from Glasgow
who were evacuated in anticipation of immediate air
raids on cities. From the railway station they were
taken to the Ice Rink, and from that assembly centre
around four thousand were distributed for billeting

in private households. The next issue of the *Advertiser*
reported 'consternation' for among the evacuees were
'slum dwellers' and P.A. Thomson, town clerk and
chief reception officer, reported that 'many of them
came only with what they stood in, and these are not
what we call clothes in the burgh of Ayr'.

When the expected air raids (and gas attacks) did
not occur, most evacuees drifted back home to the
city. The *Advertiser* could announce (2 November) that
'War Passes Almost Unnoticed in the West'. Ayr Parks
Department had (12 October) planted spring bulbs to
keep the town attractive; and the black-out had its
compensations (26 October) for Ayr's fine buildings
'appear most imposing when their dark bulk is seen
against a frosty sky'. People were urged to carry their
gas masks, and required (after national registration
on 30 September) to carry identity cards, but food
rationing was not introduced till January 1940. There
was Digging for Victory in Park Circus (2 November),
the *Advertiser* started a Famos Fund ('For Ayrshire
Men On Service'), a Canteen was opened in Sandgate
Church Hall, fund-raising concerts were organised,
Belleisle and the Old Racecourse were let for grazing, but the *Advertiser* (28 December) found it was
'Christmas As Usual' though with theatre treats for
evacuees as an additional good cause.

1940 opened with a heavy January snowfall (which
could not be reported in the press till the following
month). Several local men had been 'lost at sea' but
there was no action involving the RSF, which was with
the BEF in France. The Ayrshire Yeomanry, stationed
at the Dam Park, was in process of conversion from a
cavalry unit into 151 and 152 Field Regiments of the
Royal Artillery. A 10th battalion RSF raised in 1938
for home defence moved its headquarters from Ayr
to Stranraer. 'Ayr is the safest place in the country',
a local travel agent advised (8 February), forecasting
that 'Ayrshire should have a Bumper Holiday Season'.
There were only 745 evacuees left in Ayr by March;
reports of others to come were countered by pleas that
inland towns should be used, to leave the resorts available for summer visitors. The town council in March
arranged for the usual summer amusements at the
shore and in July at the Glasgow Fair there were indeed
'unprecedented crowds', despite dramatic change in
conduct of the war.

The end of the 'Phoney War' was marked by
military action, reverses in Norway and Belgium
(April-May), the appointment of a National Government under Churchill for the more effective
prosecution of the war (11 May), the evacuation
of British forces from Dunkirk (27 May–4 June),

Threatened invasion in 1940 resulted in the formation of the Home Guard, which provided for local defence.

and the collapse of France (25 June). With invasion threatened, there was a call in May for Local Defence Volunteers: by the end of June 7,000 Ayrshiremen had responded, armed with 250 rifles; later, with a complement of 14,000, organised into 8 Home Guard battalions and a South Carrick company attached to the RSF, including the 7th (Ayr) battalion HG. Road blocks were manned, surface air raid shelters erected, fire watchers organised. The *Advertiser* reported (22 August) some incendiary bombs dropped on a farm 'near a south-west of Scotland town, belonging to a well-known auctioneer'. But only London and the south of England faced the air raids and aerial combats of the Battle of Britain (10 July–15 September). One solitary outbreak of war hysteria followed the entry of Italy into the war (10 June); there were demonstrations against local Italians and shop windows smashed at Lochside and South Harbour Street.

The war was extended in 1941 by German invasion of Russia (June), and the Japanese attack on Pearl Harbour (December) brought in the USA. Some units of the RSF were engaged in fighting in the Far East and Middle East. Others were meantime required for home defence, including the Ayrshire Yeomanry and the 4/5 RSF. The west of Scotland was suitable for training and equipping a variety of units. At Ayr harbour mine-sweeping and escort vessels were berthed, repaired, and fitted out: ironically as late as December 1939 the closure of the Ailsa Shipbuilding Company yard was scheduled. In January 1942 *HMS Scotia* was commissioned – a naval barracks erected south of Doonfoot able to accommodate 4,000 ratings undergoing communications training. The first Commando units formed were stationed at Ayr, Troon, and Largs. Throughout the county there were ten military training centres with capacity for 20,000 soldiers. The tide of war began to turn after the American naval victory at Midway (June 1942), the British desert victory at El Alamein (October 1942), and the Russian recovery of Stalingrad (January 1943). In 1942 the newly-formed 6th Armoured Division was moved into this area; 152 (Ayrshire Yeomanry) Regt. RA, which was attached to it, returned to familiar ground at Doonfoot, then Ayr Racecourse; and as part of the 1st Army left the Clyde in December 1942 for an invasion of North Africa and thereafter Italy. 151 (AY) Regt. RA, attached from 1942 to the 11th Armoured Division, was stationed in England in preparation for the invasion of Normandy in June 1944 and advance through France and the Netherlands into Germany. The territorial 4/5 RSF was attached to the 52nd (Lowland) Division and would assist in the liberation of Holland. In Ayrshire the 6th Armoured Division was followed by the 1st Infantry Division and the 47th Division. Some units were accommodated in seven hutted camps at Dam Park, Dalmilling, and Fulshawwood beyond Whitletts; the mansion houses of Craigie and Belleisle were also available; there was billetting in private households; at Doonfoot there was a camp for Italian prisoners-of-war. The number of servicemen frequenting Ayr was augmented after 1941 when the grass air-strip beyond Prestwick was converted into an air terminal into which planes were ferried across the Atlantic for service with the RAF and the US 8th Air Force; and there was a smaller airfield at Heathfield.

Ayr remained a 'safe area' undamaged by air raids, though with Prestwick handling an estimated 40,000 transatlantic flights between 1940 and 1945, there were inevitable crashes, as at Whitletts in 1941 with 22 victims and at Prestwick in 1944 when another 25 were killed. The Clydebank blitz of 13–14 March 1941 brought homeless families to rest centres prepared in

Ayr Barracks, dating from 1794, depot for the Royal Scots Fusiliers, was in 1942 designated Churchill Barracks after the premier who had served with the regiment in the First World War.

Ayr, and others from England also found accommodation in the town. One result was the expansion of Ayr Academy roll to 1,223 by taking in pupils from no fewer than 72 other schools.

For the civilian population, apart from obvious concern for relatives on active service, the principal problems were those of discomfort and inconvenience. Rationing was extended in 1941 to most groceries and to clothing. Direction of labour was introduced. There was constant criticism in the local press of inadequate bus services. Waste materials had to be salvaged, and in 1942 Ayr produced 247 tons of scrap iron from gates and railings which were compulsorily removed. One golf course at Belleisle had to be ploughed up to grow vegetables. Paper restrictions forced the *Ayr Advertiser* and the *Ayrshire Post* in 1941 to reduce their sizes. The *Advertiser* took the opportunity then (April 1941) to initiate news on the front page; the *Post* (which in 1943 passed into control of George Outram & Co.) did not make that change till 1968. To provide ameliorating facilities of one kind and another, a British Restaurant was opened in Limond's Wynd in 1942, the Women's Voluntary Service operated from Kyle Street, the YWCA took over a girls hostel in Charlotte Street in 1943, and the Rents Tribunal for South Ayrshire was authorised in 1944 to deal with cases within the county

town. The sheriff court had to deal with various new offences – ranging from dealing in the black market to refusal to billet war workers, with a stowaway on a plane fined £10 (*Advertiser* 17.2.1944) and smuggling of cigarettes and silk stockings through 'an airport in Ayrshire' (8.6.1944). The drabness of wartime life was relieved somewhat by periodic parades. There were parades during the successive National Savings campaigns for Spitfire Fund, War Weapons Week, Warship Week, Tanks for Attack, Wings for Victory, Salute the Soldier, and ultimately Thanksgiving Week. There were parades to celebrate United Nations Day and Battle of Britain Sunday. There were parades of the Ayrshire Cadet battalion RSF, Air Training Corps, and Sea Cadets. There were Home Guard anniversary parades and their final Stand Down parade on a wet Sunday in December 1944.

Everyday life contrived to continue. The New Year in 1941 was brought in 'quietly' and the *Advertiser* remarked also that 'To many Englishmen who are in the district it was their first experience of the traditional Scottish New year celebrations'. By 1944 'weary hours in a queue at a well known licensed grocer's in High Street for the reward of a half-bottle for Hogmanay ... has become an annual phenomenon of war-time Ayr'. The usual Christmas treats were provided at the County Hospital, Heathfield Hospital, and Kyle Home, with ARP workers now arranging some children's parties. In summer a programme of band concerts on the Low Green was continued. Day trippers continued to patronise the shore. Burns Cottage was sometimes quite busy, and one day in October 1943 Clark Gable and Irving Berlin called in. Another celebrity, Harry Lauder, was in Ayr on various occasions raising funds for war charities. The routine of ordinary existence is reflected by assorted news items: St Andrews House purchased by the Scottish Horse and Motormen's Association as a convalescent home (31.7.1941); Rev J.Strathearn McNab at a St Andrew's Day dinner declared that Scotland had 'the status of a crown colony' (4.12.1941); Ayr and District Young Farmers Club formed at Auchincruive (4.12.1941); D.E.Edwards retired after thirty years in charge of the Carnegie Library (19.3.42); to be succeeded by James W. Forsyth (28.5.1942); death of Rev W. Phin Gillieson at the age of 63, 'one of the town's most popular ministers' (2.4.1942); Whitletts Fete and Gala Day in Meadow Park (20.8.1942); Scottish Educational Films Association awards to local film-makers (1.4.1943, 9.3.1944); Ayr Presbytery debated if women should be admitted as elders (7.10.1943); Tam O'Shanter Inn purchased by Ayr Town Council for £4,000 (14.10.1943); Ayr's first woman minister when Rev May Findlay was inducted to the EU Congregational Church (22.6.1944); a public meeting organised by Ayr Spiritualist Association (27.7.1944); Students Charities Day (5.4.1945).

While some local organisations had necessarily to curtail or suspend activities for the duration of the war, others could busily involve themselves in entertaining troops or raising money for comforts. Ayr's cultural life was enhanced from August 1941 when the Council for Encouragement of Music and the Arts sponsored the first of a series of classical concerts in Sandgate Church. Adult education classes in Ayr Academy, sponsored by the Education Committee and by the Workers Educational Association, attracted those interested in history, economics, and current affairs. The Ministry of Information provided popular War Commentaries in the Odeon Cinema on Sunday evenings. When in June 1942 the Home Guard organised a sports meeting on a Sunday there were, however, objections from Ayr Presbytery; and the town council in June 1943 turned down proposals for Sunday tennis because, as one councillor asserted, 'the world needed a more spiritual basis'.

As early as 1942 plans were being made for the post-war world. In November 1942 Housing Convener Thomas Paterson presented a Report on Ayr's Post-War Housing Policy and anticipated the need for 2,000 new council houses. In December 1942 the government published the Beveridge Report which promised a future Welfare State. The *Advertiser* could announce (23.9.1943) 'Ayrshire Man's "Miracle" Cures' with a report on Professor Alexander Fleming's 'Wonder Drug' called penicillin. It was revealed (20.4.1944) that Butlin's Ltd would at the end of the war open an Ayr holiday camp; that firm's subsequent proposal (25.1.1945) to convert the entire Low Green into an fair-ground was mercifully rejected by the town council. 'Prestwick's Great Future' as the 'Aerial Cross Roads of the World' was publicised (24.2.1944) and Ayr's hopes for involvement no doubt prompted a renewed suggestion (19.4.1945) for amalgamation of the two burghs. 1944 brought the partial de-requisitioning of parts of Craigie and Belleisle, and permission to complete council houses left half-built at the outbreak of war. The Ayrshire Cattle Herd Book Society was reported (11.1.1945) to be considering the dehorning of cattle at birth.

There were some stirrings of dissatisfaction. In August 1943 the town council received a deputation of shipyard workers objecting to Admiralty proposals to return Ayr Shipyard to the company which had previously let it run down. A month later Ayr fishermen protested when the Ministry of Food ordered them to dump one million herring which could not be distributed or processed. In January 1944 2,000 miners went on strike at Glenburn, Mossblown, Tofts, and Annbank pits; the following January it was Enterkine and Mossblown with 1,500 involved. In December 1944 militant action of another kind occurred when a number of homeless families moved as 'squatters' into empty condemned houses at Whitletts.

As victory in Europe approached, Ayr town council in February 1945 inaugurated a Provost's Welcome Home Fund, but realised it would be awkward to plan in advance how to expend it with servicemen and women likely to be demobilised over an extended period. In April there arrived home some who had been released from prisoner of war camps in occupied Europe; the territorial gunners of 130 Field Regiment RA were still fighting in Burma. With a long continuing war against Japan expected, the council proposed that the imminent defeat of Germany required only a 'quiet' celebration. In the event, VE Day on 8 May was greeted with 'Crowds, bells, flags, cheers, and greetings'. On the eve, a bonfire on Newton Green was extinguished by a zealous unit of the National Fire Service, for the ban on illuminations within five miles of the coast still applied, though the possibility of Japanese submarines in the Firth was surely remote! On 14 August Japan surrendered: the early-morning news was welcomed by shouting, singing, dancing in the streets, and an impromptu bonfire was (without interference) made of herring boxes at the South Harbour, all in advance of official celebration of VJ Day on 2 September.

After the end of the war in Europe, a general election was held on 5 July but, with service votes to be included, results were not announced till 26 July, when Labour victory replaced Churchill with Attlee as prime minister. The constituency of Ayr Burghs had an electoral roll of 55,610 civilian and 5,441 service voters. Of these there were within the burgh of Ayr 23,454 and 2,397 respectively, apart from 2,837 and 295 from those parts of the burgh which were still part of the South Ayrshire constituency. Alexander Sloan who had held South Ayrshire for Labour in a by-election after James Brown's death in 1939 was re-elected with an increased majority. Sir Thomas Moore (who had been knighted in 1937) was able to hold Ayr Burghs, which he had represented for twenty years already. But his previous majority of 13,274 was reduced to 728. 21,865 votes went to 34 year old Major William Ross, schoolteacher son of an Ayr railwayman who would enter Parliament the following year at a by-election and represent Kilmarnock till 1979, serving as Secretary of State for Scotland in two Labour administrations, created a life peer in 1979 with the title of Lord Ross of Marnock, and died in 1988.

Municipal elections were recommenced in November 1945. During their wartime suspension casual vacancies had been filled by cooption, and during this period two provosts had died in office, James Wills in 1940 and Robert Bowman in 1943. Thomas Murray would occupy the chair from 1943 till 1949, for the Moderates retained control of the council. At the 1945 election there were contests in five wards, with seventeen candidates for ten vacant seats. The first postwar council comprised ten Moderate councillors, seven Labour, and as an Independent Ayr's first woman councillor, a social worker Miss Louisa McIntyre, one of two candidates sponsored by the Standing Conference of Women's organisations.

Ayr Town council addressed itself to a variety of urgent issues. The most critical was housing. Plans were made for future developments at Castlehill, Belmont, and Fenwickland; sites already acquired at Dalmilling and Thornyflat could not be fully utilised so long as they lay within the flight path of Heathfield airfield, which the Fleet Air Arm contemplated retaining as a training school. Such houses as the town council could build in this era of postwar shortages were supplemented by others provided by the Scottish Special Housing Association. Temporary 'prefab' houses were also erected. But so severe was the shortage that in August 1946 there was an 'Invasion of Vacant Camps' and in 1950 there were still 161 families of 'squatters' in seven war-time camps within the burgh, living in conditions then described as 'deplorable'. A second issue to concern the council was that of local industry. The town's engineering and textile firms which had been involved in war work had to adjust to peacetime conditions. In 1945 the town council made plans for an industrial area at South Sanquhar farm. It also agreed to make work available where possible for demobilised men who were unemployed. To provide for cases of hardship there was the Council's Social Welfare Department – as the former Public Assistance Office was renamed in 1944. A return to the normal way of life for the town was promised in July 1945 when Glasgow holidaymakers arrived and the *Advertiser* was pleased to announce 'Ayr Crowded for Fair Week'.

As post-script, on 11 November 1956 at the War Memorial in Wellington Square were unveiled panels listing the names of those 263 who had died on service. Far fewer than the 817 of the First War, the distribution was also different, including 71 RAF, 31 RN or merchant navy, and 27 RSF. In 1960 an RSF memorial was erected on the seafront to all members of that regiment who died in the Second World War, with battalions fighting in Europe, Africa, and Asia.

NINETEEN

Mid-Century

When the Third Statistical Account was being compiled between 1947 and 1950, local informants (responding to questionnaires from the present author) provided a detailed picture of the county town still not quite recovered from war, and attempting to retain its prewar identity in the midst of social changes whose impact would only later become apparent.

The extent of the housing shortage was revealed by a series of statistics. In 1946 there were 2,000 families on the housing list currently living in furnished rooms, and an estimated need for 3,800 houses. It was calculated in 1948 that of Ayr's 10,765 houses, 4,063 had been erected since 1919, 2,605 of those by public authority. Of the older houses, 4,097 needed to be modernised or replaced, 721 of them being unfit for habitation. 3,717 houses were overcrowded. The Census Report of 1951 provided a more detailed analysis. Over twenty years the number of one- and two-roomed houses had been reduced, replaced by three- and four-roomed houses which now accommodated 56.9% of the burgh population. The average number of persons per room had improved from 1.24 to 1.04. But much remained to be done. There were still 743 persons living in 325 single-ends – in three cases six to a room. A new census enquiry indicated that of the 10,753 households in the burgh, 3,882 were without a fixed bath; 3,595 had to share a water closet (and 43 had none); 90 were without indoor piped water and another 1,484 had to share. There were 1,567 cases of families having to share homes, involving 4,538 persons, amounting to 10.7% of Ayr's population of 42,377.

Council house developments at Braehead, Dalmilling, Thorneyflat, Forehill, Belmont, and Craigie went only some way towards accommodating those in need. Because of shortages of labour and materials, the government had to impose quotas. Private building was limited to 10% of the total till 1952 when it was increased to 20%. Some larger houses which could be split into separate homes were in 1948 'selling at fantastic prices'. In August 1953 the *Advertiser* reported that property prices in Ayr were higher than in any other Scottish town. 4-room bungalows were in keenest demand and fetching 'astronomical' sums between £4,000 and £4,500. (For purposes of comparison, anyone then earning over £1,000 per annum was accounted well-off.)

The government required to continue other restrictions. Indeed, bread rationing had to be introduced in 1946 and it was July 1954 before all food rationing ended. Despite difficulties, Attlee's Labour government (1945–51) implemented its socialist policies. The mines were nationalised in 1947 and the National Coal Board became responsible for 36 Ayrshire pits. On the northern edge of Ayr parish were Mossblown (Auchincruive 1/2/3) and Glenburn (Auchincruive 4/5) collieries, and 500 of the 1,800 miners employed in them lived in Ayr, most of them in Whitletts. In 1948 British Railways took over the LMS railway lines, stock, and ownership of Ayr harbour. In 1948 electricity and in 1949 gas were similarly brought into public ownership. In 1948 the foundations of the welfare state were laid. The National Health Service involved, as far as Ayr was concerned, 24 local doctors, 21 dentists, 16 chemists, and 13 opticians, who would operate under a County of Ayr Executive Council. South Ayrshire Hospitals Board acquired responsibility for Ayr County Hospital, Glengall, Seafield, Kyle Welfare Home, Crofthead, Heathfield, and Thorneyflat. Seafield, operated by the County Council from 1920 as a maternity home, was in 1944 converted into a sick children's hospital; Thorneyflat Maternity Home, built by Ayr town council, was opened just two days before the take-over. The Ministry of National Insurance made new comprehensive provision, resulting in the decay or demise of friendly societies which previously had been involved in distribution of benefits. A National Assistance Board took over from Ayr town council responsibility for social security, which had hitherto been known as social welfare and before that poor relief. The town council similarly lost control of its fire brigade when a National Fire Service was formed in 1948 from the wartime coordinated organisation of that name.

In 1950 Sir Thomas Moore completed twenty five years as Conservative MP for Ayr Burghs; his success in the general election early that year involved a drastically altered constituency. The creation of a new Central Ayrshire constituency severed Irvine's 243-year link with Ayr Burghs, which became that more compact area around the county town. For Sir Thomas it meant the loss of many supporters in north Ayrshire, and it was dubious compensation for him to acquire instead the miners of Annbank as constituents. Yet he continued to hold the seat till he retired in 1964, serving as a government back-bencher during the ministries of Churchill (1951–55), Eden (1955–57), Macmillan (1957–63) and Home (1963–64). The Moderates continued to retain effective control of Ayr Town Council. Labour representation dwindled from a maximum of eight in 1946 to four from 1949. There were vigorous campaigns in the 'Fighting Fifth' Ward; in the Sixth Ward a by-election in 1948 retained a seat for Labour only after a dramatic recount the following morning; in 1951 the same candidate won after an equality of votes and decision by lot. When in 1953 it became Labour Party policy to prohibit members accepting conversHIPS on councils which they did not control, Thomas Paterson resigned from Ayr Town Council. He had been Housing Convener for most of his 34 years as councillor. His departure was regretted even by his political opponents for, as the *Advertiser* declared, 'his views almost invariably commanded respect ... if ever a man deserved to have the honour of becoming civic chief of the royal burgh conferred on him that man was surely he'. Since 1933 he had been one of Ayr's twelve representatives on the county council, and chairman of its Education Committee 1947–49; though no longer a town councillor, he returned to the county education committee in 1955 as one of its coopted members, and served till retiral through ill health in 1963.

Other changes affecting the council occurred in 1946 when 80-year-old P.A.Thomson retired as town clerk, having served over forty years since 1905; and T.L.Robb as Town Chamberlain after 32 years since 1914. Then in 1949 John Lowdon retired, Chief Constable of the Burgh Police Force, Britain's senior holder of such a post, as he had been the youngest when appointed in 1903 at the age of 29. Other innovations were – evening meetings in 1945, but with reversion to the traditional morning meetings a

year later; the appointment of Miss Louisa McIntyre in 1947 as the burgh's first woman magistrate; in 1949 by statutory requirement municipal elections moved from November to May; in 1950 the practice of ringing the steeple bell before council meetings was given up. Tradition was maintained when the freedom of the burgh was presented in 1946 to the RSF, and in 1947 to Winston Churchill. In 1952 Queen Elizabeth was proclaimed at the County Buildings by Sheriff Principal J. F. Gordon Thomson, then at the site of the malt cross by Provost James Smith. Later in 1952 the 750th anniversary of the royal burgh was celebrated by a Pageant in the Ice Rink, a Service of Thanksgiving at the Tower of St John, an Auld Ayr Exhibition in the Carnegie Library, plaques on historic sites, special features in the local press (including 'The Story of Ayr' in an *Advertiser* cartoon series), and the publication the following year of a historical volume on *The Royal Burgh of Ayr*. Later in July 1956 when Queen Elizabeth and the Duke of Edinburgh made a tour of Ayrshire, the royal burgh enjoyed its first official royal visit since Mary Queen of Scots passed through in 1563.

One chronic concern was the rise in rates which for the year 1952–53 reached 5/9 in the £ for owners of property and 10/5 plus 8d water rate on occupiers, based on the rateable value of property. The Burgh's estimated expenditure for the year was almost £400,000 and a third of that – £139,000 – was the county requisition for education. Protests from the town council about that were ineffective, for it was represented by only twelve members who sat among 79 others on Ayr County Council. In the year 1956–57 rates were 7/3 on owners and 11/1 plus 10d water rate on occupiers, and the following year following abolition of the charge on owners it was 20/– on all householders plus a water rate of 1/–; the burgh's estimated expenditure was £613,373, of which £187,256 was the county requisition for education.

The massive postwar increases in educational expenditure were due to several causes. The statutory school leaving age was raised to fifteen in 1947. New schools were required to supplement and replace overcrowded older buildings. The scope of education was extended – stimulating some Ayr councillors (and others) to grumble about expensive nursery schools and Further Education classes in country dancing. Within the burgh of Ayr 7,000 pupils were taught in twelve schools maintained by Ayr County Council Education Committee – as compared with fewer than 300 in five private schools. Three of these accommodated boarders and local pupils: Wellington

Burns Statue Square: Though traffic was increasing, in the immediate postwar years parking was not yet a problem.

(girls and some younger boys), Hartfield (boys and girls), Cambusdoon (boys); plus Hartree (boarding boys) and the Convent private school (for local boys and girls).

Ayr Academy remained the town's premier school. The primary department was phased out between 1953 and 1960 following the abolition of fees in 1947. Thereafter under J.Douglas Cairns (1945–65) this became a selective secondary school, catering for all parts of Ayr, Prestwick, Tarbolton, and the Doon valley; entry being determined by performance in a county promotions test; and providing a full academic course, as well as a continuing range of extra-mural activities. There were around the town purely primary schools at Heathfield, Newtonhead, Wallacetown, Whitletts, Holmston, and Alloway. The Grammar School, Newton Academy, Newton Park, and Russell Street as junior secondary schools pro-

vided for primary children within their own districts, plus all those older pupils considered to be 'less able' and likely to leave school aged fifteen. St Margaret's School in Whitletts Road took Catholic pupils up to the age of fifteen; boys wishing to go further had to travel to Kilmarnock and girls to Irvine. The Education Committee also administered St Leonard's Home for mentally and physically defective children, with accommodation for 120. The provision of additional schools was delayed by shortages, by priority being given to the building of houses, and costs were steadily soaring. The first local postwar school was Braehead primary opened in 1951.

The County Education Committee also appointed full-time youth organisers, one responsible for a Burgh of Ayr Youth Panel, to which were affiliated most of the town's 94 youth groups, which had a combined membership of nearly 5,000. The most recently-formed groups, like five promoted by the Education Committee and some attached to churches, included both sexes, unlike the older uniformed organisations which still predominated. There were companies of Boys Brigade (14), Life Boys (10), Boy Scouts (6), Girl Guides (14), Brownies (7), Girls Guildry (2) and others like the Army Cadet Force, Air Training Corps, and Sea Cadets.

The immediate post-war years witnessed the revival of societies many of which had been dormant in wartime, and the formation of a number of organisations catering for other special interests. In some cases there was an overlapping or even duplication of purpose, indicating how wide was the support obtained from the local burgh population of 43,000 and in some cases from other parts of the county – whose total population in 1951 amounted to 321,000. For those keen on music there was Ayr Choral Union, Ayr Burgh Choir, Ayr Amateur Orchestral Society, Ayr Amateur Opera Society, Ayr Philharmonic Opera Company, Land of Burns Caledonia Strathspey and Reel Society, Scottish Country Dance Society, Ayr Burgh Band, Ayr Pipe Band, a Recorded Music Club, and a Swing and Rhythm Club. For drama enthusiasts, Ayr Amateur Players were joined by the Fort Players (1946) and the Compass Club (1953), and there was a Playgoers Club. There were the Ayr Sketch Club, Ayr Art Circle, and Ayr Photographic Society. There were two Film Societies, four Burns Clubs, and the various Masonic lodges (with Ayr St Paul celebrating its 150th anniversary in 1949). There were Ayr and District Field Club, a local branch of the Scotish Youth Hostels Association, Ayr Chess Club, Ayr Bridge Club, Ayr Magic Circle, a Philatelists Society, the International Club, Electrical Association for Women, Workers Educational Association. The Ayrshire Archaeological and Natural History Society was formed in 1947, reviving a former organisation after exactly fifty years. The Saltire Society spent nine years in restoring Loudoun Hall, completed in 1956. Clubs of a social nature were Rotary, Soroptimists, Business and Professional Women, Townswomen's Guild, Women Citizens Association, Toastmasters, BP Guild of Old Scouts, various regimental clubs, and an Comunn Gaidhealach. Bodies which had their own premises were the County Club which moved from Sandgate to Wellington Square in 1949, the Ayr Club in Academy Street, the Ex-Servicemen's Club which in 1955 moved from Cathcart Street into new premises in Barns Park purchased in 1943 but only now derequisitioned by the Ministry of Food, the British Legion in Limonds Wynd from 1948, and the

YMCA in Prestwick Road. The Carnegie Library, still managed by a joint committee of councillors and other ratepayers, had now a stock of 43,000 books, in one year attracted 30,000 visitors to thirteen exhibitions, and opened a branch library at Whitletts in 1949. From about 1950 there was written an increasing number of studies of local history. For almost half a century from 1934 Elizabeth Kyle (Mrs Agnes Dunlop) continued to produce nearly a hundred historical novels and similar works. Another book deserving mention is *Bairnsangs* by Sandy Thomas Ross, pseudonym for Alexander (Sandy) Macmillan (teacher), Thomas Limond (Town Chamberlain), and A.L. (Ross) Taylor (another teacher), a book of original Scots nursery rhymes which went through many editions from 1955.

In sports, association football remained popular. At Somerset Park up to 20,000 spectators watched Ayr United, promoted into the First Division briefly in 1956–7 and 1959–61. Ayr Newton Rovers failed to survive, but the other junior team, Whitletts Victoria, continued in Voluntary Park which was opened in 1949. There were numerous juvenile teams associated with youth organisations. Rugby, cricket, and hockey retained their limited clientele. Golf, tennis, and bowling continued to attract residents and summer visitors. Badminton was played (usually in church halls) and darts (usually in pubs). At the Ayr Stadium in Limekiln Road there was greyhound racing twice weekly. At the Ice Rink the transatlantic sport of ice hockey was played by the Ayr Raiders team and the junior Ayr Spitfires. For cyclists there was the Ayr Road Club, the Ayr Argonauts, and the Ayr Motor Cycling Club – which last had dirt track races on Prestwick beach, just as the Ayr Amateur Swimming Club had to use Prestwick Bathing Lake. Ayr Athletic Club which had been founded in 1932 merged in 1953 with a group of runners based at Seaforth Road to form Ayr Seaforth Athletic Club. Athletic meetings were held in Dam Park, which the town council purchased in 1948 from the Ayrshire Agricultural Association, whose annual shows were now held on the Racecourse. Ayr Races, restored after the war, from 1950 with separate tracks for flat racing, hurdling, and steeplechases, could attract a daily attendance of over 20,000 to the more popular of its meetings in May, June, July, September (flat) and January, March, October (steeplechase). In 1948 Ayr town council awarded a £150 Plate to celebrate the reputed 250th anniversary of the Western Meeting. More leisurely recreational interests were those of the Ayr Angling Club, Ayr Allotment Holders and Horticultural Association, Ayr Gardeners Mutual

Improvement Association (established 1815, with annual exhibitions since 1868), Ayr Chrysanthemum Society, Scottish Rock Garden Club, Ayrshire Beekeepers Association, Ayr and District Canine Club, a Homing Pigeon Society, and Ayr Cage Bird Society.

The range of other types of recreation included dancing at the Bobby Jones Ballroom, the Pavilion, and in various halls; private classes in tap dancing, Highland dancing, ballet; Scottish country dancing; even an Ayr Figure Skating and Dancing Club at the Ice Rink. Ayr's six cinemas were still crowded with filmgoers. The Gaiety was so busy in summertime that the Robertson Memorial OS Church which closed in 1944 was purchased by the town council to be opened in 1952 as a Civic Theatre. The council also extended the area of public open spaces to more than 600 acres. At Belleisle after the war there were restored the two golf courses, gardens, aviary, miniature deer park and pets corner, with the mansion house as hotel and restaurant. Craigie, acquired in 1940, provided gardens, a caravan park, a restaurant (for a time) in the mansion house, and from 1952 an extension to the River Walk. Dam Park, acquired in 1948, was available for athletics. In 1949 the Tower of St John was taken over by the council (thus atoning for the councils of 1903 and 1911 which had refused to save that historic site). The Low Green (having in 1945 escaped Butlin's clutches) provided a choice of quiet relaxation or more active pleasures.

Lest it be presumed from what has just been written that all appeared perfect, reference may be made to a discussion within the Saltire Society (*Advertiser*, 5 June 1947) on 'Good features – also bad ones – of the town of Ayr'. Francis B. Dunbar, a local architect, remarked on the river separating the two parts of the town, with 'the two sides turning their backs on each other', and another split from which Ayr suffered was a cultural one for though there were numerous organisations 'there was no mixing of interests'. The local report in the *Third Statistical Account* (in the preparation of which the Saltire Society played an important part) emphasised this social division which had long been apparent. In housing 'there is a sharp contrast between conditions in different parts of the town ... The same contrast exists in general conditions of health in the different areas.' And later, 'There is not a great deal of coming and going between the working class folk, who are domiciled in the industrial area north of the River, and the middle class folk who live south of the town centre'. It was from the latter group 'that support comes for Ayr's many clubs and societies, and its influence is very evident in local government'.

South of the river there was a continuing division of interest between those whose livelihood depended on the holiday trade and other residents for whom crowds of tourists and trippers brought only inconvenience. North of the river 'many of the working folks rarely cross the bridges ... They live in Ayr but are not quite of it'. Newton-upon-Ayr and Wallacetown were 'complete local townships' at one time. 'Social life still goes on in them but with a narrowing of interests'. Further off, Whitletts seemed 'in danger of being swallowed up by the eastwards expansion of Ayr'. The last old rows of the mining village would soon be replaced by new council houses, and the long road into town was already lined with bungalows. Yet Whitletts retained its separate identity, acquiring from the town council in 1949 a community centre, a branch library, and Voluntary Park. Football with Whitletts Victoria was just one of a number of continuing local activities. Despite divisions in the community, the *Third Statistical Account* decided that 'there is no great sense of class antagonism', noted that 'in the planning of new housing areas steps have been taken to bring different sections together', but as the local press throughout the fifties and sixties reported, families in the new housing schemes like Craigie found themselves in unfamiliar surroundings and isolated by irregular and often expensive local bus services. Another less obvious feature of demographic change was at that time noted by the present author: 'In the last hundred years Ayr has experienced those general trends which are resulting in an ageing of the population. The decline in the birth rate has resulted in a decrease in the proportion of children and young people; while in the declining death rate more people are surviving till later ages and the proportion of older people has been growing and is continuing to grow. The average age of the population is rising. There are not very many more children in Ayr than there were a century ago; but the numbers in the higher age groups have increased very considerably. While this trend is being effected by the processes of natural growth, in Ayr it is being accentuated by the kind of migration Ayr has been experiencing. There has been an influx of older, middle-aged and retired people into the town, as in the case of all the coast residential towns of Ayrshire, and consequently the proportions of old folk in these towns are higher than is normally found in the inland industrial towns. And on the other hand, many of the outgoers are young folk, sons and daughters of the small middle class families, going into business and the professions, outside Ayr'. The percentage of the local population aged 65 and over increased from 4%

Whitletts was included within Ayr burgh in 1935, but not till twenty years later were its sub-standard dwellings demolished, and new council housing estates formed in this part of Ayr.

in 1841 to 7% in 1931; and there was a continuing trend to 10.5% (1951) and 11.8% (1961).

The *Third Statistical Account* assessed Ayr's standing as a holiday town. There were the attractions of the beach, sporting facilities, shops, theatres and cinemas, and pleasure cruises from the harbour were recommended in 1947. There were 23 restaurants and cafes, 41 hotels, a large number of boarding houses, hundreds of apartments let by householders. In 1947 Butlin's Holiday Camp was opened at the former naval camp in a secluded bay a couple of miles south of the burgh boundary. This promised 3,500 visitors each season. Many arrived at the Heads of Ayr station on special trains from England. Regular passenger services on this line between Ayr and Girvan had ceased in 1930; the fifteen mile coastal stretch from Turnberry was lifted in 1956 and planted with caravans; the Heads of Ayr – Alloway – Ayr line was itself closed in 1968. In retrospect it is easy to comment that later generations of tourists would have enjoyed trips by steam train along this scenic route to Culzean and to Turnberry. In the fifties more people than before were travelling by private car. Glasgow Fair Monday of 1955 brought an estimated 20,000 day trippers to Ayr, some in ten special trains, others by eighty special buses, many more by cars which crawled in a continuous line from Monkton through Prestwick and crossed the New Bridge at 1,300 in one hour. But while Ayr remained popular for day trips, ominously the *Advertiser* reported that hotel bookings were down that summer; holidaymakers were travelling further

afield – on charter flights to Italy, Austria, and Spain. Later that year a hotelier criticised Ayr town council for failing in enterprise and publicity – 'nothing is ever done to improve the town'.

The town council and the churches were of one mind in opposing certain developments which others felt desirable. The presbytery of Ayr in general and Rev W.H.Whalley of Newton-on-Ayr Old Church in particular opposed applications by hotels and restaurants for drinks licences. In 1947 he announced that 'When I came to Ayr two years ago as a stranger I was repelled and disgusted by the scenes of drunkenness and the attitude towards drink of many members of the Church.' There were about fifty public houses or licensed grocers where spirits could be purchased, and four wholesale wine merchants, but as late as 1955 only nine of the town's 51 hotels were licensed. In 1956 Rev W.H.Whalley continued his campaign by refusing to attend any wedding reception at which alcoholic drink was served. The town council (whose Belleisle hotel remained unlicensed) also maintained a policy of sabbatarianism by continuing to prohibit golf, putting, boating, or the seafront fairground entertainments on Sundays. In 1948 when the gambling game of bingo was popularised locally by American families stationed at Prestwick, the council banned it from any of its halls. The continuing influence of the Church was evidenced in the Registrar's statistics for Ayr district indicating 368 church weddings in 1958 as compared with only 96 civil marriages. He noted that the number of marriages of local girls to US servicemen had declined to 10 from 32 in the peak year of 1956.

The Church of Scotland was adjusting to new conditions. The declining population in the central areas allowed Darlington Place and Wallacetown South congregations to unite in 1948 as Darlington New Church – with the Christian Brethren of Victoria Hall in 1952 taking over the disused church in John Street. In 1951 Cathcart Church moved from its old and unsafe premises into the adjacent New Church, most of whose congregation chose to move to the Old Church. The two charges were united as the Auld Kirk of Ayr, with the designation of St John the Baptist added after some debate. The Church Extension charge at Lochside received full status in 1945. In 1952 services were begun in Forehill farmhouse as a prelude to the dedication of Castlehill Church in 1958. Further provision for new housing areas was a hall church opened at Dalmilling in 1953 as an adjunct to St Quivox parish church. The *Third Statistical Account* estimated in 1948 that the 15 Church of Scotland congregations held around 11,000 communicant members. Another 1,100 were attached to other protestant churches – UF, Free, Congregational Union (2), Baptist (2), with the OS congregation disbanded in 1944. There were almost 3,000 adult Catholics, and about 700 Episcopalians belonging to Holy Trinity and (until it closed in 1952) its St John's Mission. Perhaps 1,500 were members of the numerous and various smaller assemblies – some of 19th century origin, like the Salvation Army, Ayrshire Christian Union, Wooden Kirk Mission, Seamen's Mission, and the Christian Brethren with two assemblies of Open Brethren and much smaller dissident groups, two of Exclusive Brethren and two of Church of God; more recent sects like the Church of the Nazarene, Pentecostal Church, Elim Foursquare Gospel, Ayr Spiritualist Association, Psychic Church, Christian Science Society, British Israelites, and Jehovah's Witnesses (whose proselytising caused some concern in 1956); and about 30 families of practising Jews. Altogether about 60% of the population was estimated to have some definite church connection, which was accounted reasonable in view of the distance of many new households from old places of worship, the presence of so many incomers, and secular interests in a holiday town limiting church attendances.

The disillusionment which had followed the end of the First World War was not repeated after 1945, if only because postwar expectations were this time more realistic. There was however a certain optimism about industrial prospects. 'Ayr is not commonly regarded as an important industrial town. Actually it is now one of the main manufacturing centres in the county.' The *Third Statistical Account* added that 'New firms are finding Ayr a good place in which to settle, and some of the older firms are extending their activities.' Ayr's engineering works remained busy after the war – the Scottish Stamping and Engineering Co., James Dickie & Co., the smaller Kyle Foundry of J.M.Rodger and the long-established Vulcan Foundry in Newton, John Wallace and Sons, Wallacetown Engineering Company; these were joined by Ayr Engineering and Constructional Company, and by Scottish Mechanical Light Industries which was formed in 1946 for the manufacture of household and domestic items. The Stamp Works especially had been expanded during the war, acquiring Britain's largest drop forge hammers (which would continue to disturb Newton Park School and other adjacent properties). Dickie's in 1952 planned a new foundry. Ayr Engineering and Constructional Company acquired the Victoria Bridge Works in 1941, and in 1947 took over the shipyard to

add repair and conversion of small vessels to its other light engineering work. Of the town's other principal branch of manufacture, the *Third Statistical Account* boasted that 'Textiles is a growing industry in Ayr'. James Templeton & Sons continued to produce yarns, and was in the immediate postwar years joined by two small new firms. Gray's carpet factory was the largest local business. It employed 1,300 during the war, and in 1948 as a constituent part of the newly-formed nation-wide combine of Gray's Carpet and Textiles Ltd there were ambitious plans to expand the local labour force from 800 to 4,000. The town's remaining manufacturing firms all continued making fertilisers (SAI, with large-scale expansion planned in 1949), asphalt (W.G.Walker), leather (Harry Beebee), boots and shoes (Andrew Lees, Alexander Cuthbert), aerated water (Turners). Among long-established businesses were sawmills and one surviving sailmaker in Newton. But it was in this era that corn milling ceased in the town mills. An era ended with the demolition of the Nether Mill in 1941 and the Over Mills in 1963.

In addition to manufacturing, which employed about 3,000 men and 1,300 women in the various factories, Ayr contained in Westfield the initial headquarters of the Ayr and Dumfries Area of the National Coal Board, responsible for 36 pits, four brick works, over three thousand dwelling houses, and employing 11,500 workers. The Auchincruive pits of Glenburn and Mossblown in Ayr parish and Annbank colliery just beyond formed a most productive sub-area with 2,400 miners producing 700,000 tons annually, approximately 3% of the Scottish total output. The export of coal through Ayr harbour passed a peak of 1,740,000 tons in 1939. That volume could not be maintained, and British Railways (which now owned the port) handled around 920,000 tons in 1950 and 610,000 tons ten years later, most of this going to Ireland. Coal was virtually Ayr's only export, apart from general cargo carried by Burns-Laird vessels in their regular service between Ayr and Belfast five days each week. Imports of timber and potash were resumed after the war. There was growth in the fish trade. Though there were only half a dozen local fishing vessels, Ayr handled the bulk of landings by the rest of the Ayrshire fleet and by other craft fishing in the Firth of Clyde. Nearly 5,000 tons were landed in 1947; a decade later with the trade booming, a Fish Salesmen's Association was formed in Ayr; and in 1960 a new £30,000 covered fish market was opened at the south harbour.

Behind the town lay a hinterland of farmland, with the county specialising in dairying and a production

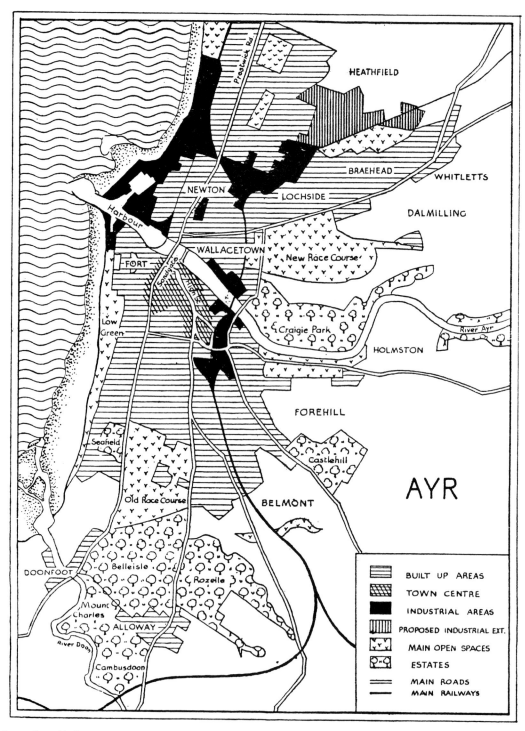

This map from the *Third Statistical Account* emphasised a continued division within the town, with industrial and working class areas in the north, while south of the river was the principal middle class residential district and most of the facilities.

of more than 30 million gallons of milk in 1946. Ayr parish, extending to 12,493 acres, contained 8,269 acres devoted to agriculture and including some of the best farmland in the west of Scotland. Within the burgh itself were 2,630 acres in agricultural use, with 13 farms from 50 to 100 acres concerned with cropping, dairying, and grazing of cattle for the market, as well as 16 market gardens. In the St Quivox area 12 farms from 100 to 150 acres were mainly arable. South of the river and beyond Alloway were 25 farms from 50 to 250 acres, the largest on high ground by Loch Fergus taking sheep as well as cattle. At Brickrow, Mainholm, and Belston were a total of 42 small holdings created after the First World War by the Department of Agriculture for Scotland. In the St Quivox area at Auchincruive were located since 1931 the West of Scotland Agricultural College and the Hannah Dairy Research Institute. The light soils and relatively dry climate allowed arable farming on 38% of the parish's farm land. Crops raised were marketed or went to maintain (in 1947) 3,711 dairy cattle, 371 beef cattle, 2,262 sheep, and 697 pigs (these last fed by swill from the town). For the farm folk of the whole of Ayrshire Ayr was a mecca on the traditional Tuesday market days, when Messrs James Craig conducted what were sometimes Scotland's largest cattle sales, with special auctions also of horses and sheep at appropriate seasons. Each April the annual Show organised by the Ayrshire Agricultural Association met on Ayr Racecourse (from 1946) for two days. In June 1958 the Royal Highland Show was held on the Old Racecourse.

Ayr retained the character of a county town because of its market, its shops, its holiday traffic, and its continuing importance as an important administrative centre. Ayr County Council, with its headquarters in the County Buildings, was now one of Ayrshire's biggest employers, with nearly 5,000 persons staffing its extending services. In the original part of these Buildings the Law Courts still dispensed justice. In the adjoining area around Wellington Square many of the old terrace houses had been converted into offices for various public, private, and voluntary bodies. The Royal Scots Fusiliers retained their depot in Ayr – designated Churchill Barracks in 1942 after the premier who had commanded the 6th battalion in the previous war. In 1958 an amalgamation with the Highland Light Infantry created the Royal Highland Fusiliers, which was in that year granted the Freedom of Ayr. The Ayrshire Yeomanry was reformed in 1947, converted into an armoured tank regiment affiliated to the Royal Scots Greys, retaining its separate identity despite various amalgamations in 1956. Other territorials were attached to the Royal Artillery or to a Port Task Force.

In this royal burgh, celebrating its 750th anniversary, old institutions like the Guildry, the Incorporations of Shoemakers and Squaremen, and the Whipmen's Society continued to function alongside more recent bodies like Ayr Chamber of Commerce, and associations representing grocers, hoteliers, and other interests. The Directory of 1955–56 continued to list the Palm Fair (on the last Friday of April), Midsummer Fair (Thursday before the second Monday of July), Michaelmas Fair (second Tuesday of October), and four Hiring Fairs (third Tuesday of April and October, first Tuesday after 28th in May and November); but the holidays which now really mattered were those for shopkeepers and the others for factory workers; and the Glasgow Holidays were also listed because these meant the busiest days of the year for Ayr.

TWENTY

Finale

The writing of contemporary history is notoriously dangerous. Pitfalls include overemphasising items which will later prove to have been unimportant, ignoring others which hindsight will discover as significant, making statements and judgments of a sort which in earlier chapters would normally be accepted without question, but here are likely to be subject to more critical examination, are open to challenge by those who have been personally involved, and which despite careful checking may be proved erroneous, though hopefully only in minor details. Despite such misgivings, an attempt must be made to examine some of the social changes which have affected Ayr within the last thirty years.

Extinction of the royal burgh in the local government reorganisation of 1975 might have been a fitting conclusion to this book. Yet that event, however important, was only one episode in the continuing development of the town. It marked one further step in a process of centralisation initiated by the Local Government (Scotland) Act of 1929, and accelerated as the century advanced, with Ayr burgh losing control of various undertakings. In 1948 hospitals were taken over by the Western Regional Hospitals Board as part of the new National Health Service; social welfare was transferred to the Ministry of National Insurance; a South West Fire Service took over the local fire service. Also in 1948 the South West of Scotland Electricity Board absorbed the Ayrshire Electricity Board which Ayr had helped create in 1924, and in 1949 gas was also nationalised. In 1968, though local Moderates and Labour were united in opposition, the police forces of Ayr, Kilmarnock and the County were amalgamated, which was followed by opening of Ayr's new police station in King Street in 1975. In 1968 an Ayrshire and Bute Water Board took over from the various local authorities. In 1974, Ayrshire and Arran Health Board became responsible for those duties previously undertaken in the county and large burghs by their medical officers of health. Then in 1975 the county council and all the burghs were abolished and local government reorganised. The existing authorities were deemed to be obsolete, though local opinion suggested Ayr Town Council and Ayr County Council had each a satisfactory record in providing the town with services and necessary improvements.

Ayr town council, after some indecision in the thirties and difficulties thereafter, addressed itself to dealing with the housing problem. By 1948 it had erected only 2,605 council houses – compared with 4,430 in Kilmarnock, a town of comparable size, and 1,630 in Irvine which had less than a third of Ayr's population. By 1961 the number was 6,287, thus filling up the remaining spaces in Lochside, Braehead, Dalmilling, and Craigie. For those three thousand families still on the waiting list further major programmes were undertaken. One hundred acres of Wallacetown were scheduled for clearance and redevelopment, with over a thousand new houses, including 3 blocks of multi-storey flats fronting the river, which were built in 1968. A second major scheme followed at Kincaidston. At the same time Ayr town council had to provide the necessary environmental services for the private houses which were being built. 1,458 of these had been erected between 1919 and 1948. For a few years thereafter there were post-war restrictions on private building, and with the demolition of rented slum properties, the number of private dwellings in the town by 1961 actually decreased to 7,473 – 5,003 of these being owner-occupied. There followed a mushrooming of private housing estates – to the east from Holmston past Masonhill and Castlehill; to the south by Rozelle, Alloway, Doonbank, Cunningpark, and beyond at Doonfoot and Burton. In the period 1952–72 there were built 2,260 private houses and 4,600 by the council. The 1971 Census indicated a total of 8,115 council houses and 7,610 privately-owned. Of the latter, 6,330 were owner-occupied, 375 rented furnished, and 905 rented unfurnished from private landlords.

In 1956 Ayr enjoyed its first official royal visit since Mary Queen of Scots in 1563.

There remained over a thousand on the waiting list for council houses, and the census showed 1,725 persons in 645 households sharing accommodation. Comparison with the figures for 1951 (as noted at the beginning of Chapter 19) indicates what progress had been made, and what still had to be done. Though by 1971 out of 15,750 households in the burgh there were 14,535 whose facilities could be regarded as adequate, there remained 835 without fixed bath or shower, 530 sharing a water closet (and 15 with none), and 435 without a hot water supply. The number of single-end dwellings in the town had been reduced in the previous ten years from 153 to 80. There were a few slum properties to be cleared, particularly in the Newton Green area. Renovations were required in the older council schemes, with Lochside indeed designated as one of Scotland's areas of multiple deprivation. James Brown Avenue – dubbed as 'Jabba' – had problems of a sort which would have distressed the man after whom it was named. Overcrowding remained with 12,770 persons in 2,360 households of more than one person per room. For the burgh there was by 1971 an average of 0.72 persons per room, a decided advance from 1.04 in 1951, and now ranging from 0.52 in Ward 2 to 0.98 in Ward 6. The overall picture was one of improvement, and decent living conditions for all but a diminishing few.

To make provision for a population increasing from 42,377 (1951) to 45,276 (1961), and 47,896 (1971) the town council was involved in steadily increasing expenditure, reaching £7½ million net in its final year. Of this over £4 million had to be paid to the county council as a contribution for education, and smaller sums to other statutory bodies which provided various services in the town. In most years it proved necessary for the town council to present an increased bill for rates, which in the burgh's final years amounted to a levy on householders of one pound for every pound of the rateable value of property.

The town council and Ayr County Council shared

In 1958 the RSF and HLI were amalgamated to form the Royal Highland Fusiliers, which was granted the Freedom of Ayr. But Churchill Barracks were closed and Ayr ceased to be a garrison town.

a common problem in providing roads capable of coping with the vast increase in traffic. The number of motor vehicles registered in Ayrshire, around 18,000 in 1948, by 1974 passed 98,000. With private cars becoming so popular, the flow of traffic through Ayr was augmented not only by people travelling in to work and to shop, but by day trippers heading for Ayr beach or through the town for the south Ayrshire coast. Each Glasgow holiday weekend there were continuous streams of traffic. There were jams at Monkton Cross where traffic coming down the coast converged with that from Kilmarnock, with hold-ups as the road crossed the airport runway. After slow progress through Prestwick and Newton, this massive stream merged at River Street with another coming down from Lanarkshire via Galston and through Whitletts, creating a bottleneck at the New Bridge approach to High Street and Sandgate. In the evenings there was a slow-moving returning

stream with a tailback to Doonfoot. In 1961 opening of the first stage of a bypass, dual carriageway from Monkton to Whitletts roundabout, brought no immediate relief, since it simply channelled a greater proportion of traffic down Whitletts Road. The second stage, single carriageway from Whitletts to Holmston roundabout, crossing the River Ayr by a new bridge at the former Overmills, was opened in 1963. That diverted some traffic down Holmston Road only to increase congestion at Burns Statue Square. There followed the completion in 1964 of a loop road from Monkton to Prestwick around the western perimeter of the airport. Not till 1971 was the final stage of Ayr bypass opened, with a single carriageway past Kincaidston roundabout and on towards Maybole. This at last freed the town of through traffic, both the heavy daily commercial traffic of long-distance lorries and the holiday peak traffic of cars and coaches. While the bypass was being constructed under the aegis of

New developments involved destruction of old features. Newton Old Church and Churchyard were removed in 1964 for widening of King Street.

Ayr County Council, the town council addressed itself to improving local traffic movements. The widening of Victoria Bridge (1961) was first stage of an inner ring road which would extend from Tam's Bridge by dual carriageway along Allison Street and John Street, with two pedestrian underpasses and a new railway bridge (1971), and by Station Road and another widened bridge over the railway by the station (1974) to reach Burns Statue Square which had been converted into a one-way system (1971). Concurrently, the redevelopment of Wallacetown suggested an improved route into town from Whitletts Road, superseding George Street and River Street, each of which was closed at both ends. King Street was widened to provide a dual carriageway, with a new bridge over the railway, taking away part of the Secession cemetery, and reaching Main Street after removal of the old Newton Church and Townhouse (1964). While the flow of traffic was thus assisted, it proved less easy to provide sufficient car parking facilities. From 1967 traffic wardens had to be employed to regulate parking in the main shopping streets and those near the beach; a multi-storey car park off Carrick Street (1970) alleviated but did not solve this continuing problem.

This was of particular concern for a town which was the principal shopping centre for central and south Ayrshire, and a holiday resort now catering especially for day trippers and short-stay visitors. So many people were now seeking the sun overseas, that fewer would patronise Clyde coast hotels and boarding houses for the traditional week or fortnight's summer holiday. In 1960 there was much public discussion of this situation. Ayr had been 'the Queen of Scotland's Holiday Towns' but it had become 'the Resort that ought to die for shame' if it did not provide sufficient

new amenities to restore its attraction. The opinion of Provost Lanham that 'Ayr shouldn't try to be a Blackpool' found widespread support as against expensive 'new look' plans of improvement. Developments were undertaken which would be appreciated by residents as well as visitors. A third municipal golf course was laid out (1960) at Dalmilling. The estate of Rozelle was gifted to the town (1966) by Lieutenant Commander John Hamilton, providing an additional public park (1969), with a nature trail (1970), art and exhibition galleries thanks to a bequest from Mrs Mary Ellen MacLaurin (1973), and a Regalia Room (1975). Cambusdoon was purchased by the council (1967). In 1974 a Craigholm footbridge linked Craigie and Holmston and enhanced the River Ayr Walk. The north end of the beach was improved by removal of the slipway and the gas works, and after the Royal Highland Fusiliers abandoned the barracks in 1961 the site was acquired by the town council, providing a new location for Codona's showground amusement and for the long-anticipated Ayr Baths, which were opened in 1972. In that year, when Ayr Gaiety theatre was threatened with closure, Ayr town council stepped in and it opened its 1974 season under municipal ownership. Earlier in 1960 was opened the Dam Park Hall which would prove to be of prime importance by offering facilities for major exhibitions and assemblies, able to take up to 2,000 conference delegates. It provided that year the venue for a three-day Flower Show which in succeeding seasons would expand to become Scotland's premier horticultural event. A range of national organisations chose this for conferences. In 1973 it brought the annual Mod of An Comunn Gaidhealach and an estimated 20,000 visitors. Other events were organised after the council in 1964 appointed a Publicity and Entertainments Officer, enticing groups to spend a few days in Ayr. A competition in 1964 to find 'Ayr's Bonnie Lass' was followed by other beauty contests to elect a 'Miss Ayr'. A World Pipe Band Championship at Dam Park in 1964 was followed from 1966 by annual Highland Gatherings. The numbers who came on pilgrimage to the birthplace of Burns were augmented. Visitors to Burns Cottage were over 100,000 each year. There was a Burns Pageant in 1959. In 1970 a Tam O'Shanter Ride was inaugurated and repeated each following June. In 1973 when a Burns Heritage Trail was planned for tours of the Burns Country, Ayr was the obvious centre. In 1976 a Land of Burns Interpretion Centre was opened at Alloway on the site of the former railway goods yard. Throughout the seventies and eighties public, private,

256	*The History of Ayr*

and voluntary efforts combined to extend the tourist season. In April 1975 there was celebrated the 50th annual Ayrshire Musical Festival. In the same month each year was the annual Ayrshire Agricultural Association Show. In June an open Golf Week with championship matches supplemented the established August Bowls Week. Also in June the Tam O'Shanter ride was joined by a Holy Fair fete with sideshows, bands, and displays, extended into a Burns Festival, latterly associated with an Ayrshire Arts Festival of plays, films, and concerts. In August Ayr Flower Show continued to extend its reputation, and from 1987 had to move to a more commodious site at Rozelle. Throughout the year Ayr Races were held on what was now Scotland's premier horse-racing circuit, with appropriately reconstructed Craigie, Carrick, and Eglinton Stands (1965–71). There were National Hunt and Flat races on 31 days of the year, including the Scottish Grand National in April and the Western Meeting in September. Day trippers and others continued to enjoy the town and the shore. In 1973 Ayr Parks Department received the first of a series of 'Britain in Bloom' awards, commended for 'imaginative landscaping and varied planning'. The continued attractions of the beach were advertised in 1988: 'All the traditional seaside amusements are here with children's playground, paddling pool, miniature railway, crazy golf, boating pond, and entertainers on the front at peak periods.' There were facilities for yachts at Blackburn and the South Harbour, with trips for sea angling also available. Though summer cruises from Ayr ceased for three seasons, after 1974 these were provided by the Paddle Steamer Preservation Society on the *Waverley*. The nature of Ayr's continuing popularity was summed up by one who was impelled to write to the *Advertiser* (17.9.1970) that 'What is natural for the resident can amaze or amuse the visitor ... we really felt we had received value for money ... I think we'll be back.' The catering trade succeeded in adapting to new circumstances. The 1968 Directory listed 41 hotels, 20 boarding houses, and 11 guest houses. An Ayrshire and Burns Country brochure twenty years later included 56 hotels and 61 other premises offering bed and breakfast accommodation. Though these lists are not exactly comparable, they indicated 28 smaller and older establishments which had ceased trading, but compensated by 25 newer alternatives. Included was the 114-bedroom Caledonian Hotel built in Dalblair Road in 1971, Ayr's first purpose-built hotel since the Station Hotel opened in 1886. Many of the hotels benefitted from increased numbers partaking

As part of the Wallacetown redevelopment scheme, three blocks of multi-storey flats were completed in 1968. On one side, a riverside walk replaced old dilapidated premises; on the other, the dual carriageway was part of a new inner ring road.

of bar lunches or dining-out in the evening. The town centre also saw a mushrooming of new eating places, superseding some of the 19 restaurants listed in 1968. More holidaymakers were brought to Ayr when Butlin's holiday camp adapted to new demands and after massive conversion reopened in 1988 as a Holiday Wonderworld. In its first season it attracted 100,000 who came to stay, and 190,000 day visitors. For those others who now enjoyed caravanning or camping, there were sites at Craigie, Crofthead, Ayr Racecourse, Heads of Ayr, Sundrum, and several others throughout the district.

As the town expanded, Ayr County Council extended the educational provision. To begin with, Ayr Academy remained the only senior secondary school providing courses leading to the Higher Grade of the Scottish Certificate of Education. But it was joined by two new high schools – Belmont (1960) and Mainholm (1965). These took all other secondary pupils from the town (and some adjacent areas), presented candidates for the new Ordinary Grade of the Scottish Certificate of Education instituted in 1961, and coped with the increased numbers when the school leaving age was raised to sixteen in 1973. The former junior secondary schools – Grammar, Russell Street, Newton Park, and Newton Academy – continued with primary pupils only. The other older primary schools – Alloway, Whitletts, Holmston, Newtonhead, Heathfield – were joined by new schools. Braehead (1951) was followed by Dalmilling (1959), Forehill (1964), Castlehill (1968), Doonfoot (1974) and Kincaidston (1975). Newton Academy was closed in 1970, serving for a time thereafter as an annexe for Ayr Academy, then as the Newton Centre for Education Advisers and a base for a Schools Library and Resource Service. Wallacetown was converted into a nursery school. For

Local government reorganisation in 1975 involved the demise of Ayr town council after a life of 770 years. The last Kirking of the Council marked the end of an era.

Roman Catholic boys and girls, complete secondary courses were for the first time provided locally when Queen Margaret's was built at Mainholm (1966). Primary pupils continued in the former school building, now St John's, and in a new St Catherine's (1957) at Dalmilling. Catering for the minority of parents who chose to pay fees, Wellington School for girls attracted sufficient numbers to extend from Carlton Turrets and acquire Westfield for boarders, Sleaford for juniors, and Hartfield for nursery and kindergarten girls. But Cambusdoon School for boys had to close in 1967.

Expansion of education took various forms. Craigie College of Education was established in 1964, a government measure to train new primary teachers at a time of severe staffing shortage. In 1966 Ayr Technical College was opened by Ayr County Council, a new building at Dam Park superseding the limited facilities previously available within the old St Leonard's school. Extra-mural education was extended further in that year when evening classes in schools were supplemented by afternoon adult classes. Educational advances were sometimes limited by shortage of funds

in this period of inflation – which contributed to Scottish teachers' strikes in 1965, 1974, 1980, and 1985. Ayr County Council was however able to implement plans made in 1967 for the introduction of comprehensive education throughout Ayrshire. This was initiated in Ayr, accompanied by acrimonious argument and bitter complaint made in Ayr town council that it was 'a direct attempt to destroy Ayr Academy'. With abolition of primary promotion examinations, all pupils from primary schools in and around Ayr would be allocated by zoning to Ayr Academy, or to Belmont Academy and Mainholm Academy (as these were now designated). In each academy the new intakes of 1968 and thereafter, of whatever abilities, followed initially a two-year common course, then had the opportunity of a choice of subjects and possible presentation for Ordinary and Higher grade certificates and Sixth Year Studies. Certain teachers were appointed as Guidance staff to attend to the welfare of individual pupils in secondary schools which were larger than previously experienced. The new academies in modern buildings developed their own range of extra-mural activities and achieved recognised acceptance; Ayr Academy adapted itself, with a peak roll of 1350 pupils and ninety teachers in 1971 overflowing from its over-crowded premises into the former Newton Academy.

Between town and county council there was continued antagonism. It was inevitable as the county budget for education rose to £23 million in 1974 (out of its total of £34 million) and Ayr had to pay £4 million as its share, with twelve of its councillors having limited influence in a county council which contained (after 1952) 95 members. That council from 1957 had always a Labour majority, while Ayr town council remained Moderate apart from three years. Ward changes in 1961 did not immediately alter the balance of parties, but in the 1964 municipal election Labour increased its representation to nine of the eighteen seats. After a tied vote for selection of a new provost, the Labour nominee Charles O'Halloran was chosen by lot and his party exercised power for the next three years by virtue of his casting vote. In parliamentary elections, the Ayr constituency continued to return a Conservative member (the designation of Unionist was abandoned after 1965). Sir Thomas Moore, after thirty nine years as Ayr's MP, retired in 1964 and died in 1971. His successor George Younger, whose grandfather had been Ayr Burghs MP from 1906 till 1922, served in opposition during the ministries of Wilson (1964–70, 74–76) and Callaghan (1976–79), and on the government benches under Heath (1970–74) and Thatcher (since 1979), as Secretary of State for Scotland (1979–86), thereafter as Secretary of State for Defence.

In 1971 Ayr Junior Chamber of Commerce produced a report on local government which included some adverse comments on town councillors and officials. At an angry council meeting thereafter the report was taken to imply that 'the present Council were a lot of ill-educated gentlemen, lacking in expertise, and that they were on the fiddle to boot'. One valid point the report made was that all eighteen members were members of each of the twelve statutory committees and many also represented the council on outside bodies: so it was difficult for individual councillors to become expert in anything when they were involved with everything. It can be appreciated that, with so much business involved and with day-time meetings, service on the council could be undertaken only by persons able and willing to interrupt regularly a normal work pattern. Because many occupations would not allow this, council membership could never accurately represent a cross section of the community. It may be added that the provost who had to attend various ceremonies and functions by virtue of his

Ayr cattle sales perpetuate the weekly markets authorised by William the Lion's charter of 1205.

office was kept so busy that none since 1949 was prepared to attempt more than one three-year term. Curiously, many were incomers to the town, including Provosts Lanham and O'Halloran who were English. Appropriately however the last provost, Campbell Howie, was born within the royal burgh, educated at Ayr Academy, lived and worked locally, as an architectural assistant, all within the 4th Ward which he represented.

The last council made some final arrangements. To the roll of thirteen Freemen created during the 20th century it was unanimously agreed to add the provost and the five living ex-provosts, his immediate predecessors. Two councillors felt it inappropriate to accept as a gift the quaichs which it had been decided to present to each member of the last council. There was turned down a proposal to hand over £10,000 from the Common Good and Council fund for relief of distress, to be held in trust by Ayr Guildry, that 650-year-old relic of the royal burgh. £700 was donated to provide a commemorative trophy at Ayr Races. It was agreed to contribute £500 towards a chain of office for its successor, Kyle and Carrick District Council; the treasured relics of the royal burgh were transferred from the Town Hall to be included in a public display at Rozelle. On 15 May 1975 Ayr town council met for the last time, and that evening the end of an era of 770 years was celebrated by a 'Clamjamfray' in High Street, the festivities including dramatic and dancing displays, music provided by six bands, and a parade by the Royal Highland Fusiliers.

Already in May 1974 elections for the new local authorities had been held. Some continuity was assured by several town councillors becoming successful candidates. Provosts Howie and O'Halloran be-

The site of the Malt Cross is marked on the roadway at the junction of High Street and Sandgate.

came Ayr's two representatives on the Strathclyde Regional Council of 103 members. Four other town councillors were among Ayr's seven representatives on the 25-strong Kyle and Carrick District Council. The District Council provided continuity by inheriting most of the town council's responsibilities, by making Burns House in Ayr its headquarters, and by deciding that its chairman should be entitled provost. There was a certain continuity also in political alignments. The first District Council comprised sixteen Conservative and nine Labour members. Those who had previously been denominated as Moderates were now enrolled as members of the Conservative Party. National issues more closely than ever before impinged on local politics. Divisions within the council were highlighted in press reports, and can be followed in the published memoirs of one of the councillors. Each of the party groups found itself on occasion involved in factional disputes, and discord could also occur because parochial interests ranged from those of busy coastal resorts to quiet rural villages. There were complaints as in 1976 of 'too much cash spent on Ayr'. The Conservative administration under Provost Alexander Paton of Troon (1975–80) was ousted when Labour gained a majority with thirteen members under Provost Dr James Boyle of Girvan (1980–84). Divisions within Labour ranks (as when Provost Boyle on occasion refused to vote according to group dictate) contributed to electoral defeat. The Conservative group was increased to thirteen, but split over leadership, and Provost Gibson Macdonald of Ayr held office (1984–88) as an Independent Conservative appointed with the votes of the Labour group. After a term which all concerned must at times have found

awkward, in 1988 Labour recovered control with a 16–7 majority and formed an administration under Provost Dan McNeill of Maybole.

The financing of local services was a continuing problem in a period of inflation, latterly aggravated by government cut-backs. In 1975 householders' rates in Ayr rose from £1 to £1.21 to pay for District and Regional demands. Periodic revaluations of property caused anxiety. The district's increased valuation might allow reduction of the rate levied (which was 85p per £1 for 1988–89); but most years householders were faced with a bigger bill. The impact on businesses was also considerable: one High Street superstore had its rates demand increased in 1985 from £132,000 to £216,000; the rates burden contributed to the failure of some smaller retailers. Another financial issue concerned council housing. Periodic increases of rents provoked resentment among tenants, and there was argument about sale of council houses to tenants. Economies ranged from restrictions on building works to closure of public libraries on Saturdays. The District Council was however able to extend the provision of sheltered housing for elderly people. Ayr Carnegie Library now provided not only for branches at Whitletts, Forehill, and Alloway but for others throughout the district. The council had responsibility for cleansing; for cemeteries, and the Masonhill crematorium which had been opened by Ayr County Council in 1966. It continued to operate the extensive range of facilities which Ayr town council had provided for residents and visitors, publicised the district's attractions, and helped operate an Ayrshire and Burns Country Tourist Board.

Strathclyde Regional Council, centred in Glasgow, was dominated by the Labour Party, which enabled Charles O'Halloran to become Strathclyde's Convener 1978–82. Ayr County Buildings, headquarters of the now-defunct Ayr County Council, became Regional Offices. Here were located the Divisional Education Office, and some other departments including Roads, Finance, Architects, related services, and Archives. Other regional services had administrative centres elsewhere in Ayr: in Wellington Square, Assessment and Electoral Registration; in Charlotte Street for Water supply; in Sandgate, Sewerage, also Registration of births, marriages and deaths; in King Street, Police headquarters; the Fire Station in Station Road; Consumer and Trading Standards, River Terrace; Reporter to the Children's Panel, in Alloway Place. Regional responsibilities extended to car parks, street lighting, and social work included provision of centres for adult training (Holmston Road), for the

Ayr's oldest dwelling is Barns House, a little 18th century mansion added to the 17th century portion on its left. Once surrounded by a considerable estate, which is now a built-up area in the heart of the town.

deaf (Peebles Street), for the elderly (Carrick Street), for voluntary services (Holmston Road), plus three homes for the elderly, and five units of sheltered housing.

Educational provision required a new Queen Margaret Academy (1975) located near Kincaidston. Its former premises were incorporated within the adjacent Mainholm Academy. An additional secondary school was provided when Kyle Academy was opened (1979) at Holmston. The building of Newton Primary School (1984) made it possible to replace the older Russell Street, Newton Park, and Newtonhead schools. Westwood Nursery School, built on ground beside Dalmilling primary school, was opened in 1977. Two special schools for pupils with learning difficulties were opened in 1980. Southpark at Belmont provided for those with serious difficulties; Craigpark at Mainholm for others whose difficulties were designated as profound. Rosebank School also at Belmont replaced St Leonard's School for those who were mildly mentally handicapped. Beyond supplying formal schooling for pupils of all ages and abilities, there was a widened range of educational provision: the schools meals service, a child guidance centre (Wills Road), careers offices (Boswell Park), Ayr Technical College for further education, Community Centres at Lochside and Whitletts, other Community Education provision at Wellington Square Leisure Centre and at Whitletts Road, recreational wings at Belmont

and Queen Margaret academies, training workshop (Limonds Wynd).

The period when there was an urgent demand for additional accommodation was followed by one when a national trend of reduced child numbers affected the rolls of primary then secondary schools. As a result, by 1988 Ayr had 4,300 pupils in primary schools which had a capacity of 5,700, and 3,900 secondary pupils in academies with capacity for 6,800. The 14 primary schools were Alloway, Forehill, Heathfield (each with rolls between 400 and 500), Kincaidston, Grammar, and Dalmilling (300–400), Doonfoot, Castlehill, Holmston, Braehead, Newton, St John's (200–300), Whitletts (about 150). St Catherine's (below 100) was in 1988 moved into part of the old Queen Margaret's Academy and renamed Good Shepherd School. Of the five secondary schools, Belmont with 1,300 pupils remained three-quarters full, while the smaller Kyle Academy with a full quota of nearly 800 took nearly all the others from the south side of the town. Mainholm, with a capacity of 1,800 able to accommodate as many as Belmont, catered for an area which had a reduced school population, and now took in fewer than 700, which included pupils from Tarbolton. Queen Margaret Academy with a similar number was only half full. By the eighties, government policy favoured parental choice, which required relaxation of regional council policy of school zoning. This affected the secondary schools

Belleisle estate, purchased by the town council in 1925, provides facilities for residents as well as visitors.

in particular, and especially Ayr Academy. Though it could accommodate 1,100 and had indeed in 1971 been overcrowded with 1,350 pupils, its roll sharply declined to 500 by 1988. Among these were pupils from Annbank and Coylton, so that only a handful from Ayr were now enrolled in what had once been the town's premier school. The newer academies on the outskirts of the town seemed preferable to older premises with less modern facilities, situated near the busy town centre. Ayr Academy however was particularly well placed to cater for academic and leisure courses for adults during the normal school day, these being now available in all secondary schools. The extensive scope of educational provision in each school is exhibited in their 'Handbooks' which the Regional Council had prepared for parents. One typical primary school described its aims as 'to provide a broad education for each pupil, relevant to his/her age, aptitude, and ability. We wish to foster an acceptable attitude towards work and develop a considerate and caring attitude for other people and our environment'; and described its courses as designed not only to 'produce numerate, literate children' but also 'develop and stimulate personal skills and interests' and 'strengthen character and compensate for weaknesses'. The handbooks stress concern for extra-curricular activities, parental involvement, and attend to such diverse matters as assessment, learning difficulties, discipline, school meals, transport, and

health care. One feature of the primary schools was that by 1988 six of them had women as head teachers. The handbooks for secondary schools indicate the variety of courses available and provide details of presentations in the Scottish Certificate of Education Examinations. By the eighties, for a variety of social and economic reasons, a majority of pupils in each school now continued beyond the statutory school leaving age of sixteen. Again for a variety of reasons, numbers in each school varied of those presented for and obtaining passes in Scottish Certificate of Education examinations. Numbers of subject-passes in 1988 at the Higher Grade were as follows: Belmont 446, Kyle 330, Queen Margaret 260, Ayr Academy 136, Mainholm 121. Wellington School, with a roll around 500, 360 of them in the senior school, took 214; and further education students at Ayr Technical College had 271 passes. In the five academies of Ayr there were 744 fifth and sixth year pupils, taking among them 1,193 Higher subject-passes; just forty years earlier there were, in the whole of Ayrshire, only 447 such pupils, of whom 271 received Higher passes in two or more subjects – an indication of how educational opportunity had been extended in this part of the 20th century.

While local authorities could do little about the market forces which affected the fortunes of local industry, planning policies did contribute to relocation of businesses in the second half of the century, by the town council acquiring land at Heathfield for an industrial estate from 1967, and the county council helping set up another just outwith the burgh at Mosshill in 1973. Manufacturing premises virtually disappeared from the old Townhead with removal of the slaughterhouse, tannery, several engineering firms, while James Templeton and Son did little spinning after 1968. The sea front was enhanced by removal of the shipyard and gas works. The town centre lost Gilchrist's bakery and the printing works of the two local papers. At Doonfoot in 1971 there was demolished the 100-foot chimney of the former Greenan laundry. Even north of the River Ayr, businesses were displaced by clearances in Newton and the Wallacetown redevelopment. Alexander's Sawmills and Walter Mitchell's bacon factory both moved to Heathfield. While nearly all the major manufacturing firms of mid-century were still listed in the Directory published in 1968, there had closed down those two making boots and shoes; followed in ensuing years by the long-established makers of leather and of aerated waters. The textile industry went into eclipse. Templeton's which employed 240 in 1967 ceased thereafter to be a major manufacturer of yarns. Gray's Carpet and Textiles Ltd. which had expanded to become the town's second largest employer, suddenly closed down in 1974, with the loss of 1,100 jobs. Those two diverse branches of the chemicals industry continued, W.G.Walker producing asphalt and SAI in 1961 expanding its output of fertilisers. The important engineering industry survived periodic difficulties. The Scottish Stamping and Engineering Company expanded its production of forgings for motor vehicles as a member of the Guest, Keen, and Nettleford Group, with a workforce of 1,800 in 1968, but reduced to 1,450 in 1979, then drastically cut to 1,000 (1980), 700 (1981), 400 (1984), and 270 (1985). Wallacetown Engineering Company, also under new owners, moved to Heathfield to employ 700 workers in 1975, thereafter reduced to 500 in 1982. James Dickie & Co. extended from its Victoria Works with an additional Heathfield Foundry in Seaforth Road, but employed only 140 workers in 1974. More than a dozen smaller engineering businesses listed in the 1968 Directory failed to survive, leaving the Vulcan Engineering Company in Green Street and two others in Newton Green. The closure of old businesses was partially compensated by the establishment of new ones. At Mosshill the first tenant in 1973 was Prestwick Circuits Ltd, established four years earlier to produce electronic circuit boards and after ten years at Mosshill employing 240 workers there. They were followed in 1976 by Digital Equipment (Scotland) Ltd,

a US subsidiary which by 1983 employed 570 workers there. Coincidentally the year that brought electronics to Mosshill saw also the demise of local coal mining. The decline of Ayrshire's coal industry was marked in 1962 by the closure of the NCB area offices at Prestwick after only three years there. Mossblown pit was closed and Glenburn, the last local pit, run down and ceased production in 1973. Deep mining in Ayrshire ceased in 1989 with closure of Barony colliery at Auchinleck. But there was continued export of coal to Ireland through Ayr harbour. Opencast mining required reopening for goods traffic of the Mauchline – Ayr railway line in 1987. Coal exports from Ayr in the postwar period declined to less than 500,000 tons in 1970, followed by recovery and hopes (in 1980) of reaching 1 million tons, though amounting to 658,000 tons in 1987. In that year, the harbour (now managed by Associated British Ports Holdings) handled other exports of only 51,000 tons and total imports were 109,000 tons. Fish landings, 15,000 tons in one good year (1966), were 7,850 tons in 1985, including whitefish (4,603), herrings (2,050), mackerel (185), and shellfish (1,012). The fishing trade suffered from bad seasons, fears of foreign competition which early in 1975 produced a token blockade of Ayr harbour as part of a protest by Scottish fishermen, and there were quota limitations on catches. The other traditional local trade continued to be operated by James Craig Ltd whose firm still provided livestock auctions at their cattle market, and managed the new abattoir at Heathfield.

One responsibility which the district council inherited from Ayr burgh was for town planning and building control. After the passing of the Town and Country Planning Act of 1932, Ayr town council prepared an over-all plan for future development; a further Act of 1947 required development plans to be regularly reviewed and provided added powers of enforcement. But not till the Civic Amenities Act of 1967 was there special recognition of the need to protect historic towns whose character was under threat from housing, shopping, and traffic redevelopments. Post-war Ayr suffered the loss of some fine old houses with the demolition of Belmont, Cambusdoon, Castlehill, Content, Corsehill, Dalblair, Doonside, Milrig, and Sandgate House, and (with less regret) the destruction by fire of the Trades Hotel in Newton in 1969. It was particularly unfortunate that new building often was undistinguished. As far back as 1941 Rev J.S.McNab had complained that the town 'was becoming more and more nondescript', indicating especially 'that incredible collocation of ugliness that

Kyle Academy, opened in 1979, exemplifies the range of modern facilities acquired by a town of 50,000 inhabitants.

stands at the south side of Burns Statue Square'. His comments followed the construction there of the Odeon Cinema (1938) and Ice Rink (1939). A new layout of the Square in 1951 was described in the *Advertiser* as 'an eyesore'; a further conversion in 1971, however necessary for traffic purposes, transformed it into a busy roundabout with the central monumental features dwarfed by the cinema and the new Burns House office block which was erected in 1973. High Street by 1967 was in the words of the burgh surveyor 'already a conglomeration of various types and periods of buildings' so it was then felt pointless to oppose replacement of the Gaumont Picture House by Littlewoods superstore. The John Welch memorial garden to the rear was lost in the process – just as a new Marks and Spencer store opened in 1974 would require destruction of the 15th century Blair's tenement at 70 High Street which, though derelict, was Ayr's oldest house. What did arouse more public concern was the town council's proposal in 1961 to remove the 18th century Newton kirk and townhouse 'to bulldoze a way through for the planned new road in King Street'. It required a Public Inquiry in 1963 before a compromise was reached, involving the destruction of the main building, leaving an isolated Newton Steeple, whose restoration was completed in 1968. In 1974 there was a threat to that prominent 18th century building commanding the entrance by the New Bridge to the town centre; costs of repair were so great that the town council considered demolition; but that threat was averted. By this time concepts of conservation had become more widely recognised. A local Civic Society was formed in 1967. In 1968 Ayr Town Council adopted those powers conferred by the recent Civic Amenities Act to designate three Conservation Areas within the town – Wellington Square, Alloway Place, the Fort

area – to which part of Sandgate and adjuncts was added as a fourth the following year. New awareness of responsibility resulted in some later redevelopments exhibiting more pleasing features. In High Street old frontages were sometimes retained and restored in process of rebuilding. Those new buildings erected alongside the Auld Brig by Marks and Spencer and by British Home Stores allowed the River Ayr Walk to proceed from that bridge upriver past their premises. It was also possible now to walk by the riverside on the other bank. There was exposed to view across the river a range of modern building extending downriver from the multi-storey flats past the housing department's Riverside House and the Gateway store to new flats of private dwellings at the North Harbour, where the old railway bridge had been dismantled in 1978. Though of diverse character, new buildings flanking the river on both sides were an advance on some of the nondescript erections they superseded. The elimination of most of the older manufacturing premises from the town centre, as noticed in a previous paragraph, was another advance. Sufficient memorable features survived to justify the production in 1972 of *Round Old Ayr, A Guided Walk*, a joint production of the Archaeological and Civic societies which went through several editions. In 1984 the Scottish Urban Archaeological Trust initiated the excavation of 15 sites. Conservation policies continued in 1988, when the disused 19th century lighthouse at the North Harbour was restored; and the District Council rejected proposals to demolish the Tam O'Shanter Museum and sell the Wallace Tower. In 1988, Lady Cathcart's House in the Sandgate seemed doomed. That building, presumed to be of 18th or early 19th century date, had a shabby and nondescript facade, and its only claim to note was as the birthplace of John Loudon McAdam. The Bank of Scotland purchased the property and believing it to be in dangerous condition proposed to replace it by a modern extension to its premises. Demolition plans were under way, and halted only when the Civic Society commissioned an investigation which revealed that the buildings at 22 Sandgate and the adjoining 2–4 Cathcart Street actually dated from the late 16th or early 17th century, were 'of outstanding national importance', 'not liable to collapse, nor ... in danger of imminent failure', but 'capable of being repaired, restored to a most handsome appearance'.

Altogether, despite blemishes, Ayr remained an attractive town. High Street, subtly changing direction along its way, provided a succession of perspectives, a series of intimate precincts rather than an impersonally continuous sequence of shops. Though marred by certain garish modern shopfronts, many of the buildings exhibit attractive 19th century features if one raises one's eyes. Behind the street, only a few of the centuries-old long burgage plots survived 20th century redevelopments. The Sandgate retained more of its erstwhile dignity, from the Town Hall as far as the Queens Court where the former County Club was occupied by little shops; though beyond the old Sandgate Port the narrower street had no special features, even with the new Post Office opened in 1968. Wellington Square, now mainly surrounded by offices, retained its imposing character, as well as providing the main access to the beach beyond. From the Fort area and southwards towards the old racecourse the extensive residential area ranged from terraces to villas in a wide variety of architectural styles, and including Barns House as Ayr's oldest inhabited dwelling.

For the people of Ayr and district, the town's shopping facilities were extended. In High Street, Woolworth's and Boots' from the twenties, Marks and Spencer's from the thirties were joined by new superstores – Littlewoods (1969), Safeway at the former Ice Rink, Tesco in Boswell Park, a new Marks and Spencer (all in 1974), British Home Stores (1983), and Gateway (1987). These and smaller more-specialised new shops displaced many old-established firms. In 1980 the *Ayrshire Post* in commemorating its centenary noted a dozen such still surviving. Some like P.B.Hill, fishmongers (1830–1961), had recently disappeared; others would follow, as Afflecks the house furnishers (1801–1981). By 1988 half-a-dozen remaining were Whighams the wine merchants (originating as Alexander Oliphant's, 1766), Thomas Imrie & Son, seedsman (1820), Alexander Cuthbert & Sons, children's shoes (1845), two jewellers – Matthew Mark (1863) and Wallace Allan (1872); also, from Newton, A. Picken & Sons, butcher (1870). One establishment which continued was the draper's emporium set up by David Hourston in Alloway Street in 1896, which was taken over by the House of Fraser in 1949. Another enterprise ended its local career when the Coop pulled out of Ayr by closing its last shop in Main Street in 1984. The principal shopping areas remained those busy streets from Sandgate as far as Burns Statue Square. It proved possible to pedestrianise Newmarket Street and Carrick Street in 1979, while off-street shopping was provided in Dalblair Arcade (1967), some smaller malls, and especially the impressive Kyle Centre between High Street and Carrick Street which was completed in 1988. The shopping week was extended when a

ballot of shopkeepers decided in 1974 to abolish the Wednesday half-day, following the example of the superstores, which themselves a decade later introduced seven-day opening. Other notable changes were the proliferation of shops dealing in electrical, television, and video items; also travel agencies, estate agents, and building societies. The banks continued to present their image of architecturally-secure solidity, but amalgamations reduced the number of firms to the Bank of Scotland (5 branches), Clydesdale Bank (3), Royal Bank of Scotland (3), and the Trustee Savings Bank (1). Other professional services were provided by solicitors, architects, accountants, and insurance companies, physicians, chiropodists, veterinary surgeons; many of these found convenient and substantial accommodation in what had once been terraced homes, so that there was mercifully no need to deface the skyline with new office blocks.

In recreational activities, the most dramatic change was the appeal of television, following its introduction into Scotland in 1952, with colour from 1967, and improved local reception from the Darvel mast after 1973. This had its drastic effect on the cinemas, with the Odeon alone surviving, and two of the other five continuing as bingo halls. There was surprisingly little adverse effect on reading, for the Carnegie Library reported no diminution in issues. The last of the old-established local booksellers, Stephen and Pollock, was sold in 1972 and closed in 1975; but reading demand was met in 1988 by four more modern bookshops, as well as a dozen newsagents in the town centre and suburbs. Cultural opportunities were extended. Facilities ranged from the massive Dam Park Hall to the intimacy of Loudoun Hall; the Town Hall, Gaiety and Civic Theatres; the Pavilion accommodating multi-purpose entertainment from opera to boxing bouts; Craigie College and the newer schools. Ayr now enjoyed concerts performed by visiting orchestras as well as amateur groups; drama presented by professional companies and by local players; light opera from the two established local societies complemented from 1986 by Opera West. The Maclaurin Galleries at Rozelle offered touring exhibitions and displays of impressive local talent; and in addition to art and photographic clubs there was after 1970 a Writers Club. Nearly all the other societies listed in Chapter 19 continued active, though uniformed youth organisations attracted fewer recruits. Fusilier House in Seaforth Road, opened in 1965, provided new headquarters for the Territorial and Army Volunteer Reserve, with the Ayrshire Yeomanry at Chalmers Road. TV increased the popularity of some sports. Association football after a century still had its mass following. Ayr United's fortunes fluctuated, sometimes in the Second Division (1961–66, 1967–69, 1986–88), for a spell promoted into the Premier League (1975–78), but played most seasons in the First Division of Scottish football. Whitletts Victoria continued as a junior club. Ayr Boswell Boys Football Club formed in 1963 flourished, and could field nine teams in 1988. More limited numbers enjoyed rugby at Millbrae, cricket at Cambusdoon, and other active sports like hockey, volleyball, ice hockey, and curling. Though the Ice Rink at Parkhouse closed, another one was opened soon afterwards in 1974 at Limekiln Road, and greyhound racing moved from there to Whitletts. Ayr Baths opened in 1972 proved widely popular. A revived enthusiasm for athletics was signified variously by the efforts of Ayr Seaforth, the provision by the district council of an all-weather running track at Dam Park Stadium, and the introduction in 1984 of an annual Land of Burns Half-Marathon race. Others less energetic could enjoy public parks in the estates of Belleisle, Rozelle, and Craigie, the Low Green, the River Ayr Walk, smaller features like Corsehill and Ramsay Gardens; and the Ayrshire local authorities in 1969 collaborated in establishing Culzean Country Park.

With so many secular pursuits, the churches now occupied a less prominent part in the life of the community. The Auld Kirk of Ayr (St John the Baptist) was certainly a more noticeable feature after opening of the riverside to pedestrians in the sixties. The 16th century church set in its graveyard was adjoined by a new church hall in 1968. It continued to attract a large congregation, and its kirk session from 1966 included women as elders. The interior of the church was enhanced in 1952 by restoration work when an organ brought from the New Church replaced one whose installation in 1882 had destroyed some of the old fabric. The Church of Scotland remained the leading establishment with 10 congregations and still nearly 11,000 communicant members. In 1988 the largest congregation was St Columba's, as Trinity was now known (nearly 1,800 members), followed by Alloway (1,500), Castlehill (1,400), the Auld Kirk (1,200) and St Andrew's (1,000). The others (each between 700 and 800) were St Leonard's and those north of the river – Newton on Ayr, St James', Wallacetown, and St Quivox. The next largest denomination was the Roman Catholic Church which shepherded an estimated Catholic population of 4,000 of all ages. St Margaret's in John Street (with 1,600) was joined in 1957 by the Cathedral of the Good Shepherd

in Dalmilling (with 1,100), seat of the Bishop of Galloway; and in 1967 by St Paul's in Belmont (with 1,600). Of the other denominations, the largest remained the Scottish Episcopalian congregation in Holy Trinity Church. The two Baptist churches had a combined membership just over 400. North of the river were the separate congregations of the Free and the United Free churches, the Salvation Army, and six out of seven evangelical assemblies. More recently established groups were the Mormons of the Church of Jesus Christ of Latter Day Saints, and Jehovah's Witnesses.

Some former church buildings were disposed of. Newton on Ayr Old Church was demolished following the union of the Old and New congregations in 1962; that nearby kirk built by the Burgher congregation in 1799 was demolished later to make way for the Gateway superstore; others survived to be utilised for various secular purposes – the former Robertson Memorial Church had become the Civic Theatre; Cathcart Church became a shop; the New Church which was taken over by Cathcart congregation was later converted into a dance studio; Sandgate Church into auction rooms; Darlington Church became a workshop for the Borderline Theatre group; St John's Mission housed a railway club; the kirk built in George Street by the Anti-burghers in 1779 now stored theatrical costumes; St John's Mission housed a railway club; the much more recent Lochside Church became a community centre. Most, including those nearest the town centre, had been closed to allow congregations to unite. There remained about as many people with a church connection as in mid-century; the population however had grown, and secular ideas more influential. The proportion of couples choosing a civil wedding rose from less than 20% in the fifties to more than 40% a generation later. The census report of 1971 listed Ayr as containing 130 men and 225 women who were divorced persons. In 1961, after many years of debate, the town council agreed to Sunday golf, but only at Dalmilling. In 1962 the seafront amusements were allowed for the first time to operate on Sundays. Sunday sport was extended to Belleisle golf course in 1964 and to certain bowling greens in 1966. Sabbatarianism lost again in 1970 when it was decided to hold the annual Highland Gathering on Sunday, and advocates of temperance were distressed when relaxation of the licensing laws allowed all-day drinking to be introduced in 1978.

Communications remained particularly important for Ayr. Though travel by private car was now so popular for business and pleasure, public transport was still an essential service. Western SMT's Sandgate bus depot, modernised in 1978, continued to provide services to all corners of Ayrshire, though rural routes were proving less economic to maintain at former frequency. Express coaches to Glasgow were introduced as part of a City Link network. AA Motor Services still ran their green buses from Boswell Park to Annbank and along the coast to Ardrossan. Western SMT in its operation of local services within the town found it sometimes difficult to satisfy demands of the outlying housing schemes; a private operator in 1987 made an unsuccessful effort to provide competition; that year Western SMT augmented local services with a fleet of 40 new mini-buses known as 'buzzers'. British Rail, faced with competition from road traffic, withdrew services to Mauchline, Cumnock, and Muirkirk (1951), Dalmellington (1964), the Heads of Ayr (1968), and Kilmarnock (1968). On the busy main line to Glasgow, diesels replaced steam trains in 1959; in 1983 work was commenced on massive alterations required for electrification of the route; and in 1986 'Ayrline' electric trains began operating from a modernised Ayr railway station. Closure of the line to Girvan and Stranraer was averted in 1964, and Ayr continued to be served by direct overnight trains between Stranraer and London. Closer links with the outside world were promised by the designation of Prestwick as an international airport in 1946, and the construction of a modern terminal in 1964, but Glasgow airport monopolised internal and European flights and most international companies chose to fly direct to London, though leaving Prestwick still with several regular transatlantic services.

Communications of another sort were provided by the local press. The *Ayr Advertiser* and the *Ayrshire Post* each passed into new ownership and ceased to be printed in Ayr. In 1974 the *Advertiser* was sold by T.M.Gemmell & Son Ltd, owners since 1850, to the Guthrie Newspaper Group and was printed in Ardrossan. The *Post* was acquired in 1972 by Scottish and Universal Newspapers Ltd and from 1978 printed by the SUN press in Irvine. The *Post* in 1968 began printing news on its front page, as the *Advertiser* had done since 1941; each increased its number of pages, but most space was devoted to advertisements, especially for houses and cars; and popular fashion for tabloid presentation meant briefer reports, and neglect of many items previously covered. Yet the editorial staffs were still sited in Ayr town centre, and the papers attended to special events, provided occasional features on local history, and continued to attract a readership in Ayr and a wide

surrounding district. These established weeklies were supplemented by new free newspapers deriving their revenue entirely from advertisements – *Ayrshire World* from 1980, *Ayr Free Press* 1982–88, *Ayrshire Extra* from 1987, and *Ayrshire Leader* from 1988. Media coverage was extended from October 1981 when Westsound commercial radio began broadcasting from a studio in Holmston Road.

In the eighties the population of Ayr passed 50,000. In the 1971 census report (the last to provide figures for the burgh area) there were 47,896 inhabitants. Incomers who contributed to the town's continuing growth did not significantly change its character. Most came from other parts of Scotland and were included in those 91% of the population noted as born in Scotland. Of the remaining 4,360, there were 2,880 from England and Wales; 250 from Northern Ireland and 150 from Eire; 115 from Canada and 40 from other old dominions; 275 from what was described as 'the new commonwealth', mainly Asians, and including restaurateurs, with 80 from India and 45 from Hong Kong; among 555 aliens there were 120 Italians, 95 Germans, and 100 Americans. The character of the town was more radically changed by the demographic trend towards an ageing population, which particularly affected Ayr, as remarked in Chapter 19. Between 1961 and 1971 the proportion of persons aged 65 and more increased from 11.8% to 14.3% and, with most women living longer than men, the ratio of the sexes was further distorted in that decade from 113 to 116 women per 100 men. The 1971 census report analysed those 8,540 over pensionable age (women above 60, men above 65) and found 2,030 of them living on their own, and another 500 in hospitals and nursing homes. To cope with increased numbers requiring help, a local branch of Age Concern was formed in 1978, while Opportunities in Retirement began in 1985 to provide programmes of active leisure pursuits. Homes for the elderly were maintained by Strathclyde Regional Council (Content House, South Lodge, and Templeton House) and by the Church of Scotland (Cumnor Hall and Broomfield Road); some hotels and boarding houses were converted to provide by 1988 twelve privately-run retirement and nursing homes – a trend affecting Ayrshire coastal resorts which tourist interests viewed with some misgiving. For general needs, a new hospital with 286 beds was sited at Glengall, to be opened in 1990 and replacing the County Hospital, Heathfield, and Seafield. Voluntary efforts in five years of fund-raising created an Ayrshire Hospice for the terminally-ill, opened in 1989.

As in any other town, there were divided interests within the community – the generation gap between aged and youth, council tenants versus owner-occupiers. As a historic town, there were conflicts between developers and conservationists. As in other holiday resorts, a proportion of the residents felt inconvenienced by crowds of visitors, especially by that minority who might be rowdy, vandals, or litter-louts. In the summer of 1986 the *Advertiser* reported 'traffic chaos' before the busiest weekend in Ayr's history as 250,000 visitors were expected when the Open Golf championship at Turnberry coincided with Ayr Races at the beginning of the Glasgow Fair fortnight. Two groups who regarded the town from different points of view were commuters who were only in Ayr at evenings and week-ends, and those others from the surrounding district who spent only their working hours in town. Sectional interests of course often contributed to divided opinions within the District Council and even within the constituent political groups; and conversely certain Council decisions stimulated inevitable public responses. When a superstore at the Racecourse was proposed by Asda in 1985 and permission obtained by Tesco in 1988, opponents included town-centre shopkeepers and residents in Whitletts Road. Differences of one kind or another were unavoidable in a town so heterogeneous in its interests. The growth of Ayr also necessarily involved a loss of that cohesion found in some smaller places. Five Community Councils, first elected in 1977 to represent opinion in different parts of the town, were lacking in powers, though they did collaborate to sponsor a town-twinning association which in 1984 formally initiated a link with Saint-Germain-en-Laye near Paris. Community Associations formed in Craigie (1979) and Kincaidston (1980) organised popular galas. Whitletts and Alloway, once separate communities outwith Ayr, retained their own identities and some of their own organisations.

In 1988 Ayr's further expansion seemed limited. No significant increase in stock of council houses was envisaged. What was described as 'a private sector housing explosion' involved construction of another 2,000 houses by building firms, but after that no further sites would be available without encroaching on farmland or threatening environmentally sensitive places. With Ayr regarded as such a desirable place to live, it became 'a Mecca for the house hunter'. Continued demand for scarce accommodation forced house prices well above the Scottish average. In late 1988 the local press carried advertisements for flats about £30,000, newly-built small bungalows around £50,000 and larger villas at and above £100,000. Many prospective purchasers moved instead to new housing estates in the several villages of the vicinity which were now suburban satellites of the county town.

Despite a generation of change, it remains true what was written in the *Third Statistical Account* as an assessment of the continuing community. 'Here, more than in most places, the past lives on. ... There is much in the town to remind the people of their rich heritage and make them appreciate the goodly place in which they live. Within the comparatively small area of what was once the old town and is still the centre of the new, there is a wonderful variety of things ancient and modern charged with significance. ... Here before the eyes of everyone is the essential Ayr, the Ayr of which its people are proud, that makes even the incomers who are always joining the civic company conscious that they have come to no mean city. In this integrating sentiment is the assurance that however much Ayr may change and grow it will still be Ayr.'

Sources of Information

The Bibliography includes books and articles dealing specifically with the history of Ayr, some others which contain significant relevant material, and several typescripts held in Ayr Carnegie Library (ACL); additional items are included subsequently in the Notes on Chapters. Other sources are indicated in the sections on Libraries and Archives; Newspapers; Maps and Plans. Cue titles used in the Chapter Notes are shown in this list.

Bibliography

AANHS: Ayrshire Archaeological and Natural History Society has published the books and booklets as noted; see also *AC*.

AC: Ayrshire Collections of AANHS, Volumes 1, 1950; 2, 1953; 3, 1955; 4, 1958; 5, 1959; 6, 1961; 7, 1966; 8, 1969; 9, 1970; 10, 1972; 11, 1976; 12, 1983 – containing articles, some of which as indicated have also been published separately.

AHC: Archaeological and Historical Collections, 18 vols., 1878–1890, include items separately listed under 'Gild Court', *Charters*, *Friars*, and *Protocol Books* (Mason).

Alexander, R.W., 'Conservation and Development in Ayr', unpublished thesis, Heriot-Watt University, 1967, copy in ACL 671 JE.

Allan, Hugh L. 'Ayr Half a Century Ago and Since' series from *Ayr Advertiser* 1889, in bound volume ACL 671 BL.

Allan, Wallace, *Auld Ayr Reminiscences*, from articles in *Ayr Advertiser* 1929.

Anderson, Miss E.E., *Sparks from an Old Anvil*, 1919.

Andrew, Ken, *Guide to the Kyle and Carrick District of Ayrshire*, 1981. See also Strawhorn.

anon., *Short Account of the Town of Ayr*, Edinburgh, 1828.

anon., *Ayr as a Holiday Residence*, 1870.

anon., *Ayrshire, Historical, Commercial, and Descriptive*, pub. F.W.Sears, London, 1894.

anon., *Discovering Ayr's Past*, Scottish Urban Archaeological Trust publication 1988, 4 pages with separate leaflet listing excavations 1984–88; see also Lindsay for 1982 excavation.

Archaeological Sites in North Kyle, Royal Commission on the Ancient and Historical Monuments of Scotland, No. 15, 1985.

ATB: Ayrshire at the Time of Burns, ed. John Strawhorn, AANHS, 1959; *AC* Vol.5.

Baird, William, *Sixty Years of Church Life in Ayr*, 1896.

Barrow, G.W.S., 'The Gilbertine House at Dalmilling', *AC* Vol.4. 'Ayr's Charter, 1205', *AC* Vol. 8, p.152. *Regesta Regnum Scottorum II, the Acts of William I*, 1971. *Robert the Bruce and the Community of the Realm of Scotland*, 1976. *Robert Bruce and Ayrshire*, AANHS, 1980; in *AC* Vol.12.

Bone, H., *The Book of the Auld Kirk of Ayr 1654–1954*, with a section by John M.Short on the kirk session records, 1954.

Boyd, William, *Education in Ayrshire Through Seven Centuries*, 1961. See also *TSA*.

Boyle, Andrew, *The Ayrshire Book of Burns Lore*, 1985.

Brady, Frank, *So Fast to Ruin: the Ayr Bank Crash*, AANHS, 1973; in *AC* Vol.11.

Brash, Ronald, *The Tramways of Ayr*, 1983. *Round Old Ayr*, 1972 and 1977 with Allan Leach; revised edition, 1986.

Broad, Harry, *Rails to Ayr*, AANHS, 1981; in *AC* Vol.12.

Broadie, Alexander, *George Lokert of Ayr*, AANHS 1987.

Brownlie, W.S., *The Proud Trooper, the History of the Ayrshire Yeomanry*, 1964.

Bryden, Robert, *Etchings of Auld Ayr*, 1898.

Burn, W.L., 'The General Election of 1761 at Ayr', *English Historical Review*, Vol.52, 1937.

Bute, Marquess of, *The Burning of the Barns of Ayr*, 1878.

Caldwell, David, *Poor Law Administration: History of the Parish of Ayr from 1756 to 1895*, 1895. *The Kipper Fair and Cadger Races*, 1903. *Leaves from my Notebook*, 1904.

Campbell, Jane, ed. *Air Academy and Burgh Schule, 1233–1895*, with historical survey by David Patrick, 1895.

Carrick, J.C, *Ayr Fort: the Tower of St John*, 1913.

Chalmers, George, *Caledonia*, 4 vols., 1807–24; 8 vols., 1887–1902.

Charters: Charters of the Royal Burgh of Ayr, ed. W.S.Cooper, *AHC*, 1883.

Corbett, R.Y., *Ayr, Prestwick and District Historical Guide*, 1965.

Crathorne, Nancy, *Tennant's Stalk*, 1973.

Cunninghame, J., see *Reports*.

Dillon, William, 'The Streets in Early Times', 'Pre-Reformation Church', 'Witchcraft', 'Fairs and Markets' in *RB*. 'The Origins of Feudal Ayrshire', *AC* Vol.3. *Catholic Ayrshire*, Catholic Truth Society pamphlet, 1958. 'The Spittals of Ayrshire', *AC* Vol.6. 'Ayrshire Clergy before 1600', 3 typescript volumes in ACL 4 FA.

Directories: 1830, 1832, pub. by Wm McCarter (qv); 1837,*Pigot's Directory of Scotland*; 1842, 1846, by C. Lockhart, *Ayr Observer*; 1849, *Ayr Advertiser*; 1851, Ayrshire Directory, *Ayr Advertiser*; 1857, *Directory of Noblemen and Gentlemen's Seats*; 1858, 1861, 1864, 1867, 1870, 1873, 1876, *Ayr Observer*; 1878,1880, 1882, 1884, *Ayr Advertiser*; 1886, 1888, 1890, 1892, *Ayr Observer*; 1894, 1896, *Ayrshire Post*; 1898, *Ayr Observer*; 1900, *Ayrshire Post*; 1903, 1904, 1906, 1907, 1908, Ferguson & Co. 1909, 1910, 1911, 1912, *Ayr Observer*; 1912, *County Directory of Scotland*; 1913, 1914, 1915, 1918, 1922, 1924, 1926, 1928, 1930, *Ayrshire Post*; 1934, 1936, 1938, 1940, John Browning & Co.; 1949, Dallas Advertising Agency; 1953, T.M.Gemmell & Son Ltd.; 1956, Border Publicity Co., Carlisle; 1968, Civic Publications, Blackpool.

Dixon, Jean, see Jackson.

Dodd, William, 'Ayr, a Study in Urban Growth', *AC* Vol.10; which is an abbreviated version of unpublished thesis, University of Strathclyde, copy in ACL 671 JE.

Dougall, Charles, *The Burns Country*, 1904.

Duncan, Peter C., 'Ayr and District 1830–50', unpublished dissertation, University of Lancaster, 1973, copy in ACL 671 BL.

Dunlop, Annie I., see RB.

Durkan, John, 'Chaplains in late Medieval Scotland', *Scottish Church History Society Records*, Vol. XX, 1980; 'The Bishops Barony of Glasgow', *ibid* Vol. XXII, 1986.

Ferguson, James M., *Auld Ayr, Sketches and Reminiscences*, 1884. *Reminiscences of Auld Ayr*, 1907.

Fergusson, Sir James, *William Wallace, Guardian of Scotland*, 1938, 1948. 'Loudoun Hall and its Owners', *AC* Vol.1. See also *Protocol Books*. 'A Wine Merchant's Letter Book', *AC*, Vol.4. See also *ATB. The White Hind*, 1963.

Forsyth, James, 'Provosts' and 'General Bibliography' in *RB*.

Fowler, J.J., 'The Presbytery of Ayr: Its Schools and Schoolmasters 1642–1746', *AC* Vol.6. With McNab, J.S., 'The Churches after 1800' in *RB*.

Friars: Charters of the Friars Preachers of Ayr, ed. R.W.Cochran-Patrick, *AHC*, 1881.

Gairdner, C.D., *Autobiography*, reprinted from *Kilmarnock Standard*, 1902.

Gardner, Careen, *Printing in Ayr and Kilmarnock*, AANHS 1976; in *AC* Vol.12.

'Gild Court': 'Proceedings of the Gild Court of Ayr' ed. Thomas Dickson, *AHC*, Vol. 1, 1878.

Goodwin, Alexander, 'Road Development in Ayrshire 1750–1835', unpublished thesis, University of Strathclyde, 1970, copy in ACL 4MB.

Gourlay, Robert and Turner, Anne, *Historic Ayr*, Scottish Burgh Survey 1977.

Graham, Angus, *Old Ayrshire Harbours*, AANHS 1984.

Gray, Henry C., *The Auld Toon o' Ayr and its History since 1800*, 1872.

Groome, Francis H., ed., *Ordnance Gazetteer of Scotland*, 6 vols., 1885–86.

Grose, Francis, *The Antiquities of Scotland*, 2 vols., 1789, 1791.

Guide Books: *Guide to the Glasgow and Ayrshire railway ... to Ayr and Its Environs and to the Land of Burns*, 1841. Young's *Guide to Ayr and the Land of Burns*, post 1860. *New Guide to Ayr and the land of Burns*, pub. Henry and Grant, p.1860. *Penny Guide to Ayr and Alloway*, 1885. *Guide to Ayr and the Land of Burns*, pub. H.Henry, revised edition, p.1883. *Guide to Ayr and the Land of Burns*, pub. H.Henry, new edition, p.1898. *Guide to Ayr and the Land of Burns*, pub. H.Henry, revised edition, p.1901. *The Original Guide to Ayr and the Land of Burns*, pub. H.Henry, revised edition, c.1901. *Ayr and the Birthplace of Burns*, James Ferguson, Argus Office, 1886. See also above under 'anon.' For these and later guide books see ACL 671 BY.

Hamilton, Thomas, *Poor Relief in South Ayrshire 1700–1845*, 1942. 'How the Burgh Helped the Poor' in *RB*. 'Local Administration in Ayrshire 1750–1800' in *ATB*.

Hewat, Kirkwood, *In the Olden Times*, 1898.

Howie, James, *An Historical Account of the Town of Ayr for the past Fifty Years*, 1861.

Hughes, Isobel, see Morrison.

Hume, John, 'Mills of the River Ayr', *AC* Vol.8.

Hunter, Andrew, *The Pedigree of Hunter of Abbothill and Barjarg*, 1905, copy in NLS.

Hunter, James, *The House of John Blair*, AANHS 1976; in *AC* Vol. 11.

Ivory, J., see *Reports*.

Jackson, John and Dixon, Jean, 'The Plague' in *RB*.

Kennedy, A., 'Some Economic Developments' in *RB*.

Kirkwood, James, 'Auchincruive House', *AC*, Vol.3.

Leach, Allan, *Libraries in Ayr 1762–1975*, AANHS 1975; in *AC* Vol.11. See also Brash.

Limond, Thomas, 'Roup of the Lands of Alloway' and 'Enclosure of the Town's Common' in *ATB*.

Lindsay, W.J., *Digging Up Auld Ayr: An Excavation at 102–104 High Street*, AANHS 1985.

Lyon: D.Murray Lyon, *Ayr in the Olden Times*, 1928, reprinted from *Ayr Advertiser* 1874–77. Unpublished Notes in ACL 671 BG. 'Ayr Burgh Schools', printed extracts supplied to James Grant for his *History of the Burgh and Parish Schools of Scotland*, in ACL 671 PB.

McCarter, William, *Brief Historical Reminiscences of the County and Town of Ayr ... to which is added ... a Post Office*

Directory ... by a Burgess (Guild Brother), 1830; revised edition entitled *Ayrshire*, 1832.

McCartney, John, 'Some Eminent Men' in *RB*.

McClelland, James, 'Schools' in *RB*.

McGhee, Hugh, 'The Old Harbour of Ayr', *AC* Vol.1. 'The Harbour' in *RB*.

McGloin, J., 'Catholic Education in Ayr 1823–1918', *Innes Review*, Vol. 13, 1962. 'The Abbé Nicholas', *Innes Review*, Vol.14, 1963.

Mackenzie, Archibald, *William Adair and his Kirk*, 1933. *An Old Kirk and Burns Memories*, 1934. *An Ancient Church*, 1935. 'John Welch and his Garden', *AC* Vol.1. 'Church from Reformation till 1800' in *RB*. 'Extracts from the Kirk Session Book of John Welch', *AC* Vol.7.

MacKenzie, Ross, *Ayr's Export Trade at the End of the 16th Century*, AANHS 1988.

McNab, J.S., see Fowler.

Macnair, John Ferguson, 'Newspapers' in *RB*.

Manson, J.R., 'Topography' in *RB*.

Mason, John, see *Protocol Books*.

Millar, A.H., *The Castles and Mansions of Ayrshire*, with plates by Messrs Annand, Glasgow, 1885.

Moore, John, *Ayr Gaiety*, 1976.

Morris, James, *Ayr Theatricals from 1809*, 1872.

Morris, James A., 'The Church of St John', Scottish Ecclesiological Society Transactions, 1912. *The Brig of Ayr*, 1912. *The Auld Toon o' Ayr*, 1928.

Morrison, Alex, *The Bronze Age in Ayrshire*, AANHS 1978; in *AC* Vol. 12. With Hughes, Isobel, *The Stone Ages in Ayrshire*, AANHS 1989.

Murdoch, John, 'Notable Ayrshire Folk' series from *Ayrshire Post* 1913 in bound volume ACL 4 CG.

Murray, David, *Legal Practice in the West of Scotland in the Fifteenth and Sixteenth Centuries*, 1910. *Early Burgh Organisation in Scotland*, Vol.2, 1932, deals with Ayr and Newton.

NSA: New Statistical Account of Scotland, Vol. V, Ayrshire, 1842.

Obit Book: James Paterson, *The Obit Book of the Church of St John the Baptist, Ayr*, 1848.

Ordnance Survey Card Index of Ayrshire Sites, in ACL.

OSA: The Old Statistical Account. *The Statistical Account of Scotland*, ed. Sir John Sinclair, 21 vols., 1790–99; Ayrshire parishes reprinted as Vol. VI, 1982, with Introduction by John Strawhorn.

Pagan, John, *Annals of Ayr in the Olden Times, 1560–1692*, 1897.

Paterson, James, *History of the County of Ayr*, 2 vols., 1847, 1852; in 5 vols., 1863–66; re-issued in 2 vols. with addenda, 1871. See also *Obit Book*. *Reminiscences of Auld Ayr*, pub. T.Stillie, Edinburgh, 1864 (by Paterson though author not named). *Autobiographical Reminiscences*, 1871. *Contemporaries of Burns*, 1840.

Paterson, Thomas, 'Modern Development of the Burgh' in *RB*.

Patrick, David, see Campbell.

Prestoun, Henry, see *Protocol Books*.

Protocol Books: 1512–32: Ros, Gavin, *The Protocol Book of Gavin Ros*, ed. J. Anderson and F.J.Grant, 1908. 1547–51: Prestoun, Henry: 'The Protocol Book of Henry Prestoun' ed. Sir James Fergusson, *AC* Vol.3, 1955. 1582–1612: Mason, John: 'Mason's Protocol Book, Abstracts' and 'Notorial Note Book of John Mason', ed. John Shedden-Dobbie, *AHC*, Vol.VI, 1889.

Pryde, George, *Ayr Burgh Accounts 1534–1624*, Scottish History Society, 1937. 'Ayr Burgh Accounts 1428–29', *Scottish Historical Review*, Vol. XXXI, 1952. 'Charter of Foundation' in *RB*. 'Development of the Burgh' in *RB*. 'The Burghs of Ayrshire', *AC* Vol.4. *The Burghs of Scotland, A Critical List*, 1965.

RB: The Royal Burgh of Ayr, ed. Annie I. Dunlop, *AC* Vol.2, 1953.

Report on the Royal Burgh of Ayr Boundaries, 1832, in ACL 671 GF.

Reports from the Commissioners on Municipal Corporations in Scotland, Ayr and Newton-upon-Ayr by J.Ivory and John Cuninghame, 1836.

Robertson, William, *Ayrshire, Its History and Historic Families*, 2 vols., 1908. *Historical Tales and Legends of Ayrshire*, 1889. *The Kings of Carrick*, 1890. *The Lords of Cuninghame*, 1891. *Historic Ayrshire*, 2 vols., 1891, 1894. *The Second Volunteer Battalion R.S.F.*, 1897. *Auld Ayr*, 1901. *The Dule Tree of Cassillis*, 1903. *Old Ayrshire Days*, 1905. *The Annals of Drumsmudden*, 1903.

Robinson, W. Stitt, 'Richard Oswald the Peacemaker', *AC* Vol. 3.

Ros, Gavin, see *Protocol Books*.

Sanderson, Margaret, 'Some Aspects of the Church in Scottish Society in the Era of the Reformation, illustrated from the Sheriffdom of Ayr', *Scottish Church History Society Records*, Vol. XVII, 1970. *Scottish Rural Life in the 16th Century*, 1982. *Mary Stewart's People*, 1987. *The People of Sixteenth Century Ayrshire*, AANHS 1987.

Sasines: Index to Register of Sasines for Ayrshire, 3 vols. 1599–1660; also *Register of Sasines for Ayrshire, 1781–1868*, 10 vols.

Shaw, James E., *Ayrshire 1745–1950*, 1953.

Shaw, John, *The Dalrymples of Langlands*, Bath, n.d., copy in Edinburgh Public Library.

Shearer, Joseph D., *The Dwelling House of James Shearer*, n.d.

Short, John M., 'Street Names' in *RB*. See also Bone, H.

Slezer, J., *Theatrum Scotiae*, 1693.

Smith, John, *Prehistoric Man in Ayrshire*, 1895.

Smith, John, *Records of the Burgh of Prestwick*, 1834. *Memorabilia of the City of Glasgow*, 1835.

Smout, T.C., 'Overseas Trade of Ayrshire 1660–1700', *AC* Vol. 6.

Stevenson, David, 'The Battle of Mauchline Moor, 1648', AANHS, 1973; in *AC* Vol.11. 'The Covenanters and the Western Association 1648–1650', AANHS, 1982; in *AC* Vol. 12.

Stillie, T., see Paterson, James.

Strawhorn, John, 'How Ayr has grown' in *RB*. 'Ayrshire's Changing Population', *AC* Vol. 8. See also *ATB; OSA;* and *TSA. Ayrshire, the Story of a County,* 1975. 'Life's Deceitful Morning', *Burns Chronicle* 1980. 'The Litigation at Lochlea,' *Burns Chronicle* 1985. *750 Years of a Scottish School: Ayr Academy 1233–1983,* 1983. With Andrew, Ken, *Discovering Ayrshire,* 1988.

Stuart, Sir James, see Bute, Marquess of.

Taylor, A.L., 'Tam's Road' in *ATB*. 'The Braw New Coat – the Building of Ayr New Brig', *AC* Vol.6. 'The Grammar School of Ayr 1746–96', *AC* Vol.7.

TSA: Third Statistical Account of Scotland, ed. John Strawhorn and William Boyd, 1951.

Turner, Anne, see Gourlay.

Wallace, Edwin, 'Shipping Through the Port of Ayr 1745–1815', Research Project in Scottish Social and Economic History, University of St Andrews, 1987, copy in ACL.

Walton, David, 'Ayr at War', newspaper items relating to World War One compiled for use in Ayr Academy, 1981.

Waterson, Duncan, *An Ayrshire Family 1526–1900,* AANHS 1978; in *AC* Vol. 12.

Whatley, C.A., 'The Process of Industrialisation in Ayrshire, c.1707–1871', unpublished thesis, University of Strathclyde, 1975, copy in ACL. *The Finest Place for a Lasting Colliery c.1600–1840,* AANHS 1983.

Wilson, Alexander, 'Dr John Taylor, the Ayrshire Chartist', *AC* Vol.1. *The Chartist Movement in Scotland,* 1970.

Young, John, *Some of the Municipal Works of Ayr,* reprinted from the *Ayr Observer* 1908, ACL 671 GJ.

Libraries and Archives

ACL: Ayr Carnegie Library, being Kyle and Carrick District Library Headquarters, 12 Main Street, Ayr, contains in its Reference Department a Local Collection; Burns Collection; files of maps, plans, photographs; local newspapers; Ayr Town Council Minutes (cited subsequently as ATC Minutes), other burgh papers, and those of Newton-upon-Ayr, as listed in 'Inventory of SRO Records'; there is an 'Inventory of other Locally-held Records' (both in ACL 671 CB).

ATC: Ayr Town Council Minutes and other papers in ACL.

SRA: Strathclyde Regional Archivist's Office, County Buildings, Wellington Square, Ayr, contains records relating to education, roads, and other functions exercised by the Regional Council, Ayr County Council, and authorities whom they superseded. Certain church records transferred from SRO.

SRO: Scottish Record Office. The Keeper of the Records, H.M.General Register House, Princes Street, Edinburgh, retains certain records mainly of a legal nature; West Register House, Charlotte Square, Edinburgh, holds maps, plans, and other papers.

New Register House, Edinburgh. The Registrar General for Scotland has records of births, marriages, and deaths since compulsory registration was introduced in 1855; plus surviving earlier parish registers; also decennial census returns, some of which are open to inspection. For this and other genealogical inquiries see *Family History: a Guide to Ayrshire Sources,* ed. Jane Jamieson or MacLean, AANHS, 1984.

NLS: National Library of Scotland, George IV Bridge, Edinburgh, and also NLS Map Room, Causewayside Building, 33 Salisbury Place, Edinburgh.

Other libraries with relevant material include Mitchell Library, Glasgow; Edinburgh Public Library; Edinburgh University Library; Glasgow University Library; and the International Genealogical Index (IGI) as held by the Church of Jesus Christ of Latter Day Saints, Campbell Street, Johnstone, with microfiches in ACL.

Ayrshire Sound Archive, in library of Craigie College of Education, Ayr – tape-recording project sponsored by Ayrshire Federation of Historical Societies.

Scottish Film Archive in premises of Scottish Film Council, 74 Victoria Crescent Road, Glasgow, has items on Ayr 1937; Pageant of Ayrshire 1934; Home Guard Stand-Down 1944; Pageant of Ayr 1948; Ayr From the Auld Brig 1961; with sequences in A Life of Burns 1933; Immortal Memory 1946; Lowlands of Scotland c.1946; Fair County of Ayr c.1950; the Power and Pulse of Scotland, at Butlins 1968; for other local films see A.J.Nelson, 'Films on Ayrshire' (1947–1957) in *AC* Vol. 4; and references in *AA* 1.4.1943, 9.3.1944, 27.3.1952, 15.6.67.

Photographic collections in ACL as above; Scottish Photography Archive, Scottish National Portrait Gallery, 1 Queen Street, Edinburgh; National Monuments Record of Scotland, 54 Melville Street, Edinburgh; Aberdeen University Library (George Washington Wilson series c.1875–1908); St Andrews University Library (Valentine postcard series 1878–1962); Francis Frith Collection, Andover, Hampshire (1897, 1900); Aerofilms Ltd., Gate Studios, Station Road, Boreham Wood, Herts. (1927 and later).

Newspapers

Files of the local press supply not only reports of contemporary events, but obituary notices of prominent persons, features on anniversaries, reminiscences and other historical articles and series.

AA: Ayr Advertiser from 1803.

AP: Ayrshire Post from 1880.

ACL has *AA, AP,* also *Ayr Observer* from 1832 till absorption by *AA* in 1930; and copies of other shorter-lived papers. *Directory of Scottish Newspapers,* ed. Joan Ferguson, NLS, 1984, gives complete list, also location of other repositories.

Maps and Plans

ACL has an extensive collection of maps and plans, including copies of originals held in SRO, etc. The more important items listed are mostly in Map Drawer entitled 'Ayr, Development and Growth'; there are numerous other plans, especially RH Plans from SRO, for which see Ian H. Adam, *Descriptive List of Plans in SRO,* 1960 and later volumes.

Blaeu 1654: *The Province of Kyle,* from Vol.5 of the *Atlas Novus.* Published by W. and J. Blaeu, Amsterdam; reprinted by John Bartholomew and Son, Edinburgh, 1967. Based on information collected locally c.1600 by Timothy Pont, and collated by Robert Gordon, whose manuscript map of Kyle (Gordon Map 60) is held in NLS Map Room. Scale 13/4 miles to one inch, 1:79200.

Tessin 1654: 'Citadell at Ayre', by Hans Ewald Tessin, from the Clarke Papers in Worcester College Library – included in C.H.Firth, *Scotland and the Protectorate,* Scottish History Society, 1899; copy in ACL – Scale 180 feet to one inch, 1: 2100.

Another version in Krigsarkivet, Stockholm, with inscriptions in German, entitled 'Die Stadt und das Fort zu Ayre'; scale 15 Ruten (approximately 225 feet) to one inch, 1:2700; ACL copy on scale 1:2100.

Another copy inscribed 'Plan of the Town and Citadell of Air', by T.Walker, apparently 18th century, is reduced to 300 feet to one inch, 1:3600.

early 18th century: The Citadel. anon. Shows brewery, saltpans, and My Lady's house, possibly referring to Lady Eglinton, owner 1727–55. Scale 60 feet to one inch, 1:720.

Roy 1747–55: Military Survey of Scotland by General William Roy. Manuscript maps in the British Library, Map Library, Great Russell Street, London. Photocopies and colour slide in ACL. Scale 13/4 inches to one mile, 1:36000.

1768: Map of the Common Grounds Belonging to Ayr, by J.Gregg. Scale 4 Scots chains to one inch, 1:3550.

Armstrong 1775: *Plan of the Town of Ayr.* One of six sheets of *A New Map of Ayrshire* by A. & M. Armstrong; reprinted by AANHS 1959. Scale 133/4 inches to one mile, 1:4600.

1784: Craigie House and Lands of Mill Quarter. anon. Scale 2 Scots chains to one inch, 1:1800.

1786: Plan of Ayr Common, by W.Millar. Scale 31/2 Scots chains to one inch, 1:3150.

1792: Sketch of the Common of Ayr, by J.Gregg. Scale 2 Scots chains to one inch, 1:1800.

1799: Plan of the Green. anon. Scale 1 Scots chain to one inch, 1:900.

Wood 1818: *Plan of the Towns and Part of the Parishes of Ayr, Newton upon Ayr, and St Quivox.* Included in John Wood's *Town Atlas,* 1819. Scale 4 Scots chains to one inch, 1:3550.

1818: Lands of Greenfield and Alloway Crofts, by James Milliken. Scale 2 Scots chains to one inch, 1:1800.

1819: Plan of Ayr Barracks, by Gavin Rowatt. Scale 30 feet to one inch, 1:360.

1821: Plan of Barracks and Coal Works, by the Barrack Master. Scale 12 inches to one mile, 1:5280.

Milliken 1824: Plan of Part of the Town of Ayr, by James Milliken. Scale 80 feet to one inch, 1:960.

1826: Ayr Harbour. anon. Scale 100 feet to one inch, 1:1200.

1826: The Lands of Newton. anon. Surveyed 1826, versions dated 1833, 1846, 1877. Scale 6.7 Imperial chains to one inch, 1:5360.

Milliken 1832: *Plan and Views of Ayr.* Based on Wood 1818 and included in McCarter's *Directory.* Scale approx 6 inches to one mile, 1:10560.

Boundaries 1832: from *Report on Royal Burgh of Ayr Boundaries,* 1832. Scale 6 inches to one mile, 1: 10560.

1841: Plan of the Lands of Barns, by James Milliken. For the heirs of Patrick McNeight, who died in 1840. Scale 100 yards to one inch, 1:3600.

1845: Plan of Feuing of Barns, by Alex E. Thomson. Scale 280 yards to one inch, 1:10,000.

1845: Lime Kilns and Coal Yards, by Alex Thomson. Scale 40 feet to one inch, 1:480.

1846: New Turnpike Road ... Widening of Alloway Street. By James Campbell and John Paterson. Scale 200 feet to one inch, 1:2400.

1849: Proposed slip and dam dyke at Ayr Mill. anon. Scale 25 feet to one inch, 1:300.

1850: Farm of Greenfield, by John Bell. Scale 2 Imperial Chains to one inch, 1:1600.

n.d.: Estate of Blackhouse. anon. Scale 6 Imperial chains to one inch, 1:4800.

1852: District of Ayr, Turnpike Roads, by James McDerment and Sons. Scale 3/4 miles to one inch, 1:47520.

OS 1855: *Ordnance Survey First Edition.* Scale 6 inches to one mile, 1:10560; also 25 inches to one mile, 1:2500; also 60 inches to one mile, 1:1056. Surveyed 1855–57, published 1856–60.

1885: Widening of High Street. Based on OS, scale 60 inches to one mile, 1:1056.

OS 1886: *Ordnance Survey,* 1857 survey revision. Scale 25 inches to one mile, 1:2500.

OS 1895: *Ordnance Survey Second Edition.* Scale 6 inches to one mile, 1: 10560; also 25 inches to one mile, 1: 2500. Revised and published 1895.

n.d. Ground to be feued at Victoria Park. orig. in SRA. Scale 65 feet to one inch, 1:780.

OS 1908: *Ordnance Survey Third Edition*. Scale 6 inches to one mile, 1: 10560; also 25 inches to one mile, 1: 2500; also 60 inches to one mile, 1:1056. Revised 1905–08, published 1905–11. Also later OS editions.

1970: Ayr Census of Distribution Map. Based on OS, Scale 88 feet to one inch, 1:1060.

Also numerous 20th century street guides.

Notes

Currency

Before decimalisation in 1971, £1 was divided into twenty shillings and each shilling contained twelve pennies; thus £1.2.6, 12/6, 10/–, 6d equalled respectively £1.12$^1/_2$, 62$^1/_2$, 50p, 2$^1/_2$p. For earlier currency, £1 Scots was valued at one twelfth of £1 Sterling, and a mark was worth two-thirds of £1 Scots.

Dates

The New Year commenced on 25 March in Scotland until 1600 (and until 1752 in England); this has required the conversion of certain previous dates, e.g. a document dated 1 January 1588 would by modern usage refer to 1 January 1589. The United Kingdom converted from the Julian to the Gregorian calendar in 1752 by following 2 September by 14 September that year; after which New Style dates were used, but certain traditional events continued to follow the Old Style calendar. e.g. Old New Year, Old Hallowe'en.

Spellings

Quotations from earlier periods have been given in original spellings, save where clarity has suggested minor alterations. Personal and place names, which show no uniformity in spelling, have been standardised where it seemed essential.

For authors and cue titles included in the following *Notes on Chapters* reference should be made to *Bibliography*.

Chapter 1 – Origins

For etymology of the place name see *OSA*, 18; Chalmers, VI, 445; *NSA*, 1; Paterson, 1; Lyon's Unpublished Notes; and, more reliably, W. F. H. Nicolaisen, *Scottish Place-Names*, 1976, esp. 187, also articles by that author in *Scottish Studies*. For archaeological evidence, Smith has been superseded by an Ordnance Survey Card Index (in ACL), also *Archaeological Sites in North Kyle* and Morrison's recent studies. The Bronze Age site at Content (34272168, 342218) was first recorded in *NSA*, 119; that at Greenfield (32961862), as noted in Burns's 'Tam O'Shanter' line 93, and recorded in *NSA*, 40, is marked by a stone cairn erected in 1965. Remains said to be Roman are mentioned in Chalmers, I, 154; *NSA*, 20, 40; Paterson, 5. The 'Roman Road' as traced by Joseph Train is described in Chalmers, VI, 449; *NSA*, 39; Paterson, xxvii and 5; Smith, 159; but dismissed in *Proceedings of the Society of Antiquaries of Scotland*, XXVII, 1893, 417; *Transactions of Dumfriesshire and Galloway Society*, 1921, 88; *Journal of Roman Studies*, 1939, 201; O.G.S.Crawford, *Topography of Roman Scotland*, 1949, 6; see also *AC* Vol.3, 30; Vol.4, 239; Vol.6, 244. For Dark Ages stories and references, Chalmers, VI, 455; *NSA*, 40, 315;

Paterson, xi,v. That the legendary Arthur was a historical figure based in SW Scotland was argued in J.S.S.Glennie, *Arthurian Localities*, 1869; the first of his twelve battles located near Darvel as noted in John Macintosh, *Ayrshire Nights Entertainments*, 1894; Burke's Peerage press release entitled 'Discovery of Camelot' (*Glasgow Herald* 31.10.1988) reported the earthworks on the site of the 15th century Greenan Castle identified by Professor Norma Goodrich, Claremont College, California, as 'one of many Camelots' for 'It was the custom of the king to refer to the castle he was using at the time as Camelot' and 'Greenan probably derives from the word "Grianan" meaning a sunny place, a summer fort'. Legends relating to Coilus are in *OSA*, 24; *NSA*, 41, 655, 751; Paterson, xi, xv, 759; it may be worth remark that Burns opened his Kilmarnock Edition with 'The Twa Dogs' commencing "Twas in that place o' Scotland's isle,/ That bears the name o' auld king Coil'. The circumstances in which the Castle of Ayr was built in 1197 (as reported in *Chron. de Mailros*, 103) have been discussed in Chalmers, VI, 481; *NSA*, 21; Paterson, 6; Murray, *Early Burgh Organisation*, II, 299; Pryde in *RB*, 5; also Pryde in *AC* Vol.4, 10; and Dodd, 310. Dillon's 'Origins of Feudal Ayrshire' summarises much useful detail; Durkan, 'The Bishop's Barony of Glasgow' includes mention of Sanchar and Carcluie c.1166. G.W.S.Barrow, *Kingship and Unity: Scotland 1000–1306*, 1981, is an authoritative study of the background; A.A.M.Duncan, *Scotland: the Making of the Kingdom*, 1975, is especially useful for the situation in Galloway which made so urgent the building of a castle at Ayr in 1197 as is explained (p.187). For the recession of the sea in prehistoric and later times, see *British Regional Geology: Midland Valley of Scotland*, 1948, and *Geological Survey; Central Ayrshire*, 1949; information supplied by Dr William Boyd (as noted in my *History of Irvine*, 1985, 2, 238) I have adapted to apply to this part of the Ayrshire coast. That the River Doon changed its course has been considered in *OSA*, 29; *NSA*, 8; Paterson, 3; Lyon, 51; correspondence in *AA*, September 1875; *Charters*, xxi; David Murray, 303; Pryde in *RB*, 11; Manson in *RB*, 66; Dillon in *AP*, 3.8.1956. Some material for this and later chapters comes from Strawhorn in *RB* and *AC* Vol.8; and McNeill and Nicholson, *An Historic Atlas of Scotland c.400–c.1600*, 1975. T.A.Hendry provided information and constructive criticism of this chapter; he does not agree with certain of my conclusions.

Chapter 2 – Foundation of the Burgh

For the area north of the river in the 13th century, see Barrow in *AC* Vol.4. William the Lion's charter was noted by Chalmers, who dated it as 1202 × 1207 in his *Caledonia*, 1824 edition, III, 499; first printed by McCarter, 1830; considered in *NSA*, 19; in *Charters*, where it was printed with annotations; Paterson, 1–6; Murray, II, 303. Paterson believed (p.5) 'That Ayr existed as a town or hamlet at a much earlier period than the date of King William's charter is abundantly evident'. Murray also imagined (p.305) a community of freemen 'holding an extensive territory ... from time immemorial'. Pryde dated the charter as 1203 x 1206 (*SHR*, XXIX, 1950, 215–6); provided a corrected transcript with detailed commentary in *RB*, 1–18, arguing there (p. 17) that it was 'the written record of an act of creation' as quoted in the text of this chapter; Pryde further described 'The Development of the Burgh' *RB*, 19–52; also in *AC* Vol.4; and his findings are included in his *Burghs of Scotland, A Critical List* – thus concluding that research into Ayr's history he had commenced with his *Ayr Burgh Accounts* in 1937. More recently Barrow has fixed the charter date as 1205, this noted in *AC* Vol.8, 152; also in his *Regesta* of 1971, which again transcribes the Ayr charter, pp. 426–8. Barrow's *Kingship and Unity: Scotland 1000–1306*, 1981, 84–104, sums up current views on the origins and development of Scottish burghs. The morphology of the burgh of Ayr was investigated by Dodd in *AC* Vol. 10, and some of his observations have been quoted. Lindsay's *Digging Up Auld Ayr* postulates (p.195) the 'possible presence of an early church or chapel which may have ante-dated the creation of Ayr burgh'. More recent work by the Scottish Urban Archaeological Trust is briefly listed in their anonymous *Discovering Ayr's Past*. The streets and other places of the early burgh have been considered by Paterson, 7, 11, 56, etc.; Murray, 322; Pryde in his *Accounts*, cxxiii; and especially by Dillon in *RB*, 68–77; the 'Roll of Ground Annualis'

in ATC Minutes 23.9.1656 has been useful for this and other purposes. Other relevant sources are (with dates of documents shown in brackets): *Charters* (1205–1715); *Friars* (1242–1614), *Obit Book* (1306–1599); *Protocol Books* of Gavin Ros (1517–32), Henry Prestoun (1547–51), and John Mason (1582–1612). 'Ayr Burgh Accounts 1428–29' were noted in *SHR*, XXIX, 1950, and transcribed with comments by Pryde in *SHR*, XXXI, 1952, 139–146. 'Gild Court Proceedings for 1428–31' appeared in *AHC*. For early trade see also McGhee on 'The Old Harbour of Ayr', in *AC* Vol. 1, esp. p. 78; and Bain's *Calendar of Documents*, I, 249. For other national records see notes on Chapter 4.

Chapter 3 – The Medieval Church

Some basic details were supplied by Chalmers; *NSA*, 34–39; Paterson, 42–56. Primary sources are listed in notes for Chapter 2, especially *Obit Book* and *Friars*; with references in *Charters* and *Protocol Books*. The structure of the Church of St John was examined by McGibbon and Ross, *Ecclesiastical Architecture of Scotland*, 3 vols., 1896; by Morris, 'The Church of St John'; by a Scottish Urban Archaeology unit in 1987. Carrick's *Tower of St John* was followed by the more reliable and informative Mackenzie's *An Ancient Church*. Most admirable are Dillon's 'Pre-Reformation Church' in *RB*, quoted in this chapter; his *Catholic Ayrshire* pamphlet, 1958, also quoted; 'The Spittals of Ayrshire', *AC* Vol. 6; and his unpublished typescript of 'Ayrshire Clergy before 1600'; this meticulous reference work is held in ACL, as are other Dillon papers. Various relevant studies are D.A.Mackay, 'Ayrshire Parish Clerks', *AC* Vol.7; D.E.Easson, *Medieval Religious Houses: Scotland*, 1957; I.B.Cowan et al., *The Knights of St John of Jerusalem in Scotland*, Scottish History Society, 1983; W.M.Bryce, *The Scottish Grey Friars*, 2 vols., 1909, assembled what information is available about their house in Ayr, but missed Mason, 120, 132.

Chapter 4 – Local Scene

Essential information is found in the published national records – Bain's *Calendar of Documents relating to Scotland* (with items from 1108), including supplementary volume published 1986 with corrections and addenda; *Acts of the Parliaments of Scotland* (from 1124); *Exchequer Rolls* (from 1264); *Register of the Great Seal* (from 1306); *Accounts of the Lord High Treasurer* (from 1473); *Register of the Privy Seal* (from 1488); *Register of the Privy Council* (from 1545). Sketches of medieval events as they affected Ayr were attempted by Chalmers, Paterson, and Robertson. Various accounts of the Wars of Independence relying principally on Blind Harry and Barbour have been superseded by Fergusson's biography of Wallace and more recently Barrow on Bruce. Professor Barrow read this chapter in draft and kindly corrected some errors of detail. Older histories by Hill Burton and Hume Brown are now supplemented by W.C.Dickinson, *Scotland from the Earliest*

Times to 1603, 1961, revised by A.A.M.Duncan, 1977; the first two volumes of *A Source Book of Scottish History*, ed. Dickinson et al., 1952, 1953; R.Nicolson, *Scotland: The Later Middle Ages*, 1974; and the latest series which includes G.W.S.Barrow, *Kingship and Unity*, 1981, A.Grant, *Independence and Nationhood*, 1985, and J. Wormald, *Court, King, and Community*, 1981. Details of the Ayrshire Feuds are contained in Chalmers; throughout Paterson's accounts of Cunninghame, Kyle, and Carrick; and among the many works of William Robertson. Robertson's *Historic Ayrshire* reprints various original sources and includes items relating to Ayrshire from Pitcairn's *Criminal Trials*; to which may be added Pitcairn's edition of the *Historie of the Kennedyis*, 1830; and – returning to historical fiction – S.R.Crocket's *The Grey Man*, numerous editions and still in print. For Ayr itself, Pryde in *RB*, 19–52, has been augmented by local sources previously noted, plus various special studies: Morris, *The Brig of Ayr*; Marquess of Bute, *The Burning of the Barns of Ayr*; Fergusson, 'Loudoun Hall and its Owners' and his *The White Hind*; Hunter, *The House of John Blair*.

Chapter 5 – The 16th Century Royal Burgh

This detailed account of 16th century Ayr is based almost entirely on the surviving burgh records. The fragmentary evidence for earlier times as listed in notes for Chapter 2 is succeeded by the more complete series of manuscript records retained by Ayr town council, transferred to the Scottish Record Office, and now returned to Ayr Carnegie Library. 'The Book of the Common Comptis of the Commoun Gude of the Burgh of Air' described (by Anna Mill, *Inventory of MS Records of the Older Royal Burghs*, 1923) as 'probably the most complete set of early Town Accounts extant in Scotland' has been magnificently transcribed, edited, and introduced by George S. Pryde in *Ayr Burgh Accounts 1534–1624*. There are also in ACL 'Court Books' for 1547–53, 1549–60; 'Court and Council Records' for 1580–89, 1590–96, 1596–1606; 'Council Minutes' 1596–1611; 'Court Book of Alloway' 1582–1607. Such records have been scrutinised by several writers and quoted, often extensively in their works: John Smith, *Memorabilia of the City of Glasgow*, contains extracts from Ayr records 1550–59; Paterson in his Ayrshire History, chapter on 'The Parish of Ayr'; Lyon; Pagan; Murray; Archibald Mackenzie; Pryde in *RB*, esp. pp. 33–35, and in *AC* Vol. 4, esp. pp. 23–24 where he estimates the population. Other specialised topics in *RB* using burgh records are Dillon on 'Fairs and Markets' and Jackson and Dickson on 'The Plague' which last topic is also dealt with by Lyon, and by Pryde in his *Accounts* pp. c–ciii. Sanderson, *Scottish Rural Life in the 16th Century*, makes use of the Alloway court book. Most recent is Ross MacKenzie's study of export trade, based on the Coquet Book. For tenure of lands, see notes on Chapters 2, 3, and 4. Murray, *Legal Practice*, is based on Ros's protocol book. *Inquisitionum Retornatum Abbreviato*, 3 vols., 1811–16; and the relevant index of *Sasines* provide some details. A draft inventory of lands compiled in the

making of this book has been deposited in ACL, perhaps useful even though incomplete. Newton-upon-Ayr and St Quivox are covered by Paterson, and some families associated find mention also in his sections on Craigie, Ochiltree, and other parishes. Charles Rogers, *The Book of Wallace*, 2 vols., 1889, has some useful local references. For William Hamilton see *RMS* and *Accounts of the Lord High Treasurer*; for James Stewart, *RMS* and *Scots Peerage*. The Burgh of Newton is dealt with at length by Murray, *Early Burgh Organisation*, Vol. 2; Pryde offers more sober assessment in *AC* Vol. 4, pp.20, 24, 43, 49. The manuscript records of the Burgh of Newton-upon-Ayr from 1596 are in ACL, with a transcription of the earliest years by Jane MacLean. *Records of the Burgh of Prestwick*, ed. John Smith, has some mentions of Newton and Ayr. Finally, for this period cartographic evidence becomes available with Blaeu's *Atlas Novus*, based on surveys made by Timothy Pont at the very beginning of the 17th century.

Chapter 6 – The Church Reformed

For the Reformation period, Pagan provides the principal local study, supplemented by Chalmers, Paterson, and Robertson; *Charters*, *Friars*, and Smith's *Memorabilia* include some relevant documents. For more recent local details, see Pryde's *Accounts*, especially his Introduction, pp.lxi–lxvi; also several works by Mackenzie. Gordon Donaldson, *Thirds of Benefices*, Scottish History Society, 1949, deals with post-Reformation church finances. All these precede more recent and specific studies which have revolutionised the historical view of the Reformation: Gordon Donaldson, *The Scottish Reformation*, 1960, has been followed by W.C.Dickinson, *Scotland from the Earliest Times to 1603*, 1961; Gordon Donaldson, *Scotland, James V–James VII*, 1965; T.C.Smout, *History of the Scottish People 1560–1830*, 1969; Jenny Wormald, *Court, Kirk, and Community, 1470–1625*, 1981; Ian B. Cowan, *The Scottish Reformation*, 1982. New material relating to Ayrshire is to be found in Scottish Record Society publications, especially Ian B. Cowan, *The Parishes of Medieval Scotland*, 1967; D.E.R.Watt, *Fasti Ecclesiae Scoticanae Medii Aevi*, 1967; C.H.Hawes, *Scottish Parish Clergy at the Reformation*, 1972; the *Records of the Scottish Church History Society* contain articles by Durkan, Vol. XX, 1980; and of prime importance, Sanderson, Vol. XVII, this last supplemented by *Mary Stewart's People*, with its chapter on Robert Leggat and a splendid appreciation of the local situation in Ayr and Prestwick. Dr Sanderson also supplied some helpful suggestions after reading a draft of this present chapter. Iain Fraser contributed a useful copy of his Edinburgh University seminar paper on 'The Later Medieval Clergy of Ayrshire', 1986. Alexander Broadie, *George Lokert, Late Scholastic Logician*, 1983, is an impressive example of recent research, with biographical details made more accessible by the author in his AANHS monograph. One source not yet fully utilised but which has proved invaluable is the typescript magnum opus of the late lamented William Dillon, 'Ayrshire Clergy before

1600'. It should be noted also that *Fasti* ed. Scott, 1868, provides for this and later chapters particulars of ministers of the protestant Church of Scotland, with supplementary details about earlier ministers in some of its more recent volumes. Anyone wishing to follow the intricate pattern of legislative change and examine the text of important national documents should make use of *A Source Book of Scottish History*, ed. W.C.Dickinson and G. Donaldson, 5 vols., 1952–54 and later editions. For the religious conflicts of the 17th century older (and usually partisan) accounts have been overtaken by G.S.Pryde, *Scotland from 1603 to the Present Day*, 1962, and superseded by David Stevenson, *The Scottish Revolution 1637–1644*, 1973, and his *Revolution and Counter Revolution in Scotland*, 1978; Ian B. Cowan, *The Scottish Covenanters 1660–1688*, 1976; Rosalind Mitchison, *Lordship and Patronage 1603–1745*, 1983. For the Cromwellian occupation of Ayr see Paterson, 103–104 and *Scotland and the Protectorate*, ed. C.H.Firth, Scottish History Society, 1899, which gives details of the Citadel and its garrison. Local 17th century details are supplied by Pagan, and by Mackenzie in his several works, with some particulars from Paterson, Lyon, Bone, and Stevenson. The role of Ayr council and councillors in the religious crises between 1660 and 1689 has often been misunderstood: a clearer picture for this and the following chapter is afforded by study of the *Register of the Privy Council* in conjunction with Ayr Town Council minutes for the same period – these last meticulously transcribed, to my great advantage, by Alistair Lindsay of Glasgow. George Hickes, *The Spirit of Enthusiasm*, 1680 (ACL 671 BJ) should not be relied upon for its information regarding John Welch.

Chapter 7 – *17th Century Social Aspects*

Traditional emphasis on 17th century problems, as by McGhee in *RB*, is revised by Smout in *AC* Vol. 6. For the text of contemporary descriptions: see Hume Brown, *Scotland before 1700*, 1893, for Leslie 1578; his *Early Travellers in Scotland*, 1891, for Brereton 1636, Tucker 1655, Morer 1689; *Miscellany of the Scottish Burgh Records Society*, 1881, gives Tucker 1655, and the Report on Condition of Burghs in 1692. Extracts from council minutes dealing with social conditions are given by Paterson (in his long chapter on Ayr); also by Pagan and Lyon; see also Pryde's *Accounts* and his article in *AC* Vol.4. Material from kirk session records appears in the several works of Mackenzie, and in Bone. For other topics see *RB*, especially Jackson and Dixon on 'The Plague' and Dillon on 'Witchcraft'; Fergusson, 'Loudoun Hall and its Owners', *AC* Vol.1; Hunter, *The House of John Blair*; for family history see Hunter's *Pedigree*; *AA* 21.2.1974 has note of a silver quaich by Matthew Colquhoun. On the burgh school, Campbell, Lyon, Taylor, and Strawhorn – Lyon's 'Ayr Burgh Schools' quotes under Oct. 1602 'Aggreis wt Johne Osburne for his hous in the Sandgait to be ane schulehous for ane yeir for x lb of maill'; this requires me now to reject Taylor's argument in *AC* Vol.7 that 'from the time that it ceased

to be held in one of the Kirk buildings near the Old Fort, the Grammar School was roughly where its successor, Ayr Academy, stands today'. Michael Lynch's inspiring article, 'Whatever happened to the Medieval Burgh?' in *Scottish Economic and Social History*, Vol. 4, 1984, suggested among other things an analysis of the stent roll, transcribed for me by Alistair Lindsay (originals and transcripts in ACL). Additional material comes from 'Roll of Ground Annualis' in ATC Minutes 23.9.1656; and 'List of Seamen' (and ships) in ATC Minutes 23.2.1665. For a number of provosts local sources have been supplemented by 'History of the Parliament of Scotland: Biographies of Commissioners of Shires and Burghs', draft in two parts, SRO 493.01 (GA 371.06). For a particularly interesting period, the Council Book 1678–1690 has been fully transcribed by Alistair Lindsay, providing (in ACL which holds also the originals) a set of photocopied pages with transcriptions to correspond, a most useful palaeographic project. The briefer Minutes of the burgh of Newton-upon-Ayr for the period 1596–1686 (also in ACL) have been transcribed by Jane McLean. *The Register of the Privy Council* contains much detail about local politics and politicians, whose complaints about their rivals' activities offer a necessary corrective to the burgh minutes which preserve the views only of the faction then in power.

Chapter 8 – *The 18th Century Burgh Council*

ATC Minutes and other papers (now in ACL) have been used by Paterson and Lyon, also by Pryde in *RB* and in *AC* Vol.4. The sett of the burgh in 1713 is from *Miscellany of the Scottish Burgh Records Society*, 1881. W.L.Burn's article is discussed in Lenman, *infra*. ATB has a 'Directory of Ayrshire 1750–1800' with details of peers, freeholders, members of parliament, etc., including tables of 18th century weights and measures; also relevant articles by Hamilton and Limond. Details about Thomas Garvine come from J.H.Appleby and from an article by Renate Burgess in *Medical History*, Wellcome Institute, Vol. 19, no.1, 1975; also Paterson, pp. 251–3, 282; *Scottish Notes and Queries*, Vol. IV, no.9, 1891. For Ayr Library Society, see notes on Chapter 10. *OSA* provides contemporary comment, and observations on 18th century practices are to be found also in *NSA* and *Report from the Commissioners on Municipal Corporations*. Background information for this and subsequent chapters from G.S.Pryde, *Scotland from 1603 to the Present Day*, 1962; William Ferguson, *Scotland, 1689 to the Present*, 1968; T.C.Smout, *A History of the Scottish People, 1560–1830*, 1969; Rosalind Mitchison, *Lordship and Patronage, Scotland 1603–1745*, 1983; Bruce Lenman, *Integration, Enlightenment, and Industrialisation, Scotland 1745–1832*, 1981.

Chapter 9 – *18th Century Commerce*

Economic aspects of the 18th century are sometimes noted in ATC Minutes; some such items have been abstracted by Paterson and Lyon; and noted by Kennedy in *RB*.

Trade and the harbour are also dealt with by Smout in *AC* Vol. 6; McGhee, in *RB*; Graham, *Old Ayrshire Harbours*; and Wallace, 'Shipping through the Port of Ayr 1745–1815'. For one special aspect, see Fergusson, 'A Wine Merchant's Letter Book' and also, by Billy Kay and Cailean Maclean, *Knee Deep in Claret*, 1983. Smuggling is examined by Strawhorn in *AC* Vol 4, with new material from L.M.Cullen, 'Smuggling in the North Channel in the 18th Century', *Scottish Economic and Social History*, Vol. 7, 1987. The authority on industry and especially the coal trade is Whatley, who has a thesis, a pamphlet, plus articles on the associated salt industry in *Scottish Industrial History*, 1977 and 1982. Primary sources for coal are Minute Book of Undertakers of Coal at Alloway (B6/28/5 in ACL) and Newton-upon-Ayr Council Minute Books (B6/27). James Hutton's visit to Blackhouse colliery is noted in John Clerk's Notebook of 1786 (SRO, GD 18/2120). For waggonways see Broad; also William Aiton, *General View of the Agriculture of the County of Ayr*, 1811, section on 'Iron Railways'. For the two financial crises affecting Ayr merchants see *The Darien Papers*, ed. Hill Burton, Bannatyne Club, 1849, with its list of names; the collapse of the Ayr Bank is dealt with by Brady, with lists of shareholders in *Scots Magazine*, January 1774, and in Paterson, *Contemporaries of Burns*. The bank of Douglas and Heron was situated in the Sandgate where the Ayrshire Banking Company building was later erected (McCarter, 1832 Directory, p.116); compare High Street site of the previous bank of John McAdam and the later Hunter's Bank (McCarter, 1830 Directory, pp.82, 101). For developments in manufacturing as well as many other topics *OSA* gives details for Ayr, Newton-upon-Ayr, and St Quivox in several of its 21 volumes, now more conveniently edited in county volumes, as Vol. VI, Ayrshire. Strawhorn has several articles specially relating to the 18th century. Relevant materials include *RB*, with two contributions by Limond and Dillon on 'Fairs and Markets'; R.H.Campbell and J.B.A.Dow, *Source Book of Scottish Economic and Social History*, 1968, p.78, prints a letter of 1790 proposing conversion of the Sugar House to a cotton spinning factory; Robinson, 'Richard Oswald the Peacemaker', and James Kirkwood, 'Auchincruive House' both appear in *AC* Vol. 3; Goodwin, 'Road Development in Ayrshire 1750–1835' is based largely on Minute Books of Ayr County Road Trustees (SRA: CO3/41); A.R.B.Haldane, *Three Centuries of Scottish Posts*, 1971, is supplemented by some local details in *OSA*.

Chapter 10 – Auld Ayr and Its Honest Men

The maps of Roy and especially Armstrong are essential primary sources; so too are ATC Minutes and other burgh papers in ACL as later detailed; *OSA* reports on the parishes of Ayr, Newton-upon-Ayr, and St Quivox are filled with masses of information on assorted subjects; and much historical detail is contained in *The Poems and Songs of Robert Burns*, edited with notes by James Kinsley, 3 vols., 1968; *Letters of Robert Burns*, edited by J. De Lancey

Ferguson, 2 vols., 1931; extended version edited by G. Ross Roy, 2 vols., 1986; while James Currie's much-maligned *Life of Burns*, 1800 and later editions, contains the indispensable accounts by Gilbert Burns and John Murdoch of the poet's childhood in the parish of Ayr. Paterson's *Reminiscences* has a section on Burns Cottage and Miller Goudie, who spoke of a return visit of Burns to Alloway (p.99). For the earliest Burns Clubs, see Chapter 11 Notes. Secondary studies on aspects of Ayr in the 18th century are to be found in Paterson, *RB*, *ATB*, and *AC*; see especially Limond, Strawhorn, and Taylor. For family histories, see Paterson; *ATB*; Shaw, *The Dalrymples of Langlands* (which includes also full details of Governor Macrae and the McGuire family); Hunter, *The Hunters of Abbothill and Barjarg*; Crathorne, *Tennant's Stalk*; with additional details of the Tennant family from Taylor in *AC* Vol.7; Gairdner's *Autobiography*; for William McClure, see *Dictionary of American Biography*, sources therein cited, and McJannet Papers, Boxes 1–3 in strong-room of Irvine Burns Club, Wellwood, Irvine; information on McNeights and their Barns estate from Mr T.R.Bruen, Barns House; for John Loudon McAdam, *AA* 8.12.1836, 5.11.1936; for various particulars, *Sasines*. For poor relief see Minute Book of Ayr Poorhouse (ACL: 674 GQ); Caldwell, *Poor Law Administration*; and Hamilton. For the Church, Mackenzie, Bone, and Ayr Session Minutes (SRA: CH2/751); *Fasti*; *ATB*; articles in *RB*; on Rev John Hunter, letter to Rev John Black from George Dunlop, 29 Feb. 1820 (Edinburgh University Library MSS, La. IV. 17 (Black); ACL contains copies of publications by Dalrymple, McGill, et al, and has *Procedure in the Case against Dr William McGill* (ACL: 672 FF). For education, McClelland in *RB*; Fowler in *AC* Vol.6; A.L.Taylor also in AC Vol. 6; Strawhorn; and Boyd. Note also *Ayr Faculty of Solicitors, Extracts from Minute Books 1710–1824*, 1824.

Chapter 11 – Old into New

Chapters 11, 12, and part of Chapter 13 are devoted to the early 19th century. ATC Minutes are suddenly augmented by a wealth of other sources (equally available in ACL). There are files of the *Air Advertiser* from 1803, the *Ayr Observer* from 1832, and some Ayr Magazines (ACL – 671 LE). Maps include the Plan of Ayr made by John Wood in 1818. J.Pigot and Co.'s *Commercial Directory of Scotland*, 1820, with an informative section on Ayr was followed by William McCarter's 1830 publication entitled *Brief Historical Reminiscences of the County and Town of Ayr ... to which is added ... a Post Office Directory ... by a Burgess (Guild Brother)* and by his *Ayrshire*, 1832, which contains similar material with more illustrations. There are official *Reports*; an anonymous *Short Account*, 1828; *NSA* with 85 pages on the parish of Ayr by Rev. Alexander Cuthill, plus Newton-upon-Ayr by Rev. James Stevenson, and St Quivox by Rev. Stair McQuhae, all written in 1837. There are memoirs by Howie, dealing with 'the last fifty years, with notable occurrences during that time from personal recollection'; reference to the *AA* however indicates that Howie's details are not always quite exact. Gray deals rather with social changes 'since 1800'. James Paterson, who lived in Ayr briefly, has little contemporary detail in his anonymous *Reminiscences* of 1864, simply repeated in his later autobiography. Ayrshire's other historian William Robertson has some information on 19th century Ayr, but in his *Auld Ayr* he took 'two charitable liberties' with persons mentioned, because he had 'not recalled them by their own proper names' and excluded what might 'give pain to their descendants'. Ferguson, Hugh Allan, and Wallace Allan deal mainly with late 19th century, but the first in his 1907 book included reprints of Paterson's *Reminiscences* and Morris's *Ayr Theatricals*. Various writers on the Ayr Theatre have deduced from Morris a date of 1812, when Henry Johnstone is supposed to have moved to new premises; but the theatre in Content was noticed in the local press after that; the feu was not taken till 1815; this is confirmed by 'State of the Town in 1828' manuscript deposited under the foundation of the Town Building, with copy in folder (ACL 671 GBC); for theatre building refer to Stephen Walsh's 'The Queens Rooms', University of Strathclyde paper, 1980 (ACL 672 UL). For Barns Street and adjacent developments, I am indebted to Mr T.R.Bruen of Barns House and Mr John A. Hay of D. & J. Dunlop, solicitors, who both generously allowed access to relevant private documents. Among secondary works, *RB* has chapters on Population (Strawhorn), Streets (Dillon, Short), the Churches (Fowler and McNab), Economic Developments (Kennedy), Fairs and Markets (Dillon), Harbour (McGhee), Schools (McClelland), Poor Relief (Hamilton), Newspapers (McNair), and Eminent Men (McCartney). Other information comes from Strawhorn on *Ayr Academy; Fasti; Process of Rev. Dr Robert Auld v Magistrates and Heritors of Ayr and Alloway*, 1821 (ACL 672HH); McGloin in the *Innes Review*; Shaw's *Ayrshire*, especially on Churches and Banking; Dodd on urban growth; Broad on waggonways; Graham on the harbour; Whatley on coal; Leach on libraries; Duncan on urban developments and resort facilities; A.R.B.Haldane, *Three Centuries of Scottish Posts*, 1971. For early Burns Clubs, see *AA*, 2.2.1804, 31.1.1828, 4.2.1836; Hamilton Paul's edition of the *Poems and Songs of R.B.*, 1819, p.295; also Boyle. For the Kipper Fair, see Hugh Allan, p.23, and especially Caldwell.

Chapter 12 – The Coming of Reform

Of those sources listed for Chapter 11, *NSA*, the directories, and Gray are most useful in analysing the social classes. Cholera is referred to by Gray, Lyon, and with confirmatory and supplementary material in ATC Minutes, Board of Health Minutes (ACL B6/29/41), *AA* news items and report (7.3.1833). Howie has chapters on the meal mob (VIII), radicals and 1820 (IX), Caroline riot (X), Resurrectionists (XI), Election riots (XII, XIII), though other evidence (esp. Brownlie, p.67) shows the Battle of River Street occurred after the 1834 by-election. References

in ATC Minutes are supplemented by Guildry Record Book (B6/24/8) and Papers relating to Burgh Reform (B6/39/54). ACL has several volumes surviving from this period, e.g. *Memoir on Royal Burghs Reform*, 1819, from Ayr Mechanics Institution library (ACL 1 GH QH); *Letter on the Reform Bill* by James Dobie, 1831, with other papers bound in (ACL O GG 1832). Brownlie recalls Ayrshire Yeomanry's dealing with various political disturbances, and Gairdner tells of his role as a Yeoman in 1820. Ferguson has details of parliamentary elections. For Dr John Taylor, see Wilson; additional details from Whatley, 'Process', p.168, and *Finest Place*, p.72; *Sasines*, references for 1810; *AA* 16.9.1805 for birth notice; 21.12.1826 advertisement for sale of Blackhouse; 8.12. 1842 for obituary; 'Register of Incarcerations 1832–35' (ACL B6/15/20) has (p.200) 'John Taylor of the Ayr Chemical Works and residing in Newton upon Ayr' incarcerated on 12 September 1833 'for Breach of the peace by reason of a Challenge to fight a Duel' and liberated (p.207) on 25 September 1833 after signing a pledge to keep the peace for two years; cf. Tom Johnston, *History of the Working Classes in Scotland*, fourth edition 1946, p. 246. ACL holds Taylor's *Christian Lyrics*, 1851 (665 NG); copy with comments of a *Letter to the Editor of the Ayr Observer*, 1832, which 'appeared in a garbled state in that most contemptible of all papers' (672 LB DON); and a volume of miscellaneous *Pamphlets* (4 ZZ) by various authors including Taylor's *Case of Duel*, 1833, and *Cloudshire Political Gazette* attributed to Taylor. Charitable bequests are noted in *NSA*, also in David Caldwell, *Poor Law Administration*.

Chapter 13 – The 19th Century Burgh Council

ATC Minutes, Minutes of Police Commissioners from 1850 (B6/21), *Ayr Burgh Acts 1873–1908* (O GC 1873); Minutes of Newton Freemen (B6/27); Ferguson; Allan; *AA* and *Ayr Observer* – these primary sources can be supplemented by Hamilton on Commissioners of Supply (*AC* Vol. 1) and Poor Relief (in *RB*); Pryde on Burghs (*AC* Vol.4), McNair on Newspapers (in *RB*). For the survival of the Burgh of Newton after 1874 see directories, valuation rolls, ATC Minutes 1940–41, *AP* 13.12.1940. For the local situation in a national context see *Dod's Electoral Facts 1832–58*, ed. H.J.Hanham, 1972, also F.W.S.Craig, *British Parliamentary Election Results 1832–85*, 1977, and later volumes in that series. For this and subsequent chapters, each of the following general histories emphasises certain aspects: G.S.Pryde, *Scotland from 1603*, 1962; W.Ferguson, *Scotland, 1689 to the present*, 1968; S. & O. Checkland, *Industry and Ethos, Scotland 1832–1914*, 1984; T.C.Smout, *A Century of the Scottish People 1830–1950*, 1986.

Chapter 14 – The Railway Age

For the coming of the railway, C.J.A.Robertson, *The Origins of the Scottish Railway System 1744–1844*, 1983; *Guide to the Glasgow and Ayrshire Railway*, published by McCormick and Gemmell, 1841; *The Glasgow and South Western Railway*, Stephenson Society, 1950; *AA* 28.4.1814 and esp. 13.8.1840; *Ayr Observer*, 11.8.1840; William Robertson's *Ayrshire*, Vol 1. For the harbour, McGhee in *RB*; also Groome; for the lifeboats, *AA*, 16. 6. 1910. For coal industry, Broad is most informative; supplemented by Barbara Paterson, 'Social and Working Conditions of the Ayrshire Mining Population 1840–1875', *AC* Vol.10; other details from Howie; Allan; OS maps. For industries in general, Kennedy and Dillon in *RB*; the anonymous *Ayrshire* commercial guide of 1894; Directories, including that of the National Telephone Company for 1892–3 (ACL 4AP).

Chapter 15 – The Victorian Town

For expansion of the town see OS maps of 1855 and 1895; Directories; the Railway Guide as noted above for Chapter 14; later Guide Books (ACL 671 BY); the anonymous *Ayr as a Holiday Residence*, 1870; the reminiscences of Hugh Allan, Wallace Allan, Ferguson, and Anderson. A.H.Miller, *The Castles and Mansions of Ayrshire*, 1885, with plates by Messrs Annand, Glasgow, has sections on Auchincruive, Auchendrane, Belleisle, Cambusdoon, Craigie, and Mount Charles. For estates see also *Scotland: Owners of Lands and Heritages 1872–73*; for James Baird see J.T.Ward, 'Ayrshire Landed Estates, 19th Century' in *AC* Vol. 8, and *AA* 29.6.1876; Sir Robert Purvis, *Sir William Arrol, a Memoir*, 1913; John Watson 'Baron' Miller, *AP* 24.6.1910. Information on public health from Dr Ian Levitt and his subsequent *Government and Social Conditions in Scotland 1845–1919*, Scottish History Society, 1988; see also *AA* 11.2.1892 and *AP* 12.2.1892. Boyle supplies more information on places associated with Burns; Andrew for architectural and other details of a variety of buildings. *RB* has a meticulous study of the Churches after 1800 by Fowler and McNab (who list other sources). Hugh Allan, Wallace Allan, and Ferguson in their reminiscences are informative about many of the ministers, and also some schoolmasters. Schools are particularly dealt with by Campbell, McClelland, Boyd, and Strawhorn; and libraries by Leach. For population see decennial *Census Reports* and articles by Strawhorn in *RB* and *AC* Vol.8. For eminent persons see McCartney in *RB*; Shaw's *Ayrshire*; John Murdoch, 'Notable Ayrshire Folk' from *AP* 1913 (ACL 4 CG); John Macintosh, *The Poets of Ayrshire*, 1910; Stanley Cursiter, *Scottish Art*, 1949; and relevant volumes of *Who's Who* and *Who Was Who*. For the sculptor James Thom (whose date of birth is uncertain) see *AA* 28.5.1970, 4.6.1970. For Dr John McCosh see John Hannavy, *A Moment in Time, Scottish Contributions to Photography 1840–1920*, 1983; also articles by Peter Russell-Jones in *Photographic Journal*, January 1968, and by Ray MacKenzie in *Bulletin of the Scottish Society for the History of Photography*, Spring 1986; there are books by McCosh in ACL – *Topography of Assam*, 1837 (672 QD), *Advice to Officers in India*, 2nd edition 1856 (721 ZZ), *Nuova Italia*, 1872. Vol. 2 1875, and *Grand Tours in Many*

Lands, 1881 (all in 672 QN); other books donated by him are held by the Mitchell Library, Glasgow; the only known set of photographs by McCosh is in the National Army Museum, London. For Regiments, etc., see Shaw's *Ayrshire*; Robertson, *Second Volunteer Battalion R.S.F.*; and Brownlie. For sports, much information is from directories, and J.G.McIlvean, *The Birth of Football in the Burns Country*, 1980. Ephemeral papers include *I.O.R.Souvenir*, 1913 (ACL 455 Rec); Ayr Choral Union (ACL box 671 VN), Catalogues of Fine Art Exhibitions (ACL 671 VA). For various aspects of social life, the local newspapers are an essential source; also ATC Minutes, Minutes of ATC committees, and printed Minutes of Ayr School Board (SRA, some in ACL). For Ayr overseas see *AP* 3.6.1988 for Virginia and Ontario; for Queensland, *A History of the Burdekin*, 1952 (ACL 994 BA). For visitors to Ayr sources worth exploring are the Burns Cottage Visitors Books (now in ACL): eg. 'Dec. 18. 1856: Kossuth in exile to the memory of Burns in immortality'.

Chapter 16 – A New Age

For this and the other chapters in Part 4, background information from G.S.Pryde, *Scotland from 1603 to the Present Day*, 1962; W.Ferguson, *Scotland 1689 to the Present*, 1968; Sydney and Olive Checkland, *Industry and Ethos, Scotland 1832–1914*, 1984; C.Harvie, *No Gods and Precious Few Heroes, Scotland 1914–1980*, 1981; and T.C.Smout, *A Century of the Scottish People, 1830–1950*, 1986. ATC Minutes from 1902 appear in annual printed volumes, each with a convenient index; there are annual Directories and also Guide Books; the local newspapers with the *Ayr Advertiser* and *Ayrshire Post* presenting Unionist and Liberal points of view. The *Census Reports* for 1901 and 1911 and the third (1911) edition of the Ordnance Survey map are essential, especially in relation to housing and industry. ACL has Valuation Rolls for the County (1899–) and the Burgh (1906–) and Voters' Rolls for the Burgh (1905–). Miscellaneous details come from John Young on *Municipal Works*; Morris on *The Brig of Ayr*; Brash on *Tramways*; Moore on *Ayr Gaiety*, also D.S.Allan's University of Strathclyde paper, 1978 (ACL 672 UL); McNab and Fowler on churches, also *Fasti* and *Presbytery of Ayr v Rev W.C.Duncan, 1908* (ACL 672 HH); F.W.S.Craig, *British Parliamentary Election Results 1885–1918*, 1974; *Kilmarnock Equitable Cooperative Society, A Fifty Years Record*, 1910 (ACL 4LI); details of trade unions from *TSA*, 138, 874, and Ian MacDougall, *Catalogue of Labour Records in Scotland*, 1978; for Mary Macarthur, obituary in *AP* 7.1.1921; for John Neil, *AP* 29.5.1941. On schools, McClelland in *RB*, Boyd, Strawhorn, and *Handbook of the EIS Congress in Ayr, 1905* (ACL 4PA); Drew Cochrane, *The Story of Ayrshire Junior Football*, 1976; and 'Carrick Hill' on *The Ayr United Story*, 1960 (ACL 663 UB); *The Glasgow and South Western Railway Company 1850–1923*, Stephenson Society, 1950. For Ayrshire regiments see Shaw's *Ayrshire*; John Buchan, *History of the Royal Scots Fusiliers (1678–1918)*, 1925; and Brownlie's *Proud Trooper*.

Chapter 17 – The First War and After

As for Chapter 16, plus *Census Report* for 1931; *TSA*; McGhee in *RB*; Walton; F.W.S.Craig, *British Parliamentary Election Results 1918–1949*, 1969 and 1977; Alexander Gammie, *From Pit to Palace*, biography of James Brown, 1931. For buses, see directories; *Scottish Transport Magazine*, No.28, 1976; Neil MacDonald, *The Western Way*, 1983; Bill McGregor, *Dodds of Troon and AA Motor Services*, 1985; and Appendix III of Brash on *Tramways*. ACL holds miscellaneous papers relating to the War Memorial, with names of the Fallen (672 HN); the General Strike (6 GP); Wellington School (681 PH). This and subsequent chapters were read and useful comments made by John Pollock: a son of Bailie Pollock, he was educated at Heathfield School and Ayr Academy, and later became first head teacher of Mainholm Academy, then General Secretary of the EIS.

Chapter 18 – The Large Burgh and the Second War

As for Chapters 16 and 17, especially ATC Minutes, Directories, and local press; also *Ayrshire* brochure of Ayrshire Development Council, 1939; ed A.Allan, *Theatre in Ayr*, typescript, 1972 (ACL 672 UL); J.C.Kemp, *The History of the Royal Scots Fusiliers 1919–1959*, 1963; Brownlie's *Proud Trooper*; Shaw's *Ayrshire*, pp. 165–168 on Ayrshire war work. For list of the fallen, ATC Minutes 1956–7, p.207.

Chapter 19 – Mid Century

TSA is principal source; supplemented by *Census Report* for 1951; *RB*, esp. Strawhorn on 'How Ayr Has Grown' (which is quoted) and Thomas Paterson on 'Modern Development of the Burgh'; ATC Minutes; Directories; local press.

Chapter 20 – Finale

Based principally on the local press, including *Presenting the Ayr Advertiser* (1803–1953) in ACL 672 LD, and the centenary edition of the *Ayrshire Post* (1880–1980); articles in *AP* by Archie Venters on aspects of Auld Ayr have provided details for some earlier chapters, e.g. *AP* 25.11.1988 for Tam's Brig. *Census Reports*, with 1971 the last to provide details of the burgh as such; the Ayr and District Directory of 1968, the last published; supplemented by more recent telephone directories, valuation rolls, church directories, etc. Minutes of ATC and KCDC; with Alec M. Sloan, *Those were the Days*, 1988, providing a personal inside view of district council politics 1977–1984. For planning and other developments, Paterson in *RB*, Dodd in *AC* Vol.10; R.W.Alexander's 'Conservation and Development', 1967; 'The County Council and Ayrshire's Progress' by the present author in *Ayrshire, A Comprehensive Guide*, ACC brochure, 1975. For places of note, see Lists of Buildings compiled by the Civic Society, 1968; and more recently Brash, *Round Old Ayr*; two books by Ken Andrew; Report on Lady Cathcart's House prepared for the Civic Society, 1988. For Ayr's housing boom, *AP* 11.11.1988. Other information from SRC, KCDC, and British Ports Federation. Useful comments on parts of this chapter were made by Sheena Andrew, Bob Blain, Donald MacLean, and John Pollock.

Drafts of the entire book were read by Ian R.D.Smillie, Chief Executive of KCDC, and Peter Hemphill, Director of Libraries and Museums. Any omissions, errors, or misinterpretions in this published version remain the responsibility of the author.

Illustrations

For black and white illustrations acknowledgements are due to the following:

ACL: Ayr Carnegie Library provided most of the black and white photographs. Its considerable collection has been assembled over a long period, so that it has proved impossible to indicate date or photographer of individual items; documents reproduced are from originals in ACL: pp. 3, 4, 11, 13, 17, 21, 30, 31, 34, 43, 56, 60, 85, 86, 87, 89, 104, 110, 111, 114, 121, 122, 123, 125, 133, 141, 150, 151, 152, 166, 169, 171, 174, 175, 176, 177, 179, 181, 182, 189, 190, 191, 192, 193, 195, 196, 198, 199, 200, 201, 203, 212, 213, 214, 218, 225, 227, 228, 233, 234, 235, 236, 239, 240, 245, 248, 253, 254, 255, 256, 257, 260, 261.

For details of certain illustrations subsequently listed see *Bibliography* p. 268 and *Maps and Plans* p. 272.

pp. 6, 15, 22, 39, 69: from *AC* Vol. 10 by W.A. Dodd for AANHS.

pp. 12, 20, 49, 74, 75: from Slezer, *Theatrum Scotiae*.

pp. 23, 28: from ACH *Friars* and *Charters*.

pp. 27, 33, 41, 62, 64, 109, 113, 145, 162, 164: from Bryden, *Etchings of Auld Ayr*.

pp. 29, 101, 120, 142, 154, 197, 229, 258, 259, 263: specially photographed by Norman Cunningham and supplied by the *Ayr Advertiser*;

pp. 32, 116: from Grose, *The Antiquities of Scotland*.

pp. 46, 99, 138, 168, 184, 205, 211, 215, 216, 217, 224: from Postcard Collection of Jean and Robert Kennedy.

p. 55: from Alexander Broadie for AANHS.

p. 58: Tessin's Plan from Clarke Papers in the Worcester College Library, as published by Scottish History Society.

pp. 69, 71, 103, 139, 140, 143, 178: from McCarter's *Directory*, 1832.

p. 91: portrait of Garvine by courtesy of the Wellcome Institute.

pp. 92, 144: from Ayr Academy.

p. 92: Armstrong 1775.

p. 106: by D.O.Hill from Wilson and Chambers, *The Land of Burns*, 1840.

p. 118: by Stephen Hunter for *ATB*.

p. 127: from *The American Journal of Science and Arts*, Vol. XLVII, 1844.

pp. 136, 136: Wood 1818.
p. 156: Boundaries 1832.
pp. 160, 180, 187: OS 1855.
p. 219: OS 1911.
p. 226: from *Directory* 1920–21.
p. 237: from *Pageant of Ayrshire* brochure 1936.
p. 250: by Stephen Hunter for *TSA*.
At end: Street Plans by Messrs M.V. Nicolson, Largs.

For colour illustrations:
C1, C2, C3, C6, C10, C11, C12: base map copyright Ordnance Survey; detail supplied by author.
C4, C7: details by author.
C5, C9 from Blaeu 1654 and McDerment, 1852.
C8 by courtesy of the British Library;
C13, C14, C15, C16: photographs from Ayrshire and Burns Country Tourist Board per Jack Wild, Tourist Officer; Kyle and Carrick District Council, Planning and Estates Departments, per Nancy Brown, Chief Technician; and from author.

List of Provosts

The burgh was originally administered by royal officials like the sheriff or governor of the castle. Fiscal, commercial, and some judicial duties were delegated to certain burgesses, these royal nominees being made responsible for securing the cooperation of the general body of burgesses. The burgesses were required to assemble at Yule, Easter, and Michaelmas, on which last occasion annual appointments were made of the *prepositi* who were later known as *ballivi* or bailies. The first mention of the prepositi is in a mandate of Alexander II in 1242 (*prepositi suis de Are*); the first whose names were recorded were Simon Colinson and Adam Petit in 1327. Quite soon afterwards the two prepositi (or bailies) were joined by a third magistrate known originally as alderman and latterly as provost. The first mention of a council was in 1471 (*The alderman, bailyeis, counsale, and communite*). All who were burgesses had a hand in elections, despite royal disapproval of such popular participation. Sometime in the 16th century before 1580, Ayr was compelled to adopt a new *sett* or constitution which excluded the general mass of burgesses from participation. Until 1833 there was a complicated system whereby retiring magistrates and councillors chose their successors.

Appointment of the provost and other magistrates was (until 1949) made shortly after Michaelmas each year. Any date given, e.g. 1480, signifies the period from Michaelmas 1480 till Michaelmas 1481; 1488–90 indicates a re-election at Michaelmas 1489. For earlier periods the evidence is incomplete, or of uncertain reliability. Spelling of surnames is rarely uniform. The 'History of the Parliament of Scotland: Biographies of Commissioners of Shires and Burghs', unpublished draft in two parts, SRO 493.01 (GA 371.06) supplements the List of Provosts compiled by James W. Forsyth for *The Royal Burgh of Ayr*, ed. Dunlop, 1953, which forms the basis for this present List.

ALDERMEN

Adam Mure, sheriff of Ayr, 1329, 1340, 1342
Robert Small, 1359
Reginald de Fynwyke, 1401, 1406
Nicholas de Fynwyke, 1415–17
Patrick Hair, 1430, 1438
Thomas Mason, 1431
John Campbell of Skeldon, 1435
John Multrar, 1450, 1458–67, 1471–76, 1481
John Petyt, 1454
Alexander Otterburn, 1469
James Blair, 1477, 1494
David Blair of Adamton, 1480
Andrew Busby, 1488–90, 1491–94, 1495–97, 1498
Allan Boyman, 1497
Robert Clerk of Auldhall, 1499–1501, 1502, 1505, 1509, 1511
John Brown, 1501, 1510, 1514–16
Matthew Wallace of Craigie, 1503–05, 1506–09
John Dalrymple, 1519
James Tait, 1521, 1527–29
Thomas Brown, 1532
Richard Bannatyne, 1534–38, 1543

PROVOSTS

William Hamilton of Sanchar, with title of alderman 1539–43, 1547; continuing as provost 1548–53, 1559
Michael Wallace of Cunning Park, 1560–63, 1573, 1575
John Lockhart of Boghall, 1568–70, 1574, 1577, 1589
Hugh Campbell, younger, of Loudoun, 1578
John Jamieson, 1580, 1583
George Jamieson, 1581, 1590–92, 1593–96, 1602
Robert Campbell, 1582
Adam Stewart, 1584, 1592, 1604, 1606, 1608
Sir William Stewart of Monkton, 1585

Archibald Fergushill, 1586–89

David Fergushill, his son, 1596–1601, 1603, 1605, 1607

Alexander Lockhart of Boghall, 1601

John Lockhart of Bar, 1609, 1611

John Osborne, 1612, 1616, 1620, 1626

Adam Ritchie, 1613, 1615, 1618, 1621, 1623, 1625, 1629, 1631

Hew Kennedy, 1610, 1614, 1617, 1619

Hew Kennedy, his son, 1643–1645, 1648, 1650, 1657, 1659

James Blair, 1622, 1624, 1627, 1633

William Cunningham, 1628

John Stewart, 1630, 1632, 1635

John Osborne, younger, 1634, 1636, 1638, 1640, 1642, 1645, 1656, 1658

Robert Gordon, 1637, 1639, 1641, 1647, 1651

John Kennedy, 1646

Gilbert Richard, 1649

William Cunningham of Brounhill, 1655, 1660–67, 1669–71

Thomas Knight, 1667–69, 1671–73

John Mure, 1673–75, 1688–91, 1692, 1696, 1698, 1701, 1706

John Cunningham, 1675

Robert Doock, 1676–78

William Cunningham, younger, of Brounhill, 1678–81, 1686

Vaxley Robson, vice-provost 1654, provost 1681–83

William Brisbane, 1683

Robert Hunter, 1684–86

Sir William Wallace, 1687

John Osborne, 1691, 1694

Hugh Crauford, 1693

Robert Mure of Blairston, son of John Mure, 1695, 1697, 1699, 1707, 1709–11, 1712–14, 1715–17, 1718–20

Samuel Mure, 1700, 1702, 1708, 1711, 1714

Hew McHutcheon, 1703

John Ballantine, 1704

David Fergusson, 1705

Mungo Campbell, 1717

Joseph Wilson, 1720–22

James Montgomery, 1722–24, 1726–28, 1730–32, 1734–36, 1742

Thomas Garvine, 1724–26, 1728–30, 1732–34, 1738–40, 1745–47, 1749–51, 1753–55

James Hunter, 1736–38, 1740–42

John Campbell, 1743–45

Andrew Sloan, 1747–49, 1751–53, 1755–57

Elias Cathcart, 1757–59

William Fergusson, 1759–61, 1763–65

David Bannatyne, 1761–63, 1767–69

David Fergusson, 1766, 1769–71, 1773–75, 1778–80, 1781–83, 1785–87, 1789–91

James Fergusson, 1771–73

James Hutcheson, 1775–77

John Nimmo, 1780

William Campbell of Fairfield, 1783–85

John Ballantine, 1787–89, 1793–95, 1796–98

John Murdoch, 1791–93

Charles Shaw, 1795

George Charles, 1798–1800, 1802–04, 1808–10, 1812–14

William Bowie, 1800–02, 1804–06

George Dunlop, 1806–08

William Cowan, 1810–12, 1814–16, 1818–20, 1822–24

Hugh Cowan, 1816–18

David Limond, 1820–22, 1824, 1834–41

Quintin Kennedy, 1825–27, 1829–31

William Fullarton, 1827–29, 1831–34

Hugh Miller, 1841–55

Primrose William Kennedy, 1855–61

Andrew Paterson, 1861–64

John Macneille, 1864–73

Thomas Steele, 1876–82

William Kilpatrick, 1882–88

James Murray Ferguson, 1888–91

Robert Shankland, 1891–94

Hugh Douglas Willock, 1894–97

Thomas Templeton, 1897–1903

William Allan, 1903–09

James S. Hunter, 1909–12

John Mitchell, 1912–18

John M. Mathie Morton, 1918–22

Donald McDonald, 1922–24

James R. Gould, 1924–27

John S. Stewart, 1927–30

Thomas Wilson, 1930–32

Thomas Galloway, 1933–36

James Wills, 1936–40

Robert Bowman, 1940–42

Thomas Murray, 1942–49

James Smith 1949–52

Adam Hart, 1952–55

William M. Anderson, 1955–58

William S. Lanham, 1958–61

William Cowan, 1961–64

Charles O'Halloran, 1964–67

Alexander Handyside, 1967–70

Donald C. McLean, 1970–73

Campbell Howie, 1973–75

PROVOSTS OF KYLE AND CARRICK

Alexander D. Paton, 1975–80
James L. Boyle, 1980–84
Gibson T. Macdonald, 1984–88
Dan McNeill, 1988–

List of Events

1731	Auld Tour improved	1707	Union of Scots and English Parliaments
1747	Street lamps installed	1715, 1745	Jacobite rebellions
1754	Alloway feued	1740–95	James Boswell
1756	John L. McAdam born	1752	Change in calendar
1758	Poorshouse opened	1757	Plassey: British defeat French in India
1759	Robert Burns born	1759	Quebec: British defeat French in Canada
1760	Wallacetown planned	1767	First Ayrshire Turnpike Act
1762	Ayr Library Society formed	1768	Captain Cook in the Pacific
1770	Racecourse inaugurated	1769	Murder of 10th Earl of Eglinton
1772	Harbour Improvement Act	1769	James Watt's steam engine
1772	Collapse of Ayr Bank	1770–1827	Beethoven
1779	Newton Townhouse built	1776	Declaration of American Independence
1788	New Bridge opened	1779	John Galt born in Irvine
1794	Barracks established	1789	French Revolution
1796	Ayr Academy opened	1796	Robert Burns died in Dumfries

1803	first issue of *Ayr Advertiser*	1808	Kilmarnock-Troon railway
1823	Burns Monument at Alloway	1815	Battle of Waterloo ends Napoleonic Wars
1830	Town Buildings opened	1818–83	Karl Marx
1832	Cholera, 205 deaths	1832	Great Reform Act
1833	First municipal elections	1837–1901	Reign of Queen Victoria
1834	Wallace Tower rebuilt	1840	Penny Postage introduced
1840	Water company formed	1843	Disruption and formation of Free Church
1840	Glasgow-Ayr railway opened	1854	Crimean War
1850	Police and Improvement Act	1857	Indian Mutiny
1873	Ayr Burgh Act takes in Newton	1861–65	American Civil War
1878	New Bridge rebuilt after flood	1869	Suez Canal opened
1880	First esplanade provided	1871	German Empire founded
1883	County Hospital opened	1885	Motor automobile built by Karl Benz
1893	Carnegie Library opened	1888	Dunlop invents pneumatic tyre
1898	Electricity Works completed	1899	Boer War begins

1901–32	Ayr Tramways	1903	Wright brothers' flight
1902	Gaiety Theatre opened	1909	Introduction of old age pensions
1907	New Racecourse	1914–18	First World War
1910	Auld Brig restored	1917	Russian Revolution
1911	Pavilion opened	1922	BBC begin broadcasts
1921	First council houses built	1926	General Strike
1929	Local government reorganisation	1928	Fleming discovers penicillin
1935	Ayr absorbs Alloway and Whitletts	1939–45	Second World War
1949	Butlin's Holiday Camp opened	1946	Prestwick designated international airport
1964	Craigie College opened	1951	First nuclear power stations
1968	Multi-storey flats built	1956	Suez crisis
1971	Ayr by-pass completed	1957–73	Vietnam War
1972	Ayr Baths opened	1962	Cuban missile crisis
1975	Burgh ceased to exist	1969	First landing on the moon
1986	Glasgow-Ayr railway electrified	1973	Britain joins the European Economic Community

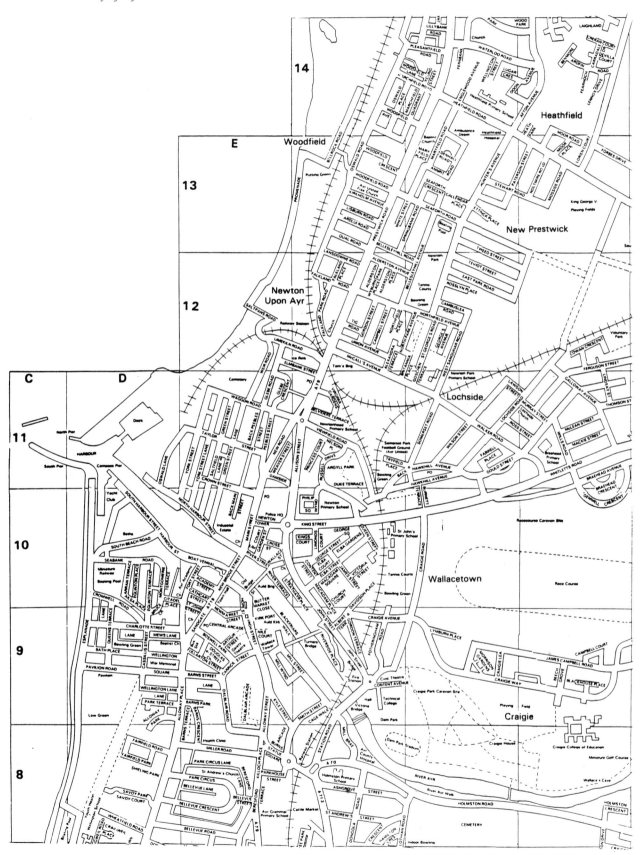

Street Plan, North West

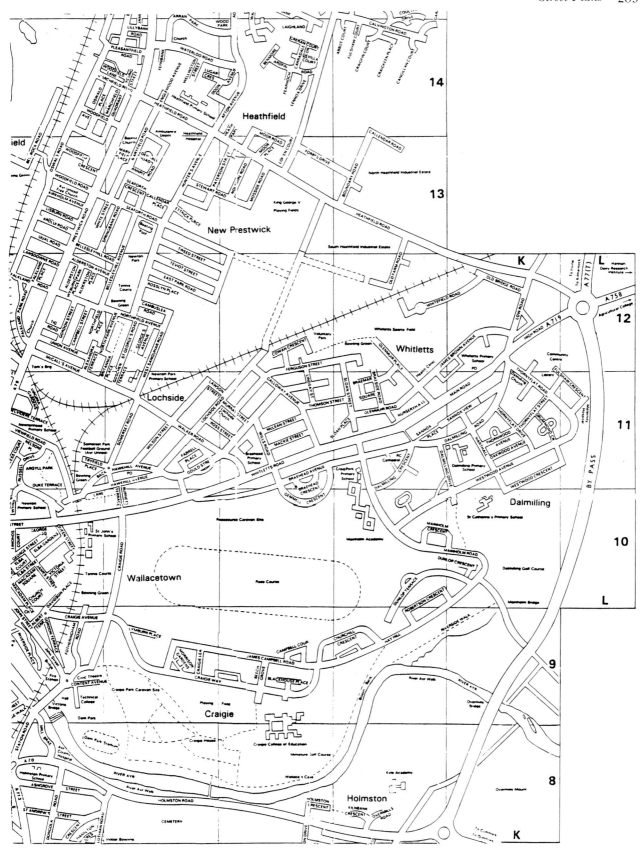

Street Plan, North East

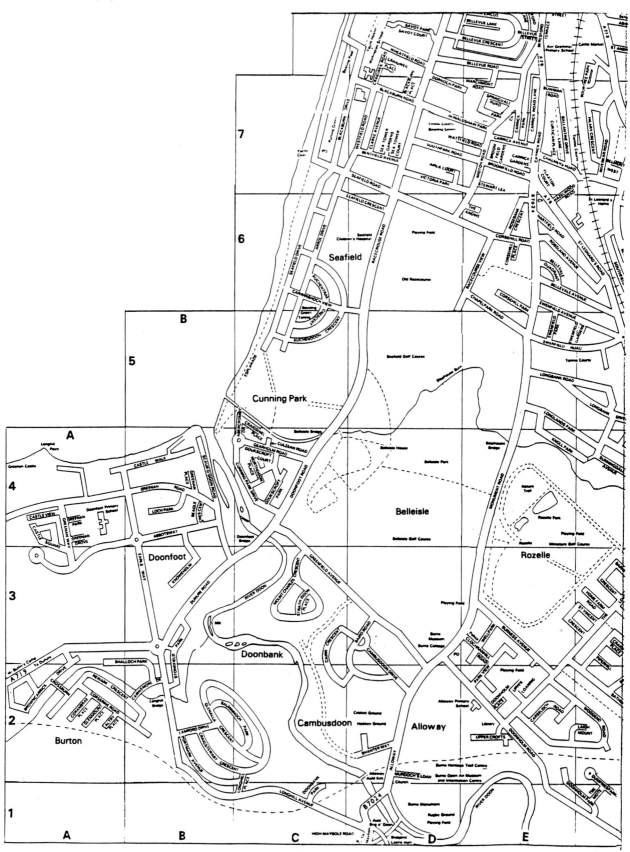

Street Plan, South West

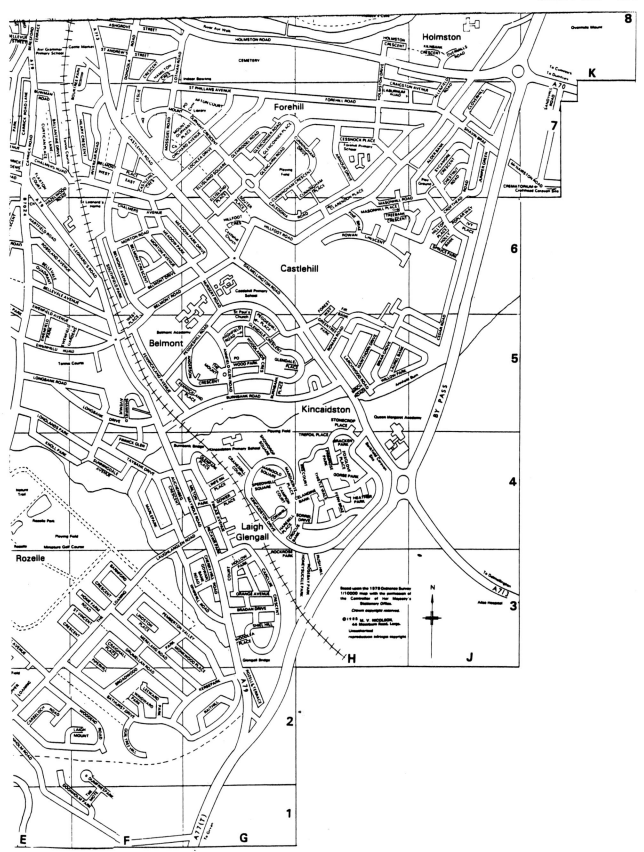

Street Plan, South East

Index